Genetic Disorders

SOURCEBOOK

Sixth Edition

Health Reference Series

Sixth Edition

Genetic Disorders
SOURCEBOOK

*Basic Consumer Health Information about Heritable
Disorders, including Disorders Resulting from
Abnormalities in Specific Genes, Such as Cystic Fibrosis,
Sickle Cell Disease, Hemophilia, and Complex Disorders
with Environmental and Genetic Components, Such as
Alzheimer Disease, Cancer, Heart Disease, and Obesity,
Chromosomal Disorders, Such as Down Syndrome,
Fragile X Syndrome, and Klinefelter Syndrome*

*Along with Information about the Human Genome Project,
Genetic Testing and Newborn Screening, Gene Therapy and
Other Current Research Initiatives, the Special Needs of
Children with Genetic Disorders, a Glossary of Terms, and a
Directory of Resources for Further Help and Information*

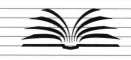

OMNIGRAPHICS

615 Griswold, Ste. 901, Detroit, MI 48226

Bibliographic Note

Because this page cannot legibly accommodate all the copyright notices, the Bibliographic Note portion of the Preface constitutes an extension of the copyright notice.

* * *

Omnigraphics, Inc.

Editorial Services provided by Omnigraphics, Inc.,
a division of Relevant Information, LLC

Keith Jones, *Managing Editor*

* * *

Library of Congress Cataloging-in-Publication Data

Names: Omnigraphics, Inc.

Title: Genetic disorders sourcebook: basic consumer health information about heritable disorders, including disorders resulting from abnormalities in specific genes, such as hemophilia, sickle cell disease, and cystic fibrosis, chromosomal disorders, such as down syndrome, fragile x syndrome, and klinefelter syndrome, and complex disorders with environmental and genetic components, such as alzheimer disease, cancer, heart disease, and obesity; along with information about the human genome project, genetic testing and newborn screening, gene therapy and other current research initiatives, the special needs of children with genetic disorders, a glossary of terms, and a directory of resources for further help and information.

Description: Sixth edition. | Detroit, MI: Omnigraphics, [2016] | Series: Health reference series | Includes bibliographical references and index. | Description based on print version record and CIP data provided by publisher; resource not viewed.

Identifiers: LCCN 2016019419 (print) | LCCN 2016018972 (ebook) | ISBN 9780780815230 (eBook) | ISBN 9780780815223 (hardcover: alk. paper) | ISBN 9780780815230 (ebook)

Subjects: LCSH: Human chromosome abnormalities--Popular works.

Classification: LCC RB155.5 (print) | LCC RB155.5 .G455 2016 (ebook) | DDC 616/.042--dc23

LC record available at https://lccn.loc.gov/2016019419

This book is printed on acid-free paper meeting the ANSI Z39.48 Standard. The infinity symbol that appears above indicates that the paper in this book meets that standard.

Printed in the United States

Table of Contents

Part II: Disorders Resulting from Abnormalities in Specific Genes

Part III: Chromosome Abnormalities

Part IV: Complex Disorders with Genetic and Environmental Components

Part V: Genetic Research

Part VI: Information for Parents of Children with Genetic Disorders

Part VII: Additional Help and Information

Preface

About This Book

Genes provide the information that directs the human body's basic cellular activities. Research on the human genome has shown that the DNA sequences of any two individuals are 99.9 percent identical. That 0.1 percent variation, however, is profoundly important. It contributes to visible differences, like height and hair color, and also to invisible differences, such as increased risk for—or protection from—a myriad of diseases and disorders.

As medical researchers unlock the secrets of the human genome, they are learning that nearly all diseases have a genetic component. Some are caused by a mutation in a gene or group of genes. Such mutations can occur randomly or as the result of exposure to hazardous conditions or substances. Other disorders are hereditary. These can be passed down from generation to generation within a family. Finally, many—perhaps most—genetic disorders are caused by a combination of small variations in genes operating in concert with environmental factors.

Genetic Disorders Sourcebook, Sixth Edition, offers updated information on how genes work and how genetic mutations affect health. It provides facts about the most common genetic disorders, including those that arise from mutations in specific genes—for example, muscular dystrophy, sickle cell anemia, and cystic fibrosis—as well as those arising from chromosomal abnormalities—such as Down syndrome and fragile X syndrome. A section on disorders with genetic and environmental components explains the hereditary components of Alzheimer disease, cancer, diabetes, mental illness, obesity, addiction, and others. Reports on current research initiatives provide detailed information on the newest breakthroughs in the causes and treatments of genetic disorders, including strategies, like gene therapy, nutrigenomics, and pharmacogenetics that could radically change how we treat these disorders in the future. A section for parents of children with genetic disorders offers information about assistive technologies, educational options, transition to adulthood, and estate planning. Information about genetic counseling, prenatal testing, newborn screening, and preventing genetic discrimination is also provided. The book concludes with a glossary of genetic terms and a list of resources for additional help and information.

How to Use This Book

This book is divided into parts and chapters. Parts focus on broad areas of interest. Chapters are devoted to single topics within a part.

Part I: Introduction to Genetics describes how genes work and explains what is known about how genetic mutations affect health. It details how genetic inheritance works, explains when genetic counseling might be advisable, and describes how genetic testing works and the type of information it can provide. Information on family history and the risk of genetic disorders is provided, as well as information on diagnosing and treating genetic conditions. The part concludes with a discussion on how to prevent genetic discrimination.

Part II: Disorders Resulting from Abnormalities in Specific Genes provides basic information about the types of disorders that are caused by changes in one or more genes. Individual chapters include information about the inheritance, symptoms, diagnosis, and treatment of each disorder. These include albinism, alpha-1 antitrypsin deficiency, anhidrotic ectodermal dysplasia with immune deficiency, blood and clotting disorders, CHARGE syndrome, connective tissue disorders, cystic fibrosis, endocrine disorders, heart rhythm disorders, kidney and urinary system disorders, neuromuscular disorders, and Wilson disease.

Part III: Chromosome Abnormalities offers detailed information about the types of disorders caused by changes in chromosomes. It explains how Angleman syndrome, Down syndrome, fragile X syndrome, Prader-Willi syndrome, and other chromosomal disorders are inherited and describes the diagnostic tests and treatment techniques used.

Part IV: Complex Disorders with Genetic and Environmental Components explains what is known about the causes of addiction, Alzheimer disease, cancer, diabetes, heart disease, hypertension, obesity, stroke, and other disorders with both genetic and environmental components. It describes the genetic associations related to each disorder and discusses the research advances that may lead to improved prevention efforts and treatment outcomes.

Part V: Genetic Research describes recent advances in the field of genetics as doctors seek ways to use knowledge of an individual's genetic background to target disease prevention and treatment techniques. It discusses the Human Genome Project and describes promising new avenues of research, including pharmacogenomics, and gene therapy. The part concludes with information on the Precision Medicine Initiative Cohort Program and genomic medicine.

Part VI: Information for Parents of Children with Genetic Disorders discusses birth defects and addresses the challenges of raising special needs children. It discusses early interventions, educational concerns of children with special needs and the transition into adulthood. The part also explains government benefits available to children and adults with disabilities, keeping children with disabilities safe, and offers estate planning information for families of children with special needs.

Part VII: Additional Help and Information includes a glossary of terms related to human genetics and a directory of resources offering additional help and support.

Bibliographic Note

This volume contains documents and excerpts from publications issued by the following U.S. government agencies: Centers for Disease Control and Prevention (CDC); *Eunice Kennedy Shriver* National Institute of Child Health and Human Development (NICHD); Genetics Home Reference (GHR); National Cancer Institute (NCI); National Center for Advancing Translational Sciences (NCATS); National Heart, Lung, and Blood Institute (NHLBI); National Human Genome Research Institute (NHGRI); National Institute of Arthritis and Musculoskeletal and Skin Diseases (NIAMS); National Institute of Diabetes and Digestive and Kidney Diseases (NIDDK); National Institute of General Medical Sciences (NIGMS); National Institute of Neurological Disorders and Stroke (NINDS); National Institute on Alcohol Abuse and Alcoholism (NIAAA); National Institute on Deafness and Other Communication Disorders (NIDCD); National Institutes of Health (NIH); Social Security Administration (SSA); U.S. Department of Education (ED); U.S. Department of Health and Human Services (HHS); U.S. Office of Personnel Management (OPM); and U.S. Social Security Administration.

About the Health Reference Series

The *Health Reference Series* is designed to provide basic medical information for patients, families, caregivers, and the general public. Each volume takes a particular topic and provides comprehensive coverage. This is especially important for people who may be dealing with a newly diagnosed disease or a chronic disorder in themselves or in a family member. People looking for preventive guidance, information about disease warning signs, medical statistics, and risk factors for health problems will also find answers to their questions in the *Health Reference Series*. The *Series*, however, is not intended to serve as a tool for diagnosing illness, in prescribing treatments, or as a substitute for the physician/patient relationship. All people concerned about medical symptoms or the possibility of disease are encouraged to seek professional care from an appropriate health care provider.

A Note about Spelling and Style

Health Reference Series editors use *Stedman's Medical Dictionary* as an authority for questions related to the spelling of medical terms and the *Chicago Manual of Style* for questions related to grammatical structures, punctuation, and other editorial concerns. Consistent adherence is not always possible, however, because the individual volumes within the *Series* include many documents from a wide variety of different producers, and the editor's primary goal is to present material from each source as accurately as is possible. This sometimes means that information in different chapters or sections may follow other guidelines and alternate spelling authorities.

Medical Review

Omnigraphics contracts with a team of qualified, senior medical professionals who serve as medical consultants for the *Health Reference Series*. As necessary, medical consultants review reprinted and originally written material for currency and accuracy. Citations including the phrase, "Reviewed (month, year)" indicate material reviewed by this team. Medical consultation services are provided to the *Health Reference Series* editors by:

Dr. Vijayalakshmi, MBBS, DGO, MD
Dr. Senthil Selvan, MBBS, DCH, MD
Dr. K. Sivanandham, MBBS, DCH, MS (Research), PhD

Our Advisory Board

We would like to thank the following board members for providing initial guidance on the development of this series:

- Dr. Lynda Baker, Associate Professor of Library and Information Science, Wayne State University, Detroit, MI

- Nancy Bulgarelli, William Beaumont Hospital Library, Royal Oak, MI

- Karen Imarisio, Bloomfield Township Public Library, Bloomfield Township, MI

- Karen Morgan, Mardigian Library, University of Michigan-Dearborn, Dearborn, MI

- Rosemary Orlando, St. Clair Shores Public Library, St. Clair Shores, MI

Health Reference Series *Update Policy*

The inaugural book in the *Health Reference Series* was the first edition of *Cancer Sourcebook* published in 1989. Since then, the *Series* has been enthusiastically received by librarians and in the medical community. In order to maintain the standard of providing high-quality health information for the layperson the editorial staff at Omnigraphics felt it was necessary to implement a policy of updating volumes when warranted.

Medical researchers have been making tremendous strides, and it is the purpose of the *Health Reference Series* to stay current with the most recent advances. Each decision to update a volume is made on an individual basis. Some of the considerations include how much new information is available and the feedback we receive from people who use the books. If there is a topic you would like to see added to the update list, or an area of medical concern you feel has not been adequately addressed, please write to:

Managing Editor
Health Reference Series
Omnigraphics, Inc.
615 Griswold, Ste. 901
Detroit, MI 48226

Part One

Introduction to Genetics

Chapter 1

Cells and DNA: The Basics

What Are Cells?

Cells are the basic building blocks of all living things. The human body is composed of trillions of cells. They provide structure for the body, take in nutrients from food, convert those nutrients into energy, and carry out specialized functions. Cells also contain the body's hereditary material and can make copies of themselves.

Cells have many parts, each with a different function. Some of these parts, called organelles, are specialized structures that perform certain tasks within the cell. Human cells contain the following major parts, listed in alphabetical order:

- **Cytoplasm**. Within cells, the cytoplasm is made up of a jelly-like fluid (called the cytosol) and other structures that surround the nucleus.

- **Cytoskeleton**. The cytoskeleton is a network of long fibers that make up the cell's structural framework. The cytoskeleton has several critical functions, including determining cell shape, participating in cell division, and allowing cells to move. It also provides a track-like system that directs the movement of organelles and other substances within cells.

This chapter includes text excerpted from "Cells and DNA," Genetics Home Reference (GHR), National Institutes of Health (NIH), March 7, 2016.

- **Endoplasmic reticulum (ER).** This organelle helps process molecules created by the cell. The endoplasmic reticulum also transports these molecules to their specific destinations either inside or outside the cell.

- **Golgi apparatus**. The Golgi apparatus packages molecules processed by the endoplasmic reticulum to be transported out of the cell.

- **Lysosomes and peroxisomes**. These organelles are the recycling center of the cell. They digest foreign bacteria that invade the cell, rid the cell of toxic substances, and recycle worn-out cell components.

- **Mitochondria**. Mitochondria are complex organelles that convert energy from food into a form that the cell can use. They have their own genetic material, separate from the DNA in the nucleus, and can make copies of themselves.

- **Nucleus**. The nucleus serves as the cell's command center, sending directions to the cell to grow, mature, divide, or die. It also houses DNA (deoxyribonucleic acid), the cell's hereditary material. The nucleus is surrounded by a membrane called the nuclear envelope, which protects the DNA and separates the nucleus from the rest of the cell.

- **Plasma membrane**. The plasma membrane is the outer lining of the cell. It separates the cell from its environment and allows materials to enter and leave the cell.

- **Ribosomes**. Ribosomes are organelles that process the cell's genetic instructions to create proteins. These organelles can float freely in the cytoplasm or be connected to the endoplasmic reticulum.

What Is DNA?

DNA, or deoxyribonucleic acid, is the hereditary material in humans and almost all other organisms. Nearly every cell in a person's body has the same DNA. Most DNA is located in the cell nucleus (where it is called nuclear DNA), but a small amount of DNA can also be found in the mitochondria (where it is called mitochondrial DNA or mtDNA).

The information in DNA is stored as a code made up of four chemical bases: adenine (A), guanine (G), cytosine (C), and thymine (T). Human DNA consists of about 3 billion bases, and more than 99 percent of those bases are the same in all people. The order, or sequence, of these bases determines the information available for building and maintaining an organism, similar to the way in which letters of the alphabet appear in a certain order to form words and sentences.

DNA bases pair up with each other, A with T and C with G, to form units called base pairs. Each base is also attached to a sugar molecule and a phosphate molecule. Together, a base, sugar, and phosphate are called a nucleotide. Nucleotides are arranged in two long strands that form a spiral called a double helix. The structure of the double helix is somewhat like a ladder, with the base pairs forming the ladder's rungs and the sugar and phosphate molecules forming the vertical sidepieces of the ladder.

An important property of DNA is that it can replicate, or make copies of itself. Each strand of DNA in the double helix can serve as a pattern for duplicating the sequence of bases. This is critical when cells divide because each new cell needs to have an exact copy of the DNA present in the old cell.

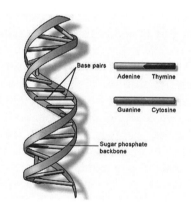

Figure 1.1. *DNA Structure*

What Is Mitochondrial DNA?

Although most DNA is packaged in chromosomes within the nucleus, mitochondria also have a small amount of their own DNA. This genetic material is known as mitochondrial DNA or mtDNA.

Mitochondria are structures within cells that convert the energy from food into a form that cells can use. Each cell contains hundreds to thousands of mitochondria, which are located in the fluid that surrounds the nucleus (the cytoplasm).

Mitochondria produce energy through a process called oxidative phosphorylation. This process uses oxygen and simple sugars to create adenosine triphosphate (ATP), the cell's main energy source. A set of enzyme complexes, designated as complexes I-V, carry out oxidative phosphorylation within mitochondria.

In addition to energy production, mitochondria play a role in several other cellular activities. For example, mitochondria help regulate the self-destruction of cells (apoptosis). They are also necessary for the production of substances such as cholesterol and heme (a component of hemoglobin, the molecule that carries oxygen in the blood).

Mitochondrial DNA contains 37 genes, all of which are essential for normal mitochondrial function. Thirteen of these genes provide instructions for making enzymes involved in oxidative phosphorylation. The remaining genes provide instructions for making molecules called transfer RNAs (tRNAs) and ribosomal RNAs (rRNAs), which are chemical cousins of DNA. These types of RNA help assemble protein building blocks (amino acids) into functioning proteins.

What Is a Gene?

A gene is the basic physical and functional unit of heredity. Genes, which are made up of DNA, act as instructions to make molecules called proteins. In humans, genes vary in size from a few hundred DNA bases to more than 2 million bases. The Human Genome Project has estimated that humans have between 20,000 and 25,000 genes.

Every person has two copies of each gene, one inherited from each parent. Most genes are the same in all people, but a small number of genes (less than 1 percent of the total) are slightly different between people. Alleles are forms of the same gene with small differences in their sequence of DNA bases. These small differences contribute to each person's unique physical features.

What Is a Chromosome?

In the nucleus of each cell, the DNA molecule is packaged into thread-like structures called chromosomes. Each chromosome is made up of DNA tightly coiled many times around proteins called histones that support its structure.

Chromosomes are not visible in the cell's nucleus—not even under a microscope—when the cell is not dividing. However, the DNA that makes up chromosomes becomes more tightly packed during cell division and is then visible under a microscope. Most of what researchers know about chromosomes was learned by observing chromosomes during cell division.

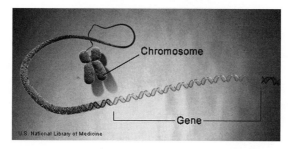

Figure 1.2. *Gene and Chromosome*

Each chromosome has a constriction point called the centromere, which divides the chromosome into two sections, or "arms." The short arm of the chromosome is labeled the "p arm." The long arm of the chromosome is labeled the "q arm." The location of the centromere on each chromosome gives the chromosome its characteristic shape, and can be used to help describe the location of specific genes.

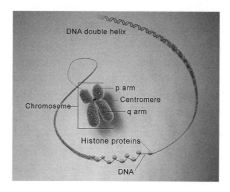

Figure 1.3. *Chromosome Structure*

How Many Chromosomes Do People Have?

In humans, each cell normally contains 23 pairs of chromosomes, for a total of 46. Twenty-two of these pairs, called autosomes, look the same in both males and females. The 23rd pair, the sex chromosomes, differ between males and females. Females have two copies of the X chromosome, while males have one X and one Y chromosome.

The 22 autosomes are numbered by size. The other two chromosomes, X and Y, are the sex chromosomes. This picture of the human chromosomes lined up in pairs is called a karyotype.

Chapter 2

How Genes Work

What Are Proteins and What Do They Do?

Proteins are large, complex molecules that play many critical roles in the body. They do most of the work in cells and are required for the structure, function, and regulation of the body's tissues and organs.

Proteins are made up of hundreds or thousands of smaller units called amino acids, which are attached to one another in long chains. There are 20 different types of amino acids that can be combined to make a protein. The sequence of amino acids determines each protein's unique 3-dimensional structure and its specific function.

Proteins can be described according to their large range of functions in the body, listed in alphabetical order:

Table 2.1. Examples of Protein Functions

Function	Description	Example
Antibody	Antibodies bind to specific foreign particles, such as viruses and bacteria, to help protect the body.	Immunoglobulin G (IgG)
Enzyme	Enzymes carry out almost all of the thousands of chemical reactions that take place in cells. They also assist with the formation of new molecules by reading the genetic information stored in DNA.	Phenylalanine hydroxylase

This chapter includes text excerpted from "How Genes Work," Genetics Home Reference (GHR), National Institutes of Health (NIH), March 7, 2016.

Table 2.1. Continued

Function	Description	Example
Messenger	Messenger proteins, such as some types of hormones, transmit signals to coordinate biological processes between different cells, tissues, and organs.	Growth hormone
Structural component	These proteins provide structure and support for cells. On a larger scale, they also allow the body to move.	Actin
Transport/storage	These proteins bind and carry atoms and small molecules within cells and throughout the body.	Ferritin

How Do Genes Direct the Production of Proteins?

Most genes contain the information needed to make functional molecules called proteins. (A few genes produce other molecules that help the cell assemble proteins.) The journey from gene to protein is complex and tightly controlled within each cell. It consists of two major steps: transcription and translation. Together, transcription and translation are known as gene expression.

During the process of transcription, the information stored in a gene's DNA is transferred to a similar molecule called RNA (ribonucleic acid) in the cell nucleus. Both RNA and DNA are made up of a chain of nucleotide bases, but they have slightly different chemical properties. The type of RNA that contains the information for making a protein is called messenger RNA (mRNA) because it carries the information, or message, from the DNA out of the nucleus into the cytoplasm.

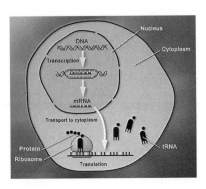

Figure 2.1. *Protein Synthesis*

10

Translation, the second step in getting from a gene to a protein, takes place in the cytoplasm. The mRNA interacts with a specialized complex called a ribosome, which "reads" the sequence of mRNA bases. Each sequence of three bases, called a codon, usually codes for one particular amino acid. (Amino acids are the building blocks of proteins.) A type of RNA called transfer RNA (tRNA) assembles the protein, one amino acid at a time. Protein assembly continues until the ribosome encounters a "stop" codon (a sequence of three bases that does not code for an amino acid).

The flow of information from DNA to RNA to proteins is one of the fundamental principles of molecular biology. It is so important that it is sometimes called the "central dogma."

Through the processes of transcription and translation, information from genes is used to make proteins.

Can Genes Be Turned On and Off in Cells?

Each cell expresses, or turns on, only a fraction of its genes. The rest of the genes are repressed, or turned off. The process of turning genes on and off is known as gene regulation. Gene regulation is an important part of normal development. Genes are turned on and off in different patterns during development to make a brain cell look and act different from a liver cell or a muscle cell, for example. Gene regulation also allows cells to react quickly to changes in their environments. Although we know that the regulation of genes is critical for life, this complex process is not yet fully understood.

Gene regulation can occur at any point during gene expression, but most commonly occurs at the level of transcription (when the information in a gene's DNA is transferred to mRNA). Signals from the environment or from other cells activate proteins called transcription factors. These proteins bind to regulatory regions of a gene and increase or decrease the level of transcription. By controlling the level of transcription, this process can determine the amount of protein product that is made by a gene at any given time.

How Do Cells Divide?

DNA modifications that do not change the DNA sequence can affect gene activity. Chemical compounds that are added to single genes can regulate their activity; these modifications are known as epigenetic changes. The epigenome comprises all of the chemical compounds that have been added to the entirety of one's DNA (genome) as a way to regulate the activity (expression) of all the genes within the genome. The chemical compounds of the epigenome are not part of the DNA sequence, but are on or attached to DNA ("epi-" means above in Greek). Epigenomic modifications remain as cells divide and in some cases can be inherited through the generations. Environmental influences, such as a person's diet and exposure to pollutants, can also impact the epigenome.

Epigenetic changes can help determine whether genes are turned on or off and can influence the production of proteins in certain cells, ensuring that only necessary proteins are produced. For example, proteins that promote bone growth are not produced in muscle cells. Patterns of epigenome modification vary among individuals, different tissues within an individual, and even different cells.

A common type of epigenomic modification is called methylation. Methylation involves attaching small molecules called methyl groups, each consisting of one carbon atom and three hydrogen atoms, to segments of DNA. When methyl groups are added to a particular gene, that gene is turned off or silenced, and no protein is produced from that gene.

Because errors in the epigenetic process, such as modifying the wrong gene or failing to add a compound to a gene, can lead to abnormal gene activity or inactivity, they can cause genetic disorders. Conditions including cancers, metabolic disorders, and degenerative disorders have all been found to be related to epigenetic errors.

Scientists continue to explore the relationship between the genome and the chemical compounds that modify it. In particular, they are studying what effect the modifications have on gene function, protein production, and human health.

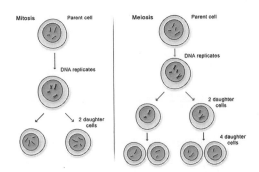

Figure 2.2. *Mitosis and Meiosis*

What Is the Epigenome?

The *epigenome* is a multitude of chemical compounds that can tell the *genome* what to do. The human genome is the complete assembly of DNA (deoxyribonucleic acid)—about 3 billion base pairs—that makes each individual unique. DNA holds the instructions for building the proteins that carry out a variety of functions in a cell. The epigenome is made up of chemical compounds and proteins that can attach to DNA and direct such actions as turning genes on or off, controlling the production of proteins in particular cells.

When epigenomic compounds attach to DNA and modify its function, they are said to have "marked" the genome. These marks do not change the sequence of the DNA. Rather, they change the way cells use the DNA's instructions. The marks are sometimes passed on from cell to cell as cells divide. They also can be passed down from one generation to the next.

How Do Genes Control the Growth and Division of Cells?

A variety of genes are involved in the control of cell growth and division. The cell cycle is the cell's way of replicating itself in an organized, step-by-step fashion. Tight regulation of this process ensures that a dividing cell's DNA is copied properly, any errors in the DNA are repaired, and each daughter cell receives a full set of chromosomes. The cycle has checkpoints (also called restriction points), which allow certain genes to check for mistakes and halt the cycle for repairs if something goes wrong.

If a cell has an error in its DNA that cannot be repaired, it may undergo programmed cell death (apoptosis). Apoptosis is a common process throughout life that helps the body get rid of cells it doesn't need. Cells that undergo apoptosis break apart and are recycled by a type of white blood cell called a macrophage. Apoptosis protects the body by removing genetically damaged cells that could lead to cancer, and it plays an important role in the development of the embryo and the maintenance of adult tissues.

Cancer results from a disruption of the normal regulation of the cell cycle. When the cycle proceeds without control, cells can divide without order and accumulate genetic defects that can lead to a cancerous tumor.

How Do Geneticists Indicate the Location of a Gene?

Geneticists use maps to describe the location of a particular gene on a chromosome. One type of map uses the cytogenetic location to describe a gene's position. The cytogenetic location is based on a dis-tinctive pattern of bands created when chromosomes are stained with certain chemicals. Another type of map uses the molecular location, a precise description of a gene's position on a chromosome. The molecular location is based on the sequence of DNA building blocks (base pairs) that make up the chromosome.

Cytogenetic Location

Geneticists use a standardized way of describing a gene's cytoge-netic location. In most cases, the location describes the position of a particular band on a stained chromosome:

17q12

It can also be written as a range of bands, if less is known about the exact location:

17q12-q21

The combination of numbers and letters provide a gene's "address" on a chromosome. This address is made up of several parts:

The chromosome on which the gene can be found. The first number or letter used to describe a gene's location represents the chromosome. Chromosomes 1 through 22 (the autosomes) are designated by their chromosome number. The sex chromosomes are designated by X or Y.

- The arm of the chromosome. Each chromosome is divided into two sections (arms) based on the location of a narrowing (con-striction) called the centromere. By convention, the shorter arm is called p, and the longer arm is called q. The chromosome arm is the second part of the gene's address. For example, 5q is the long arm of chromosome 5, and Xp is the short arm of the X chromosome.

- The position of the gene on the p or q arm. The position of a gene is based on a distinctive pattern of light and dark bands that appear when the chromosome is stained in a certain way. The position is usually designated by two digits (representing a region and a band), which are sometimes followed by a decimal point and one or more additional digits (representing sub-bands within a light or dark area). The number indicating the gene position increases with distance from the centromere. For exam-ple: 14q21 represents position 21 on the long arm of chromosome 14. 14q21 is closer to the centromere than 14q22.

Sometimes, the abbreviations "cen" or "ter" are also used to describe a gene's cytogenetic location. "Cen" indicates that the gene is very close to the centromere. For example, 16pcen refers to the short arm of chromosome 16 near the centromere. "Ter" stands for terminus, which indicates that the gene is very close to the end of the p or q arm. For example, 14qter refers to the tip of the long arm of chromosome 14. ("Tel" is also sometimes used to describe a gene's location. "Tel" stands for telomeres, which are at the ends of each chromosome. The abbreviations "tel" and "ter" refer to the same location.)

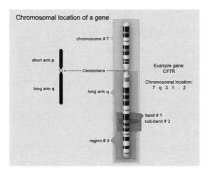

Figure 2.3. *Chromosome Allocation*

Molecular Location

The Human Genome Project, an international research effort completed in 2003, determined the sequence of base pairs for each human chromosome. This sequence information allows researchers to provide a more specific address than the cytogenetic location for many genes. A gene's molecular address pinpoints the location of that gene in terms of base pairs. It describes the gene's precise position on a chromosome and indicates the size of the gene. Knowing the molecular location also allows researchers to determine exactly how far a gene is from other genes on the same chromosome.

Different groups of researchers often present slightly different values for a gene's molecular location. Researchers interpret the sequence of the human genome using a variety of methods, which can result in small differences in a gene's molecular address.

What Are Gene Families?

A gene family is a group of genes that share important characteristics. In many cases, genes in a family share a similar sequence of

DNA building blocks (nucleotides). These genes provide instructions for making products (such as proteins) that have a similar structure or function. In other cases, dissimilar genes are grouped together in a family because proteins produced from these genes work together as a unit or participate in the same process.

Classifying individual genes into families helps researchers describe how genes are related to each other. Researchers can use gene families to predict the function of newly identified genes based on their similarity to known genes. Similarities among genes in a family can also be used to predict where and when a specific gene is active (expressed). Additionally, gene families may provide clues for identifying genes that are involved in particular diseases.

Sometimes not enough is known about a gene to assign it to an established family. In other cases, genes may fit into more than one family. No formal guidelines define the criteria for grouping genes together. Classification systems for genes continue to evolve as scientists learn more about the structure and function of genes and the relationships between them.

Chapter 3

Genetic Mutations and Health

What Is a Gene Mutation and How Do Mutations Occur?

A gene mutation is a permanent alteration in the DNA sequence that makes up a gene, such that the sequence differs from what is found in most people. Mutations range in size; they can affect anywhere from a single DNA building block (base pair) to a large segment of a chromosome that includes multiple genes.

Gene mutations can be classified in two major ways:

1. Hereditary mutations are inherited from a parent and are present throughout a person's life in virtually every cell in the body. These mutations are also called germline mutations because they are present in the parent's egg or sperm cells, which are also called germ cells. When an egg and a sperm cell unite, the resulting fertilized egg cell receives DNA from both parents. If this DNA has a mutation, the child that grows from the fertilized egg will have the mutation in each of his or her cells.

2. Acquired (or somatic) mutations occur at some time during a person's life and are present only in certain cells, not in every cell in the body. These changes can be caused by environmental

This chapter includes text excerpted from "Mutations and Health," Genetics Home Reference (GHR), National Institutes of Health (NIH), March 7, 2016.

factors such as ultraviolet radiation from the sun, or can occur if a mistake is made as DNA copies itself during cell division. Acquired mutations in somatic cells (cells other than sperm and egg cells) cannot be passed on to the next generation.

Genetic changes that are described as de novo (new) mutations can be either hereditary or somatic. In some cases, the mutation occurs in a person's egg or sperm cell but is not present in any of the person's other cells. In other cases, the mutation occurs in the fertilized egg shortly after the egg and sperm cells unite. (It is often impossible to tell exactly when a de novo mutation happened.) As the fertilized egg divides, each resulting cell in the growing embryo will have the mutation. De novo mutations may explain genetic disorders in which an affected child has a mutation in every cell in the body but the parents do not, and there is no family history of the disorder.

Somatic mutations that happen in a single cell early in embryonic development can lead to a situation called mosaicism. These genetic changes are not present in a parent's egg or sperm cells, or in the fertilized egg, but happen a bit later when the embryo includes several cells. As all the cells divide during growth and development, cells that arise from the cell with the altered gene will have the mutation, while other cells will not. Depending on the mutation and how many cells are affected, mosaicism may or may not cause health problems.

Most disease-causing gene mutations are uncommon in the general population. However, other genetic changes occur more frequently. Genetic alterations that occur in more than 1 percent of the population are called polymorphisms. They are common enough to be considered a normal variation in the DNA. Polymorphisms are responsible for many of the normal differences between people such as eye color, hair color, and blood type. Although many polymorphisms have no negative effects on a person's health, some of these variations may influence the risk of developing certain disorders.

How Can Gene Mutations Affect Health and Development?

To function correctly, each cell depends on thousands of proteins to do their jobs in the right places at the right times. Sometimes, gene mutations prevent one or more of these proteins from working properly. By changing a gene's instructions for making a protein, a mutation can cause the protein to malfunction or to be missing entirely. When a mutation alters a protein that plays a critical role in the body, it can disrupt normal development or cause a medical condition. A condition caused by mutations in one or more genes is called a genetic disorder.

In some cases, gene mutations are so severe that they prevent an embryo from surviving until birth. These changes occur in genes that are essential for development, and often disrupt the development of an embryo in its earliest stages. Because these mutations have very serious effects, they are incompatible with life.

It is important to note that genes themselves do not cause disease— genetic disorders are caused by mutations that make a gene function improperly. For example, when people say that someone has "the cystic fibrosis gene," they are usually referring to a mutated version of the *CFTR* gene, which causes the disease. All people, including those without cystic fibrosis, have a version of the *CFTR* gene.

Do All Gene Mutations Affect Health and Development?

No; only a small percentage of mutations cause genetic disorders— most have no impact on health or development. For example, some mutations alter a gene's DNA sequence but do not change the function of the protein made by the gene.

Often, gene mutations that could cause a genetic disorder are repaired by certain enzymes before the gene is expressed and an altered protein is produced. Each cell has a number of pathways through which enzymes recognize and repair mistakes in DNA. Because DNA can be damaged or mutated in many ways, DNA repair is an important process by which the body protects itself from disease.

A very small percentage of all mutations actually have a positive effect. These mutations lead to new versions of proteins that help an individual better adapt to changes in his or her environment. For example, a beneficial mutation could result in a protein that protects an individual and future generations from a new strain of bacteria.

Because a person's genetic code can have a large number of mutations with no effect on health, diagnosing genetic conditions can be difficult. Sometimes, genes thought to be related to a particular genetic condition have mutations, but whether these changes are involved in development of the condition has not been determined; these genetic changes are known as variants of unknown significance (VOUS). Sometimes, no mutations are found in suspected disease-related genes, but mutations are found in other genes whose relationship to a particular genetic condition is unknown. It is difficult to know whether these variants are involved in the disease.

What Kinds of Gene Mutations Are Possible?

The DNA sequence of a gene can be altered in a number of ways. Gene mutations have varying effects on health, depending on where they occur and whether they alter the function of essential proteins. The types of mutations include:

Missense Mutation

This type of mutation is a change in one DNA base pair that results in the substitution of one amino acid for another in the protein made by a gene.

Nonsense Mutation

A nonsense mutation is also a change in one DNA base pair. Instead of substituting one amino acid for another, however, the altered DNA sequence prematurely signals the cell to stop building a protein. This type of mutation results in a shortened protein that may function improperly or not at all.

Insertion

An insertion changes the number of DNA bases in a gene by adding a piece of DNA. As a result, the protein made by the gene may not function properly.

Deletion

A deletion changes the number of DNA bases by removing a piece of DNA. Small deletions may remove one or a few base pairs within a gene, while larger deletions can remove an entire gene or several neighboring genes. The deleted DNA may alter the function of the resulting protein(s).

Duplication

A duplication consists of a piece of DNA that is abnormally copied one or more times. This type of mutation may alter the function of the resulting protein.

Frameshift Mutation

This type of mutation occurs when the addition or loss of DNA bases changes a gene's reading frame. A reading frame consists of groups of

3 bases that each code for one amino acid. A frameshift mutation shifts the grouping of these bases and changes the code for amino acids. The resulting protein is usually nonfunctional. Insertions, deletions, and duplications can all be frameshift mutations.

Repeat Expansion

Nucleotide repeats are short DNA sequences that are repeated a number of times in a row. For example, a trinucleotide repeat is made up of 3-base-pair sequences, and a tetranucleotide repeat is made up of 4-base-pair sequences. A repeat expansion is a mutation that increases the number of times that the short DNA sequence is repeated. This type of mutation can cause the resulting protein to function improperly.

Can a Change in the Number of Genes Affect Health and Development?

People have two copies of most genes, one copy inherited from each parent. In some cases, however, the number of copies varies—meaning that a person can be born with one, three, or more copies of particular genes. Less commonly, one or more genes may be entirely missing. This type of genetic difference is known as copy number variation (CNV).

Copy number variation results from insertions, deletions, and duplications of large segments of DNA. These segments are big enough to include whole genes. Variation in gene copy number can influence the activity of genes and ultimately affect many body functions.

Researchers were surprised to learn that copy number variation accounts for a significant amount of genetic difference between people. More than 10 percent of human DNA appears to contain these differences in gene copy number. While much of this variation does not affect health or development, some differences likely influence a person's risk of disease and response to certain drugs. Future research will focus on the consequences of copy number variation in different parts of the genome and study the contribution of these variations to many types of disease.

Can Changes in the Number of Chromosomes Affect Health and Development?

Human cells normally contain 23 pairs of chromosomes, for a total of 46 chromosomes in each cell. A change in the number of chromosomes can cause problems with growth, development, and function of the body's systems. These changes can occur during the formation of reproductive cells (eggs and sperm), in early fetal development, or in any cell after birth. A gain or loss of chromosomes from the normal 46 is called aneuploidy.

A common form of aneuploidy is trisomy, or the presence of an extra chromosome in cells. "Tri-" is Greek for "three"; people with trisomy have three copies of a particular chromosome in cells instead of the normal two copies. Down syndrome is an example of a condition caused by trisomy. People with Down syndrome typically have three copies of chromosome 21 in each cell, for a total of 47 chromosomes per cell.

Monosomy, or the loss of one chromosome in cells, is another kind of aneuploidy. "Mono-" is Greek for "one"; people with monosomy have one copy of a particular chromosome in cells instead of the normal two copies. Turner syndrome is a condition caused by monosomy. Women with Turner syndrome usually have only one copy of the X chromosome in every cell, for a total of 45 chromosomes per cell.

Rarely, some cells end up with complete extra sets of chromosomes. Cells with one additional set of chromosomes, for a total of 69 chromosomes, are called triploid. Cells with two additional sets of chromosomes, for a total of 92 chromosomes, are called tetraploid. A condition in which every cell in the body has an extra set of chromosomes is not compatible with life.

In some cases, a change in the number of chromosomes occurs only in certain cells. When an individual has two or more cell populations with a different chromosomal makeup, this situation is called chromosomal mosaicism. Chromosomal mosaicism occurs from an error in cell division in cells other than eggs and sperm. Most commonly, some cells end up with one extra or missing chromosome (for a total of 45 or 47 chromosomes per cell), while other cells have the usual 46 chromosomes. Mosaic Turner syndrome is one example of chromosomal mosaicism. In females with this condition, some cells have 45 chromosomes because they are missing one copy of the X chromosome, while other cells have the usual number of chromosomes.

Many cancer cells also have changes in their number of chromosomes. These changes are not inherited; they occur in somatic cells (cells other than eggs or sperm) during the formation or progression of a cancerous tumor.

Can Changes in the Structure of Chromosomes Affect Health and Development?

Changes that affect the structure of chromosomes can cause problems with growth, development, and function of the body's systems. These changes can affect many genes along the chromosome and disrupt the proteins made from those genes.

Structural changes can occur during the formation of egg or sperm cells, in early fetal development, or in any cell after birth. Pieces of DNA can be rearranged within one chromosome or transferred between two or more chromosomes. The effects of structural changes depend on their size and location, and whether any genetic material is gained or lost. Some changes cause medical problems, while others may have no effect on a person's health.

Changes in chromosome structure include:

Translocations

A translocation occurs when a piece of one chromosome breaks off and attaches to another chromosome. This type of rearrangement is described as balanced if no genetic material is gained or lost in the cell. If there is a gain or loss of genetic material, the translocation is described as unbalanced.

Deletions

Deletions occur when a chromosome breaks and some genetic material is lost. Deletions can be large or small, and can occur anywhere along a chromosome.

Duplications

Duplications occur when part of a chromosome is copied (duplicated) too many times. This type of chromosomal change results in extra copies of genetic material from the duplicated segment.

Inversions

An inversion involves the breakage of a chromosome in two places; the resulting piece of DNA is reversed and re-inserted into the chromosome. Genetic material may or may not be lost as a result of the chromosome breaks. An inversion that involves the chromosome's constriction point (centromere) is called a pericentric inversion. An inversion that occurs in the long (q) arm or short (p) arm and does not involve the centromere is called a paracentric inversion.

Isochromosomes

An isochromosome is a chromosome with two identical arms. Instead of one long (q) arm and one short (p) arm, an isochromosome has two long arms or two short arms. As a result, these abnormal chromosomes have an extra copy of some genes and are missing copies of other genes.

Dicentric Chromosomes

Unlike normal chromosomes, which have a single constriction point (centromere), a dicentric chromosome contains two centromeres. Dicentric chromosomes result from the abnormal fusion of two chromosome pieces, each of which includes a centromere. These structures are unstable and often involve a loss of some genetic material.

Ring Chromosomes

Ring chromosomes usually occur when a chromosome breaks in two places and the ends of the chromosome arms fuse together to form a circular structure. The ring may or may not include the chromosome's constriction point (centromere). In many cases, genetic material near the ends of the chromosome is lost.

Many cancer cells also have changes in their chromosome structure. These changes are not inherited; they occur in somatic cells (cells other than eggs or sperm) during the formation or progression of a cancerous tumor.

Can Changes in Mitochondrial DNA Affect Health and Development?

Mitochondria are structures within cells that convert the energy from food into a form that cells can use. Although most DNA is packaged in chromosomes within the nucleus, mitochondria also have a small amount of their own DNA (known as mitochondrial DNA or mtDNA). In some cases, inherited changes in mitochondrial DNA can cause problems with growth, development, and function of the body's systems. These mutations disrupt the mitochondria's ability to generate energy efficiently for the cell.

Conditions caused by mutations in mitochondrial DNA often involve multiple organ systems. The effects of these conditions are most pronounced in organs and tissues that require a lot of energy (such as the heart, brain, and muscles). Although the health consequences of inherited mitochondrial DNA mutations vary widely, frequently observed features include muscle weakness and wasting, problems with movement, diabetes, kidney failure, heart disease, loss of intellectual functions (dementia), hearing loss, and abnormalities involving the eyes and vision.

Mitochondrial DNA is also prone to somatic mutations, which are not inherited. Somatic mutations occur in the DNA of certain cells during a person's lifetime and typically are not passed to future generations. Because mitochondrial DNA has a limited ability to repair itself when it is damaged, these mutations tend to build up over time. A buildup of somatic mutations in mitochondrial DNA has been associated with some forms of cancer and an increased risk of certain age-related disorders such as heart disease, Alzheimer disease, and Parkinson disease. Additionally, research suggests that the progressive accumulation of these mutations over a person's lifetime may play a role in the normal process of aging.

What Are Complex or Multifactorial Disorders?

Researchers are learning that nearly all conditions and diseases have a genetic component. Some disorders, such as sickle cell disease and cystic fibrosis, are caused by mutations in a single gene. The causes of many other disorders, however, are much more complex. Common medical problems such as heart disease, diabetes, and obesity do not have a single genetic cause—they are likely associated with the effects of multiple genes in combination with lifestyle and environmental factors. Conditions caused by many contributing factors are called complex or multifactorial disorders.

Although complex disorders often cluster in families, they do not have a clear-cut pattern of inheritance. This makes it difficult to determine a person's risk of inheriting or passing on these disorders. Complex disorders are also difficult to study and treat because the specific factors that cause most of these disorders have not yet been identified. Researchers continue to look for major contributing genes for many common complex disorders.

What Does It Mean to Have a Genetic Predisposition to a Disease?

A genetic predisposition (sometimes also called genetic susceptibility) is an increased likelihood of developing a particular disease based on a person's genetic makeup. A genetic predisposition results from specific genetic variations that are often inherited from a parent. These genetic changes contribute to the development of a disease but do not directly cause it. Some people with a predisposing genetic variation will never get the disease while others will, even within the same family.

Genetic variations can have large or small effects on the likelihood of developing a particular disease. For example, certain mutations in the *BRCA1* or *BRCA2* genes greatly increase a person's risk of developing breast cancer and ovarian cancer. Variations in other genes, such as *BARD1* and *BRIP1*, also increase breast cancer risk, but the contribution of these genetic changes to a person's overall risk appears to be much smaller.

Current research is focused on identifying genetic changes that have a small effect on disease risk but are common in the general population. Although each of these variations only slightly increases a person's risk, having changes in several different genes may combine to increase disease risk significantly. Changes in many genes, each with a small effect, may underlie susceptibility to many common diseases, including cancer, obesity, diabetes, heart disease, and mental illness.

In people with a genetic predisposition, the risk of disease can depend on multiple factors in addition to an identified genetic change. These include other genetic factors (sometimes called modifiers) as well as lifestyle and environmental factors. Diseases that are caused by a combination of factors are described as multifactorial. Although a person's genetic makeup cannot be altered, some lifestyle and environmental modifications (such as having more frequent disease screenings and maintaining a healthy weight) may be able to reduce disease risk in people with a genetic predisposition.

What Information about a Genetic Condition Can Statistics Provide?

Statistical data can provide general information about how common a condition is, how many people have the condition, or how likely it is that a person will develop the condition. Statistics are not personalized, however—they offer estimates based on groups of people. By taking into account a person's family history, medical history, and other factors, a genetics professional can help interpret what statistics mean for a particular patient.

Some statistical terms are commonly used when describing genetic conditions and other disorders.

How Are Genetic Conditions and Genes Named?

Naming Genetic Conditions

Genetic conditions are not named in one standard way (unlike genes, which are given an official name and symbol by a formal committee). Doctors who treat families with a particular disorder are often the first to propose a name for the condition. Expert working groups may later revise the name to improve its usefulness. Naming is important because it allows accurate and effective communication about particular conditions, which will ultimately help researchers find new approaches to treatment.

Disorder names are often derived from one or a combination of sources:

- The basic genetic or biochemical defect that causes the condition (for example, alpha-1 antitrypsin deficiency);

- One or more major signs or symptoms of the disorder (for example, hypermanganesemia with dystonia, polycythemia, and cirrhosis);

- The parts of the body affected by the condition (for example, craniofacial-deafness-hand syndrome);

- The name of a physician or researcher, often the first person to describe the disorder (for example, Marfan syndrome, which was named after Dr. Antoine Bernard-Jean Marfan);

- A geographic area (for example, familial Mediterranean fever, which occurs mainly in populations bordering the Mediterranean Sea); or

- The name of a patient or family with the condition (for example, amyotrophic lateral sclerosis, which is also called Lou Gehrig disease after the famous baseball player who had the condition).

Disorders named after a specific person or place are called eponyms. There is debate as to whether the possessive form (e.g., Alzheimer disease) or the nonpossessive form (Alzheimer disease) of eponyms is preferred. As a rule, medical geneticists use the nonpossessive form, and this form may become the standard for doctors in all fields of medicine.

Naming Genes

The HUGO Gene Nomenclature Committee (HGNC) designates an official name and symbol (an abbreviation of the name) for each known human gene. Some official gene names include additional information in parentheses, such as related genetic conditions, subtypes of a condition, or inheritance pattern. The HGNC is a non-profit organization funded by the U.K. Medical Research Council and the U.S. National Institutes of Health. The Committee has named more than 13,000 of the estimated 20,000 to 25,000 genes in the human genome.

During the research process, genes often acquire several alternate names and symbols. Different researchers investigating the same gene may each give the gene a different name, which can cause confusion. The HGNC assigns a unique name and symbol to each human gene, which allows effective organization of genes in large databanks, aiding the advancement of research.

Chapter 4

Genetic Inheritance

What Does It Mean If a Disorder Seems to Run in My Family?

A particular disorder might be described as "running in a family" if more than one person in the family has the condition. Some disorders that affect multiple family members are caused by gene mutations, which can be inherited (passed down from parent to child). Other conditions that appear to run in families are not caused by mutations in single genes. Instead, environmental factors such as dietary habits or a combination of genetic and environmental factors are responsible for these disorders.

It is not always easy to determine whether a condition in a family is inherited. A genetics professional can use a person's family history (a record of health information about a person's immediate and extended family) to help determine whether a disorder has a genetic component. He or she will ask about the health of people from several generations of the family, usually first-, second-, and third-degree relatives.

This chapter includes text excerpted from "Inheriting Genetic Conditions," Genetics Home Reference (GHR), National Institutes of Health (NIH), March 14, 2016.

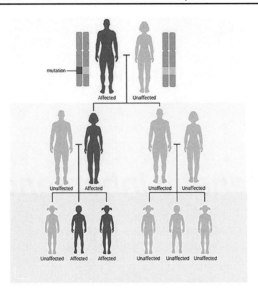

Figure 4.1. *Pedigree—Multigenerational Conditions*

Why Is It Important to Know My Family Medical History?

A family medical history is a record of health information about a person and his or her close relatives. A complete record includes information from three generations of relatives, including children, brothers and sisters, parents, aunts and uncles, nieces and nephews, grandparents, and cousins.

Families have many factors in common, including their genes, environment, and lifestyle. Together, these factors can give clues to medical conditions that may run in a family. By noticing patterns of disorders among relatives, healthcare professionals can determine whether an individual, other family members, or future generations may be at an increased risk of developing a particular condition.

A family medical history can identify people with a higher-than-usual chance of having common disorders, such as heart disease, high blood pressure, stroke, certain cancers, and diabetes. These complex disorders are influenced by a combination of genetic factors, environmental conditions, and lifestyle choices. A family history also can provide information about the risk of rarer conditions caused by mutations in a single gene, such as cystic fibrosis and sickle cell anemia.

While a family medical history provides information about the risk of specific health concerns, having relatives with a medical condition does not mean that an individual will definitely develop that condition. On the other hand, a person with no family history of a disorder may still be at risk of developing that disorder.

Knowing one's family medical history allows a person to take steps to reduce his or her risk. For people at an increased risk of certain cancers, healthcare professionals may recommend more frequent screening (such as mammography or colonoscopy) starting at an earlier age. Healthcare providers may also encourage regular checkups or testing for people with a medical condition that runs in their family. Additionally, lifestyle changes such as adopting a healthier diet, getting regular exercise, and quitting smoking help many people lower their chances of developing heart disease and other common illnesses.

The easiest way to get information about family medical history is to talk to relatives about their health. Have they had any medical problems, and when did they occur? A family gathering could be a good time to discuss these issues. Additionally, obtaining medical records and other documents (such as obituaries and death certificates) can help complete a family medical history. It is important to keep this information up-to-date and to share it with a healthcare professional regularly.

What Are the Different Ways in Which a Genetic Condition Can Be Inherited?

Many health conditions are caused by the combined effects of multiple genes or by interactions between genes and the environment. Such disorders usually do not follow the patterns of inheritance described above. Examples of conditions caused by multiple genes or gene/environment interactions include heart disease, diabetes, schizophrenia, and certain types of cancer.

Disorders caused by changes in the number or structure of chromosomes also do not follow the straightforward patterns of inheritance listed above.

Other genetic factors sometimes influence how a disorder is inherited.

Some genetic conditions are caused by mutations in a single gene. These conditions are usually inherited in one of several patterns, depending on the gene involved:

Table 4.1. Patterns of Inheritance

Inheritance pattern	Description	Examples
Autosomal dominant	One mutated copy of the gene in each cell is sufficient for a person to be affected by an autosomal dominant disorder. In some cases, an affected person inherits the condition from an affected parent. In others, the condition may result from a new mutation in the gene and occur in people with no history of the disorder in their family.	Huntington disease, Marfan syndrome
Autosomal recessive	In autosomal recessive inheritance, both copies of the gene in each cell have mutations. The parents of an individual with an autosomal recessive condition each carry one copy of the mutated gene, but they typically do not show signs and symptoms of the condition. Autosomal recessive disorders are typically not seen in every generation of an affected family.	cystic fibrosis, sickle cell disease
X-linked dominant	X-linked dominant disorders are caused by mutations in genes on the X chromosome, one of the two sex chromosomes in each cell. In females (who have two X chromosomes), a mutation in one of the two copies of the gene in each cell is sufficient to cause the disorder. In males (who have only one X chromosome), a mutation in the only copy of the gene in each cell causes the disorder. In most cases, males experience more severe symptoms of the disorder than females. A characteristic of X-linked inheritance is that fathers cannot pass X-linked traits to their sons (no male-to-male transmission).	fragile X syndrome

Table 4.1. Continued

Inheritance pattern	Description	Examples
X-linked recessive	X-linked recessive disorders are also caused by mutations in genes on the X chromosome. In males (who have only one X chromosome), one altered copy of the gene in each cell is sufficient to cause the condition. In females (who have two X chromosomes), a mutation would have to occur in both copies of the gene to cause the disorder. Because it is unlikely that females will have two altered copies of this gene, males are affected by X-linked recessive disorders much more frequently than females. A characteristic of X-linked inheritance is that fathers cannot pass X-linked traits to their sons (no male-to-male transmission).	hemophilia, Fabry disease
Y-linked	A condition is considered Y-linked if the mutated gene that causes the disorder is located on the Y chromosome, one of the two sex chromosomes in each of a male's cells. Because only males have a Y chromosome, in Y-linked inheritance, a mutation can only be passed from father to son.	Y chromosome infertility, some cases of Swyer syndrome
Codominant	In codominant inheritance, two different versions (alleles) of a gene are expressed, and each version makes a slightly different protein. Both alleles influence the genetic trait or determine the characteristics of the genetic condition.	ABO blood group,alpha-1 antitrypsin deficiency
Mitochondrial	Mitochondrial inheritance, also known as maternal inheritance, applies to genes in mitochondrial DNA. Mitochondria, which are structures in each cell that convert molecules into energy, each contain a small amount of DNA. Because only egg cells contribute mitochondria to the developing embryo, only females can pass on mitochondrial mutations to their children. Conditions resulting from mutations in mitochondrial DNA can appear in every generation of a family and can affect both males and females, but fathers do not pass these disorders to their daughters or sons.	Leber hereditary optic neuropathy(LHON)

If a Genetic Disorder Runs in My Family, What Are the Chances That My Children Will Have the Condition?

When a genetic disorder is diagnosed in a family, family members often want to know the likelihood that they or their children will develop the condition. This can be difficult to predict in some cases because many factors influence a person's chances of developing a genetic condition. One important factor is how the condition is inherited. For example:

- **Autosomal dominant inheritance**: A person affected by an autosomal dominant disorder has a 50 percent chance of passing the mutated gene to each child. The chance that a child will not inherit the mutated gene is also 50 percent. However, in some cases an autosomal dominant disorder results from a new (de novo) mutation that occurs during the formation of egg or sperm cells or early in embryonic development. In these cases, the child's parents are unaffected, but the child may pass on the condition to his or her own children.

- **Autosomal recessive inheritance**: Two unaffected people who each carry one copy of the mutated gene for an autosomal recessive disorder (carriers) have a 25 percent chance with each pregnancy of having a child affected by the disorder. The chance with each pregnancy of having an unaffected child who is a carrier of the disorder is 50 percent, and the chance that a child will not have the disorder and will not be a carrier is 25 percent.

- **X-linked dominant inheritance**: The chance of passing on an X-linked dominant condition differs between men and women because men have one X chromosome and one Y chromosome, while women have two X chromosomes. A man passes on his Y chromosome to all of his sons and his X chromosome to all of his daughters. Therefore, the sons of a man with an X-linked dominant disorder will not be affected, but all of his daughters will inherit the condition. A woman passes on one or the other of her X chromosomes to each child. Therefore, a woman with an X-linked dominant disorder has a 50 percent chance of having an affected daughter or son with each pregnancy.

- **X-linked recessive inheritance**: Because of the difference in sex chromosomes, the probability of passing on an X-linked recessive disorder also differs between men and women. The sons of a man with an X-linked recessive disorder will not be affected, and his daughters will carry one copy of the mutated gene. With each pregnancy, a woman who carries an X-linked recessive disorder has a 50 percent chance of having sons who are affected and a 50 percent chance of having daughters who carry one copy of the mutated gene.

- **Y-linked inheritance**: Because only males have a Y chromosome, only males can be affected by and pass on Y-linked disorders. All sons of a man with a Y-linked disorder will inherit the condition from their father.

- **Codominant inheritance**: In codominant inheritance, each parent contributes a different version of a particular gene, and both versions influence the resulting genetic trait. The chance of developing a genetic condition with codominant inheritance, and the characteristic features of that condition, depend on which versions of the gene are passed from parents to their child.

- **Mitochondrial inheritance**: Mitochondria, which are the energy-producing centers inside cells, each contain a small amount of DNA. Disorders with mitochondrial inheritance result from mutations in mitochondrial DNA. Although these disorders can affect both males and females, only females can pass mutations in mitochondrial DNA to their children. A woman with a disorder caused by changes in mitochondrial DNA will pass the mutation to all of her daughters and sons, but the children of a man with such a disorder will not inherit the mutation.

It is important to note that the chance of passing on a genetic condition applies equally to each pregnancy. For example, if a couple has a child with an autosomal recessive disorder, the chance of having another child with the disorder is still 25 percent. Having one child with a disorder does not "protect" future children from inheriting the condition. Conversely, having a child without the condition does not mean that future children will definitely be affected.

Although the chances of inheriting a genetic condition appear straightforward, factors such as a person's family history and the results of genetic testing can sometimes modify those chances. In addition, some people with a disease-causing mutation never develop any health problems or may experience only mild symptoms of the disorder. If a disease that runs in a family does not have a clear-cut inheritance pattern, predicting the likelihood that a person will develop the condition can be particularly difficult.

Estimating the chance of developing or passing on a genetic disorder can be complex. Genetics professionals can help people understand these chances and help them make informed decisions about their health.

What Are Reduced Penetrance and Variable Expressivity?

Reduced penetrance and variable expressivity are factors that influence the effects of particular genetic changes. These factors usually affect disorders that have an autosomal dominant pattern of inheritance, although they are occasionally seen in disorders with an autosomal recessive inheritance pattern.

Reduced Penetrance

Penetrance refers to the proportion of people with a particular genetic change (such as a mutation in a specific gene) who exhibit signs and symptoms of a genetic disorder. If some people with the mutation do not develop features of the disorder, the condition is said to have reduced (or incomplete) penetrance. Reduced penetrance often occurs with familial cancer syndromes. For example, many people with a mutation in the *BRCA1* or *BRCA2* gene will develop cancer during their lifetime, but some people will not. Doctors cannot predict which people with these mutations will develop cancer or when the tumors will develop.

Reduced penetrance probably results from a combination of genetic, environmental, and lifestyle factors, many of which are unknown. This phenomenon can make it challenging for genetics professionals to interpret a person's family medical history and predict the risk of passing a genetic condition to future generations.

Variable Expressivity

Although some genetic disorders exhibit little variation, most have signs and symptoms that differ among affected individuals. Variable expressivity refers to the range of signs and symptoms that can occur in different people with the same genetic condition. For example, the features of Marfan syndrome vary widely—some people have only mild symptoms (such as being tall and thin with long, slender fingers), while others also experience life-threatening complications involving the heart and blood vessels. Although the features are highly variable, most people with this disorder have a mutation in the same gene (*FBN1*).

As with reduced penetrance, variable expressivity is probably caused by a combination of genetic, environmental, and lifestyle factors, most of which have not been identified. If a genetic condition has highly variable signs and symptoms, it may be challenging to diagnose.

What Do Geneticists Mean by Anticipation?

The signs and symptoms of some genetic conditions tend to become more severe and appear at an earlier age as the disorder is passed from one generation to the next. This phenomenon is called anticipation. Anticipation is most often seen with certain genetic disorders of the nervous system, such as Huntington disease, myotonic dystrophy, and fragile X syndrome.

Anticipation typically occurs with disorders that are caused by an unusual type of mutation called a trinucleotide repeat expansion. A trinucleotide repeat is a sequence of three DNA building blocks (nucleotides) that is repeated a number of times in a row. DNA segments with an abnormal number of these repeats are unstable and prone to errors during cell division. The number of repeats can change as the gene is passed from parent to child. If the number of repeats increases, it is known as a trinucleotide repeat expansion. In some cases, the trinucleotide repeat may expand until the gene stops functioning normally. This expansion causes the features of some disorders to become more severe with each successive generation.

Most genetic disorders have signs and symptoms that differ among affected individuals, including affected people in the same family. Not all of these differences can be explained by anticipation. A combination of genetic, environmental, and lifestyle factors is probably responsible for the variability, although many of these factors have not been identified. Researchers study multiple generations of affected family members and consider the genetic cause of a disorder before determining that it shows anticipation.

What Are Genomic Imprinting and Uniparental Disomy?

Genomic imprinting and uniparental disomy are factors that influence how some genetic conditions are inherited.

Genomic Imprinting

People inherit two copies of their genes—one from their mother and one from their father. Usually both copies of each gene are active, or "turned on," in cells. In some cases, however, only one of the two copies is normally turned on. Which copy is active depends on the parent of origin: some genes are normally active only when they are inherited from a person's father; others are active only when inherited from a person's mother. This phenomenon is known as genomic imprinting.

In genes that undergo genomic imprinting, the parent of origin is often marked, or "stamped," on the gene during the formation of egg and sperm cells. This stamping process, called methylation, is a chemical reaction that attaches small molecules called methyl groups to certain segments of DNA. These molecules identify which copy of a gene was inherited from the mother and which was inherited from the father. The addition and removal of methyl groups can be used to control the activity of genes.

Only a small percentage of all human genes undergo genomic imprinting. Researchers are not yet certain why some genes are imprinted and others are not. They do know that imprinted genes tend to cluster together in the same regions of chromosomes. Two major clusters of imprinted genes have been identified in humans, one on the short (p) arm of chromosome 11 (at position 11p15) and another on the long (q) arm of chromosome 15 (in the region 15q11 to 15q13).

Uniparental Disomy

Uniparental disomy (UPD) occurs when a person receives two copies of a chromosome, or part of a chromosome, from one parent and no copies from the other parent. UPD can occur as a random event during the formation of egg or sperm cells or may happen in early fetal development.

In many cases, UPD likely has no effect on health or development. Because most genes are not imprinted, it doesn't matter if a person inherits both copies from one parent instead of one copy from each parent. In some cases, however, it does make a difference whether a gene is inherited from a person's mother or father. A person with UPD may lack any active copies of essential genes that undergo genomic imprinting. This loss of gene function can lead to delayed development, intellectual disability, or other health problems.

Several genetic disorders can result from UPD or a disruption of normal genomic imprinting. The most well-known conditions include Prader-Willi syndrome, which is characterized by uncontrolled eating and obesity, and Angelman syndrome, which causes intellectual disability and impaired speech. Both of these disorders can be caused by UPD or other errors in imprinting involving genes on the long arm of chromosome 15. Other conditions, such as Beckwith-Wiedemann syndrome (a disorder characterized by accelerated growth and an increased risk of cancerous tumors), are associated with abnormalities of imprinted genes on the short arm of chromosome 11.

Are Chromosomal Disorders Inherited?

Although it is possible to inherit some types of chromosomal abnormalities, most chromosomal disorders (such as Down syndrome and Turner syndrome) are not passed from one generation to the next.

Some chromosomal conditions are caused by changes in the number of chromosomes. These changes are not inherited, but occur as random events during the formation of reproductive cells (eggs and sperm). An error in cell division called nondisjunction results in reproductive cells with an abnormal number of chromosomes. For example, a reproductive cell may accidentally gain or lose one copy of a chromosome. If one of these atypical reproductive cells contributes to the genetic makeup of a child, the child will have an extra or missing chromosome in each of the body's cells.

Changes in chromosome structure can also cause chromosomal disorders. Some changes in chromosome structure can be inherited, while others occur as random accidents during the formation of reproductive cells or in early fetal development. Because the inheritance of these changes can be complex, people concerned about this type of chromosomal abnormality may want to talk with a genetics professional.

Some cancer cells also have changes in the number or structure of their chromosomes. Because these changes occur in somatic cells (cells other than eggs and sperm), they cannot be passed from one generation to the next.

Why Are Some Genetic Conditions More Common in Particular Ethnic Groups?

Some genetic disorders are more likely to occur among people who trace their ancestry to a particular geographic area. People in an ethnic group often share certain versions of their genes, which have been passed down from common ancestors. If one of these shared genes contains a disease-causing mutation, a particular genetic disorder may be more frequently seen in the group.

Examples of genetic conditions that are more common in particular ethnic groups are sickle cell anemia, which is more common in people of African, African American, or Mediterranean heritage; and Tay-Sachs disease, which is more likely to occur among people of Ashkenazi (eastern and central European) Jewish or French Canadian ancestry. It is important to note, however, that these disorders can occur in any ethnic group.

Chapter 5

Family History and Risk of Genetic Disorders

Why Is It Important to Know My Family Medical History?

A family medical history is a record of health information about a person and his or her close relatives. A complete record includes information from three generations of relatives, including children, brothers and sisters, parents, aunts and uncles, nieces and nephews, grandparents, and cousins.

Families have many factors in common, including their genes, environment, and lifestyle. Together, these factors can give clues to medical conditions that may run in a family. By noticing patterns of disorders among relatives, healthcare professionals can determine whether an individual, other family members, or future generations may be at an increased risk of developing a particular condition.

A family medical history can identify people with a higher-than-usual chance of having common disorders, such as heart disease, high

This chapter contains text excerpted from the following sources: Text beginning with the heading "Why Is It Important to Know My Family Medical History?" is excerpted from "Why Is It Important to Know My Family Medical History?" Genetics Home Reference (GHR), National Institutes of Health (NIH), March 14, 2016; Text under the heading "Frequently Asked Questions on Family History" is excerpted from "Public Health Genomics," Centers for Disease Control and Prevention (CDC), December 6, 2015.

blood pressure, stroke, certain cancers, and diabetes. These complex disorders are influenced by a combination of genetic factors, environmental conditions, and lifestyle choices. A family history also can provide information about the risk of rarer conditions caused by mutations in a single gene, such as cystic fibrosis and sickle cell anemia.

While a family medical history provides information about the risk of specific health concerns, having relatives with a medical condition does not mean that an individual will definitely develop that condition. On the other hand, a person with no family history of a disorder may still be at risk of developing that disorder.

Knowing one's family medical history allows a person to take steps to reduce his or her risk. For people at an increased risk of certain cancers, healthcare professionals may recommend more frequent screening (such as mammography or colonoscopy) starting at an earlier age. Healthcare providers may also encourage regular checkups or testing for people with a medical condition that runs in their family. Additionally, lifestyle changes such as adopting a healthier diet, getting regular exercise, and quitting smoking help many people lower their chances of developing heart disease and other common illnesses.

The easiest way to get information about family medical history is to talk to relatives about their health. Have they had any medical problems, and when did they occur? A family gathering could be a good time to discuss these issues. Additionally, obtaining medical records and other documents (such as obituaries and death certificates) can help complete a family medical history. It is important to keep this information up-to-date and to share it with a healthcare professional regularly.

Frequently Asked Questions on Family History

What Is Family Health History?

Family health history refers to health information about you and your close relatives. Family health history is one of the most important risk factors for health problems like heart disease, stroke, diabetes and cancer. (A risk factor is anything that increases your chance of getting a disease.)

Why Is Knowing My Family Health History Important?

Family members share their genes, as well as their environment, lifestyles and habits. A family health history helps identify people at increased risk for disease because it reflects both a person's genes and these other shared risk factors.

My Mother Had Breast Cancer. Does This Mean I Will Get Cancer, Too?

Having a family member with a disease suggests that you may have a higher chance of developing that disease than someone without a similar family history. It does not mean that you will definitely develop the disease. Genes are only one of many factors that contribute to disease. Other factors to consider include lifestyle habits, such as diet and physical activity.

If you are at risk for breast cancer, consider following national guidelines for a healthy diet and regular exercise. It is also important to talk with your physician about your risk and follow recommendations for screening tests (such as mammograms) that may help to detect disease early, when it is most treatable.

Because Both of My Parents Had Heart Disease, I Know I Have "Bad" Genes. Is There Anything I Can Do to Protect Myself?

First of all, there are no "good" or "bad" genes. Most human diseases, especially common diseases such as heart disease, result from the interaction of genes with environmental and behavioral risk factors that can be changed. The best disease prevention strategy for anyone, especially for someone with a family health history, includes reducing risky behaviors (such as smoking) and increasing healthy behaviors (such as regular exercise).

How Can Knowing My Family Health History Help Lower My Risk of Disease?

You can't change your genes, but you can change behaviors that affect your health, such as smoking, inactivity and poor eating habits. People with a family health history of chronic disease may have the most to gain from making lifestyle changes. In many cases, making these changes can reduce your risk of disease even if the disease runs in your family.

Another change you can make is to participate in screening tests, such as mammograms and colorectal cancer screening, for early detection of disease. People who have a family history of a chronic disease

43

may benefit the most from screening tests that look for risk factors or early signs of disease. Finding disease early, before symptoms appear, can mean better health in the long run.

How Can I Learn about My Family Health History?

The best way to learn about your family health history is to ask questions, talk at family gatherings, draw a family tree and record health information. If possible, look at death certificates and family medical records.

How Do I Learn about My Family Health History If I'm Adopted?

Learning about your family health history may be hard if you are adopted. Some adoption agencies collect medical information on birth relatives. This is becoming more common but is not routine. Laws concerning collection of information vary by state. Contact the health and social service agency in your state for information about how to access medical or legal records. The National Adoption Clearinghouse offers information on adoption and could be helpful if you decide to search for your birth parents.

What Should I Do with the Information?

First, write down the information you collect about your family health history and share it with your doctor. Second, remember to keep your information updated and share it with your siblings and children. Third, pass it on to your children, so that they too will have a family health history record.

If I Don't Have a Family Health History of Disease, Does That Mean I Am Not at Risk?

Even if you don't have a history of a particular health problem in your family, you could still be at risk. This is because you may be unaware of disease in some family members, or you could have family members who died young, before they had a chance to develop chronic conditions. Your risk of developing a chronic disease is also influenced by many other factors, including your habits and personal health history.

Chapter 6

Genetic Counseling

Genetic Conditions and Counseling

In genetic counseling, specially-trained professionals help people learn about genetic conditions, find out their chances of being affected by or having a child or other family member with a genetic condition, and make informed decisions about testing and treatment.

Reasons for Genetic Counseling

There are many reasons that people go for genetic counseling, such as:

- A family history of a genetic condition

- To learn about genetic screening for diseases that are more common in certain ethnic groups (e.g., sickle cell disease in African Americans and Tay-Sachs disease in Ashkenazi Jews)

- To discuss abnormal results from tests during pregnancy (such as a blood test, ultrasound, chorionic villus sampling (CVS), or amniocentesis)

This chapter contains text excerpted from the following sources: Text beginning with the heading "Genetic Conditions and Counseling" is excerpted from "Genetic Counseling," Centers for Disease Control and Prevention (CDC), March 3, 2015; Text under the heading "What Is Genetic Counseling and Evaluation?" is excerpted from "Frequently Asked Questions about Genetic Counseling," National Human Genome Research Institute (NHGRI), November 20, 2013.

- To learn about the higher chance for certain types of genetic conditions (such as Down syndrome) in the baby if mother-to-be is 35 years of age or more, or is concerned at any age about her chances of having a child with a genetic condition

- To learn about the effects of being exposed to X-rays, chemicals, illness, or prescribed or illicit drugs while pregnant

- A woman has had several miscarriages or infant deaths

- Trouble getting pregnant (infertility)

- A genetic condition or birth defect occurred in a previous pregnancy

- A child has birth defects, disabilities, or conditions found by newborn screening

- To find out if there is a genetic cause for developmental delays or health problems

- Steps to get ready for a healthy pregnancy and baby (such as screening for genetic conditions)

About Genetics Professionals

Clinical geneticists and genetic counselors often work together as part of a health care team. They diagnose and care for people with genetic conditions and give information and support to people with genetic conditions and their families.

Clinical Geneticists

Clinical geneticists are medical doctors with special training in genetics. In addition to educating families about genetic conditions, they perform clinical exams and order lab tests to diagnose the causes of birth defects and other genetic conditions. They can explain how a genetic condition may affect a person and give advice about treatment options and recurrence risks for future pregnancies.

Genetic Counselors

Genetic counselors are professionals who have special training to help people and families cope with and understand genetic conditions. They are also trained to provide counseling and support for people and families with genetic conditions.

What Genetics Professionals Do?

Some of the things a genetic counselor or clinical geneticist might do during a clinical visit include:

- Ask questions about medical, family, and pregnancy history
- Talk about birth defects and genetic conditions
- Explain chances of a genetic condition occurring or recurring within the family
- Discuss how genetic conditions are passed down in the family
- Talk about illnesses and chemicals that can cause birth defects
- Recommend and order tests that can help diagnose a condition, and explain test results
- Discuss treatment options for a genetic condition
- Help people deal with feelings about how genetic conditions affect their families
- Answer medical questions and address emotional concerns
- Explore reproductive options
- Refer people to other resources for help

How to Find a Genetics Professional?

- Healthcare providers can help their patients find a genetic counselor or clinical geneticist in their area.
- The nearest medical school or university medical center will usually have information about finding a genetic professional. Search for "genetics" at the medical center's website or call the main telephone number.

What Is Genetic Counseling and Evaluation?

Genetic professionals work as members of health care teams providing information and support to individuals or families who have genetic disorders or may be at risk for inherited conditions. Genetic professionals:

- Assess the risk of a genetic disorder by researching a family's history, evaluating medical records, and conducting a physical examination of the patient and other family members when indicated.

- Weigh the medical, social and ethical decisions surrounding genetic testing.

- Provide support and information to help a person make a decision about testing.

- Interpret the results of genetic tests and medical data.

- Provide counseling or refer individuals and families to support services.

- Serve as patient advocates.

- Explain possible treatments or preventive measures.

- Discuss reproductive options.

How Do I Decide Whether I Need to See a Geneticist or Other Specialist?

Your healthcare provider may refer you to a geneticist-a medical doctor or medical researcher-who specializes in your disease or disorder. A medical geneticist has completed a fellowship or has other advanced training in medical genetics. While a genetic counselor or genetic nurse may help you with testing decisions and support issues, a medical geneticist will make the actual diagnosis of a disease or condition. Many genetic diseases are so rare that only a geneticist can provide the most complete and current information about your condition.

Along with a medical geneticist, you may also be referred to a physician who is a specialist in the type of disorder you have. For example, if a genetic test is positive for colon cancer, you might be referred to an oncologist. For a diagnosis of Huntington disease, you may be referred to a neurologist.

Chapter 7

How Are Genetic Conditions Diagnosed and Treated?

How Are Genetic Conditions Diagnosed?

A doctor may suspect a diagnosis of a genetic condition on the basis of a person's physical characteristics and family history, or on the results of a screening test.

Genetic testing is one of several tools that doctors use to diagnose genetic conditions. The approaches to making a genetic diagnosis include:

- **A physical examination**: Certain physical characteristics, such as distinctive facial features, can suggest the diagnosis of a genetic disorder. A geneticist will do a thorough physical examination that may include measurements such as the distance around the head (head circumference), the distance between the eyes, and the length of the arms and legs. Depending on the situation, specialized examinations such as nervous system

This chapter contains text excerpted from the following sources: Text under the heading "How Are Genetic Conditions Diagnosed?" is excerpted from "How Are Genetic Conditions Diagnosed?" Genetics Home Reference (GHR), National Institutes of Health (NIH), March 14, 2016; Text under the heading "How Are Genetic Conditions Treated or Managed?" is excerpted from "How Are Genetic Conditions Treated or Managed?" Genetics Home Reference (GHR), National Institutes of Health (NIH), March 14, 2016.

(neurological) or eye (ophthalmologic) exams may be performed. The doctor may also use imaging studies including x-rays, computerized tomography (CT) scans, or magnetic resonance imaging (MRI) to see structures inside the body.

- **Personal medical history**: Information about an individual's health, often going back to birth, can provide clues to a genetic diagnosis. A personal medical history includes past health issues, hospitalizations and surgeries, allergies, medications, and the results of any medical or genetic testing that has already been done.

- **Family medical history**: Because genetic conditions often run in families, information about the health of family members can be a critical tool for diagnosing these disorders. A doctor or genetic counselor will ask about health conditions in an individual's parents, siblings, children, and possibly more distant relatives. This information can give clues about the diagnosis and inheritance pattern of a genetic condition in a family.

- **Laboratory tests, including genetic testing**: Molecular, chromosomal, and biochemical genetic testing are used to diagnose genetic disorders. Other laboratory tests that measure the levels of certain substances in blood and urine can also help suggest a diagnosis.

Genetic testing is currently available for many genetic conditions. However, some conditions do not have a genetic test; either the genetic cause of the condition is unknown or a test has not yet been developed. In these cases, a combination of the approaches listed above may be used to make a diagnosis. Even when genetic testing is available, the tools listed above are used to narrow down the possibilities (known as a differential diagnosis) and choose the most appropriate genetic tests to pursue.

A diagnosis of a genetic disorder can be made anytime during life, from before birth to old age, depending on when the features of the condition appear and the availability of testing. Sometimes, having a diagnosis can guide treatment and management decisions. A genetic diagnosis can also suggest whether other family members may be affected by or at risk of a specific disorder. Even when no treatment is available for a particular condition, having a diagnosis can help people know what to expect and may help them identify useful support and advocacy resources.

How Are Genetic Conditions Treated or Managed?

Many genetic disorders result from gene changes that are present in essentially every cell in the body. As a result, these disorders often affect many body systems, and most cannot be cured. However, approaches may be available to treat or manage some of the associated signs and symptoms.

For a group of genetic conditions called inborn errors of metabolism, which result from genetic changes that disrupt the production of specific enzymes, treatments sometimes include dietary changes or replacement of the particular enzyme that is missing. Limiting certain substances in the diet can help prevent the buildup of potentially toxic substances that are normally broken down by the enzyme. In some cases, enzyme replacement therapy can help compensate for the enzyme shortage. These treatments are used to manage existing signs and symptoms and may help prevent future complications.

For other genetic conditions, treatment and management strategies are designed to improve particular signs and symptoms associated with the disorder. These approaches vary by disorder and are specific to an individual's health needs. For example, a genetic disorder associated with a heart defect might be treated with surgery to repair the defect or with a heart transplant. Conditions that are characterized by defective blood cell formation, such as sickle cell disease, can sometimes be treated with a bone marrow transplant. Bone marrow transplantation can allow the formation of normal blood cells and, if done early in life, may help prevent episodes of pain and other future complications.

Some genetic changes are associated with an increased risk of future health problems, such as certain forms of cancer. One well-known example is familial breast cancer related to mutations in the *BRCA1* and *BRCA2* genes. Management may include more frequent cancer screening or preventive (prophylactic) surgery to remove the tissues at highest risk of becoming cancerous.

Genetic disorders may cause such severe health problems that they are incompatible with life. In the most severe cases, these conditions may cause a miscarriage of an affected embryo or fetus. In other cases, affected infants may be stillborn or die shortly after birth. Although few treatments are available for these severe genetic conditions, health professionals can often provide supportive care, such as pain relief or mechanical breathing assistance, to the affected individual.

Most treatment strategies for genetic disorders do not alter the underlying genetic mutation; however, a few disorders have been treated with gene therapy. This experimental technique involves changing a person's genes to prevent or treat a disease. Gene therapy, along with many other treatment and management approaches for genetic conditions, are under study in clinical trials.

Chapter 8

Testing for Genetic Disorders

Chapter Contents

Section 8.1

What You Need to Know about Genetic Testing

This section includes text excerpted from "Frequently Asked Questions about Genetic Testing," National Human Genome Research Institute (NHGRI), August 27, 2015; text under heading "What Are the Different Types of Genetic Tests?" is excerpted from "What Are the Types of Genetic Tests?" Genetics Home Reference (GHR), National Institutes of Health (NIH), March 28, 2016.

What Is Genetic Testing?

Genetic testing uses laboratory methods to look at your genes, which are the DNA instructions you inherit from your mother and your father. Genetic tests may be used to identify increased risks of health problems, to choose treatments, or to assess responses to treatments.

What Can I Learn from Testing?

There are many different types of genetic tests. Genetic tests can help to:

- Diagnose disease
- Identify gene changes that are responsible for an already diagnosed disease
- Determine the severity of a disease
- Guide doctors in deciding on the best medicine or treatment to use for certain individuals
- Identify gene changes that may increase the risk to develop a disease
- Identify gene changes that could be passed on to children
- Screen newborn babies for certain treatable conditions

Genetic test results can be hard to understand, however specialists like geneticists and genetic counselors can help explain what results might mean to you and your family. Because genetic testing tells you information about your DNA, which is shared with other family members, sometimes a genetic test result may have implications for blood relatives of the person who had testing.

What Are the Different Types of Genetic Tests?

Genetic testing can provide information about a person's genes and chromosomes. Available types of testing include:

Newborn screening

Newborn screening is used just after birth to identify genetic disorders that can be treated early in life. Millions of babies are tested each year in the United States. All states currently test infants for phenylketonuria (a genetic disorder that causes intellectual disability if left untreated) and congenital hypothyroidism (a disorder of the thyroid gland). Most states also test for other genetic disorders.

Diagnostic testing

Diagnostic testing is used to identify or rule out a specific genetic or chromosomal condition. In many cases, genetic testing is used to confirm a diagnosis when a particular condition is suspected based on physical signs and symptoms. Diagnostic testing can be performed before birth or at any time during a person's life, but is not available for all genes or all genetic conditions. The results of a diagnostic test can influence a person's choices about health care and the management of the disorder.

Carrier testing

Carrier testing is used to identify people who carry one copy of a gene mutation that, when present in two copies, causes a genetic disorder. This type of testing is offered to individuals who have a family history of a genetic disorder and to people in certain ethnic groups with an increased risk of specific genetic conditions. If both parents are tested, the test can provide information about a couple's risk of having a child with a genetic condition.

Prenatal testing

Prenatal testing is used to detect changes in a fetus's genes or chromosomes before birth. This type of testing is offered during pregnancy if there is an increased risk that the baby will have a genetic or chromosomal disorder. In some cases, prenatal testing can lessen a couple's uncertainty or help them make decisions about a pregnancy. It cannot identify all possible inherited disorders and birth defects, however.

Preimplantation testing

Preimplantation testing, also called preimplantation genetic diagnosis (PGD), is a specialized technique that can reduce the risk of having a child with a particular genetic or chromosomal disorder. It is used to detect genetic changes in embryos that were created using assisted reproductive techniques such as in-vitro fertilization. In-vitro fertilization involves removing egg cells from a woman's ovaries and fertilizing them with sperm cells outside the body. To perform preimplantation testing, a small number of cells are taken from these embryos and tested for certain genetic changes. Only embryos without these changes are implanted in the uterus to initiate a pregnancy.

Predictive and presymptomatic testing

Predictive and presymptomatic types of testing are used to detect gene mutations associated with disorders that appear after birth, often later in life. These tests can be helpful to people who have a family member with a genetic disorder, but who have no features of the disorder themselves at the time of testing. Predictive testing can identify mutations that increase a person's risk of developing disorders with a genetic basis, such as certain types of cancer. Presymptomatic testing can determine whether a person will develop a genetic disorder, such as hereditary hemochromatosis (an iron overload disorder), before any signs or symptoms appear. The results of predictive and presymptomatic testing can provide information about a person's risk of developing a specific disorder and help with making decisions about medical care.

Forensic testing

Forensic testing uses DNA sequences to identify an individual for legal purposes. Unlike the tests described above, forensic testing is not used to detect gene mutations associated with disease. This type of testing can identify crime or catastrophe victims, rule out or implicate a crime suspect, or establish biological relationships between people (for example, paternity).

What Are the Benefits and Drawbacks of Genetic Testing?

Benefits: Genetic testing may be beneficial whether the test identifies a mutation or not. For some people, test results serve as a relief, eliminating some of the uncertainty surrounding their health. These results may also help doctors make recommendations for treatment or monitoring, and give people more information for making decisions about their and their family's health, allowing them to take steps to lower his/her chance of developing a disease. For example, as the result of such a finding, someone could be screened earlier and more frequently for the disease and/or could make changes to health habits like diet and exercise. Such a genetic test result can lower a person's feelings of uncertainty, and this information can also help people to make informed choices about their future, such as whether to have a baby.

Drawbacks: Genetic testing has a generally low risk of negatively impacting your physical health. However, it can be difficult financially or emotionally to find out your results.

- *Emotional:* Learning that you or someone in your family has or is at risk for a disease can be scary. Some people can also feel guilty, angry, anxious, or depressed when they find out their results.

- *Financial:* Genetic testing can cost anywhere from less than $100 to more than $2,000. Health insurance companies may cover part or all of the cost of testing. Many people are worried about discrimination based on their genetic test results. In 2008, Congress enacted the Genetic Information Nondiscrimination Act (GINA) to protect people from discrimination by their health insurance provider or employer. GINA does not apply to long-term care, disability, or life insurance providers.

- *Limitations of testing:* Genetic testing cannot tell you everything about inherited diseases. For example, a positive result does not always mean you will develop a disease, and it is hard to predict how severe symptoms may be. Geneticists and genetic counselors can talk more specifically about what a particular test will or will not tell you, and can help you decide whether to undergo testing.

How Do I Decide Whether to Be Tested?

There are many reasons that people might get genetic testing. Doctors might suggest a genetic test if patients or their families have certain patterns of disease. Genetic testing is voluntary and the decision about whether to have genetic testing is complex.

A geneticist or genetic counselor can help families think about the benefits and limitations of a particular genetic test. Genetic counselors help individuals and families understand the scientific, emotional, and ethical factors surrounding the decision to have genetic testing and how to deal with the results of those tests.

Section 8.2

Prenatal Genetic Testing

This section includes text excerpted from "Birth Defects,"
Centers for Disease Control and Prevention (CDC), October 20, 2014.

Diagnosis

Birth defects can be diagnosed during pregnancy or after the baby is born, depending on the specific type of birth defect.

During Pregnancy: Prenatal Testing

Screening Tests

A screening test is a procedure or test that is done to see if a woman or her baby might have certain problems. A screening test does not provide a specific diagnosis—that requires a diagnostic test. A screening test can sometimes give an abnormal result even when there is nothing wrong with the mother or her baby. Less often, a screening test result can be normal and miss a problem that does exist. During pregnancy, women are usually offered these screening tests to check for birth defects or other problems for the woman or her baby. Talk to your doctor about any concerns you have about prenatal testing.

First Trimester Screening

First trimester screening is a combination of tests completed between weeks 11 and 13 of pregnancy. It is used to look for certain birth defects related to the baby's heart or chromosomal disorders, such as Down syndrome. This screen includes a maternal blood test and an ultrasound.

- **Maternal Blood Screen.** The maternal blood screen is a simple blood test. It measures the levels of two proteins, human chorionic gonadotropin (hCG) and pregnancy associated plasma protein A (PAPP-A). If the protein levels are abnormally high or low, there could be a chromosomal disorder in the baby.

- **Ultrasound.** An ultrasound creates pictures of the baby. The ultrasound for the first trimester screen looks for extra fluid behind the baby's neck. If there is increased fluid found on the ultrasound, there could be a chromosomal disorder or heart defect in the baby.

Second Trimester Screening

Second trimester screening tests are completed between weeks 15 and 20 of pregnancy. They are used to look for certain birth defects in the baby. Second trimester screening tests include a maternal serum screen and a comprehensive ultrasound evaluation of the baby looking for the presence of structural anomalies (also known as an anomaly ultrasound).

- **Maternal Serum Screen.** The maternal serum screen is a simple blood test used to identify if a woman is at increased risk for having a baby with certain birth defects, such as neural tube defects or chromosomal disorders such as Down syndrome. It is also known as a "triple screen" or "quad screen" depending on the number of proteins measured in the mother's blood. For example, a quad screen tests the levels of 4 proteins AFP (alpha-fetoprotein), hCG, estriol, and inhibin-A. Generally, the maternal serum screen is completed during the second trimester.

- **Anomaly Ultrasound**. An ultrasound creates pictures of the baby. This test is usually completed around 18–20 weeks of pregnancy. The ultrasound is used to check the size of the baby and looks for birth defects or other problems with the baby.

Diagnostic Tests

If the result of a screening test is abnormal, doctors usually offer further diagnostic tests to determine if birth defects or other possible problems with the baby are present. These diagnostic tests are also offered to women with higher risk pregnancies, which may include women who are 35 years of age or older; women who have had a previous pregnancy affected by a birth defect; women who have chronic diseases such as lupus, high blood pressure, diabetes, or epilepsy; or women who use certain medications.

High Resolution Ultrasound

An ultrasound creates pictures of the baby. This ultrasound, also known as a level II ultrasound, is used to look in more detail for possible birth defects or other problems with the baby that were suggested in the previous screening tests. It is usually completed between weeks 18 and 22 of pregnancy.

Chorionic Villus Sampling (CVS)

CVS is a test where the doctor collects a tiny piece of the placenta, called chorionic villus, which is then tested to check for chromosomal or genetic disorders in the baby. Generally, a CVS test is offered to women who received an abnormal result on a first trimester screening test or to women who could be at higher risk. It is completed between 10 and 12 weeks of pregnancy, earlier than an amniocentesis.

Amniocentesis

An amniocentesis is test where the doctor collects a small amount of amniotic fluid from the area surrounding the baby. The fluid is then tested to measure the baby's protein levels, which might indicate certain birth defects. Cells in the amniotic fluid can be tested for chromosomal disorders, such as Down syndrome, and genetic problems, such as cystic fibrosis or Tay-Sachs disease. Generally, an amniocentesis is offered to women who received an abnormal result on a screening test or to women who might be at higher risk. It is completed between 15 and 18 weeks of pregnancy. Below are some of the proteins for which an amniocentesis tests.

- **AFP**. AFP stands for alpha-fetoprotein, a protein the unborn baby produces. A high level of AFP in the amniotic fluid might mean that the baby has a defect indicating an opening in the tissue, such as a neural tube defect (anencephaly or spina bifida), or a body wall defect, such as omphalocele or gastroschisis.

- **AChE**. AChE stands for acetylcholinesterase, an enzyme that the unborn baby produces. This enzyme can pass from the unborn baby to the fluid surrounding the baby if there is an opening in the neural tube.

Section 8.3

Newborn Screening

This section includes text excerpted from "Newborn Screening," Centers for Disease Control and Prevention (CDC), February 23, 2016.

What Is Newborn Screening?

Soon after birth, all babies born in the United States are checked for certain medical conditions. This is called newborn screening.

Importance of Newborn Screening

All babies are screened, even if they look healthy, because some medical conditions cannot be seen by just looking at the baby. Finding these conditions soon after birth can help prevent some serious problems, such as brain damage, organ damage, and even death.

For example, a test for phenylketonuria (PKU) checks if the baby's body can process phenylalanine. Phenylalanine is found in many protein-rich foods and some sweeteners and can build up in the blood and tissues of a baby with PKU, resulting in brain damage. This can be prevented if a baby with PKU is put on a special diet early. Babies are also tested for hypothyroidism, which means that their bodies do not make enough thyroid hormone. Babies with hypothyroidism can take medication with the hormone to avoid the slowed growth and brain damage that can happen if their hypothyroidism is not treated.

Even though some conditions cannot be treated as easily as PKU and hypothyroidism, it is still helpful to know about the condition as soon as possible. For example, a baby with sickle cell disease is at risk for harmful infections. These babies can take a daily dose of penicillin, an antibiotic medicine, to help prevent infections. Although the penicillin will not change the fact that the baby has sickle cell disease, it can help prevent serious problems.

When and How Babies Are Screened

Babies that are born in a hospital should be screened before they leave the hospital. Parents should take babies that are not born in a hospital or those that were not screened before leaving the hospital to a hospital or clinic to be checked within a few days of birth. In some states all babies are screened a second time, about two weeks after birth.

Blood Test

A health professional will take a few drops of blood from the baby's heel. The blood sample is sent to a newborn screening lab for testing.

Hearing Screening

Hearing screening is a short test to tell if people might have hearing loss. Hearing screening is easy and not painful. In fact, babies are often asleep while being screened. All babies should be screened for hearing loss no later than 1 month of age. It is best if they are screened before leaving the hospital after birth.

Screening for Critical Congenital Heart Defects

Babies with a critical congenital heart defect (CCHD) are at significant risk of disability or death if their condition is not diagnosed soon after birth. Newborn screening using pulse oximetry can identify some infants with a CCHD before they show signs of the condition. Once identified, babies with a CCHD can be seen by cardiologists (doctors that know a lot about the heart) and can receive special care and treatment that can prevent disability and death early in life.

Many hospitals routinely screen all newborns for CCHDs. However, CCHD screening is not currently included in all state newborn screening panels.

Conditions Tested

Each state runs its own newborn screening program. The conditions include sickle cell disease and other hemoglobin disorders, conditions where a child is unable to process certain nutrients (such as PKU), or conditions where there is a hormonal insufficiency (such as hypothyroidism). Most states screen for a standard number of conditions, but some states may screen for more. That means that there are differences in the screening process and the number and types of conditions included in screening in each state.

Baby's First Test provides a current list of conditions included in newborn screening in each state.

Screening Results

- If the results are "negative" ("pass" or in-range result) it means that the baby's test results did not show signs of any of the conditions included in the screening.

- If the results are "positive" ("fail" or out-of-range result) it means that the baby's test results showed signs of one or more of the conditions included in the newborn screening. This does not always mean that the baby has the condition. It may just mean that more testing is needed.

The child's doctor might recommend that the child get screened again or have more specific tests to diagnose a condition. For example, all babies who do not pass a hearing screening should have a full hearing test by three months and sometimes also at six months of age to confirm if there is a hearing loss.

Get Help!

If your baby's newborn screening tests show that there could be a problem, work with your baby's doctor to get any needed follow-up tests as soon as possible – don't wait!

Finding and treating some of the conditions at an early age can prevent serious problems, such as brain damage, organ damage, and even death. Many of the conditions can be treated with medication or changes to the baby's diet.

In order to make sure your baby reaches his or her full potential, it is very important to get help for any medical condition as soon as possible.

Section 8.4

Screening for Critical Congenital Heart Defects

This section includes text excerpted from "Facts about Critical Congenital Heart Defects," Centers for Disease Control and Prevention (CDC), December 22, 2015.

Facts about Critical Congenital Heart Defects

About 1 in every 4 babies born with a heart defect has a critical congenital heart defect (critical CHD, also known as critical congenital heart disease). Babies with a critical CHD need surgery or other procedures in the first year of life.

What Are Critical Congenital Heart Defects (Critical CHDs)?

In the United States, about 7,200 babies born every year have critical CHDs. Typically, these types of heart defects lead to low levels of oxygen in a newborn and may be identified using pulse oximetry screening at least 24 hours after birth. Some specific types of critical CHDs are listed in the box to the right. Babies with a critical CHD need surgery or other procedures in the first year of life. Other heart defects can be just as severe as critical CHDs and may also require treatment soon after birth.

Importance of Newborn Screening for Critical CHDs

Some CHDs may be diagnosed during pregnancy using a special type of ultrasound called a fetal *echocardiogram*, which creates pictures of the heart of the developing baby. However, some heart defects are not found during pregnancy. In these cases, heart defects may be detected at birth or as the child ages.

Some babies born with a critical CHD appear healthy at first, and they may be sent home before their heart defect is detected. These babies are at risk of having serious complications within the first few days or weeks of life, and often require emergency care. Newborn screening is a tool that can identify some of these babies so they can receive prompt care and treatment. Timely care may prevent disability or death early in life.

How Newborn Screening for Critical CHDs Is Done

Newborn screening for critical CHDs involves a simple bedside test called pulse oximetry. This test estimates the amount of oxygen in a baby's blood. Low levels of oxygen in the blood can be a sign of a critical CHD. The test is done using a machine called a pulse oximeter, with sensors placed on the baby's skin. The test is painless and takes only a few minutes.

Pulse oximetry screening does not replace a complete history and physical examination, which sometimes can detect a critical CHD before oxygen levels in the blood become low. Pulse oximetry screening, therefore, should be used along with the physical examination.

Timing of Critical CHD Screening

Screening is done when a baby is at least 24 hours of age, or as late as possible if the baby is to be discharged from the hospital before he or she is 24 hours of age.

Pulse Oximetry Screening Results

Pulse oximetry screening is most likely to detect seven of the critical CHDs. These seven main screening targets are hypoplastic left heart syndrome, pulmonary atresia, tetralogy of Fallot, total anomalous pulmonary venous return, transposition of the great arteries, tricuspid atresia, and truncus arteriosus. Other heart defects can be just as severe as the main screening targets and also require treatment soon after birth. However, pulse oximetry screening may not detect these heart defects as consistently as the seven disorders listed as the main screening targets.

Pass

If the baby passes the screen (also called "negative" or "in-range" result), it means that the baby's test results did not show signs of a low level of oxygen in the blood. A baby that passes the screen is unlikely to have a critical CHD. However, not all babies with a critical CHD will have a low level of oxygen in the blood that is detected during newborn screening. Thus, it is possible for a baby who passes the screen to still have a critical CHD or other CHD.

Fail

If the baby fails the screen (also known as "positive" or "out-of-range" result), it means that the baby's test results showed low levels of oxygen in the blood, which could be a sign of a critical CHD. This does not always mean that the baby has a critical CHD but could mean that more testing is needed. There may be other causes, such as breathing problems, for low levels of oxygen in the blood. The baby's doctor might recommend that the baby get screened again or have more specific tests, like an echocardiogram (an ultrasound picture of the heart), to diagnose a critical CHD.

Chapter 9

Preventing Genetic Discrimination

Overview

Many Americans fear that participating in research or undergoing genetic testing will lead to them being discriminated against based on their genetics. Such fears may dissuade patients from volunteering to participate in the research necessary for the development of new tests, therapies and cures, or refusing genomics-based clinical tests. To address this, in 2008 the Genetic Information Nondiscrimination Act (GINA) was passed into law, prohibiting discrimination in the workplace and by health insurance issuers. In addition, there are other legal protections against genetic discrimination by employers, issuers of health insurance, and others.

The Genetic Information Nondiscrimination Act of 2008

GINA protects Americans from discrimination based on their genetic information in both health insurance (Title I) and employment (Title II). Title I amends the Employee Retirement Income Security Act of 1974 (ERISA), the Public Health Service Act (PHSA), and the Internal Revenue Code (IRC), through the Health Insurance Portability and

This chapter includes text excerpted from "Genetic Discrimination," National Human Genome Research Institute (NHGRI), July 31, 2014.

Accountability Act of 1996 (HIPAA), as well as the Social Security Act, to prohibit health insurers from engaging in genetic discrimination.

Health Insurance (Title I)

GINA prohibits issuers of health insurance from discrimination on the basis of the genetic information of enrollees. Specifically, health insurance issuers may not use genetic information to make eligibility, coverage, underwriting or premium-setting decisions. Furthermore, issuers may not request or require individuals or their family members to undergo genetic testing or to provide genetic information. As defined in the law, genetic information includes family medical history and information regarding individuals' and family members' genetic tests.

The regulations governing implementation of GINA in health insurance took effect on December 7, 2009 and are implemented by the Internal Revenue Service, Department of Labor, and Department of Health and Human Services. GINA amends HIPAA to clarify that genetic information is health information and provides a finalized rule that went into effect March 26, 2013.

Employment (Title II)

GINA prevents employers from using genetic information in employment decisions such as hiring, firing, promotions, pay, and job assignments. Furthermore, GINA prohibits employers or other covered entities (employment agencies, labor organizations, joint labor-management training programs, and apprenticeship programs) from requiring or requesting genetic information and/or genetic tests as a condition of employment. The regulation governing implementation of GINA in employment took effect on January 10, 2011 and are implemented by the Equal Employment Opportunity Commission (EEOC).

GINA and Clinical Research

GINA has implications for individuals participating in research studies. The Office of Human Research Protections (OHRP) within the Department of Health and Human Services has issued guidance on integrating GINA into clinical research, including information on GINA's research exemption, considerations for Institutional Review Boards, and integrating information on GINA into informed consents.

Informed Consent Forms

To comply with GINA, informed consent forms should include information on any risks associated with participation in the research project and a statement describing how the confidentiality of records will be maintained. NHGRI has developed guidance for informed consent forms for participants in genomics research.

GINA in Action

GINA tasks the Equal Employment Opportunity Commission with protecting workers from genetic discrimination in the workplace. According to the EEOC, over 1,000 charges have been filed under GINA as of December 2013. In 2013 the Commission announced the settlement of the first lawsuit it had filed for a GINA violation (EEOC v. Fabricut Inc.), and a second suit was settled in 2014 (EEOC v. Founders Pavilion Inc).

Both cases alleged that the employer illegally included questions about family medical histories in pre-employment medical exams. In the first, the fabrics manufacturer Fabricut agreed to pay $50,000 compensation and provide anti discrimination training to employees after a prospective employee was asked for their family medical history during a post-offer medical exam. In the second suit, a New York nursing and rehabilitation center, Founders Pavilion Inc., was similarly accused of requesting family medical histories during medical exams. Under GINA, it is illegal for companies to ask their employees for genetic information, which includes family medical history.

Where GINA Does Not Apply

GINA does not apply to employers with fewer than 15 employees. GINA's protections in employment do not extend to the U.S. military. Nor does it apply to health insurance through the TRICARE military health system, the Indian Health Service, the Veterans Health Administration, or the Federal Employees Health Benefits Program. Lastly, the law does not cover long term care insurance, life insurance or disability insurance.

Reporting a Violation of GINA

An individual who believes they have been discriminated against at work can file a charge with the Equal Employment Opportunity Commission (EEOC).

Genetic Discrimination and Other Laws

Bill Clinton's Executive Order Prohibiting the Use of Genetic Information in Federal Worker Employment (2000)

On February 8, 2000, Bill Clinton issued Executive Order 13145, prohibiting discrimination in Federal employment based on genetic information. The Executive Order prohibits federal employers from requesting or requiring any genetic information from their employees, or the use of genetic information in any employment decision. (At the time of releasing this executive order, he expressed support for a federal law prohibiting genetic discrimination by private employers or health insurance issuers.)

As of November 21, 2009, GINA affords federal employees the same protections as they had under Bill Clinton's executive order.

The Affordable Care Act

A major provision of The Affordable Care Act of 2010 (ACA) [healthcare.gov] is to establish 'guaranteed issue'; issuers offering insurance in either the group or individual market must provide coverage for all individuals who request it. The law therefore prohibits issuers of health insurance from discriminating against patients with genetic diseases by refusing coverage because of 'pre-existing conditions'. ACA further provides additional protections for patients with genetic diseases by establishing that certain health insurance issuers may only vary premiums based on a few specified factors such as age or geographic area, thereby prohibiting the adjustment of premiums because of medical conditions.

Note: *Under GINA, health insurance issuers are prohibited from using a person's genetic information for underwriting, but GINA provides no such protections for individuals with a "manifest disease"-requiring a provider of health insurance to issue coverage for an individual with a genetic disease.*

The Americans with Disabilities Act

The Americans with Disabilities Act (ADA) prohibits discrimination in employment, public services, accommodations, and communications based on a disability. In 1995, the Equal Employment Opportunity Commission (EEOC) issued an interpretation that discrimination based on genetic information relating to illness, disease, or other disorders is prohibited by the ADA. In a subsequent Senate hearing in

2000, EEOC Commissioner Paul Miller further affirmed that the ADA "can be interpreted to prohibit employment discrimination based on genetic information." However, these EEOC opinions are not legally binding, and whether the ADA protects against genetic discrimination in the workplace has never been tested in court.

The ADA has, however, been used to challenge genetic testing practices by an employer. In 2001, EEOC filed a suit against the Burlington Northern Santa Fe (BNSF) Railroad for secretly testing its employees for a rare genetic condition (hereditary neuropathy with liability to pressure palsies—HNPP) that causes carpal tunnel syndrome as one of its many symptoms. BNSF claimed that the testing was a way of determining whether the high incidence of repetitive-stress injuries among its employees was work-related. Besides testing for HNPP, company-paid doctors also were instructed to screen for several other medical conditions such as diabetes and alcoholism. A medicated settlement was announced by the EEOC and BNSF in 2002.

Policies Pertaining to Federal Employees, U.S. Military, Veterans, and the Indian Health Service

GINA does not apply to individuals who receive their insurance through the Federal Employees Health Benefits, the Veterans Health Administration, the U.S. Military (TRICARE), and the Indian Health Service because Title I of GINA amends laws that do not have jurisdiction over these groups. However, some of these programs have internal policies that prohibit or restrict genetic discrimination.

Federal Employees Health Benefits

The Office of Personnel Management, which administers the FEHB program, requires all participating insurers and plans to accept all enrollees regardless of health status.

Veterans Health Administration and the U.S. Military

For many years, the Department of Defense could deny benefits to a soldier or veteran who developed an illness of a known genetic basis after enlistment. In 1990, the Veterans Health Administration changed its policy and began covering genetic or hereditary conditions that manifest after enrollment, because they could be "service aggravated." In 2008, the U.S. Military followed suit and adopted the same policy for service members under TRICARE coverage.

Indian Health Affairs

The Department of Indian Health Affairs is tasked with providing healthcare to all American Indians and Alaskan Natives under its treaty obligations. However, Indian Health Affairs often experiences shortfalls in funding, meaning that some services are not available in practice.

State Laws

A patchwork of state laws exists to protect Americans from genetic discrimination, although these laws vary widely in the scope, applicability, and amount of protection provided. The earliest state laws focused on particular genetic conditions. For example, North Carolina was the first state to prohibit discrimination based on the presence of the sickle cell trait. In 1991, Wisconsin was the first state to prevent whole-sale discrimination based on genetic tests. At present, 48 states and the District of Columbia have passed laws preventing genetic discrimination in health insurance providers and 35 states and the District of Columbia prevent genetic discrimination in employment. GINA sets a floor of minimum protection against genetic discrimination and does not preempt state laws with stricter protections. At present, 15 states have additional laws restricting the use of genetic information in determining coverage for life insurance, 17 states for disability insurance, and nine states for long-term care insurance.

Part Two

Disorders Resulting from Abnormalities in Specific Genes

Chapter 10

Albinism

Chapter Contents

Section 10.1

Ocular Albinism

This section includes text excerpted from "Ocular
Albinism," Genetics Home Reference (GHR), National
Institutes of Health (NIH), March 7, 2016.

What Is Ocular Albinism?

Ocular albinism is a genetic condition that primarily affects the
eyes. This condition reduces the coloring (pigmentation) of the iris,
which is the colored part of the eye, and the retina, which is the
light-sensitive tissue at the back of the eye. Pigmentation in the eye
is essential for normal vision.

Ocular albinism is characterized by severely impaired sharpness
of vision (visual acuity) and problems with combining vision from
both eyes to perceive depth (stereoscopic vision). Although the vision
loss is permanent, it does not worsen over time. Other eye abnormalities associated with this condition include rapid, involuntary eye
movements (nystagmus); eyes that do not look in the same direction
(strabismus); and increased sensitivity to light (photophobia). Many
affected individuals also have abnormalities involving the optic nerves,
which carry visual information from the eye to the brain.

Unlike some other forms of albinism, ocular albinism does not significantly affect the color of the skin and hair. People with this condition may have a somewhat lighter complexion than other members of
their family, but these differences are usually minor.

The most common form of ocular albinism is known as the Net-
tleship-Falls type or type 1. Other forms of ocular albinism are much
rarer and may be associated with additional signs and symptoms,
such as hearing loss.

How Common Is Ocular Albinism?

The most common form of this disorder, ocular albinism type 1,
affects at least 1 in 60,000 males. The classic signs and symptoms of
this condition are much less common in females.

What Genes Are Related to Ocular Albinism?

Ocular albinism type 1 results from mutations in the *GPR143* gene. This gene provides instructions for making a protein that plays a role in pigmentation of the eyes and skin. It helps control the growth of melanosomes, which are cellular structures that produce and store a pigment called melanin. Melanin is the substance that gives skin, hair, and eyes their color. In the retina, this pigment also plays a role in normal vision.

Most mutations in the *GPR143* gene alter the size or shape of the *GPR143* protein. Many of these genetic changes prevent the protein from reaching melanosomes to control their growth. In other cases, the protein reaches melanosomes normally but mutations disrupt the protein's function. As a result of these changes, melanosomes in skin cells and the retina can grow abnormally large. Researchers are uncertain how these giant melanosomes are related to vision loss and other eye abnormalities in people with ocular albinism.

Rare cases of ocular albinism are not caused by mutations in the *GPR143* gene. In these cases, the genetic cause of the condition is often unknown.

How Do People Inherit Ocular Albinism?

Ocular albinism type 1 is inherited in an X-linked pattern. A condition is considered X-linked if the mutated gene that causes the disorder is located on the X chromosome, one of the two sex chromosomes. In males (who have only one X chromosome), one altered copy of the *GPR143* gene in each cell is sufficient to cause the characteristic features of ocular albinism. Because females have two copies of the X chromosome, women with only one copy of a *GPR143* mutation in each cell usually do not experience vision loss or other significant eye abnormalities. They may have mild changes in retinal pigmentation that can be detected during an eye examination.

Section 10.2

Oculocutaneous Albinism

This section includes text excerpted from "Oculocutaneous
Albinism," Genetics Home Reference (GHR), National
Institutes of Health (NIH), March 7, 2016.

What Is Oculocutaneous Albinism?

Oculocutaneous albinism is a group of conditions that affect coloring
(pigmentation) of the skin, hair, and eyes. Affected individuals typically have very fair skin and white or light-colored hair. Long-term sun
exposure greatly increases the risk of skin damage and skin cancers,
including an aggressive form of skin cancer called melanoma, in people
with this condition. Oculocutaneous albinism also reduces pigmentation
of the colored part of the eye (the iris) and the light-sensitive tissue at
the back of the eye (the retina). People with this condition usually have
vision problems such as reduced sharpness; rapid, involuntary eye movements (nystagmus); and increased sensitivity to light (photophobia).

Researchers have identified multiple types of oculocutaneous albinism,
which are distinguished by their specific skin, hair, and eye color changes
and by their genetic cause. Oculocutaneous albinism type 1 is characterized by white hair, very pale skin, and light-colored irises. Type 2 is
typically less severe than type 1; the skin is usually a creamy white color
and hair may be light yellow, blond, or light brown. Type 3 includes a form
of albinism called rufous oculocutaneous albinism, which usually affects
dark-skinned people. Affected individuals have reddish-brown skin, gin-
ger or red hair, and hazel or brown irises. Type 3 is often associated with
milder vision abnormalities than the other forms of oculocutaneous albinism. Type 4 has signs and symptoms similar to those seen with type 2.

Several additional types of this disorder have been proposed, each
affecting one or a few families.

How Common Is Oculocutaneous Albinism?

Overall, an estimated 1 in 20,000 people worldwide are born with
oculocutaneous albinism. The condition affects people in many ethnic

groups and geographical regions. Types 1 and 2 are the most common forms of this condition; types 3 and 4 are less common. Type 2 occurs more frequently in African Americans, some Native American groups, and people from sub-Saharan Africa. Type 3, specifically rufous oculocutaneous albinism, has been described primarily in people from southern Africa. Studies suggest that type 4 occurs more frequently in the Japanese and Korean populations than in people from other parts of the world.

What Genes Are Related to Oculocutaneous Albinism?

Oculocutaneous albinism can result from mutations in several genes, including *TYR, OCA2, TYRP1,* and *SLC45A2.* Changes in the *TYR* gene cause type 1; mutations in the *OCA2* gene are responsible for type 2; *TYRP1* mutations cause type 3; and changes in the SLC45A2 gene result in type 4. Mutations in additional genes likely underlie the other forms of this disorder. The genes associated with oculocutaneous albinism are involved in producing a pigment called melanin, which is the substance that gives skin, hair, and eyes their color. In the retina, melanin also plays a role in normal vision. Mutations in any of these genes disrupt the ability of cells to make melanin, which reduces pigmentation in the skin, hair, and eyes. A lack of melanin in the retina leads to the vision problems characteristic of oculocutaneous albinism.

Alterations in the *MC1R* gene can change the appearance of people with oculocutaneous albinism type 2. This gene helps regulate melanin production and is responsible for some normal variation in pigmentation. People with genetic changes in both the *OCA2* and *MC1R* genes have many of the usual features of oculocutaneous albinism type 2, including light-colored eyes and vision problems; however, they typically have red hair instead of the usual yellow, blond, or light brown hair seen with this condition.

Some individuals with oculocutaneous albinism do not have mutations in any of the known genes. In these people, the genetic cause of the condition is unknown.

How Do People Inherit Oculocutaneous Albinism?

Oculocutaneous albinism is inherited in an autosomal recessive pattern, which means both copies of a gene in each cell have mutations. Most often, the parents of an individual with an autosomal recessive condition each carry one copy of the mutated gene, but they do not show signs and symptoms of the condition.

Chapter 11

Alpha-1 Antitrypsin Deficiency

What Is Alpha-1 Antitrypsin Deficiency?

Alpha-1 antitrypsin deficiency is an inherited disorder that may cause lung disease and liver disease. The signs and symptoms of the condition and the age at which they appear vary among individuals.

People with alpha-1 antitrypsin deficiency usually develop the first signs and symptoms of lung disease between ages 20 and 50. The earliest symptoms are shortness of breath following mild activity, reduced ability to exercise, and wheezing. Other signs and symptoms can include unintentional weight loss, recurring respiratory infections, fatigue, and rapid heartbeat upon standing. Affected individuals often develop emphysema, which is a lung disease caused by damage to the small air sacs in the lungs (alveoli). Characteristic features of emphysema include difficulty breathing, a hacking cough, and a barrel-shaped chest. Smoking or exposure to tobacco smoke accelerates the appearance of emphysema symptoms and damage to the lungs.

About 10 percent of infants with alpha-1 antitrypsin deficiency develop liver disease, which often causes yellowing of the skin and

This chapter includes text excerpted from "Alpha-1 Antitrypsin Deficiency," Genetics Home Reference (GHR), National Institutes of Health (NIH), March 7, 2016.

whites of the eyes (jaundice). Approximately 15 percent of adults with alpha-1 antitrypsin deficiency develop liver damage (cirrhosis) due to the formation of scar tissue in the liver. Signs of cirrhosis include a swollen abdomen, swollen feet or legs, and jaundice. Individuals with alpha-1 antitrypsin deficiency are also at risk of developing a type of liver cancer called hepatocellular carcinoma.

In rare cases, people with alpha-1 antitrypsin deficiency develop a skin condition called panniculitis, which is characterized by hardened skin with painful lumps or patches. Panniculitis varies in severity and can occur at any age.

How Common Is Alpha-1 Antitrypsin Deficiency?

Alpha-1 antitrypsin deficiency occurs worldwide, but its prevalence varies by population. This disorder affects about 1 in 1,500 to 3,500 individuals with European ancestry. It is uncommon in people of Asian descent. Many individuals with alpha-1 antitrypsin deficiency are likely undiagnosed, particularly people with a lung condition called chronic obstructive pulmonary disease (COPD). COPD can be caused by alpha-1 antitrypsin deficiency; however, the alpha-1 antitrypsin deficiency is often never diagnosed. Some people with alpha-1 antitrypsin deficiency are misdiagnosed with asthma.

What Genes Are Related to Alpha-1 Antitrypsin Deficiency?

Mutations in the *SERPINA1* gene cause alpha-1 antitrypsin deficiency. This gene provides instructions for making a protein called alpha-1 antitrypsin, which protects the body from a powerful enzyme called neutrophil elastase. Neutrophil elastase is released from white blood cells to fight infection, but it can attack normal tissues (especially the lungs) if not tightly controlled by alpha-1 antitrypsin.

Mutations in the *SERPINA1* gene can lead to a shortage (deficiency) of alpha-1 antitrypsin or an abnormal form of the protein that cannot control neutrophil elastase. Without enough functional alpha-1 antitrypsin, neutrophil elastase destroys alveoli and causes lung disease. Abnormal alpha-1 antitrypsin can also accumulate in the liver and damage this organ.

Environmental factors, such as exposure to tobacco smoke, chemicals, and dust, likely impact the severity of alpha-1 antitrypsin deficiency.

How Do People Inherit Alpha-1 Antitrypsin Deficiency?

This condition is inherited in an autosomal codominant pattern. Codominance means that two different versions of the gene may be active (expressed), and both versions contribute to the genetic trait.

The most common version (allele) of the *SERPINA1* gene, called M, produces normal levels of alpha-1 antitrypsin. Most people in the general population have two copies of the M allele (MM) in each cell. Other versions of the *SERPINA1* gene lead to reduced levels of alpha-1 antitrypsin. For example, the S allele produces moderately low levels of this protein, and the Z allele produces very little alpha-1 antitrypsin. Individuals with two copies of the Z allele (ZZ) in each cell are likely to have alpha-1 antitrypsin deficiency. Those with the SZ combination have an increased risk of developing lung diseases (such as emphysema), particularly if they smoke.

Worldwide, it is estimated that 161 million people have one copy of the S or Z allele and one copy of the M allele in each cell (MS or MZ). Individuals with an MS (or SS) combination usually produce enough alpha-1 antitrypsin to protect the lungs. People with MZ alleles, however, have a slightly increased risk of impaired lung or liver function.

Chapter 12

Anhidrotic Ectodermal Dysplasia with Immune Deficiency

What Is Anhidrotic Ectodermal Dysplasia with Immune Deficiency?

Anhidrotic ectodermal dysplasia with immune deficiency (EDA-ID) is a form of ectodermal dysplasia, which is a group of conditions characterized by abnormal development of ectodermal tissues including the skin, hair, teeth, and sweat glands. In addition, immune system function is reduced in people with EDA-ID. The signs and symptoms of EDA-ID are evident soon after birth.

Skin abnormalities in people with EDA-ID include areas that are dry, wrinkled, or darker in color than the surrounding skin. Affected individuals tend to have sparse scalp and body hair (hypotrichosis). EDA-ID is also characterized by missing teeth (hypodontia) or teeth that are small and pointed. Most people with EDA-ID have a reduced ability to sweat (hypohidrosis) because they have fewer sweat glands than normal or their sweat glands do not function properly. An inability

This chapter includes text excerpted from "Anhidrotic Ectodermal Dysplasia with Immune Deficiency," Genetics Home Reference (GHR), National Institutes of Health (NIH), March 7, 2016.

to sweat (anhidrosis) can lead to a dangerously high body temperature (hyperthermia), particularly in hot weather.

The immune deficiency in EDA-ID varies among people with this condition. People with EDA-ID often produce abnormally low levels of proteins called antibodies or immunoglobulins. Antibodies help protect the body against infection by attaching to specific foreign particles and germs, marking them for destruction. A reduction in antibodies makes it difficult for people with this disorder to fight off infections. In EDA-ID, immune system cells called T cells and B cells have a decreased ability to recognize and respond to foreign invaders (such as bacteria, viruses, and yeast) that have sugar molecules attached to their surface (glycan antigens). Other key aspects of the immune system may also be impaired, leading to recurrent infections.

People with EDA-ID commonly get infections in the lungs (pneumonia), ears (otitis media), sinuses (sinusitis), lymph nodes (lymphadenitis), skin, bones, and GI tract. Approximately one quarter of individuals with EDA-ID have disorders involving abnormal inflammation, such as inflammatory bowel disease or rheumatoid arthritis.

The life expectancy of affected individuals depends of the severity of the immune deficiency; most people with this condition do not live past childhood.

There are two forms of this condition that have similar signs and symptoms and are distinguished by the modes of inheritance: X-linked recessive or autosomal dominant.

How Common Is Anhidrotic Ectodermal Dysplasia with Immune Deficiency?

The prevalence of the X-linked recessive type of EDA-ID is estimated to be 1 in 250,000 individuals. Only a few cases of the autosomal dominant form have been described in the scientific literature.

What Genes Are Related to Anhidrotic Ectodermal Dysplasia with Immune Deficiency?

Mutations in the *IKBKG* gene cause X-linked recessive EDA-ID, and mutations in the *NFKBIA* gene cause autosomal dominant EDA-ID. The proteins produced from these two genes regulate nuclear factor-kappa-B. Nuclear factor-kappa-B is a group of related proteins (a protein complex) that binds to DNA and controls the activity of other genes, including genes that direct the body's immune responses and inflammatory reactions. It also protects cells from certain signals that would otherwise cause them to self-destruct (undergo apoptosis).

The *IKBKG* and *NFKBIA* gene mutations responsible for EDA-ID result in the production of proteins with impaired function, which reduces activation of nuclear factor-kappa-B. These changes disrupt certain signaling pathways within immune cells, resulting in immune deficiency. It is unclear how gene mutations alter the development of the skin, teeth, sweat glands, and other tissues, although it is likely caused by abnormal nuclear factor-kappa-B signaling in other types of cells.

How Do People Inherit Anhidrotic Ectodermal Dysplasia with Immune Deficiency?

When EDA-ID is caused by mutations in the *IKBKG* gene, it is inherited in an X-linked recessive pattern. The *IKBKG* gene is located on the X chromosome, which is one of the two sex chromosomes. In males (who have only one X chromosome), one altered copy of the gene in each cell is sufficient to cause the condition. In females (who have two X chromosomes), a mutation would have to occur in both copies of the gene to cause the disorder. Because it is unlikely that females will have two altered copies of the *IKBKG* gene, males are affected by X-linked recessive disorders much more frequently than females. A characteristic of X-linked inheritance is that fathers cannot pass X-linked traits to their sons.

When EDA-ID is caused by mutations in the *NFKBIA* gene, the condition is inherited in an autosomal dominant pattern, which means one copy of the altered gene in each cell is sufficient to cause the disorder. Most cases result from new mutations in the gene and occur in people with no history of the disorder in their family.

Chapter 13

Blood Clotting Deficiency Disorders

Chapter Contents

Section 13.1

Factor V Leiden Thrombophilia

This section contains text excerpted from the following sources:
Text beginning with the heading "What Is Factor V Leiden
Thrombophilia?" is excerpted from "Factor V Leiden Thrombophilia,"
Genetics Home Reference (GHR), National Institutes of
Health (NIH), March 7, 2016; Text under the heading "How
Might Factor V Leiden Gene Mutation Affect a Person with Type
1 Diabetes?" is excerpted from "Factor V Leiden Thrombophilia,"
National Center for Advancing Translational Sciences (NCATS),
National Institutes of Health (NIH), August 28, 2015.

What Is Factor V Leiden Thrombophilia?

Factor V Leiden thrombophilia is an inherited disorder of blood clotting. Factor V Leiden is the name of a specific gene mutation that results in thrombophilia, which is an increased tendency to form abnormal blood clots that can block blood vessels.

People with factor V Leiden thrombophilia have a higher than average risk of developing a type of blood clot called a deep venous thrombosis (DVT). DVTs occur most often in the legs, although they can also occur in other parts of the body, including the brain, eyes, liver, and kidneys. Factor V Leiden thrombophilia also increases the risk that clots will break away from their original site and travel through the bloodstream. These clots can lodge in the lungs, where they are known as pulmonary emboli. Although factor V Leiden thrombophilia increases the risk of blood clots, only about 10 percent of individuals with the factor V Leiden mutation ever develop abnormal clots.

The factor V Leiden mutation is associated with a slightly increased risk of pregnancy loss (miscarriage). Women with this mutation are two to three times more likely to have multiple (recurrent) miscarriages or a pregnancy loss during the second or third trimester. Some research suggests that the factor V Leiden mutation may also increase the risk of other complications during pregnancy, including pregnancy-induced high blood pressure (preeclampsia), slow fetal growth, and early separation of the placenta from the uterine wall (placental abruption). However, the association between the factor V Leiden mutation and these complications has not been confirmed. Most women with factor V Leiden thrombophilia have normal pregnancies.

How Common Is Factor V Leiden Thrombophilia?

Factor V Leiden is the most common inherited form of thrombophilia. Between 3 and 8 percent of people with European ancestry carry one copy of the factor V Leiden mutation in each cell, and about 1 in 5,000 people have two copies of the mutation. The mutation is less common in other populations.

What Genes Are Related to Factor V Leiden Thrombophilia?

A particular mutation in the *F5* gene causes factor V Leiden thrombophilia. The *F5* gene provides instructions for making a protein called coagulation factor V. This protein plays a critical role in the coagulation system, which is a series of chemical reactions that forms blood clots in response to injury.

The coagulation system is controlled by several proteins, including a protein called activated protein C (APC). APC normally inactivates coagulation factor V, which slows down the clotting process and prevents clots from growing too large. However, in people with factor V Leiden thrombophilia, coagulation factor V cannot be inactivated normally by APC. As a result, the clotting process remains active longer than usual, increasing the chance of developing abnormal blood clots.

Other factors also increase the risk of developing blood clots in people with factor V Leiden thrombophilia. These factors include increasing age, obesity, injury, surgery, smoking, pregnancy, and the use of oral contraceptives (birth control pills) or hormone replacement therapy. The risk of abnormal clots is also much higher in people who have a combination of the factor V Leiden mutation and another mutation in the *F5* gene. Additionally, the risk is increased in people who have the factor V Leiden mutation together with a mutation in another gene involved in the coagulation system.

How Do People Inherit Factor V Leiden Thrombophilia?

The chance of developing an abnormal blood clot depends on whether a person has one or two copies of the factor V Leiden mutation in each cell. People who inherit two copies of the mutation, one from each parent, have a higher risk of developing a clot than people who inherit one copy of the mutation. Considering that about 1 in 1,000 people per year in the general population will develop an abnormal blood clot, the presence of one copy of the factor V Leiden mutation increases that risk to 3 to 8 in 1,000, and having two copies of the mutation may raise the risk to as high as 80 in 1,000.

How Are Factor V Leiden and Elevated Levels of Activated Protein C Associated?

Elevated protein C levels are not usually associated with medical problems or considered clinically significant.

Factor V is a coagulation factor, a protein essential for proper blood clot formation. When an injury occurs and bleeding starts, a process called hemostasis begins to form a plug at the injury site to help stop the bleeding. Blood cells called platelets adhere to and aggregate at the injury site, and a coagulation cascade begins to activate coagulation factors in sequence. Eventually, a blood clot forms. Once the area has healed, the blood clot dissolves.

During hemostasis, factor V is normally inactivated by a protein called activated protein C (APC) to prevent the blood clot from growing too large. But a factor V Leiden genetic mutation can lead to an altered factor V protein that resists inactivation by APC. The result is that clotting remains more active than usual, increasing risks of a blood clot forming in the deep veins of legs (DVT) or breaking off and blocking a vein (venous thromboembolism or VTE).

Testing for factor V Leiden can be done in one of two ways: using a second generation Activate Protein C (APC) resistance assay (and confirming positive results with genetic testing) or using genetic testing. The normal reference value for the APC resistance (APCR) ratio is greater than 2. People with one factor V Leiden gene mutation typically have APCR ratios in the range of 1.5 -1.8. People with two factor V Leiden gene mutations typically have APCR ratios of less than 1.5.

How Might Factor V Leiden Be Treated?

The management of individuals with factor V Leiden depends on the clinical circumstances. People with factor V Leiden who have had a deep venous thrombosis (DVT) or pulmonary embolism (PE) are usually treated with blood thinners, or anticoagulants. Anticoagulants such as heparin and warfarin are given for varying amounts of time depending on the person's situation. It is not usually recommended that people with factor V Leiden be treated lifelong with anticoagulants if they have had only one DVT or PE, unless there are additional risk factors present.

Having had a DVT or PE in the past increases a person's risk for developing another one in the future, but having factor V Leiden does not seem to add to the risk of having a second clot. In general, individuals who have factor V Leiden but have never had a blood clot are not routinely treated with an anticoagulant. Rather, these individuals are counseled about reducing or eliminating other factors that may add to one's risk of developing a clot in the future. In addition, these individuals may require temporary treatment with an anticoagulant during periods of particularly high risk, such as major surgery.

Factor V Leiden increases the risk of developing a DVT during pregnancy by about seven-fold. Women with factor V Leiden who are planning pregnancy should discuss this with their obstetrician and/ or hematologist. Most women with factor V Leiden have normal pregnancies and only require close follow-up during pregnancy. For those with a history of DVT or PE, treatment with an anticoagulant during a subsequent pregnancy can prevent recurrent problems.

Section 13.2

Hemophilia

This section contains text excerpted from the following sources: Text beginning with the heading "What Is Hemophilia?" is excerpted from "Hemophilia," Genetics Home Reference (GHR), National Institutes of Health (NIH), March 7, 2016; Text under the heading "Causes" is excerpted from "Hemophilia," Centers for Disease Prevention and Control (CDC), August 26, 2014.

What Is Hemophilia?

Hemophilia is a bleeding disorder that slows the blood clotting process. People with this condition experience prolonged bleeding or oozing following an injury, surgery, or having a tooth pulled. In severe cases of hemophilia, continuous bleeding occurs after minor trauma or even in the absence of injury (spontaneous bleeding).

Serious complications can result from bleeding into the joints, muscles, brain, or other internal organs. Milder forms of hemophilia do not necessarily involve spontaneous bleeding, and the condition may not become apparent until abnormal bleeding occurs following surgery or a serious injury.

The major types of this condition are hemophilia A (also known as classic hemophilia or factor VIII deficiency) and hemophilia B (also known as Christmas disease or factor IX deficiency). Although the two types have very similar signs and symptoms, they are caused by mutations in different genes. People with an unusual form of hemophilia B, known as hemophilia B Leyden, experience episodes of excessive bleeding in childhood but have few bleeding problems after puberty.

How Common Is Hemophilia?

The two major forms of hemophilia occur much more commonly in males than in females. Hemophilia A is the most common type of the condition; 1 in 4,000 to 1 in 5,000 males worldwide are born with this disorder. Hemophilia B occurs in approximately 1 in 20,000 newborn males worldwide.

What Genes Are Related to Hemophilia?

Changes in the *F8* gene are responsible for hemophilia A, while mutations in the *F9* gene cause hemophilia B. The *F8* gene provides instructions for making a protein called coagulation factor VIII. A related protein, coagulation factor IX, is produced from the *F9* gene. Coagulation factors are proteins that work together in the blood clotting process. After an injury, blood clots protect the body by sealing off damaged blood vessels and preventing excessive blood loss.

Mutations in the *F8* or *F9* gene lead to the production of an abnormal version of coagulation factor VIII or coagulation factor IX, or reduce the amount of one of these proteins. The altered or missing protein cannot participate effectively in the blood clotting process. As a result, blood clots cannot form properly in response to injury. These problems with blood clotting lead to continuous bleeding that can be difficult to control. The mutations that cause severe hemophilia almost completely eliminate the activity of coagulation factor VIII or coagulation factor IX. The mutations responsible for mild and moderate hemophilia reduce but do not eliminate the activity of one of these proteins.

Another form of the disorder, known as acquired hemophilia, is not caused by inherited gene mutations. This rare condition is characterized by abnormal bleeding into the skin, muscles, or other soft tissues, usually beginning in adulthood. Acquired hemophilia results when the body makes specialized proteins called autoantibodies that attack and disable coagulation factor VIII. The production of autoantibodies is sometimes associated with pregnancy, immune system disorders, cancer, or allergic reactions to certain drugs. In about half of cases, the cause of acquired hemophilia is unknown.

How Do People Inherit Hemophilia?

Hemophilia A and hemophilia B are inherited in an X-linked recessive pattern. The genes associated with these conditions are located on the X chromosome, which is one of the two sex chromosomes. In males (who have only one X chromosome), one altered copy of the gene in each cell is sufficient to cause the condition. In females (who have two X chromosomes), a mutation would have to occur in both copies of the gene to cause the disorder. Because it is unlikely that females will have two altered copies of this gene, it is very rare for females to have hemophilia. A characteristic of X-linked inheritance is that fathers cannot pass X-linked traits to their sons.

In X-linked recessive inheritance, a female with one altered copy of the gene in each cell is called a carrier. Carrier females have about half the usual amount of coagulation factor VIII or coagulation factor IX, which is generally enough for normal blood clotting. However, about 10 percent of carrier females have less than half the normal amount of one of these coagulation factors; these individuals are at risk for abnormal bleeding, particularly after an injury, surgery, or tooth extraction.

Causes

Hemophilia is caused by a mutation or change, in one of the genes, that provides instructions for making the clotting factor proteins needed to form a blood clot. This change or mutation can prevent the clotting protein from working properly or to be missing altogether. These genes are located on the X chromosome. Males have one X and one Y chromosome (XY) and females have two X chromosomes (XX). Males inherit the X chromosome from their mothers and the Y chromosome from their fathers. Females inherit one X chromosome from each parent.

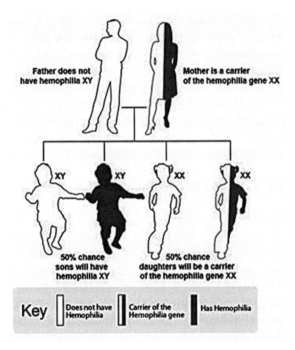

Figure 13.1. *Hemophilia-genes*

The X chromosome contains many genes that are not present on the Y chromosome. This means that males only have one copy of most of the genes on the X chromosome, whereas females have 2 copies. Thus, males can have a disease like hemophilia if they inherit an affected X chromosome that has a mutation in either the factor VIII or factor IX gene. Females can also have hemophilia, but this is much rarer. In such cases both X chromosomes are affected or one is affected and the other is missing or inactive. In these females, bleeding symptoms may be similar to males with hemophilia.

A female with one affected X chromosome is a "carrier" of hemophilia. Sometimes a female who is a carrier can have symptoms of hemophilia. In addition, she can pass the affected X chromosome with the clotting factor gene mutation on to her children.

Even though hemophilia runs in families, some families have no prior history of family members with hemophilia. Sometimes, there are carrier females in the family, but no affected boys, just by chance. However, about one-third of the time, the baby with hemophilia is the first one in the family to be affected with a mutation in the gene for the clotting factor.

Hemophilia can result in:

- Bleeding within joints that can lead to chronic joint disease and pain
- Bleeding in the head and sometimes in the brain which can cause long term problems, such as seizures and paralysis
- Death can occur if the bleeding cannot be stopped or if it occurs in a vital organ such as the brain.

Types

There are several different types of hemophilia. The following two are the most common:

1. **Hemophilia A (Classic Hemophilia).** This type is caused by a lack or decrease of clotting factor VIII.

2. **Hemophilia B (Christmas Disease).** This type is caused by a lack or decrease of clotting factor IX.

Signs and Symptoms

Common signs of hemophilia include:

- Bleeding into the joints. This can cause swelling and pain or tightness in the joints; it often affects the knees, elbows, and ankles.
- Bleeding into the skin (which is bruising) or muscle and soft tissue causing a build-up of blood in the area (called a hematoma).
- Bleeding of the mouth and gums, and bleeding that is hard to stop after losing a tooth.
- Bleeding after circumcision (surgery performed on male babies to remove the hood of skin, called the foreskin, covering the head of the penis).
- Bleeding after having shots, such as vaccinations.
- Bleeding in the head of an infant after a difficult delivery.
- Blood in the urine or stool.
- Frequent and hard-to-stop nosebleeds.

Diagnosis

Many people who have or have had family members with hemophilia will ask that their baby boys get tested soon after birth.

About one-third of babies who are diagnosed with hemophilia have a new mutation not present in other family members. In these cases, a doctor might check for hemophilia if a newborn is showing certain signs of hemophilia.

To make a diagnosis, doctors would perform certain blood tests to show if the blood is clotting properly. If it does not, then they would do clotting factor tests, also called factor assays, to diagnose the cause of the bleeding disorder. These blood tests would show the type of hemophilia and the severity.

Treatment

The best way to treat hemophilia is to replace the missing blood clotting factor so that the blood can clot properly. This is done by infusing (administering through a vein) commercially prepared factor concentrates. People with hemophilia can learn how to perform these infusions themselves so that they can stop bleeding episodes and, by performing the infusions on a regular basis, can even prevent most bleeding episodes.

Good quality medical care from doctors and nurses who know a lot about the disorder can help prevent some serious problems. Often the best choice for care is to visit a comprehensive Hemophilia Treatment Center (HTC). An HTC not only provides care to address all issues related to the disorder, but also provides health education that helps people with hemophilia stay healthy.

Inhibitors

About 15-20 percent of people with hemophilia develop an antibody (called an inhibitor) that stops the clotting factors from being able to clot the blood and stop bleeding. Treatment of bleeding episodes becomes extremely difficult, and the cost of care for a person with an inhibitor can skyrocket because more clotting factor or a different type of clotting factor is needed. People with inhibitors often experience more joint disease and other problems from bleeding that result in a reduced quality of life.

Section 13.3

Von Willebrand Disease

This section contains text excerpted from the following sources:
Text beginning with the heading "What Is Von Willebrand
Disease?" is excerpted from "Von Willebrand Disease," Genetics
Home Reference (GHR), National Institutes of Health (NIH),
March 7, 2016; Text under the heading "Types of VWD" is excerpted
from "Von Willebrand Disease (VWD)," Centers for Disease
Prevention and Control (CDC), March 2, 2016.

What Is Von Willebrand Disease?

Von Willebrand disease is a bleeding disorder that slows the blood
clotting process, causing prolonged bleeding after an injury. People
with this condition often experience easy bruising, long-lasting nosebleeds, and excessive bleeding or oozing following an injury, surgery,
or dental work. Mild forms of von Willebrand disease may become
apparent only when abnormal bleeding occurs following surgery or a
serious injury.

Women with this condition typically have heavy or prolonged bleeding during menstruation (menorrhagia), and some may also experience reproductive tract bleeding during pregnancy and childbirth. In
severe cases of von Willebrand disease, heavy bleeding occurs after
minor trauma or even in the absence of injury (spontaneous bleeding).
Symptoms of von Willebrand disease may change over time. Increased
age, pregnancy, exercise, and stress may cause bleeding symptoms to
become less frequent.

How Common Is Von Willebrand Disease?

Von Willebrand disease is estimated to affect 1 in 100 to 10,000
individuals. Because people with mild signs and symptoms may not
come to medical attention, it is thought that this condition is underdiagnosed. Most researchers agree that von Willebrand disease is the
most common genetic bleeding disorder.

What Genes Are Related to Von Willebrand Disease?

Mutations in the *VWF* gene cause von Willebrand disease. The *VWF* gene provides instructions for making a blood clotting protein called von Willebrand factor, which is essential for the formation of blood clots. After an injury, clots protect the body by sealing off damaged blood vessels and preventing further blood loss. Von Willebrand factor acts as a glue to hold blood clots together and prevents the breakdown of other blood clotting proteins. If von Willebrand factor does not function normally or too little of the protein is available, blood clots cannot form properly. Abnormally slow blood clotting causes the prolonged bleeding episodes seen in von Willebrand disease.

The three types of von Willebrand disease are based upon the amount of von Willebrand factor that is produced. Mutations in the *VWF* gene that reduce the amount of von Willebrand factor cause type 1 von Willebrand disease. People with type 1 have varying amounts of von Willebrand factor in their bloodstream. Some people with a mild case of type 1 never experience a prolonged bleeding episode. Mutations that disrupt the function of von Willebrand factor cause the four subtypes of type 2 von Willebrand disease. People with type 2 von Willebrand disease have bleeding episodes of varying severity depending on the extent of von Willebrand factor dysfunction, but the bleeding episodes are typically similar to those seen in type 1. Mutations that result in an abnormally short, nonfunctional von Willebrand factor generally cause type 3 von Willebrand disease. Because there is no functional protein, people with type 3 von Willebrand disease usually have severe bleeding episodes.

How Do People Inherit Von Willebrand Disease?

Von Willebrand disease can have different inheritance patterns. Most cases of type 1 and type 2 von Willebrand disease are inherited in an autosomal dominant pattern, which means one copy of the altered gene in each cell is sufficient to cause the disorder. Type 3, some cases of type 2, and a small number of type 1 cases of von Willebrand disease are inherited in an autosomal recessive pattern, which means both copies of the gene in each cell have mutations. Most often, the parents of an individual with an autosomal recessive condition each carry one copy of the mutated gene, but they do not show signs and symptoms of the condition.

Types of Von Willebrand Disease

Type 1

This is the most common and mildest form of VWD, in which a person has lower than normal levels of VWF. A person with Type 1 VWD also might have low levels of factor VIII, another type of blood-clotting protein. This should not be confused with hemophilia, in which there are low levels or a complete lack of factor VIII but normal levels of VWF.

Type 2

With this type of VWD, although the body makes normal amounts of the VWF, the factor does not work the way it should. Type 2 is further broken down into four subtypes; 2A, 2B, 2M, and 2N, depending on the specific problem with the person's VWF. Because the treatment is different for each type, it is important that a person know which subtype he or she has.

Type 3

This is the most severe form of VWD, in which a person has very little or no VWF and low levels of factor VIII.

Causes

Most people who have VWD are born with it. It almost always is inherited, or passed down, from a parent to a child. VWD can be passed down from either the mother or the father, or both, to the child.

While rare, it is possible for a person to get VWD without a family history of the disease. This happens when a "spontaneous mutation" occurs. That means there has been a change in the person's gene. Whether the child received the affected gene from a parent or as a result of a mutation, once the child has it, the child can later pass it along to his or her children. Rarely, a person who is not born with VWD can acquire it or have it first occur later in life. This can happen when a person's own immune system destroys his or her VWF, often as a result of use of a medication or as a result of another disease. If VWD is acquired, meaning it was not inherited from a parent, it cannot be passed along to any children.

Signs and Symptoms

The major signs of VWD are:

Frequent or Hard-to-Stop Nosebleeds. People with VWD might have nosebleeds that:

- Start without injury (spontaneous)

- Occur often, usually five times or more in a year

- Last more than 10 minutes

- Need packing or cautery to stop the bleeding

Easy Bruising. People with VWD might experience easy bruising that:

- Occurs with very little or no trauma or injury

- Occurs often (one to four times per month)

- Is larger than the size of a quarter

- Is not flat and has a raised lump

Heavy Menstrual Bleeding. Women with VWD might have heavy menstrual periods during which:

- Clots larger than the size of a quarter are passed

- More than one pad is soaked through every 2 hours

- A diagnosis of anemia (not having enough red blood cells) is made as a result of bleeding from heavy periods

Longer than Normal Bleeding After Injury, Surgery, Childbirth, or Dental Work. People with VWD might have longer than normal bleeding after injury, surgery, or childbirth, for example:

- After a cut to the skin, the bleeding lasts more than 5 minutes

- Heavy or longer bleeding occurs after surgery. Bleeding sometimes stops, but starts up again hours or days later.

- Heavy bleeding occurs during or after childbirth

People with VWD might have longer than normal bleeding during or after dental work, for example:

- Heavy bleeding occurs during or after dental surgery

- The surgery site oozes blood longer than 3 hours after the surgery

- The surgery site needs packing or cautery to stop the bleeding

The amount of bleeding depends on the type and severity of VWD. Other common bleeding events include:

- Blood in the stool (feces) from bleeding into the stomach or intestines

- Blood in the urine from bleeding into the kidneys or bladder

- Bleeding into joints or internal organs in severe cases (Type 3)

Diagnosis

To find out if a person has VWD, the doctor will ask questions about personal and family histories of bleeding. The doctor also will check for unusual bruising or other signs of recent bleeding and order some blood tests that will measure how the blood clots. The tests will provide information about the amount of clotting proteins present in the blood and if the clotting proteins are working properly. Because certain medications can cause bleeding, even among people without a bleeding disorder, the doctor will ask about recent or routine medications taken that could cause bleeding or make bleeding symptoms worse.

Treatments

The type of treatment prescribed for VWD depends on the type and severity of the disease. For minor bleeds, treatment might not be needed.

The most commonly used types of treatment are:

- **Desmopressin Acetate Injection:** This medicine (DDAVP®) is injected into a vein to treat people with milder forms of VWD (mainly type 1). It works by making the body release more VWF into the blood. It helps increase the level of factor VIII in the blood as well.

- **Desmopressin Acetate Nasal Spray:** This high-strength nasal spray (Stimate®) is used to treat people with milder forms of VWD. It works by boosting the levels of VWF and factor VIII in the blood.

- **Factor Replacement Therapy:** The medicines used in this treatment are rich in VWF and factor VIII (for example, Humate P®, Alphanate®, or Koate DVI®) and are used to treat people with more severe forms of VWD or people with milder forms of

VWD who do not respond well to the nasal spray. These medicines are injected into a vein in the arm to replace the missing factor in the blood.

- **Antifibrinolytic Drugs:** These drugs (for example, Amicar®, Lysteda®) are either injected or taken orally to help slow or prevent the breakdown of blood clots.

- **Birth Control Pills:** Birth control pills can increase the levels of VWF and factor VIII in the blood and reduce menstrual blood loss. A doctor can prescribe these pills for women who have heavy menstrual bleeding.

Chapter 14

Blood Disorders (Hemoglobinopathies)

Chapter Contents

105

Section 14.1

Fanconi Anemia

This section includes text excerpted from "Fanconi
Anemia," Genetics Home Reference (GHR), National
Institutes of Health (NIH), March 7, 2016.

What Is Fanconi Anemia?

Fanconi anemia is a condition that affects many parts of the body. People with this condition may have bone marrow failure, physical abnormalities, organ defects, and an increased risk of certain cancers.

The major function of bone marrow is to produce new blood cells. These include red blood cells, which carry oxygen to the body's tissues; white blood cells, which fight infections; and platelets, which are necessary for normal blood clotting. Approximately 90 percent of people with Fanconi anemia have impaired bone marrow function that leads to a decrease in the production of all blood cells (aplastic anemia). Affected individuals experience extreme tiredness (fatigue) due to low numbers of red blood cells (anemia), frequent infections due to low numbers of white blood cells (neutropenia), and clotting problems due to low numbers of platelets (thrombocytopenia). People with Fanconi anemia may also develop myelodysplastic syndrome, a condition in which immature blood cells fail to develop normally.

More than half of people with Fanconi anemia have physical abnormalities. These abnormalities can involve irregular skin coloring such as unusually light-colored skin (hypopigmentation) or café-au-lait spots, which are flat patches on the skin that are darker than the surrounding area. Other possible symptoms of Fanconi anemia include malformed thumbs or forearms and other skeletal problems including short stature; malformed or absent kidneys and other defects of the urinary tract; gastrointestinal abnormalities; heart defects; eye abnormalities such as small or abnormally shaped eyes; and malformed ears and hearing loss. People with this condition may have abnormal genitalia or malformations of the reproductive system. As a result, most affected males and about half of affected females cannot have biological children (are infertile). Additional signs and symptoms can include abnormalities of the brain and spinal cord (central nervous system), including increased fluid in the center of the brain (hydrocephalus) or an unusually small head size (microcephaly).

Individuals with Fanconi anemia have an increased risk of developing a cancer of blood-forming cells in the bone marrow called acute myeloid leukemia (AML) or tumors of the head, neck, skin, gastrointestinal system, or genital tract. The likelihood of developing one of these cancers in people with Fanconi anemia is between 10 and 30 percent.

How Common Is Fanconi Anemia?

Fanconi anemia occurs in 1 in 160,000 individuals worldwide. This condition is more common among people of Ashkenazi Jewish descent, the Roma population of Spain, and black South Africans.

What Genes Are Related to Fanconi Anemia?

Mutations in at least 15 genes can cause Fanconi anemia. Proteins produced from these genes are involved in a cell process known as the FA pathway. The FA pathway is turned on (activated) when the process of making new copies of DNA, called DNA replication, is blocked due to DNA damage. The FA pathway sends certain proteins to the area of damage, which trigger DNA repair so DNA replication can continue.

The FA pathway is particularly responsive to a certain type of DNA damage known as interstrand cross-links (ICLs). ICLs occur when two DNA building blocks (nucleotides) on opposite strands of DNA are abnormally attached or linked together, which stops the process of DNA replication. ICLs can be caused by a buildup of toxic substances produced in the body or by treatment with certain cancer therapy drugs.

Eight proteins associated with Fanconi anemia group together to form a complex known as the FA core complex. The FA core complex activates two proteins, called FANCD and FANCI. The activation of these two proteins brings DNA repair proteins to the area of the ICL so the cross-link can be removed and DNA replication can continue.

Eighty to 90 percent of cases of Fanconi anemia are due to mutations in one of three genes, *FANCA, FANCC,* and *FANCG.* These genes provide instructions for producing components of the FA core complex. Mutations in any of the many genes associated with the FA core complex will cause the complex to be nonfunctional and disrupt the entire FA pathway. As a result, DNA damage is not repaired efficiently and

ICLs build up over time. The ICLs stall DNA replication, ultimately resulting in either abnormal cell death due to an inability make new DNA molecules or uncontrolled cell growth due to a lack of DNA repair processes. Cells that divide quickly, such as bone marrow cells and cells of the developing fetus, are particularly affected. The death of these cells results in the decrease in blood cells and the physical abnormalities characteristic of Fanconi anemia. When the buildup of errors in DNA leads to uncontrolled cell growth, affected individuals can develop acute myeloid leukemia or other cancers.

How Do People Inherit Fanconi Anemia?

Fanconi anemia is most often inherited in an autosomal recessive pattern, which means both copies of the gene in each cell have mutations. The parents of an individual with an autosomal recessive condition each carry one copy of the mutated gene, but they typically do not show signs and symptoms of the condition.

Very rarely, this condition is inherited in an X-linked recessive pattern. The gene associated with X-linked recessive Fanconi anemia is located on the X chromosome, which is one of the two sex chromosomes. In males (who have only one X chromosome), one altered copy of the gene in each cell is sufficient to cause the condition. In females (who have two X chromosomes), a mutation would have to occur in both copies of the gene to cause the disorder. Because it is unlikely that females will have two altered copies of this gene, males are affected by X-linked recessive disorders much more frequently than females. A characteristic of X-linked inheritance is that fathers cannot pass X-linked traits to their sons.

Section 14.2

Hemochromatosis

This section contains text excerpted from the following
sources: Text beginning with the heading "What Is
Hereditary Hemochromatosis?" is excerpted from "Hereditary
Hemochromatosis," Genetics Home Reference (GHR), National
Institutes of Health (NIH), March 7, 2016; Text under the heading
"Signs and Symptoms" is excerpted from "Hemochromatosis
(Iron Storage Disease)," Centers for Disease Control and
Prevention (CDC), June 19, 2015; Text under the heading "What
Are the Complications of Hemochromatosis?" is excerpted from
"Hemochromatosis," National Institute of Diabetes and
Digestive and Kidney Diseases (NIDDK), March 2014.

What Is Hereditary Hemochromatosis?

Hereditary hemochromatosis is a disorder that causes the body to
absorb too much iron from the diet. The excess iron is stored in the
body's tissues and organs, particularly the skin, heart, liver, pancreas,
and joints. Because humans cannot increase the excretion of iron,
excess iron can overload and eventually damage tissues and organs.
For this reason, hereditary hemochromatosis is also called an iron
overload disorder.

Early symptoms of hereditary hemochromatosis are nonspecific
and may include fatigue, joint pain, abdominal pain, and loss of sex
drive. Later signs and symptoms can include arthritis, liver disease,
diabetes, heart abnormalities, and skin discoloration. The appearance
and progression of symptoms can be affected by environmental and
lifestyle factors such as the amount of iron in the diet, alcohol use,
and infections.

Hereditary hemochromatosis is classified by type depending on
the age of onset and other factors such as genetic cause and mode of
inheritance. Type 1, the most common form of the disorder, and type
4 (also called ferroportin disease) begin in adulthood. Men with type
1 or type 4 hemochromatosis typically develop symptoms between
the ages of 40 and 60, and women usually develop symptoms after
menopause.

Type 2 hemochromatosis is a juvenile-onset disorder. Iron accumulation begins early in life, and symptoms may appear in childhood. By age 20, decreased or absent secretion of sex hormones is evident. Females usually begin menstruation in a normal manner, but menses stop after a few years. Males may experience delayed puberty or symptoms related to a shortage of sex hormones. If the disorder is untreated, heart disease becomes evident by age 30.

The onset of type 3 hemochromatosis is usually intermediate between types 1 and 2. Symptoms of type 3 hemochromatosis generally begin before age 30.

How Common Is Hereditary Hemochromatosis?

Type 1 hemochromatosis is one of the most common genetic disorders in the United States, affecting about 1 million people. It most often affects people of Northern European descent. The other types of hemochromatosis are considered rare and have been studied in only a small number of families worldwide.

What Genes Are Related to Hereditary Hemochromatosis?

Mutations in the *HAMP, HFE, HFE2, SLC40A1*, and *TFR2* genes cause hereditary hemochromatosis. Type 1 hemochromatosis results from mutations in the *HFE* gene, and type 2 hemochromatosis results from mutations in either the *HFE2* or *HAMP* gene. Mutations in the *TFR2* gene cause type 3 hemochromatosis, and mutations in the *SLC40A1* gene cause type 4 hemochromatosis.

The proteins produced from these genes play important roles in regulating the absorption, transport, and storage of iron. Mutations in any of these genes impair the control of iron absorption during digestion and alter the distribution of iron to other parts of the body. As a result, iron accumulates in tissues and organs, which can disrupt their normal functions.

How Do People Inherit Hereditary Hemochromatosis?

Types 1, 2, and 3 hemochromatosis are inherited in an autosomal recessive pattern, which means both copies of the gene in each cell have mutations. Most often, the parents of an individual with an autosomal recessive condition each carry one copy of the mutated gene but do not show signs and symptoms of the condition.

Type 4 hemochromatosis is distinguished by its autosomal dominant inheritance pattern. With this type of inheritance, one copy of the altered gene in each cell is sufficient to cause the disorder. In most cases, an affected person has one parent with the condition.

Signs and Symptoms

Hemochromatosis can have a variety of symptoms and symptoms may be different for men and women. Hemochromatosis can be hard to identify because early symptoms are similar to those of many other common diseases.

Although most people reach middle-age before they have symptoms of hemochromatosis, some people may have symptoms at a younger age. The symptoms depend on which organs are being affected by the iron buildup.

Early Symptoms

- Fatigue (feeling very tired)
- Weakness
- Weight loss
- Abdominal (belly) pain
- Joint pain

As iron builds up in the body organs, hemochromatosis may also produce the following symptoms:

- Loss of menstrual periods or early menopause
- Loss of sex drive (libido) or impotence
- Loss of body hair
- Shortness of breath
- Although not a physical symptom, another possible indication of hemochromatosis is having an elevated liver enzyme test.

Advanced Symptoms

As the disease progresses, hemochromatosis may cause the following more serious problems:

- Arthritis

- Liver problems, such as cirrhosis (or scarring of the liver) and liver cancer

- High blood sugar and diabetes

- Abdominal (belly) pain that does not go away

- Severe fatigue (feeling extremely tired and having a lack of energy)

- Heart problems (such as a heartbeat that is not regular)

- Heart failure (such as the heart not pumping blood as well as it did previously)

- Gray-colored or bronze-colored skin

Risk Factors and Causes

Although hemochromatosis can have other causes, in the United States the disease is usually caused by a genetic disorder. A person who inherits the defective gene from both parents may develop hemochromatosis. The genetic defect of hemochromatosis is present at birth, but symptoms rarely appear before adulthood. Because people inherit genes from their parents, this type of the disease is also called hereditary hemochromatosis.

How Is Hemochromatosis Diagnosed?

Health care providers use medical and family history, a physical exam, and routine blood tests to diagnose hemochromatosis or other conditions that could cause the same symptoms or complications.

- **Medical and family history.** Taking a medical and family history is one of the first things a health care provider may do to help diagnose hemochromatosis. The health care provider will look for clues that may indicate hemochromatosis, such as a family history of arthritis or unexplained liver disease.

- **Physical exam.** After taking a medical history, a health care provider will perform a physical exam, which may help diagnose hemochromatosis. During a physical exam, a health care provider usually

  - examines a patient's body

  - uses a stethoscope to listen to bodily sounds

  - taps on specific areas of the patient's body

- **Blood tests.** A blood test involves drawing blood at a health care provider's office or a commercial facility and sending the sample to a lab for analysis. Blood tests can determine whether the amount of iron stored in the body is higher than normal:

- The **transferrin saturation test** shows how much iron is bound to the protein that carries iron in the blood. Transferrin saturation values above or equal to 45 percent are considered abnormal.

- The **serum ferritin test** detects the amount of ferritin—a protein that stores iron—in the blood. Levels above 300 μg/L in men and 200 μg/L in women are considered abnormal. Levels above 1,000 μg/L in men or women indicate a high chance of iron overload and organ damage.

If either test shows higher-than-average levels of iron in the body, health care providers can order a special blood test that can detect two copies of the *C282Y* mutation to confirm the diagnosis. If the mutation is not present, health care providers will look for other causes.

- **Liver biopsy.** Health care providers may perform a liver biopsy, a procedure that involves taking a piece of liver tissue for examination with a microscope for signs of damage or disease. The health care provider may ask the patient to temporarily stop taking certain medications before the liver biopsy. The health care provider may ask the patient to fast for 8 hours before the procedure.

During the procedure, the patient lies on a table, right hand resting above the head. The health care provider applies a local anesthetic to the area where he or she will insert the biopsy needle. If needed, a healthcare provider will also give sedatives and pain medication. The health care provider uses a needle to take a small piece of liver tissue. He or she may use ultrasound, computerized tomography scans, or other imaging techniques to guide the needle. After the biopsy, the patient must lie on the right side for up to 2 hours and is monitored an additional 2 to 4 hours before being sent home.

A health care provider performs a liver biopsy at a hospital or an outpatient center. The health care provider sends the liver sample to a pathology lab where the pathologist—a doctor who specializes in diagnosing disease—looks at the tissue with a microscope and sends a report to the patient's health care provider. The biopsy shows how much iron has accumulated in the liver and whether the patient has liver damage.

Hemochromatosis is rare, and healthcare providers may not think to test for this disease. Thus, the disease is often not diagnosed or treated. The initial symptoms can be diverse, vague, and similar to the symptoms of many other diseases. Health care providers may focus on the symptoms and complications caused by hemochromatosis rather than on the underlying iron overload. However, if a healthcare provider diagnoses and treats the iron overload caused by hemochromatosis before organ damage has occurred, a person can live a normal, healthy life.

What Are the Complications of Hemochromatosis?

Without treatment, iron may build up in the organs and cause complications, including

- cirrhosis, or scarring of liver tissue

- diabetes

- irregular heart rhythms or weakening of the heart muscle

- arthritis

- erectile dysfunction

The complication most often associated with hemochromatosis is liver damage. Iron buildup in the liver causes cirrhosis, which increases the chance of developing liver cancer.

For some people, complications may be the first sign of hemochromatosis. However, not everyone with hemochromatosis will develop complications.

Who Should Be Tested for Hemochromatosis?

Experts recommend testing for hemochromatosis in people who have symptoms, complications, or a family history of the disease.

Some researchers have suggested widespread screening for the *C282Y* mutation in the general population. However, screening is not cost-effective. Although the *C282Y* mutation occurs quite frequently, the disease caused by the mutation is rare, and many people with two copies of the mutation never develop iron overload or organ damage.

Researchers and public health officials suggest the following:

- Siblings of people who have hemochromatosis should have their blood tested to see if they have the *C282Y* mutation.

- Parents, children, and other close relatives of people who have hemochromatosis should consider being tested.

- Health care providers should consider testing people who have severe and continuing fatigue, unexplained cirrhosis, joint pain or arthritis, heart problems, erectile dysfunction, or diabetes because these health issues may result from hemochromatosis.

How Is Hemochromatosis Treated?

Healthcare providers treat hemochromatosis by drawing blood. This process is called phlebotomy. Phlebotomy rids the body of extra iron. This treatment is simple, inexpensive, and safe.

Based on the severity of the iron overload, a patient will have phlebotomy to remove a pint of blood once or twice a week for several months to a year, and occasionally longer. Healthcare providers will test serum ferritin levels periodically to monitor iron levels. The goal is to bring serum ferritin levels to the low end of the average range and keep them there. Depending on the lab, the level is 25 to 50 μg/L.

After phlebotomy reduces serum ferritin levels to the desired level, patients may need maintenance phlebotomy treatment every few months. Some patients may need phlebotomies more often. Serum ferritin tests every 6 months or once a year will help determine how often a patient should have blood drawn. Many blood donation centers provide free phlebotomy treatment for people with hemochromatosis.

Treating hemochromatosis before organs are damaged can prevent complications such as cirrhosis, heart problems, arthritis, and diabetes. Treatment cannot cure these conditions in patients who already have them at diagnosis. However, treatment will help most of these conditions improve. The treatment's effectiveness depends on the degree of organ damage. For example, treating hemochromatosis can stop the progression of liver damage in its early stages and lead to a normal life expectancy. However, if a patient develops cirrhosis, his or her chance of developing liver cancer increases, even with phlebotomy treatment. Arthritis usually does not improve even after phlebotomy removes extra iron.

Eating, Diet, and Nutrition

Iron is an essential nutrient found in many foods. Healthy people usually absorb less than 10 percent of iron in the food they eat. People with hemochromatosis absorb up to 30 percent of that iron. People with hemochromatosis can help prevent iron overload by

- eating only moderate amounts of iron-rich foods, such as red meat and organ meat

- avoiding supplements that contain iron

- avoiding supplements that contain vitamin C, which increases iron absorption

- People with hemochromatosis can take steps to help prevent liver damage, including

- limiting the amount of alcoholic beverages they drink because alcohol increases their chance of cirrhosis and liver cancer

- avoiding alcoholic beverages entirely if they already have cirrhosis

Section 14.3

Sickle Cell Disease

This section contains text excerpted from the following sources: Text beginning with the heading "What Is Sickle Cell Disease?" is excerpted from "Sickle Cell Disease," Genetics Home Reference (GHR), National Institutes of Health (NIH), March 7, 2016; Text under the heading "Types of SCD" is excerpted from "Sickle Cell Disease (SCD)," Centers for Disease Control and Prevention (CDC), September 14, 2015; Text under the heading "What Are the Signs and Symptoms of Sickle Cell Disease?" is excerpted from "Sickle Cell Disease," National Heart, Lung and Blood Institute (NHLBI), June 12, 2015.

What Is Sickle Cell Disease?

Sickle cell disease is a group of disorders that affects hemoglobin, the molecule in red blood cells that delivers oxygen to cells throughout the body. People with this disorder have atypical hemoglobin molecules called hemoglobin S, which can distort red blood cells into a sickle, or crescent, shape.

Signs and symptoms of sickle cell disease usually begin in early childhood. Characteristic features of this disorder include a low number of red blood cells (anemia), repeated infections, and periodic episodes of pain. The severity of symptoms varies from person to person. Some people have mild symptoms, while others are frequently hospitalized for more serious complications.

The signs and symptoms of sickle cell disease are caused by the sickling of red blood cells. When red blood cells sickle, they break down prematurely, which can lead to anemia. Anemia can cause shortness of breath, fatigue, and delayed growth and development in children. The rapid breakdown of red blood cells may also cause yellowing of the eyes and skin, which are signs of jaundice. Painful episodes can occur when sickled red blood cells, which are stiff and inflexible, get stuck in small blood vessels. These episodes deprive tissues and organs of oxygen-rich blood and can lead to organ damage, especially in the lungs, kidneys, spleen, and brain. A particularly serious complication of sickle cell disease is high blood pressure in the blood vessels that supply the lungs (pulmonary hypertension). Pulmonary hypertension occurs in about one-third of adults with sickle cell disease and can lead to heart failure.

How Common Is Sickle Cell Disease?

Sickle cell disease affects millions of people worldwide. It is most common among people whose ancestors come from Africa; Mediterranean countries such as Greece, Turkey, and Italy; the Arabian Peninsula; India; and Spanish-speaking regions in South America, Central America, and parts of the Caribbean.

Sickle cell disease is the most common inherited blood disorder in the United States, affecting 70,000 to 80,000 Americans. The disease is estimated to occur in 1 in 500 African Americans and 1 in 1,000 to 1,400 Hispanic Americans.

What Genes Are Related to Sickle Cell Disease?

Mutations in the *HBB* gene cause sickle cell disease.

Hemoglobin consists of four protein subunits, typically, two subunits called alpha-globin and two subunits called beta-globin. The *HBB* gene provides instructions for making beta-globin. Various versions of beta-globin result from different mutations in the *HBB* gene. One particular *HBB* gene mutation produces an abnormal version of beta-globin known as hemoglobin S (HbS). Other mutations in the HBB gene lead to additional abnormal versions of beta-globin such as hemoglobin C (HbC) and hemoglobin E (HbE). *HBB* gene mutations can also result in an unusually low level of beta-globin; this abnormality is called beta thalassemia.

In people with sickle cell disease, at least one of the beta-globin subunits in hemoglobin is replaced with hemoglobin S. In sickle cell anemia, which is a common form of sickle cell disease, hemoglobin S replaces both beta-globin subunits in hemoglobin. In other types of sickle cell disease, just one beta-globin subunit in hemoglobin is replaced with hemoglobin S. The other beta-globin subunit is replaced with a different abnormal variant, such as hemoglobin C. For example, people with sickle-hemoglobin C (HbSC) disease have hemoglobin molecules with hemoglobin S and hemoglobin C instead of beta-globin. If mutations that produce hemoglobin S and beta thalassemia occur together, individuals have hemoglobin S-beta thalassemia (HbSBetaThal) disease.

Abnormal versions of beta-globin can distort red blood cells into a sickle shape. The sickle-shaped red blood cells die prematurely, which can lead to anemia. Sometimes the inflexible, sickle-shaped cells get stuck in small blood vessels and can cause serious medical complications.

How Do People Inherit Sickle Cell Disease?

This condition is inherited in an autosomal recessive pattern, which means both copies of the gene in each cell have mutations. The parents of an individual with an autosomal recessive condition each carry one copy of the mutated gene, but they typically do not show signs and symptoms of the condition.

Types of SCD

Following are the most common types of SCD:

- **HbSS:** People who have this form of SCD inherit two sickle cell genes ("S"), one from each parent. This is commonly called sickle cell anemia and is usually the most severe form of the disease.

- **HbSC:** People who have this form of SCD inherit a sickle cell gene ("S") from one parent and from the other parent a gene for an abnormal hemoglobin called "C." Hemoglobin is a protein that allows red blood cells to carry oxygen to all parts of the body. This is usually a milder form of SCD.

- **HbS beta thalassemia:** People who have this form of SCD inherit one sickle cell gene ("S") from one parent and one gene for beta thalassemia, another type of anemia, from the other parent. There are two types of beta thalassemia: "0" and "+." Those with HbS beta 0-thalassemia usually have a severe form of SCD. People with HbS beta +-thalassemia tend to have a milder form of SCD.

There also are a few rare types of SCD:

- **HbSD, HbSE, and HbSO:** People who have these forms of SCD inherit one sickle cell gene ("S") and one gene from an abnormal type of hemoglobin ("D," "E," or "O") Hemoglobin is a protein that allows red blood cells to carry oxygen to all parts of the body. The severity of these rarer types of SCD varies.

What Are the Signs and Symptoms of Sickle Cell Disease?

Early Signs and Symptoms

If a person has sickle cell disease (SCD), it is present at birth. But most infants do not have any problems from the disease until they are about 5 or 6 months of age. Every state in the United States, the District of Columbia, and the U.S. territories requires that all newborn babies receive screening for SCD. When a child has SCD, parents are notified before the child has symptoms.

Some children with SCD will start to have problems early on, and some later. Early symptoms of SCD may include:

- Painful swelling of the hands and feet, known as *dactylitis*

- Fatigue or fussiness from anemia

- A yellowish color of the skin, known as *jaundice*, or whites of the eyes, known as *icteris*, that occurs when a large number of red cells hemolyze

The signs and symptoms of SCD will vary from person to person and can change over time. Most of the signs and symptoms of SCD are related to complications of the disease.

Major Complications of Sickle Cell Disease

Acute Pain (Sickle Cell or Vaso-occlusive) Crisis. Pain episodes (crises) can occur without warning when sickle cells block blood flow and decrease oxygen delivery. People describe this pain as sharp, intense, stabbing, or throbbing. Severe crises can be even more uncomfortable than post-surgical pain or childbirth.

Pain can strike almost anywhere in the body and in more than one spot at a time. But the pain often occurs in the,

- Lower back
- Legs
- Arms
- Abdomen
- Chest

A crisis can be brought on by

- Illness
- Temperature changes
- Stress
- Dehydration (not drinking enough)
- Being at high altitudes

But often a person does not know what triggers, or causes, the crisis.

Chronic Pain. Many adolescents and adults with SCD suffer from chronic pain. This kind of pain has been hard for people to describe, but it is usually different from crisis pain or the pain that results from organ damage.

Chronic pain can be severe and can make life difficult. Its cause is not well understood.

Severe Anemia. People with SCD usually have mild to moderate anemia. At times, however, they can have severe anemia. Severe anemia can be life threatening. Severe anemia in an infant or child with SCD may be caused by:

- **Splenic sequestration crisis.** The spleen is an organ that is located in the upper left side of the belly. The spleen filters germs in the blood, breaks up blood cells, and makes a kind of white blood cell. A splenic sequestration crisis occurs when red blood cells get stuck in the spleen, making it enlarge quickly. Since the red blood cells are trapped in the spleen, there are fewer cells to circulate in the blood. This causes severe anemia. A big spleen may also cause pain in the left side of the belly.

A parent can usually palpate or feel the enlarged spleen in the belly of his or her child.

- **Aplastic crisis.** This crisis is usually caused by a parvovirus B19 infection, also called fifth disease or slapped cheek syndrome. Parvovirus B19 is a very common infection, but in SCD it can cause the bone marrow to stop producing new red cells for a while, leading to severe anemia.

Splenic sequestration crisis and aplastic crisis most commonly occur in infants and children with SCD. Adults with SCD may also experience episodes of severe anemia, but these usually have other causes.

No matter the cause, severe anemia may lead to symptoms that include:

- Shortness of breath

- Being very tired

- Feeling dizzy

- Having pale skin

Babies and infants with severe anemia may feed poorly and seem very sluggish.

Infections. The spleen is important for protection against certain kinds of germs. Sickle cells can damage the spleen and weaken or destroy its function early in life.

People with SCD who have damaged spleens are at risk for serious bacterial infections that can be life-threatening. Some of these bacteria include:

- Pneumococcus

- Hemophilus influenza type B

- Meningococcus

- Salmonella

- Staphylococcus

- Chlamydia

- Mycoplasma pneumoniae

Bacteria can cause:

- Blood infection (septicemia)

- Lung infection (pneumonia)

- Infection of the covering of the brain and spinal cord (meningitis)

- Bone infection (osteomyelitis)

Acute Chest Syndrome. Sickling in blood vessels of the lungs can deprive a person's lungs of oxygen. When this happens, areas of lung tissue are damaged and cannot exchange oxygen properly. This condition is known as acute chest syndrome. In acute chest syndrome, at least one segment of the lung is damaged. This condition is very serious and should be treated right away at a hospital.

Acute chest syndrome often starts a few days after a painful crisis begins. A lung infection may accompany acute chest syndrome.

Symptoms may include:

- **Chest pain**

- **Fever**

- **Shortness of breath**

- **Rapid breathing**

- **Cough**

Brain Complications. Clinical Stroke. A stroke occurs when blood flow is blocked to a part of the brain. When this happens, brain cells can be damaged or can die. In SCD, a clinical stroke means that a person shows outward signs that something is wrong. The symptoms depend upon what part of the brain is affected. Symptoms of stroke may include:

- Weakness of an arm or leg on one side of the body

- Trouble speaking, walking, or understanding

- Loss of balance

- Severe headache

As many as 24 percent of people with hemoglobin SS and 10 percent of people with hemoglobin Sβ0 may suffer a clinical stroke by age 45. In children, clinical stroke occurs most commonly between the ages of 2 and 9, but recent prevention strategies have lowered the risk. When people with SCD show symptoms of stroke, their families or friends should call 9-1-1 right away.

Silent Stroke and Thinking Problems. Brain imaging and tests of thinking (cognitive studies) have shown that children and adults with hemoglobin SS and hemoglobin Sβ0 thalassemia often have signs of silent brain injury, also called silent stroke. Silent brain injury is damage to the brain without showing outward signs of stroke. This injury is common. Silent brain injury can lead to learning problems or trouble making decisions or holding down a job.

Eye Problems. Sickle cell disease can injure blood vessels in the eye.

The most common site of damage is the retina, where blood vessels can overgrow, get blocked, or bleed. The retina is the light-sensitive layer of tissue that lines the inside of the eye and sends visual messages through the optic nerve to the brain.

Detachment of the retina can occur. When the retina detaches, it is lifted or pulled from its normal position. These problems can cause visual impairment or loss.

Heart Disease. People with SCD can have problems with blood vessels in the heart and with heart function. The heart can become enlarged. People can also develop pulmonary hypertension.

People with SCD who have received frequent blood transfusions may also have heart damage from iron overload.

Pulmonary Hypertension. In adolescents and adults, injury to blood vessels in the lungs can make it hard for the heart to pump blood through them. This causes the pressure in lung blood vessels to rise. High pressure in these blood vessels is called pulmonary hypertension. Symptoms may include shortness of breath and fatigue. When this condition is severe, it has been associated with a higher risk of death.

Kidney Problems. The kidneys are sensitive to the effects of red blood cell sickling. SCD causes the kidneys to have trouble making the urine as concentrated as it should be. This may lead to a need to urinate often and to have bedwetting or uncontrolled urination during the night (nocturnal enuresis). This often starts in childhood. Other problems may include:

- Blood in the urine

- Decreased kidney function

- Kidney disease

- Protein loss in the urine

Priapism. Males with SCD can have unwanted, sometimes prolonged, painful erections. This condition is called priapism. Priapism happens when blood flow out of the erect penis is blocked by sickled cells. If it goes on for a long period of time, priapism can cause permanent damage to the penis and lead to impotence. If priapism lasts for more than 4 hours, emergency medical care should be sought to avoid complications.

Gallstones. When red cells hemolyze, they release hemoglobin. Hemoglobin gets broken down into a substance called bilirubin. Bilirubin can form stones that get stuck in the gallbladder. The gallbladder is a small, sac-shaped organ beneath the liver that helps with digestion. Gallstones are a common problem in SCD.

Gallstones may be formed early on but may not produce symptoms for years. When symptoms develop, they may include:

- Right-sided upper belly pain

- Nausea

- Vomiting

If problems continue or recur, a person may need surgery to remove the gallbladder.

Liver Complications. There are a number of ways in which the liver may be injured in SCD. Sickle cell intrahepatic cholestasis is an uncommon, but severe, form of liver damage that occurs when sickled red cells block blood vessels in the liver. This blockage prevents enough oxygen from reaching liver tissue. These episodes are usually sudden and may recur. Children often recover, but some adults may have chronic problems that lead to liver failure. People with SCD who have received frequent blood transfusions may develop liver damage from iron overload.

Leg Ulcers. Sickle cell ulcers are sores that usually start small and then get larger and larger. The number of ulcers can vary from one to many. Some ulcers will heal quickly, but others may not heal and may last for long periods of time. Some ulcers come back after healing. People with SCD usually don't get ulcers until after the age of 10.

Joint Complications. Sickling in the bones of the hip and, less commonly, the shoulder joints, knees, and ankles, can decrease oxygen flow and result in severe damage. This damage is a condition called avascular or aseptic necrosis. This disease is usually found in adolescents and adults. Symptoms include pain and problems with walking and joint movement. A person may need pain medicines, surgery, or joint replacement if symptoms persist.

Delayed Growth and Puberty. Children with SCD may grow and develop more slowly than their peers because of anemia. They will reach full sexual maturity, but this may be delayed.

Pregnancy. Pregnancies in women with SCD can be risky for both the mother and the baby. Mothers may have medical complications including:

- Infections
- Blood clots
- High blood pressure
- Increased pain episodes

They are also at higher risk for:

- Miscarriages
- Premature births
- "Small-for-dates babies" or underweight babies

Mental Health. As in other chronic diseases, people with SCD may feel sad and frustrated at times. The limitations that SCD can impose on a person's daily activities may cause them to feel isolated from others. Sometimes they become depressed.

People with SCD may also have trouble coping with pain and fatigue, as well as with frequent medical visits and hospitalizations.

How Can Sickle Cell Disease Be Prevented?

People who do not know whether they carry an abnormal hemoglobin gene can ask their doctor to have their blood tested.

Couples who are planning to have children and know that they are at risk of having a child with sickle cell disease (SCD) may want to meet with a genetics counselor. A genetics counselor can answer questions about the risk and explain the choices that are available.

How Is Sickle Cell Disease Diagnosed?

Screening Tests

People who do not know whether they make sickle hemoglobin (hemoglobin S) or another abnormal hemoglobin (such as C, β thalassemia, E) can find out by having their blood tested. This way, they can learn whether they carry a gene (i.e., have the trait) for an abnormal hemoglobin that they could pass on to a child.

When each parent has this information, he or she can be better informed about the chances of having a child with some type of sickle cell disease (SCD), such as hemoglobin SS, SC, Sβ thalassemia, or others.

Newborn Screening

When a child has SCD, it is very important to diagnose it early to better prevent complications. Every state in the United States, the District of Columbia, and the U.S. territories require that every baby is tested for SCD as part of a newborn screening program.

In newborn screening programs, blood from a heel prick is collected in "spots" on a special paper. The hemoglobin from this blood is then analyzed in special labs. Newborn screening results are sent to the doctor who ordered the test and to the child's primary doctor.

If a baby is found to have SCD, health providers from a special follow-up newborn screening group contact the family directly to make sure that the parents know the results. *The child is always retested to be sure that the diagnosis is correct.*

Newborn screening programs also find out whether the baby has an abnormal hemoglobin trait. If so, parents are informed, and counseling is offered.

Remember that when a child has sickle cell trait or SCD, a future sibling, or the child's own future child, may be at risk. These possibilities should be discussed with the primary care doctor, a blood specialist called a *hematologist*, and/or a genetics counselor.

Prenatal Screening

Doctors can also diagnose SCD before a baby is born. This is done using a sample of *amniotic fluid*, the liquid in the sac surrounding a growing embryo, or tissue taken from the *placenta*, the organ that attaches the umbilical cord to the mother's womb.

Testing before birth can be done as early as 8–10 weeks into the pregnancy. This testing looks for the sickle hemoglobin gene rather than the abnormal hemoglobin.

How Is Sickle Cell Disease Treated?

Babies with sickle cell disease (SCD) should be referred to a doctor or provider group that has experience taking care of people with this disease. The doctor might be a hematologist (a doctor with special training in blood diseases) or an experienced general pediatrician, internist, or family practitioner.

For infants, the first SCD visit should take place before 8 weeks of age.

If someone was born in a country that doesn't perform newborn SCD screening, he or she might be diagnosed with SCD later in childhood. These people should also be referred as soon as possible for special SCD care.

All people who have SCD should see their SCD care providers regularly. Regularly means every 3 to 12 months, depending on the person's age. The SCD doctor or team can help to prevent problems by:

- Examining the person

- Giving medicines and immunizations

- Performing tests

- Educating families about the disease and what to watch out for

Section 14.4

Thalassemia

This section includes text excerpted from "Thalassemia," Centers for Disease Control and Prevention (CDC), October 30, 2015.

What Is Thalassemia?

Thalassemia is an inherited (i.e., passed from parents to children through genes) blood disorder caused when the body doesn't make enough of a protein called hemoglobin, an important part of red blood cells. When there isn't enough hemoglobin, the body's red blood cells don't function properly and they last shorter periods of time, so there are fewer healthy red blood cells traveling in the bloodstream.

Red blood cells carry oxygen to all the cells of the body. Oxygen is a sort of food that cells use to function. When there are not enough healthy red blood cells, there is also not enough oxygen delivered to all the other cells of the body, which may cause a person to feel tired, weak or short of breath. This is a condition called anemia. People with thalassemia may have mild or severe anemia. Severe anemia can damage organs and lead to death.

What Are the Different Types of Thalassemia?

When we talk about different "types" of thalassemia, we might be talking about one of two things: the specific part of hemoglobin that is affected (usually either "alpha" or "beta"), or the severity of thalassemia, which is noted by words like trait, carrier, intermedia, or major.

Hemoglobin, which carries oxygen to all cells in the body, is made of two different parts, called alpha and beta. When thalassemia is called "alpha" or "beta," this refers to the part of hemoglobin that isn't being made. If either the alpha or beta part is not made, there aren't enough building blocks to make normal amounts of hemoglobin. Low alpha is called alpha thalassemia. Low beta is called beta thalassemia.

When the words "trait," "minor," "intermedia," or "major" are used, these words describe how severe the thalassemia is. A person who has thalassemia trait may not have any symptoms at all or may have only mild anemia, while a person with thalassemia major may have severe symptoms and may need regular blood transfusions.

In the same way that traits for hair color and body structure are passed down from parents to children, thalassemia traits are passed from parents to children. The type of thalassemia that a person has depends on how many and what type of traits for thalassemia a person has inherited, or received from their parents. For instance, if a person receives a beta thalassemia trait from his father and another from his mother, he will have beta thalassemia major. If a person received an alpha thalassemia trait from her mother and the normal alpha parts from her father, she would have alpha thalassemia trait (also called alpha thalassemia minor). Having a thalassemia trait means that you may not have any symptoms, but you might pass that trait on to your children and increase their risk for having thalassemia.

Sometimes, thalassemias have other names, like Constant Spring, Cooley's Anemia, or hemoglobin Bart hydrops fetalis. These names are specific to certain thalassemias – for instance, Cooley's Anemia is the same thing as beta thalassemia major.

How Do I Know If I Have Thalassemia?

People with moderate and severe forms of thalassemia usually find out about their condition in childhood, since they have symptoms of severe anemia early in life. People with less severe forms of thalassemia may only find out because they are having symptoms of anemia, or maybe because a doctor finds anemia on a routine blood test or a test done for another reason.

Because thalassemias are inherited, the condition sometimes runs in families. Some people find out about their thalassemia because they have relatives with a similar condition.

People who have family members from certain parts of the world have a higher risk for having thalassemia. Traits for thalassemia are more common in people from Mediterranean countries, like Greece and Turkey, and in people from Asia, Africa, and the Middle East. If you have anemia and you also have family members from these areas, your doctor might test your blood further to find out if you have thalassemia.

How Can I Prevent Thalassemia?

Because thalassemia is passed from parents to children, it is very hard to prevent. However, if you or your partner knows of family members with thalassemia, or if you both have family members from places in the world where thalassemia is common, you can speak to a genetic counselor to determine what your risk would be of passing thalassemia to your children.

If I Have Thalassemia, How Does It Affect My Body?

Since your body has fewer red blood cells when you have thalassemia, you may have symptoms of a low blood count, or anemia. When you have anemia, you might feel tired or weak. You might also experience:

- Dizziness
- Shortness of breath
- A fast heart beat
- Headache
- Leg cramps
- Difficulty concentrating
- Pale skin

Your body will try very hard to make more red blood cells. The main place where blood cells are made is the bone marrow, the dark spongy part in the middle of bones. Because your bone marrow may be working harder than normal, it might grow bigger. This causes your bones to expand, and may stretch your bones and make them thinner and more easily broken.

Another place where blood is made is an organ called the spleen. It sits on the left side of your abdomen, just under your lower ribs. The spleen has many other jobs. Two of the major ones are filtering the blood and monitoring the blood for certain infections. When it finds these infections, it can start the process of fighting them. When you have thalassemia, the spleen can get very big as it tries to make blood cells. Because it is working so hard on this job, it can't work as hard to filter blood or monitor for and fight infections. Because of this, people with thalassemia are said to be "immunocompromised," which means that some of the body's defenses against infection aren't working. When you are immunocompromised, it is easier for you to get infections and you sometimes need extra protection, like flu shots and other vaccines.

How Is Thalassemia Treated?

The type of treatment a person receives depends on how severe the thalassemia is. The more severe the thalassemia, the less hemoglobin the body has, and the more severe the anemia may be.

One way to treat anemia is to provide the body with more red blood cells to carry oxygen. This can be done through a blood transfusion, a safe, common procedure in which you receive blood through a small plastic tube inserted into one of your blood vessels. Some people with thalassemia —usually with thalassemia major— need regular blood transfusions because their body makes such low amounts of hemoglobin. People with thalassemia intermedia (not as severe as major, but not as mild as trait) may need blood transfusions sometimes, such as when they have an infection or an illness. People with thalassemia minor or trait usually do not need blood transfusions because they either do not have anemia or have only a mild anemia.

Many times people with thalassemia are prescribed a supplemental B vitamin, known as folic acid, to help treat anemia. Folic acid can help red blood cells develop. Treatment with folic acid is usually done in addition to other therapies.

How Do Blood Transfusions Affect My Body?

People who receive a lot of blood transfusions are at risk for iron overload. Red blood cells contain a lot of iron, and over time, the iron from all of the transfusions can build up in the body. When it builds up, the iron collects in places like the heart, liver, and brain, and can make it hard for these organs to work properly. To prevent iron overload, people with thalassemia may need chelation therapy, which is when doctors give a medicine—either a pill or a shot under the skin – to remove excess iron before it builds up in the organs.

Every time a person gets a blood transfusion, their risk for a problem called "alloimmunization" goes up. Alloimmunization happens when a person's body reacts to blood from a transfusion because it is seen as harmful by their immune system, and tries to destroy it. Persons with alloimmunization can still receive blood transfusions, but the blood they receive has to be checked and compared to their own blood to make sure that it won't be destroyed by their immune system. This takes time and can mean that persons with alloimmunization have to wait longer for blood, or may have a harder time finding blood that won't be destroyed by their body.

Another concern for people who receive a lot of blood transfusions is the safety of the blood they receive. Some infections, like hepatitis, can be carried in blood. In the United States, the blood supply is screened and monitored for safety, and the risk of getting an infection from a blood transfusion is very low. Nevertheless, there is still a very small risk of getting an infection through a blood transfusion.

What Can a Person Living with Thalassemia Do to Stay Healthy?

A healthy lifestyle is important for everyone. For people living with thalassemia, it is especially important to know that a healthy lifestyle means "managing the disorder," as well as making healthy choices.

Managing Thalassemia

Thalassemia is a treatable disorder that can be well-managed with blood transfusions and chelation therapy. A person with thalassemia will need to receive medical care on a regular basis from a hematologist (a medical specialist who treats diseases or disorders of the blood) or a doctor who specializes in treating patients with thalassemia. If a doctor has prescribed either blood transfusions or chelation therapy, the most important thing a person with thalassemia can do is stick to their transfusion and chelation schedules to prevent severe anemia and possible organ damage from iron overload, respectively.

Healthy Choices for People Living with Thalassemia

Other healthy choices a person with thalassemia should consider include keeping vaccinations up-to-date, eating nutritious meals, exercising, and developing positive relationships.

Chapter 15

CHARGE Syndrome

What Is CHARGE Syndrome?

CHARGE syndrome is a disorder that affects many areas of the body. CHARGE stands for coloboma, heart defect, atresia choanae (also known as choanal atresia), retarded growth and development, genital abnormality, and ear abnormality. The pattern of malformations varies among individuals with this disorder, and infants often have multiple life-threatening medical conditions. The diagnosis of CHARGE syndrome is based on a combination of major and minor characteristics.

The major characteristics of CHARGE syndrome are more specific to this disorder than are the minor characteristics. Many individuals with CHARGE syndrome have a hole in one of the structures of the eye (coloboma), which forms during early development. A coloboma may be present in one or both eyes and can affect a person's vision, depending on its size and location. Some people also have small eyes (microphthalmia). One or both nasal passages may be narrowed (choanal stenosis) or completely blocked (choanal atresia). Individuals with CHARGE syndrome frequently have cranial nerve abnormalities.

This chapter contains text excerpted from the following sources: Text beginning with the heading "What Is CHARGE Syndrome?" is excerpted from "CHARGE Syndrome," Genetics Home Reference (GHR), National Institutes of Health (NIH), March 7, 2016; Text under the heading "What Causes CHARGE Syndrome?" is excerpted from "CHARGE Syndrome," National Center for Advancing Translational Sciences (NCATS), March 8, 2013.

The cranial nerves emerge directly from the brain and extend to various areas of the head and neck, controlling muscle movement and transmitting sensory information. Abnormal function of certain cranial nerves can cause swallowing problems, facial paralysis, a sense of smell that is diminished (hyposmia) or completely absent (anosmia), and mild to profound hearing loss. People with CHARGE syndrome also typically have middle and inner ear abnormalities and unusually shaped ears.

The minor characteristics of CHARGE syndrome are not specific to this disorder; they are frequently present in people without CHARGE syndrome. The minor characteristics include heart defects, slow growth starting in late infancy, developmental delay, and an opening in the lip (cleft lip) with or without an opening in the roof of the mouth (cleft palate).

Individuals frequently have hypogonadotropic hypogonadism, which affects the production of hormones that direct sexual development. Males are often born with an unusually small penis (micropenis) and undescended testes (cryptorchidism). External genitalia abnormalities are seen less often in females with CHARGE syndrome. Puberty can be incomplete or delayed. Individuals may have a tracheoesophageal fistula, which is an abnormal connection (fistula) between the esophagus and the trachea.

People with CHARGE syndrome also have distinctive facial features, including a square-shaped face and difference in the appearance between the right and left sides of the face (facial asymmetry). Individuals have a wide range of cognitive function, from normal intelligence to major learning disabilities with absent speech and poor communication.

How Common Is CHARGE Syndrome?

CHARGE syndrome occurs in approximately 1 in 8,500 to 10,000 individuals.

What Genes Are Related to CHARGE Syndrome?

Mutations in the *CHD7* gene cause more than half of all cases of CHARGE syndrome. The *CHD7* gene provides instructions for making a protein that most likely regulates gene activity (expression) by a process known as chromatin remodeling. Chromatin is the complex of DNA and protein that packages DNA into chromosomes. The structure of chromatin can be changed (remodeled) to alter how tightly

DNA is packaged. Chromatin remodeling is one way gene expression is regulated during development. When DNA is tightly packed, gene expression is lower than when DNA is loosely packed.

Most mutations in the *CHD7* gene lead to the production of an abnormally short, nonfunctional *CHD7* protein, which presumably disrupts chromatin remodeling and the regulation of gene expression. Changes in gene expression during embryonic development likely cause the signs and symptoms of CHARGE syndrome.

About one-third of individuals with CHARGE syndrome do not have an identified mutation in the *CHD7* gene. Researchers suspect that other genetic and environmental factors may be involved in these individuals.

How Do People Inherit CHARGE Syndrome?

CHARGE syndrome is inherited in an autosomal dominant pattern, which means one copy of the altered gene in each cell is sufficient to cause the disorder. Most cases result from new mutations in the *CHD7* gene and occur in people with no history of the disorder in their family. In rare cases, an affected person inherits the mutation from an affected parent.

What Causes CHARGE Syndrome?

CHARGE syndrome is caused by mutations in the *CHD7* gene in the majority of cases. Almost all mutations in affected individuals are de novo, which means they occur for the first time as new mutations and are not inherited from a parent. However, autosomal dominant inheritance with transmission from parent to child has been reported in rare cases.

The *CHD7* gene provides instructions for making a protein that most likely regulates gene activity (expression). Most mutations in the *CHD7* gene lead to the production of an abnormally short, nonfunctional *CHD7* protein, which is thought to disrupt the regulation of gene expression. Changes in gene expression during embryonic development likely cause the signs and symptoms of CHARGE syndrome.

About one-third of individuals with CHARGE syndrome do not have an identified mutation in the *CHD7* gene. The cause is unknown in these individuals, but researchers suspect that other genetic and/or environmental factors may be involved.

Is Genetic Testing Available for CHARGE Syndrome?

Genetic testing is available for CHARGE syndrome. The *CHD7* gene is the only gene in which mutations are known to cause CHARGE syndrome. The *CHD7* mutation detection rate when sequence analysis is performed is estimated to be 65—70% for all typical and suspected cases combined.

Chapter 16

Connective Tissue Disorders

Chapter Contents

Section 16.1

Beals Syndrome
(Congenital Contractural Arachnodactyly)

This section contains text excerpted from the following sources:
Text beginning with the heading "What Is Congenital Contractural
Arachnodactyly?" is excerpted from "Congenital Contractural
Arachnodactyly," Genetics Home Reference (GHR), National
Institutes of Health (NIH), March 7, 2016; Text under the
heading "What Are the Signs and Symptoms of Congenital
Contractural Arachnodactyly?" is excerpted from "Congenital
Contractural Arachnodactyly," National Centers for Advancing
Transitional Sciences (NCATS), February 9, 2015.

What Is Congenital Contractural Arachnodactyly?

Congenital contractural arachnodactyly is a disorder that affects
many parts of the body. People with this condition typically are tall
with long limbs (dolichostenomelia) and long, slender fingers and
toes (arachnodactyly). They often have permanently bent joints (contractures) that can restrict movement in their hips, knees, ankles, or
elbows. Additional features of congenital contractural arachnodactyly include underdeveloped muscles, a rounded upper back that also
curves to the side (kyphoscoliosis), permanently bent fingers and toes
(camptodactyly), ears that look "crumpled," and a protruding chest
(pectus carinatum).

Rarely, people with congenital contractural arachnodactyly have
heart defects such as an enlargement of the blood vessel that distributes blood from the heart to the rest of the body (aortic root dilatation)
or a leak in one of the valves that control blood flow through the heart
(mitral valve prolapse). The life expectancy of individuals with congenital contractural arachnodactyly varies depending on the severity
of symptoms but is typically not shortened.

A rare, severe form of congenital contractural arachnodactyly
involves both heart and digestive system abnormalities in addition
to the skeletal features described above; individuals with this severe
form of the condition usually do not live past infancy.

How Common Is Congenital Contractural Arachnodactyly?

The prevalence of congenital contractural arachnodactyly is estimated to be less than 1 in 10,000 worldwide.

What Genes Are Related to Congenital Contractural Arachnodactyly?

Mutations in the *FBN2* gene cause congenital contractural arachnodactyly. The *FBN2* gene provides instructions for producing the fibrillin-2 protein. Fibrillin-2 binds to other proteins and molecules to form threadlike filaments called microfibrils. Microfibrils become part of the fibers that provide strength and flexibility to connective tissue that supports the body's joints and organs. Additionally, microfibrils regulate the activity of molecules called growth factors. Growth factors enable the growth and repair of tissues throughout the body.

Mutations in the *FBN2* gene can decrease fibrillin-2 production or result in the production of a protein with impaired function. As a result, microfibril formation is reduced, which probably weakens the structure of connective tissue and disrupts regulation of growth factor activity. The resulting abnormalities of connective tissue underlie the signs and symptoms of congenital contractural arachnodactyly.

How Do People Inherit Congenital Contractural Arachnodactyly?

This condition is inherited in an autosomal dominant pattern, which means one copy of the altered gene in each cell is sufficient to cause the disorder.

What Are the Signs and Symptoms of Congenital Contractural Arachnodactyly?

Congenital contractural arachnodactyly represents a broad spectrum of characteristics. The features are quite variable, both within and between families. The classic form is characterized by a Marfan-like appearance (tall and slender with arm span exceeding height), arachnodactyly (long slender fingers and toes), 'crumpled' ears, contractures of major joints from birth (particularly knees, elbows, fingers, toes, and hips), bowed long bones, muscular hypoplasia (underdeveloped muscles), kyphosis/scoliosis, aortic root dilation, and various craniofacial abnormalities (such as micrognathia, high arched palate, scaphocephaly (premature fusion of the sagittal suture of the skull leading to a long, narrow head), brachycephaly (premature fusion of the coronal suture, leading to a short skull), and frontal bossing).

At the most severe end of the spectrum is a rare type with very few reported cases. In addition to the typical skeletal findings (arachnodactyly, joint contractures, scoliosis) and abnormally shaped ears, infants with the severe/lethal form have multiple cardiovascular and gastrointestinal abnormalities.

How Might Congenital Contractural Arachnodactyly Be Treated?

Physical therapy for joint contractures helps increase joint mobility and ameliorate the effects of muscle hypoplasia (usually in the calf muscles). In severe cases, surgical release may be necessary. Since the kyphosis/scoliosis tends to be progressive, bracing and/or surgical correction is often needed. Consultation with an orthopedist is encouraged. Other symptoms, if present, should be addressed as they arise and in the standard manner. Regular physician visits should be scheduled to monitor symptom progression and development.

What Is the Prognosis for Individuals with Congenital Contractural Arachnodactyly?

Individuals with congenital contractural arachnodactyly may live normal lives unless complications involving cardiac issues or severe deformity of the vertebrae arise. In general, life span does not appear to be shortened.

Section 16.2

Ehlers-Danlos Syndrome

This section contains text excerpted from the following sources:
Text beginning with the heading "What Is Ehlers-Danlos
Syndrome?" is excerpted from "Ehlers-Danlos Syndrome," Genetics
Home Reference (GHR), National Institutes of Health (NIH),
March 7, 2016; Text under the heading "What Are the Signs and
Symptoms of Ehlers-Danlos Syndrome?" is excerpted from
"Ehlers-Danlos Syndrome," National Center for Advancing
Transitional Sciences (NCATS), May 21, 2015.

What Is Ehlers-Danlos Syndrome?

Ehlers-Danlos syndrome is a group of disorders that affect the connective tissues that support the skin, bones, blood vessels, and many other organs and tissues. Defects in connective tissues cause the signs and symptoms of Ehlers-Danlos syndrome, which vary from mildly loose joints to life-threatening complications.

Previously, there were more than 10 recognized types of Ehlers-Danlos syndrome, differentiated by Roman numerals. In 1997, researchers proposed a simpler classification that reduced the number of major types to six and gave them descriptive names: the classical type (types I and II), the hypermobility type (type III), the vascular type (type IV), the kyphoscoliosis type (formerly type VIA), the arthrochalasia type (formerly types VIIA and VIIB), and the dermatosparaxis type (type VIIC). This six-type classification, known as the Villefranche nomenclature, is still commonly used. The types are distinguished by their signs and symptoms, their underlying genetic causes, and their patterns of inheritance. Since 1997, several additional forms of the condition have been described. These additional forms appear to be rare, affecting a small number of families, and most have not been well characterized.

Although all types of Ehlers-Danlos syndrome affect the joints and skin, additional features vary by type. An unusually large range of joint movement (hypermobility) occurs with most forms of Ehlers-Danlos syndrome, particularly the hypermobility type. Infants with hypermobile joints often have weak muscle tone, which can delay the development of motor skills such as sitting, standing, and walking. The loose joints are unstable and prone to dislocation and chronic pain. Hypermobility and dislocations of both hips at birth are characteristic features in infants with the arthrochalasia type of Ehlers-Danlos syndrome.

Many people with Ehlers-Danlos syndrome have soft, velvety skin that is highly stretchy (elastic) and fragile. Affected individuals tend to bruise easily, and some types of the condition also cause abnormal scarring. People with the classical form of Ehlers-Danlos syndrome experience wounds that split open with little bleeding and leave scars that widen over time to create characteristic "cigarette paper" scars. The dermatosparaxis type of the disorder is characterized by skin that sags and wrinkles. Extra (redundant) folds of skin may be present as affected children get older.

Some forms of Ehlers-Danlos syndrome, notably the vascular type and to a lesser extent the kyphoscoliosis and classical types, can involve serious and potentially life-threatening complications due to unpredictable tearing (rupture) of blood vessels. This rupture can cause internal bleeding, stroke, and shock. The vascular type of Ehlers-Danlos syndrome is also associated with an increased risk of organ rupture, including tearing of the intestine and rupture of the uterus (womb) during pregnancy. People with the kyphoscoliosis form of Ehlers-Danlos syndrome experience severe, progressive curvature of the spine that can interfere with breathing.

How Common Is Ehlers-Danlos Syndrome?

Although it is difficult to estimate the overall frequency of Ehlers-Danlos syndrome, the combined prevalence of all types of this condition may be about 1 in 5,000 individuals worldwide. The hypermobility and classical forms are most common; the hypermobility type may affect as many as 1 in 10,000 to 15,000 people, while the classical type probably occurs in 1 in 20,000 to 40,000 people.

Other forms of Ehlers-Danlos syndrome are very rare. About 30 cases of the arthrochalasia type and about 60 cases of the kyphoscoliosis type have been reported worldwide. About a dozen infants and children with the dermatosparaxis type have been described. The vascular type is also rare; estimates vary widely, but the condition may affect about 1 in 250,000 people.

What Genes Are Related to Ehlers-Danlos Syndrome?

Mutations in more than a dozen genes have been found to cause Ehlers-Danlos syndrome. The classical type results most often from mutations in either the *COL5A1* gene or the *COL5A2* gene. Mutations in the TNXB gene have been found in a very small percentage of cases of the hypermobility type (although in most cases, the cause of this type is unknown). The vascular type results from mutations in the *COL3A1* gene. *PLOD1* gene mutations cause the kyphoscoliosis type. Mutations in the *COL1A1* gene or the *COL1A2* gene result in the arthrochalasia type. The dermatosparaxis type is caused by mutations in the *ADAMTS2* gene. The other, less well-characterized forms of Ehlers-Danlos syndrome result from mutations in other genes, some of which have not been identified.

Some of the genes associated with Ehlers-Danlos syndrome, including *COL1A1, COL1A2, COL3A1, COL5A1,* and *COL5A2,* provide instructions for making pieces of several different types of collagen. These pieces assemble to form mature collagen molecules that give structure and strength to connective tissues throughout the body. Other genes, including *ADAMTS2, PLOD1,* and *TNXB*, provide instructions for making proteins that process or interact with collagen. Mutations that cause the different forms of Ehlers-Danlos syndrome disrupt the production or processing of collagen, preventing these molecules from being assembled properly. These defects weaken connective tissues in the skin, bones, and other parts of the body, resulting in the characteristic features of this condition.

How Do People Inherit Ehlers-Danlos Syndrome?

The inheritance pattern of Ehlers-Danlos syndrome varies by type. The arthrochalasia, classical, hypermobility, and vascular forms of the disorder have an autosomal dominant pattern of inheritance. Autosomal dominant inheritance means that one copy of the altered gene in each cell is sufficient to cause the disorder. In some cases, an affected person inherits the mutation from one affected parent. Other cases result from new (sporadic) gene mutations and occur in people with no history of the disorder in their family.

The dermatosparaxis and kyphoscoliosis types of Ehlers-Danlos syndrome, as well as some of the rare, less well-characterized types of the disorder, are inherited in an autosomal recessive pattern. In autosomal recessive inheritance, two copies of the gene in each cell are altered. Most often, the parents of an individual with an autosomal recessive disorder are carriers of one copy of the altered gene but do not show signs and symptoms of the disorder.

What Are the Signs and Symptoms of Ehlers-Danlos Syndrome?

There are six major types of Ehlers-Danlos syndrome (EDS). Although there is significant overlap in associated features, the subtypes are classified based on their unique signs and symptoms:

1. **Hypermobility type**—characterized primarily by joint hypermobility affecting both large (elbows, knees) and small (fingers, toes) joints which may lead to recurrent joint dislocations and subluxations (partial dislocation). Affected people generally experience skin involvement (soft, smooth and velvety skin with easy bruising) and chronic pain of the muscles and/or bones, as well.

2. **Classic type**—associated with extremely elastic (stretchy), smooth skin that is fragile and bruises easily; wide, atrophic scars (flat or depressed scars); and joint hypermobility. Molluscoid pseudotumors (calcified hematomas over pressure points such as the elbow) and spheroids (fat-containing cysts on forearms and shins) are frequently diagnosed in affected people. Hypotonia and delayed motor development may occur, as well.

3. **Vascular type**—characterized by thin, translucent skin that is extremely fragile and bruises easily. Arteries and certain organs such as the intestines and uterus are also fragile and prone to rupture. Affected people typically have short stature; thin scalp hair; and characteristic facial features including large eyes, a thin nose and lobeless ears. Joint hypermobility is present, but generally confined to the small joints (fingers, toes). Other common features include club foot; tendon and/or muscle rupture; acrogeria (premature aging of the skin of the hands and feet); early onset varicose veins; pneumothorax (collapse of a lung); gingival (gums) recession; and a decreased amount of subcutaneous (under the skin) fat.

4. **Kyphoscoliosis type**—associated with severe hypotonia at birth, delayed motor development, progressive scoliosis (present from birth), and scleral fragility. Affected people may also have easy bruising; fragile arteries that are prone to rupture; unusually small cornia; and osteopenia (low bone density). Other common features include a "marfanoid habitus" which is characterized by long, slender fingers (arachnodactyly);

144

unusually long limbs; and a sunken chest (pectus excavatum) or protruding chest (pectus carinatum).

5. **Arthrochalasia type**—characterized by severe joint hypermobility and congenital hip dislocation. Other common features include fragile, elastic skin with easy bruising; hypotonia; kyphoscoliosis (kyphosis and scoliosis); and mild osteopenia.

6. **Dermatosparaxis type**—associated with extremely fragile skin leading to severe bruising and scarring; saggy, redundant skin, especially on the face; and hernias.

Although other forms of the condition exist, they are extremely rare and are not well-characterized.

How Might Ehlers-Danlos Syndrome Be Treated?

There is no specific cure for Ehlers-Danlos syndrome (EDS). The treatment and management is focused on preventing serious complications and relieving associated signs and symptoms. Because the features of EDS vary by subtype, management strategies differ slightly.

What Is the Long-Term Outlook for People with Ehlers-Danlos Syndrome?

The long-term outlook (prognosis) for people with Ehlers-Danlos syndrome (EDS) varies by subtype. The vascular type is typically the most severe form of EDS and is often associated with a shortened lifespan. People affected by vascular EDS have a median life expectancy of 48 years and many will have a major event by age 40. The lifespan of people with the kyphoscoliosis form is also decreased, largely due to the vascular involvement and the potential for restrictive lung disease.

Other forms of EDS are typically not as dangerous and can be associated with normal lifespans. Affected people can often live healthy if somewhat restricted lives.

Section 16.3

Heritable Disorders of Connective Tissue

This section includes text excerpted from "Questions and
Answers about Heritable Disorders of Connective Tissue,"
National Institute of Arthritis and Musculoskeletal
and Skin Diseases (NIAMS), May 2013.

What Are Heritable Disorders of Connective Tissue?

Heritable (genetic) disorders of connective tissue are a family of
more than 200 disorders that affect connective tissues. These disorders result from alterations (mutations) in genes, and thus are called
"heritable." All of these diseases are directly related to mutations in
genes that are responsible for building tissues. Alterations in these
genes may change the structure and development of skin, bones, joints,
the heart, blood vessels, lungs, eyes, and ears. Some mutations also
change how these tissues work.

Some other connective tissue problems are not directly linked to
mutations in tissue-building genes, although some people may be
genetically predisposed to becoming affected.

Some Common Heritable Disorders of Connective Tissue

Physicians and scientists have identified more than 200 heritable
connective tissue disorders. Some of the more common ones are listed
below. Some of these are really groups of disorders and may be known
by other names.

Ehlers-Danlos syndrome. The problems present in the group of
disorders known as Ehlers-Danlos syndrome (EDS) include changes
in the physical properties of skin, joints, blood vessels, and other tissues such as ligaments and tendons. People with Ehlers-Danlos syndrome have some degree of joint looseness; fragile, small blood vessels;
abnormal scar formation and wound healing; and soft, velvety skin
that stretches excessively but returns to normal after being pulled.

Some forms can cause problems with the eyes and spine. Ehlers-Danlos syndrome can also lead to weak internal organs, including the uterus, intestines, and large blood vessels. Mutations in several different genes are responsible for varying symptoms in the several types of Ehlers-Danlos syndrome. In most cases, the genetic defect involves collagen, the major protein-building material of bone.

Epidermolysis bullosa. The characteristic feature of epidermolysis bullosa (EB) is blistering of the skin, which results when skin layers separate after minor trauma. People with a mild form of the disease may have just a few blisters on skin, whereas others may have many blisters. In some forms, blisters may form in the mouth, stomach, esophagus, bladder, and other parts of the body. Epidermolysis bullosa can be both disabling and disfiguring, and some forms may lead to early death. Defects in several proteins within the skin are at fault.

Marfan syndrome. People with Marfan syndrome tend to have a tall, thin build with long arms and legs and "spider-like" fingers. Other problems include a sideways curve of the spine (scoliosis); crowded teeth; flat feet; abnormal position of the lens of the eye; and enlargement of the beginning part of the aorta, the major vessel carrying blood away from the heart. If left untreated, an enlarged aorta can lead to hemorrhage and even death. Marfan syndrome results from mutations in the gene that determines the structure of fibrillin-1, a protein important to connective tissue.

Osteogenesis imperfecta. Osteogenesis imperfecta (OI) is characterized by fragile bones, low muscle mass, and loose joints and ligaments. There are several identified types of osteogenesis imperfecta, ranging in severity from mild to lethal. The appearance of people with osteogenesis imperfecta varies considerably, depending on the particular form they have and its severity. Some may have a blue or gray tint to the sclera (whites of the eyes), thin skin, growth deficiencies, and fragile teeth. They may develop scoliosis, respiratory problems, and hearing loss. Also known as "brittle bone disease," this disorder is caused by a mutation in one of several genes that play a role in how the body makes collagen, the main component of connective tissue.

What Is Connective Tissue and What Does Heritable Disorders Mean?

Connective tissue is the material between the cells of the body that gives tissues form and strength. This "cellular glue" is also involved in delivering nutrients to the tissue, and in the special functioning of certain tissues. Connective tissue is made up of dozens of proteins, including collagens, proteoglycans, and glycoproteins. The combination of these proteins can vary between tissues.

The genes that encode these proteins can harbor defects or mutations, which can affect the functioning of certain properties of connective tissue in selected tissues. When this occurs, the result can be a heritable disorder—one that can be inherited, or passed from parent to child—of connective tissue.

How Do People Get Gene Alterations?

People with heritable disorders of connective tissue inherit an altered gene either from one or from both parents. We have two copies of most genes: one inherited from each parent. Males have one copy of each gene on the X chromosome, because they have only one X chromosome, and one copy of each gene on the Y chromosome. In contrast, females have two copies of X chromosome genes because they have two X chromosomes.

Some genetic disorders require that only a single copy of a gene be altered. These disorders can be seen in many generations of a family because the altered copy of the gene is passed from parent to child (dominant inheritance). The same disorder can occur in a person without a family history of the condition if there is a new mutation in the right gene at conception. Some disorders are seen only when the person has received an altered copy of the gene from each parent (recessive inheritance); in these families, the person with only a single copy is called a "carrier" and is not actually affected.

If a mutation occurs on an X chromosome, it generally produces a condition in which the pattern of affected individuals in a family is unusual. Often, women are carriers (that is, they have only a single altered copy of the gene), but males show the condition because they do not have a second protective copy of the gene. Such a condition is referred to as "X-linked."

Who Gets Heritable Disorders of Connective Tissue?

Heritable disorders of connective tissue can affect people of all ethnic groups. All ages, and both sexes are affected. Many of these disorders are rare. Some may not be evident at birth, but only appear after a certain age or after exposure to a particular environmental stress.

Does Anything Increase the Chances of Having a Genetic Disease?

Several factors increase the likelihood that a person will inherit an alteration in a gene. If you are concerned about your risk—or the risk to your children or future children—you should talk to your healthcare provider or a genetic counselor.

The following factors may increase the chance of getting or passing on a genetic disease:

- parents who have a genetic disease

- a family history of a genetic disease

- parents who are closely related or part of a distinct ethnic or geographic community

- parents who do not show disease symptoms, but "carry" a disease gene in their genetic makeup (this can be discovered through genetic testing).

How Does Genetic Counseling Help?

People seek genetic counseling to make better decisions about their lives and families. Because genetic counselors understand how genetic disorders are passed on through families, they can help couples estimate the risks of having children with genetic diseases. They can also tell parents about tests to determine if they are carrying certain altered genes, tests for newborns who may have inherited certain altered genes, and tests that can be done in early pregnancy to determine if a fetus either carries an altered copy of a gene or is affected with a disorder. The information derived from all these studies can facilitate family planning.

Your healthcare team can help you find genetic counseling if you wish to better understand your or your child's disease or risk of disease.

What Are the Symptoms of a Heritable Disorder of Connective Tissue?

The symptoms are different for different disorders. Some of them cause bone growth problems. People with bone growth disorders may have brittle bones or bones that are too long or too short. Some cause people to be unusually tall (Marfan syndrome) or short (chondrodysplasias, osteogenesis imperfecta), or to have head and facial structure

149

malformations (Apert syndrome, Pfeiffer syndrome). In others, joints may be stiff or immobile (fibrodysplasia ossificans progressiva or FOP).

Some disorders affect the skin. For example, Ehlers-Danlos syndrome results in stretchy or loose skin, while in another connective tissue disorder, cutis laxa, deficient elastic fibers cause the skin to hang in folds. Epidermolysis bullosa results in blistered skin.

Other tissues can be affected as well. Pseudoxanthoma elasticum (PXE) causes skin, eye, and heart problems, and closed-off or blocked blood vessels. Marfan syndrome and some forms of Ehlers-Danlos syndrome lead to weak blood vessels.

It is critical for people with these disorders and their family members to work closely with their healthcare teams to get a proper diagnosis and the best treatment. Symptoms of heritable disorders of connective tissue are extremely variable, and some disorders can pose severe health risks even when affected individuals have no symptoms.

How Do Doctors Diagnose Heritable Disorders of Connective Tissue?

Diagnosis always rests first on a combination of family history, medical history, and physical examination. Because many of these conditions are uncommon, the family physician may suspect a diagnosis but be uncertain about how to confirm it. At this point, referral to experienced clinicians, often medical geneticists, can be extremely valuable to either confirm or exclude the suspected diagnosis. Laboratory tests are available to confirm the diagnosis for many heritable disorders of connective tissue, but not for all. Once a diagnosis is made, laboratory studies may be available to provide some or all of the following:

- Prenatal testing to identify an affected fetus and assist in family planning.

- Newborn screening to spot a condition that may become evident later in life.

- Carrier testing to identify adults who, without symptoms, carry a genetic mutation for a disease.

- Predictive testing to spot people at risk for developing a genetic connective tissue disease later in life.

These tests are helpful for diseases that run in the family.

What Treatments Are Available?

The term heritable disorders of connective tissue refers to a wide range of disorders, each requiring a specific program for management and treatment. In most instances, regular monitoring is important to assess, for example, the diameter of the aorta in people with Marfan syndrome, the extent of scoliosis (spine curvature) in people with osteogenesis imperfecta and those with some forms of Ehlers-Danlos syndrome, and whether there is protrusion of the spine into the base of the skull in people with osteogenesis imperfecta.

For some conditions, specific metabolic treatment is useful, for example, vitamin B6 in people with homocystinuria, a metabolic disorder resulting from a liver enzyme deficiency. In others, drugs like beta-blockers are useful for slowing the dilation of the aorta, and bone-building drugs called bisphosphonates may be help strengthen fragile bones. Maintaining general health though a nutritious diet, exercise, and healthy lifestyle habits is also important for people with all heritable disorders of connective tissue.

Section 16.4

Marfan Syndrome

This section contains text excerpted from the following sources:
Text beginning with the heading "What Is Marfan Syndrome?"
is excerpted from "Marfan Syndrome," Genetics Home Reference
(GHR), National Institutes of Health (NIH), March 7, 2016;
Text under the heading "What Are the Symptoms of Marfan
Syndrome?" is excerpted from "Questions and Answers about Marfan
Syndrome," National Institute of Arthritis and Musculoskeletal
and Skin Diseases (NIAMS), October 2015.

What Is Marfan Syndrome?

Marfan syndrome is a disorder that affects the connective tissue in many parts of the body. Connective tissue provides strength and flexibility to structures such as bones, ligaments, muscles, blood vessels, and heart valves. The signs and symptoms of Marfan syndrome vary widely in severity, timing of onset, and rate of progression.

The two primary features of Marfan syndrome are vision problems caused by a dislocated lens (ectopia lentis) in one or both eyes and defects in the large blood vessel that distributes blood from the heart to the rest of the body (the aorta). The aorta can weaken and stretch, which may lead to a bulge in the blood vessel wall (an aneurysm). Stretching of the aorta may cause the aortic valve to leak, which can lead to a sudden tearing of the layers in the aorta wall (aortic dissection). Aortic aneurysm and dissection can be life threatening.

Many people with Marfan syndrome have additional heart problems including a leak in the valve that connects two of the four chambers of the heart (mitral valve prolapse) or the valve that regulates blood flow from the heart into the aorta (aortic valve regurgitation). Leaks in these valves can cause shortness of breath, fatigue, and an irregular heartbeat felt as skipped or extra beats (palpitations).

Individuals with Marfan syndrome are usually tall and slender, have elongated fingers and toes (arachnodactyly), and have an arm span that exceeds their body height. Other common features include a long and narrow face, crowded teeth, an abnormal curvature of the spine (scoliosis or kyphosis), and either a sunken chest (pectus excavatum) or a protruding chest (pectus carinatum). Some individuals develop an abnormal accumulation of air in the chest cavity that can result in the collapse of a lung (spontaneous pneumothorax). A membrane called the dura, which surrounds the brain and spinal cord, can be abnormally enlarged (dural ectasia) in people with Marfan syndrome. Dural ectasia can cause pain in the back, abdomen, legs, or head. Most individuals with Marfan syndrome have some degree of nearsightedness (myopia). Clouding of the lens (cataract) may occur in mid-adulthood, and increased pressure within the eye (glaucoma) occurs more frequently in people with Marfan syndrome than in those without the condition.

The features of Marfan syndrome can become apparent anytime between infancy and adulthood. Depending on the onset and severity of signs and symptoms, Marfan can be fatal early in life; however, the majority of affected individuals survive into mid- to late adulthood.

How Common Is Marfan Syndrome?

The incidence of Marfan syndrome is approximately 1 in 5,000 worldwide.

What Genes Are Related to Marfan Syndrome?

Mutations in the *FBN1* gene cause Marfan syndrome. The *FBN1* gene provides instructions for making a protein called fibrillin-1. Fibrillin-1 attaches (binds) to other fibrillin-1 proteins and other molecules to form threadlike filaments called microfibrils. Microfibrils become part of the fibers that provide strength and flexibility to connective tissue. Additionally, microfibrils store molecules called growth factors and release them at various times to control the growth and repair of tissues and organs throughout the body. A mutation in the *FBN1* gene can reduce the amount of functional fibrillin-1 that is available to form microfibrils, which leads to decreased microfibril formation. As a result, excess growth factors are released and elasticity in many tissues is decreased, leading to overgrowth and instability of tissues.

How Do People Inherit Marfan Syndrome?

This condition is inherited in an autosomal dominant pattern, which means one copy of the altered gene in each cell is sufficient to cause the disorder. At least 25 percent of Marfan syndrome cases result from a new mutation in the *FBN1* gene. These cases occur in people with no history of the disorder in their family.

What Are the Symptoms of Marfan Syndrome?

Marfan syndrome affects different people in different ways. Some people have only mild symptoms, while others are more severely affected. In most cases, the symptoms progress as the person ages. The body systems most often affected by Marfan syndrome are:

- **Skeleton.** People with Marfan syndrome are typically very tall, slender, and loose-jointed. Because Marfan syndrome affects the long bones of the skeleton, a person's arms, legs, fingers, and toes may be disproportionately long in relation to the rest of the body. A person with Marfan syndrome often has a long, narrow face, and the roof of the mouth may be arched, causing the teeth to be crowded. Other skeletal problems include a sternum (breastbone) that is either protruding or indented, curvature of the spine (scoliosis), and flat feet.

- **Eyes.** More than half of all people with Marfan syndrome experience dislocation of one or both lenses of the eye. The lens may be slightly higher or lower than normal, and may be shifted off to one side. The dislocation may be minimal, or it may be pronounced and obvious. One serious complication that may occur with this disorder is retinal detachment. Many people with Marfan syndrome are also nearsighted (myopic), and some can develop early glaucoma (high pressure within the eye) or cataracts (the eye's lens loses its clearness).

- **Heart and blood vessels (cardiovascular system).** Most people with Marfan syndrome have problems associated with the heart and blood vessels. Because of faulty connective tissue, the wall of the aorta (the large artery that carries blood from the heart to the rest of the body) may be weakened and stretch, a process called aortic dilatation. Aortic dilatation increases the risk that the aorta will tear (aortic dissection) or rupture, causing serious heart problems or sometimes sudden death. Sometimes, defects in heart valves can also cause problems. In some cases, certain valves may leak, creating a "heart murmur," which a doctor can hear with a stethoscope. Small leaks may not result in any symptoms, but larger ones may cause shortness of breath, fatigue, and palpitations (a very fast or irregular heart rate).

- **Nervous system.** The brain and spinal cord are surrounded by fluid contained by a membrane called the dura, which is composed of connective tissue. As someone with Marfan syndrome gets older, the dura often weakens and stretches, then begins to weigh on the vertebrae in the lower spine and wear away the bone surrounding the spinal cord. This is called dural ectasia. These changes may cause only mild discomfort; or they may lead to radiated pain in the abdomen; or to pain, numbness, or weakness in the legs.

- **Skin.** Many people with Marfan syndrome develop stretch marks on their skin, even without any weight change. These stretch marks can occur at any age and pose no health risk. However, people with Marfan syndrome are also at increased risk for developing an abdominal or inguinal hernia, in which a bulge develops that contains part of the intestines.

- **Lungs.** Although connective tissue problems make the tiny air sacs within the lungs less elastic, people with Marfan syndrome generally do not experience noticeable problems with their lungs. If, however, these tiny air sacs become stretched or swollen, the risk of lung collapse may increase. Rarely, people with Marfan syndrome may have sleep-related breathing disorders such as snoring or sleep apnea (which is characterized by brief periods when breathing stops).

What Causes Marfan Syndrome?

Marfan syndrome is caused by a defect, or mutation, in the gene that determines the structure of fibrillin-1, a protein that is an important part of connective tissue. A person with Marfan syndrome is born with the disorder, even though it may not be diagnosed until later in life.

The defective gene that causes Marfan syndrome can be inherited; the child of a person who has Marfan syndrome has a 50 percent chance of inheriting the disease. Sometimes a new gene defect occurs during the formation of sperm or egg cells, making it possible for two parents without the disease to have a child with the disease. But this is rare. Two unaffected parents have only a 1 in 10,000 chance of having a child with Marfan syndrome. Possibly 25 percent of cases are due to a spontaneous mutation at the time of conception.

Although everyone with Marfan syndrome has a defect in the same gene, different mutations are found in different families, and not everyone experiences the same characteristics to the same degree. In other words, the defective gene expresses itself in different ways in different people. This phenomena is known as variable expression. Scientists do not yet understand why variable expression occurs in people with Marfan syndrome.

How Is Marfan Syndrome Diagnosed?

There is no specific laboratory test, such as a blood test or skin biopsy, to diagnose Marfan syndrome. The doctor and/or geneticist (a doctor with special knowledge about inherited diseases) relies on observation and a complete medical history, including:

- Information about any family members who may have the disorder or who had an early, unexplained, heart-related death.

- A thorough physical examination, including an evaluation of the skeletal frame for the ratio of arm/leg size to trunk size.

- An eye examination, including a "slit lamp" evaluation.

- Heart tests such as an echocardiogram (a test that uses ultrasound waves to examine the heart and aorta).

The doctor may diagnose Marfan syndrome if the patient has a family history of the disease, and if there are specific problems in at least two of the body systems known to be affected. For a patient with no family history of the disease, at least three body systems must be affected before a diagnosis is made. Moreover, two of the systems must show clear signs that are relatively specific for Marfan syndrome.

In some cases, a genetic analysis may be useful in making a diagnosis of Marfan syndrome, but such analyses are often time consuming and may not provide any additional helpful information. Family members of a person diagnosed with Marfan syndrome should not assume they are not affected if there is no knowledge that the disorder existed in previous generations of the family. After a clinical diagnosis of a family member, a genetic study might identify the specific mutation for which a test can be performed to determine if other family members are affected.

In 2005, doctors discovered a connective tissue disorder known as Loeys-Dietz syndrome, which has several characteristics that overlap with those of Marfan syndrome. When making a diagnosis, it is important to distinguish between the two disorders: Loeys-Dietz is more likely to cause fatal aortic aneurysms, and treatment for the two is different. A diagnostic test for Loeys-Dietz syndrome is available.

What Types of Doctors Treat Marfan Syndrome?

Because a number of body systems may be affected, a person with Marfan syndrome should be cared for by several different types of doctors. A general practitioner or pediatrician may oversee routine healthcare and refer the patient to specialists such as a cardiologist (a doctor who specializes in heart disorders), an orthopaedist (a doctor who specializes in bones), or an ophthalmologist (a doctor who specializes in eye disorders), as needed. Some people with Marfan syndrome also go to a geneticist.

What Treatment Options Are Available?

There is no cure for Marfan syndrome. To develop one, scientists may have to identify and change the specific gene responsible for the disorder before birth. However, a range of treatment options can minimize and sometimes prevent complications. The appropriate specialists will develop an individualized treatment program; the approach the doctors use, depends on which systems have been affected.

- **Skeletal.** Annual evaluations are important to detect any changes in the spine or sternum. This is particularly important in times of rapid growth, such as adolescence. A serious malformation not only can be disfiguring, but also can prevent the heart and lungs from functioning properly. In some cases, an orthopaedic brace or surgery may be recommended to limit damage and disfigurement.

- **Eyes.** Early, regular eye examinations are essential for identifying and correcting any vision problems associated with Marfan syndrome. In most cases, eyeglasses or contact lenses can correct the problem, although surgery may be necessary in some cases.

- **Heart and blood vessels.** Regular checkups and echocardiograms help the doctor evaluate the size of the aorta and the way the heart is working. The earlier a potential problem is identified and treated, the lower the risk of life-threatening complications. Those with heart problems are encouraged to wear a medical alert bracelet and to go to the emergency room if they experience chest, back, or abdominal pain. Some heart-valve problems can be managed with drugs such as beta-blockers, which may help decrease stress on the aorta. In other cases, surgery to replace a valve or repair the aorta may be necessary.

- **Nervous system.** If dural ectasia (swelling of the covering of the spinal cord) develops, medication may help minimize any associated pain.

- **Lungs.** It is especially important that people with Marfan syndrome not smoke, as they are already at increased risk for lung damage. Any problems with breathing during sleep should be assessed by a doctor.

Pregnancy poses a particular concern due to the stress on the body, particularly the heart. A pregnancy should be undertaken only under conditions specified by obstetricians and other specialists familiar with Marfan syndrome. In some cases, valve surgery prior to pregnancy may be warranted. The pregnancy should be monitored as a high-risk condition. Women with Marfan syndrome may also seek genetic counseling concerning the likelihood that they will pass the disease on to their children.

Although eating a balanced diet is important for maintaining a healthy lifestyle, no vitamin or dietary supplement has been shown to help slow, cure, or prevent Marfan syndrome.

For most people with Marfan syndrome, engaging in moderate aerobic exercise is important for promoting skeletal and cardiovascular health and a sense of well-being. However, because of the risk of aortic dissection, people with the syndrome should not engage in contact sports, competitive athletics, or isometric exercise.

What Are Some of the Emotional and Psychological Effects of Marfan Syndrome?

Being diagnosed and learning to live with a genetic disorder can cause social, emotional, and financial stress. It often requires a great deal of adjustment in outlook and lifestyle. A person who is an adult when Marfan syndrome is diagnosed may feel angry or afraid. There may also be concerns about passing the disorder to future generations or about its physical, emotional, and financial implications.

The parents and siblings of a child diagnosed with Marfan syndrome may feel sadness, anger, and guilt. It is important for parents to know that nothing that they did caused the fibrillin-1 gene to mutate. Parents may be concerned about the genetic implications for siblings or have questions about the risk to future children.

Some children with Marfan syndrome are advised to restrict their activities. This may require a lifestyle adjustment that is hard for a child to understand or accept.

For both children and adults, appropriate medical care, accurate information, and social support make it easier to live with the disease. Genetic counseling may also be helpful for understanding the disease and its potential impact on future generations.

While Marfan syndrome is a lifelong disorder, the outlook has improved in recent years. As early as the 1970s, the life expectancy of a person with Marfan syndrome was two-thirds that of a person without the disease; however, with improvements in recognition and treatment, people with Marfan syndrome now have a life expectancy similar to that of the average person.

Section 16.5

Osteogenesis Imperfecta

This section contains text excerpted from the following sources:
Text beginning with the heading "What Is Osteogenesis Imperfecta?"
is excerpted from "Osteogenesis Imperfecta," Genetics Home
Reference (GHR), National Institutes of Health (NIH), March 7,
2016; Text under the heading "What Causes Osteogenesis Imperfecta
(OI)?" is excerpted from "Questions and Answers about Marfan
Syndrome," *Eunice Kennedy Shriver* National Institute of Child
Health and Human Development (NICHD), December 16, 2013.

What Is Osteogenesis Imperfecta?

Osteogenesis imperfecta (OI) is a group of genetic disorders that
mainly affect the bones. The term "osteogenesis imperfecta" means
imperfect bone formation. People with this condition have bones that
break easily, often from mild trauma or with no apparent cause. Multiple fractures are common, and in severe cases, can occur even before
birth. Milder cases may involve only a few fractures over a person's
lifetime.

There are at least eight recognized forms of osteogenesis imperfecta,
designated type I through type VIII. The types can be distinguished
by their signs and symptoms, although their characteristic features
overlap. Type I is the mildest form of osteogenesis imperfecta and type
II is the most severe; other types of this condition have signs and symptoms that fall somewhere between these two extremes. Increasingly,
genetic factors are used to define the different forms of osteogenesis
imperfecta.

The milder forms of osteogenesis imperfecta, including type I, are
characterized by bone fractures during childhood and adolescence
that often result from minor trauma. Fractures occur less frequently
in adulthood. People with mild forms of the condition typically have a
blue or grey tint to the part of the eye that is usually white (the sclera),
and may develop hearing loss in adulthood. Affected individuals are
usually of normal or near normal height.

Other types of osteogenesis imperfecta are more severe, causing
frequent bone fractures that may begin before birth and result from

little or no trauma. Additional features of these conditions can include blue sclerae, short stature, hearing loss, respiratory problems, and a disorder of tooth development called dentinogenesis imperfecta. The most severe forms of osteogenesis imperfecta, particularly type II, can include an abnormally small, fragile rib cage and underdeveloped lungs. Infants with these abnormalities have life-threatening problems with breathing and often die shortly after birth.

How Common Is Osteogenesis Imperfecta?

This condition affects an estimated 6 to 7 per 100,000 people worldwide. Types I and IV are the most common forms of osteogenesis imperfecta, affecting 4 to 5 per 100,000 people.

What Genes Are Related to Osteogenesis Imperfecta?

Mutations in the *COL1A1, COL1A2, CRTAP,* and *P3H1* genes cause osteogenesis imperfecta.

Mutations in the *COL1A1* and *COL1A2* genes are responsible for more than 90 percent of all cases of osteogenesis imperfecta. These genes provide instructions for making proteins that are used to assemble type I collagen. This type of collagen is the most abundant protein in bone, skin, and other connective tissues that provide structure and strength to the body.

Most of the mutations that cause osteogenesis imperfecta type I occur in the *COL1A1* gene. These genetic changes reduce the amount of type I collagen produced in the body, which causes bones to be brittle and to fracture easily. The mutations responsible for most cases of osteogenesis imperfecta types II, III, and IV occur in either the *COL1A1* or *COL1A2* gene. These mutations typically alter the structure of type I collagen molecules. A defect in the structure of type I collagen weakens connective tissues, particularly bone, resulting in the characteristic features of osteogenesis imperfecta.

Mutations in the *CRTAP* and *P3H1* genes are responsible for rare, often severe cases of osteogenesis imperfecta. Cases caused by *CRTAP* mutations are usually classified as type VII; when *P3H1* mutations underlie the condition, it is classified as type VIII. The proteins produced from these genes work together to process collagen into its mature form. Mutations in either gene disrupt the normal folding, assembly, and secretion of collagen molecules. These defects weaken connective tissues, leading to severe bone abnormalities and problems with growth.

In cases of osteogenesis imperfecta without identified mutations in one of the genes described above, the cause of the disorder is unknown. These cases include osteogenesis imperfecta types V and VI. Researchers are working to identify additional genes that may be responsible for these conditions.

How Do People Inherit Osteogenesis Imperfecta?

Most cases of osteogenesis imperfecta have an autosomal dominant pattern of inheritance, which means one copy of the altered gene in each cell is sufficient to cause the condition. Many people with type I or type IV osteogenesis imperfecta inherit a mutation from a parent who has the disorder. Most infants with more severe forms of osteogenesis imperfecta (such as type II and type III) have no history of the condition in their family. In these infants, the condition is caused by new (sporadic) mutations in the *COL1A1* or *COL1A2* gene.

Less commonly, osteogenesis imperfecta has an autosomal recessive pattern of inheritance. Autosomal recessive inheritance means two copies of the gene in each cell are altered. The parents of a child with an autosomal recessive disorder typically are not affected, but each carry one copy of the altered gene. Some cases of osteogenesis imperfecta type III are autosomal recessive; these cases usually result from mutations in genes other than *COL1A1* and *COL1A2*. When osteogenesis imperfecta is caused by mutations in the *CRTAP* or *P3H1* gene, the condition also has an autosomal recessive pattern of inheritance.

What Causes Osteogenesis Imperfecta (OI)?

OI is caused by defects in or related to a protein called type 1 collagen. Collagen is an essential building block of the body. The body uses type 1 collagen to make bones strong and to build tendons, ligaments, teeth, and the whites of the eyes.

Certain gene changes, or mutations, cause the collagen defects. Mutations in several genes can lead to OI. About 80%–90% of OI cases are caused by autosomal dominant mutations in the type 1 collagen genes, *COL1A1* and *COL1A2*. Mutations in one or the other of these genes cause the body to make either abnormally formed collagen or too little collagen. Mutations in these genes cause OI Types I through IV.

The remaining cases of OI (types VI–XI) are caused by autosomal recessive mutations in any of six genes (*SERPINF1, CRTAP, LEPRE1, PPIB, SERPINH1,* and *FKBP10*) that code for proteins that help make collagen. These mutations also cause the body to make too little collagen or abnormally formed collagen.

These gene changes are inherited, or passed down from parents to their children; people who have OI are born with it. However, in some cases, the gene mutation is not inherited and occurs after conception.

What Are the Symptoms of Osteogenesis Imperfecta (OI)?

All types of OI have some degree of bone fragility and fracturing, and many have some degree of bone deformity.

The symptoms of OI vary by type:

Type I

- Most common and mildest form of OI. It can be so mild that healthcare providers do not diagnose it in some people until they are adults.

- Bone fractures occur mostly in years before puberty and decrease in frequency after puberty

- Normal height; a few inches shorter than same gender relatives

- Little or no bone deformity

- Brittle teeth in rare cases

- Hearing loss in some cases

- Blue sclera (whites of the eyes)

- Easy bruising

- Mild delay in motor skills

Type II

- Severe; usually results in stillborn birth or death in the first months of life

- Severe bone deformity

Type III

- Most severe, nonlethal form

- Hundreds of fractures starting very early in life

- Severe bone deformities and physical disability that worsen over time

- Sclera may be blue or grey
- Triangular face and prominent forehead
- Scoliosis (abnormal curving of the spine)
- Sunken or protruding chest wall
- Brittle teeth
- Hearing loss
- Very short height
- Motor skill delays
- Usually need wheelchairs

Type IV

- Similar to type I but with mild to moderate bone deformity
- Dozens of fractures on average, most of which occur before puberty or after middle age
- Motor skill delays
- People with type IV often need braces or crutches to walk
- Short height
- Brittle teeth
- Hearing loss in some cases
- White or blue sclera
- Scoliosis
- Large head
- Easy bruising

Type V

- Identical symptoms to Type IV except:
  - Normal sclera
  - Normal teeth
- Severely limited ability to twist forearms clockwise or counterclockwise
- Distinguished from Type IV by differing bone features at microscopic level

Type VI

- Identical symptoms to Type IV except:
  - Normal teeth
  - Greater frequency of fractures
- Distinguished from Type IV by differing bone features at microscopic level

Types VII and VIII

- Similar to Types II and III
- Severe or lethal bone deformity
- Type VII can also involve small head, blue sclera, bulging eyes
- Some people with Type VIII have lived into their second or third decade

Type IX

- Moderate to severe bone deformity and similar to Types III and IV
- White sclera
- Short height

Type X

- Severe and often leads to death

Type XI

- Bone deformities worsen over time

The bone deformities and collagen defects common to OI can affect various internal organs, leading to secondary problems. These include:

Lung Problems. People with OI are more vulnerable to lung problems, including asthma and pneumonia. Viral and bacterial infections can become severe. In fact, respiratory failure is the most common cause of death in people with OI.

Lung problems result from a combination of factors. If the ribs and spine do not develop normally, there may be less space for the lungs to expand. Collagen also is an important building block of connective tissue in the lungs. If the body does not make enough collagen, or makes abnormal collagen, the lungs do not work properly. This makes it difficult for people with OI to get enough oxygen through their bodies. In addition, they may have problems coughing effectively to clear away mucus.

Heart Problems. Heart problems, such as incorrectly working valves and arteries, sometimes occur in people with OI.

Neurological Problems. People with OI often have enlarged heads, called macrocephaly. They can also have a condition called hydrocephalus, in which fluid builds up inside the skull, causing the brain to swell.

People with severe OI often have basilar invagination, a malformation of the spinal column that puts pressure on the spinal cord and brain stem. It worsens over time and can cause severe headaches, changes in facial sensation, lack of control over muscle movements, and difficulty swallowing. If untreated, basilar invagination can lead to rapid neurological decline and inability to breathe.

How Do Health Care Providers Diagnose Osteogenesis Imperfecta (OI)?

If OI is moderate or severe, healthcare providers usually diagnose it during prenatal ultrasound at 18 to 24 weeks of pregnancy.

If a parent or sibling has OI, a healthcare provider can test the DNA of the fetus for the presence of an OI mutation. In this case, a healthcare provider obtains a sample of fetal cells by chorionic villus sampling (CVS) or amniocentesis. The fetal cells can also be tested for the presence of abnormal collagen.

For amniocentesis, a healthcare provider takes a small amount of fluid from the sac surrounding the fetus for testing. He or she takes the sample by inserting a thin needle into the uterus through the abdomen. For CVS, a healthcare provider uses a similar procedure to take a sample of tissue from the placenta for testing.

If OI is not detected prenatally, parents or a healthcare provider may notice symptoms in an infant or child. The healthcare provider may perform the following:

- Physical exam, which includes:
  - Measuring the length of limbs
  - Measuring the head circumference
  - Examining the eyes and teeth

- Examining the spine and rib cage
- Personal and family medical history, which include questions about:
  - Broken bones
  - Hearing loss
  - Brittle teeth
  - Adult height
  - Racial background
  - Whether close relatives have had children together
  - X-ray
  - Bone density test
  - Bone biopsy, in some cases

The healthcare providers may send blood or skin samples to a lab for collagen or genetic testing. These tests usually confirm whether a person has OI.

What Are the Treatments for Osteogenesis Imperfecta (OI)?

OI treatments are designed to prevent or control symptoms and vary from person to person. Early intervention is important to ensure optimal quality of life and outcomes. Treatment for OI and its related symptoms may include:

- **Fracture Care.** Casting, splinting, and bracing fractured bones can help them heal properly. However, bones may weaken if they are held in one place for long periods. healthcare providers try to strike a balance between healing fractures and maintaining bone strength.

- **Physical Therapy.** Physical therapy aims to maintain functioning in as many aspects of life as possible. A usual program combines muscle strengthening with aerobic conditioning. Many children with OI have delayed motor skills because their muscles are weak. A physical rehabilitation program can include strengthening of deltoids, biceps, and important lower muscles, such as the gluteus maximus, gluteus medius, and trunk extensors. When these muscles are strong, children can lift their arms and legs against the pull of gravity and get around independently.

- **Bracing.** For some people with OI, wearing braces on the legs can provide support for weak muscles, decrease pain, and keep joints properly aligned. Braces can allow people to get around and function more easily.

- **Surgical Procedures.** Some people with OI undergo surgery to correct bone deformities, including scoliosis and basilar invagination. A common surgical procedure for OI patients, "rodding," is the placement of metal rods in the long bones of the legs. This strengthens them and helps prevent fractures. Some rods get longer as the legs grow. But they also can work their way out of the bone. Surgery can also be performed to improve hearing loss.

- **Medication.** Bisphosphonates are drugs used to treat osteoporosis. They also are useful for OI, especially in children. These drugs do not build new bone, but they slow the loss of existing bone. They have been shown to reduce vertebral compressions and some long bone fractures. However, controlled trials show no improvement in motor skill or decrease in bone pain.

Treatments for Related Conditions

- Although these treatments are not specifically for OI, individuals with OI might rely on the following to address conditions related to OI:

  - Hearing aids for hearing loss

  - Crowns and similar dental devices for brittle teeth

  - Oxygen administration for people with lung problems

Can OI Lead to Cancer?

Studies comparing people with and without OI have found no differences in cancer risks between the two groups.

What If I Have OI and Want to Get Pregnant?

OI does not affect fertility. However, about one-half of women with OI give birth by cesarean section. This is because they often have pelvic bone abnormalities that prevent vaginal birth. Women with OI also are more likely to have infants who present in the breech position (feet first).

Women who have OI, have partners with OI, or have already had a child with OI should consider genetic counseling. A genetic counselor is a healthcare professional who understands the risks of having an infant with OI and can explain prenatal tests that can identify this disorder so that the family can provide care.

Section 16.6

Stickler Syndrome

This section includes text excerpted from "Stickler Syndrome," Genetic Home Reference (GHR), March 2016.

Stickler syndrome is a group of hereditary conditions characterized by a distinctive facial appearance, eye abnormalities, hearing loss, and joint problems. These signs and symptoms vary widely among affected individuals.

A characteristic feature of Stickler syndrome is a somewhat flattened facial appearance. This appearance results from underdeveloped bones in the middle of the face, including the cheekbones and the bridge of the nose. A particular group of physical features called Pierre Robin sequence is also common in people with Stickler syndrome. Pierre Robin sequence includes an opening in the roof of the mouth (a cleft palate), a tongue that is placed further back than normal (glossoptosis), and a small lower jaw (micrognathia). This combination of features can lead to feeding problems and difficulty breathing.

Many people with Stickler syndrome have severe nearsightedness (high myopia). In some cases, the clear gel that fills the eyeball (the vitreous) has an abnormal appearance, which is noticeable during an eye examination. Other eye problems are also common, including increased pressure within the eye (glaucoma), clouding of the lens of the eyes (cataracts), and tearing of the lining of the eye (retinal detachment). These eye abnormalities cause impaired vision or blindness in some cases.

In people with Stickler syndrome, hearing loss varies in degree and may become more severe over time. The hearing loss may be sensorineural, meaning that it results from changes in the inner ear, or conductive, meaning that it is caused by abnormalities of the middle ear.

Most people with Stickler syndrome have skeletal abnormalities that affect the joints. The joints of affected children and young adults may be loose and very flexible (hypermobile), though joints become less flexible with age. Arthritis often appears early in life and may cause joint pain or stiffness. Problems with the bones of the spine (vertebrae) can also occur, including abnormal curvature of the spine (scoliosis or kyphosis) and flattened vertebrae (platyspondyly). These spinal abnormalities may cause back pain.

Researchers have described several types of Stickler syndrome, which are distinguished by their genetic causes and their patterns of signs and symptoms. In particular, the eye abnormalities and severity of hearing loss differ among the types. Type I has the highest risk of retinal detachment. Type II also includes eye abnormalities, but type III does not (and is often called non-ocular Stickler syndrome). Types II and III are more likely than type I to have significant hearing loss. Types IV, V, and VI are very rare and have each been diagnosed in only a few individuals.

A condition similar to Stickler syndrome, called Marshall syndrome, is characterized by a distinctive facial appearance, eye abnormalities, hearing loss, and early-onset arthritis. Marshall syndrome can also include short stature. Some researchers have classified Marshall syndrome as a variant of Stickler syndrome, while others consider it to be a separate disorder.

Frequency

Stickler syndrome affects an estimated 1 in 7,500 to 9,000 newborns. Type I is the most common form of the condition.

Genetic Changes

Mutations in several genes cause the different types of Stickler syndrome. Between 80 and 90 percent of all cases are classified as type I and are caused by mutations in the COL2A1 gene. Another 10 to 20 percent of cases are classified as type II and result from mutations in the COL11A1 gene. Marshall syndrome, which may be a variant of Stickler syndrome, is also caused by COL11A1 gene mutations. Stickler syndrome types III through VI result from mutations in other, related genes.

All of the genes associated with Stickler syndrome provide instructions for making components of collagens, which are complex molecules that give structure and strength to the connective tissues that support the body's joints and organs. Mutations in any of these genes impair the production, processing, or assembly of collagen molecules. Defective collagen molecules or reduced amounts of collagen impair the development of connective tissues in many different parts of the body, leading to the varied features of Stickler syndrome.

Not all individuals with Stickler syndrome have mutations in one of the known genes. Researchers believe that mutations in other genes may also cause this condition, but those genes have not been identified.

Inheritance Pattern

Stickler syndrome types I, II, and III are inherited in an autosomal dominant pattern, which means one copy of the altered gene in each cell is sufficient to cause the disorder. In some cases, an affected person inherits a gene mutation from one affected parent. Other cases result from new mutations. These cases occur in people with no history of Stickler syndrome in their family.

Marshall syndrome also typically has an autosomal dominant pattern of inheritance.

Stickler syndrome types IV, V, and VI are inherited in an autosomal recessive pattern. Autosomal recessive inheritance means both copies of the gene in each cell have mutations. The parents of an individual with an autosomal recessive condition each carry one copy of the mutated gene, but they typically do not show signs and symptoms of the condition.

Other Names for This Condition

- Hereditary arthro-ophthalmo-dystrophy
- Hereditary arthro-ophthalmopathy
- Stickler dysplasia

Chapter 17

Cornelia de Lange Syndrome

What Is Cornelia de Lange Syndrome?

Cornelia de Lange syndrome is a developmental disorder that affects many parts of the body. The features of this disorder vary widely among affected individuals and range from relatively mild to severe.

Cornelia de Lange syndrome is characterized by slow growth before and after birth leading to short stature; intellectual disability that is usually moderate to severe; and abnormalities of bones in the arms, hands, and fingers. Most people with Cornelia de Lange syndrome also have distinctive facial features, including arched eyebrows that often meet in the middle (synophrys), long eyelashes, low-set ears, small and widely spaced teeth, and a small and upturned nose. Many affected individuals also have behavior problems similar to autism, a developmental condition that affects communication and social interaction.

This chapter contains text excerpted from the following sources: Text beginning with the heading "What Is Cornelia de Lange Syndrome?" is excerpted from "Cornelia de Lange Syndrome," Genetics Home Reference (GHR), National Institutes of Health (NIH), March 7, 2016; Text under the heading "What Causes Cornelia de Lange Syndrome?" is excerpted from "Cornelia de Lange syndrome," National Center for Advancing Translational Sciences (NCATS), National Institutes of Health (NIH), July 28, 2015.

Additional signs and symptoms of Cornelia de Lange syndrome can include excessive body hair (hypertrichosis), an unusually small head (microcephaly), hearing loss, and problems with the digestive tract. Some people with this condition are born with an opening in the roof of the mouth called a cleft palate. Seizures, heart defects, and eye problems have also been reported in people with this condition.

How Common Is Cornelia de Lange Syndrome?

Although the exact incidence is unknown, Cornelia de Lange syndrome likely affects 1 in 10,000 to 30,000 newborns. The condition is probably underdiagnosed because affected individuals with mild or uncommon features may never be recognized as having Cornelia de Lange syndrome.

What Genes Are Related to Cornelia de Lange Syndrome?

Cornelia de Lange syndrome can result from mutations in at least five genes: *NIPBL, SMC1A, HDAC8, RAD21,* and *SMC3.*

Mutations in the *NIPBL* gene have been identified in more than half of all people with this condition; mutations in the other genes are much less common.

The proteins produced from all five genes contribute to the structure or function of the cohesin complex, a group of proteins with an important role in directing development before birth. Within cells, the cohesin complex helps regulate the structure and organization of chromosomes, stabilize cells' genetic information, and repair damaged DNA. The cohesin complex also regulates the activity of certain genes that guide the development of limbs, face, and other parts of the body.

Mutations in the *NIPBL, SMC1A, HDAC8, RAD21,* and *SMC3* genes cause Cornelia de Lange syndrome by impairing the function of the cohesin complex, which disrupts gene regulation during critical stages of early development.

The features of Cornelia de Lange syndrome vary widely, and the severity of the disorder can differ even in individuals with the same gene mutation. Researchers suspect that additional genetic or environmental factors may be important for determining the specific signs and symptoms in each individual. In general, *SMC1A, RAD21,* and *SMC3* gene mutations cause milder signs and symptoms than *NIPBL* gene mutations. Mutations in the *HDAC8* gene cause a somewhat different set of features, including delayed closure of the "soft spot" on the head (the anterior fontanelle) in infancy, widely spaced eyes, and dental abnormalities. Like affected individuals with *NIPBL* gene mutations, those with *HDAC8* gene mutations may have significant intellectual disability.

In about 30 percent of cases, the cause of Cornelia de Lange syndrome is unknown. Researchers are looking for additional changes in the five known genes, as well as mutations in other genes, that may cause this condition.

How Do People Inherit Cornelia de Lange Syndrome?

When Cornelia de Lange syndrome is caused by mutations in the *NIPBL, RAD21,* or *SMC3* gene, the condition is considered to have an autosomal dominant pattern of inheritance. Autosomal dominant inheritance means one copy of the altered gene in each cell is sufficient to cause the disorder. Most cases result from new gene mutations and occur in people with no history of the condition in their family.

When Cornelia de Lange syndrome is caused by mutations in the *HDAC8* or *SMC1A* gene, the condition has an X-linked dominant pattern of inheritance. A condition is considered X-linked if the mutated gene that causes the disorder is located on the X chromosome, one of the two sex chromosomes. Studies of X-linked Cornelia de Lange syndrome indicate that one copy of the altered gene in each cell may be sufficient to cause the condition. Unlike X-linked recessive conditions, in which males are more frequently affected or experience more severe symptoms than females, X-linked dominant Cornelia de Lange syndrome appears to affect males and females similarly. Most cases result from new mutations in the *HDAC8* or *SMC1A* gene and occur in people with no history of the condition in their family.

What Causes Cornelia de Lange Syndrome?

Most cases (approximately 65%) of Cornelia de Lange syndrome (CdLS) are caused by changes (mutations) in the NIPBL gene. An additional 5% of people affected by the condition have mutations in one of four known genes (*SMC1A, SMC3, HDAC8,* and *RAD21*). Many of the genes associated with CdLS encode proteins that play an important role in human development before birth. Mutations in these genes may result in an abnormal protein that is not able to carry out its normal function. This is thought to interfere with early development leading to the many signs and symptoms of CdLS.

What Are the Signs and Symptoms of Cornelia de Lange Syndrome?

The signs and symptoms of Cornelia de Lange syndrome (CdLS) vary widely among affected people and can range from relatively mild to severe. Affected people may experience:

- Slowed growth before and after birth
- Intellectual disability
- Developmental delay
- Autistic and/or self-destructive behaviors
- Skeletal abnormalities of the arms and hands
- Gastrointestinal problems
- Hirsutism (excess hair growth)
- Hearing loss
- Myopia
- Congenital heart defects
- Genital abnormalities (i.e., cryptorchidism)
- Seizures

Affected people typically have distinctive craniofacial features, as well, which may include microcephaly; arched eyebrows that often grow together in the middle (synophrys); long eyelashes; low-set ears; small, widely spaced teeth; and a small, upturned nose.

How Is Cornelia de Lange Syndrome Diagnosed?

A diagnosis of Cornelia de Lange syndrome (CdLS) is generally based on the presence of characteristic signs and symptoms during a thorough medical evaluation. In some cases, genetic testing can be ordered to confirm the diagnosis; however, it may not be informative in all people affected by CdLS as the underlying genetic cause is unknown in approximately 30% of cases.

How Might Cornelia de Lange Syndrome Be Treated?

Because Cornelia de Lange syndrome (CdLS) affects many different systems of the body, medical management is often provided by a team of doctors and other healthcare professionals. Treatment for this condition varies based on the signs and symptoms present in each person. For example, many people affected by CdLS have poor growth after birth and may require supplemental formulas and/or gastrostomy tube placement to meet nutritional needs. Ongoing physical, occupational, and speech therapies are often recommended to optimize developmental potential. Surgery may be necessary to treat skeletal abnormalities, gastrointestinal problems, congenital heart defects and other health problems. Medications may be prescribed to prevent or control seizures.

What Is the Life Expectancy for People with Cornelia de Lange Syndrome?

Life expectancy is relatively normal for people with Cornelia de Lange syndrome and most affected children live well into adulthood. For example, one article mentioned a woman with Cornelia de Lange syndrome who lived to age 61 and an affected man who lived to age 54. However, certain features of this condition, particularly severe malformations of the heart or throat, may decrease life expectancy in some affected people.

Chapter 18

Cystic Fibrosis

What Is Cystic Fibrosis?

Cystic fibrosis is an inherited disease characterized by the buildup of thick, sticky mucus that can damage many of the body's organs. The disorder's most common signs and symptoms include progressive damage to the respiratory system and chronic digestive system problems. The features of the disorder and their severity varies among affected individuals.

Mucus is a slippery substance that lubricates and protects the linings of the airways, digestive system, reproductive system, and other organs and tissues. In people with cystic fibrosis, the body produces mucus that is abnormally thick and sticky. This abnormal mucus can clog the airways, leading to severe problems with breathing and bacterial infections in the lungs. These infections cause chronic coughing, wheezing, and inflammation. Over time, mucus buildup and infections result in permanent lung damage, including the formation of scar tissue (fibrosis) and cysts in the lungs.

Most people with cystic fibrosis also have digestive problems. Some affected babies have meconium ileus, a blockage of the intestine that

This chapter contains text excerpted from the following sources: Text beginning with the heading "What Is Cystic Fibrosis?" is excerpted from "Cystic Fibrosis," Genetics Home Reference (GHR), National Institutes of Health (NIH), March 7, 2016; Text under the heading "What Causes Cystic Fibrosis?" is excerpted from "Cystic Fibrosis," National Heart, Lung, and Blood Institute (NHLBI), December 26, 2013.

occurs shortly after birth. Other digestive problems result from a buildup of thick, sticky mucus in the pancreas. The pancreas is an organ that produces insulin (a hormone that helps control blood sugar levels). It also makes enzymes that help digest food. In people with cystic fibrosis, mucus blocks the ducts of the pancreas, reducing the production of insulin and preventing digestive enzymes from reaching the intestines to aid digestion. Problems with digestion can lead to diarrhea, malnutrition, poor growth, and weight loss. In adolescence or adulthood, a shortage of insulin can cause a form of diabetes known as cystic fibrosis-related diabetes mellitus (CFRDM).

Cystic fibrosis used to be considered a fatal disease of childhood. With improved treatments and better ways to manage the disease, many people with cystic fibrosis now live well into adulthood. Adults with cystic fibrosis experience health problems affecting the respiratory, digestive, and reproductive systems. Most men with cystic fibrosis have congenital bilateral absence of the vas deferens (CBAVD), a condition in which the tubes that carry sperm (the vas deferens) are blocked by mucus and do not develop properly. Men with CBAVD are unable to father children (infertile) unless they undergo fertility treatment. Women with cystic fibrosis may experience complications in pregnancy.

How Common Is Cystic Fibrosis?

Cystic fibrosis is a common genetic disease within the white population in the United States. The disease occurs in 1 in 2,500 to 3,500 white newborns. Cystic fibrosis is less common in other ethnic groups, affecting about 1 in 17,000 African Americans and 1 in 31,000 Asian Americans.

What Genes Are Related to Cystic Fibrosis?

Mutations in the *CFTR* gene cause cystic fibrosis. The *CFTR* gene provides instructions for making a channel that transports negatively charged particles called chloride ions into and out of cells. Chloride is a component of sodium chloride, a common salt found in sweat. Chloride also has important functions in cells; for example, the flow of chloride ions helps control the movement of water in tissues, which is necessary for the production of thin, freely flowing mucus.

Mutations in the *CFTR* gene disrupt the function of the chloride channels, preventing them from regulating the flow of chloride ions and water across cell membranes. As a result, cells that line the passageways of the lungs, pancreas, and other organs produce mucus that is unusually thick and sticky. This mucus clogs the airways and various ducts, causing the characteristic signs and symptoms of cystic fibrosis.

Other genetic and environmental factors likely influence the severity of the condition. For example, mutations in genes other than *CFTR* might help explain why some people with cystic fibrosis are more severely affected than others. Most of these genetic changes have not been identified, however.

How Do People Inherit Cystic Fibrosis?

This condition is inherited in an autosomal recessive pattern, which means both copies of the gene in each cell have mutations. The parents of an individual with an autosomal recessive condition each carry one copy of the mutated gene, but they typically do not show signs and symptoms of the condition.

What Causes Cystic Fibrosis?

A defect in the *CFTR* gene causes cystic fibrosis (CF). This gene makes a protein that controls the movement of salt and water in and out of your body's cells. In people who have CF, the gene makes a protein that doesn't work well. This causes thick, sticky mucus and very salty sweat.

Research suggests that the *CFTR* protein also affects the body in other ways. This may help explain other symptoms and complications of CF.

More than a thousand known defects can affect the *CFTR* gene. The type of defect you or your child has may affect the severity of CF. Other genes also may play a role in the severity of the disease.

What Are the Signs and Symptoms of Cystic Fibrosis?

The signs and symptoms of cystic fibrosis (CF) vary from person to person and over time. Sometimes you'll have few symptoms. Other times, your symptoms may become more severe.

One of the first signs of CF that parents may notice is that their baby's skin tastes salty when kissed, or the baby doesn't pass stool when first born. Most of the other signs and symptoms of CF happen later. They're related to how CF affects the respiratory, digestive, or reproductive systems of the body.

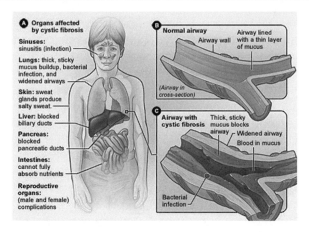

Figure 18.1. *(A) shows the organs that cystic fibrosis can affect. (B) shows a cross-section of a normal airway. (C) shows an airway with cystic fibrosis. The widened airway is blocked by thick, sticky mucus that contains blood and bacteria.*

Respiratory System Signs and Symptoms

People who have CF have thick, sticky mucus that builds up in their airways. This buildup of mucus makes it easier for bacteria to grow and cause infections. Infections can block the airways and cause frequent coughing that brings up thick sputum (spit) or mucus that's sometimes bloody.

People who have CF tend to have lung infections caused by unusual germs that don't respond to standard antibiotics. For example, lung infections caused by bacteria called mucoid Pseudomonas are much more common in people who have CF than in those who don't. An infection caused by these bacteria may be a sign of CF.

People who have CF have frequent bouts of sinusitis, an infection of the sinuses. The sinuses are hollow air spaces around the eyes, nose, and forehead. Frequent bouts of bronchitis and pneumonia also can occur. These infections can cause long-term lung damage.

As CF gets worse, you may have more serious problems, such as pneumothorax or bronchiectasis. Some people who have CF also develop nasal polyps (growths in the nose) that may require surgery.

Digestive System Signs and Symptoms

In CF, mucus can block tubes, or ducts, in your pancreas (an organ in your abdomen). These blockages prevent enzymes from reaching your intestines.

As a result, your intestines can't fully absorb fats and proteins. This can cause ongoing diarrhea or bulky, foul-smelling, greasy stools. Intestinal blockages also may occur, especially in newborns. Too much gas or severe constipation in the intestines may cause stomach pain and discomfort.

A hallmark of CF in children is poor weight gain and growth. These children are unable to get enough nutrients from their food because of the lack of enzymes to help absorb fats and proteins.

As CF gets worse, other problems may occur, such as:

- Pancreatitis. This is a condition in which the pancreas become inflamed, which causes pain.

- Rectal prolapse. Frequent coughing or problems passing stools may cause rectal tissue from inside you to move out of your rectum.

- Liver disease due to inflamed or blocked bile ducts.

- Diabetes.

- Gallstones.

Reproductive System Signs and Symptoms

Men who have CF are infertile because they're born without a vas deferens. The vas deferens is a tube that delivers sperm from the testes to the penis. Women who have CF may have a hard time getting pregnant because of mucus blocking the cervix or other CF complications.

Other Signs, Symptoms, and Complications

Other signs and symptoms of CF are related to an upset of the balance of minerals in your blood.

CF causes your sweat to become very salty. As a result, your body loses large amounts of salt when you sweat. This can cause dehydration (a lack of fluid in your body), increased heart rate, fatigue (tiredness), weakness, decreased blood pressure, heat stroke, and, rarely, death.

CF also can cause clubbing and low bone density. Clubbing is the widening and rounding of the tips of your fingers and toes. This sign develops late in CF because your lungs aren't moving enough oxygen into your bloodstream.

Low bone density also tends to occur late in CF. It can lead to bone-thinning disorders called osteoporosis and osteopenia.

How Is Cystic Fibrosis Diagnosed?

Doctors diagnose cystic fibrosis (CF) based on the results from various tests.

Newborn Screening

All States screen newborns for CF using a genetic test or a blood test. The genetic test shows whether a newborn has faulty CFTR genes. The blood test shows whether a newborn's pancreas is working properly.

Sweat Test

If a genetic test or blood test suggests CF, a doctor will confirm the diagnosis using a sweat test. This test is the most useful test for diagnosing CF. A sweat test measures the amount of salt in sweat.

For this test, the doctor triggers sweating on a small patch of skin on an arm or leg. He or she rubs the skin with a sweat-producing chemical and then uses an electrode to provide a mild electrical current. This may cause a tingling or warm feeling.

Sweat is collected on a pad or paper and then analyzed. The sweat test usually is done twice. High salt levels confirm a diagnosis of CF.

Other Tests

If you or your child has CF, your doctor may recommend other tests, such as:

- **Genetic tests** to find out what type of CFTR defect is causing your CF.

- **A chest X-ray.** This test creates pictures of the structures in your chest, such as your heart, lungs, and blood vessels. A chest X-ray can show whether your lungs are inflamed or scarred, or whether they trap air.

- **A sinus X-ray.** This test may show signs of sinusitis, a complication of CF.

- **Lung function tests.** These tests measure how much air you can breathe in and out, how fast you can breathe air out, and how well your lungs deliver oxygen to your blood.

- **A sputum culture.** For this test, your doctor will take a sample of your sputum (spit) to see whether bacteria are growing in it.

If you have bacteria called mucoid Pseudomonas, you may have more advanced CF that needs aggressive treatment.

Prenatal Screening

If you're pregnant, prenatal genetic tests can show whether your fetus has CF. These tests include amniocentesis and chorionic villus sampling (CVS).

In amniocentesis, your doctor inserts a hollow needle through your abdominal wall into your uterus. He or she removes a small amount of fluid from the sac around the baby. The fluid is tested to see whether both of the baby's CFTR genes are normal.

In CVS, your doctor threads a thin tube through the vagina and cervix to the placenta. The doctor removes a tissue sample from the placenta using gentle suction. The sample is tested to see whether the baby has CF.

Cystic Fibrosis Carrier Testing

People who have one normal *CFTR* gene and one faulty *CFTR* gene are CF carriers. CF carriers usually have no symptoms of CF and live normal lives. However, carriers can pass faulty *CFTR* genes on to their children.

If you have a family history of CF or a partner who has CF (or a family history of it) and you're planning a pregnancy, you may want to find out whether you're a CF carrier. A genetics counselor can test a blood or saliva sample to find out whether you have a faulty CF gene. This type of testing can detect faulty CF genes in 9 out of 10 cases.

How Is Cystic Fibrosis Treated?

Cystic fibrosis (CF) has no cure. However, treatments have greatly improved in recent years. The goals of CF treatment include:

- Preventing and controlling lung infections
- Loosening and removing thick, sticky mucus from the lungs
- Preventing or treating blockages in the intestines
- Providing enough nutrition
- Preventing dehydration (a lack of fluid in the body)

Depending on the severity of CF, you or your child may be treated in a hospital.

Specialists Involved

If you or your child has CF, you may be treated by a CF specialist. This is a doctor who is familiar with the complex nature of CF.

Often, a CF specialist works with a medical team of nurses, physical therapists, dietitians, and social workers. CF specialists often are located at major medical centers.

The United States also has more than 100 CF Care Centers. These centers have teams of doctors, nurses, dietitians, respiratory therapists, physical therapists, and social workers who have special training related to CF care. Most CF Care Centers have pediatric and adult programs or clinics.

Treatment for Lung Problems

The main treatments for lung problems in people who have CF are chest physical therapy (CPT), exercise, and medicines. Your doctor also may recommend a pulmonary rehabilitation (PR) program.

Chest Physical Therapy. CPT also is called chest clapping or percussion. It involves pounding your chest and back over and over with your hands or a device to loosen the mucus from your lungs so that you can cough it up.

You might sit down or lie on your stomach with your head down while you do CPT. Gravity and force help drain the mucus from your lungs.

Some people find CPT hard or uncomfortable to do. Several devices have been developed that may help with CPT, such as:

- An electric chest clapper, known as a mechanical percussor.

- An inflatable therapy vest that uses high-frequency airwaves to force the mucus that's deep in your lungs toward your upper airways so you can cough it up.

- A small, handheld device that you exhale through. The device causes vibrations that dislodge the mucus.

- A mask that creates vibrations that help break the mucus loose from your airway walls.

Breathing techniques also may help dislodge mucus so you can cough it up. These techniques include forcing out a couple of short breaths or deeper breaths and then doing relaxed breathing. This may help loosen the mucus in your lungs and open your airways.

Exercise. Aerobic exercise that makes you breathe harder can help loosen the mucus in your airways so you can cough it up. Exercise also helps improve your overall physical condition.

However, CF causes your sweat to become very salty. As a result, your body loses large amounts of salt when you sweat. Thus, your doctor may recommend a high-salt diet or salt supplements to maintain the balance of minerals in your blood.

If you exercise regularly, you may be able to cut back on your CPT. However, you should check with your doctor first.

Medicines. If you have CF, your doctor may prescribe antibiotics, anti-inflammatory medicines, bronchodilators, or medicines to help clear the mucus. These medicines help treat or prevent lung infections, reduce swelling and open up the airways, and thin mucus. If you have mutations in a gene called G551D, which occurs in about 5 percent of people who have CF, your doctor may prescribe the oral medicine ivacaftor (approved for people with CF who are 6 years of age and older).

Antibiotics are the main treatment to prevent or treat lung infections. Your doctor may prescribe oral, inhaled, or intravenous (IV) antibiotics.

Oral antibiotics often are used to treat mild lung infections. Inhaled antibiotics may be used to prevent or control infections caused by the bacteria mucoid Pseudomonas. For severe or hard-to-treat infections, you may be given antibiotics through an IV tube (a tube inserted into a vein). This type of treatment may require you to stay in a hospital.

Anti-inflammatory medicines can help reduce swelling in your airways due to ongoing infections. These medicines may be inhaled or oral.

Bronchodilators help open the airways by relaxing the muscles around them. These medicines are inhaled. They're often taken just before CPT to help clear mucus out of your airways. You also may take bronchodilators before inhaling other medicines into your lungs.

Your doctor may prescribe medicines to reduce the stickiness of your mucus and loosen it up. These medicines can help clear out mucus, improve lung function, and prevent worsening lung symptoms.

Treatments for Advanced Lung Disease. If you have advanced lung disease, you may need oxygen therapy. Oxygen usually is given through nasal prongs or a mask.

If other treatments haven't worked, a lung transplant may be an option if you have severe lung disease. A lung transplant is surgery to remove a person's diseased lung and replace it with a healthy lung from a deceased donor.

185

Pulmonary Rehabilitation. Your doctor may recommend PR as part of your treatment plan. PR is a broad program that helps improve the well-being of people who have chronic (ongoing) breathing problems.

PR doesn't replace medical therapy. Instead, it's used with medical therapy and may include:

- Exercise training

- Nutritional counseling

- Education on your lung disease or condition and how to manage it

- Energy-conserving techniques

- Breathing strategies

- Psychological counseling and/or group support

PR has many benefits. It can improve your ability to function and your quality of life. The program also may help relieve your breathing problems. Even if you have advanced lung disease, you can still benefit from PR.

Treatment for Digestive Problems

CF can cause many digestive problems, such as bulky stools, intestinal gas, a swollen belly, severe constipation, and pain or discomfort. Digestive problems also can lead to poor growth and development in children.

Nutritional therapy can improve your strength and ability to stay active. It also can improve growth and development in children. Nutritional therapy also may make you strong enough to resist some lung infections. A nutritionist can help you create a nutritional plan that meets your needs.

In addition to having a well-balanced diet that's rich in calories, fat, and protein, your nutritional therapy may include:

- Oral pancreatic enzymes to help you digest fats and proteins and absorb more vitamins.

- Supplements of vitamins A, D, E, and K to replace the fat-soluble vitamins that your intestines can't absorb.

- High-calorie shakes to provide you with extra nutrients.

- A high-salt diet or salt supplements that you take before exercising.

- A feeding tube to give you more calories at night while you're sleeping. The tube may be threaded through your nose and throat and into your stomach. Or, the tube may be placed directly into your stomach through a surgically made hole. Before you go to bed each night, you'll attach a bag with a nutritional solution to the entrance of the tube. It will feed you while you sleep.

Other treatments for digestive problems may include enemas and mucus-thinning medicines to treat intestinal blockages. Sometimes surgery is needed to remove an intestinal blockage.

Your doctor also may prescribe medicines to reduce your stomach acid and help oral pancreatic enzymes work better.

Treatments for Cystic Fibrosis Complications

A common complication of CF is diabetes. The type of diabetes associated with CF often requires different treatment than other types of diabetes. Another common CF complication is the bone-thinning disorder osteoporosis. Your doctor may prescribe medicines that prevent your bones from losing their density.

Chapter 19

Endocrine Disorders

Chapter Contents

Section 19.1

Congenital Adrenal Hyperplasia

This section includes text excerpted from "Congenital Adrenal Hyperplasia," *Eunice Kennedy Shriver* National Institute of Child Health and Human Development (NICHD), September 7, 2013.

What Is Congenital Adrenal Hyperplasia?

Congenital Adrenal Hyperplasia (CAH) refers to a group of genetic disorders that affect the adrenal glands. These glands sit on top of the kidneys and release hormones the body needs to function. CAH is caused by three disturbances:

- **Too little cortisol.** The adrenal glands of infants born with CAH cannot make enough of the hormone cortisol. This hormone affects energy levels, blood sugar levels, blood pressure, and the body's response to stress, illness, and injury.

- **Too little aldosterone.** In about 75% of cases, infants born with CAH cannot make enough of the hormone aldosterone, which helps the body maintain the proper level of sodium (salt) and water and helps maintain blood pressure.

- **Too much androgens.** In certain cases, infants born with CAH produce too much of male hormones, androgens. Proper levels of these hormones are needed for normal growth and development in both boys and girls.

CAH can also cause imbalances in the hormone adrenaline, which affects blood sugar levels, blood pressure, and the body's response to stress.

The hormone imbalances in most cases of CAH (about 95%) are caused by too little of a substance called 21-hydroxylase. The adrenal glands need 21-hydroxylase to make proper amounts of hormones. This type of CAH is sometimes referred to as 21-hydroxylase deficiency. In CAH due to 21-hydroxylase deficiency, the adrenal glands cannot make enough cortisol or aldosterone. In addition, the glands make too much androgen. People with 21-hydroxylase deficiency also may not produce enough adrenaline.

About 5% of cases of CAH are caused by deficiency in a substance similar to 21-hydroxylase, called 11-hydroxylase. This type of CAH is sometimes referred to as 11-hydroxylase deficiency. In CAH due to 11-hydroxylase deficiency, the adrenal glands make too little cortisol and too many androgens. This type of CAH does not result in aldosterone deficiency.

Other very rare types of CAH include 3-betahydroxy-steroid dehydrogenase deficiency, lipoid CAH, and 17-hydroxylase deficiency. They are not discussed here.

CAH can be categorized as classic or nonclassic types based on severity:

- **Classic CAH** is more severe than the nonclassic form. It can be life threatening in newborns if it is not diagnosed. Classic CAH can be caused by either 21-hydroxylase or 11-hydroxylase deficiency.

- **Nonclassic CAH** is sometimes called late-onset CAH. It is a milder form of the disorder that usually is diagnosed in late childhood or early adolescence. Sometimes, people have nonclassic CAH and never know it. This form of CAH is almost always caused by 21-hydroxylase deficiency.

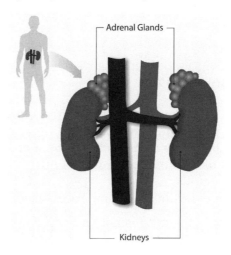

Figure 19.1. *Adrenal Glands*

What Causes Congenital Adrenal Hyperplasia (CAH)?

CAH is caused by changes (mutations) in one of several genes. These changes lead to deficiencies in 21-hydroxylase or, less

191

commonly, 11-hydroxylase. Both of these are chemicals called enzymes. The adrenal glands need these enzymes to make proper amounts of the hormones: cortisol, aldosterone, androgens, and adrenaline.

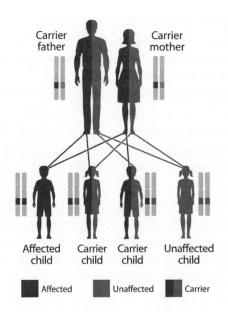

Figure 19.2. *Inheritance*

How Is CAH Inherited?

The genes for CAH are passed down from parents to their children. In general, people have two copies of every gene in their bodies. They receive one copy from each parent. For an infant to have CAH, both copies must have an error that affects an adrenal-gland enzyme.

CAH is an example of an autosomal recessive disorder:

• Autosomal means the gene is not on the X chromosome or Y chromosome.

• Recessive means that both copies of the gene must have the error for the disease or disorder to occur.

If both parents have CAH, all of their children will also have it. If each parent carries one affected gene and one normal gene (called a "carrier"), there is a one-in-four chance of their child having CAH.

How Many People Are Affected by or at Risk for Congenital Adrenal Hyperplasia (CAH)?

Classic CAH occurs in about one of every 15,000 births worldwide. It occurs in about one of every 1,000 people, but could occur in as many as 1 in 20 people in some communities. It is more common in Ashkenazi Jews, Hispanics, Italians, and Yugoslavians.

What Are the Symptoms of Congenital Adrenal Hyperplasia (CAH)?

Classic CAH

Symptoms of classic CAH due to 21-hydroxylase deficiency (95% of classic CAH cases) can be grouped into two types according to their severity: salt wasting and simple virilizing (also called non-salt wasting).

Symptoms of classic CAH due to 11-hydroxylase deficiency (5% of classic CAH cases) are similar to those of simple virilizing CAH. About two-thirds of people with classic 11-hydroxylase deficiency also have high blood pressure (hypertension).

Salt-wasting CAH: Salt-wasting CAH is the severe form of classic 21-hydroxylase deficiency. In this type of CAH, the adrenal glands make too little aldosterone, causing the body to be unable to retain enough sodium (salt). Too much sodium is lost in urine (thus the name, "salt-wasting"). If undiagnosed, symptoms of classic salt-wasting CAH appear within days or weeks of birth and, in some cases, death occurs. Symptoms may include:

- Dehydration
- Poor feeding
- Diarrhea
- Vomiting
- Heart rhythm problems (arrhythmias)
- Low blood pressure
- Very low blood sodium levels
- Low blood glucose
- Too much acid in the blood, called metabolic acidosis
- Weight loss

Shock, a condition where not enough blood gets to the brain and other organs. Shock in infants with salt-wasting is called adrenal crisis. Signs include confusion, irritability, rapid heart rate, and/or coma.

Even when carefully treated, children with salt-wasting CAH are still at risk for adrenal crises when they become ill or are under physical stress. The body needs more than the usual amount of adrenal hormones during illness, injury, or physical stress. This means a child with CAH must be given more medication during these times to prevent an adrenal crisis.

Salt-wasting CAH also involves symptoms caused by low cortisol and high androgens. These symptoms may include:

- In female newborns, external genitalia can be ambiguous, i.e., not typical female appearing, with normal internal reproductive organs (ovaries, uterus, and fallopian tubes)

- Enlarged genitalia in male newborns

- Development of certain qualities called virilization in boys or girls before the normal age of puberty, sometimes as early as age 2 or 3. This is a condition characterized by:

  - Rapid growth

  - Appearance of pubic and armpit hair

  - Deep voice

  - Failure to menstruate, or abnormal or irregular menstrual periods (females)

  - Well-developed muscles

  - Enlarged penis (males)

  - Unusually tall height as children, but being shorter than normal as adults

  - Possible difficulties getting pregnant (females)

  - Excess facial hair (females)

  - Early beard (males)

  - Severe acne

  - Benign testicular tumors and infertility (males)

- **Simple virilizing (non-salt wasting) CAH:** Simple virilizing CAH is the moderate form of classic 21-hydroxylase deficiency.

This type of CAH involves less severe aldosterone deficiency. Therefore, there are no severe or life-threatening sodium-deficiency symptoms in newborns. Like salt-wasting CAH, simple virilizing CAH involves too little cortisol and too much androgen. Female newborns have ambiguous genitalia and young children display virilization.

Nonclassic CAH

Almost all cases of nonclassic CAH are caused by a mild 21-hydroxylase deficiency. Most symptoms of nonclassic CAH are related to increased androgens. Symptoms can show up in childhood, adolescence, or early adulthood.

Symptoms of nonclassic CAH can include:

- Rapid growth in childhood and early teens but shorter height than both parents

- Early signs of puberty

- Acne

- Irregular menstrual periods (females)

- Fertility problems (in about 10% to 15% of women)

- Excess facial or body hair in women

- Male-pattern baldness (hair loss near the temples)

- Enlarged penis (males)

- Small testicles (males)

Some people have nonclassic CAH and never know it because the symptoms are so mild.

How Do Health Care Providers Diagnose Congenital Adrenal Hyperplasia (CAH)?

During Pregnancy

If a woman already has a child with CAH and becomes pregnant with the same partner, her fetus has a one in four chance of having CAH. For this reason, prenatal testing can be done for some forms of CAH. A health care provider checks for the disorder by using techniques called amniocentesis or chorionic villus sampling.

- **Amniocentesis.** This involves inserting a needle into the womb, through the abdomen, to withdraw a small amount of fluid from the sac that surrounds the fetus. The procedure is usually done between the 15th and 20th week of pregnancy.

- **Chorionic villus sampling.** This is similar to amniocentesis. A health care provider inserts a needle into the womb, either through the abdomen or the cervix, and extracts a small piece of tissue from the chorionic villi (the tissue that will later become the placenta). This procedure is usually done between the 10th and 12th week of pregnancy.

After a health care provider takes a sample using one of these techniques, he or she will perform a genetic test on the sample. This test will reveal whether the fetus has a gene change that causes CAH.

Parents may also choose to wait until birth to have the newborn tested. Talking to their health care providers may help parents identify the option that is right for them.

At Birth

All U.S. states have neonatal screening for CAH. Infants who test positive need to have follow-up testing done to confirm the diagnosis. If, for some reason, the neonatal screening is negative but there is high suspicion for CAH (such as ambiguous genitalia), further evaluation is also indicated.

Later in Life

Newborns do not show symptoms of nonclassic CAH, and the test done on newborns does not detect nonclassic CAH. Nonclassic CAH is diagnosed in childhood or adulthood, when symptoms appear. To diagnose nonclassic CAH, a health care provider may:

- Ask whether family members have CAH.

- Do a physical exam.

- Take blood and urine to measure hormone levels.

- Do a genetic test to determine if the patient has the gene change that causes CAH.

An X-ray can help to diagnose CAH in children. Because some children with CAH grow too quickly, their bones will be more developed than normal for their age.

What Are the Treatments for Congenital Adrenal Hyperplasia (CAH)?

Treatments for CAH include medication and surgery as well as psychological support.

Medication

Classic CAH. Newborns with classic CAH should start treatment very soon after birth to reduce the effects of CAH. Classic CAH is treated with steroids that replace the low hormones.

- Infants and children usually take a form of cortisol called hydrocortisone.

- Adults take hydrocortisone, prednisone, or dexamethasone, which also replace cortisol.

- Patients with classic CAH also take another medicine, fludrocortisone, to replace aldosterone.

- Eating salty foods or taking salt pills may also help salt-wasters retain salt.

The body needs more cortisol when it is under physical stress. Adults and children with classic CAH need close medical attention and may need to take more of their medication during these times. They may also need more medication if they:

- Have an illness with a high fever.

- Undergo surgery.

- Sustain a major injury.

People who have classic CAH need to wear a medical alert identification (ID) bracelet or necklace. To alert medical professionals in case of an emergency, the bracelet or necklace should read: "adrenal insufficiency, requires hydrocortisone." Adults or parents also need to learn how to give an injection of hydrocortisone if there is an emergency.

Patients with classic CAH need to take medication daily for their entire lives. If a patient stops taking his or her medication, symptoms will return.

The body makes different amounts of cortisol at different times in life, so sometimes a patient's dose of medication may be too high or too low. Taking too much medication to replace cortisol can cause symptoms of Cushing's syndrome. These include:

- Weight gain

- Slowed growth

- Stretch marks on the skin

- Rounded face

- High blood pressure

- Bone loss

- High blood sugar

It is important to alert the health care provider if these symptoms appear so that he or she can adjust the medication dose.

Nonclassic CAH. People with nonclassic CAH may not need treatment if they do not have symptoms. Individuals with symptoms are given low doses of the same cortisol replacing medication taken by people with classic CAH.

Symptoms of nonclassic CAH that signal that the patient may need treatment are:

- Early puberty

- Excess body hair

- Irregular menstrual periods (females)

- Infertility

It may be possible for patients with nonclassic CAH to stop medication as adults if their symptoms go away.

Surgery

Classic CAH. Girls who are born with ambiguous external genitalia usually have surgery. For example, surgery is necessary if changes to the genitals have affected urine flow. Surgery to make the genitals look more female also can be done.

The Endocrine Society, which supports hormonal research and clinical practice, recommends that this feminizing surgery be considered during infancy. If it is done, the group recommends choosing an experienced surgeon who practices in a center that sees many CAH cases.

The Congenital Adrenal Hyperplasia Research, Education and Support (CARES) Foundation strongly recommends delaying surgery until:

- The child is medically stable,

- Parents are fully informed of the risks and benefits, and

- A surgeon with expertise in this type of procedure is found.

Parents should also find a psychologist, social worker, or other mental health professional to support them in their decision making. It is important to find an experienced mental health provider whose expertise includes working with children who have CAH and their special needs.

Nonclassic CAH. CAH Girls with nonclassic CAH have normal genitals, so they do not need surgery.

If My Children Have CAH Can They Go to Day Care and School?

Yes, children with CAH can attend day care and school. Before enrolling children in day care, parents should explain that the child has adrenal insufficiency, which might require the administration of emergency medication. Parents should discuss the day care provider's policy on giving medications to children. They should also provide a set of written instructions, as well as a list of emergency contact names and numbers.

Before a child starts school, parents should consider meeting with the teacher, principal, and school nurse to explain the child's condition. Parents can also discuss precautions to take if the child becomes ill.

I Have CAH and Want to Start a Family. What Should I Be Thinking About?

Anyone with CAH, or from a family in which CAH has been diagnosed, should consider genetic counseling. Genetic counselors discuss all options for having a child. They explain the risks and benefits of each option.

The genes for CAH are passed down from parents to their children. In general, people have two copies of every gene in their bodies. They receive one copy from each parent. For an infant to have CAH, both copies must have an error that affects an adrenal-gland enzyme.

CAH is an example of an autosomal recessive disorder:

- Autosomal means the gene is not on the X chromosome or Y chromosome.

- Recessive means that both copies of the gene must have the error for the disease or disorder to occur.

If both parents have CAH, all of their children also will have it. If each parent carries one affected gene and one normal gene, there is a one in four chance of a child having CAH.

For Women

Women with CAH can get pregnant. In some of the women, high levels of androgens disrupt the regular release of the egg from the ovary, a process known as ovulation. Some women also have irregular menstrual cycles. These problems can make it more difficult to get pregnant. These women often can be helped with medicines. Women with CAH who want to become pregnant can meet with a reproductive endocrinologist. This is a health care provider who specializes in fertility issues.

Women with CAH who become pregnant should continue taking their medications.

For Men

Men with CAH can father children. The main challenges for these men are low testosterone (a hormone important for male fertility and sexual function), and growths in the testicles called adrenal rest tissue. These problems can cause reduced sperm production. These issues tend to occur when hormone imbalances are not well controlled with medicines. Men who wish to father children should take all medicines as directed. A health care provider may recommend that males with CAH who have gone through puberty get an ultrasound of the testicles. The ultrasound provides a picture of the inside of the testicle and can help a health care provider detect abnormal growths. Future ultrasounds can be compared with the original to quickly identify any problems.

Section 19.2

Congenital Hypothyroidism

This section includes text excerpted from "Congenital
Hypothyroidism," Genetics Home Reference (GHR), National
Institutes of Health (NIH), March 7, 2016.

What Is Congenital Hypothyroidism?

Congenital hypothyroidism is a partial or complete loss of function of the thyroid gland (hypothyroidism) that affects infants from birth (congenital). The thyroid gland is a butterfly-shaped tissue in the lower neck. It makes iodine-containing hormones that play an important role in regulating growth, brain development, and the rate of chemical reactions in the body (metabolism). People with congenital hypothyroidism have lower-than-normal levels of these important hormones.

Congenital hypothyroidism occurs when the thyroid gland fails to develop or function properly. In 80 to 85 percent of cases, the thyroid gland is absent, severely reduced in size (hypoplastic), or abnormally located. These cases are classified as thyroid dysgenesis. In the remainder of cases, a normal-sized or enlarged thyroid gland (goiter) is present, but production of thyroid hormones is decreased or absent. Most of these cases occur when one of several steps in the hormone synthesis process is impaired; these cases are classified as thyroid dyshormonogenesis. Less commonly, reduction or absence of thyroid hormone production is caused by impaired stimulation of the production process (which is normally done by a structure at the base of the brain called the pituitary gland), even though the process itself is unimpaired. These cases are classified as central (or pituitary) hypothyroidism.

Signs and symptoms of congenital hypothyroidism result from the shortage of thyroid hormones. Affected babies may show no features of the condition, although some babies with congenital hypothyroidism are less active and sleep more than normal. They may have difficulty feeding and experience constipation. If untreated, congenital hypothyroidism can lead to intellectual disability and slow growth. In the

United States and many other countries, all hospitals test newborns for congenital hypothyroidism. If treatment begins in the first two weeks after birth, infants usually develop normally.

Congenital hypothyroidism can also occur as part of syndromes that affect other organs and tissues in the body. These forms of the condition are described as syndromic. Some common forms of syndromic hypothyroidism include Pendred syndrome, Bamforth-Lazarus syndrome, and brain-lung-thyroid syndrome.

How Common Is Congenital Hypothyroidism?

Congenital hypothyroidism affects an estimated 1 in 2,000 to 4,000 newborns. For reasons that remain unclear, congenital hypothyroidism affects more than twice as many females as males.

What Genes Are Related to Congenital Hypothyroidism?

Congenital hypothyroidism can be caused by a variety of factors, only some of which are genetic. The most common cause worldwide is a shortage of iodine in the diet of the mother and the affected infant. Iodine is essential for the production of thyroid hormones. Genetic causes account for about 15 to 20 percent of cases of congenital hypothyroidism.

The cause of the most common type of congenital hypothyroidism, thyroid dysgenesis, is usually unknown. Studies suggest that 2 to 5 percent of cases are inherited. Two of the genes involved in this form of the condition are PAX8 and TSHR. These genes play roles in the proper growth and development of the thyroid gland. Mutations in these genes prevent or disrupt normal development of the gland. The abnormal or missing gland cannot produce normal amounts of thyroid hormones.

Thyroid dyshormonogenesis results from mutations in one of several genes involved in the production of thyroid hormones. These genes include DUOX2, SLC5A5, TG, and TPO. Mutations in each of these genes disrupt a step in thyroid hormone synthesis, leading to abnormally low levels of these hormones. Mutations in the TSHB gene disrupt the synthesis of thyroid hormones by impairing the stimulation of hormone production. Changes in this gene are the primary cause of central hypothyroidism. The resulting shortage of thyroid hormones disrupts normal growth, brain development, and metabolism, leading to the features of congenital hypothyroidism.

Mutations in other genes that have not been as well character-ized can also cause congenital hypothyroidism. Still other genes are involved in syndromic forms of the disorder.

How Do People Inherit Congenital Hypothyroidism?

Most cases of congenital hypothyroidism are sporadic, which means they occur in people with no history of the disorder in their family.

When inherited, the condition usually has an autosomal recessive inheritance pattern, which means both copies of the gene in each cell have mutations. Typically, the parents of an individual with an auto-somal recessive condition each carry one copy of the mutated gene, but they do not show signs and symptoms of the condition.

When congenital hypothyroidism results from mutations in the PAX8 gene or from certain mutations in the TSHR or DUOX2 gene, the condition has an autosomal dominant pattern of inheritance, which means one copy of the altered gene in each cell is sufficient to cause the disorder. In some of these cases, an affected person inherits the mutation from one affected parent. Other cases result from new (de novo) mutations in the gene that occur during the formation of repro-ductive cells (eggs or sperm) or in early embryonic development. These cases occur in people with no history of the disorder in their family.

Section 19.3

Kallmann Syndrome

This section includes text excerpted from "Kallmann Syndrome," Genetics Home Reference (GHR), National Institutes of Health (NIH), March 7, 2016.

What Is Kallmann Syndrome?

Kallmann syndrome is a condition characterized by delayed or absent puberty and an impaired sense of smell.

This disorder is a form of hypogonadotropic hypogonadism (HH), which is a condition affecting the production of hormones that direct sexual development. Males with hypogonadotropic hypogonadism are often born with an unusually small penis (micropenis) and undescended testes (cryptorchidism). At puberty, most affected individuals do not develop secondary sex characteristics, such as the growth of facial hair and deepening of the voice in males. Affected females usually do not begin menstruating at puberty and have little or no breast development. In some people, puberty is incomplete or delayed.

In Kallmann syndrome, the sense of smell is either diminished (hyposmia) or completely absent (anosmia). This feature distinguishes Kallmann syndrome from most other forms of hypogonadotropic hypogonadism, which do not affect the sense of smell. Many people with Kallmann syndrome are not aware that they are unable to detect odors until the impairment is discovered through testing.

The features of Kallmann syndrome vary, even among affected people in the same family. Additional signs and symptoms can include a failure of one kidney to develop (unilateral renal agenesis), a cleft lip with or without an opening in the roof of the mouth (a cleft palate), abnormal eye movements, hearing loss, and abnormalities of tooth development. Some affected individuals have a condition called bimanual synkinesis, in which the movements of one hand are mirrored by the other hand. Bimanual synkinesis can make it difficult to do tasks that require the hands to move separately, such as playing a musical instrument.

Researchers have identified four forms of Kallmann syndrome, designated types 1 through 4, which are distinguished by their genetic cause. The four types are each characterized by hypogonadotropic hypogonadism and an impaired sense of smell. Additional features, such as a cleft palate, seem to occur only in types 1 and 2.

How Common Is Kallmann Syndrome?

Kallmann syndrome is estimated to affect 1 in 10,000 to 86,000 people and occurs more often in males than in females. Kallmann syndrome 1 is the most common form of the disorder.

What Genes Are Related to Kallmann Syndrome?

Mutations in the *ANOS1, FGFR1, PROKR2,* and *PROK2* genes cause Kallmann syndrome. *ANOS1* gene mutations are responsible for Kallmann syndrome 1. Kallmann syndrome 2 results from mutations in the *FGFR1* gene. Mutations in the *PROKR2* and *PROK2* genes cause Kallmann syndrome types 3 and 4, respectively.

The genes associated with Kallmann syndrome play a role in the development of certain areas of the brain before birth. Although some of their specific functions are unclear, these genes appear to be involved in the formation and movement (migration) of a group of nerve cells that are specialized to process smells (olfactory neurons). These nerve cells come together into a bundle called the olfactory bulb, which is critical for the perception of odors. The *ANOS1, FGFR1, PROKR2,* and PROK2 genes also play a role in the migration of neurons that produce a hormone called gonadotropin-releasing hormone (GnRH). GnRH controls the production of several other hormones that direct sexual development before birth and during puberty. These hormones are important for the normal function of the gonads (ovaries in women and testes in men).

Studies suggest that mutations in the *ANOS1, FGFR1, PROKR2,* or *PROK2* gene disrupt the migration of olfactory nerve cells and GnRH-producing nerve cells in the developing brain. If olfactory nerve cells do not extend to the olfactory bulb, a person's sense of smell will be impaired or absent. Misplacement of GnRH-producing neurons prevents the production of certain sex hormones, which interferes with normal sexual development and causes the characteristic features of hypogonadotropic hypogonadism. It is unclear how gene mutations lead to the other possible signs and symptoms of Kallmann syndrome. Because the features of this condition vary among individuals, researchers suspect that additional genetic and environmental factors may be involved.

Together, mutations in the *ANOS1, FGFR1, PROKR2,* and *PROK2* genes account for 25 percent to 30 percent of all cases of Kallmann syndrome. In cases without an identified mutation in one of these genes, the cause of the condition is unknown. Researchers are looking for other genes that can cause this disorder.

How Do People Inherit Kallmann Syndrome?

Kallmann syndrome (caused by *ANOS1* gene mutations) has an X-linked recessive pattern of inheritance. The *ANOS1* gene is located on the X chromosome, which is one of the two sex chromosomes. In males (who have only one X chromosome), one altered copy of the gene in each cell is sufficient to cause the condition. In females (who have two X chromosomes), a mutation must be present in both copies of the gene to cause the disorder. Males are affected by X-linked recessive disorders much more frequently than females. A characteristic of X-linked inheritance is that fathers cannot pass X-linked traits to their sons.

Most cases of Kallmann syndrome are described as simplex, which means only one person in a family is affected. Some affected people inherit *ANOS1* gene mutation from their mothers, who carry a single mutated copy of the gene in each cell. Other people have the condition as a result of a new mutation in the *ANOS1* gene.

Other forms of Kallmann syndrome can be inherited in an autosomal dominant pattern, which means one copy of the altered gene in each cell is sufficient to cause the disorder. In some cases, an affected person inherits the mutation from one affected parent. Other cases result from new mutations in the gene and occur in people with no history of the disorder in their family.

In several families, Kallmann syndrome has shown an autosomal recessive pattern of inheritance. Autosomal recessive inheritance means both copies of the gene in each cell have mutations. The parents of an individual with an autosomal recessive condition each carry one copy of the mutated gene, but they typically do not show signs and symptoms of the condition.

Chapter 20

Hypercholesterolemia

What Is Hypercholesterolemia?

Hypercholesterolemia is a condition characterized by very high levels of cholesterol in the blood. Cholesterol is a waxy, fat-like substance that is produced in the body and obtained from foods that come from animals (particularly egg yolks, meat, poultry, fish, and dairy products). The body needs this substance to build cell membranes, make certain hormones, and produce compounds that aid in fat digestion. Too much cholesterol, however, increases a person's risk of developing heart disease.

People with hypercholesterolemia have a high risk of developing a form of heart disease called coronary artery disease. This condition occurs when excess cholesterol in the bloodstream is deposited in the walls of blood vessels, particularly in the arteries that supply blood to the heart (coronary arteries). The abnormal buildup of cholesterol forms clumps (plaque) that narrow and harden artery walls. As the clumps get bigger, they can clog the arteries and restrict the flow of blood to the heart. The buildup of plaque in coronary arteries causes a form of chest pain called angina and greatly increases a person's risk of having a heart attack.

Inherited forms of hypercholesterolemia can also cause health problems related to the buildup of excess cholesterol in other tissues. If

---

This chapter includes text excerpted from "Hypercholesterolemia," Genetics Home Reference (GHR), National Institutes of Health (NIH), March 7, 2016.

cholesterol accumulates in tendons, it causes characteristic growths called tendon xanthomas. These growths most often affect the Achilles tendons and tendons in the hands and fingers. Yellowish cholesterol deposits under the skin of the eyelids are known as xanthelasmata. Cholesterol can also accumulate at the edges of the clear, front surface of the eye (the cornea), leading to a gray-colored ring called an arcus cornealis.

How Common Is Hypercholesterolemia?

More than 34 million American adults have elevated blood cholesterol levels (higher than 240 mg/dL). Inherited forms of hypercholesterolemia, which cause even higher levels of cholesterol, occur less frequently. The most common inherited form of high cholesterol is called familial hypercholesterolemia. This condition affects about 1 in 500 people in most countries. Familial hypercholesterolemia occurs more frequently in certain populations, including Afrikaners in South Africa, French Canadians, Lebanese, and Finns.

What Genes Are Related to Hypercholesterolemia?

Mutations in the *APOB, LDLR, LDLRAP1,* and *PCSK9* genes cause hypercholesterolemia.

High blood cholesterol levels typically result from a combination of genetic and environmental risk factors. Lifestyle choices including diet, exercise, and tobacco smoking strongly influence the amount of cholesterol in the blood. Additional factors that impact cholesterol levels include a person's gender, age, and health problems such as diabetes and obesity. A small percentage of all people with high cholesterol have an inherited form of hypercholesterolemia. The most common cause of inherited high cholesterol is a condition known as familial hypercholesterolemia, which results from mutations in the *LDLR* gene.

The *LDLR* gene provides instructions for making a protein called a low-density lipoprotein receptor. This type of receptor binds to particles called low-density lipoproteins (LDLs), which are the primary carriers of cholesterol in the blood. By removing low-density lipoproteins from the bloodstream, these receptors play a critical role in regulating cholesterol levels. Some *LDLR* mutations reduce the number of low-density lipoprotein receptors produced within cells. Other mutations disrupt the receptors' ability to remove low-density lipoproteins from the bloodstream. As a result, people with mutations in the *LDLR* gene have very high levels of blood cholesterol. As the excess cholesterol circulates through the bloodstream, it is deposited abnormally in tissues such as the skin, tendons, and arteries that supply blood to the heart.

Less commonly, hypercholesterolemia can be caused by mutations in the *APOB, LDLRAP1,* or *PCSK9* gene. Changes in the *APOB* gene result in a form of inherited hypercholesterolemia known as familial defective apolipoprotein B-100 (FDB). *LDLRAP1* mutations are responsible for another type of inherited high cholesterol, autosomal recessive hypercholesterolemia (ARH). Proteins produced from the *APOB, LDLRAP1,* and *PCSK9* genes are essential for the normal function of low-density lipoprotein receptors. Mutations in any of these genes prevent the cell from making functional receptors or alter the receptors' function. Hypercholesterolemia results when low-density lipoprotein receptors are unable to remove cholesterol from the blood effectively.

Researchers are working to identify and characterize additional genes that may influence cholesterol levels and the risk of heart disease in people with hypercholesterolemia.

How Do People Inherit Hypercholesterolemia?

Most cases of high cholesterol are not caused by a single inherited condition, but result from a combination of lifestyle choices and the effects of variations in many genes.

Inherited forms of hypercholesterolemia resulting from mutations in the *LDLR, APOB,* or *PCSK9* gene have an autosomal dominant pattern of inheritance. Autosomal dominant inheritance means one copy of an altered gene in each cell is sufficient to cause the disorder. An affected person typically inherits one altered copy of the gene from an affected parent and one normal copy of the gene from the other parent.

Rarely, a person with familial hypercholesterolemia is born with two mutated copies of the *LDLR* gene. This situation occurs when the person has two affected parents, each of whom passes on one altered copy of the gene. The presence of two *LDLR* mutations results in a more severe form of hypercholesterolemia that usually appears in childhood.

When hypercholesterolemia is caused by mutations in the *LDL-RAP1* gene, the condition is inherited in an autosomal recessive pattern. Autosomal recessive inheritance means the condition results from two altered copies of the gene in each cell. The parents of an individual with autosomal recessive hypercholesterolemia each carry one copy of the altered gene, but their blood cholesterol levels are usually in the normal range.

Chapter 21

Growth Disorders

Chapter Contents

Section 21.1

Achondroplasia

This section contains text excerpted from the following sources: Text
beginning with the heading "What Is Achondroplasia?" is excerpted
from "Achondroplasia," Genetics Home Reference (GHR),
National Institutes of Health (NIH), March 7, 2016; Text
under the heading "What Causes Achondroplasia?" is excerpted
from "Achondroplasia," National Center for Advancing
Translational Sciences (NCATS), January 26, 2016.

What Is Achondroplasia?

Achondroplasia is a form of short-limbed dwarfism. The word achondroplasia literally means "without cartilage formation." Cartilage is a
tough but flexible tissue that makes up much of the skeleton during
early development. However, in achondroplasia the problem is not in
forming cartilage but in converting it to bone (a process called ossifi-
cation), particularly in the long bones of the arms and legs. Achondroplasia is similar to another skeletal disorder called hypochondroplasia,
but the features of achondroplasia tend to be more severe.

All people with achondroplasia have short stature. The average
height of an adult male with achondroplasia is 131 centimeters (4 feet,
4 inches), and the average height for adult females is 124 centimeters (4 feet, 1 inch). Characteristic features of achondroplasia include
an average-size trunk, short arms and legs with particularly short
upper arms and thighs, limited range of motion at the elbows, and
an enlarged head (macrocephaly) with a prominent forehead. Fingers
are typically short and the ring finger and middle finger may diverge,
giving the hand a three-pronged (trident) appearance. People with
achondroplasia are generally of normal intelligence.

Health problems commonly associated with achondroplasia include
episodes in which breathing slows or stops for short periods (apnea),
obesity, and recurrent ear infections. In childhood, individuals with
the condition usually develop a pronounced and permanent sway of
the lower back (lordosis) and bowed legs. Some affected people also
develop abnormal front-to-back curvature of the spine (kyphosis) and
back pain. A potentially serious complication of achondroplasia is

spinal stenosis, which is a narrowing of the spinal canal that can pinch (compress) the upper part of the spinal cord. Spinal stenosis is associated with pain, tingling, and weakness in the legs that can cause difficulty with walking. Another uncommon but serious complication of achondroplasia is hydrocephalus, which is a buildup of fluid in the brain in affected children that can lead to increased head size and related brain abnormalities.

How Common Is Achondroplasia?

Achondroplasia is the most common type of short-limbed dwarfism. The condition occurs in 1 in 15,000 to 40,000 newborns.

What Genes Are Related to Achondroplasia?

Mutations in the *FGFR3* gene cause achondroplasia. The *FGFR3* gene provides instructions for making a protein that is involved in the development and maintenance of bone and brain tissue. Two specific mutations in the *FGFR3* gene are responsible for almost all cases of achondroplasia. Researchers believe that these mutations cause the *FGFR3* protein to be overly active, which interferes with skeletal development and leads to the disturbances in bone growth seen with this disorder.

How Do People Inherit Achondroplasia?

Achondroplasia is inherited in an autosomal dominant pattern, which means one copy of the altered gene in each cell is sufficient to cause the disorder. About 80 percent of people with achondroplasia have average-size parents; these cases result from new mutations in the *FGFR3* gene. In the remaining cases, people with achondroplasia have inherited an altered *FGFR3* gene from one or two affected parents. Individuals who inherit two altered copies of this gene typically have a severe form of achondroplasia that causes extreme shortening of the bones and an underdeveloped rib cage. These individuals are usually stillborn or die shortly after birth from respiratory failure.

What Causes Achondroplasia?

Achondroplasia is caused by mutations in the *FGFR3* gene. This gene provides instructions for making a protein that is involved in the development and maintenance of bone and brain tissue. Two specific mutations in the *FGFR3* gene are responsible for almost all cases of achondroplasia. Researchers believe that these mutations cause the *FGFR3* protein to be overly active, which interferes with skeletal development and leads to the disturbances in bone growth seen in this condition.

What Are the Signs and Symptoms of Achondroplasia?

In babies, apnea occurs when breathing stops for more than 15 seconds. Snoring is often a sign of apnea, however most children with achondroplasia snore. Obstructive apnea or disordered breathing in sleep may be suspected if the child has increased retraction, glottal stops, choking, intermittent breathing, deep compensatory sighs, secondary bed wetting, recurrent night-time awakening or vomiting. If these signs are present then additional lung and sleep studies are recommended.

How Might Children with Achondroplasia Be Treated?

Recommendations for management of children with achondroplasia were outlined by the American Academy of Pediatrics Committee on Genetics in the article, *Health Supervision for Children with Achondroplasia*. These recommendations include:

- Monitoring of height, weight, and head circumference using growth curves standardized for achondroplasia
- Measures to avoid obesity starting in early childhood
- Careful neurologic examinations, with referral to a pediatric neurologist as necessary
- MRI or CT of the foramen magnum region for evaluation of severe hypotonia or signs of spinal cord compression
- Obtaining history for possible sleep apnea, with sleep studies as necessary
- Evaluation for low thoracic or high lumbar gibbus if truncal weakness is present
- Referral to a pediatric orthopedist if bowing of the legs interferes with walking
- Management of frequent middle-ear infections
- Speech evaluation by age two years
- Careful monitoring of social adjustment

Section 21.2

Microcephalic Osteodysplastic Primordial Dwarfism Type II

This section includes text excerpted from "Microcephalic Osteodysplastic Primordial Dwarfism Type II," Genetics Home Reference (GHR), National Institutes of Health (NIH), March 7, 2016

What Is MOPDII?

Microcephalic osteodysplastic primordial dwarfism type II (MOP-DII) is a condition characterized by short stature (dwarfism) with other skeletal abnormalities (osteodysplasia) and an unusually small head size (microcephaly). The growth problems in MOPDII are primordial, meaning they begin before birth, with affected individuals showing slow prenatal growth (intrauterine growth retardation). After birth, affected individuals continue to grow at a very slow rate. The final adult height of people with this condition ranges from 20 inches to 40 inches. Other skeletal abnormalities in MOPDII include abnormal development of the hip joints (hip dysplasia), thinning of the bones in the arms and legs, an abnormal side-to-side curvature of the spine (scoliosis), and shortened wrist bones. In people with MOPDII head growth slows over time; affected individuals have an adult brain size comparable to that of a three-month-old infant. However, intellectual development is typically normal.

People with this condition typically have a high-pitched, nasal voice that results from a narrowing of the voicebox (subglottic stenosis). Facial features characteristic of MOPDII include a prominent nose, full cheeks, a long midface, and a small jaw. Other signs and symptoms seen in some people with MOPDII include small teeth (microdontia) and farsightedness. Over time, affected individuals may develop areas of abnormally light or dark skin coloring (pigmentation).

Many individuals with MOPDII have blood vessel abnormalities. For example, some affected individuals develop a bulge in one of the blood vessels at the center of the brain (intracranial aneurysm). These aneurysms are dangerous because they can burst, causing bleeding within the brain. Some affected individuals have Moyamoya disease, in which arteries at the base of the brain are narrowed, leading to restricted blood flow. These vascular abnormalities are often treatable, though they increase the risk of stroke and reduce the life expectancy of affected individuals.

How Common Is MOPDII?

MOPDII appears to be a rare condition, although its prevalence is unknown.

What Genes Are Related to MOPDII?

Mutations in the *PCNT* gene cause MOPDII. The *PCNT* gene provides instructions for making a protein called pericentrin. Within cells, this protein is located in structures called centrosomes. Centrosomes play a role in cell division and the assembly of microtubules. Microtubules are fibers that help cells maintain their shape, assist in the process of cell division, and are essential for the transport of materials within cells. Pericentrin acts as an anchoring protein, securing other proteins to the centrosome. Through its interactions with these proteins, pericentrin plays a role in regulation of the cell cycle, which is the cell's way of replicating itself in an organized, step-by-step fashion.

PCNT gene mutations lead to the production of a nonfunctional pericentrin protein that cannot anchor other proteins to the centrosome. As a result, centrosomes cannot properly assemble microtubules, leading to disruption of the cell cycle and cell division. Impaired cell division causes a reduction in cell production, while disruption of the cell cycle can lead to cell death. This overall reduction in the number of cells leads to short bones, microcephaly, and the other signs and symptoms of MOPDII.

How Do People Inherit MOPDII?

This condition is inherited in an autosomal recessive pattern, which means both copies of the gene in each cell have mutations. The parents of an individual with an autosomal recessive condition each carry one copy of the mutated gene, but they typically do not show signs and symptoms of the condition.

Section 21.3

Multiple Epiphyseal Dysplasia

This section includes text excerpted from "Multiple
Epiphyseal Dysplasia," Genetics Home Reference (GHR),
National Institutes of Health (NIH), March 7, 2016.

What Is Multiple Epiphyseal Dysplasia?

Multiple epiphyseal dysplasia is a disorder of cartilage and bone
development primarily affecting the ends of the long bones in the
arms and legs (epiphyses). There are two types of multiple epiphyseal
dysplasia, which can be distinguished by their pattern of inheritance.
Both the dominant and recessive types have relatively mild signs and
symptoms, including joint pain that most commonly affects the hips
and knees, early-onset arthritis, and a waddling walk. Although some
people with multiple epiphyseal dysplasia have mild short stature
as adults, most are of normal height. The majority of individuals are
diagnosed during childhood; however, some mild cases may not be
diagnosed until adulthood.

Recessive multiple epiphyseal dysplasia is distinguished from the
dominant type by malformations of the hands, feet, and knees and
abnormal curvature of the spine (scoliosis). About 50 percent of individuals with recessive multiple epiphyseal dysplasia are born with at
least one abnormal feature, including an inward- and upward-turning
foot (clubfoot), an opening in the roof of the mouth (cleft palate), an
unusual curving of the fingers or toes (clinodactyly), or ear swelling.
An abnormality of the kneecap called a double-layered patella is also
relatively common.

How Common Is Multiple Epiphyseal Dysplasia?

The incidence of dominant multiple epiphyseal dysplasia is estimated to be at least 1 in 10,000 newborns. The incidence of recessive
multiple epiphyseal dysplasia is unknown. Both forms of this disorder
may actually be more common because some people with mild symptoms are never diagnosed.

What Genes Are Related to Multiple Epiphyseal Dysplasia?

Mutations in the *COMP, COL9A1, COL9A2, COL9A3,* or *MATN3* gene can cause dominant multiple epiphyseal dysplasia. These genes provide instructions for making proteins that are found in the spaces between cartilage-forming cells (chondrocytes). These proteins interact with each other and play an important role in cartilage and bone formation. Cartilage is a tough, flexible tissue that makes up much of the skeleton during early development. Most cartilage is later converted to bone, except for the cartilage that continues to cover and protect the ends of bones and is present in the nose and external ears.

The majority of individuals with dominant multiple epiphyseal dysplasia have mutations in the *COMP* gene. About 10 percent of affected individuals have mutations in the *MATN3* gene. Mutations in the *COMP* or *MATN3* gene prevent the release of the proteins produced from these genes into the spaces between the chondrocytes. The absence of these proteins leads to the formation of abnormal cartilage, which can cause the skeletal problems characteristic of dominant multiple epiphyseal dysplasia.

The *COL9A1, COL9A2,* and *COL9A3* genes provide instructions for making a protein called type IX collagen. Collagens are a family of proteins that strengthen and support connective tissues, such as skin, bone, cartilage, tendons, and ligaments. Mutations in the *COL9A1, COL9A2,* or *COL9A3* gene are found in less than five percent of individuals with dominant multiple epiphyseal dysplasia. It is not known how mutations in these genes cause the signs and symptoms of this disorder. Research suggests that mutations in these genes may cause type IX collagen to accumulate inside the cell or interact abnormally with other cartilage components.

Some people with dominant multiple epiphyseal dysplasia do not have a mutation in the *COMP, COL9A1, COL9A2, COL9A3,* or *MATN3* gene. In these cases, the cause of the condition is unknown.

Mutations in the *SLC26A2* gene cause recessive multiple epiphyseal dysplasia. This gene provides instructions for making a protein that is essential for the normal development of cartilage and for its conversion to bone. Mutations in the *SLC26A2* gene alter the structure of developing cartilage, preventing bones from forming properly and resulting in the skeletal problems characteristic of recessive multiple epiphyseal dysplasia.

How Do People Inherit Multiple Epiphyseal Dysplasia?

Multiple epiphyseal dysplasia can have different inheritance patterns.

This condition can be inherited in an autosomal dominant pattern, which means one copy of the altered gene in each cell is sufficient to cause the disorder. In some cases, an affected person inherits the mutation from one affected parent. Other cases may result from new mutations in the gene. These cases occur in people with no history of the disorder in their family.

Multiple epiphyseal dysplasia can also be inherited in an autosomal recessive pattern, which means both copies of the gene in each cell have mutations. Most often, the parents of an individual with an autosomal recessive condition each carry one copy of the mutated gene, but do not show signs and symptoms of the condition.

Section 21.4

Russell-Silver Syndrome

This section contains text excerpted from the following
sources: Text beginning with the heading "What Is Russell-
Silver Syndrome?" is excerpted from "Russell-Silver Syndrome,"
Genetics Home Reference (GHR), National Institutes of Health
(NIH), March 7, 2016; Text under the heading "What Causes
Russell-Silver Syndrome?" is excerpted from "Russell-Silver
Syndrome," National Center for Advancing Translational
Sciences (NCATS), March 3, 2016.

What Is Russell-Silver Syndrome?

Russell-Silver syndrome is a growth disorder characterized by slow growth before and after birth. Babies with this condition have a low birth weight and often fail to grow and gain weight at the expected rate (failure to thrive). Head growth is normal, however, so the head may appear unusually large compared to the rest of the body. Affected children are thin and have poor appetites, and some develop low blood sugar (hypoglycemia) as a result of feeding difficulties. Adults with Russell-Silver syndrome are short; the average height for affected males is about 151 centimeters (4 feet, 11 inches) and the average height for affected females is about 140 centimeters (4 feet, 7 inches).

Many children with Russell-Silver syndrome have a small, triangular face with distinctive facial features including a prominent forehead, a narrow chin, a small jaw, and down-turned corners of the mouth. Other features of this disorder can include an unusual curving of the fifth finger (clinodactyly), asymmetric or uneven growth of some parts of the body, and digestive system abnormalities. Russell-Silver syndrome is also associated with an increased risk of delayed development and learning disabilities.

How Common Is Russell-Silver Syndrome?

The exact incidence of Russell-Silver syndrome is unknown, but the condition is estimated to affect 1 in 75,000 to 100,000 people.

What Are the Genetic Changes Related to Russell-Silver Syndrome?

The genetic causes of Russell-Silver syndrome are complex. The disorder often results from the abnormal regulation of certain genes that control growth. Research has focused on genes located in particular regions of chromosome 7 and chromosome 11.

People normally inherit one copy of each chromosome from their mother and one copy from their father. For most genes, both copies are expressed, or "turned on," in cells. For some genes, however, only the copy inherited from a person's father (the paternal copy) is expressed. For other genes, only the copy inherited from a person's mother (the maternal copy) is expressed. These parent-specific differences in gene expression are caused by a phenomenon called genomic imprinting. Both chromosome 7 and chromosome 11 contain groups of genes that normally undergo genomic imprinting. Abnormalities involving these genes appear to be responsible for many cases of Russell-Silver syndrome.

Researchers suspect that at least one third of all cases of Russell-Silver syndrome result from changes in a process called methylation. Methylation is a chemical reaction that attaches small molecules called methyl groups to certain segments of DNA. In genes that undergo genomic imprinting, methylation is one way that a gene's parent of origin is marked during the formation of egg and sperm cells.

Russell-Silver syndrome has been associated with changes in methylation involving the *H19* and *IGF2* genes, which are located near one another on chromosome 11. These genes are thought to be involved in directing normal growth. A loss of methylation disrupts the regulation of these genes, which leads to slow growth and the other characteristic features of this disorder.

Abnormalities involving genes on chromosome 7 also cause Russell-Silver syndrome. In 7 percent to 10 percent of cases, people inherit both copies of chromosome 7 from their mother instead of one copy from each parent. This phenomenon is called maternal uniparental disomy (UPD). Maternal UPD causes people to have two active copies of maternally expressed imprinted genes rather than one active copy from the mother and one inactive copy from the father. These individuals do not have a paternal copy of chromosome 7 and therefore do not have any copies of genes that are active only on the paternal copy. In cases of Russell-Silver syndrome caused by maternal UPD, an imbalance in active paternal and maternal genes on chromosome 7 underlies the signs and symptoms of the disorder.

In at least 40 percent of people with Russell-Silver syndrome, the cause of the condition is unknown. It is possible that changes in chromosomes other than 7 and 11 may play a role. Researchers are working to identify additional genetic changes that underlie this disorder.

Can Russell-Silver Syndrome Be Inherited?

Most cases of Russell-Silver syndrome are sporadic, which means they occur in people with no history of the disorder in their family.

Less commonly, Russell-Silver syndrome can run in families. In some affected families, the condition appears to have an autosomal dominant pattern of inheritance. Autosomal dominant inheritance means one copy of a genetic change in each cell is sufficient to cause the disorder. In other families, the condition has an autosomal recessive pattern of inheritance. Autosomal recessive inheritance means both copies of a gene are altered in each cell. The parents of an individual with an autosomal recessive condition each carry one copy of the mutated gene, but they typically do not show signs and symptoms of the condition.

What Causes Russell-Silver Syndrome?

Russell-Silver syndrome (RSS) is a genetic disorder that usually results from the abnormal regulation of certain genes that control growth. Two genetic causes have been found to result in the majority of cases:

- Abnormalities at an imprinted region on chromosome 11p15–for some genes, only the copy inherited from a person's father (paternal copy) or mother (maternal copy) is "turned on," or expressed. These parent-specific differences in gene expression are caused by a phenomenon called genomic imprinting. Abnormalities involving genes that undergo imprinting are responsible for many cases of RSS.

- Maternal disomy of chromosome 7 (written as matUPD7)–this occurs when a child inherits both copies of chromosome 7 from the mother, instead of one copy from the mother and one copy from the father.

Other chromosome abnormalities involving any of several chromosomes have also been described as causing RSS, or RSS-like syndromes. In some people with RSS, the underlying cause remains unknown.

What Are the Signs and Symptoms of Russell-Silver Syndrome?

Signs and symptoms of Russell-Silver syndrome (RSS) can vary and may include:

- intrauterine growth restriction
- low birth weight
- poor growth
- short stature
- curving of the pinky finger (clinodactyly)
- characteristic facial features (wide forehead; small, triangular face; and small, narrow chin)
- arms and legs of different lengths
- cafe-au-lait spots (birth marks)
- delayed bone age
- gastroesophageal reflux disease
- kidney problems
- "stubby" fingers and toes
- developmental delay
- learning disabilities

Section 21.5

Thanatophoric Dysplasia

This section includes text excerpted from "Thanatophoric Dysplasia," Genetics Home Reference (GHR), National Institutes of Health (NIH), March 7, 2016.

What Is Thanatophoric Dysplasia?

Thanatophoric dysplasia is a severe skeletal disorder characterized by extremely short limbs and folds of extra (redundant) skin on the arms and legs. Other features of this condition include a narrow chest, short ribs, underdeveloped lungs, and an enlarged head with a large forehead and prominent, wide-spaced eyes.

Researchers have described two major forms of thanatophoric dysplasia, type I and type II. Type I thanatophoric dysplasia is distinguished by the presence of curved thigh bones and flattened bones of the spine (platyspondyly). Type II thanatophoric dysplasia is characterized by straight thigh bones and a moderate to severe skull abnormality called a cloverleaf skull.

The term thanatophoric is Greek for "death bearing." Infants with thanatophoric dysplasia are usually stillborn or die shortly after birth from respiratory failure; however, a few affected individuals have survived into childhood with extensive medical help.

How Common Is Thanatophoric Dysplasia?

This condition occurs in 1 in 20,000 to 50,000 newborns. Type I thanatophoric dysplasia is more common than type II.

What Genes Are Related to Thanatophoric Dysplasia?

Mutations in the *FGFR3* gene cause thanatophoric dysplasia. Both types of this condition result from mutations in the *FGFR3* gene. This gene provides instructions for making a protein that is involved in the development and maintenance of bone and brain tissue. Mutations in this gene cause the *FGFR3* protein to be overly active, which leads to the severe disturbances in bone growth that are characteristic of thanatophoric dysplasia. It is not known how *FGFR3* mutations cause the brain and skin abnormalities associated with this disorder.

How Do People Inherit Thanatophoric Dysplasia?

Thanatophoric dysplasia is considered an autosomal dominant disorder because one mutated copy of the *FGFR3* gene in each cell is sufficient to cause the condition. Virtually all cases of thanatophoric dysplasia are caused by new mutations in the *FGFR3* gene and occur in people with no history of the disorder in their family. No affected individuals are known to have had children; therefore, the disorder has not been passed to the next generation.

Chapter 22

Heart Rhythm Disorders

Chapter Contents

Section 22.1

Brugada Syndrome

This section includes text excerpted from "Brugada Syndrome,"
Genetics Home Reference (GHR), National Institutes
of Health (NIH), March 7, 2016.

What Is Brugada Syndrome?

Brugada syndrome is a condition that causes a disruption of the heart's normal rhythm. Specifically, this disorder can lead to irregular heartbeats in the heart's lower chambers (ventricles), which is an abnormality called ventricular arrhythmia. If untreated, the irregular heartbeats can cause fainting (syncope), seizures, difficulty breathing, or sudden death. These complications typically occur when an affected person is resting or asleep.

Brugada syndrome usually becomes apparent in adulthood, although it can develop any time throughout life. Signs and symptoms related to arrhythmias, including sudden death, can occur from early infancy to late adulthood. Sudden death typically occurs around age 40. This condition may explain some cases of sudden infant death syndrome (SIDS), which is a major cause of death in babies younger than 1 year. SIDS is characterized by sudden and unexplained death, usually during sleep.

Sudden unexplained nocturnal death syndrome (SUNDS) is a condition characterized by unexpected cardiac arrest in young adults, usually at night during sleep. This condition was originally described in Southeast Asian populations, where it is a major cause of death. Researchers have determined that SUNDS and Brugada syndrome are the same disorder.

How Common Is Brugada Syndrome?

The exact prevalence of Brugada syndrome is unknown, although it is estimated to affect 5 in 10,000 people worldwide. This condition occurs much more frequently in people of Asian ancestry, particularly in Japanese and Southeast Asian populations.

Although Brugada syndrome affects both men and women, the condition appears to be 8 to 10 times more common in men. Researchers suspect that testosterone, a sex hormone present at much higher levels in men, may account for this difference.

What Genes Are Related to Brugada Syndrome?

Brugada syndrome can be caused by mutations in one of several genes. The most commonly mutated gene in this condition is *SCN5A*, which is altered in approximately 30 percent of affected individuals. This gene provides instructions for making a sodium channel, which normally transports positively charged sodium atoms (ions) into heart muscle cells. This type of ion channel plays a critical role in maintaining the heart's normal rhythm. Mutations in the *SCN5A* gene alter the structure or function of the channel, which reduces the flow of sodium ions into cells. A disruption in ion transport alters the way the heart beats, leading to the abnormal heart rhythm characteristic of Brugada syndrome.

Mutations in other genes can also cause Brugada syndrome. Together, these other genetic changes account for less than two percent of cases of the condition. Some of the additional genes involved in Brugada syndrome provide instructions for making proteins that ensure the correct location or function of sodium channels in heart muscle cells. Proteins produced by other genes involved in the condition form or help regulate ion channels that transport calcium or potassium into or out of heart muscle cells. As with sodium channels, proper flow of ions through calcium and potassium channels in the heart muscle helps maintain a regular heartbeat. Mutations in these genes disrupt the flow of ions, impairing the heart's normal rhythm.

In affected people without an identified gene mutation, the cause of Brugada syndrome is often unknown. In some cases, certain drugs may cause a nongenetic (acquired) form of the disorder. Drugs that can induce an altered heart rhythm include medications used to treat some forms of arrhythmia, a condition called angina (which causes chest pain), high blood pressure, depression, and other mental illnesses. Abnormally high blood levels of calcium (hypercalcemia) or potassium (hyperkalemia), as well as unusually low potassium levels (hypokalemia), also have been associated with acquired Brugada syndrome. In addition to causing a nongenetic form of this disorder, these factors may trigger symptoms in people with an underlying mutation in *SCN5A* or another gene.

How Do People Inherit Brugada Syndrome?

This condition is inherited in an autosomal dominant pattern, which means one copy of the altered gene in each cell is sufficient to cause the disorder. In most cases, an affected person has one parent with the condition. Other cases may result from new mutations in the gene. These cases occur in people with no history of the disorder in their family.

Section 22.2

Familial Atrial Fibrillation

This section includes text excerpted from "Familial Atrial Fibrillation," Genetics Home Reference (GHR), National Institutes of Health (NIH), March 7, 2016.

What Is Familial Atrial Fibrillation?

Familial atrial fibrillation is an inherited condition that disrupts the heart's normal rhythm. This condition is characterized by uncoordinated electrical activity in the heart's upper chambers (the atria), which causes the heartbeat to become fast and irregular. If untreated, this abnormal heart rhythm can lead to dizziness, chest pain, a sensation of fluttering or pounding in the chest (palpitations), shortness of breath, or fainting (syncope). Atrial fibrillation also increases the risk of stroke and sudden death. Complications of familial atrial fibrillation can occur at any age, although some people with this heart condition never experience any health problems associated with the disorder.

How Common Is Familial Atrial Fibrillation?

Atrial fibrillation is the most common type of sustained abnormal heart rhythm (arrhythmia), affecting more than 3 million people in the United States. The risk of developing this irregular heart rhythm increases with age. The incidence of the familial form of atrial fibrillation is unknown; however, recent studies suggest that up to 30 percent of all people with atrial fibrillation may have a history of the condition in their family.

What Genes Are Related to Familial Atrial Fibrillation?

A small percentage of all cases of familial atrial fibrillation are associated with changes in the *KCNE2, KCNJ2,* and *KCNQ1* genes. These genes provide instructions for making proteins that act as channels across the cell membrane. These channels transport positively charged atoms (ions) of potassium into and out of cells. In heart (cardiac) muscle, the ion channels produced from the *KCNE2, KCNJ2,* and *KCNQ1* genes play critical roles in maintaining the heart's normal rhythm. Mutations in these genes have been identified in only a few families worldwide. These mutations increase the activity of the channels, which changes the flow of potassium ions between cells. This disruption in ion transport alters the way the heart beats, increasing the risk of syncope, stroke, and sudden death.

Most cases of atrial fibrillation are not caused by mutations in a single gene. This condition is often related to structural abnormalities of the heart or underlying heart disease. Additional risk factors for atrial fibrillation include high blood pressure (hypertension), diabetes mellitus, a previous stroke, or an accumulation of fatty deposits and scar-like tissue in the lining of the arteries (atherosclerosis). Although most cases of atrial fibrillation are not known to run in families, studies suggest that they may arise partly from genetic risk factors. Researchers are working to determine which genetic changes may influence the risk of atrial fibrillation.

How Do People Inherit Familial Atrial Fibrillation?

Familial atrial fibrillation appears to be inherited in an autosomal dominant pattern, which means one copy of the altered gene in each cell is sufficient to cause the disorder.

Section 22.3

Romano-Ward Syndrome (Long QT Syndrome)

This section contains text excerpted from the following sources:
Text under the heading "What Is Romano-Ward Syndrome?" is
excerpted from "Romano-Ward Syndrome," Genetics Home Reference
(GHR), National Institutes of Health (NIH), March 7, 2016; Text
under the heading "What Are the Signs and Symptoms?" is
excerpted from "Long QT Syndrome," National Institutes of
Health (NIH), September 21, 2011. Reviewed May 2016.

What Is Romano-Ward Syndrome?

Romano-Ward syndrome is a condition that causes a disruption of
the heart's normal rhythm (arrhythmia). This disorder is a form of
long QT syndrome, which is a heart condition that causes the heart
(cardiac) muscle to take longer than usual to recharge between beats.
The irregular heartbeats can lead to fainting (syncope) or cardiac
arrest and sudden death.

How Common Is Romano-Ward Syndrome?

Romano-Ward syndrome is the most common form of inherited long
QT syndrome, affecting an estimated 1 in 7,000 people worldwide. The
disorder may actually be more common than this estimate, however,
because some people never experience any symptoms associated with
arrhythmia and therefore may not have been diagnosed.

What Genes Are Related to Romano-Ward Syndrome?

Mutations in the *KCNE1, KCNE2, KCNH2, KCNQ1*, and *SCN5A*
genes cause Romano-Ward syndrome. These genes provide instructions
for making proteins that act as channels across the cell membrane.
These channels transport positively charged atoms (ions), such as
potassium and sodium, into and out of cells. In cardiac muscle, ion
channels play critical roles in maintaining the heart's normal rhythm.
Mutations in any of these genes alter the structure or function of these
channels, which changes the flow of ions between cells. A disruption in

ion transport alters the way the heart beats, leading to the abnormal heart rhythm characteristic of Romano-Ward syndrome.

Unlike most genes related to Romano-Ward syndrome, the *ANK2* gene does not provide instructions for making an ion channel. The *ANK2* protein, ankyrin-2, ensures that certain other proteins (particularly ion channels) are inserted into the cell membrane appropriately. A mutation in the *ANK2* gene likely alters the flow of ions between cells in the heart, which disrupts the heart's normal rhythm. *ANK2* mutations can cause a variety of heart problems, including the irregular heartbeat often found in Romano-Ward syndrome. It is unclear whether mutations in the *ANK2* gene cause Romano-Ward syndrome or lead to another heart condition with some of the same signs and symptoms.

How Do People Inherit Romano-Ward Syndrome?

This condition is typically inherited in an autosomal dominant pattern, which means one copy of the altered gene in each cell is sufficient to cause the disorder. In most cases, an affected person inherits the mutation from one affected parent. A small percentage of cases result from new mutations in one of the genes described above. These cases occur in people with no history of Romano-Ward syndrome in their family.

What Are the Signs and Symptoms?

Major Signs and Symptoms

If you have long QT syndrome (LQTS), you can have sudden and dangerous arrhythmias (abnormal heart rhythms). Signs and symptoms of LQTS-related arrhythmias often first occur during childhood and include:

- Unexplained fainting. This happens because the heart isn't pumping enough blood to the brain. Fainting may occur during physical or emotional stress. Fluttering feelings in the chest may occur before fainting.

- Unexplained drowning or near drowning. This may be due to fainting while swimming.

- Unexplained sudden cardiac arrest (SCA) or death. SCA is a condition in which the heart suddenly stops beating for no obvious reason. People who have SCA die within minutes unless they receive treatment. In about 1 out of 10 people who have LQTS, SCA or sudden death is the first sign of the disorder.

Other Signs and Symptoms

Often, people who have LQTS 3 develop an abnormal heart rhythm during sleep. This may cause noisy gasping while sleeping.

Silent Long QT Syndrome

Sometimes long QT syndrome doesn't cause any signs or symptoms. This is called silent LQTS. For this reason, doctors often advise family members of people who have LQTS to be tested for the disorder, even if they have no symptoms.

Medical and genetic tests may reveal whether these family members have LQTS and what type of the condition they have.

How Is It Diagnosed?

Cardiologists diagnose and treat long QT syndrome (LQTS). Cardiologists are doctors who specialize in diagnosing and treating heart diseases and conditions. To diagnose LQTS, your cardiologist will consider your:

- EKG (electrocardiogram) results
- Medical history and the results from a physical exam
- Genetic test results

EKG (Electrocardiogram)

An EKG is a simple test that detects and records the heart's electrical activity. This test may show a long QT interval and other signs that suggest LQTS. Often, doctors first discover a long QT interval when an EKG is done for another suspected heart problem.

Not all people who have LQTS will always have a long QT interval on an EKG. The QT interval may change from time to time; it may be long sometimes and normal at other times. Thus, your doctor may want you to have several EKG tests over a period of days or weeks. Or, your doctor may have you wear a device called a Holter monitor.

A Holter monitor records the heart's electrical activity for a full 24- or 48-hour period. It can detect heart problems that occur for only a few minutes out of the day.

You wear small patches called electrodes on your chest. Wires connect the patches to a small, portable recorder. You can clip the recorder to a belt, keep it in a pocket, or hang it around your neck.

While you wear the monitor, you do your usual daily activities. You also keep a notebook, noting any symptoms you have and the time they occur. You then return both the recorder and the notebook to your doctor to read the results. Your doctor can see how your heart was beating at the time you had symptoms.

Some people have a long QT interval only while they exercise. For this reason, your doctor may recommend that you have a stress test.

During a stress test, you exercise to make your heart work hard and beat fast. An EKG is done while you exercise. If you can't exercise, you may be given medicine to increase your heart rate.

Medical History and Physical Exam

Your doctor will ask whether you've had any symptoms of an abnormal heart rhythm. Symptoms may include:

- Unexplained fainting

- A fluttering feeling in your chest, which is the result of your heart beating too fast

- Loud gasping during sleep

Your doctor may ask what over-the-counter, prescription, or other drugs you take. He or she also may want to know whether anyone in your family has been diagnosed with or has had signs of LQTS. Signs of LQTS include unexplained fainting, drowning, sudden cardiac arrest, or sudden death.

Your doctor will check you for signs of conditions that may lower blood levels of potassium or sodium. These conditions include the eating disorders anorexia nervosa and bulimia, excessive vomiting or diarrhea, and certain thyroid disorders.

Genetic Tests

Genetic blood tests can detect some forms of inherited LQTS. If your doctor thinks that you have LQTS, he or she may suggest genetic testing. Genetic blood tests usually are suggested for family members of people who have LQTS as well.

However, genetic tests don't always detect LQTS. So, even if you have the disorder, the tests may not show it.

Also, some people who test positive for LQTS don't have any signs or symptoms of the disorder. These people may have silent LQTS. Less than 10 percent of these people will faint or suddenly die from an abnormal heart rhythm.

Even if you have silent LQTS, you may be at increased risk of having an abnormal heart rhythm while taking medicines that affect potassium ion channels or blood levels of potassium.

Types of Inherited Long QT Syndrome

If you have inherited LQTS, it may be helpful to know which type you have. This will help you and your doctor plan your treatment and decide which lifestyle changes you should make.

To find out what type of LQTS you have, your doctor will consider:

- Genetic test results

- The types of situations that trigger an abnormal heart rhythm

- How well you respond to medicine

The goal of treating long QT syndrome (LQTS) is to prevent life-threatening, abnormal heart rhythms and fainting spells.

Treatment isn't a cure for the disorder and may not restore a normal QT interval on an EKG (electrocardiogram). However, treatment greatly improves the chances of survival.

How Is It Treated?

Specific Types of Treatment

Your doctor will recommend the best treatment for you based on:

- Whether you've had symptoms, such as fainting or sudden cardiac arrest (SCA)

- What type of LQTS you have

- How likely it is that you'll faint or have SCA

- What treatment you feel most comfortable with

People who have LQTS without symptoms may be advised to:

- Make lifestyle changes that reduce the risk of fainting or SCA. Lifestyle changes may include avoiding certain sports and strenuous exercise, such as swimming, which can cause abnormal heart rhythms.

- Avoid medicines that may trigger abnormal heart rhythms. This may include some medicines used to treat allergies, infections, high blood pressure, high blood cholesterol, depression, and arrhythmias.

- Take medicines such as beta-blockers, which reduce the risk of symptoms by slowing the heart rate.

The type of medicine you take will depend on the type of LQTS you have. For example, doctors usually will prescribe sodium channel blocker medicines only for people who have LQTS 3.

If your doctor thinks you're at increased risk for LQTS complications, he or she may suggest more aggressive treatments (in addition to medicines and lifestyle changes). These treatments may include:

- A surgically implanted device, such as a pacemaker or implantable cardioverter defibrillator (ICD). These devices help control abnormal heart rhythms.

- Surgery on the nerves that regulate your heartbeat.

People at increased risk are those who have fainted or who have had dangerous heart rhythms from their LQTS.

Lifestyle Changes

If possible, try to avoid things that can trigger abnormal heart rhythms. For example, people who have LQTS should avoid medicines that lengthen the QT interval or lower potassium blood levels.

Many people who have LQTS also benefit from adding more potassium to their diets. Check with your doctor about eating more potassium-rich foods (such as bananas) or taking potassium supplements daily.

Medicines

Beta blockers are medicines that prevent the heart from beating faster in response to physical or emotional stress. Most people who have LQTS are treated with beta blockers.

Doctors may suggest that people who have LQTS 3 take sodium channel blockers, such as mexiletine. These medicines make sodium ion channels less active.

Medical Devices

Pacemakers and ICDs are small devices that help control abnormal heart rhythms. Both devices use electrical currents to prompt the heart to beat normally. Surgeons implant pacemakers and ICDs in the chest or belly with a minor procedure.

The use of these devices is similar in children and adults. However, because children are still growing, other issues may arise. For example, as children grow, they may need to have their devices replaced.

Surgery

People who are at high risk of death from LQTS sometimes are treated with surgery. During surgery, the nerves that prompt the heart to beat faster in response to physical or emotional stress are cut.

This type of surgery keeps the heart beating at a steady pace and lowers the risk of dangerous heart rhythms in response to stress or exercise.

Section 22.4

Short QT Syndrome

This section includes text excerpted from "Short QT Syndrome,"
Genetic Home Reference (GHR), June 2013.

What Is Short QT Syndrome?

Short QT syndrome is a condition that can cause a disruption of the heart's normal rhythm (arrhythmia). In people with this condition, the heart (cardiac) muscle takes less time than usual to recharge between beats. The term "short QT" refers to a specific pattern of heart activity that is detected with an electrocardiogram (EKG), which is a test used to measure the electrical activity of the heart. In people with this condition, the part of the heartbeat known as the QT interval is abnormally short.

If untreated, the arrhythmia associated with short QT syndrome can lead to a variety of signs and symptoms, from dizziness and fainting (syncope) to cardiac arrest and sudden death. These signs and symptoms can occur any time from early infancy to old age. This condition may explain some cases of sudden infant death syndrome (SIDS), which is a major cause of unexplained death in babies younger than 1 year. However, some people with short QT syndrome never experience any health problems associated with the condition.

Frequency

Short QT syndrome appears to be rare. At least 70 cases have been identified worldwide since the condition was discovered in 2000. However, the condition may be underdiagnosed because some affected individuals never experience symptoms.

Genetic Changes

Mutations in the KCNH2, KCNJ2, and KCNQ1 genes can cause short QT syndrome. These genes provide instructions for making channels that transport positively charged atoms (ions) of potassium out of cells. In cardiac muscle, these ion channels play critical roles in maintaining the heart's normal rhythm. Mutations in the KCNH2, KCNJ2, or KCNQ1 gene increase the activity of the channels, which enhances the flow of potassium ions across the membrane of cardiac muscle cells. This change in ion transport alters the electrical activity of the heart and can lead to the abnormal heart rhythms characteristic of short QT syndrome.

Some affected individuals do not have an identified mutation in the KCNH2, KCNJ2, or KCNQ1 gene. Changes in other genes that have not been identified may cause the disorder in these cases.

Inheritance Pattern

Short QT syndrome appears to have an autosomal dominant pattern of inheritance, which means one copy of the altered gene in each cell is sufficient to cause the disorder. Some affected individuals have a family history of short QT syndrome or related heart problems and sudden cardiac death. Other cases of short QT syndrome are classified as sporadic and occur in people with no apparent family history of related heart problems.

Chapter 23

Hereditary Deafness

Chapter Contents

Section 23.1

Usher Syndrome

This section contains text excerpted from the following sources:
Text beginning with the heading "What Is Usher Syndrome?"
is excerpted from "Usher Syndrome," Genetics Home Reference
(GHR), National Institutes of Health (NIH), March 7, 2016; Text
under the heading "What Causes Usher Syndrome?" is excerpted
from "Usher Syndrome," National Institute on Deafness and
Other Communication Disorders (NIDCD), April 30, 2014.

What Is Usher Syndrome?

Usher syndrome is a condition characterized by hearing loss or
deafness and progressive vision loss. The loss of vision is caused by an
eye disease called retinitis pigmentosa (RP), which affects the layer
of light-sensitive tissue at the back of the eye (the retina). Vision loss
occurs as the light-sensing cells of the retina gradually deteriorate.
Night vision loss begins first, followed by blind spots that develop in
the side (peripheral) vision. Over time, these blind spots enlarge and
merge to produce tunnel vision. In some cases of Usher syndrome,
vision is further impaired by clouding of the lens of the eye (cataracts).
Many people with retinitis pigmentosa retain some central vision
throughout their lives, however.

Researchers have identified three major types of Usher syndrome,
designated as types I, II, and III. These types are distinguished by
their severity and the age when signs and symptoms appear. Type I
is further divided into seven distinct subtypes, designated as types
IA through IG. Usher syndrome type II has at least three described
subtypes, designated as types IIA, IIB, and IIC.

Individuals with Usher syndrome type I are typically born completely deaf or lose most of their hearing within the first year of life.
Progressive vision loss caused by retinitis pigmentosa becomes apparent in childhood. This type of Usher syndrome also includes problems
with the inner ear that affect balance. As a result, children with the
condition begin sitting independently and walking later than usual.

Usher syndrome type II is characterized by hearing loss from birth
and progressive vision loss that begins in adolescence or adulthood.

The hearing loss associated with this form of Usher syndrome ranges from mild to severe and mainly affects high tones. Affected children have problems hearing high, soft speech sounds, such as those of the letters d and t. The degree of hearing loss varies within and among families with this condition. Unlike other forms of Usher syndrome, people with type II do not have difficulties with balance caused by inner ear problems.

People with Usher syndrome type III experience progressive hearing loss and vision loss beginning in the first few decades of life. Unlike the other forms of Usher syndrome, infants with Usher syndrome type III are usually born with normal hearing. Hearing loss typically begins during late childhood or adolescence, after the development of speech, and progresses over time. By middle age, most affected individuals are profoundly deaf. Vision loss caused by retinitis pigmentosa also develops in late childhood or adolescence. People with Usher syndrome type III may also experience difficulties with balance due to inner ear problems. These problems vary among affected individuals, however.

How Common Is Usher Syndrome?

Usher syndrome is thought to be responsible for 3 percent to 6 percent of all childhood deafness and about 50 percent of deaf-blindness in adults. Usher syndrome type I is estimated to occur in at least 4 per 100,000 people. It may be more common in certain ethnic populations, such as people with Ashkenazi (central and eastern European) Jewish ancestry and the Acadian population in Louisiana. Type II is thought to be the most common form of Usher syndrome, although the frequency of this type is unknown. Type III Usher syndrome accounts for only a small percentage of all Usher syndrome cases in most populations. This form of the condition is more common in the Finnish population, however, where it accounts for about 40 percent of all cases.

What Genes Are Related to Usher Syndrome?

Mutations in the *ADGRV1, CDH23, CLRN1, MYO7A, PCDH15, USH1C, USH1G,* and *USH2A* genes can cause Usher syndrome.

The genes related to Usher syndrome provide instructions for making proteins that play important roles in normal hearing, balance, and vision. They function in the development and maintenance of hair cells, which are sensory cells in the inner ear that help transmit sound and motion signals to the brain. In the retina, these genes are also involved in determining the structure and function of light-sensing cells called rods and cones. In some cases, the exact role of these genes in hearing and vision is unknown. Most of the mutations responsible for Usher syndrome lead to a loss of hair cells in the inner ear and a gradual loss of rods and cones in the retina. Degeneration of these sensory cells causes hearing loss, balance problems, and vision loss characteristic of this condition.

Usher syndrome type I can result from mutations in the *CDH23, MYO7A, PCDH15, USH1C,* or *USH1G* gene. At least two other unidentified genes also cause this form of Usher syndrome.

Usher syndrome type II is caused by mutations in at least four genes. Only two of these genes, *ADGRV1* and *USH2A,* have been identified. Mutations in at least two genes are responsible for Usher syndrome type III; however, *CLRN1* is the only gene that has been identified.

How Do People Inherit Usher Syndrome?

This condition is inherited in an autosomal recessive pattern, which means both copies of the gene in each cell have mutations. The parents of an individual with an autosomal recessive condition each carry one copy of the mutated gene, but they typically do not show signs and symptoms of the condition.

What Causes Usher Syndrome?

Usher syndrome is inherited, which means that it is passed from parents to their children through genes. Genes are located in almost every cell of the body. Genes contain instructions that tell cells what to do. Every person inherits two copies of each gene, one from each parent. Sometimes genes are altered, or mutated. Mutated genes may cause cells to act differently than expected.

Usher syndrome is inherited as an autosomal recessive trait. The term autosomal means that the mutated gene is not located on either of the chromosomes that determine a person's sex; in other words, both males and females can have the disorder and can pass it along to a child. The word recessive means that, to have Usher syndrome, a person must receive a mutated form of the Usher syndrome gene from each parent. If a child has a mutation in one Usher syndrome gene but the other gene is normal, he or she is predicted to have normal vision and hearing. People with a mutation in a gene that can cause an autosomal recessive disorder are called carriers, because they "carry" the gene with a mutation, but show no symptoms of the disorder. If both parents are carriers of a mutated gene for Usher syndrome, they will have a one-in-four chance of having a child with Usher syndrome with each birth.

Usually, parents who have normal hearing and vision do not know if they are carriers of an Usher syndrome gene mutation. Currently, it is not possible to determine whether a person who does not have a family history of Usher syndrome is a carrier. Scientists at the National Institute on Deafness and Other Communication Disorders are hoping to change this, however, as they learn more about the genes responsible for Usher syndrome.

What Are the Characteristics of the Three Types of Usher Syndrome?

Type 1. Children with type 1 Usher syndrome are profoundly deaf at birth and have severe balance problems. Many of these children obtain little or no benefit from hearing aids. Parents should consult their doctor and other hearing health professionals as early as possible to determine the best communication method for their child. Intervention should be introduced early, during the first few years of life, so that the child can take advantage of the unique window of time during which the brain is most receptive to learning language, whether spoken or signed. If a child is diagnosed with type 1 Usher syndrome early on, before he or she loses the ability to see, that child is more likely to benefit from the full spectrum of intervention strategies that can help him or her participate more fully in life's activities.

Because of the balance problems associated with type 1 Usher syndrome, children with this disorder are slow to sit without support and typically don't walk independently before they are 18 months old. These children usually begin to develop vision problems in early childhood, almost always by the time they reach age 10. Vision problems most often begin with difficulty seeing at night, but tend to progress rapidly until the person is completely blind.

Type 2. Children with type 2 Usher syndrome are born with moderate to severe hearing loss and normal balance. Although the severity of hearing loss varies, most of these children can benefit from hearing aids and can communicate orally. The vision problems in type 2 Usher syndrome tend to progress more slowly than those in type 1, with the onset of RP often not apparent until the teens.

Type 3. Children with type 3 Usher syndrome have normal hearing at birth. Although most children with the disorder have normal to near-normal balance, some may develop balance problems later on. Hearing and sight worsen over time, but the rate at which they decline can vary from person to person, even within the same family. A person with type 3 Usher syndrome may develop hearing loss by the teens, and he or she will usually require hearing aids by mid- to late adulthood. Night blindness usually begins sometime during puberty. Blind spots appear by the late teens to early adulthood, and, by mid-adulthood, the person is usually legally blind.

Table 23.1. Characteristics of Usher Syndrome

	Type 1	Type 2	Type 3
Hearing	Profound deafness in both ears from birth	Moderate to severe hearing loss from birth	Normal at birth; progressive loss in childhood or early teens
Vision	Decreased night vision before age 10	Decreased night vision begins in late childhood or teens	Varies in severity; night vision problems often begin in teens
Vestibular function (balance)	Balance problems from birth	Normal	Normal to near-normal, chance of later problems

How Is Usher Syndrome Diagnosed?

Because Usher syndrome affects hearing, balance, and vision, diagnosis of the disorder usually includes the evaluation of all three senses. Evaluation of the eyes may include a visual field test to measure a person's peripheral vision, an electroretinogram (ERG) to measure the electrical response of the eye's light-sensitive cells, and a retinal examination to observe the retina and other structures in the back of the eye. A hearing (audiologic) evaluation measures how loud sounds at a range of frequencies need to be before a person can hear them. An electronystagmogram (ENG) measures involuntary eye movements that could signify a balance problem.

Early diagnosis of Usher syndrome is very important. The earlier that parents know if their child has Usher syndrome, the sooner that child can begin special educational training programs to manage the loss of hearing and vision.

Is Genetic Testing for Usher Syndrome Available?

So far, 11 genetic loci (a segment of chromosome on which a certain gene is located) have been found to cause Usher syndrome, and nine genes have been pinpointed that cause the disorder. They are:

- Type 1 Usher syndrome: *MYO7A, USH1C, CDH23, PCDH15, SANS*

- Type 2 Usher syndrome: *USH2A, VLGR1, WHRN*

- Type 3 Usher syndrome: *USH3A*

With so many possible genes involved in Usher syndrome, genetic tests for the disorder are not conducted on a widespread basis. Diagnosis of Usher syndrome is usually performed through hearing, balance, and vision tests. Genetic testing for a few of the identified genes is clinically available.

How Is Usher Syndrome Treated?

Currently, there is no cure for Usher syndrome. The best treatment involves early identification so that educational programs can begin as soon as possible. The exact nature of these programs will depend on the severity of the hearing and vision loss as well as the age and abilities of the person. Typically, treatment will include hearing aids, assistive listening devices, cochlear implants, or other communication methods such as American Sign Language; orientation and mobility training; and communication services and independent-living training that may include Braille instruction, low-vision services, or auditory training.

Some ophthalmologists believe that a high dose of vitamin A palmitate may slow, but not halt, the progression of retinitis pigmentosa. This belief stems from the results of a long-term clinical trial supported by the National Eye Institute and the Foundation for Fighting Blindness. Based on these findings, the researchers recommend that most adult patients with the common forms of RP take a daily supplement of 15,000 IU (international units) of vitamin A in the palmitate form under the supervision of their eye care professional. (Because people with type 1 Usher syndrome did not take part in the study, high-dose vitamin A is not recommended for these patients.) People who are considering taking vitamin A should discuss this treatment option with their healthcare provider before proceeding. Other guidelines regarding this treatment option include:

- Do not substitute vitamin A palmitate with a beta-carotene supplement.

- Do not take vitamin A supplements greater than the recommended dose of 15,000 IU or modify your diet to select foods with high levels of vitamin A.

- Women who are considering pregnancy should stop taking the high-dose supplement of vitamin A three months before trying to conceive due to the increased risk of birth defects.

- Women who are pregnant should stop taking the high-dose supplement of vitamin A due to the increased risk of birth defects.

In addition, according to the same study, people with RP should avoid using supplements of more than 400 IU of vitamin E per day.

Section 23.2

Waardenburg Syndrome

This section contains text excerpted from the following sources: Text beginning with the heading "What Is Waardenburg Syndrome?" is excerpted from "Waardenburg Syndrome," Genetics Home Reference (GHR), National Institutes of Health (NIH), March 7, 2016; Text under the heading "How Is Waardenburg Syndrome Diagnosed?" is excerpted from "Waardenburg Syndrome," National Center for Advancing Translational Sciences (NCATS), February 11, 2016.

What Is Waardenburg Syndrome?

Waardenburg syndrome is a group of genetic conditions that can cause hearing loss and changes in coloring (pigmentation) of the hair, skin, and eyes. Although most people with Waardenburg syndrome have normal hearing, moderate to profound hearing loss can occur in one or both ears. The hearing loss is present from birth (congenital). People with this condition often have very pale blue eyes or different colored eyes, such as one blue eye and one brown eye. Sometimes one eye has segments of two different colors. Distinctive hair coloring (such as a patch of white hair or hair that prematurely turns gray) is another common sign of the condition. The features of Waardenburg syndrome vary among affected individuals, even among people in the same family.

The four known types of Waardenburg syndrome are distinguished by their physical characteristics and sometimes by their genetic cause. Types I and II have very similar features, although people with type I almost always have eyes that appear widely spaced and people with type II do not. In addition, hearing loss occurs more often in people with type II than in those with type I. Type III (sometimes called Klein-Waardenburg syndrome) includes abnormalities of the upper limbs in addition to hearing loss and changes in pigmentation. Type IV (also known as Waardenburg-Shah syndrome) has signs and symptoms of both Waardenburg syndrome and Hirschsprung disease, an intestinal disorder that causes severe constipation or blockage of the intestine.

How Common Is Waardenburg Syndrome?

Waardenburg syndrome affects an estimated 1 in 40,000 people. It accounts for 2 to 5 percent of all cases of congenital hearing loss. Types I and II are the most common forms of Waardenburg syndrome, while types III and IV are rare.

What Genes Are Related to Waardenburg Syndrome?

Mutations in the *EDN3, EDNRB, MITF, PAX3, SNAI2*, and *SOX10* genes can cause Waardenburg syndrome. These genes are involved in the formation and development of several types of cells, including pigment-producing cells called melanocytes. Melanocytes make a pigment called melanin, which contributes to skin, hair, and eye color and plays an essential role in the normal function of the inner ear. Mutations in any of these genes disrupt the normal development of melanocytes, leading to abnormal pigmentation of the skin, hair, and eyes and problems with hearing.

Types I and III Waardenburg syndrome are caused by mutations in the *PAX3* gene. Mutations in the *MITF* and *SNAI2* genes are responsible for type II Waardenburg syndrome.

Mutations in the *SOX10, EDN3*, or *EDNRB* genes cause type IV Waardenburg syndrome. In addition to melanocyte development, these genes are important for the development of nerve cells in the large intestine. Mutations in any of these genes result in hearing loss, changes in pigmentation, and intestinal problems related to Hirschsprung disease.

How Do People Inherit Waardenburg Syndrome?

Waardenburg syndrome is usually inherited in an autosomal dominant pattern, which means one copy of the altered gene in each cell is sufficient to cause the disorder. In most cases, an affected person has one parent with the condition. A small percentage of cases result from new mutations in the gene; these cases occur in people with no history of the disorder in their family.

Some cases of type II and type IV Waardenburg syndrome appear to have an autosomal recessive pattern of inheritance, which means both copies of the gene in each cell have mutations. Most often, the parents of an individual with an autosomal recessive condition each carry one copy of the mutated gene, but do not show signs and symptoms of the condition.

How Is Waardenburg Syndrome Diagnosed?

A diagnosis of Waardenburg syndrome (WS) is made based on signs and symptoms present. In 1992, the Waardenburg Consortium proposed diagnostic criteria, which includes both major and minor criteria. A clinical diagnosis of WS type 1 (the most common type) needs 2 major, or 1 major and 2 minor criteria.

Major criteria:

- Congenital sensorineural hearing loss

- Iris pigmentary (coloration) abnormality, such as heterochromia iridis (complete, partial, or segmental); pale blue eyes (isohypochromia iridis); or pigmentary abnormalities of the fundus (part of the eye opposite the pupil)

- Abnormalities of hair pigmentation, such as white forelock (lock of hair above the forehead), or loss of hair color

- Dystopia canthorum – lateral displacement of inner angles (canthi) of the eyes (in WS types 1 and 3 only)

- Having a 1st degree relative with Waardenburg syndrome

Minor criteria:

- Congenital leukoderma (hypopigmented patches of skin)
- Synophrys (connected eyebrows or "unibrow") or medial eyebrow flare
- Broad or high nasal bridge (uppermost part of the nose)
- Hypoplasia of the nostrils
- Premature gray hair (under age 30)

WS type 2 has similar features to WS type 1, but the inner canthi are normal (no dystopia cantorum present).

WS type 3 also has similar features to WS type 1, but is additionally characterized by musculoskeletal abnormalities such as muscle hypoplasia (underdevelopment); flexion contractures (inability to straighten joints); or syndactyly (webbed or fused fingers or toes).

WS type 4 has similar features to WS type 2, but with Hirschsprung disease (a condition resulting from missing nerve cells in the muscles of part or all of the large intestine).

Chapter 24

Huntington Disease

What Is Huntington Disease?

Huntington disease is a progressive brain disorder that causes uncontrolled movements, emotional problems, and loss of thinking ability (cognition).

Adult-onset Huntington disease, the most common form of this disorder, usually appears in a person's thirties or forties. Early signs and symptoms can include irritability, depression, small involuntary movements, poor coordination, and trouble learning new information or making decisions. Many people with Huntington disease develop involuntary jerking or twitching movements known as chorea. As the disease progresses, these movements become more pronounced. Affected individuals may have trouble walking, speaking, and swallowing. People with this disorder also experience changes in personality and a decline in thinking and

This chapter contains text excerpted from the following sources: Text beginning with the heading "What Is Huntington Disease?" is excerpted from "Huntington Disease," Genetics Home Reference (GHR), National Institutes of Health (NIH), March 7, 2016; Text under the heading "What Causes Huntington Disease?" is excerpted from "Huntington Disease," National Center for Advancing Translational Sciences (NCATS), July 8, 2015; Text under the heading "Is There Any Treatment?" is excerpted from "NINDS Huntington Disease Information Page," National Institute of Neurological Disorders and Stroke (NINDS), January 28, 2016.

reasoning abilities. Individuals with the adult-onset form of Huntington disease usually live about 15 to 20 years after signs and symptoms begin.

A less common form of Huntington disease known as the juvenile form begins in childhood or adolescence. It also involves movement problems and mental and emotional changes. Additional signs of the juvenile form include slow movements, clumsiness, frequent falling, rigidity, slurred speech, and drooling. School performance declines as thinking and reasoning abilities become impaired. Seizures occur in 30 percent to 50 percent of children with this condition. Juvenile Huntington disease tends to progress more quickly than the adult-onset form; affected individuals usually live 10 to 15 years after signs and symptoms appear.

How Common Is Huntington Disease?

Huntington disease affects an estimated 3 to 7 per 100,000 people of European ancestry. The disorder appears to be less common in some other populations, including people of Japanese, Chinese, and African descent.

What Genes Are Related to Huntington Disease?

Mutations in the *HTT* gene cause Huntington disease. The *HTT* gene provides instructions for making a protein called huntingtin. Although the function of this protein is unknown, it appears to play an important role in nerve cells (neurons) in the brain.

The *HTT* mutation that causes Huntington disease involves a DNA segment known as a CAG trinucleotide repeat. This segment is made up of a series of three DNA building blocks (cytosine, adenine, and guanine) that appear multiple times in a row. Normally, the CAG segment is repeated 10 to 35 times within the gene. In people with Huntington disease, the CAG segment is repeated 36 to more than 120 times. People with 36 to 39 CAG repeats may or may not develop the signs and symptoms of Huntington disease, while people with 40 or more repeats almost always develop the disorder.

An increase in the size of the CAG segment leads to the production of an abnormally long version of the huntingtin protein. The elongated protein is cut into smaller, toxic fragments that bind together and accumulate in neurons, disrupting the normal functions of these cells. The dysfunction and eventual death of neurons in certain areas of the brain underlie the signs and symptoms of Huntington disease.

How Do People Inherit Huntington Disease?

This condition is inherited in an autosomal dominant pattern, which means one copy of the altered gene in each cell is sufficient to cause the disorder. An affected person usually inherits the altered gene from one affected parent. In rare cases, an individual with Huntington disease does not have a parent with the disorder.

As the altered *HTT* gene is passed from one generation to the next, the size of the CAG trinucleotide repeat often increases in size. A larger number of repeats is usually associated with an earlier onset of signs and symptoms. This phenomenon is called anticipation. People with the adult-onset form of Huntington disease typically have 40 to 50 CAG repeats in the *HTT* gene, while people with the juvenile form of the disorder tend to have more than 60 CAG repeats.

Individuals who have 27 to 35 CAG repeats in the *HTT* gene do not develop Huntington disease, but they are at risk of having children who will develop the disorder. As the gene is passed from parent to child, the size of the CAG trinucleotide repeat may lengthen into the range associated with Huntington disease (36 repeats or more).

What Causes Huntington Disease?

Huntington disease (HD) is caused by a change (mutation) in the *HTT* gene. This gene gives instructions for making a protein called huntingtin. The exact function of this protein is unclear, but it appears to be important to nerve cells (neurons) in the brain.

The *HTT* gene mutation that causes HD involves a DNA segment known as a CAG trinucleotide repeat. This segment is made up of three DNA building blocks that repeat multiple times in a row. The CAG segment in a normal *HTT* gene repeats about 10 to 35 times. In people with HD, it may repeat from 36 to over 120 times. People with 36 to 39 CAG repeats (an intermediate size) may or may not develop HD, while people with 40 or more repeats almost always develop HD.

An increased number of CAG repeats leads to an abnormally long version of the huntingtin protein. The long protein is then cut into smaller, toxic pieces that end up sticking together and accumulating in neurons. This disrupts the function of the neurons, ultimately causing the features of HD.

What Are the Signs and Symptoms of Huntington Disease?

Huntington disease (HD) is a progressive disorder that causes motor, cognitive, and psychiatric signs and symptoms. On average, most people begin developing features of HD between ages 35 and 44. Signs and symptoms vary by stage and may include:

Early stage:

- Behavioral disturbances
- Clumsiness
- Moodiness
- Irritability
- Paranoia
- Apathy
- Anxiety
- Hallucinations
- Abnormal eye movements
- Depression
- Impaired ability to detect odors

Middle stage:

- Dystonia
- Involuntary movements
- Trouble with balance and walking
- Chorea with twisting and writhing motions
- Unsteady gait (style of walking)
- Slow reaction time
- General weakness
- Weight loss
- Speech difficulties
- Stubbornness

Late stage:

- Rigidity (continual tension of the muscles)
- Bradykinesia (difficulty initiating and continuing movements)
- Severe chorea
- Serious weight loss

- Inability to speak

- Inability to walk

- Swallowing problems

- Inability to care for oneself

There is also a less common, early-onset form of HD which begins in childhood or adolescence.

Is Genetic Testing Available for Huntington Disease?

Yes. Testing of adults at risk for Huntington disease (HD) who have no symptoms of the disease is called predictive testing. Whether to have predictive testing requires careful thought, including pre-test and post-test genetic counseling. This is particularly important because there is currently no cure. Furthermore, predictive testing cannot accurately predict the age a person with an HD mutation will develop symptoms, the severity or type of symptoms they will experience, or the future rate of disease progression. A person may want to have predictive testing because they feel they need to know, or to make personal decisions involving having children, finances, and/or career planning. Other people decide they do not want to know whether they will develop HD.

Testing is appropriate to consider in symptomatic people of any age in a family with a confirmed diagnosis of HD. However, testing of asymptomatic people younger than age 18 is not considered appropriate. A main reason is that it takes *away the choice of whether the person wants to know, while there is no major benefit to knowing at that age.*

People who are interested in learning more about genetic testing for HD should speak with a genetics professional.

How Is Huntington Disease Diagnosed?

A diagnosis of Huntington disease is typically suspected in people with characteristic signs and symptoms of the condition and a family history consistent with autosomal dominant inheritance. The diagnosis can then be confirmed with genetic testing that identifies a specific type of change (mutation) in the *HTT* gene.

Is There Any Treatment?

There is no treatment that can stop or reverse the course of HD. Tetrabenazine is prescribed for treating Huntington's-associated chorea. It is the only drug approved by the U.S. Food and Drug Administration specifically for use against HD. Antipsychotic drugs may help to alleviate chorea and may also be used to help control hallucinations, delusions, and violent outbursts. Drugs may be prescribed to treat depression and anxiety. Drugs used to treat the symptoms of HD may have side effects such as fatigue, sedation, decreased concentration, restlessness, or hyperexcitability, and should be only used when symptoms create problems for the individual.

What Is the Prognosis?

Huntington disease causes disability that gets worse over time. People with this disease usually die within 15 to 20 years following diagnosis. At this time, no treatment is available to slow, stop or reverse the course of HD.

Chapter 25

Hypohidrotic Ectodermal Dysplasia

What Is Hypohidrotic Ectodermal Dysplasia?

Hypohidrotic ectodermal dysplasia is one of about 150 types of ectodermal dysplasia in humans. Before birth, these disorders result in the abnormal development of structures including the skin, hair, nails, teeth, and sweat glands.

Most people with hypohidrotic ectodermal dysplasia have a reduced ability to sweat (hypohidrosis) because they have fewer sweat glands than normal or their sweat glands do not function properly. Sweating is a major way that the body controls its temperature; as sweat evaporates from the skin, it cools the body. An inability to sweat can lead to a dangerously high body temperature (hyperthermia), particularly in hot weather. In some cases, hyperthermia can cause life-threatening medical problems.

Affected individuals tend to have sparse scalp and body hair (hypotrichosis). The hair is often light-colored, brittle, and slow-growing.

This chapter contains text excerpted from the following sources: Text beginning with the heading "What Is Hypohidrotic Ectodermal Dysplasia?" is excerpted from "Hypohidrotic Ectodermal Dysplasia," Genetics Home Reference (GHR), National Institutes of Health (NIH), March 7, 2016; Text under the heading "Is Genetic Testing Available for Hypohidrotic Ectodermal Dysplasia?" is excerpted from "Hypohidrotic Ectodermal Dysplasia," National Center for Advancing Translational Sciences (NCATS), January 21, 2014.

This condition is also characterized by absent teeth (hypodontia) or teeth that are malformed. The teeth that are present are frequently small and pointed.

Hypohidrotic ectodermal dysplasia is associated with distinctive facial features including a prominent forehead, thick lips, and a flattened bridge of the nose. Additional features of this condition include thin, wrinkled, and dark-colored skin around the eyes; chronic skin problems such as eczema; and a bad-smelling discharge from the nose (ozena).

How Common Is Hypohidrotic Ectodermal Dysplasia?

Hypohidrotic ectodermal dysplasia is the most common form of ectodermal dysplasia in humans. It is estimated to affect at least 1 in 17,000 people worldwide.

What Genes Are Related to Hypohidrotic Ectodermal Dysplasia?

Mutations in the *EDA, EDAR,* and *EDARADD* genes cause hypohidrotic ectodermal dysplasia.

The *EDA, EDAR,* and *EDARADD* genes provide instructions for making proteins that work together during embryonic development. These proteins form part of a signaling pathway that is critical for the interaction between two cell layers, the ectoderm and the mesoderm. In the early embryo, these cell layers form the basis for many of the body's organs and tissues. Ectoderm-mesoderm interactions are essential for the formation of several structures that arise from the ectoderm, including the skin, hair, nails, teeth, and sweat glands.

Mutations in the *EDA, EDAR,* or *EDARADD* gene prevent normal interactions between the ectoderm and the mesoderm and impair the normal development of hair, sweat glands, and teeth. The improper formation of these ectodermal structures leads to the characteristic features of hypohidrotic ectodermal dysplasia.

How Do People Inherit Hypohidrotic Ectodermal Dysplasia?

Hypohidrotic ectodermal dysplasia has several different inheritance patterns. Most cases are caused by mutations in the *EDA* gene, which are inherited in an X-linked recessive pattern. A condition is considered X-linked if the mutated gene that causes the disorder is located on the X chromosome, one of the two sex chromosomes. In males (who have only one X chromosome), one altered copy of the gene in each cell is sufficient to cause the condition. In females (who have two X chromosomes), a mutation must be present in both copies of the gene to cause the disorder. Males are affected by X-linked recessive disorders much more frequently than females. A characteristic of X-linked inheritance is that fathers cannot pass X-linked traits to their sons.

In X-linked recessive inheritance, a female with one altered copy of the gene in each cell is called a carrier. In about 70 percent of cases, carriers of hypohidrotic ectodermal dysplasia experience some features of the condition. These signs and symptoms are usually mild and include a few missing or abnormal teeth, sparse hair, and some problems with sweat gland function. Some carriers, however, have more severe features of this disorder.

Less commonly, hypohidrotic ectodermal dysplasia results from mutations in the *EDAR* or *EDARADD* gene. *EDAR* mutations can have an autosomal dominant or autosomal recessive pattern of inheritance, and *EDARADD* mutations have an autosomal recessive pattern of inheritance. Autosomal dominant inheritance means one copy of the altered gene in each cell is sufficient to cause the disorder. Autosomal recessive inheritance means two copies of the gene in each cell are altered. Most often, the parents of an individual with an autosomal recessive disorder are carriers of one copy of the altered gene but do not show signs and symptoms of the disorder.

Is Genetic Testing Available for Hypohidrotic Ectodermal Dysplasia?

Yes. Genetic testing for hypohidrotic ectodermal dysplasia is available. In most cases, hypohidrotic ectodermal dysplasia can be diagnosed after infancy based upon the physical features in the affected child. Genetic testing may be ordered to confirm the diagnosis. Other reasons for testing may include to identify carriers or for prenatal diagnosis.

Clinical testing is available for detection of disease causing mutations in the *EDA, EDAR,* and *EDARADD* genes. It's recommended recommend that you speak with a health care provider or a genetics professional to learn more about your testing options.

The Genetic Testing Registry (GTR) provides information about the genetic tests for this condition. The intended audience for the GTR is health care providers and researchers. Patients and consumers with specific questions about a genetic test should contact a health care provider or a genetics professional.

How Might Hypohidrotic Ectodermal Dysplasia Be Treated?

There is no specific treatment for HED. The condition is managed by treating the various symptoms. For patients with abnormal or no sweat glands, it is recommended that they live in places with air conditioning at home, school and work. In order to maintain normal body temperature, they should frequently drink cool liquids and wear cool clothing. Dental defects can be managed with dentures and implants. Artificial tears are used to prevent cornea damage for patients that do not produce enough tears. Surgery to repair a cleft palate is also helpful in improving speech and facial deformities.

Chapter 26

Inborn Errors of Metabolism

Chapter Contents

Section 26.1

Introduction to Inborn Errors of Metabolism

This section includes text excerpted from "General
Information about Inborn Errors of Metabolism," National
Human Genome Research Institute (NHGRI), February 22, 2013.

What Are Inborn Errors of Metabolism?

Metabolism is a sequence of chemical reactions that take place in cells in the body. These reactions are responsible for the breakdown of nutrients and the generation of energy in our bodies. Inborn errors of metabolism (IEM) are a group of disorders that causes a block in a metabolic pathway leading to clinically significant consequences.

Specific chemical compounds, called enzymes, are responsible for the reactions that make up metabolism. There are also 'co-factors', or compounds that help enzymes carry out their reactions.

What Are the Different Forms of IEM?

The different IEM are usually named for the enzyme that is not working properly. For example, if the enzyme carbamoyl phosphate synthetase 1 (CPS1) is not working, the IEM is called "CPS1 deficiency." A list of broad categories of IEM and some examples are listed below.

Table 26.1. Forms of IEM

IEM	Examples
Urea cycle disorders	Ornithine transcarbamylase deficiency, citrullinemia, argininosuccinic aciduria, argininemia
Organic acidemias	Propionic acidemia, methylmalonic aciduria, isovaleric acidemia, glutaric acidemia, maple syrup urine disease
Fatty acid oxidation defects	Medium chain acyl-CoA dehydrogenase deficiency, carnitine palmitoyl transferase 1 deficiency, long chain hydroxyacyl-CoA dehydrogenase deficiency
Amino acidopathies	Tyrosinemia, phenylketonuria, homocysteinuria

Table 26.1. Continued

IEM	Examples
Carbohydrate disorders	Galactosemia, fructosemia
Mitochondrial disorders	MELAS, MERFF, pyruvate dehydrogenase deficiency

What Causes the IEM and How Are the Different Forms Inherited?

The IEM are caused by mutations (or alterations) in the genes that tell our cells how to make the enzymes and the co-factors for metabolism. A mutation causes a gene to not function at all or not to function as well as it should. Most often these altered genes are inherited from parent(s), but they may also occur spontaneously.

When discussing how genetic conditions are passed on in a family, it is important to understand that we have two copies of most genes, with one copy inherited from our mother and one copy inherited from our father. This is not the case for the genes that are on our sex chromosomes (the "X" and "Y" chromosomes). These are different in men and women: men have only one X chromosome and therefore only one copy of the genes on that chromosome, while women have two X chromosomes and therefore have two copies of the genes on that chromosome. A father passes on his X chromosome to all of his daughters and his Y chromosome on to all of his sons. A mother passes on an X chromosome to each child.

What Is the Chance of Having an IEM If Someone Else in the Family Has It?

The chance that someone else in the family has the same IEM as their relative depends on the inheritance pattern of the IEM, whether the at-risk family member is male or female, and the rest of the family history (how many relatives have been diagnosed with the disorder already and whether genetic testing has been performed in other relatives). In some cases, the age of the at-risk family member and whether or not they have shown any signs or symptoms of the disorder is helpful in estimating the chances that they also have the disorder.

It's recommended talking to your metabolic specialist and/or genetic counselor to determine those relatives who may be at risk for having an IEM and for coordination of genetic testing, when appropriate. We are happy to talk with you about this.

What Are the Symptoms of IEM and How Are They Diagnosed?

In general, the earlier someone develops symptoms of an IEM, the more severe their disorder. The severity of symptoms is generally based on

1. the position of the defective enzyme within the metabolic pathway; and

2. whether or not there is any functional enzyme or co-factor being produced.

However, other environmental and genetic factors may play a role in determining the severity of symptoms for a given patient.

IEM are multisystemic diseases and thus patients may present with a variety of symptoms, many of which depend on the specific metabolic pathway(s) involved. Some findings in patients with IEM may include elevated acid levels in the blood, low blood sugar, high blood ammonia, abnormal liver function tests, and blood cell abnormalities. Certain patients may also have neurologic abnormalities such as seizures and developmental delays. Growth may also be affected.

How Are IEM Treated?

Treatment of IEM is tailored to the specific disorder once a diagnosis is made. In general, the goals of treatment are to minimize or eliminate the buildup of toxic metabolites that result from the block in metabolism while maintaining growth and development. This may be accomplished by special modified diets, supplements and medications.

A doctor who specializes in metabolic disorders should see IEM patients on a regular basis. Severely affected patients will likely be seen on a more frequent basis than mild or moderately affected patients.

Section 26.2

Argininosuccinic Acidemia

This section includes text excerpted from "Argininosuccinic Acidemia," Genetics Home Reference (GHR), National Institutes of Health (NIH), March 7, 2016.

What Is Argininosuccinic Aciduria?

Argininosuccinic aciduria is an inherited disorder that causes ammonia to accumulate in the blood. Ammonia, which is formed when proteins are broken down in the body, is toxic if the levels become too high. The nervous system is especially sensitive to the effects of excess ammonia.

Argininosuccinic aciduria usually becomes evident in the first few days of life. An infant with argininosuccinic aciduria may be lacking in energy (lethargic) or unwilling to eat, and have poorly controlled breathing rate or body temperature. Some babies with this disorder experience seizures or unusual body movements, or go into a coma. Complications from argininosuccinic aciduria may include developmental delay and intellectual disability. Progressive liver damage, skin lesions, and brittle hair may also be seen.

Occasionally, an individual may inherit a mild form of the disorder in which ammonia accumulates in the bloodstream only during periods of illness or other stress.

How Common Is Argininosuccinic Aciduria?

Argininosuccinic aciduria occurs in approximately 1 in 70,000 newborns.

What Genes Are Related to Argininosuccinic Aciduria?

Mutations in the *ASL* gene cause argininosuccinic aciduria.

Argininosuccinic aciduria belongs to a class of genetic diseases called urea cycle disorders. The urea cycle is a sequence of reactions that occur in liver cells. It processes excess nitrogen, generated when protein is used by the body, to make a compound called urea that is excreted by the kidneys.

In argininosuccinic aciduria, the enzyme that starts a specific reaction within the urea cycle is damaged or missing. The urea cycle cannot proceed normally, and nitrogen accumulates in the bloodstream in the form of ammonia.

Ammonia is especially damaging to the nervous system, so argininosuccinic aciduria causes neurological problems as well as eventual damage to the liver.

How Do People Inherit Argininosuccinic Aciduria?

This condition is inherited in an autosomal recessive pattern, which means both copies of the gene in each cell have mutations. The parents of an individual with an autosomal recessive condition each carry one copy of the mutated gene, but they typically do not show signs and symptoms of the condition.

Section 26.3

Biotinidase Deficiency

This section includes text excerpted from "Biotinidase Deficiency," Genetics Home Reference (GHR), National Institutes of Health (NIH), March 7, 2016.

What Is Biotinidase Deficiency?

Biotinidase deficiency is an inherited disorder in which the body is unable to recycle the vitamin biotin. If this condition is not recognized and treated, its signs and symptoms typically appear within the first few months of life, although it can also become apparent later in childhood.

Profound biotinidase deficiency, the more severe form of the condition, can cause seizures, weak muscle tone (hypotonia), breathing problems, hearing and vision loss, problems with movement and balance (ataxia), skin rashes, hair loss (alopecia), and a fungal infection called candidiasis. Affected children also have delayed development. Lifelong treatment can prevent these complications from occurring or improve them if they have already developed.

Partial biotinidase deficiency is a milder form of this condition. Without treatment, affected children may experience hypotonia, skin rashes, and hair loss, but these problems may appear only during illness, infection, or other times of stress.

How Common Is Biotinidase Deficiency?

Profound or partial biotinidase deficiency occurs in approximately 1 in 60,000 newborns

What Genes Are Related to Biotinidase Deficiency?

Mutations in the *BTD* gene cause biotinidase deficiency. The *BTD* gene provides instructions for making an enzyme called biotinidase. This enzyme recycles biotin, a B vitamin found in foods such as liver, egg yolks, and milk. Biotinidase removes biotin that is bound to proteins in food, leaving the vitamin in its free (unbound) state. Free biotin is needed by enzymes called biotin-dependent carboxylases to break down fats, proteins, and carbohydrates. Because several of these enzymes are impaired in biotinidase deficiency, the condition is considered a form of multiple carboxylase deficiency.

Mutations in the *BTD* gene reduce or eliminate the activity of biotinidase. Profound biotinidase deficiency results when the activity of biotinidase is reduced to less than 10 percent of normal. Partial biotinidase deficiency occurs when biotinidase activity is reduced to between 10 percent and 30 percent of normal. Without enough of this enzyme, biotin cannot be recycled. The resulting shortage of free biotin impairs the activity of biotin-dependent carboxylases, leading to a buildup of potentially toxic compounds in the body. If the condition is not treated promptly, this buildup damages various cells and tissues, causing the signs and symptoms described above.

How Do People Inherit Biotinidase Deficiency?

This condition is inherited in an autosomal recessive pattern, which means both copies of the *BTD* gene in each cell have mutations. The parents of an individual with biotinidase deficiency each carry one copy of the mutated gene, but they typically do not have any health problems associated with the condition.

Section 26.4

Citrullinemia

This section includes text excerpted from "Citrullinemia,"
Genetics Home Reference (GHR), National Institutes
of Health (NIH), March 7, 2016.

What Is Citrullinemia?

Citrullinemia is an inherited disorder that causes ammonia and other toxic substances to accumulate in the blood. Two forms of citrullinemia have been described; they have different signs and symptoms and are caused by mutations in different genes.

Type I citrullinemia (also known as classic citrullinemia) usually becomes evident in the first few days of life. Affected infants typically appear normal at birth, but as ammonia builds up in the body they experience a progressive lack of energy (lethargy), poor feeding, vomiting, seizures, and loss of consciousness. These medical problems are life-threatening in many cases. Less commonly, a milder form of type I citrullinemia can develop later in childhood or adulthood. This later-onset form is associated with intense headaches, partial loss of vision, problems with balance and muscle coordination (ataxia), and lethargy. Some people with gene mutations that cause type I citrullinemia never experience signs and symptoms of the disorder.

Type II citrullinemia chiefly affects the nervous system, causing confusion, restlessness, memory loss, abnormal behaviors (such as aggression, irritability, and hyperactivity), seizures, and coma. In some cases, the signs and symptoms of this disorder appear during adulthood (adult-onset). These signs and symptoms can be life-threatening, and are known to be triggered by certain medications, infections, surgery, and alcohol intake in people with adult-onset type II citrullinemia.

The features of adult-onset type II citrullinemia may also develop in people who as infants had a liver disorder called neonatal intrahepatic cholestasis caused by citrin deficiency (NICCD). This liver condition is also known as neonatal-onset type II citrullinemia. NICCD blocks the flow of bile (a digestive fluid produced by the liver) and prevents the body from processing certain nutrients properly. In many cases, the signs and symptoms of NICCD resolve within a year. Years or even decades later, however, some of these people develop the characteristic features of adult-onset type II citrullinemia.

How Common Is Citrullinemia?

Type I citrullinemia is the most common form of the disorder, affecting about 1 in 57,000 people worldwide. Type II citrullinemia is found primarily in the Japanese population, where it occurs in an estimated 1 in 100,000 to 230,000 individuals. Type II also has been reported in other populations, including people from East Asia and the Middle East.

What Genes Are Related to Citrullinemia?

Mutations in the *ASS1* and *SLC25A13* genes cause citrullinemia.

Citrullinemia belongs to a class of genetic diseases called urea cycle disorders. The urea cycle is a sequence of chemical reactions that takes place in liver cells. These reactions process excess nitrogen that is generated when protein is used by the body. The excess nitrogen is used to make a compound called urea, which is excreted in urine.

Mutations in the *ASS1* gene cause type I citrullinemia. This gene provides instructions for making an enzyme, argininosuccinate synthase 1, that is responsible for one step of the urea cycle. Mutations in the *ASS1* gene reduce the activity of the enzyme, which disrupts the urea cycle and prevents the body from processing nitrogen effectively. Excess nitrogen (in the form of ammonia) and other byproducts of the urea cycle accumulate in the bloodstream. Ammonia is particularly toxic to the nervous system, which helps explain the neurologic symptoms (such as lethargy, seizures, and ataxia) that are often seen in type I citrullinemia.

Mutations in the *SLC25A13* gene are responsible for adult-onset type II citrullinemia and NICCD. This gene provides instructions for making a protein called citrin. Within cells, citrin helps transport molecules used in the production and breakdown of simple sugars, the production of proteins, and the urea cycle. Molecules transported by citrin are also involved in making nucleotides, which are the building blocks of DNA and its chemical cousin, RNA. Mutations in the *SLC25A13* gene typically prevent cells from making any functional citrin, which inhibits the urea cycle and disrupts the production of proteins and nucleotides. The resulting buildup of ammonia and other toxic substances leads to the signs and symptoms of adult-onset type II citrullinemia. A lack of citrin also leads to the features of NICCD, although ammonia does not build up in the bloodstream of infants with this condition.

How Do People Inherit Citrullinemia?

This condition is inherited in an autosomal recessive pattern, which means both copies of the gene in each cell have mutations. The parents of an individual with an autosomal recessive condition each carry one copy of the mutated gene, but they typically do not show signs and symptoms of the condition.

Section 26.5

Galactosemia

This section contains text excerpted from the following sources: Text beginning with the heading "What Is Galactosemia?" is excerpted from "Galactosemia," Genetics Home Reference (GHR), National Institutes of Health (NIH), March 7, 2016; Text under the heading "How Might Galactosemia Be Treated?" is excerpted from "Galactosemia," National Center for Advancing Translational Sciences (NCATS), June 25, 2015.

What Is Galactosemia?

Galactosemia is a disorder that affects how the body processes a simple sugar called galactose. A small amount of galactose is present in many foods. It is primarily part of a larger sugar called lactose, which is found in all dairy products and many baby formulas. The signs and symptoms of galactosemia result from an inability to use galactose to produce energy.

Researchers have identified several types of galactosemia. These conditions are each caused by mutations in a particular gene and affect different enzymes involved in breaking down galactose.

Classic galactosemia, also known as type I, is the most common and most severe form of the condition. If infants with classic galactosemia are not treated promptly with a low-galactose diet, life-threatening complications appear within a few days after birth. Affected infants typically develop feeding difficulties, a lack of energy (lethargy), a failure to gain weight and grow as expected (failure to thrive), yellowing of the skin and whites of the eyes (jaundice), liver damage, and abnormal bleeding. Other serious complications of this condition can include overwhelming bacterial infections (sepsis) and shock. Affected children are also at increased risk of delayed development, clouding of the lens of the eye (cataract), speech difficulties, and intellectual disability. Females with classic galactosemia may develop reproductive problems caused by an early loss of function of the ovaries (premature ovarian insufficiency).

Galactosemia type II (also called galactokinase deficiency) and type III (also called galactose epimerase deficiency) cause different patterns of signs and symptoms. Galactosemia type II causes fewer medical problems than the classic type. Affected infants develop cataracts but otherwise experience few long-term complications. The signs and symptoms of galactosemia type III vary from mild to severe and can include cataracts, delayed growth and development, intellectual disability, liver disease, and kidney problems.

How Common Is Galactosemia?

Classic galactosemia occurs in 1 in 30,000 to 60,000 newborns. Galactosemia type II and type III are less common; type II probably affects fewer than 1 in 100,000 newborns and type III appears to be very rare.

What Genes Are Related to Galactosemia?

Mutations in the *GALT, GALK1,* and *GALE* genes cause galactosemia. These genes provide instructions for making enzymes that are essential for processing galactose obtained from the diet. These enzymes break down galactose into another simple sugar, glucose, and other molecules that the body can store or use for energy.

Mutations in the *GALT* gene cause classic galactosemia (type I). Most of these genetic changes almost completely eliminate the activity of the enzyme produced from the *GALT* gene, preventing the normal processing of galactose and resulting in the life-threatening signs and symptoms of this disorder. Another *GALT* gene mutation, known as the Duarte variant, reduces but does not eliminate the activity of the enzyme. People with the Duarte variant tend to have much milder features of galactosemia.

Galactosemia type II results from mutations in the *GALK1* gene, while mutations in the *GALE* gene underlie galactosemia type III. Like the enzyme produced from the *GALT* gene, the enzymes made from the *GALK1* and *GALE* genes play important roles in processing galactose. A shortage of any of these critical enzymes allows galactose and related compounds to build up to toxic levels in the body. The accumulation of these substances damages tissues and organs, leading to the characteristic features of galactosemia.

How Do People Inherit Galactosemia?

This condition is inherited in an autosomal recessive pattern, which means both copies of the gene in each cell have mutations. The parents of an individual with an autosomal recessive condition each carry one copy of the mutated gene, but they typically do not show signs and symptoms of the condition.

How Might Galactosemia Be Treated?

When treatment starts before a baby is 10 days old, there is a much better chance for normal growth, development and intelligence. Affected individuals must avoid all milk, milk-containing products (including dry milk), and other foods that contain galactose for life. It is essential to read product labels and be an informed consumer. Infants can be fed with soy formula, meat-based formula or Nutramigen (a protein hydrolysate formula), or another lactose-free formula. Calcium supplements are also recommended.

Because the body also makes some galactose, symptoms cannot be completely avoided by removing all lactose and galactose from the diet. Researchers are working on finding a treatment to lower the amount of galactose made by the body, but there is no effective method to do so at this time.

The Screening, Technology, and Research in Genetics (STAR-G) Project is a U.S.-based organization that provides information on newborn screening. They provide comprehensive information for treatment on galactosemia.

Should Sucralose or Other Sugars Be Avoided by Patients Affected with Galactosemia?

Sugars that are simple are known as monosaccharides and include glucose, galactose and fructose. When the sugar contain two monosaccharides is called disaccharide. The disaccharides include sucrose (formed by glucose and fructose), maltose (formed by two glucoses) and lactose (formed by galactose and glucose).

Basically, any food or beverage or medication containing galactose or lactose should be avoided by the patients with galactosemia. The main source of galactose is from the lactose contained in the diet.

Sucralose is an artificial sweetener. During processing, sucrose (sugar) is broken down to a compound that has the word galactose in it, but it is not broken down to simple galactose, therefore it is acceptable for patients with galactosemia.

Section 26.6

Homocystinuria

This section includes text excerpted from "Homocystinuria," Genetics Home Reference (GHR), National Institutes of Health (NIH), March 7, 2016.

What Is Homocystinuria?

Homocystinuria is an inherited disorder in which the body is unable to process certain building blocks of proteins (amino acids) properly. There are multiple forms of homocystinuria, which are distinguished by their signs and symptoms and genetic cause. The most common form of homocystinuria is characterized by nearsightedness (myopia), dislocation of the lens at the front of the eye, an increased risk of abnormal blood clotting, and brittle bones that are prone to fracture (osteoporosis) or other skeletal abnormalities. Some affected individuals also have developmental delay and learning problems.

Less common forms of homocystinuria can cause intellectual disability, failure to grow and gain weight at the expected rate (failure to thrive), seizures, problems with movement, and a blood disorder called megaloblastic anemia. Megaloblastic anemia occurs when a person has a low number of red blood cells (anemia), and the remaining red blood cells are larger than normal (megaloblastic).

The signs and symptoms of homocystinuria typically develop within the first year of life, although some people with a mild form of the disease may not develop features until later in childhood or adulthood.

How Common Is Homocystinuria?

The most common form of homocystinuria affects at least 1 in 200,000 to 335,000 people worldwide. The disorder appears to be more common in some countries, such as Ireland (1 in 65,000), Germany (1 in 17,800), Norway (1 in 6,400), and Qatar (1 in 1,800). The rarer forms of homocystinuria each have a small number of cases reported in the scientific literature.

What Genes Are Related to Homocystinuria?

Mutations in the *CBS, MTHFR, MTR, MTRR*, and *MMADHC* genes cause homocystinuria.

Mutations in the *CBS* gene cause the most common form of homocystinuria. The *CBS* gene provides instructions for producing an enzyme called cystathionine beta-synthase. This enzyme acts in a chemical pathway and is responsible for converting the amino acid homocysteine to a molecule called cystathionine. As a result of this pathway, other amino acids, including methionine, are produced. Mutations in the *CBS* gene disrupt the function of cystathionine beta-synthase, preventing homocysteine from being used properly. As a result, this amino acid and toxic byproducts substances build up in the blood. Some of the excess homocysteine is excreted in urine.

Rarely, homocystinuria can be caused by mutations in several other genes. The enzymes made by the *MTHFR, MTR, MTRR,* and *MMADHC* genes play roles in converting homocysteine to methionine. Mutations in any of these genes prevent the enzymes from functioning properly, which leads to a buildup of homocysteine in the body. Researchers have not determined how excess homocysteine and related compounds lead to the signs and symptoms of homocystinuria.

How Do People Inherit Homocystinuria?

This condition is inherited in an autosomal recessive pattern, which means both copies of the gene in each cell have mutations. Most often, the parents of an individual with an autosomal recessive condition each carry one copy of the mutated gene, but do not show signs and symptoms of the condition.

Although people who carry one mutated copy and one normal copy of the *CBS* gene do not have homocystinuria, they are more likely than people without a *CBS* mutation to have shortages (deficiencies) of vitamin B12 and folic acid.

Section 26.7

Fructose Intolerance

This section contains text excerpted from the following sources: Text beginning with the heading "What Is Hereditary Fructose Intolerance?" is excerpted from "Hereditary Fructose Intolerance," Genetics Home Reference (GHR), National Institutes of Health (NIH), March 7, 2016; Text under the heading "What Causes Hereditary Fructose Intolerance (HFI)?" is excerpted from "Hereditary Fructose Intolerance," National Center for Advancing Translational Sciences (NCATS), August 20, 2015.

What Is Hereditary Fructose Intolerance?

Hereditary fructose intolerance is a condition that affects a person's ability to digest the sugar fructose. Fructose is a simple sugar found primarily in fruits. Affected individuals develop signs and symptoms of the disorder in infancy when fruits, juices, or other foods containing fructose are introduced into the diet. After ingesting fructose, individuals with hereditary fructose intolerance may experience nausea, bloating, abdominal pain, diarrhea, vomiting, and low blood sugar (hypoglycemia). Affected infants may fail to grow and gain weight at the expected rate (failure to thrive).

Repeated ingestion of fructose-containing foods can lead to liver and kidney damage. The liver damage can result in a yellowing of the skin and whites of the eyes (jaundice), an enlarged liver (hepatomegaly), and chronic liver disease (cirrhosis). Continued exposure to fructose may result in seizures, coma, and ultimately death from liver and kidney failure. Due to the severity of symptoms experienced when fructose is ingested, most people with hereditary fructose intolerance develop a dislike for fruits, juices, and other foods containing fructose.

Hereditary fructose intolerance should not be confused with a condition called fructose malabsorption. In people with fructose malabsorption, the cells of the intestine cannot absorb fructose normally, leading to bloating, diarrhea or constipation, flatulence, and stomach pain. Fructose malabsorption is thought to affect approximately 40 percent of individuals in the Western hemisphere; its cause is unknown.

How Common Is Hereditary Fructose Intolerance?

The incidence of hereditary fructose intolerance is estimated to be 1 in 20,000 to 30,000 individuals each year worldwide.

What Genes Are Related to Hereditary Fructose Intolerance?

Mutations in the *ALDOB* gene cause hereditary fructose intolerance. The *ALDOB* gene provides instructions for making the aldolase B enzyme. This enzyme is found primarily in the liver and is involved in the breakdown (metabolism) of fructose so this sugar can be used as energy. Aldolase B is responsible for the second step in the metabolism of fructose, which breaks down the molecule fructose-1-phosphate into other molecules called glyceraldehyde and dihydroxyacetone phosphate.

ALDOB gene mutations reduce the function of the enzyme, impairing its ability to metabolize fructose. A lack of functional aldolase B results in an accumulation of fructose-1-phosphate in liver cells. This buildup is toxic, resulting in the death of liver cells over time. Additionally, the breakdown products of fructose-1-phosphase are needed in the body to produce energy and to maintain blood sugar levels. The combination of decreased cellular energy, low blood sugar, and liver cell death leads to the features of hereditary fructose intolerance.

How Do People Inherit Hereditary Fructose Intolerance?

This condition is inherited in an autosomal recessive pattern, which means both copies of the gene in each cell have mutations. The parents of an individual with an autosomal recessive condition each carry one copy of the mutated gene, but they typically do not show signs and symptoms of the condition.

What Causes Hereditary Fructose Intolerance (HFI)?

HFI is caused by alterations (mutations) in the *ALDOB* gene. This gene provides instructions for making an enzyme called aldolase B. This enzyme is primarily found in the liver and is involved in the breakdown of fructose into energy. Mutations in the *ALDOB* gene reduce the function of the enzyme, impairing its ability to metabolize fructose. This causes a toxic buildup of fructose-1-phosphate in liver cells, which results in the death of liver cells over time.

What Are the Signs and Symptoms of Hereditary Fructose Intolerance?

The symptoms of HFI include:

- Poor feeding as a baby
- Irritability
- Increased or prolonged neonatal jaundice
- Vomiting
- Convulsions
- Excessive sleepiness
- Intolerance for fruits
- Avoidance of fruits and fructose/sucrose-containing foods
- Doing well after eating foods without fructose/sucrose

The early symptoms of fructose intolerance may resemble those of galactosemia: irritability, jaundice, vomiting, convulsions and an enlarged liver and spleen. Later problems relate more to liver disease.

How Is Hereditary Fructose Intolerance (HFI) Treated?

Complete elimination of fructose and sucrose from the diet is an effective treatment for most people, although this can be challenging.

Section 26.8

Maple Syrup Urine Disease

This section includes text excerpted from "Maple Syrup
Urine Disease," Genetics Home Reference (GHR),
National Institutes of Health (NIH), March 7, 2016.

What Is Maple Syrup Urine Disease?

Maple syrup urine disease is an inherited disorder in which the
body is unable to process certain protein building blocks (amino acids)
properly. The condition gets its name from the distinctive sweet odor of
affected infants' urine and is also characterized by poor feeding, vomiting, lack of energy (lethargy), and developmental delay. If untreated,
maple syrup urine disease can lead to seizures, coma, and death.

Maple syrup urine disease is often classified by its pattern of signs
and symptoms. The most common and severe form of the disease is the
classic type, which becomes apparent soon after birth. Variant forms
of the disorder become apparent later in infancy or childhood and are
typically milder, but they still involve developmental delay and other
health problems if not treated.

How Common Is Maple Syrup Urine Disease?

Maple syrup urine disease affects an estimated 1 in 185,000 infants
worldwide. The disorder occurs much more frequently in the Old Order
Mennonite population, with an estimated incidence of about 1 in 380
newborns.

What Genes Are Related to Maple Syrup Urine Disease?

Mutations in the *BCKDHA*, *BCKDHB*, and *DBT* genes can cause
maple syrup urine disease. These three genes provide instructions for
making proteins that work together as a complex. The protein complex
is essential for breaking down the amino acids leucine, isoleucine,
and valine, which are present in many kinds of food, particularly protein-rich foods such as milk, meat, and eggs.

Mutations in any of these three genes reduce or eliminate the function of the protein complex, preventing the normal breakdown of leucine, isoleucine, and valine. As a result, these amino acids and their byproducts build up in the body. Because high levels of these substances are toxic to the brain and other organs, their accumulation leads to the serious health problems associated with maple syrup urine disease.

How Do People Inherit Maple Syrup Urine Disease?

This condition is inherited in an autosomal recessive pattern, which means both copies of the gene in each cell have mutations. The parents of an individual with an autosomal recessive condition each carry one copy of the mutated gene, but they typically do not show signs and symptoms of the condition.

Section 26.9

Medium Chain Acyl-Coenzyme A Dehydrogenase Deficiency

This section contains text excerpted from the following sources: Text beginning with the heading "What Is MCAD Deficiency?" is excerpted from "Medium Chain Acyl-Coenzyme A Dehydrogenase Deficiency," Genetics Home Reference (GHR), National Institutes of Health (NIH), March 7, 2016; Text under the heading "What Are the Signs and Symptoms of Medium-Chain Acyl-Coenzyme a Dehydrogenase Deficiency?" is excerpted from "Medium Chain Acyl-Coenzyme A Dehydrogenase Deficiency," National Center for Advancing Translational Sciences (NCATS), July 7, 2015.

What Is MCAD Deficiency?

Medium-chain acyl-CoA dehydrogenase (MCAD) deficiency is a condition that prevents the body from converting certain fats to energy, particularly during periods without food (fasting).

Signs and symptoms of MCAD deficiency typically appear during infancy or early childhood and can include vomiting, lack of energy (lethargy), and low blood sugar (hypoglycemia). In rare cases, symptoms of this disorder are not recognized early in life, and the condition is not diagnosed until adulthood. People with MCAD deficiency are at risk of serious complications such as seizures, breathing difficulties, liver problems, brain damage, coma, and sudden death.

Problems related to MCAD deficiency can be triggered by periods of fasting or by illnesses such as viral infections. This disorder is sometimes mistaken for Reye syndrome, a severe disorder that may develop in children while they appear to be recovering from viral infections such as chicken pox or flu. Most cases of Reye syndrome are associated with the use of aspirin during these viral infections.

How Common Is MCAD Deficiency?

In the United States, the estimated incidence of MCAD deficiency is 1 in 17,000 people. The condition is more common in people of northern European ancestry than in other ethnic groups.

What Genes Are Related to MCAD Deficiency?

Mutations in the *ACADM* gene cause MCAD deficiency. This gene provides instructions for making an enzyme called medium-chain acyl-CoA dehydrogenase, which is required to break down (metabolize) a group of fats called medium-chain fatty acids. These fatty acids are found in foods and the body's fat tissues. Fatty acids are a major source of energy for the heart and muscles. During periods of fasting, fatty acids are also an important energy source for the liver and other tissues.

Mutations in the *ACADM* gene lead to a shortage (deficiency) of the MCAD enzyme within cells. Without sufficient amounts of this enzyme, medium-chain fatty acids are not metabolized properly. As a result, these fats are not converted to energy, which can lead to the characteristic signs and symptoms of this disorder such as lethargy and hypoglycemia. Medium-chain fatty acids or partially metabolized fatty acids may also build up in tissues and damage the liver and brain. This abnormal buildup causes the other signs and symptoms of MCAD deficiency.

How Do People Inherit MCAD Deficiency?

This condition is inherited in an autosomal recessive pattern, which means both copies of the gene in each cell have mutations. The parents of an individual with an autosomal recessive condition each carry one copy of the mutated gene, but they typically do not show signs and symptoms of the condition.

What Are the Signs and Symptoms of Medium-Chain Acyl-Coenzyme a Dehydrogenase Deficiency?

The initial signs and symptoms of medium-chain acyl-coenzyme A dehydrogenase deficiency (MCADD) typically occur during infancy or early childhood and can include vomiting, lack of energy (lethargy), and low blood sugar (hypoglycemia). In rare cases, the first episode of problems related to MCADD occurs during adulthood. The signs and symptoms of MCADD can be triggered by periods of fasting, or during illnesses such as viral infections, particularly when eating is reduced. People with MCADD are also at risk of serious complications such as seizures, breathing difficulties, liver problems, brain damage, coma, and sudden, unexpected death.

What Causes Medium-Chain Acyl-Coenzyme a Dehydrogenase (MCAD) Deficiency?

Mutations in the ACADM gene cause medium-chain acyl-co-enzyme A dehydrogenase deficiency. Mutations in the *ACADM* gene lead to inadequate levels of an enzyme called medium-chain acyl-coenzyme A dehydrogenase. Without sufficient amounts of this enzyme, medium-chain fatty acids from food and fats stored in the body are not metabolized properly. As a result, these fats are not converted to energy, which can lead to characteristic signs and symptoms of this disorder such as lethargy and low blood sugar. Medium-chain fatty acids or partially metabolized fatty acids may accumulate in tissues and can damage the liver and brain, causing serious complications.

How Is Medium-Chain Acyl-Coenzyme a Dehydrogenase Deficiency (MCADD) Diagnosed?

MCADD is now included in many newborn screening programs. If a newborn screening result for MCADD is not in the normal range, additional testing is recommended. A diagnosis of MCADD can be made through a blood test called a plasma acylcarnitine profile and an evaluation of organic acids in the urine. The diagnosis can also be confirmed by genetic testing.

Section 26.10

Methylmalonic Acidemia

This section includes text excerpted from "Methylmalonic
Acidemia," Genetics Home Reference (GHR), National
Institutes of Health (NIH), March 7, 2016.

What Is Methylmalonic Acidemia?

Methylmalonic acidemia is an inherited disorder in which the
body is unable to process certain proteins and fats (lipids) properly.
The effects of methylmalonic acidemia, which usually appear in early
infancy, vary from mild to life-threatening. Affected infants can experience vomiting, dehydration, weak muscle tone (hypotonia), developmental delay, excessive tiredness (lethargy), an enlarged liver (hepatomegaly), and failure to gain weight and grow at the expected rate
(failure to thrive). Long-term complications can include feeding problems, intellectual disability, chronic kidney disease, and inflammation
of the pancreas (pancreatitis). Without treatment, this disorder can
lead to coma and death in some cases.

How Common Is Methylmalonic Acidemia?

This condition occurs in an estimated 1 in 50,000 to 100,000 people.

What Genes Are Related to Methylmalonic Acidemia?

Mutations in the *MUT, MMAA, MMAB, MMADHC,* and *MCEE*
genes cause methylmalonic acidemia. The long term effects of methylmalonic acidemia depend on which gene is mutated and the severity
of the mutation.

About 60 percent of methylmalonic acidemia cases are caused by
mutations in the *MUT* gene. This gene provides instructions for making an enzyme called methylmalonyl CoA mutase. This enzyme works
with vitamin B12 (also called cobalamin) to break down several protein
building blocks (amino acids), certain lipids, and cholesterol. Mutations
in the *MUT* gene alter the enzyme's structure or reduce the amount of
the enzyme, which prevents these molecules from being broken down

properly. As a result, a substance called methylmalonyl CoA and other potentially toxic compounds can accumulate in the body's organs and tissues, causing the signs and symptoms of methylmalonic acidemia.

Mutations in the *MUT* gene that prevent the production of any functional enzyme result in a form of the condition designated mut0. Mut0 is the most severe form of methylmalonic acidemia and has the poorest outcome. Mutations that change the structure of methylmalonyl CoA mutase but do not eliminate its activity cause a form of the condition designated mut-. The mut- form is typically less severe, with more variable symptoms than the mut0 form.

Some cases of methylmalonic acidemia are caused by mutations in the *MMAA, MMAB,* or *MMADHC* gene. Proteins produced from the *MMAA, MMAB*, and *MMADHC* genes are needed for the proper function of methylmalonyl CoA mutase. Mutations that affect proteins produced from these three genes can impair the activity of methylmalonyl CoA mutase, leading to methylmalonic acidemia.

A few other cases of methylmalonic acidemia are caused by mutations in the *MCEE* gene. This gene provides instructions for producing an enzyme called methylmalonyl CoA epimerase. Like methylmalonyl CoA mutase, this enzyme also plays a role in the breakdown of amino acids, certain lipids, and cholesterol. Disruption in the function of methylmalonyl CoA epimerase leads to a mild form of methylmalonic acidemia.

It is likely that mutations in other, unidentified genes also cause methylmalonic acidemia.

How Do People Inherit Methylmalonic Acidemia?

This condition is inherited in an autosomal recessive pattern, which means both copies of the *MUT, MMAA, MMAB, MMADHC*, or *MCEE* gene in each cell have mutations. Most often, the parents of an individual with an autosomal recessive condition are carriers of one copy of the mutated gene but do not show signs and symptoms of the condition.

Section 26.11

Methylmalonic Acidemia with Homocystinuria

This section includes text excerpted from "Methylmalonic Acidemia with Homocystinuria," Genetics Home Reference (GHR), National Institutes of Health (NIH), March 7, 2016.

What Is Methylmalonic Acidemia with Homocystinuria?

Methylmalonic acidemia with homocystinuria is an inherited disorder in which the body is unable to properly process protein building blocks (amino acids), certain fats (lipids), and a waxy fat-like substance called cholesterol. Individuals with this disorder have a combination of features from two separate conditions, methylmalonic acidemia and homocystinuria. The signs and symptoms of the combined condition, methylmalonic acidemia with homocystinuria, usually develop in infancy, although they can begin at any age.

When the condition begins early in life, affected individuals typically have an inability to grow and gain weight at the expected rate (failure to thrive), which is sometimes recognized before birth (intrauterine growth retardation). These infants can also have difficulty feeding and an abnormally pale appearance (pallor). Neurological problems are also common in methylmalonic acidemia with homocystinuria, including weak muscle tone (hypotonia) and seizures. Most infants and children with this condition have an unusually small head size (microcephaly), delayed development, and intellectual disability. Less common features of the condition include eye problems and a blood disorder called megaloblastic anemia. Megaloblastic anemia occurs when a person has a low number of red blood cells (anemia), and the remaining red blood cells are larger than normal (megaloblastic). The signs and symptoms of methylmalonic acidemia with homocystinuria worsen over time, and the condition can be life-threatening if not treated.

When methylmalonic acidemia with homocystinuria begins in adolescence or adulthood, the signs and symptoms usually include psychiatric changes and cognitive problems. Affected individuals can exhibit changes in their behavior and personality; they may become less social and may experience hallucinations, delirium, and psychosis. In addition, these individuals can begin to lose previously acquired mental and movement abilities, resulting in a decline in school or work performance, difficulty controlling movements, memory problems, speech difficulties, a decline in intellectual function (dementia), or an extreme lack of energy (lethargy). Some people with methylmalonic acidemia with homocystinuria whose signs and symptoms begin later in life develop a condition called subacute combined degeneration of the spinal cord, which leads to numbness and weakness in the lower limbs, difficulty walking, and frequent falls.

How Common Is Methylmalonic Acidemia with Homocystinuria?

The most common form of the condition, called methylmalonic acidemia with homocystinuria, cblC type, is estimated to affect 1 in 200,000 newborns worldwide. Studies indicate that this form of the condition may be even more common in particular populations. These studies estimate the condition occurs in 1 in 100,000 people in New York and 1 in 60,000 people in California. Other types of methylmalonic acidemia with homocystinuria are much less common. Fewer than 20 cases of each of the other types have been reported in the medical literature.

What Genes Are Related to Methylmalonic Acidemia with Homocystinuria?

Methylmalonic acidemia with homocystinuria can be caused by mutations in one of several genes: *MMACHC, MMADHC, LMBRD1, ABCD4,* or *HCFC1*. Mutations in these genes account for the different types of the disorder, which are known as complementation groups: cblC, cblD, cblF, cblJ, and cblX, respectively.

Each of the above-mentioned genes is involved in the processing of vitamin B12, also known as cobalamin or Cbl. Processing of the vitamin converts it to one of two molecules, adenosylcobalamin (AdoCbl) or methylcobalamin (MeCbl). AdoCbl is required for the normal function of an enzyme that helps break down certain amino acids, lipids, and cholesterol. AdoCbl is called a cofactor because it helps the enzyme carry out its function. MeCbl is also a cofactor, but for another enzyme that converts the amino acid homocysteine to another amino acid, methionine. The body uses methionine to make proteins and other important compounds.

Mutations in the *MMACHC, MMADHC, LMBRD1, ABCD4,* or *HCFC1* gene affect early steps of vitamin B12 processing, resulting in a shortage of both AdoCbl and MeCbl. Without AdoCbl, proteins and lipids are not broken down properly. This defect allows potentially toxic compounds to build up in the body's organs and tissues, causing methylmalonic acidemia. Without MeCbl, homocysteine is not converted to methionine. As a result, homocysteine builds up in the bloodstream and methionine is depleted. Some of the excess homocysteine is excreted in urine (homocystinuria). Researchers have not determined how altered levels of homocysteine and methionine lead to the health problems associated with homocystinuria.

Mutations in other genes involved in vitamin B12 processing can cause related conditions. Those mutations that impair only AdoCbl production lead to methylmalonic acidemia, and those that impair only MeCbl production cause homocystinuria.

How Do People Inherit Methylmalonic Acidemia with Homocystinuria?

Methylmalonic acidemia with homocystinuria is usually inherited in an autosomal recessive pattern, which means both copies of the gene in each cell have mutations. The parents of an individual with an autosomal recessive condition each carry one copy of the mutated gene, but they typically do not show signs and symptoms of the condition.

When caused by mutations in the *HCFC1* gene, the condition is inherited in an X-linked recessive pattern. The *HCFC1* gene is located on the X chromosome, which is one of the two sex chromosomes. In males (who have only one X chromosome), one altered copy of the gene in each cell is sufficient to cause the condition. In females (who have two X chromosomes), a mutation would have to occur in both copies of the gene to cause the disorder. Because it is unlikely that females will have two altered copies of this gene, males are affected by X-linked recessive disorders much more frequently than females. A characteristic of X-linked inheritance is that fathers cannot pass X-linked traits to their sons.

Section 26.12

Phenylketonuria (PKU)

This section includes text excerpted from "Phenylketonuria,"
Genetics Home Reference (GHR), National Institutes
of Health (NIH), March 7, 2016.

What Is Phenylketonuria?

Phenylketonuria (commonly known as PKU) is an inherited disorder that increases the levels of a substance called phenylalanine in the blood. Phenylalanine is a building block of proteins (an amino acid) that is obtained through the diet. It is found in all proteins and in some artificial sweeteners. If PKU is not treated, phenylalanine can build up to harmful levels in the body, causing intellectual disability and other serious health problems.

The signs and symptoms of PKU vary from mild to severe. The most severe form of this disorder is known as classic PKU. Infants with classic PKU appear normal until they are a few months old. Without treatment, these children develop permanent intellectual disability. Seizures, delayed development, behavioral problems, and psychiatric disorders are also common. Untreated individuals may have a musty or mouse-like odor as a side effect of excess phenylalanine in the body. Children with classic PKU tend to have lighter skin and hair than unaffected family members and are also likely to have skin disorders such as eczema.

Less severe forms of this condition, sometimes called variant PKU and non-PKU hyperphenylalaninemia, have a smaller risk of brain damage. People with very mild cases may not require treatment with a low-phenylalanine diet.

Babies born to mothers with PKU and uncontrolled phenylalanine levels (women who no longer follow a low-phenylalanine diet) have a significant risk of intellectual disability because they are exposed to very high levels of phenylalanine before birth. These infants may also have a low birth weight and grow more slowly than other children. Other characteristic medical problems include heart defects or other heart problems, an abnormally small head size (microcephaly), and behavioral problems. Women with PKU and uncontrolled phenylalanine levels also have an increased risk of pregnancy loss.

How Common Is Phenylketonuria?

The occurrence of PKU varies among ethnic groups and geographic regions worldwide. In the United States, PKU occurs in 1 in 10,000 to 15,000 newborns. Most cases of PKU are detected shortly after birth by newborn screening, and treatment is started promptly. As a result, the severe signs and symptoms of classic PKU are rarely seen.

What Genes Are Related to Phenylketonuria?

Mutations in the *PAH* gene cause phenylketonuria.

The *PAH* gene provides instructions for making an enzyme called phenylalanine hydroxylase. This enzyme converts the amino acid phenylalanine to other important compounds in the body. If gene mutations reduce the activity of phenylalanine hydroxylase, phenylalanine from the diet is not processed effectively. As a result, this amino acid can build up to toxic levels in the blood and other tissues. Because nerve cells in the brain are particularly sensitive to phenylalanine levels, excessive amounts of this substance can cause brain damage.

Classic PKU, the most severe form of the disorder, occurs when phenylalanine hydroxylase activity is severely reduced or absent. People with untreated classic PKU have levels of phenylalanine high enough to cause severe brain damage and other serious medical problems. Mutations in the *PAH* gene that allow the enzyme to retain some activity result in milder versions of this condition, such as variant PKU or non-PKU hyperphenylalaninemia.

Changes in other genes may influence the severity of PKU, but little is known about these additional genetic factors.

How Do People Inherit Phenylketonuria?

This condition is inherited in an autosomal recessive pattern, which means both copies of the gene in each cell have mutations. The parents of an individual with an autosomal recessive condition each carry one copy of the mutated gene, but they typically do not show signs and symptoms of the condition.

Section 26.13

Tyrosinemia

This section includes text excerpted from "Tyrosinemia,"
Genetics Home Reference (GHR), National
Institutes of Health (NIH), March 7, 2016.

What Is Tyrosinemia?

Tyrosinemia is a genetic disorder characterized by disruptions in the multistep process that breaks down the amino acid tyrosine, a building block of most proteins. If untreated, tyrosine and its byproducts build up in tissues and organs, which can lead to serious health problems.

There are three types of tyrosinemia, which are each distinguished by their symptoms and genetic cause. Tyrosinemia type I, the most severe form of this disorder, is characterized by signs and symptoms that begin in the first few months of life. Affected infants fail to gain weight and grow at the expected rate (failure to thrive) due to poor food tolerance because high-protein foods lead to diarrhea and vomiting. Affected infants may also have yellowing of the skin and whites of the eyes (jaundice), a cabbage-like odor, and an increased tendency to bleed (particularly nosebleeds). Tyrosinemia type I can lead to liver and kidney failure, softening and weakening of the bones (rickets), and an increased risk of liver cancer (hepatocellular carcinoma). Some affected children have repeated neurologic crises that consist of changes in mental state, reduced sensation in the arms and legs (peripheral neuropathy), abdominal pain, and respiratory failure. These crises can last from 1 to 7 days. Untreated, children with tyrosinemia type I often do not survive past the age of 10.

Tyrosinemia type II can affect the eyes, skin, and mental development. Signs and symptoms often begin in early childhood and include eye pain and redness, excessive tearing, abnormal sensitivity to light (photophobia), and thick, painful skin on the palms of their hands and soles of their feet (palmoplantar hyperkeratosis). About 50 percent of individuals with tyrosinemia type II have some degree of intellectual disability.

Tyrosinemia type III is the rarest of the three types. The characteristic features of this type include intellectual disability, seizures, and periodic loss of balance and coordination (intermittent ataxia).

About 10 percent of newborns have temporarily elevated levels of tyrosine (transient tyrosinemia). In these cases, the cause is not genetic. The most likely causes are vitamin C deficiency or immature liver enzymes due to premature birth.

How Common Is Tyrosinemia?

Worldwide, tyrosinemia type I affects about 1 in 100,000 individuals. This type is more common in Norway where 1 in 60,000 to 74,000 individuals are affected. Tyrosinemia type I is even more common in Quebec, Canada where it occurs in about 1 in 16,000 individuals. In the Saguenay-Lac St. Jean region of Quebec, tyrosinemia type I affects 1 in 1,846 people.

Tyrosinemia type II occurs in fewer than 1 in 250,000 individuals worldwide. Tyrosinemia type III is very rare; only a few cases have been reported.

What Genes Are Related to Tyrosinemia?

Mutations in the *FAH, TAT*, and *HPD* genes can cause tyrosinemia types I, II, and III, respectively.

In the liver, enzymes break down tyrosine in a five step process, resulting in molecules that are either excreted by the kidneys or used to produce energy or make other substances in the body. The *FAH* gene provides instructions for the fumarylacetoacetate hydrolase enzyme, which is responsible for the final step of tyrosine breakdown. The enzyme produced from the *TAT* gene, called tyrosine aminotransferase enzyme, is involved at the first step in the process. The *HPD* gene provides instructions for making the 4-hydroxyphenylpyruvate dioxygenase enzyme, which is responsible for the second step.

Mutations in the *FAH, TAT*, or *HPD* gene cause a decrease in the activity of one of the enzymes in the breakdown of tyrosine. As a result, tyrosine and its byproducts accumulate to toxic levels, which can cause damage and death to cells in the liver, kidneys, nervous system, and other organs.

How Do People Inherit Tyrosinemia?

This condition is inherited in an autosomal recessive pattern, which means both copies of the gene in each cell have mutations. The parents of an individual with an autosomal recessive condition each carry one copy of the mutated gene, but they typically do not show signs and symptoms of the condition.

Chapter 27

Kidney and Urinary System Disorders

Chapter Contents

Section 27.1

Cystinuria

This section contains text excerpted from the following sources: Text beginning with the heading "What Is Cystinuria?" is excerpted from "Cystinuria," Genetics Home Reference (GHR), National Institutes of Health (NIH), March 14, 2016; Text under the heading "What Causes Cystinuria?" is excerpted from "Cystinuria," National Center for Advancing Translational Sciences (NCATS), May 11, 2015.

What Is Cystinuria?

Cystinuria is a condition characterized by the buildup of the amino acid cystine, a building block of most proteins, in the kidneys and bladder. As the kidneys filter blood to create urine, cystine is normally absorbed back into the bloodstream. People with cystinuria cannot properly reabsorb cystine into their bloodstream, so the amino acid accumulates in their urine.

As urine becomes more concentrated in the kidneys, the excess cystine forms crystals. Larger crystals become stones that may lodge in the kidneys or in the bladder. Sometimes cystine crystals combine with calcium molecules in the kidneys to form large stones. These crystals and stones can create blockages in the urinary tract and reduce the ability of the kidneys to eliminate waste through urine. The stones also provide sites where bacteria may cause infections.

How Common Is Cystinuria?

Cystinuria affects approximately 1 in 10,000 people.

What Genes Are Related to Cystinuria?

Mutations in the *SLC3A1* or *SLC7A9* gene cause cystinuria. The *SLC3A1* and *SLC7A9* genes provide instructions for making the two parts (subunits) of a protein complex that is primarily found in the kidneys. Normally this protein complex controls the reabsorption of certain amino acids, including cystine, into the blood from the filtered fluid that will become urine. Mutations in either the *SLC3A1* gene or *SLC7A9* gene disrupt the ability of the protein complex to reabsorb amino acids, which causes the amino acids to become concentrated in the urine. As the levels of cystine in the urine increase, the crystals typical of cystinuria form. The other amino acids that are reabsorbed by the protein complex do not create crystals when they accumulate in the urine.

How Do People Inherit Cystinuria?

This condition is inherited in an autosomal recessive pattern, which means both copies of the gene in each cell have mutations. The parents of an individual with an autosomal recessive condition each carry one copy of the mutated gene, but they typically do not show signs and symptoms of the condition.

What Causes Cystinuria?

Cystinuria is caused by changes (mutations) in the *SLC3A1* and *SLC7A9* genes. These genes encode a protein complex that helps control the reabsorption of amino acids (such as cystine) in the kidneys. Mutations in these genes disrupt the function of the protein complex, causing cystine to become more concentrated in the urine. As the concentration of cystine increases, cystine crystals and/or stones begin to form in the urinary tract leading to the many signs and symptoms associated with cystinuria.

What Are the Signs and Symptoms of Cystinuria?

Cystinuria is primarily characterized by a buildup of the amino acid, cystine, in the kidneys and bladder. This leads to the formation of cystine crystals and/or stones which may block the urinary tract. Signs and symptoms of cystinuria are a consequence of stone formation and may include:

- Nausea
- Blood in the urine (hematuria)
- Flank pain
- Frequent urinary tract infections
- Chronic or acute renal failure (rare)

How Is Cystinuria Diagnosed?

Screening for cystinuria should be considered in people with recurrent or bilateral (i.e. affecting both kidneys) stones; those who develop stones at an early age (before age 30); and people who have a family history of cystinuria. A diagnosis is typically made after an episode of kidney stones when testing reveals that the stones are made of cystine.

The following tests may be recommended to detect kidney stones and diagnose cystinuria:

- 24-hour urine collection
- Abdominal imaging (CT scan, MRI, or ultrasound)
- Intravenous pyelogram (IVP)
- Urinalysis
- Genetic testing

How Might Cystinuria Be Treated?

Treatment of cystinuria is focused on relieving symptoms and preventing the formation of additional stones. A more conservative approach is typically tried first. This may include increasing fluid intake, regular monitoring of urinary pH, dietary restrictions (i.e. eating less salt) and increasing the pH of urine with potassium citrate supplements. If these strategies do not prevent the formation of stones, medications may be added to help dissolve the cystine crystals.

Treatment for cystinuria-related stones varies depending on the size and location of the stone, but may include:

- Extracorporeal shock wave lithotripsy (ESWL)
- Ureteroscopy
- Percutaneous nephrolithotomy
- Open surgery (in rare cases)

What Is the Long-Term Outlook for People with Cystinuria?

Cystinuria is a chronic condition and many affected people experience recurrent cystine stones in the urinary tract (kidneys, bladder and ureters). In rare cases, frequent kidney stones can lead to tissue damage or even kidney failure.

Section 27.2

Polycystic Kidney Disease

This section includes text excerpted from "Polycystic Kidney Disease (PKD)," National Institute of Diabetes and Digestive and Kidney Diseases (NIDDK), August 2015.

What Is Polycystic Kidney Disease (PKD)?

Polycystic kidney disease is a genetic disorder that causes numerous cysts to grow in the kidneys. A kidney cyst is an abnormal sac filled with fluid. PKD cysts can greatly enlarge the kidneys while replacing much of their normal structure, resulting in chronic kidney disease (CKD), which causes reduced kidney function over time. CKD may lead to kidney failure, described as end-stage kidney disease or ESRD when treated with a kidney transplant or blood-filtering treatments called dialysis. The two main types of PKD are autosomal dominant PKD and autosomal recessive PKD.

PKD cysts are different from the usually harmless "simple" cysts that often form in the kidneys later in life. PKD cysts are more numerous and cause complications, such as high blood pressure, cysts in the liver, and problems with blood vessels in the brain and heart.

What Causes Polycystic Kidney Disease?

A gene mutation, or defect, causes polycystic kidney disease. Genes provide instructions for making proteins in the body. A gene mutation is a permanent change in the deoxyribonucleic acid (DNA) sequence that makes up a gene. In most cases of PKD, a person inherits the gene mutation, meaning a parent passes it on in his or her genes. In the remaining cases, the gene mutation develops spontaneously. In spontaneous cases, neither parent carries a copy of the mutated gene.

Researchers have found three different gene mutations associated with PKD. Two of the genes are associated with autosomal dominant PKD. The third gene is associated with autosomal recessive PKD. Gene mutations that cause PKD affect proteins that play a role in kidney development.

How Common Is Polycystic Kidney Disease and Who Is More Likely to Have the Disease?

Estimates of PKD's prevalence range from one in 400 to one in 1,000 people. According to the United States Renal Data System, PKD accounts for 2.2 percent of new cases of kidney failure each year in the United States. Annually, eight people per 1 million have kidney failure as a result of PKD. Polycystic kidney disease exists around the world and in all races. The disorder occurs equally in women and men, although men are more likely to develop kidney failure from PKD. Women with PKD and high blood pressure who have had more than three pregnancies also have an increased chance of developing kidney failure.

What Are the Signs and Symptoms of Autosomal Dominant Polycystic Kidney Disease?

In many cases, PKD does not cause signs or symptoms until cysts are half an inch or larger. When present, the most common symptoms are pain in the back and sides—between the ribs and hips—and headaches. The pain can be temporary or persistent, mild or severe. Hematuria—blood in the urine—may also be a sign of autosomal dominant PKD.

What Are the Complications of Autosomal Dominant Polycystic Kidney Disease?

The complications of autosomal dominant PKD include the following:

- **Pain.** Cyst infection, other types of urinary tract infections (UTIs), bleeding into cysts, kidney stones, or stretching of the fibrous tissue around the kidney because of cyst growth can cause pain in the area of the kidneys.

- **High blood pressure.** High blood pressure is present in about half of the people with autosomal dominant PKD and normal kidney function between the ages of 20 and 35.4 Almost 100 percent of people with kidney failure and autosomal dominant PKD have high blood pressure. High blood pressure—greater than 140/90 mm Hg—increases the likelihood of heart disease and stroke, as well as adding to the damage already done to the kidneys by the cysts.

- **Kidney failure.** Kidney failure means the kidneys no longer work well enough to maintain health. A person with kidney failure may have the following symptoms:
    - little or no urination
    - edema—swelling, usually in the legs, feet, or ankles and less often in the hands or face
    - drowsiness
    - fatigue, or feeling tired
    - generalized itching or numbness
    - dry skin
    - headaches
    - weight loss
    - appetite loss
    - nausea
    - vomiting
    - sleep problems
    - trouble concentrating
    - darkened skin
    - muscle cramps
    - shortness of breath
    - chest pain

Untreated kidney failure can lead to coma and death. More than half of people with autosomal dominant PKD progress to kidney failure by age 70.

- **UTIs.** Kidney cysts block the flow of urine through the kidneys. Stagnant urine can set the stage for infection. Bacteria enter the urinary tract through the urethra and spread up to the kidneys. Sometimes, the kidney cysts become infected. UTIs may cause scarring in the kidneys.

- **Kidney stones.** About 20 percent of people with autosomal dominant PKD have kidney stones. Kidney stones can block the flow of urine and cause pain.

- **Liver cysts.** Liver cysts are the most common nonkidney complication of autosomal dominant PKD. Liver cysts generally cause no symptoms.

- **Pancreatic cysts.** PKD can also cause cysts in the pancreas. Pancreatic cysts rarely cause pancreatitis—inflammation, or swelling, of the pancreas.

- **Abnormal heart valves.** Abnormal heart valves may occur in up to 25 percent of people with autosomal dominant PKD. Insufficient blood flow in the aorta—the large artery that carries blood from the heart—may result from the abnormal heart valves.

- **Diverticula.** Diverticula are small pouches, or sacs, that push outward through weak spots in the colon wall. This complication is more common in people with PKD who have kidney failure.

- **Brain aneurysms.** An aneurysm is a bulge in the wall of a blood vessel. Aneurysms in the brain might cause headaches that are severe or feel different from other headaches. Brain aneurysms can rupture, or break open, causing bleeding inside the skull. A ruptured aneurysm in the brain is a life-threatening condition and requires immediate medical attention.

How Do Health Care Providers Diagnose Autosomal Dominant Polycystic Kidney Disease?

Health care providers diagnose autosomal dominant PKD using imaging tests and genetic testing.

Imaging Tests

A radiologist—a doctor who specializes in medical imaging—will interpret the images produced by the following imaging tests:

- **Ultrasound** uses a device, called a transducer, that bounces safe, painless sound waves off organs to create an image of their structure. An abdominal ultrasound can create images of the entire urinary tract or focus specifically on the kidneys. A specially trained technician performs the procedure in a health care provider's office, an outpatient center, or a hospital. A patient does not need anesthesia. The images can show cysts in the kidneys.

- **CT scans** use a combination of X-rays and computer technology to create images. For a CT scan, a health care provider may give the patient an injection of a special dye, called contrast medium. CT scans require the patient to lie on a table that slides into a donutshaped device where the X-rays are taken. An X-ray technician performs the procedure in an outpatient center or a hospital. Adults do not need anesthesia. A health care provider may give infants and children a sedative to help them fall asleep for the test. CT scans can show more precise images of cysts in the kidneys.

- **Magnetic resonance imaging (MRI)** machines use radio waves and magnets to produce detailed pictures of the body's internal organs and soft tissues without using X-rays. An MRI may include the injection of contrast medium. With most MRI machines, the patient lies on a table that slides into a tunnel-shaped device that is often open ended or closed at one end; some machines allow the patient to lie in a more open space. A specially trained technician performs the procedure in an outpatient center or a hospital. A patient does not need anesthesia, though a health care provider may use light sedation for people with a fear of confined spaces. A health care provider can use MRIs to measure kidney and cyst volume and monitor kidney and cyst growth, which can help track progression of the disorder.

Kidney imaging findings vary widely, depending on a person's age. Younger people usually have fewer and smaller cysts. Health care providers have therefore developed specific criteria for diagnosing the disorder with kidney imaging findings, depending on age. For example, the presence of at least two cysts in each kidney by age 30 in a person with a family history of the disorder can confirm the diagnosis of autosomal dominant PKD. A family history of autosomal dominant PKD and cysts found in other organs make the diagnosis more likely.

Genetic Testing

The health care provider may refer a person suspected of having autosomal dominant PKD to a geneticist—a doctor who specializes in genetic disorders. For a genetic test, the geneticist takes a blood or saliva sample and analyzes the DNA for gene mutations that cause autosomal dominant PKD, called PKD1 and PKD2, or autosomal recessive PKD, called PKHD1. Personnel in specialized labs generally perform all genetic testing. A patient may not receive the results for several months because of the complexity of the testing.

Genetic testing can show whether a person's cells carry a gene mutation that causes autosomal dominant PKD. A health care provider may also use genetic testing results to determine whether someone with a family history of PKD is likely to develop the disorder in the future. Prenatal testing can diagnose autosomal recessive PKD in unborn children.

Two factors limit the usefulness of genetic testing for PKD:

1. Detection of a mutated gene cannot predict the onset of symptoms or how serious the disorder will be.

2. Even if a health care provider finds a mutated gene, no specific cure for the disorder exists.

How Do Health Care Providers Treat Autosomal Dominant Polycystic Kidney Disease?

Although a cure for autosomal dominant PKD is not currently available, treatment can ease symptoms and prolong life. Treatments for the symptoms and complications of autosomal dominant PKD include the following:

Pain. A health care provider will first determine what is causing the pain and then recommend treatment. If cyst growth is causing persistent pain, the health care provider may first suggest over-the-counter pain medications such as aspirin or acetaminophen. People should consult their health care provider before taking any over-the counter medication because some may be harmful to the kidneys. For most cases of severe pain due to cyst growth, surgery to shrink cysts can temporarily relieve pain in the back and sides. However, surgery does not slow the disorder's progression toward kidney failure.

High blood pressure. Keeping blood pressure under control can slow the effects of autosomal dominant PKD. Lifestyle changes and various medications can lower high blood pressure. Some health care providers recommend blood pressure medications called angiotensin-converting enzyme (ACE) inhibitors or angiotensin receptor blockers (ARBs). Health care providers have found these medications to protect the kidneys in people with other forms of kidney disease besides autosomal dominant PKD. Sometimes a patient can control blood pressure through diet and exercise alone.

Kidney failure. After many years, PKD can cause the kidneys to fail. Kidneys are essential for life, so people with kidney failure must receive either dialysis or a kidney transplant to replace kidney function. The two forms of dialysis are hemodialysis and peritoneal dialysis. Hemodialysis uses a machine to circulate a patient's blood through a filter outside the body. Peritoneal dialysis uses the lining of the abdomen to filter the blood inside the body. A kidney transplant is surgery to place a healthy kidney from a person who has just died or a living person, most often a family member, into the patient's body. People with autosomal dominant PKD have no more complications after transplantation than people with kidney failure from other causes.

UTIs. People with autosomal dominant PKD tend to have frequent UTIs, which health care providers treat with antibiotics. People with the disorder should seek treatment for a UTI immediately because infection can spread through the urinary tract to the kidney cysts. Cyst infections are difficult to treat because many antibiotics do not reach the cysts.

Kidney stones. Treatment of kidney stones in people with autosomal dominant PKD is similar to treatment in people without the disorder. Potassium citrate, taken by mouth, is useful for treating the types of kidney stones associated with autosomal dominant PKD. Breaking up stones with shock waves and removing stones through a small incision do not cause more complications in people with autosomal dominant PKD than in people without the disorder.

Liver cysts. Most people with liver cysts do not need treatment. A health care provider may aspirate—drain with a needle through the skin—liver cysts in people who have symptoms. In the most severe cases, a patient may need a liver transplant. Infections in liver cysts can be treated with antibiotics and aspiration.

Pancreatitis. Treatment for pancreatitis usually involves a hospital stay with intravenous (IV) fluids and antibiotics.

Abnormal heart valves. Abnormal heart valves in people with autosomal dominant PKD rarely require valve replacement. A patient may need further tests if a health care provider detects a heart murmur—a blowing, whooshing, or rasping sound heard with a stethoscope during a heartbeat.

Diverticula. A high-fiber diet and pain medications help relieve symptoms when diverticula are present. Uncomplicated infection of the diverticula with mild symptoms usually requires the person to rest, take oral antibiotics, and be on a liquid diet for a period of time. Sometimes an infection is serious enough to require a hospital stay, IV antibiotics, and possibly surgery.

Brain aneurysms. People with autosomal dominant PKD should see a health care provider if they have severe or recurring headaches—even before considering over-the-counter pain medications. Small aneurysms rarely require surgery. A person with a brain aneurysm should avoid smoking and control blood pressure and lipids—fats in the blood.

What Is Autosomal Recessive Polycystic Kidney Disease?

Autosomal recessive PKD is a rare genetic disorder that affects the liver as well as the kidneys. The signs of autosomal recessive PKD frequently appear in the earliest months of life, even in the womb, so health care providers often call it "infantile PKD." In an autosomal recessive disorder, the child has to inherit the gene muta-tion from both parents to have an increased likelihood for the disor-der. The chance of a child inheriting autosomal recessive mutations from both parents with a gene mutation is 25 percent, or one in four.

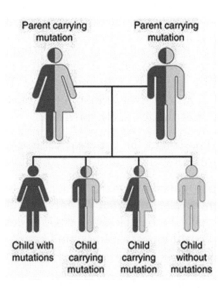

Figure 27.1. *Autosomal Recessive*

If only one parent carries the mutated gene, the child will not get the disorder, although the child may inherit the gene mutation. The child is a "carrier" of the disorder and can pass the gene mutation to the next generation. Genetic testing can show whether a parent or child is a carrier of the mutated gene. Autosomal recessive disorders do not typically appear in every generation of an affected family.

What Are the Signs and Symptoms of Autosomal Recessive Polycystic Kidney Disease?

An early sign of autosomal recessive PKD is an enlarged kidney, seen in a fetus or an infant using ultrasound. Kidney function is crucial for early physical development, so children with autosomal recessive PKD and decreased kidney function are usually smaller-than-average size, a condition called growth failure.

Some people with autosomal recessive PKD do not develop signs or symptoms until later in childhood or even adulthood.

What Are the Complications of Autosomal Recessive Polycystic Kidney Disease?

Babies with the most severe cases of autosomal recessive PKD often die hours or days after birth because they cannot breathe well enough to sustain life. Their lungs do not develop as they should during the prenatal period. Pressure from enlarged kidneys also contributes to breathing problems.

Children born with autosomal recessive PKD often develop kidney failure before reaching adulthood.

Live scarring occurs in all people with autosomal recessive PKD and is usually present at birth. However, liver problems tend to become more of a concern as people with autosomal recessive PKD grow older. Liver scarring can lead to progressive liver dysfunction and other problems.

Additional complications of autosomal recessive PKD include high blood pressure and UTIs.

How Do Health Care Providers Diagnose Autosomal Recessive Polycystic Kidney Disease?

Health care providers diagnose autosomal recessive PKD with ultrasound imaging, even in a fetus or newborn. The test can show enlarged kidneys with an abnormal appearance. However, a health care provider rarely sees large cysts such as those in autosomal dominant PKD. Ultrasound imaging can also show scarring of the liver.

How Do Health Care Providers Treat Autosomal Recessive Polycystic Kidney Disease?

Treatments for the symptoms and complications of autosomal recessive PKD include the following:

- **Enlarged kidney.** No treatment to prevent or reverse kidney enlargement is available. A patient may need removal of one or both kidneys if pressure from the enlarged kidneys makes breathing impossible. Children with removed kidneys must receive dialysis or a kidney transplant.

- **Growth failure.** A health care provider should address physical development through nutritional therapy. In severe cases of growth failure in children, a health care provider may consider human growth hormone.

- **Breathing problems.** Health care providers treat infants with breathing problems with artificial ventilation and, in urgent cases, resuscitative efforts, such as artificial respiration and heart massage.

- **Kidney failure.** Peritoneal dialysis is the preferred method of treating children with kidney failure, although health care providers also use hemodialysis. Kidney transplantation may be limited in infants because of their size.

- **High blood pressure.** A health care provider can help control blood pressure with medications.

- **UTIs.** A health care provider can treat UTIs with antibiotics.

- **Liver disease.** If serious liver disease develops, some children may need to undergo combined liver and kidney transplantation.

Can a Person Prevent Polycystic Kidney Disease?

Scientists have not yet found a way to prevent PKD. However, people with PKD may slow the progression of kidney damage caused by high blood pressure through lifestyle changes, diet, and blood pressure medications. People with PKD should be physically active 30 minutes a day most days of the week. If lifestyle and diet changes do not control a person's blood pressure, a health care provider may prescribe one or more blood pressure medications, including ACE inhibitors or ARBs.

Eating, Diet, and Nutrition

A dietitian specializes in helping people who have kidney disease choose the right foods and plan healthy meals. People with any kind of kidney disease, including PKD, should talk with a dietitian about foods that should be added to their diet and foods that might be harmful.

PKD may require diet changes for blood pressure control. Kidney disease in general also calls for certain diet changes.

Following a healthy eating plan can help lower blood pressure. A health care provider may recommend the Dietary Approaches to Stop Hypertension (DASH) eating plan, which focuses on fruits, vegetables, whole grains, and other foods that are heart healthy and lower in sodium, which often comes from salt. The DASH eating plan, is low in fat and cholesterol features fat-free or low-fat milk and dairy products, fish, poultry, and nuts suggests less red meat, sweets, added sugars, and sugar-containing beverages is rich in nutrients, protein, and fiber.

As your kidneys become more damaged, you may need to eat foods that are lower in phosphorus and potassium. The health care provider will use lab tests to watch your levels.

Foods high in potassium include:

- bananas

- oranges

- potatoes

- tomatoes

Lower-potassium foods include:

- apples

- peaches

- carrots

- green beans

Foods higher in phosphorus include:

- large portions of meat, fish and dairy foods

- bran cereals and oatmeal

- beans and nuts

- colas

Lower-phosphorus alternatives include:

- fresh fruits and vegetables

- breads

- pasta

- rice

- corn and rice cereals

- light-colored sodas

People with kidney disease and high blood pressure should also limit how much sodium they get to 2,300 mg or less each day.

People with CKD may need to watch how much protein they eat. Everyone needs protein. However, protein breaks down into wastes the kidneys must remove. Large amounts of protein make the kidneys work harder. High-quality proteins such as meat, fish, and eggs create fewer wastes than other sources of protein. Beans, whole grains, soy products, nuts and nut butters, and dairy products can also be good sources of protein. Most people eat more protein than they need. Eating high-quality protein and smaller portions of protein can help protect the kidneys.

Chapter 28

Leukodystrophies

Chapter Contents

Section 28.1

General Information on Leukodystrophy

This section includes text excerpted from "Leukodystrophy,"
National Institute of Neurological Disorders and
Stroke (NINDS), September 11, 2015.

What Is Leukodystrophy?

Leukodystrophy refers to progressive degeneration of the white matter of the brain due to imperfect growth or development of the myelin sheath, the fatty covering that acts as an insulator around nerve fiber. Myelin, which lends its color to the white matter of the brain, is a complex substance made up of at least ten different chemicals.

The leukodystrophies are a group of disorders that are caused by genetic defects in how myelin produces or metabolizes these chemicals. Each of the leukodystrophies is the result of a defect in the gene that controls one (and only one) of the chemicals. Specific leukodystrophies include metachromatic leukodystrophy, Krabbe disease, adrenoleukodystrophy, Pelizaeus-Merzbacher disease, Canavan disease, Childhood Ataxia with Central Nervous System Hypomyelination or CACH (also known as Vanishing White Matter Disease), Alexander disease, Refsum disease, and cerebrotendinous xanthomatosis.

The most common symptom of a leukodystrophy disease is a gradual decline in an infant or child who previously appeared well. Progressive loss may appear in body tone, movements, gait, speech, ability to eat, vision, hearing, and behavior. There is often a slowdown in mental and physical development. Symptoms vary according to the specific type of leukodystrophy, and may be difficult to recognize in the early stages of the disease.

Is There Any Treatment?

Treatment for most of the leukodystrophies is symptomatic and supportive, and may include medications, physical, occupational, and speech therapies; and nutritional, educational, and recreational programs. Bone marrow transplantation is showing promise for a few of the leukodystrophies.

What Is the Prognosis?

The prognosis for the leukodystrophies varies according to the specific type of leukodystrophy.

Section 28.2

Metachromatic Leukodystrophy

This section contains text excerpted from the following sources:
Text beginning with the heading "What Is Metachromatic
Leukodystrophy?" is excerpted from "Metachromatic
Leukodystrophy," Genetic Home Reference (GHR), National
Institutes of Health (NIH), March 7, 2016; Text under the heading
"Is There Any Treatment?" is excerpted from "Metachromatic
Leukodystrophy," National Institute of Neurological
Disorders and Stroke (NINDS), February 22, 2016.

What Is Metachromatic Leukodystrophy?

Metachromatic leukodystrophy is an inherited disorder characterized by the accumulation of fats called sulfatides in cells. This accumulation especially affects cells in the nervous system that produce myelin, the substance that insulates and protects nerves. Nerve cells covered by myelin make up a tissue called white matter. Sulfatide accumulation in myelin-producing cells causes progressive destruction of white matter (leukodystrophy) throughout the nervous system, including in the brain and spinal cord (the central nervous system) and the nerves connecting the brain and spinal cord to muscles and sensory cells that detect sensations such as touch, pain, heat, and sound (the peripheral nervous system).

In people with metachromatic leukodystrophy, white matter damage causes progressive deterioration of intellectual functions and motor skills, such as the ability to walk. Affected individuals also develop loss of sensation in the extremities (peripheral neuropathy), incontinence, seizures, paralysis, an inability to speak, blindness, and hearing loss. Eventually they lose awareness of their surroundings and become unresponsive. While neurological problems are the primary feature of metachromatic leukodystrophy, effects of sulfatide accumulation on other organs and tissues have been reported, most often involving the gallbladder.

The most common form of metachromatic leukodystrophy, affecting about 50 to 60 percent of all individuals with this disorder, is called the late infantile form. This form of the disorder usually appears in the second year of life. Affected children lose any speech they have developed, become weak, and develop problems with walking (gait disturbance). As the disorder worsens, muscle tone generally first decreases, and then increases to the point of rigidity. Individuals with the late infantile form of metachromatic leukodystrophy typically do not survive past childhood.

In 20 to 30 percent of individuals with metachromatic leukodystrophy, onset occurs between the age of 4 and adolescence. In this juvenile form, the first signs of the disorder may be behavioral problems and increasing difficulty with schoolwork. Progression of the disorder is slower than in the late infantile form, and affected individuals may survive for about 20 years after diagnosis.

The adult form of metachromatic leukodystrophy affects approximately 15 to 20 percent of individuals with the disorder. In this form, the first symptoms appear during the teenage years or later. Often behavioral problems such as alcoholism, drug abuse, or difficulties at school or work are the first symptoms to appear. The affected individual may experience psychiatric symptoms such as delusions or hallucinations. People with the adult form of metachromatic leukodystrophy may survive for 20 to 30 years after diagnosis. During this time there may be some periods of relative stability and other periods of more rapid decline.

Metachromatic leukodystrophy gets its name from the way cells with an accumulation of sulfatides appear when viewed under a microscope. The sulfatides form granules that are described as metachromatic, which means they pick up color differently than surrounding cellular material when stained for examination.

How Common Is Metachromatic Leukodystrophy?

Metachromatic leukodystrophy is reported to occur in 1 in 40,000 to 160,000 individuals worldwide. The condition is more common in certain genetically isolated populations: 1 in 75 in a small group of Jews who immigrated to Israel from southern Arabia (Habbanites), 1 in 2,500 in the western portion of the Navajo Nation, and 1 in 8,000 among Arab groups in Israel.

What Genes Are Related to Metachromatic Leukodystrophy?

Most individuals with metachromatic leukodystrophy have mutations in the *ARSA* gene, which provides instructions for making the enzyme arylsulfatase A. This enzyme is located in cellular structures called lysosomes, which are the cell's recycling centers. Within lysosomes, arylsulfatase A helps break down sulfatides. A few individuals with metachromatic leukodystrophy have mutations in the *PSAP* gene. This gene provides instructions for making a protein that is broken up (cleaved) into smaller proteins that assist enzymes in breaking down various fats. One of these smaller proteins is called saposin B; this protein works with arylsulfatase A to break down sulfatides.

Mutations in the *ARSA* or *PSAP* genes result in a decreased ability to break down sulfatides, resulting in the accumulation of these substances in cells. Excess sulfatides are toxic to the nervous system. The accumulation gradually destroys myelin-producing cells, leading to the impairment of nervous system function that occurs in metachromatic leukodystrophy.

In some cases, individuals with very low arylsulfatase A activity show no symptoms of metachromatic leukodystrophy. This condition is called pseudoarylsulfatase deficiency.

How Do People Inherit Metachromatic Leukodystrophy?

This condition is inherited in an autosomal recessive pattern, which means both copies of the gene in each cell have mutations. The parents of an individual with an autosomal recessive condition each carry one copy of the mutated gene, but they typically do not show signs and symptoms of the condition.

Is There Any Treatment?

There is no cure for MLD. Bone marrow transplantation may delay progression of the disease in some infantile-onset cases. Other treatment is symptomatic and supportive. Considerable progress has been made with regard to gene therapy in an animal model of MLD and in clinical trials.

What Is the Prognosis?

The prognosis for MLD is poor. Most children within the infantile form die by age 5. Symptoms of the juvenile form progress with death occurring 10 to 20 years following onset. Those persons affected by the adult form typically die within 6 to 14 years following onset of symptoms.

Section 28.3

Pol III-Related Leukodystrophy

This section includes text excerpted from "Pol III-Related Leukodystrophy," Genetic Home Reference (GHR), National Institutes of Health (NIH), March 7, 2016.

What Is Pol III-Related Leukodystrophy?

Pol III-related leukodystrophy is a disorder that affects the nervous system and other parts of the body. Leukodystrophies are conditions that involve abnormalities of the nervous system's white matter, which consists of nerve fibers covered by a fatty substance called myelin. Myelin insulates nerve fibers and promotes the rapid transmission of nerve impulses.

Pol III-related leukodystrophy is a hypomyelinating disease, which means that the nervous system of affected individuals has a reduced ability to form myelin. Hypomyelination underlies most of the neurological problems associated with Pol III-related leukodystrophy. A small number of people with this disorder also have a loss of nerve cells in a part of the brain involved in coordinating movements (cerebellar atrophy) and underdevelopment (hypoplasia) of tissue that connects the left and right halves of the brain (the corpus callosum). These brain abnormalities likely contribute to the neurological problems in affected individuals.

People with Pol III-related leukodystrophy usually have intellectual disability ranging from mild to severe, which gradually worsens over time. Some affected individuals have normal intelligence in early childhood but develop mild intellectual disability during the course of the disease.

Difficulty coordinating movements (ataxia), which begins in childhood and slowly worsens over time, is a characteristic feature of Pol

III-related leukodystrophy. Affected children typically have delayed development of motor skills such as walking. Their gait is unstable, and they usually walk with their feet wide apart for balance. Affected individuals may eventually need to use a walker or wheelchair. Involuntary rhythmic shaking (tremor) of the arms and hands may occur in this disorder. In some cases the tremor occurs mainly during movement (intentional tremor); other affected individuals experience the tremor both during movement and at rest.

Development of the teeth (dentition) is often abnormal in Pol III-related leukodystrophy, resulting in the absence of some teeth (known as hypodontia or oligodontia). Some affected infants are born with a few teeth (natal teeth), which fall out during the first weeks of life. The primary (deciduous) teeth appear later than usual, beginning at about age 2. In Pol III-related leukodystrophy, the teeth may not appear in the usual sequence, in which front teeth (incisors) appear before back teeth (molars). Instead, molars often appear first, with incisors appearing later or not at all. Permanent teeth are also delayed, and may not appear until adolescence. The teeth may also be unusually shaped.

Some individuals with Pol III-related leukodystrophy have excessive salivation and difficulty chewing or swallowing (dysphagia), which can lead to choking. They may also have speech impairment (dysarthria). People with Pol III-related leukodystrophy often have abnormalities in eye movement, such as progressive vertical gaze palsy, which is restricted up-and-down eye movement that worsens over time. Nearsightedness is common in affected individuals, and clouding of the lens of the eyes (cataracts) has also been reported. Deterioration (atrophy) of the nerves that carry information from the eyes to the brain (the optic nerves) and seizures may also occur in this disorder.

Hypogonadotropic hypogonadism, which is a condition caused by reduced production of hormones that direct sexual development, may occur in Pol III-related leukodystrophy. Affected individuals have delayed development of the typical signs of puberty, such as the growth of body hair.

People with Pol III-related leukodystrophy may have different combinations of its signs and symptoms. These varied combinations of clinical features were originally described as separate disorders. Affected individuals may be diagnosed with ataxia, delayed dentition, and hypomyelination (ADDH); hypomyelination, hypodontia, hypogonadotropic hypogonadism (4H syndrome); tremor-ataxia with central hypomyelination (TACH); leukodystrophy with oligodontia (LO); or hypomyelination with cerebellar atrophy and hypoplasia of the corpus callosum (HCAHC). Because these disorders were later found to have the same genetic cause, researchers now group them as variations of the single condition Pol III-related leukodystrophy.

How Common Is Pol III-Related Leukodystrophy?

Pol III-related leukodystrophy is a rare disorder; its prevalence is unknown. Only about 40 cases have been described in the medical literature. However, researchers believe that a significant percentage of people with an unspecified hypomyelinating leukodystrophy could have Pol III-related leukodystrophy.

What Genes Are Related to Pol III-Related Leukodystrophy?

Pol III-related leukodystrophy is caused by mutations in the *POLR3A* or *POLR3B* gene. These genes provide instructions for making the two largest parts (subunits) of an enzyme called RNA polymerase III. This enzyme is involved in the production (synthesis) of ribonucleic acid (RNA), a chemical cousin of DNA. The RNA polymerase III enzyme attaches (binds) to DNA and synthesizes RNA in accordance with the instructions carried by the DNA, a process called transcription. RNA polymerase III helps synthesize several forms of RNA, including ribosomal RNA (rRNA) and transfer RNA (tRNA). Molecules of rRNA and tRNA assemble protein building blocks (amino acids) into working proteins; this process is essential for the normal functioning and survival of cells.

Researchers suggest that mutations in the *POLR3A* or *POLR3B* gene may impair the ability of subunits of the RNA polymerase III enzyme to assemble properly or result in an RNA polymerase III with impaired ability to bind to DNA. Reduced function of the RNA polymerase III molecule likely affects development and function of many parts of the body, including the nervous system and the teeth, but the relationship between *POLR3A* and *POLR3B* gene mutations and the specific signs and symptoms of Pol III-related leukodystrophy is unknown.

How Do People Inherit Pol III-Related Leukodystrophy?

This condition is inherited in an autosomal recessive pattern, which means both copies of the gene in each cell have mutations. The parents of an individual with an autosomal recessive condition each carry one copy of the mutated gene, but they typically do not show signs and symptoms of the condition.

Section 28.4

X-Linked Adrenoleukodystrophy

This section includes text excerpted from "X-Linked
Adrenoleukodystrophy," Genetic Home Reference (GHR),
National Institutes of Health (NIH), March 7, 2016.

What Is X-Linked Adrenoleukodystrophy?

X-linked adrenoleukodystrophy is a genetic disorder that occurs
primarily in males. It mainly affects the nervous system and the adrenal glands, which are small glands located on top of each kidney. In
this disorder, the fatty covering (myelin) that insulates nerves in the
brain and spinal cord is prone to deterioration (demyelination), which
reduces the ability of the nerves to relay information to the brain. In
addition, damage to the outer layer of the adrenal glands (adrenal
cortex) causes a shortage of certain hormones (adrenocortical insufficiency). Adrenocortical insufficiency may cause weakness, weight loss,
skin changes, vomiting, and coma.

There are three distinct types of X-linked adrenoleukodystrophy: a
childhood cerebral form, an adrenomyeloneuropathy type, and a form
called Addison disease only.

Children with the cerebral form of X-linked adrenoleukodystrophy experience learning and behavioral problems that usually begin
between the ages of 4 and 10. Over time the symptoms worsen, and
these children may have difficulty reading, writing, understanding
speech, and comprehending written material. Additional signs and
symptoms of the cerebral form include aggressive behavior, vision
problems, difficulty swallowing, poor coordination, and impaired
adrenal gland function. The rate at which this disorder progresses
is variable but can be extremely rapid, often leading to total disability within a few years. The life expectancy of individuals with this
type depends on the severity of the signs and symptoms and how
quickly the disorder progresses. Individuals with the cerebral form
of X-linked adrenoleukodystrophy usually survive only a few years
after symptoms begin but may survive longer with intensive medical
support.

Signs and symptoms of the adrenomyeloneuropathy type appear between early adulthood and middle age. Affected individuals develop progressive stiffness and weakness in their legs (paraparesis), experience urinary and genital tract disorders, and often show changes in behavior and thinking ability. Most people with the adrenomyeloneuropathy type also have adrenocortical insufficiency. In some severely affected individuals, damage to the brain and nervous system can lead to early death.

People with X-linked adrenoleukodystrophy whose only symptom is adrenocortical insufficiency are said to have the Addison disease only form. In these individuals, adrenocortical insufficiency can begin anytime between childhood and adulthood. However, most affected individuals develop the additional features of the adrenomyeloneuropathy type by the time they reach middle age. The life expectancy of individuals with this form depends on the severity of the signs and symptoms, but typically this is the mildest of the three types.

Rarely, individuals with X-linked adrenoleukodystrophy develop multiple features of the disorder in adolescence or early adulthood. In addition to adrenocortical insufficiency, these individuals usually have psychiatric disorders and a loss of intellectual function (dementia). It is unclear whether these individuals have a distinct form of the condition or a variation of one of the previously described types.

For reasons that are unclear, different forms of X-linked adrenoleukodystrophy can be seen in affected individuals within the same family.

How Common Is X-Linked Adrenoleukodystrophy?

The prevalence of X-linked adrenoleukodystrophy is 1 in 20,000 to 50,000 individuals worldwide. This condition occurs with a similar frequency in all populations.

What Genes Are Related to X-Linked Adrenoleukodystrophy?

Mutations in the *ABCD1* gene cause X-linked adrenoleukodystrophy. The *ABCD1* gene provides instructions for producing the adrenoleukodystrophy protein (ALDP), which is involved in transporting certain fat molecules called very long-chain fatty acids (VLCFAs) into peroxisomes. Peroxisomes are small sacs within cells that process many types of molecules, including VLCFAs.

ABCD1 gene mutations result in a shortage (deficiency) of ALDP. When this protein is lacking, the transport and subsequent breakdown of VLCFAs is disrupted, causing abnormally high levels of these fats in the body. The accumulation of VLCFAs may be toxic to the adrenal cortex and myelin. Research suggests that the accumulation of VLCFAs triggers an inflammatory response in the brain, which could lead to the breakdown of myelin. The destruction of these tissues leads to the signs and symptoms of X-linked adrenoleukodystrophy.

How Do People Inherit X-Linked Adrenoleukodystrophy?

X-linked adrenoleukodystrophy is inherited in an X-linked pattern. A condition is considered X-linked if the mutated gene that causes the disorder is located on the X chromosome, one of the two sex chromosomes in each cell. In males (who have only one X chromosome), one altered copy of the *ABCD1* gene in each cell is sufficient to cause X-linked adrenoleukodystrophy. Because females have two copies of the X chromosome, one altered copy of the *ABCD1* gene in each cell usually does not cause any features of X-linked adrenoleukodystrophy; however, some females with one altered copy of the gene have health problems associated with this disorder. The signs and symptoms of X-linked adrenoleukodystrophy tend to appear at a later age in females than in males. Affected women usually develop features of the adrenomyeloneuropathy type.

Chapter 29

Lipid Storage Diseases

Chapter Contents

Section 29.1

An Introduction to
Lipid Storage Diseases

This section includes text excerpted from "Lipid Storage
Diseases Fact Sheet," National Institute of Neurological
Disorders and Stroke (NINDS), February 23, 2016.

What Are Lipid Storage Diseases?

Lipid storage diseases, or the lipidoses, are a group of inherited
metabolic disorders in which harmful amounts of fatty materials (lipids) accumulate in various cells and tissues in the body. People with
these disorders either do not produce enough of one of the enzymes
needed to break down (metabolize) lipids or they produce enzymes
that do not work properly. Over time, this excessive storage of fats can
cause permanent cellular and tissue damage, particularly in the brain,
peripheral nervous system, liver, spleen, and bone marrow.

What Are Lipids?

Lipids are fat-like substances that are important parts of the membranes found within and between each cell and in the myelin sheath
that coats and protects the nerves. Lipids include oils, fatty acids,
waxes, steroids (such as cholesterol and estrogen), and other related
compounds.

These fatty materials are stored naturally in the body's cells, organs,
and tissues. Minute bodies within cells called lysosomes regularly convert, or metabolize, the lipids and proteins into smaller components to
provide energy for the body. Disorders in which intracellular material
is stored are called lysosomal storage diseases. In addition to lipid
storage diseases, other lysosomal storage diseases include the muco-
lipidoses, in which excessive amounts of lipids and sugar molecules
are stored in the cells and tissues, and the mucopolysaccharidoses, in
which excessive amounts of sugar molecules are stored.

How Are Lipid Storage Diseases Inherited?

Lipid storage diseases are inherited from one or both parents who carry a defective gene that regulates a particular protein in a class of the body's cells. They can be inherited two ways:

1. **Autosomal recessive** inheritance occurs when both parents carry and pass on a copy of the faulty gene, but neither parent is affected by the disorder. Each child born to these parents has a 25 percent chance of inheriting both copies of the defective gene, a 50 percent chance of being a carrier like the parents, and a 25 percent chance of not inheriting either copy of the defective gene. Children of either gender can be affected by an autosomal recessive this pattern of inheritance.

2. **X-linked** inheritance occurs when the mother carries the affected gene on the X chromosome that determines the child's gender and passes it to her son. Sons of carriers have a 50 percent chance of inheriting the disorder. Daughters have a 50 percent chance of inheriting the X-linked chromosome but usually are not severely affected by the disorder. Affected men do not pass the disorder to their sons but their daughters will be carriers for the disorder.

How Are These Disorders Diagnosed?

Diagnosis is made through clinical examination, enzyme assays (which measure enzyme activity), biopsy, genetic testing, and molecular analysis of cells or tissues. In some forms of the disorder, a urine analysis can identify the presence of stored material. Some tests can also determine if a person carries the defective gene that can be passed on to her or his children. This process is known as genotyping.

Biopsy for lipid storage disease involves removing a small sample of the liver or other tissue and studying it under a microscope. In this procedure, a physician will administer a local anesthetic and then remove a small piece of tissue either surgically or by needle biopsy (a small piece of tissue is removed by inserting a thin, hollow needle through the skin). The latter biopsy is usually performed at an outpatient testing facility.

Genetic testing can help individuals who have a family history of lipid storage disease determine if they are carrying a mutated gene that causes the disorder. Other genetic tests can determine if a fetus has the disorder or is a carrier of the defective gene. Prenatal testing is usually done by *chorionic villus sampling,* in which a very small sample of the placenta is removed and tested during early pregnancy. The sample, which contains the same DNA as the fetus, is removed by catheter or fine needle inserted through the cervix or by a fine needle inserted through the abdomen. Results are usually available within 2 weeks.

What Are the Types of Lipid Storage Disease?

Gaucher disease is caused by a deficiency of the enzyme glucocerebrosidase. Fatty material can collect in the spleen, liver, kidneys, lungs, brain, and bone marrow. Symptoms may include enlarged spleen and liver, liver malfunction, skeletal disorders and bone lesions that may cause pain and fractures, severe neurologic complications, swelling of lymph nodes and (occasionally) adjacent joints, distended abdomen, a brownish tint to the skin, anemia, low blood platelets, and yellow spots in the eyes. Persons affected most seriously may also be more susceptible to infection. The disease affects males and females equally.

Gaucher disease has three common clinical subtypes. *Type 1* (or *nonneuropathic* type) is the most common form of the disease in the United States. It occurs most often among persons of Ashkenazi Jewish heritage. Symptoms may begin early in life or in adulthood and include enlarged liver and grossly enlarged spleen, which can rupture and cause additional complications. Skeletal weakness and bone disease may be extensive. The brain is not affected, but there may be lung and, rarely, kidney impairment. Individuals usually bruise easily due to low blood platelets and experience fatigue due to anemia.

Depending on disease onset and severity, those with type 1 may live well into adulthood. Many individuals have a mild form of the disease or may not show any symptoms. *Type 2* (or *acute infantile neuropathic Gaucher disease*) typically begins within 3 months of birth. Symptoms include an enlarged liver and spleen, abnormal eye movement, extensive and progressive brain damage, spasticity, seizures, limb rigidity, and a poor ability to suck and swallow.

Affected children usually die before age 2. *Type 3* (the *chronic neuronopathic* form) can begin at any time in childhood or even in adulthood. It is characterized by slowly progressive but milder neurological symptoms compared to the acute or *Type 2* Gaucher disease. Major symptoms include eye movement disorders, cognitive deficit, poor coordination, an enlarged spleen and/or liver, seizures, skeletal irregularities, blood disorders including anemia, and respiratory problems. Individuals who are successfully treated with enzyme replacement therapy generally live into adulthood.

For those with type 1 and most type 3 Gaucher disease, enzyme replacement treatment given intravenously every two weeks can dramatically decrease liver and spleen size, reduce skeletal abnormalities, and reverse other manifestations. Successful bone marrow transplantation cures the non-neurological manifestations of the disease. However, this procedure carries significant risk and is rarely performed in individuals with Gaucher diseases. Surgery to remove the whole or part of the spleen may be required on rare occasions (if the person is anemic or when the enlarged organ affects the person's comfort). Blood transfusion may benefit some anemic individuals. Others may require joint replacement surgery to improve mobility and quality of life. There is currently no effective treatment for the brain damage that may occur in types 2 and 3 Gaucher disease.

Niemann-Pick disease is actually a group of autosomal recessive disorders caused by an accumulation of fat and cholesterol in cells of the liver, spleen, bone marrow, lungs, and, in some patients, brain. Neurological complications may include ataxia, eye paralysis, brain degeneration, learning problems, spasticity, feeding and swallowing difficulties, slurred speech, loss of muscle tone, hypersensitivity to touch, and some corneal clouding. A characteristic cherry-red halo develops around the center of the retina in 50 percent of patients.

Niemann-Pick disease is currently subdivided into four categories. Onset of type A, the most severe form, is in early infancy. Infants appear normal at birth but develop an enlarged liver and spleen, swollen lymph nodes, nodes under the skin (xanthemas), and profound brain damage by 6 months of age. The spleen may enlarge to as much as 10 times its normal size and can rupture. These children become progressively weaker, lose motor function, may become anemic, and are susceptible to recurring infection. They rarely live beyond 18 months. This form of the disease occurs most often in Jewish families. In the second group, called *type B* (or juvenile onset), enlargement of the liver and spleen characteristically occurs in the pre-teen years.

Most patients also develop ataxia, peripheral neuropathy, and pulmonary difficulties that progress with age, but the brain is generally not affected. Type B patients may live a comparatively long time but many require supplemental oxygen because of lung involvement. Niemann-Pick types A and B result from accumulation of the fatty

323

substance called sphingomyelin, due to deficiency of an enzyme called sphingomyelinase.

Niemann-Pick disease also includes two other variant forms called *types C* and *D*. These may appear early in life or develop in the teen or even adult years. Niemann-Pick disease types C and D are not caused by a deficiency of sphlingomyelinase but by a lack of the NPC1 or NPC2 proteins. As a result, various lipids and particularly cholesterol accumulate inside nerve cells and cause them to malfunction. Patients with types C and D have only moderate enlargement of their spleens and livers. Brain involvement may be extensive, leading to inability to look up and down, difficulty in walking and swallowing, and progressive loss of vision and hearing. Type D patients typically develop neurologic symptoms later than those with type C and have a progressively slower rate of loss of nerve function. Most type D patients share a common ancestral background in Nova Scotia. The life expectancies of patients with types C and D vary considerably. Some patients die in childhood while others who appear to be less severely affected can live into adulthood.

There is currently no cure for Niemann-Pick disease. Treatment is supportive. Children usually die from infection or progressive neurological loss. Bone marrow transplantation has been attempted in a few patients with type B. Patients with types C and D are frequently placed on a low-cholesterol diet and/or cholesterol lowering drugs, although research has not shown these interventions change the abnormal cholesterol metabolism or halt progression of the disease.

Fabry disease, also known as alpha-galactosidase-A deficiency, causes a buildup of fatty material in the autonomic nervous system, eyes, kidneys, and cardiovascular system. Fabry disease is the only X-linked lipid storage disease. Males are primarily affected although a milder form is common in females. Occasionally, affected females have severe manifestations similar to those seen in males with the disorder.

Onset of symptoms is usually during childhood or adolescence. Neurological signs include burning pain in the arms and legs, which worsens in hot weather or following exercise, and the buildup of excess material in the clear layers of the cornea (resulting in clouding but no change in vision). Fatty storage in blood vessel walls may impair circulation, putting the patient at risk for stroke or heart attack. Other manifestations include heart enlargement, progressive kidney impairment leading to renal failure, gastrointestinal difficulties, decreased sweating, and fever. Angiokeratomas (small, non-cancerous, reddish-purple elevated spots on the skin) may develop on the lower part of the trunk of the body and become more numerous with age.

Patients with Fabry disease often die prematurely of complications from heart disease, renal failure, or stroke. Drugs such as phenytoin and carbamazepine are often prescribed to treat pain that accompanies Fabry disease. Metoclopramaide or Lipisorb (a nutritional supplement) can ease gastrointestinal distress that often occurs in Fabry patients, and some individuals may require kidney transplant or dialysis. Enzyme replacement can reduce storage, ease pain, and improve organ function in patients with Fabry disease.

Farber disease, also known as Farber lipogranulomatosis, describes a group of rare autosomal recessive disorders that cause an accumulation of fatty material in the joints, tissues, and central nervous system. The disorder affects both males and females. Disease onset is typically in early infancy but may occur later in life. Children who have the classic form of Farber disease develop neurological symptoms within the first few weeks of life. These symptoms may include moderately impaired mental ability and problems with swallowing. The liver, heart, and kidneys may also be affected.

Other symptoms may include vomiting, arthritis, swollen lymph nodes, swollen joints, joint contractures (chronic shortening of muscles or tendons around joints), hoarseness, and xanthemas which thicken around joints as the disease progresses. Patients with breathing difficulty may require insertion of a breathing tube. Most children with the disease die by age 2, usually from lung disease. In one of the most severe forms of the disease, an enlarged liver and spleen (hepatosplenomegaly) can be diagnosed soon after birth. Children born with this form of the disease usually die within 6 months.

Farber disease is caused by a deficiency of the enzyme called ceramidase. Currently there is no specific treatment for Farber` disease. Corticosteroids may be prescribed to relieve pain. Bone marrow transplants may improve granulomas (small masses of inflamed tissue) on patients with little or no lung or nervous system complications. Older patients may have granulomas surgically reduced or removed.

The **gangliosidoses** are comprised of two distinct groups of genetic diseases. Both are autosomal recessive and affect males and females equally.

The **GM1 gangliosidoses** are caused by a deficiency of the enzyme beta-galactosidase, resulting in abnormal storage of acidic lipid materials particularly in the nerve cells in the central and peripheral nervous systems. GM1 gangliosidosis has three clinical presentations: early infantile, late infantile, and adult. Signs of *early infantile* GM1 (the most severe subtype, with onset shortly after birth) may include neurodegeneration, seizures, liver and spleen enlargement, coarsening of facial features, skeletal irregularities, joint stiffness, distended abdomen, muscle weakness, exaggerated startle response, and problems with gait. About half of affected patients develop cherry-red spots in the eye. Children may be deaf and blind by age 1 and often die by age 3 from cardiac complications or pneumonia. Onset of *late infantile* GM1 gangliosidosis is typically between ages 1 and 3 years. Neurological signs include ataxia, seizures, dementia, and difficulties with speech. Onset of *adult* GM1 gangliosidosis is between ages 3 and 30. Symptoms include muscle atrophy, neurological complications that are less severe and progress at a slower rate than in other forms of the disorder, corneal clouding in some patients, and dystonia (sustained muscle contractions that cause twisting and repetitive movements or abnormal postures). Angiokeratomas may develop on the lower part of the trunk of the body. The size of the liver and spleen in most patients is normal.

The **GM2 gangliosidoses** also cause the body to store excess acidic fatty materials in tissues and cells, most notably in nerve cells. These disorders result from a deficiency of the enzyme beta-hexosaminidase. The GM2 disorders include:

- **Tay-Sachs disease** (also known as GM2 gangliosidosis-variant B). Tay-Sachs and its variant forms are caused by a deficiency in the enzyme hexosaminidase A. The incidence is particularly high among Eastern European and Ashkenazi Jewish populations, as well as certain French Canadians and Louisianan Cajuns. Affected children appear to develop normally for the first few months of life. Symptoms begin by 6 months of age and include progressive loss of mental ability, dementia, decreased eye contact, increased startle reflex to noise, progressive loss of hearing leading to deafness, difficulty in swallowing, blindness, cherry-red spots in the retinas, and some paralysis. Seizures may begin in the child's second year. Children may eventually need a feeding tube and they often die by age 4 from recurring infection. No specific treatment is available. Anticonvulsant medications may initially control seizures. Other supportive treatment includes proper nutrition and hydration and techniques to keep the airway open. A rarer form of the disorder, called late-onset Tay-Sachs disease, occurs in patients in their twenties and early thirties and is characterized by unsteadiness of gait and progressive neurological deterioration.

- **Sandhoff disease** (variant AB). This is a severe form of Tay-Sachs disease. Onset usually occurs at the age of 6 months and is not limited to any ethnic group. Neurological signs may include progressive deterioration of the central nervous system, motor weakness, early blindness, marked startle response to sound, spasticity, myoclonus (shock-like contractions of a muscle), seizures, macrocephaly (an abnormally enlarged head), and cherry-red spots in the eye. Other symptoms may include frequent respiratory infections, murmurs of the heart, doll-like facial features, and an enlarged liver and spleen. There is no specific treatment for Sandhoff disease. As with Tay-Sachs disease, supportive treatment includes keeping the airway open and proper nutrition and hydration. Anticonvulsant medications may initially control seizures. Children generally die by age 3 from respiratory infections.

- **Krabbe disease** (also known as globoid cell leukodystrophy and galactosylceramide lipidosis) is an autosomal recessive disorder caused by deficiency of the enzyme galactocerebrosidase. The disease most often affects infants, with onset before age 6 months, but can occur in adolescence or adulthood. The buildup of undigested fats affects the growth of the nerve's protective myelin sheath and causes severe deterioration of mental and motor skills. Other symptoms include muscle weakness, hypertonia (reduced ability of a muscle to stretch), myoclonic seizures (sudden, shock-like contractions of the limbs), spasticity, irritability, unexplained fever, deafness, optic atrophy and blindness, paralysis, and difficulty when swallowing. Prolonged weight loss may also occur. The disease may be diagnosed by its characteristic grouping of cells into globoid bodies in the white matter of the brain, demyelination of nerves and degeneration, and destruction of brain cells. In infants, the disease is generally fatal before age 2. People with a later onset form of the disease have a milder course of the disease and live significantly longer. No specific treatment for Krabbe disease has been developed, although early bone marrow transplantation may help some patients.

- **Metachromatic leukodystrophy,** or MLD, is a group of disorders marked by storage buildup in the white matter of the central nervous system and in the peripheral nerves and to some extent in the kidneys. Similar to Krabbe disease, MLD affects the myelin that covers and protects the nerves. This autosomal

327

recessive disorder is caused by a deficiency of the enzyme arylsulfatase A. Both males and females are affected by this disorder.

MLD has three characteristic phenotypes: late infantile, juvenile, and adult.

The most common form of the disease is late infantile, with onset typically between 12 and 20 months following birth. Infants may appear normal at first but develop difficulty in walking and a tendency to fall, followed by intermittent pain in the arms and legs, progressive loss of vision leading to blindness, developmental delays, impaired swallowing, convulsions, and dementia before age 2. Children also develop gradual muscle wasting and weakness and eventually lose the ability to walk.

Most children with this form of the disorder die by age 5. Symptoms of the juvenile form typically begin between ages 3 and 10. Symptoms include impaired school performance, mental deterioration, ataxia, seizures, and dementia. Symptoms are progressive with death occurring 10 to 20 years following onset. In the adult form, symptoms begin after age 16 and may include impaired concentration, depression, psychiatric disturbances, ataxia, seizures, tremor, and dementia. Death generally occurs within 6 to 14 years after onset of symptoms.

There is no cure for MLD. Treatment is symptomatic and supportive. Bone marrow transplantation may delay progression of the disease in some cases. Considerable progress has been made with regard to gene therapies in animal models of MLD.

- **Wolman disease,** also known as acid lipase deficiency, is a severe lipid storage disorder that is usually fatal by age 1. This autosomal recessive disorder is marked by accumulation of cholesteryl esters (normally a transport form of cholesterol) and triglycerides (a chemical form in which fats exist in the body) that can build up significantly and cause damage in the cells and tissues. Both males and females are affected by this disorder. Infants are normal and active at birth but quickly develop progressive mental deterioration, enlarged liver and grossly enlarged spleen, distended abdomen, gastrointestinal problems including steatorrhea (excessive amounts of fats in the stools), jaundice, anemia, vomiting, and calcium deposits in the adrenal glands, causing them to harden.

Another type of acid lipase deficiency is **cholesteryl ester storage disease.** This extremely rare disorder results from storage of cholesteryl esters and triglycerides in cells in the blood and lymph and lymphoid tissue. Children develop an enlarged liver leading to cirrhosis and chronic liver failure before adulthood. Children may also have calcium deposits in the adrenal glands and may develop jaundice late in the disorder.

Enzyme replacement for both Wolman disease and cholesteryl ester storage disease is currently under active investigation.

How Are These Disorders Treated?

At present, there is no specific treatment available for most of the lipid storage disorders but highly effective enzyme replacement therapy is available for patients with type 1 Gaucher disease and some patients with type 3 Gaucher disease. Patients with anemia may require blood transfusions. In some patients, the enlarged spleen must be removed to improve cardiopulmonary function. Medications such as gabapentin and carbamazepine may be prescribed to help treat pain (including bone pain) for patients with Fabry disease. Restricting one's diet does not prevent lipid buildup in cells and tissues.

Section 29.2

Batten Disease

This section includes text excerpted from "Batten Disease Fact Sheet," National Institute of Neurological Disorders and Stroke (NINDS), September 1, 2015.

What Is Batten Disease?

Batten disease is a fatal, inherited disorder of the nervous system that typically begins in childhood. Early symptoms of this disorder usually appear between the ages of 5 and 10 years, when parents or physicians may notice a previously normal child has begun to develop vision problems or seizures. In some cases the early signs are subtle, taking the form of personality and behavior changes, slow learning, clumsiness, or stumbling. Over time, affected children suffer cognitive impairment, worsening seizures, and progressive loss of sight and motor skills. Eventually, children with Batten disease become blind, bedridden, and demented. Batten disease is often fatal by the late teens or twenties.

Batten disease is named after the British pediatrician who first described it in 1903. Also known as Spielmeyer-Vogt-Sjogren-Batten disease, it is the most common form of a group of disorders called the neuronal ceroid lipofuscinoses, or NCLs. Although Batten disease originally referred specifically to the juvenile form of NCL (JNCL), the term Batten disease is increasingly used by pediatricians to describe all forms of NCL.

What Are the Other Forms of NCL?

There are four other main types of NCL, including three forms that begin earlier in childhood and a very rare form that strikes adults. The symptoms of these childhood types are similar to those caused by Batten disease, but they become apparent at different ages and progress at different rates.

1. **Congenital NCL** is a very rare and severe form of NCL. Babies have abnormally small heads (microcephaly) and seizures, and die soon after birth.

2. **Infantile NCL** (INCL or Santavuori-Haltia disease) begins between about ages 6 months and 2 years and progresses rapidly. Affected children fail to thrive and have microcephaly. Also typical are short, sharp muscle contractions called myoclonic jerks. These children usually die before age 5, although some have survived in a vegetative state a few years longer.

3. **Late infantile NCL** (LINCL, or Jansky-Bielschowsky disease) begins between ages 2 and 4. The typical early signs are loss of muscle coordination (ataxia) and seizures that do not respond to drugs. This form progresses rapidly and ends in death between ages 8 and 12.

4. **Adult NCL** (also known as Kufs disease, Parry's disease, and ANCL) generally begins before age 40, causes milder symptoms that progress slowly, and does not cause blindness. Although age of death varies among affected individuals, this form does shorten life expectancy.

There are also "variant" forms of late-infantile NCL (vLINCL) that do not precisely conform to classical late-infantile NCL.

How Many People Have These Disorders?

Batten disease and other forms of NCL are relatively rare, occurring in an estimated 2 to 4 of every 100,000 live births in the United States. These disorders appear to be more common in Finland, Sweden, other parts of northern Europe, and Newfoundland, Canada. Although NCLs are classified as rare diseases, they often strike more than one person in families that carry the defective genes.

How Are NCLs Inherited?

Childhood NCLs are autosomal recessive disorders; that is, they occur only when a child inherits two copies of the defective gene, one from each parent. When both parents carry one defective gene, each of their children faces a one in four chance of developing NCL. At the same time, each child also faces a one in two chance of inheriting just one copy of the defective gene. Individuals who have only one defective gene are known as carriers, meaning they do not develop the disease, but they can pass the gene on to their own children. Because the mutated genes that are involved in certain forms of Batten disease are known, carrier detection is possible in some instances.

Adult NCL may be inherited as an autosomal recessive or, less often, as an autosomal dominant disorder. In autosomal dominant inheritance, all people who inherit a single copy of the disease gene develop the disease. As a result, there are no unaffected carriers of the gene.

What Causes These Diseases?

Symptoms of Batten disease and other NCLs are linked to a buildup of substances called lipofuscins (lipopigments) in the body's tissues. These lipopigments are made up of fats and proteins. Their name comes from the technical word *lipo*, which is short for "lipid" or fat, and from the term *pigment*, used because they take on a greenish-yellow color when viewed under an ultraviolet light microscope. The lipopigments build up in cells of the brain and the eye as well as in skin, muscle, and many other tissues. The substances are found inside a part of cells called lysosomes.

Lysosomes are responsible for getting rid of things that become damaged or are no longer needed and must be cleared from inside the cell. The accumulated lipopigments in Batten disease and the other NCLs form distinctive shapes that can be seen under an electron microscope. Some look like half-moons, others like fingerprints. These deposits are what doctors look for when they examine a skin sample to diagnose Batten disease. The specific appearance of the lipopigment deposits can be useful in guiding further diagnostic tests that may identify the specific gene defect.

To date, eight genes have been linked to the varying forms of NCL. Mutations of other genes in NCL are likely since some individuals do not have mutations in any of the known genes. More than one gene may be associated with a particular form of NCL. The known NCL genes are:

- *CLN1,* also known as *PPT1,* encodes an enzyme called palmitoyl-protein thioesterase 1 that is insufficiently active in Infantile NCL.

- *CLN 2,* or TPP1, produces an enzyme called tripeptidyl peptidase 1—an acid protease that degrades proteins. The enzyme is insufficiently active in Late Infantile NCL (also referred to as *CLN2*).

- *CLN3* mutation is the major cause of Juvenile NCL. The gene codes for a protein called CLN3 or battenin, which is found in the membranes of the cell (most predominantly in lysosomes and in related structures called endosomes). The protein's function is currently unknown.

- *CLN5,* which causes variant Late Infantile NCL (vLINCL, also referred to as CLN5), produces a lysosomal protein called CLN5, whose function has not been identified.

- *CLN6,* which also causes Late Infantile NCL, encodes a protein called CLN6 or linclin. The protein is found in the membranes of the cell (most predominantly in a structure called the endoplasmic reticulum). Its function has not been identified.

- *MFSD8,* seen in variant Late Infantile NCL (also referred to as CLN7), encodes the MFSD8 protein that is a member of a protein family called the *major facilitator superfamily.* This superfamily is involved with transporting substances across the cell membranes. The precise function of MFSD8 has not been identified.

- *CLN8* causes progressive epilepsy with mental retardation. The gene encodes a protein also called CLN8, which is found in the membranes of the cell—most predominantly in the endoplasmic reticulum. The protein's function has not been identified.

- *CTSD,* involved with Congenital NCL (also referred to as CLN10), encodes cathepsin D, a lysosomal enzyme that breaks apart other proteins. A deficiency of cathepsin D causes the disorder.

How Are These Disorders Diagnosed?

Because vision loss is often an early sign, Batten disease may be first suspected during an eye exam. An eye doctor can detect a loss of cells within the eye that occurs in the childhood forms of NCL. However, because such cell loss occurs in other eye diseases, the disorder cannot be diagnosed by this sign alone. Often an eye specialist or other physician who suspects NCL may refer the child to a neurologist for additional testing.

In order to diagnose NCL, the neurologist needs the individual's medical and family history and information from various laboratory tests. Diagnostic tests used for NCLs include:

- **Blood or urine tests**. These tests can detect abnormalities that may indicate Batten disease. For example, elevated levels of a chemical called dolichol are found in the urine of many individuals with NCL. The presence of vacuolated lymphocytes—white blood cells that contain holes or cavities (observed by microscopic analysis of blood smears)—when combined with other findings that indicate NCL, is suggestive for the juvenile form caused by CLN3 mutations.

- **Skin or tissue sampling**. The doctor can examine a small piece of tissue under an electron microscope. The powerful magnification of the microscope helps the doctor spot typical NCL deposits. These deposits are common in skin cells, especially those from sweat glands.

- **Electroencephalogram or EEG**. An EEG uses special patches placed on the scalp to record electrical currents inside the brain. This helps doctors see telltale patterns in the brain's electrical activity that suggest an individual has seizures.

- **Electrical studies of the eyes**. These tests, which include visual-evoked responses and electroretinograms, can detect various eye problems common in childhood NCLs.

- **Diagnostic imaging using computed tomography (CT) or magnetic resonance imaging (MRI)**. Diagnostic imaging can help doctors look for changes in the brain's appearance. CT uses

X-rays and a computer to create a sophisticated picture of the brain's tissues and structures, and may reveal brain areas that are decaying, or "atrophic," in persons with NCL. MRI uses a combination of magnetic fields and radio waves, instead of radiation, to create a picture of the brain.

- **Measurement of enzyme activity.** Measurement of the activity of palmitoyl-protein thioesterase involved in CLN1, the acid protease involved in CLN2, and, though more rare, cathepsin D activity involved in CLN10, in white blood cells or cultured skin fibroblasts (cells that strengthen skin and give it elasticity) can be used to confirm or rule out these diagnoses.

- **DNA analysis**. If families where the mutation in the gene for CLN3 is known, DNA analysis can be used to confirm the diagnosis or for the prenatal diagnosis of this form of Batten disease. When the mutation is known, DNA analysis can also be used to detect unaffected carriers of this condition for genetic counseling. If a family mutation has not previously been identified or if the common mutations are not present, recent molecular advanced have made it possible to sequence all of the known NCL genes, increasing the chances of finding the responsible mutation(s).

Is There Any Treatment?

As yet, no specific treatment is known that can halt or reverse the symptoms of Batten disease or other NCLs. However, seizures can sometimes be reduced or controlled with anticonvulsant drugs, and other medical problems can be treated appropriately as they arise. At the same time, physical and occupational therapy may help patients retain function as long as possible.

Some reports have described a slowing of the disease in children with Batten disease who were treated with vitamins C and E and with diets low in vitamin A. However, these treatments did not prevent the fatal outcome of the disease.

Support and encouragement can help patients and families cope with the profound disability and dementia caused by NCLs. Often, support groups enable affected children, adults, and families to share common concerns and experiences.

Meanwhile, scientists pursue medical research that could someday yield an effective treatment.

Section 29.3

Fabry Disease

This section contains text excerpted from the following sources: Text beginning with the heading "What Is Fabry Disease?" is excerpted from "NINDS Fabry Disease Information Page," National Institute of Neurological Disorders and Stroke (NINDS), February 22, 2016; Text under the heading "How Common Is Fabry Disease?" is excerpted from "Fabry Disease," Genetics Home Reference (GHR), National Institutes of Health (NIH), March 21, 2016; Text under the heading "Is There Any Treatment?" is excerpted from "NINDS Fabry Disease Information Page," National Institute of Neurological Disorders and Stroke (NINDS), February 22, 2016.

What Is Fabry Disease?

Fabry disease is caused by the lack of or faulty enzyme needed to metabolize lipids, fat-like substances that include oils, waxes, and fatty acids. The disease is also called *alpha-galactosidase-A deficiency*. A mutation in the gene that controls this enzyme causes insufficient breakdown of lipids, which build up to harmful levels in the autonomic nervous system (which controls involuntary functions such as breathing and digestion), cardiovascular system, eyes, and kidneys.

Symptoms usually begin during childhood or adolescence and include burning sensations in the arms and legs that gets worse with exercise and hot weather and small, non-cancerous, raised reddish-purple blemishes on the skin. Excess material buildup can lead to clouding in the corneas. Lipid storage may lead to impaired blood circulation and increased risk of heart attack or stroke. The heart may also become enlarged and the kidneys may become progressively impaired, leading to renal failure. Other signs include decreased sweating, fever, and gastrointestinal difficulties.

Fabry disease is the only X-linked lipid storage disease (where the mother carries the affected gene on the X chromosome that determines the child's gender and passes it to her son). Boys have a 50 percent chance of inheriting the disorder and her daughters have a 50 percent chance of being a carrier. A milder form is common in females, and occasionally some affected females may have severe symptoms similar to males with the disorder.

How Common Is Fabry Disease?

Fabry disease affects an estimated 1 in 40,000 to 60,000 males. This disorder also occurs in females, although the prevalence is unknown. Milder, late-onset forms of the disorder are probably more common than the classic, severe form.

What Genes Are Related to Fabry Disease?

Fabry disease is caused by mutations in the *GLA* gene. This gene provides instructions for making an enzyme called alpha-galactosidase A. This enzyme is active in lysosomes, which are structures that serve as recycling centers within cells. Alpha-galactosidase A normally breaks down a fatty substance called globotriaosylceramide.

Mutations in the *GLA* gene alter the structure and function of the enzyme, preventing it from breaking down this substance effectively. As a result, globotriaosylceramide builds up in cells throughout the body, particularly cells lining blood vessels in the skin and cells in the kidneys, heart, and nervous system. The progressive accumulation of this substance damages cells, leading to the varied signs and symptoms of Fabry disease.

GLA gene mutations that result in an absence of alpha-galactosidase A activity lead to the classic, severe form of Fabry disease. Mutations that decrease but do not eliminate the enzyme's activity usually cause the milder, late-onset forms of Fabry disease that affect only the heart or kidneys.

How Do People Inherit Fabry Disease?

This condition is inherited in an X-linked pattern. A condition is considered X-linked if the mutated gene that causes the disorder is located on the X chromosome, one of the two sex chromosomes in each cell. In males (who have only one X chromosome), one altered copy of the *GLA* gene in each cell is sufficient to cause the condition. Because females have two copies of the X chromosome, one altered copy of the gene in each cell usually leads to less severe symptoms in females than in males, or rarely may cause no symptoms at all.

Unlike other X-linked disorders, Fabry disease causes significant medical problems in many females who have one altered copy of the

GLA gene. These women may experience many of the classic features of the disorder, including nervous system abnormalities, kidney problems, chronic pain, and fatigue. They also have an increased risk of developing high blood pressure, heart disease, stroke, and kidney failure. The signs and symptoms of Fabry disease usually begin later in life and are milder in females than in their affected male relatives.

A small percentage of females who carry a mutation in one copy of the *GLA* gene never develop signs and symptoms of Fabry disease.

Is There Any Treatment?

Enzyme replacement therapy has been approved by the U.S. Food and Drug Administration (FDA) for the treatment of Fabry disease. Enzyme replacement therapy can reduce lipid storage, ease pain, and preserve organ function in some individuals with the disorder. The pain that accompanies the disease may be treated with anticonvulsants. Gastrointestinal hyperactivity may be treated with metoclopramide. Some individuals may require dialysis or kidney transplantation. Restricting one's diet does not prevent lipid buildup in cells and tissues.

What Is the Prognosis?

Individuals with Fabry disease often die prematurely of complications from strokes, heart disease, or kidney failure.

Section 29.4

Gaucher Disease

This section contains text excerpted from the following sources: Text beginning with the heading "What Is Gaucher Disease?" is excerpted from "Gaucher Disease," Genetics Home Reference (GHR), National Institutes of Health (NIH), March 7, 2016; Text under the heading "Is There Any Treatment?" is excerpted from "NINDS Gaucher Disease Information Page," National Institute of Neurological Disorders and Stroke (NINDS), February 22, 2016.

What Is Gaucher Disease?

Gaucher disease is an inherited disorder that affects many of the body's organs and tissues. The signs and symptoms of this condition vary widely among affected individuals. Researchers have described several types of Gaucher disease based on their characteristic features.

Type 1 Gaucher disease is the most common form of this condition. Type 1 is also called non-neuronopathic Gaucher disease because the brain and spinal cord (the central nervous system) are usually not affected. The features of this condition range from mild to severe and may appear anytime from childhood to adulthood. Major signs and symptoms include enlargement of the liver and spleen (hepatosplenomegaly), a low number of red blood cells (anemia), easy bruising caused by a decrease in blood platelets (thrombocytopenia), lung disease, and bone abnormalities such as bone pain, fractures, and arthritis.

Types 2 and 3 Gaucher disease are known as neuronopathic forms of the disorder because they are characterized by problems that affect the central nervous system. In addition to the signs and symptoms described above, these conditions can cause abnormal eye movements, seizures, and brain damage. Type 2 Gaucher disease usually causes life-threatening medical problems beginning in infancy. Type 3 Gaucher disease also affects the nervous system, but it tends to worsen more slowly than type 2.

The most severe type of Gaucher disease is called the perinatal lethal form. This condition causes severe or life-threatening complications starting before birth or in infancy. Features of the perinatal lethal form can include extensive swelling caused by fluid accumulation before birth (hydrops fetalis); dry, scaly skin (ichthyosis) or other skin abnormalities; hepatosplenomegaly; distinctive facial features; and serious neurological problems. As its name indicates, most infants with the perinatal lethal form of Gaucher disease survive for only a few days after birth.

Another form of Gaucher disease is known as the cardiovascular type because it primarily affects the heart, causing the heart valves to harden (calcify). People with the cardiovascular form of Gaucher disease may also have eye abnormalities, bone disease, and mild enlargement of the spleen (splenomegaly).

How Common Is Gaucher Disease?

Gaucher disease occurs in 1 in 50,000 to 100,000 people in the general population. Type 1 is the most common form of the disorder; it occurs more frequently in people of Ashkenazi (eastern and central European) Jewish heritage than in those with other backgrounds. This form of the condition affects 1 in 500 to 1,000 people of Ashkenazi Jewish heritage. The other forms of Gaucher disease are uncommon and do not occur more frequently in people of Ashkenazi Jewish descent.

What Genes Are Related to Gaucher Disease?

Mutations in the *GBA* gene cause Gaucher disease. The *GBA* gene provides instructions for making an enzyme called beta-glucocerebrosidase. This enzyme breaks down a fatty substance called glucocerebroside into a sugar (glucose) and a simpler fat molecule (ceramide). Mutations in the *GBA* gene greatly reduce or eliminate the activity of beta-glucocerebrosidase. Without enough of this enzyme, glucocerebroside and related substances can build up to toxic levels within cells. Tissues and organs are damaged by the abnormal accumulation and storage of these substances, causing the characteristic features of Gaucher disease.

How Do People Inherit Gaucher Disease?

This condition is inherited in an autosomal recessive pattern, which means both copies of the gene in each cell have mutations. The parents of an individual with an autosomal recessive condition each carry one copy of the mutated gene, but they typically do not show signs and symptoms of the condition.

Is There Any Treatment?

Enzyme replacement therapy is available for most people with types 1 and 3 Gaucher disease. Given intravenously every two weeks, this therapy decreases liver and spleen size, reduces skeletal abnormalities, and reverses other symptoms of the disorder. The U.S. Food and Drug Administration has approved eligustat tartrate for Gaucher treatment, which works by administering small molecules that reduce the action of the enzyme that catalyzes glucose to ceramide. Surgery to remove the whole or part of the spleen may be required on rare occasions, and blood transfusions may benefit some anemic individuals. Other individuals may require joint replacement surgery to improve mobility and quality of life. There is no effective treatment for severe brain damage that may occur in persons with types 2 and 3 Gaucher disease.

What Is the Prognosis?

Enzyme replacement therapy is very beneficial for type 1 and most type 3 individuals with this condition. Successful bone marrow transplantation can reverse the non-neurological effects of the disease, but the procedure carries a high risk and is rarely performed in individuals with Gaucher disease.

Section 29.5

Niemann-Pick Disease

This section contains text excerpted from the following sources:
Text beginning with the heading "What Is Niemann-Pick
Disease?" is excerpted from "Niemann-Pick Disease," Genetics
Home Reference (GHR), National Institutes of Health (NIH),
March 7, 2016; Text under the heading "Is There Any Treatment?"
is excerpted from "NINDS Niemann-Pick Disease Information
Page," National Institute of Neurological Disorders and
Stroke (NINDS), February 22, 2016.

What Is Niemann-Pick Disease?

Niemann-Pick disease is a condition that affects many body systems. It has a wide range of symptoms that vary in severity. Niemann-Pick disease is divided into four main types: type A, type B,
type C1, and type C2. These types are classified on the basis of genetic
cause and the signs and symptoms of the condition.

Infants with Niemann-Pick disease type A usually develop an
enlarged liver and spleen (hepatosplenomegaly) by age 3 months and
fail to gain weight and grow at the expected rate (failure to thrive).
The affected children develop normally until around age 1 year when
they experience a progressive loss of mental abilities and movement
(psychomotor regression). Children with Niemann-Pick disease type
A also develop widespread lung damage (interstitial lung disease)
that can cause recurrent lung infections and eventually lead to respiratory failure. All affected children have an eye abnormality called
a cherry-red spot, which can be identified with an eye examination.
Children with Niemann-Pick disease type A generally do not survive
past early childhood.

Niemann-Pick disease type B usually presents in mid-childhood.
The signs and symptoms of this type are similar to type A, but not as
severe. People with Niemann-Pick disease type B often have hepatosplenomegaly, recurrent lung infections, and a low number of platelets
in the blood (thrombocytopenia). They also have short stature and
slowed mineralization of bone (delayed bone age). About one-third
of affected individuals have the cherry-red spot eye abnormality or

neurological impairment. People with Niemann-Pick disease type B usually survive into adulthood.

The signs and symptoms of Niemann-Pick disease types C1 and C2 are very similar; these types differ only in their genetic cause. Niemann-Pick disease types C1 and C2 usually become apparent in childhood, although signs and symptoms can develop at any time. People with these types usually develop difficulty coordinating movements (ataxia), an inability to move the eyes vertically (vertical supranuclear gaze palsy), poor muscle tone (dystonia), severe liver disease, and interstitial lung disease. Individuals with Niemann-Pick disease types C1 and C2 have problems with speech and swallowing that worsen over time, eventually interfering with feeding. Affected individuals often experience progressive decline in intellectual function and about one-third have seizures. People with these types may survive into adulthood.

How Common Is Niemann-Pick Disease?

Niemann-Pick disease types A and B is estimated to affect 1 in 250,000 individuals. Niemann-Pick disease type A occurs more frequently among individuals of Ashkenazi (eastern and central European) Jewish descent than in the general population. The incidence within the Ashkenazi population is approximately 1 in 40,000 individuals.

Combined, Niemann-Pick disease types C1 and C2 are estimated to affect 1 in 150,000 individuals; however, type C1 is by far the more common type, accounting for 95 percent of cases. The disease occurs more frequently in people of French-Acadian descent in Nova Scotia. In Nova Scotia, a population of affected French-Acadians were previously designated as having Niemann-Pick disease type D, however, it was shown that these individuals have mutations in the gene associated with Niemann-Pick disease type C1.

What Genes Are Related to Niemann-Pick Disease?

Niemann-Pick disease types A and B is caused by mutations in the *SMPD1* gene. This gene provides instructions for producing an enzyme called acid sphingomyelinase. This enzyme is found in lysosomes, which are compartments within cells that break down and recycle different types of molecules. Acid sphingomyelinase is responsible for the conversion of a fat (lipid) called sphingomyelin into another type of lipid called ceramide. Mutations in *SMPD1* lead to a shortage of acid sphingomyelinase, which results in reduced break down of sphingo-myelin, causing this fat to accumulate in cells. This fat buildup causes cells to malfunction and eventually die. Over time, cell loss impairs function of tissues and organs including the brain, lungs, spleen, and liver in people with Niemann-Pick disease types A and B.

Mutations in either the *NPC1* or *NPC2* gene cause Niemann-Pick disease type C. The proteins produced from these genes are involved in the movement of lipids within cells. Mutations in these genes lead to a shortage of functional protein, which prevents movement of choles-terol and other lipids, leading to their accumulation in cells. Because these lipids are not in their proper location in cells, many normal cell functions that require lipids (such as cell membrane formation) are impaired. The accumulation of lipids as well as the cell dysfunction eventually leads to cell death, causing the tissue and organ damage seen in Niemann-Pick disease types C1 and C2.

How Do People Inherit Niemann-Pick Disease?

This condition is inherited in an autosomal recessive pattern, which means both copies of the gene in each cell have mutations. The parents of an individual with an autosomal recessive condition each carry one copy of the mutated gene, but they typically do not show signs and symptoms of the condition.

Is There Any Treatment?

There is currently no cure for Niemann-Pick disease. Treatment is supportive. Children usually die from infection or progressive neu-rological loss. There is currently no effective treatment for persons with type A. Bone marrow transplantation has been attempted in a few individuals with type B. The development of enzyme replace-ment and gene therapies might also be helpful for those with type B. restricting one's diet does not prevent the buildup of lipids in cells and tissues.

What Is the Prognosis?

Infants with type A die in infancy. Children with Type B may live a comparatively long time, but may require supplemental oxygen because of lung impairment. The life expectancy of persons with type C varies: some individuals die in childhood while others who appear to be less severely affected can live into adulthood.

Section 29.6

Sandhoff Disease

This section contains text excerpted from the following sources: Text
beginning with the heading "What Is Sandhoff Disease?" is excerpted
from "Sandhoff Disease," Genetics Home Reference (GHR), National
Institutes of Health (NIH), March 7, 2016; Text under the heading
"Is There Any Treatment?" is excerpted from "NINDS Sandhoff
Disease Information Page," National Institute of Neurological
Disorders and Stroke (NINDS), February 22, 2016.

What Is Sandhoff Disease?

Sandhoff disease is a rare inherited disorder that progressively
destroys nerve cells (neurons) in the brain and spinal cord.

The most common and severe form of Sandhoff disease becomes
apparent in infancy. Infants with this disorder typically appear normal
until the age of 3 to 6 months, when their development slows and muscles used for movement weaken. Affected infants lose motor skills such
as turning over, sitting, and crawling. They also develop an exaggerated
startle reaction to loud noises. As the disease progresses, children with
Sandhoff disease experience seizures, vision and hearing loss, intellectual disability, and paralysis. An eye abnormality called a cherry-red
spot, which can be identified with an eye examination, is characteristic of this disorder. Some affected children also have enlarged organs
(organomegaly) or bone abnormalities. Children with the severe infantile form of Sandhoff disease usually live only into early childhood.

Other forms of Sandhoff disease are very rare. Signs and symptoms can
begin in childhood, adolescence, or adulthood and are usually milder than
those seen with the infantile form. Characteristic features include muscle
weakness, loss of muscle coordination (ataxia) and other problems with
movement, speech problems, and mental illness. These signs and symptoms vary widely among people with late-onset forms of Sandhoff disease.

How Common Is Sandhoff Disease?

Sandhoff disease is a rare disorder; its frequency varies among
populations. This condition appears to be more common in the Creole

population of northern Argentina; the Metis Indians in Saskatchewan, Canada; and people from Lebanon.

What Genes Are Related to Sandhoff Disease?

Mutations in the *HEXB* gene cause Sandhoff disease. The *HEXB* gene provides instructions for making a protein that is part of two critical enzymes in the nervous system, beta-hexosaminidase A and beta-hexosaminidase B. These enzymes are located in lysosomes, which are structures in cells that break down toxic substances and act as recycling centers. Within lysosomes, these enzymes break down fatty substances, complex sugars, and molecules that are linked to sugars. In particular, beta-hexosaminidase A helps break down a fatty substance called GM2 ganglioside.

Mutations in the *HEXB* gene disrupt the activity of beta-hexosaminidase A and beta-hexosaminidase B, which prevents these enzymes from breaking down GM2 ganglioside and other molecules. As a result, these compounds can accumulate to toxic levels, particularly in neurons of the brain and spinal cord. A buildup of GM2 ganglioside leads to the progressive destruction of these neurons, which causes many of the signs and symptoms of Sandhoff disease.

Because Sandhoff disease impairs the function of lysosomal enzymes and involves the buildup of GM2 ganglioside, this condition is sometimes referred to as a lysosomal storage disorder or a GM2-gangliosidosis.

How Do People Inherit Sandhoff Disease?

This condition is inherited in an autosomal recessive pattern, which means both copies of the gene in each cell have mutations. The parents of an individual with an autosomal recessive condition each carry one copy of the mutated gene, but they typically do not show signs and symptoms of the condition.

Is There Any Treatment?

There is no specific treatment for Sandhoff disease. Supportive treatment includes proper nutrition and hydration and keeping the airway open. Anticonvulsants may initially control seizures.

What Is the Prognosis?

The prognosis for individuals with Sandhoff disease is poor. Death usually occurs by age 3 and is generally caused by respiratory infections.

Section 29.7

Tay-Sachs Disease

> This section contains text excerpted from the following sources: Text beginning with the heading "What Is Tay-Sachs Disease?" is excerpted from "Tay-Sachs Disease," Genetics Home Reference (GHR), National Institutes of Health (NIH), March 7, 2016; Text under the heading "Is There Any Treatment?" is excerpted from "NINDS Tay-Sachs Disease Information Page," National Institute of Neurological Disorders and Stroke (NINDS), February 22, 2016.

What Is Tay-Sachs Disease?

Tay-Sachs disease is a rare inherited disorder that progressively destroys nerve cells (neurons) in the brain and spinal cord.

The most common form of Tay-Sachs disease becomes apparent in infancy. Infants with this disorder typically appear normal until the age of 3 to 6 months, when their development slows and muscles used for movement weaken. Affected infants lose motor skills such as turning over, sitting, and crawling. They also develop an exaggerated startle reaction to loud noises. As the disease progresses, children with Tay-Sachs disease experience seizures, vision and hearing loss, intellectual disability, and paralysis. An eye abnormality called a cherry-red spot, which can be identified with an eye examination, is characteristic of this disorder. Children with this severe infantile form of Tay-Sachs disease usually live only into early childhood.

Other forms of Tay-Sachs disease are very rare. Signs and symptoms can appear in childhood, adolescence, or adulthood and are usually milder than those seen with the infantile form. Characteristic features include muscle weakness, loss of muscle coordination (ataxia) and other problems with movement, speech problems, and mental illness. These signs and symptoms vary widely among people with late-onset forms of Tay-Sachs disease.

How Common Is Tay-Sachs Disease?

Tay-Sachs disease is very rare in the general population. The genetic mutations that cause this disease are more common in people of Ashkenazi (eastern and central European) Jewish heritage than in those with other backgrounds. The mutations responsible for this disease are also more common in certain French-Canadian communities of Quebec, the Old Order Amish community in Pennsylvania, and the Cajun population of Louisiana.

What Genes Are Related to Tay-Sachs Disease?

Mutations in the *HEXA* gene cause Tay-Sachs disease. The *HEXA* gene provides instructions for making part of an enzyme called beta-hexosaminidase A, which plays a critical role in the brain and spinal cord. This enzyme is located in lysosomes, which are structures in cells that break down toxic substances and act as recycling centers. Within lysosomes, beta-hexosaminidase A helps break down a fatty substance called GM2 ganglioside.

Mutations in the *HEXA* gene disrupt the activity of beta-hexosaminidase A, which prevents the enzyme from breaking down GM2 ganglioside. As a result, this substance accumulates to toxic levels, particularly in neurons in the brain and spinal cord. Progressive damage caused by the buildup of GM2 ganglioside leads to the destruction of these neurons, which causes the signs and symptoms of Tay-Sachs disease.

Because Tay-Sachs disease impairs the function of a lysosomal enzyme and involves the buildup of GM2 ganglioside, this condition is sometimes referred to as a lysosomal storage disorder or a GM2-gangliosidosis.

How Do People Inherit Tay-Sachs Disease?

This condition is inherited in an autosomal recessive pattern, which means both copies of the gene in each cell have mutations. The parents of an individual with an autosomal recessive condition each carry one copy of the mutated gene, but they typically do not show signs and symptoms of the condition.

What Causes Tay-Sachs Disease?

Tay-Sachs disease is caused by mutations in the *HEXA* gene. The *HEXA* gene provides instructions for making part of an enzyme called beta-hexosaminidase A, which plays a critical role in the brain and spinal cord. This enzyme is located in lysosomes, which are structures in cells that break down toxic substances and act as recycling centers. Within lysosomes, beta-hexosaminidase A helps break down a fatty substance called GM2 ganglioside.

Mutations in the *HEXA* gene disrupt the activity of beta-hexosaminidase A, which prevents the enzyme from breaking down GM2 ganglioside. As a result, this substance accumulates to toxic levels, particularly in neurons in the brain and spinal cord. Progressive damage caused by the buildup of GM2 ganglioside leads to the destruction of these neurons, which causes the signs and symptoms seen in Tay-Sachs disease.

What Are the Signs and Symptoms of Tay-Sachs Disease?

The most common form of Tay-Sachs disease begins in infancy. Infants with this disorder typically appear normal until the age of 3 to 6 months, when development slows and muscles used for movement weaken. Affected infants lose motor skills such as turning over, sitting, and crawling. As the disease progresses, infants develop seizures, vision and hearing loss, mental retardation, and paralysis. An eye abnormality called a cherry-red spot, which can be identified with an eye examination, is characteristic of this disorder. Children with this severe form of Tay-Sachs disease usually live only into early childhood.

Other forms of Tay-Sachs disease are much rarer. Signs and symptoms can begin in childhood, adolescence, or adulthood and are usually milder than those seen with the infantile form of Tay-Sachs disease. As in the infantile form, mental abilities and coordination are affected. Characteristic features include muscle weakness, loss of muscle coordination (ataxia) and other problems with movement, speech problems, and mental illness. These signs and symptoms vary widely among people with late-onset forms of Tay-Sachs disease.

Is There Any Treatment?

Presently there is no specific treatment for Tay-Sachs disease. Anticonvulsant medicine may initially control seizures. Other supportive treatment includes proper nutrition and hydration and techniques to keep the airway open. Children may eventually need a feeding tube.

What Is the Prognosis?

Even with the best of care, children with Tay-Sachs disease usually die by age 4, from recurring infection.

Chapter 30

Mitochondrial Diseases

What Are Mitochondrial Diseases?

Mitochondria are tiny parts of almost every cell in your body. Mitochondria are like the powerhouse of the cells. They turn sugar and oxygen into energy that the cells need to work.

In mitochondrial diseases, the mitochondria cannot efficiently turn sugar and oxygen into energy, so the cells do not work correctly.

There are many types of mitochondrial disease, and they can affect different parts of the body: the brain, kidneys, muscles, heart, eyes, ears, and others. Mitochondrial diseases can affect one part of the body or can affect many parts. They can affect those part(s) mildly or very seriously.

Not everyone with a mitochondrial disease will show symptoms. However, when discussing the group of mitochondrial diseases that tend to affect children, symptoms usually appear in the toddler and preschool years.

Mitochondrial diseases and mitochondrial disorders are the same thing.

Is there a Relationship between Mitochondrial Disease and Autism?

A child with a mitochondrial disease:

- may also have an autism spectrum disorder,

This chapter includes text excerpted from "Mitochondrial Disease-Frequently Asked Questions," Centers for Disease Control and Prevention (CDC), August 12, 2015.

- may have some of the symptoms/signs of autism, or

- may not have any signs or symptoms related to autism.

A child with autism may or may not have a mitochondrial disease. When a child has both autism and a mitochondrial disease, they sometimes have other problems as well, including epilepsy, problems with muscle tone, and/or movement disorders.

More research is needed to find out how common it is for people to have autism and a mitochondrial disorder. Right now, it seems rare. In general, more research about mitochondrial disease and autism is needed.

What Is Regressive Encephalopathy?

Encephalopathy is a medical term for a disease or disorder of the brain. It usually means a slowing down of brain function.

Regression happens when a person loses skills that they used to have like walking or talking or even being social.

Regressive encephalopathy means there is a disease or disorder in the brain that makes a person lose skills they once had.

We know that sometimes children with mitochondrial diseases seem to be developing as they should, but around toddler or preschool age, they regress. The disease was there all the time, but something happens that "sets it off". This could be something like malnutrition, an illness such as flu, a high fever, dehydration, or it could be something else.

Is There a Relationship Between Autism and Encephalopathy?

Most children with an autism spectrum disorder do not and have not had an encephalopathy. Some children with an autism spectrum disorder have had regression and some have had a regressive encephalopathy.

What Do We Know about the Relationship between Mitochondrial Disease and Other Disorders Related to the Brain?

Different parts of the brain have different functions. The area of the brain that is damaged by a mitochondrial disease determines how the person is impacted. This means that a person could have seizures; trouble talking or interacting with people; difficulty eating; muscle weakness, or other problems. They could have one issue or several.

Do Vaccines Cause or Worsen Mitochondrial Diseases?

As of now, there are no scientific studies that say vaccines cause or worsen mitochondrial diseases. We do know that certain illnesses that can be prevented by vaccines, such as the flu, can trigger the regression that is related to a mitochondrial disease. More research is needed to determine if there are rare cases where underlying mitochondrial disorders are triggered by anything related to vaccines. However, we know that for most children, vaccines are a safe and important way to prevent them from getting life-threatening diseases.

Are All Children Routinely Tested for Mitochondrial Diseases? What about Children with Autism?

Children are not routinely tested for mitochondrial diseases. This includes children with autism and other developmental delays.

Testing is not easy and may involve getting multiple samples of blood, and often samples of muscle. Doctors decide whether testing for mitochondrial diseases should be done based on a child's signs and symptoms.

Should I Have My Child Tested for a Mitochondrial Disease?

If you are worried that your child might have a mitochondrial disease, talk to your child's doctor.

Chapter 31

Neurofibromatosis

What Are the Neurofibromatoses?

The neurofibromatoses are a group of three genetically distinct disorders that cause tumors to grow in the nervous system. Tumors begin in the supporting cells that make up the nerve and the myelin sheath (the thin membrane that envelops and protects the nerves), rather than the cells that actually transmit information. The type of tumor that develops depends on the type of supporting cells involved.

Scientists have classified the disorders as **neurofibromatosis type 1** (NF1, also called von Recklinghaus disease), **neurofibromatosis type 2** (NF2), and a type that was once considered to be a variation of NF2 but is now called **schwannomatosis**. An estimated 100,000 Americans have a neurofibromatosis disorder, which occurs in both sexes and in all races and ethnic groups.

The most common nerve-associated tumors in NF1 are neurofibromas (tumors of the peripheral nerves), whereas schwannomas (tumors that begin in Schwann cells that help form the myelin sheath) are most common in NF2 and schwannomatosis. Most tumors are benign, although occasionally they may become cancerous.

Why these tumors occur still isn't completely known, but it appears to be related mainly to mutations in genes that play key roles in

This chapter includes text excerpted from "Neurofibromatosis Fact Sheet," National Institute of Neurological Disorders and Stroke (NINDS), February 3, 2016.

suppressing cell growth in the nervous system. These mutations keep the genes—identified as *NF1, NF2* and *SMARCB1/INI1*—from making normal proteins that control cell production. Without the normal function of these proteins, cells multiply out of control and form tumors.

What Is NF1?

NF1 is the most common neurofibromatosis, occurring in 1 in 3,000 to 4,000 individuals in the United States. Although many affected people inherit the disorder, between 30 and 50 percent of new cases result from a spontaneous genetic mutation of unknown cause. Once this mutation has taken place, the mutant gene can be passed to succeeding generations.

What Are the Signs and Symptoms of NF1?

To diagnose NF1, a doctor looks for two or more of the following:

- six or more light brown spots on the skin (often called "café-au-lait" spots), measuring more than 5 millimeters in diameter in children or more than 15 millimeters across in adolescents and adults;

- two or more neurofibromas, or one plexiform neurofibroma (a neurofibroma that involves many nerves);

- freckling in the area of the armpit or the groin;

- two or more growths on the iris of the eye (known as Lisch nodules or iris hamartomas);

- a tumor on the optic nerve (called an optic nerve glioma)

- abnormal development of the spine (scoliosis), the temple (sphenoid) bone of the skull, or the tibia (one of the long bones of the shin);

- a parent, sibling, or child with NF1.

When Do Symptoms Appear?

Many children with NF1 have larger than normal head circumference and are shorter than average. Hydrocephalus, the abnormal buildup of fluid in the brain, is a possible complication of the disorder. Headache and epilepsy are also more likely in individuals with NF1 than in the healthy population.

Cardiovascular complications associated with NF1 include congenital heart defects, high blood pressure (hypertension), and constricted, blocked, or damaged blood vessels (vasculopathy).

Children with NF1 may have poor language and visual-spatial skills, and perform less well on academic achievement tests, including those that measure reading, spelling, and math skills. Learning disabilities, such as attention deficit hyperactivity disorder (ADHD), are common in children with NF1. An estimated 3 to 5 percent of tumors may become cancerous, requiring aggressive treatment. These tumors are called malignant peripheral nerve sheath tumors.

What Is the Prognosis for Someone with NF1?

NF1 is a progressive disorder, which means most symptoms will worsen over time, although a small number of people may have symptoms that remain constant. It isn't possible to predict the course of an individual's disorder. In general, most people with NF1 will develop mild to moderate symptoms. Most people with NF1 have a normal life expectancy. Neurofibromas on or under the skin can increase with age and cause cosmetic and psychological issues.

How Is NF1 Treated?

Scientists don't know how to prevent neurofibromas from growing. Surgery is often recommended to remove tumors that become symptomatic and may become cancerous, as well as for tumors that cause significant cosmetic disfigurement. Several surgical options exist, but there is no general agreement among doctors about when surgery should be performed or which surgical option is best. Individuals considering surgery should carefully weigh the risks and benefits of all their options to determine which treatment is right for them. Treatment for neurofibromas that become malignant may include surgery, radiation, or chemotherapy. Surgery, radiation and/or chemotherapy may also be used to control or reduce the size of optic nerve gliomas when vision is threatened. Some bone malformations, such as scoliosis, can be corrected surgically.

Treatments for other conditions associated with NF1 are aimed at controlling or relieving symptoms. Headache and seizures are treated with medications. Since children with NF1 have a higher than average risk for learning disabilities, they should undergo a detailed neurological exam before they enter school. Once these children are in school, teachers or parents who suspect there is evidence of one or more learning disabilities should request an evaluation that includes an IQ test and the standard range of tests to evaluate verbal and spatial skills.

What Is NF2?

This rare disorder affects about 1 in 25,000 people. Approximately 50 percent of affected people inherit the disorder; in others the disorder is caused by a spontaneous genetic mutation of unknown cause. The hallmark finding in NF2 is the presence of slow-growing tumors on the eighth cranial nerves. These nerves have two branches: the acoustic branch helps people hear by transmitting sound sensations to the brain; and the vestibular branch helps people maintain their balance.

The characteristic tumors of NF2 are called vestibular schwannomas because of their location and the types of cells involved. As these tumors grow, they may press against and damage nearby structures such as other cranial nerves and the brain stem, the latter which can cause serious disability. Schwannomas in NF2 may occur along any nerve in the body, including the spinal nerves, other cranial nerves, and peripheral nerves in the body. These tumors may be seen as bumps under the skin (when the nerves involved are just under the skin surface) or can also be seen on the skin surface as small (less than 1 inch), dark, rough areas of hairy skin. In children, tumors may be smoother, less pigmented, and less hairy.

Although individuals with NF2 may have schwannomas that resemble small, flesh-colored skin flaps, they rarely have the café-au-lait spots that are seen in NF1.

Individuals with NF2 are at risk for developing other types of nervous system tumors, such as ependymomas and gliomas (two tumor types that grow in the spinal cord) and meningiomas (tumors that grow along the protective layers surrounding the brain and spinal cord). Affected individuals may develop cataracts at an earlier age or changes in the retina that may affect vision. Individuals with NF2 may also develop problems with nerve function independent of tumors, usually symmetric numbness and weakness in the extremities, due to the development of a peripheral neuropathy.

What Are the Signs and Symptoms of NF2?

To diagnose NF2, a doctor looks for the following:

- bilateral vestibular schwannomas; or

- a family history of NF2 (parent, sibling, or child) plus a unilateral vestibular schwannoma before age 30; or

- any two of the following:

  - glioma,

  - meningioma,

  - schwannoma; or

  - juvenile posterior subcapsular/lenticular opacity (cataract) or juvenile cortical cataract.

When Do Symptoms Appear?

Signs of NF2 may be present in childhood but are so subtle that they can be overlooked, especially in children who don't have a family history of the disorder. Typically, symptoms of NF2 are noticed between 18 and 22 years of age. The most frequent first symptom is hearing loss or ringing in the ears (tinnitus). Less often, the first visit to a doctor will be because of disturbances in balance, visual impairment (such as vision loss from cataracts), weakness in an arm or leg, seizures, or skin tumors.

What Is the Prognosis for Someone with NF2?

Because NF2 is so rare, few studies have been done to look at the natural progression of the disorder. The course of NF2 varies greatly among individuals, although inherited NF2 appears to run a similar course among affected family members. Generally, vestibular schwannomas grow slowly, and balance and hearing deteriorate over a period of years. A recent study suggests that an earlier age of onset and the presence of meningiomas are associated with greater mortality risk.

How Is NF2 Treated?

NF2 is best managed at a specialty clinic with an initial screening and annual follow-up evaluations (more frequent if the disease is severe). Improved diagnostic technologies, such as magnetic resonance imaging (MRI), can reveal tumors of the vestibular nerve as small as a few millimeters in diameter. Vestibular schwannomas grow slowly, but they can grow large enough to engulf one of the eighth cranial nerves and cause brain stem compression and damage to surrounding cranial nerves.

Surgical options depend on tumor size and the extent of hearing loss. There is no general agreement among doctors about when surgery should be performed or which surgical option is best. Individuals considering surgery should carefully weigh the risks and benefits of all options to determine which treatment is right for them. Surgery to remove the entire tumor while it's still small might help preserve hearing. If hearing is lost during this surgery, but the auditory nerve is maintained, the surgical placement of a cochlear implant (a device placed in the inner ear, or cochlea, that processes electronic signals from sound waves to the auditory nerve) may be an option to improve hearing.

As tumors grow larger, it becomes harder to surgically preserve hearing and the auditory nerve. The development of the penetrating auditory brain stem implant (a device that stimulates the hearing portions of the brain) can restore some hearing in individuals who have completely lost hearing and do not have an auditory nerve present. Surgery for other tumors associated with NF2 is aimed at controlling or relieving symptoms. Surgery also can correct cataracts and retinal abnormalities.

Chapter 32

Neuromuscular Disorders

Chapter Contents

Section 32.1

Charcot-Marie-Tooth Disease

This section includes text excerpted from "Charcot-Marie-
Tooth Disease Fact Sheet," National Institute of Neurological
Disorders and Stroke (NINDS), January 14, 2016.

What Is Charcot-Marie-Tooth Disease?

Charcot-Marie-Tooth disease (CMT) is one of the most common
inherited neurological disorders, affecting approximately 1 in 2,500
people in the United States. The disease is named for the three physicians who first identified it in 1886—Jean-Martin Charcot and Pierre
Marie in Paris, France, and Howard Henry Tooth in Cambridge,
England. CMT, also known as hereditary motor and sensory neuropathy (HMSN) or peroneal muscular atrophy, comprises a group
of disorders that affect peripheral nerves. The peripheral nerves lie
outside the brain and spinal cord and supply the muscles and sensory
organs in the limbs. Disorders that affect the peripheral nerves are
called peripheral neuropathies.

What Are the Symptoms of Charcot-Marie-Tooth Disease (CMT)?

The neuropathy of CMT affects both motor and sensory nerves.
(Motor nerves cause muscles to contract and control voluntary muscle activity such as speaking, walking, breathing, and swallowing.) A
typical feature includes weakness of the foot and lower leg muscles,
which may result in foot drop and a high-stepped gait with frequent
tripping or falls. Foot deformities, such as high arches and hammertoes
(a condition in which the middle joint of a toe bends upwards) are also
characteristic due to weakness of the small muscles in the feet.

In addition, the lower legs may take on an "inverted champagne
bottle" appearance due to the loss of muscle bulk. Later in the disease,
weakness and muscle atrophy may occur in the hands, resulting in
difficulty with carrying out fine motor skills (the coordination of small
movements usually in the fingers, hands, wrists, feet, and tongue).

Onset of symptoms is most often in adolescence or early adulthood, but some individuals develop symptoms in mid-adulthood. The severity of symptoms varies greatly among individuals and even among family members with the disease. Progression of symptoms is gradual. Pain can range from mild to severe, and some people may need to rely on foot or leg braces or other orthopedic devices to maintain mobility. Although in rare cases, individuals may have respiratory muscle weakness, CMT is not considered a fatal disease and people with most forms of CMT have a normal life expectancy.

What Causes Charcot-Marie-Tooth Disease?

A nerve cell communicates information to distant targets by sending electrical signals down a long, thin part of the cell called the axon. In order to increase the speed at which these electrical signals travel, the axon is insulated by myelin, which is produced by another type of cell called the Schwann cell. Myelin twists around the axon like a jelly-roll cake and prevents the loss of electrical signals. Without an intact axon and myelin sheath, peripheral nerve cells are unable to activate target muscles or relay sensory information from the limbs back to the brain.

CMT is caused by mutations in genes that produce proteins involved in the structure and function of either the peripheral nerve axon or the myelin sheath. Although different proteins are abnormal in different forms of CMT disease, all of the mutations affect the normal function of the peripheral nerves. Consequently, these nerves slowly degenerate and lose the ability to communicate with their distant targets. The degeneration of motor nerves results in muscle weakness and atrophy in the extremities (arms, legs, hands, or feet), and in some cases the degeneration of sensory nerves results in a reduced ability to feel heat, cold, and pain.

The gene mutations in CMT disease are usually inherited. Each of us normally possesses two copies of every gene, one inherited from each parent. Some forms of CMT are inherited in an autosomal dominant fashion, which means that only one copy of the abnormal gene is needed to cause the disease. Other forms of CMT are inherited in an autosomal recessive fashion, which means that both copies of the abnormal gene must be present to cause the disease. Still other forms of CMT are inherited in an X-linked fashion, which means that the abnormal gene is located on the X chromosome. The X and Y chromosomes determine an individual's sex. Individuals with two X chromosomes are female and individuals with one X and one Y chromosome are male.

In rare cases the gene mutation causing CMT disease is a new mutation which occurs spontaneously in the individual's genetic material and has not been passed down through the family.

What Are the Types of Charcot-Marie-Tooth Disease?

There are many forms of CMT disease, including CMT1, CMT2, CMT3, CMT4, and CMTX. **CMT1**, caused by abnormalities in the myelin sheath, has three main types. **CMT1A** is an autosomal dominant disease that results from a duplication of the gene on chromosome 17 that carries the instructions for producing the peripheral myelin protein-22 (PMP-22). The PMP-22 protein is a critical component of the myelin sheath. Overexpression of this gene causes the structure and function of the myelin sheath to be abnormal. Patients experience weakness and atrophy of the muscles of the lower legs beginning in adolescence; later they experience hand weakness and sensory loss. Interestingly, a different neuropathy distinct from CMT1A called **hereditary neuropathy with predisposition to pressure palsy (HNPP)** is caused by a deletion of one of the *PMP-22* genes. In this case, abnormally low levels of the *PMP-22* gene result in episodic, recurrent demyelinating neuropathy.

CMT1B is an autosomal dominant disease caused by mutations in the gene that carries the instructions for manufacturing the myelin protein zero (P0), which is another critical component of the myelin sheath. Most of these mutations are point mutations, meaning a mistake occurs in only one letter of the DNA genetic code. To date, scientists have identified more than 120 different point mutations in the P0 gene. As a result of abnormalities in P0, CMT1B produces symptoms similar to those found in CMT1A. The less common CMT1C, CMT1D, and CMT1E, which also have symptoms similar to those found in CMT1A, are caused by mutations in the *LITAF, EGR2,* and *NEFL* genes, respectively.

CMT2 results from abnormalities in the axon of the peripheral nerve cell rather than the myelin sheath. It is less common than CMT1. CMT2A, the most common axonal form of CMT, is caused by mutations in Mitofusin 2, a protein associated with mitochondrial fusion. CMT2A has also been linked to mutations in the gene that codes for the kinesin family member 1B-beta protein, but this has not been replicated in other cases. Kinesins are proteins that act as motors to help power the transport of materials along the cell. Other less common forms of CMT2 have been recently identified and are associated with various genes: *CMT2B* (associated with *RAB7*), *CMT2D* (GARS). *CMT2E* (NEFL), *CMT2H* (HSP27), and *CMT2l* (HSP22).

CMT3 or **Dejerine-Sottas disease** is a severe demyelinating neuropathy that begins in infancy. Infants have severe muscle atrophy, weakness, and sensory problems. This rare disorder can be caused by a specific point mutation in the *P0* gene or a point mutation in the *PMP-22* gene.

CMT4 comprises several different subtypes of autosomal recessive demyelinating motor and sensory neuropathies. Each neuropathy subtype is caused by a different genetic mutation, may affect a particular ethnic population, and produces distinct physiologic or clinical characteristics. Individuals with CMT4 generally develop symptoms of leg weakness in childhood and by adolescence they may not be able to walk. Several genes have been identified as causing CMT4, including *GDAP1* (CMT4A), *MTMR13* (CMT4B1), *MTMR2* (CMT4B2), *SH3TC2* (CMT4C), *NDG1* (CMT4D), *EGR2* (CMT4E), *PRX* (CMT4F), *FDG4* (CMT4H), and *FIG4* (CMT4J).

CMTX is caused by a point mutation in the *connexin-32* gene on the X chromosome. The connexin-32 protein is expressed in Schwann cells-cells that wrap around nerve axons, making up a single segment of the myelin sheath. This protein may be involved in Schwann cell communication with the axon. Males who inherit one mutated gene from their mothers show moderate to severe symptoms of the disease beginning in late childhood or adolescence (the Y chromosome that males inherit from their fathers does not have the *connexin-32* gene). Females who inherit one mutated gene from one parent and one normal gene from the other parent may develop mild symptoms in adolescence or later or may not develop symptoms of the disease at all.

How Is Charcot-Marie-Tooth Disease Diagnosed?

Diagnosis of CMT begins with a standard medical history, family history, and neurological examination. Individuals will be asked about the nature and duration of their symptoms and whether other family members have the disease. During the neurological examination a physician will look for evidence of muscle weakness in the individual's arms, legs, hands, and feet, decreased muscle bulk, reduced tendon reflexes, and sensory loss. Doctors look for evidence of foot deformities, such as high arches, hammertoes, inverted heel, or flat feet. Other orthopedic problems, such as mild scoliosis or hip dysplasia, may also be present. A specific sign that may be found in people with CMT1 is nerve enlargement that may be felt or even seen through the skin. These enlarged nerves, called hypertrophic nerves, are caused by abnormally thickened myelin sheaths.

If CMT is suspected, the physician may order electrodiagnostic tests. This testing consists of two parts: nerve conduction studies and electromyography (EMG). During nerve conduction studies, electrodes are placed on the skin over a peripheral motor or sensory nerve. These electrodes produce a small electric shock that may cause mild discomfort. This electrical impulse stimulates sensory and motor nerves and provides quantifiable information that the doctor can use to arrive at a diagnosis. EMG involves inserting a needle electrode through the skin to measure the bioelectrical activity of muscles. Specific abnormalities in the readings signify axon degeneration. EMG may be useful in further characterizing the distribution and severity of peripheral nerve involvement.

Genetic testing is available for some types of CMT and results are usually enough to confirm a diagnosis. In addition, genetic counseling is available to assist individuals in understanding their condition and plan for the future.

If all the diagnostic work-up in inconclusive or genetic testing comes back negative, a neurologist may perform a nerve biopsy to confirm the diagnosis. A nerve biopsy involves removing a small piece of peripheral nerve through an incision in the skin. This is most often done by removing a piece of the nerve that runs down the calf of the leg. The nerve is then examined under a microscope. Individuals with CMT1 typically show signs of abnormal myelination. Specifically, "onion bulb" formations may be seen which represent axons surrounded by layers of demyelinating and remyelinating Schwann cells. Individuals with CMT1 usually show signs of axon degeneration. Recently, skin biopsy has been used to study unmyelinated and myelinated nerve fibers in a minimally invasive way, but their clinical use in CMT has not yet been established.

How Is Charcot-Marie-Tooth Disease Treated?

There is no cure for CMT, but physical therapy, occupational therapy, braces and other orthopedic devices, and even orthopedic surgery can help individuals cope with the disabling symptoms of the disease.

In addition, pain-killing drugs can be prescribed for individuals who have severe pain.

Physical and occupational therapy, the preferred treatment for CMT, involves muscle strength training, muscle and ligament stretching, stamina training, and moderate aerobic exercise. Most therapists recommend a specialized treatment program designed with the approval of the person's physician to fit individual abilities and needs. Therapists also suggest entering into a treatment program early; muscle strengthening may delay or reduce muscle atrophy, so strength training is most useful if it begins before nerve degeneration and muscle weakness progress to the point of disability.

Stretching may prevent or reduce joint deformities that result from uneven muscle pull on bones. Exercises to help build stamina or increase endurance will help prevent the fatigue that results from performing everyday activities that require strength and mobility. Moderate aerobic activity can help to maintain cardiovascular fitness and overall health. Most therapists recommend low-impact or no-impact exercises, such as biking or swimming, rather than activities such as walking or jogging, which may put stress on fragile muscles and joints.

Many CMT patients require ankle braces and other orthopedic devices to maintain everyday mobility and prevent injury. Ankle braces can help prevent ankle sprains by providing support and stability during activities such as walking or climbing stairs. High-top shoes or boots can also provide support for weak ankles. Thumb splints can help with hand weakness and loss of fine motor skills. Assistive devices should be used before disability sets in because the devices may prevent muscle strain and reduce muscle weakening. Some individuals with CMT may decide to have orthopedic surgery to reverse foot and joint deformities.

Section 32.2

Early-Onset Primary Dystonia

This section includes text excerpted from "Early-Onset
Primary Dystonia," Genetic Home Reference (GHR),
National Institutes of Health (NIH), March 7, 2016.

What Is Early-Onset Primary Dystonia?

Early-onset primary dystonia is a condition characterized by progressive problems with movement, typically beginning in childhood.
Dystonia is a movement disorder that involves involuntary tensing of
the muscles (muscle contractions), twisting of specific body parts such
as an arm or a leg, rhythmic shaking (tremors), and other uncontrolled
movements. A primary dystonia is one that occurs without other neurological symptoms, such as seizures or a loss of intellectual function
(dementia). Early-onset primary dystonia does not affect a person's
intelligence.

On average, the signs and symptoms of early-onset primary dystonia appear around age 12. Abnormal muscle spasms in an arm or a
leg are usually the first sign. These unusual movements initially occur
while a person is doing a specific action, such as writing or walking. In
some affected people, dystonia later spreads to other parts of the body
and may occur at rest. The abnormal movements persist throughout
life, but they do not usually cause pain.

The signs and symptoms of early-onset primary dystonia vary from
person to person, even among affected members of the same family.
The mildest cases affect only a single part of the body, causing isolated
problems such as a writer's cramp in the hand. Severe cases involve
abnormal movements affecting many regions of the body.

How Common Is Early-Onset Primary Dystonia?

Early-onset primary dystonia is among the most common forms of
childhood dystonia. This disorder occurs most frequently in people of
Ashkenazi (central and eastern European) Jewish heritage, affecting
1 in 3,000 to 9,000 people in this population. The condition is less

common among people with other backgrounds; it is estimated to affect 1 in 10,000 to 30,000 non-Jewish people worldwide.

What Genes Are Related to Early-Onset Primary Dystonia?

A particular mutation in the *TOR1A* gene (also known as *DYT1*) is responsible for most cases of early-onset primary dystonia. The *TOR1A* gene provides instructions for making a protein called torsinA. Although little is known about its function, this protein may help process and transport other proteins within cells. It appears to be critical for the normal development and function of nerve cells in the brain.

A mutation in the *TOR1A* gene alters the structure of torsinA. The altered protein's effect on the function of nerve cells in the brain is unclear. People with early-onset primary dystonia do not have a loss of nerve cells or obvious changes in the structure of the brain that would explain the abnormal muscle contractions. Instead, the altered torsinA protein may have subtle effects on the connections between nerve cells and likely disrupts chemical signaling between nerve cells that control movement. Researchers are working to determine how a change in this protein leads to the characteristic features of this disorder.

How Do People Inherit Early-Onset Primary Dystonia?

Mutations in the *TOR1A* gene are inherited in an autosomal dominant pattern, which means one of the two copies of the gene is altered in each cell. Many people who have a mutation in this gene are not affected by the disorder and may never know they have the mutation. Only 30 to 40 percent of people who inherit a *TOR1A* mutation will ever develop signs and symptoms of early-onset primary dystonia.

Everyone who has been diagnosed with early-onset primary dystonia has inherited a *TOR1A* mutation from one parent. The parent may or may not have signs and symptoms of the condition, and other family members may or may not be affected.

Section 32.3

Friedreich Ataxia

This section contains text excerpted from the following sources: Text
beginning with the heading "What Is Friedreich Ataxia?" is excerpted
from "Friedreich Ataxia," Genetic Home Reference (GHR), National
Institutes of Health (NIH), March 7, 2016; Text under the heading
"What Are the Signs and Symptoms?" is excerpted from "Friedreich's
Ataxia Fact Sheet," National Institute of Neurological Disorders
and Stroke (NINDS), February 19, 2016.

What Is Friedreich Ataxia?

Friedreich ataxia is a genetic condition that affects the nervous system and causes movement problems. People with this condition develop
impaired muscle coordination (ataxia) that worsens over time. Other
features of this condition include the gradual loss of strength and sensation in the arms and legs, muscle stiffness (spasticity), and impaired
speech. Individuals with Friedreich ataxia often have a form of heart
disease called hypertrophic cardiomyopathy that enlarges and weakens
the heart muscle. Some affected individuals develop diabetes, impaired
vision, hearing loss, or an abnormal curvature of the spine (scoliosis).

Most people with Friedreich ataxia begin to experience the signs
and symptoms of the disorder around puberty. Poor balance when
walking and slurred speech are often the first noticeable features.
Affected individuals typically require the use of a wheelchair about
10 years after signs and symptoms appear.

About 25 percent of people with Friedreich ataxia have an atypical
form that begins after age 25. Affected individuals who develop Friedreich ataxia between ages 26 and 39 are considered to have late-onset Friedreich ataxia (LOFA). When the signs and symptoms begin after age 40
the condition is called very late-onset Friedreich ataxia (VLOFA). LOFA
and VLOFA usually progress more slowly than typical Friedreich ataxia.

How Common Is Friedreich Ataxia?

Friedreich ataxia is estimated to affect 1 in 40,000 people. This
condition is found in people with European, Middle Eastern, or North
African ancestry. It is rarely identified in other ethnic groups.

What Genes Are Related to Friedreich Ataxia?

Mutations in the *FXN* gene cause Friedreich ataxia. This gene provides instructions for making a protein called frataxin. Although its role is not fully understood, frataxin appears to be important for the normal function of mitochondria, the energy-producing centers within cells. One region of the *FXN* gene contains a segment of DNA known as a GAA trinucleotide repeat. This segment is made up of a series of three DNA building blocks (one guanine and two adenines) that appear multiple times in a row. Normally, this segment is repeated 5 to 33 times within the *FXN* gene.

In people with Friedreich ataxia, the GAA segment is repeated 66 to more than 1,000 times. The length of the GAA trinucleotide repeat appears to be related to the age at which the symptoms of Friedreich ataxia appear. People with GAA segments repeated fewer than 300 times tend to have a later appearance of symptoms (after age 25) than those with larger GAA trinucleotide repeats. The abnormally long GAA trinucleotide repeat disrupts the production of frataxin, which severely reduces the amount of this protein in cells. Certain nerve and muscle cells cannot function properly with a shortage of frataxin, leading to the characteristic signs and symptoms of Friedreich ataxia.

What Are the Signs and Symptoms?

Symptoms typically begin between the ages of 5 and 15 years, although they sometimes appear in adulthood and on rare occasions as late as age 75. The first symptom to appear is usually gait ataxia, or difficulty walking. The ataxia gradually worsens and slowly spreads to the arms and the trunk. There is often loss of sensation in the extremities, which may spread to other parts of the body. Other features include loss of tendon reflexes, especially in the knees and ankles. Most people with Friedreich ataxia develop scoliosis (a curving of the spine to one side), which often requires surgical intervention for treatment.

Dysarthria (slowness and slurring of speech) develops and can get progressively worse. Many individuals with later stages of Friedreich ataxia develop hearing and vision loss.

Other symptoms that may occur include chest pain, shortness of breath, and heart palpitations. These symptoms are the result of various forms of heart disease that often accompany Friedreich ataxia, such as hypertrophic cardiomyopathy (enlargement of the heart), myocardial fibrosis (formation of fiber-like material in the muscles of the heart), and cardiac failure. Heart rhythm abnormalities such as tachycardia (fast heart rate) and heart block (impaired conduction of cardiac impulses within the heart) are also common.

About 20 percent of people with Friedreich ataxia develop carbohydrate intolerance and 10 percent develop diabetes. Most individuals with Friedreich ataxia tire very easily and find that they require more rest and take a longer time to recover from common illnesses such as colds and flu.

The rate of progression varies from person to person. Generally, within 10 to 20 years after the appearance of the first symptoms, the person is confined to a wheelchair, and in later stages of the disease individuals may become completely incapacitated.

Friedreich ataxia can shorten life expectancy, and heart disease is the most common cause of death. However, some people with less severe features of Friedreich ataxia live into their sixties, seventies, or older.

How Is Friedreich Ataxia Diagnosed?

A diagnosis of Friedreich ataxia requires a careful clinical examination, which includes a medical history and a thorough physical exam, in particular looking for balance difficulty, loss of proprioception (joint sensation), absence of reflexes, and signs of neurological problems. Genetic testing now provides a conclusive diagnosis. Other tests that may aid in the diagnosis or management of the disorder include:

- electromyogram (EMG), which measures the electrical activity of muscle cells,

- nerve conduction studies, which measure the speed with which nerves transmit impulses,

- electrocardiogram (ECG), which gives a graphic presentation of the electrical activity or beat pattern of the heart,

- echocardiogram, which records the position and motion of the heart muscle,

- blood tests to check for elevated glucose levels and vitamin E levels, and

- magnetic resonance imaging (MRI) or computed tomography (CT) scans, tests which provide brain and spinal cord images that are useful for ruling out other neurological conditions.

How Is Friedreich Ataxia Inherited?

Friedreich ataxia is an autosomal recessive disease, meaning individuals only develop symptoms if they inherit two copies of the defective *FXN* gene, one from their father and one from their mother. A person who has only one abnormal copy of the gene is called a carrier. A carrier will not develop the disease but could pass the gene mutation on to his or her children. If both parents are carriers, their children will have a 1 in 4 chance of having the disease and a 1 in 2 chance of inheriting one abnormal gene that they, in turn, could pass on to their children. About one in 90 Americans of European ancestry carries an abnormal *FXN* gene.

In 1996, an international research team identified the Friedreich ataxia gene on chromosome 9. The *FXN* gene codes for production of a protein called "frataxin." In the normal version of the gene, a sequence of DNA (labeled "GAA") is repeated between 7 and 22 times. In the defective *FXN* gene, the repeat occurs over and over again—hundreds, even up to a thousand times.

This abnormal pattern, called a triplet repeat expansion, has been implicated as the cause of several dominantly inherited diseases, but Friedreich ataxia is the only known recessive genetic disorder caused by the problem. Almost all people with Friedreich ataxia have two copies of this mutant form of *FXN*, but it is not found in all cases of the disease. About two percent of affected individuals have other defects in the *FXN* gene that are responsible for causing the disease.

The triplet repeat expansion greatly disrupts the normal production of frataxin. Frataxin is found in the energy-producing parts of the cell called mitochondria. Research suggests that without a normal level of frataxin, certain cells in the body (especially peripheral nerve, spinal cord, brain and heart muscle cells) cannot effectively produce energy and have been hypothesized to have a buildup of toxic byproducts leading to what is called "oxidative stress." It also may lead to increased levels of iron in the mitochondria. When the excess iron reacts with oxygen, free radicals can be produced. Although free radicals are essential molecules in the body's metabolism, they can also destroy cells and harm the body. Research continues on this subject.

Can Friedreich Ataxia Be Cured or Treated?

As with many degenerative diseases of the nervous system, there is currently no cure or effective treatment for Friedreich ataxia. However, many of the symptoms and accompanying complications can be treated to help individuals maintain optimal functioning as long as possible. Doctors can prescribe treatments for diabetes, if present; some of the heart problems can be treated with medication as well. Orthopedic problems such as foot deformities and scoliosis can be corrected with braces or surgery. Physical therapy may prolong use of the arms and legs. Advances in understanding the genetics of Friedreich ataxia are leading to breakthroughs in treatment. Research has moved forward to the point where clinical trials of proposed treatments are presently occurring for Friedreich ataxia.

What Services Are Useful to Friedreich Ataxia Patients and Their Families?

Genetic testing is essential for proper clinical diagnosis, and can aid in prenatal diagnosis and determining a person's carrier status. Genetic counselors can help explain how Friedreich ataxia is inherited. Psychological counseling and support groups for people with genetic diseases may also help affected individuals and their families cope with the disease.

A primary care physician can screen people for complications such as heart disease, diabetes and scoliosis, and can refer individuals to specialists such as cardiologists, physical therapists, and speech therapists to help deal with some of the other associated problems.

Support and information for families is also available through a number of private organizations. These groups can offer ways to network and communicate with others affected by Friedreich ataxia. They can also provide access to patient registries, clinical trials information, and other useful resources.

Section 32.4

Hereditary Spastic Paraplegia

This section contains text excerpted from the following sources:
Text beginning with the heading "What Is Hereditary Spastic
Paraplegia?" is excerpted from "NINDS Hereditary Spastic
Paraplegia Information Page," National Institute of Neurological
Disorders and Stroke (NINDS), February 10, 2014; Text under the
heading "What Are the Signs and Symptoms of Hereditary Spastic
Paraplegia?" is excerpted from "Hereditary Spastic Paraplegia,"
National Center for Advancing Translational Sciences (NCATS),
March 1, 2016; Text under the heading "Is There Any Treatment?"
is excerpted from "NINDS Hereditary Spastic Paraplegia
Information Page," National Institute of Neurological
Disorders and Stroke (NINDS), February 10, 2014.

What Is Hereditary Spastic Paraplegia?

Hereditary spastic paraplegia (HSP), also called familial spastic
paraparesis (FSP), refers to a group of inherited disorders that are
characterized by progressive weakness and spasticity (stiffness) of the
legs. Early in the disease course, there may be mild gait difficulties and
stiffness. These symptoms typically slowly progress so that eventually
individuals with HSP may require the assistance of a cane, walker, or
wheelchair. Though the primary features of "pure" HSP are progressive lower limb spasticity and weakness, complicated forms may be
accompanied by other symptoms. These additional impaired vision due
to cataracts and problems with the optic nerve and retina of the eye,
ataxia (lack of muscle coordination), epilepsy, cognitive impairment,
peripheral neuropathy, and deafness.

The diagnosis of HSP is primarily by neurological examination and
testing to rule out other disorders. Brain MRI abnormalities, such as
a thin corpus callosum, may be seen in some of the complicated forms
of HSP. Several genetic mutations have been identified which underlie
various forms of HSP, and specialized genetic testing and diagnosis
are available at some medical centers. HSP has several forms of inheritance. Not all children in a family will necessarily develop symptoms,
although they may be carriers of the abnormal gene. Symptoms may

begin in childhood or adulthood, depending on the particular HSP gene involved.

What Are the Signs and Symptoms of Hereditary Spastic Paraplegia?

The main symptoms include a slow, progressive, spasticity and weakness of the legs that often gets severe, requiring assistive devices. There is also difficulty with balance, clumsiness, and often muscle spasms.

How Is Hereditary Spastic Paraplegia (HSP) Diagnosed?

HSP is diagnosed on the basis of the following:

- **Characteristic clinical symptoms** of slowly progressive weakness and stiffness in the legs often accompanied by urinary urgency

- **Neurologic examination** demonstrating damage to the nerve paths connecting the spinal cord and the brain (corticospinal tract), such as spastic weakness, exaggerated reflexes, typically associated with bilateral extensor plantar responses; often accompanied by a mild inability to sense vibration in the lower part of the legs and muscle changes of the urinary bladder

- **Family history** shows a pattern of inheritance that is either autosomal dominant, autosomal recessive, or X-linked recessive inheritance

- **Identification of a disease-causing mutation in an HSP-causing gene** (Such testing is increasingly available and can confirm the diagnosis of HSP)

Is There Any Treatment?

There are no specific treatments to prevent, slow, or reverse HSP. Symptomatic treatments used for spasticity, such as muscle relaxants, are sometimes helpful. Regular physical therapy is important for muscle strength and to preserve range of motion.

What Is the Prognosis?

The prognosis for individuals with HSP varies. Some individuals are very disabled and others have only mild disability. The majority of individuals with uncomplicated HSP have a normal life expectancy.

Section 32.5

Muscular Dystrophy

This section includes text excerpted from "Muscular Dystrophy:
Hope through Research," National Institute of Neurological
Disorders and Stroke (NINDS), March 4, 2016.

What Is Muscular Dystrophy (MD)?

Muscular dystrophy (MD) refers to a group of more than 30 genetic
diseases that cause progressive weakness and degeneration of skeletal muscles used during voluntary movement. The word dystrophy is
derived from the Greek dys, which means "difficult" or "faulty," and
troph, or "nourish." These disorders vary in age of onset, severity, and
pattern of affected muscles. All forms of MD grow worse as muscles
progressively degenerate and weaken. Many individuals eventually
lose the ability to walk.

Some types of MD also affect the heart, gastrointestinal system,
endocrine glands, spine, eyes, brain, and other organs. Respiratory
and cardiac diseases may occur, and some people may develop a swallowing disorder. MD is not contagious and cannot be brought on by
injury or activity.

What Causes MD?

All of the muscular dystrophies are inherited and involve a mutation in one of the thousands of genes that program proteins critical to
muscle integrity. The body's cells don't work properly when a protein
is altered or produced in insufficient quantity (or sometimes missing
completely). Many cases of MD occur from spontaneous mutations
that are not found in the genes of either parent, and this defect can
be passed to the next generation.

Genes are like blueprints: they contain coded messages that determine a person's characteristics or traits. They are arranged along 23
rod-like pairs of chromosomes, with one half of each pair being inherited from each parent. Each half of a chromosome pair is similar to the

other, except for one pair, which determines the sex of the individual. Muscular dystrophies can be inherited in three ways:

- **Autosomal dominant inheritance** occurs when a child receives a normal gene from one parent and a defective gene from the other parent. Autosomal means the genetic mutation can occur on any of the 22 non-sex chromosomes in each of the body's cells. Dominant means only one parent needs to pass along the abnormal gene in order to produce the disorder. In families where one parent carries a defective gene, each child has a 50 percent chance of inheriting the gene and therefore the disorder. Males and females are equally at risk and the severity of the disorder can differ from person to person.

- **Autosomal recessive inheritance** means that both parents must carry and pass on the faulty gene. The parents each have one defective gene but are not affected by the disorder. Children in these families have a 25 percent chance of inheriting both copies of the defective gene and a 50 percent chance of inheriting one gene and therefore becoming a carrier, able to pass along the defect to their children. Children of either sex can be affected by this pattern of inheritance.

- **X-linked (or sex-linked) recessive inheritance** occurs when a mother carries the affected gene on one of her two X chromosomes and passes it to her son (males always inherit an X chromosome from their mother and a Y chromosome from their father, while daughters inherit an X chromosome from each parent). Sons of carrier mothers have a 50 percent chance of inheriting the disorder. Daughters also have a 50 percent chance of inheriting the defective gene but usually are not affected, since the healthy X chromosome they receive from their father can offset the faulty one received from their mother. Affected fathers cannot pass an X-linked disorder to their sons but their daughters will be carriers of that disorder. Carrier females occasionally can exhibit milder symptoms of MD.

How Many People Have MD?

MD occurs worldwide, affecting all races. Its incidence varies, as some forms are more common than others. Its most common form in children, Duchenne muscular dystrophy, affects approximately 1 in every 3,500 to 6,000 male births each year in the United States.** Some types of MD are more prevalent in certain countries and regions of the world. Many muscular dystrophies are familial, meaning there is some family history of the disease. Duchenne cases often have no prior family history. This is likely due to the large size of the dystrophin gene that is implicated in the disorder, making it a target for spontaneous mutations.

** Source: Centers for Disease Control and Prevention, National Center on Birth Defects and Developmental Disabilities, July 17, 2013.

How Does MD Affect Muscles?

Muscles are made up of thousands of muscle fibers. Each fiber is actually a number of individual cells that have joined together during development and are encased by an outer membrane. Muscle fibers that make up individual muscles are bound together by connective tissue.

Muscles are activated when an impulse, or signal, is sent from the brain through the spinal cord and peripheral nerves (nerves that connect the central nervous system to sensory organs and muscles) to the neuromuscular junction (the space between the nerve fiber and the muscle it activates). There, a release of the chemical acetylcholine triggers a series of events that cause the muscle to contract.

The muscle fiber membrane contains a group of proteins—called the dystrophin-glycoprotein complex—which prevents damage as muscle fibers contract and relax. When this protective membrane is damaged, muscle fibers begin to leak the protein creatine kinase (needed for the chemical reactions that produce energy for muscle contractions) and take on excess calcium, which causes further harm. Affected muscle fibers eventually die from this damage, leading to progressive muscle degeneration.

Although MD can affect several body tissues and organs, it most prominently affects the integrity of muscle fibers. The disease causes muscle degeneration, progressive weakness, fiber death, fiber branching and splitting, phagocytosis (in which muscle fiber material is broken down and destroyed by scavenger cells), and, in some cases, chronic or permanent shortening of tendons and muscles. Also, overall muscle strength and tendon reflexes are usually lessened or lost due to replacement of muscle by connective tissue and fat.

Are There Other MD-like Conditions?

There are many other heritable diseases that affect the muscles, the nerves, or the neuromuscular junction. Such diseases as inflammatory myopathy, progressive muscle weakness, and cardiomyopathy (heart muscle weakness that interferes with pumping ability) may produce symptoms that are very similar to those found in some forms of MD), but they are caused by different genetic defects. The differential diagnosis for people with similar symptoms includes congenital myopathy, spinal muscular atrophy, and congenital myasthenic syndromes. The sharing of symptoms among multiple neuromuscular diseases, and the prevalence of sporadic cases in families not previously affected by MD, often makes it difficult for people with MD to obtain a quick diagnosis.

Gene testing can provide a definitive diagnosis for many types of MD, but not all genes have been discovered that are responsible for some types of MD. Some individuals may have signs of MD, but carry none of the currently recognized genetic mutations. Studies of other related muscle diseases may, however, contribute to what we know about MD.

How Do the Muscular Dystrophies Differ?

There are nine major groups of the muscular dystrophies. The disorders are classified by the extent and distribution of muscle weakness, age of onset, rate of progression, severity of symptoms, and family history (including any pattern of inheritance). Although some forms of MD become apparent in infancy or childhood, others may not appear until middle age or later. Overall, incidence rates and severity vary, but each of the dystrophies causes progressive skeletal muscle deterioration, and some types affect cardiac muscle.

1. Duchenne MD is the most common childhood form of MD, as well as the most common of the muscular dystrophies overall, accounting for approximately 50 percent of all cases. Because inheritance is X-linked recessive (caused by a mutation on the X, or sex, chromosome), Duchenne MD primarily affects boys, although girls and women who carry the defective gene may show some symptoms. About one-third of the cases reflect new mutations and the rest run in families. Sisters of boys with Duchenne MD have a 50 percent chance of carrying the defective gene.

Duchenne MD usually becomes apparent during the toddler years, sometimes soon after an affected child begins to walk. Progressive weakness and muscle wasting (a decrease in muscle strength and size) caused by degenerating muscle fibers begins in the upper legs and pelvis before spreading into the upper arms. Other symptoms include loss of some reflexes, a waddling gait, frequent falls and clumsiness (especially when running), difficulty when rising from a sitting or lying position or when climbing stairs, changes to overall posture, impaired breathing, lung weakness, and cardiomyopathy. Many children are unable to run or jump. The wasting muscles, in particular the calf muscles (and, less commonly, muscles in the buttocks, shoulders, and arms), may be enlarged by an accumulation of fat and connective tissue, causing them to look larger and healthier than they actually are (called pseudohypertrophy).

As the disease progresses, the muscles in the diaphragm that assist in breathing and coughing may weaken. Affected individuals may experience breathing difficulties, respiratory infections, and swallowing problems. Bone thinning and scoliosis (curving of the spine) are common. Some affected children have varying degrees of cognitive and behavioral impairments. Between ages 3 and 6, children may show brief periods of physical improvement followed later on by progressive muscle degeneration. Children with Duchenne MD typically lose the ability to walk by early adolescence. Without aggressive care, they usually die in their late teens or early twenties from progressive weakness of the heart muscle, respiratory complications, or infection. However, improvements in multidisciplinary care have extended the life expectancy and improved the quality of life significantly for these children; numerous individuals with Duchenne muscular dystrophy now survive into their 30s, and some even into their 40s.

Duchenne MD results from an absence of the muscle protein dystrophin. Dystrophin is a protein found in muscle that helps muscles stay healthy and strong. Blood tests of children with Duchenne MD show an abnormally high level of creatine kinase; this finding is apparent from birth.

2. Becker MD is less severe than but closely related to Duchenne MD. People with Becker MD have partial but insufficient function of the protein dystrophin. There is greater variability in the clinical course of Becker MD compared to Duchenne MD. The disorder usually appears around age 11 but may occur as late as age 25, and affected individuals generally live into middle age or later. The rate of progressive, symmetric (on both sides of the body) muscle atrophy and weakness varies greatly among affected individuals. Many individuals are able to walk until they are in their mid-thirties or later, while others are unable to walk past their teens. Some affected individuals never need to use a wheelchair. As in Duchenne MD, muscle weakness in Becker MD is typically noticed first in the upper arms and shoulders, upper legs, and pelvis.

Early symptoms of Becker MD include walking on one's toes, frequent falls, and difficulty rising from the floor. Calf muscles may appear large and healthy as deteriorating muscle fibers are replaced by fat, and muscle activity may cause cramps in some people. Cardiac complications are not as consistently present in Becker MD compared to Duchenne MD, but may be as severe in some cases. Cognitive and behavioral impairments are not as common or severe as in Duchenne MD, but they do occur.

3. Congenital MD refers to a group of autosomal recessive muscular dystrophies that are either present at birth or become evident before age 2. They affect both boys and girls. The degree and progression of muscle weakness and degeneration vary with the type of disorder. Weakness may be first noted when children fail to meet landmarks in motor function and muscle control. Muscle degeneration may be mild or severe and is restricted primarily to skeletal muscle. The majority of individuals are unable to sit or stand without support, and some affected children may never learn to walk. There are three groups of congenital MD:

- merosin-negative disorders, where the protein merosin (found in the connective tissue that surrounds muscle fibers) is missing;

- merosin-positive disorders, in which merosin is present but other needed proteins are missing; and

- neuronal migration disorders, in which very early in the development of the fetal nervous system the migration of nerve cells (neurons) to their proper location is disrupted.

Defects in the protein merosin cause nearly half of all cases of congenital MD.

People with congenital MD may develop contractures (chronic shortening of muscles or tendons around joints, which prevents the joints from moving freely), scoliosis, respiratory and swallowing difficulties, and foot deformities. Some individuals have normal intellectual development while others become severely impaired. Weakness in diaphragm muscles may lead to respiratory failure. Congenital MD may also affect the central nervous system, causing vision and speech problems, seizures, and structural changes in the brain. Some children with the disorders die in infancy while others may live into adulthood with only minimal disability.

4. Distal MD, also called distal myopathy, describes a group of at least six specific muscle diseases that primarily affect distal muscles (those farthest away from the shoulders and hips) in the forearms, hands, lower legs, and feet. Distal dystrophies are typically less severe, progress more slowly, and involve fewer muscles than other forms of MD, although they can spread to other muscles, including the proximal ones later in the course of the disease. Distal MD can affect the heart and respiratory muscles, and individuals may eventually require the use of a ventilator. Affected individuals may not be able to perform fine hand movement and have difficulty extending the fingers. As leg muscles become affected, walking and climbing stairs become difficult and some people may be unable to hop or stand on their heels. Onset of distal MD, which affects both men and women, is typically between the ages of 40 and 60 years. In one form of distal MD, a muscle membrane protein complex called dysferlin is known to be lacking.

Although distal MD is primarily an autosomal dominant disorder, autosomal recessive forms have been reported in young adults. Symptoms are similar to those of Duchenne MD but with a different pattern of muscle damage. An infantile-onset form of autosomal recessive distal MD has also been reported. Slow but progressive weakness is often first noticed around age 1, when the child begins to walk, and continues to progress very slowly throughout adult life.

5. Emery-Dreifuss MD primarily affects boys. The disorder has two forms: one is X-linked recessive and the other is autosomal dominant.

Onset of Emery-Dreifuss MD is usually apparent by age 10, but symptoms can appear as late as the mid-twenties. This disease causes slow but progressive wasting of the upper arm and lower leg muscles and symmetric weakness. Contractures in the spine, ankles, knees, elbows, and back of the neck usually precede significant muscle weakness, which is less severe than in Duchenne MD. Contractures may cause elbows to become locked in a flexed position. The entire spine may become rigid as the disease progresses. Other symptoms include shoulder deterioration, toe-walking, and mild facial weakness. Serum creatine kinase levels may be moderately elevated. Nearly all people with Emery-Dreifuss MD have some form of heart problem by age 30, often requiring a pacemaker or other assistive device. Female carriers of the disorder often have cardiac complications without muscle weakness. Affected individuals often die in mid-adulthood from progressive pulmonary or cardiac failure. In some cases, the cardiac symptoms may be the earliest and most significant symptom of the disease, and may appear years before muscle weakness does.

6. Facioscapulohumeral MD (FSHD) initially affects muscles of the face (facio), shoulders (scapulo), and upper arms (humera) with progressive weakness. Also known as Landouzy-Dejerine disease, this third most common form of MD is an autosomal dominant disorder. Most individuals have a normal life span, but some individuals become severely disabled. Disease progression is typically very slow, with intermittent spurts of rapid muscle deterioration. Onset is usually in the teenage years but may occur as early as childhood or as late as age 40.

One hallmark of FSHD is that it commonly causes asymmetric weakness. Muscles around the eyes and mouth are often affected first, followed by weakness around the shoulders, chest, and upper arms. A particular pattern of muscle wasting causes the shoulders to appear to be slanted and the shoulder blades to appear winged. Muscles in the lower extremities may also become weakened. Reflexes are diminished, typically in the same distribution as the weakness. Changes in facial appearance may include the development of a crooked smile, a pouting look, flattened facial features, or a mask-like appearance. Some individuals cannot pucker their lips or whistle and may have difficulty swallowing, chewing, or speaking. In some individuals, muscle weakness can spread to the diaphragm, causing respiratory problems. Other symptoms may include hearing loss (particularly at high frequencies) and lordosis, an abnormal swayback curve in the spine. Contractures are rare. Some people with FSHD feel severe pain in the affected limb. Cardiac muscles are not usually affected, and significant weakness of the pelvic girdle is less common than in other forms of MD. An infant-onset form of FSHD can also cause retinal disease and some hearing loss.

7. Limb-girdle MD (LGMD) refers to more than 20 inherited conditions marked by progressive loss of muscle bulk and symmetrical weakening of voluntary muscles, primarily those in the shoulders and around the hips. At least 5 forms of autosomal dominant limb-girdle MD (known as type 1) and 17 forms of autosomal recessive limb-girdle MD (known as type 2) have been identified. Some autosomal recessive forms of the disorder are now known to be due to a deficiency of any of four dystrophin-glycoprotein complex proteins called the sarcoglycans. Deficiencies in dystroglycan, classically associated with congenital muscular dystrophies, may also cause LGMD.

The recessive LGMDs occur more frequently than the dominant forms, usually begin in childhood or the teenage years, and show dramatically increased levels of serum creatine kinase. The dominant

LGMDs usually begin in adulthood. In general, the earlier the clinical signs appear, the more rapid the rate of disease progression. Limb-girdle MD affects both males and females. Some forms of the disease progress rapidly, resulting in serious muscle damage and loss of the ability to walk, while others advance very slowly over many years and cause minimal disability, allowing a normal life expectancy. In some cases, the disorder appears to halt temporarily, but progression then resumes.

The pattern of muscle weakness is similar to that of Duchenne MD and Becker MD. Weakness is typically noticed first around the hips before spreading to the shoulders, legs, and neck. Individuals develop a waddling gait and have difficulty when rising from chairs, climbing stairs, or carrying heavy objects. They fall frequently and are unable to run. Contractures at the elbows and knees are rare but individuals may develop contractures in the back muscles, which gives them the appearance of a rigid spine. Proximal reflexes (closest to the center of the body) are often impaired. Some individuals also experience cardiomyopathy and respiratory complications, depending in part on the specific subtype. Intelligence remains normal in most cases, though exceptions do occur. Many individuals with limb-girdle MD become severely disabled within 20 years of disease onset.

8. Myotonic dystrophy (DM1), also known as Steinert disease and dystrophia myotonica, is another common form of MD. Myotonia, or an inability to relax muscles following a sudden contraction, is found only in this form of MD, but is also found in other non-dystrophic muscle diseases. People with DM1 can live a long life, with variable but slowly progressive disability. Typical disease onset is between ages 20 and 30, but childhood onset and congenital onset are well-documented. Muscles in the face and the front of the neck are usually first to show weakness and may produce a haggard, "hatchet" face and a thin, swan-like neck. Wasting and weakness noticeably affect forearm muscles. DM1 affects the central nervous system and other body systems, including the heart, adrenal glands and thyroid, eyes, and gastrointestinal tract. Other symptoms include cardiac complications, difficulty swallowing, droopy eyelids (called ptosis), cataracts, poor vision, early frontal baldness, weight loss, impotence, testicular atrophy, mild mental impairment, and increased sweating. Individuals may also feel drowsy and have an excess need to sleep. There is a second form of the disease that is similar to the classic form, but usually affects proximal muscles more significantly. This form is known as myotonic dystrophy type 2 (DM2).

This autosomal dominant disease affects both men and women. Females may have irregular menstrual periods and are sometimes infertile. The disease may occur earlier and be more severe in successive generations. A childhood-onset form of myotonic MD may become apparent between ages 5 and 10. Symptoms include general muscle weakness (particularly in the face and distal muscles), lack of muscle tone, and mental impairment.

A woman with DM1 can give birth to an infant with a rare congenital form of the disorder. Symptoms at birth may include difficulty swallowing or sucking, impaired breathing, absence of reflexes, skeletal deformities and contractures (such as club feet), and muscle weakness, especially in the face. Children with congenital myotonic MD may also experience mental impairment and delayed motor development. This severe infantile form of myotonic MD occurs almost exclusively in children who have inherited the defective gene from their mother, whose symptoms may be so mild that she is sometimes not aware that she has the disease until she has an affected child.

The inherited gene defect that causes DM1 is an abnormally long repetition of a three-letter "word" in the genetic code. In unaffected people, the word is repeated a number of times, but in people with DM1, it is repeated many more times. This triplet repeat gets longer with each successive generation. The triplet repeat mechanism has now been implicated in at least 15 other disorders, including Huntington disease and the spinocerebellar ataxias.

9. Oculopharyngeal MD (OPMD) generally begins in a person's forties or fifties and affects both men and women. In the United States, the disease is most common in families of French-Canadian descent and among Hispanic residents of northern New Mexico. People first report drooping eyelids, followed by weakness in the facial muscles and pharyngeal muscles in the throat, causing difficulty swallowing. The tongue may atrophy and changes to the voice may occur. Eyelids may droop so dramatically that some individuals compensate by tilting back their heads. Affected individuals may have double vision and problems with upper gaze, and others may have retinitis pigmentosa (progressive degeneration of the retina that affects night vision and peripheral vision) and cardiac irregularities. Muscle weakness and wasting in the neck and shoulder region is common. Limb muscles may also be affected. Persons with OPMD may find it difficult to walk, climb stairs, kneel, or bend. Those persons most severely affected will eventually lose the ability to walk.

How Are the Muscular Dystrophies Diagnosed?

Both the individual's medical history and a complete family history should be thoroughly reviewed to determine if the muscle disease is secondary to a disease affecting other tissues or organs or is an inherited condition. It is also important to rule out any muscle weakness resulting from prior surgery, exposure to toxins, or current medications that may affect the person's functional status or rule out many acquired muscle diseases. Thorough clinical and neurological exams can rule out disorders of the central and/or peripheral nervous systems, identify any patterns of muscle weakness and atrophy, test reflex responses and coordination, and look for contractions.

Various laboratory tests may be used to confirm the diagnosis of MD.

Blood and urine tests can detect defective genes and help identify specific neuromuscular disorders.

Exercise tests can detect elevated rates of certain chemicals following exercise and are used to determine the nature of the MD or other muscle disorder. Some exercise tests can be performed bedside while others are done at clinics or other sites using sophisticated equipment. These tests also assess muscle strength. They are performed when the person is relaxed and in the proper position to allow technicians to measure muscle function against gravity and detect even slight muscle weakness. If weakness in respiratory muscles is suspected, respiratory capacity may be measured by having the person take a deep breath and count slowly while exhaling.

Genetic testing looks for genes known to either cause or be associated with inherited muscle disease. DNA analysis and enzyme assays can confirm the diagnosis of certain neuromuscular diseases, including MD. Genetic linkage studies can identify whether a specific genetic marker on a chromosome and a disease are inherited together. They are particularly useful in studying families with members in different generations who are affected. An exact molecular diagnosis is necessary for some of the treatment strategies that are currently being developed. Advances in genetic testing include whole exome and whole genome sequencing, which will enable people to have all of their genes screened at once for disease-causing mutations, rather than have just one gene or several genes tested at a time. Exome sequencing looks at the part of the individual's genetic material, or genome, that "code for" (or translate) into proteins.

Genetic counseling can help parents who have a family history of MD determine if they are carrying one of the mutated genes that cause the disorder. Two tests can be used to help expectant parents find out if their child is affected.

1. **Amniocentesis**, done usually at 14–16 weeks of pregnancy, tests a sample of the amniotic fluid in the womb for genetic defects (the fluid and the fetus have the same DNA). Under local anesthesia, a thin needle is inserted through the woman's abdomen and into the womb. About 20 milliliters of fluid (roughly 4 teaspoons) is withdrawn and sent to a lab for evaluation. Test results often take 1–2 weeks.

2. **Chorionic villus sampling**, or CVS, involves the removal and testing of a very small sample of the placenta during early pregnancy. The sample, which contains the same DNA as the fetus, is removed by catheter or a fine needle inserted through the cervix or by a fine needle inserted through the abdomen. The tissue is tested for genetic changes identified in an affected family member. Results are usually available within 2 weeks.

Diagnostic imaging can help determine the specific nature of a disease or condition. One such type of imaging, called magnetic resonance imaging (MRI), is used to examine muscle quality, any atrophy or abnormalities in size, and fatty replacement of muscle tissue, as well as to monitor disease progression. Ultrasound may be used to measure muscle bulk. MRI scans of the brain may be useful in diagnosing certain forms of congenital muscular dystrophy where structural brain abnormalities are typically present.

Muscle biopsies are used for diagnostic purposes, and in research settings, to monitor the course of disease and treatment effectiveness. Muscle biopsies can sometimes also assist in carrier testing. With the advent of accurate molecular techniques, muscle biopsy is less frequently needed to diagnose muscular dystrophies. Muscle biopsy is still necessary to make the diagnosis in most of the acquired muscle diseases.

Immunofluorescence testing can detect specific proteins such as dystrophin within muscle fibers. Following biopsy, fluorescent markers are used to stain the sample that has the protein of interest.

Electron microscopy can identify changes in subcellular components of muscle fibers. Electron microscopy can also identify changes that characterize cell death, mutations in muscle cell mitochondria, and an increase in connective tissue seen in muscle diseases such as MD. Changes in muscle fibers that are evident in a rare form of distal MD can be seen using an electron microscope.

Neurophysiology studies can identify physical and/or chemical changes in the nervous system.

- **Nerve conduction velocity** studies measure the speed and strength with which an electrical signal travels along a nerve.

- **Repetitive stimulation** studies involve electrically stimulating a motor nerve several times in a row to assess the function of the neuromuscular junction.

- **Electromyography (EMG)** can record muscle fiber and motor unit activity. Results may reveal electrical activity characteristic of MD or other neuromuscular disorders.

How Are the Muscular Dystrophies Treated?

There is no specific treatment that can stop or reverse the progression of any form of MD. All forms of MD are genetic and cannot be prevented at this time, aside from the use of prenatal screening interventions. However, available treatments are aimed at keeping the person independent for as long as possible and prevent complications that result from weakness, reduced mobility, and cardiac and respiratory difficulties. Treatment may involve a combination of approaches, including physical therapy, drug therapy, and surgery. The available treatments are sometimes quite effective and can have a significant impact on life expectancy and quality of life.

Assisted ventilation is often needed to treat respiratory muscle weakness that accompanies many forms of MD, especially in the later stages. Air that includes supplemental oxygen is fed through a flexible mask (or, in some cases, a tube inserted through the esophagus and into the lungs) to help the lungs inflate fully. Since respiratory difficulty may be most extreme at night, some individuals may need overnight ventilation. Many people prefer non-invasive ventilation, in which a mask worn over the face is connected by a tube to a machine that generates intermittent bursts of forced air that may include supplemental oxygen. Some people with Duchenne MD, especially those who are overweight, may develop obstructive sleep apnea and require nighttime ventilation. Individuals on a ventilator may also require the use of a gastric feeding tube.

Drug therapy may be prescribed to delay muscle degeneration. Corticosteroids such as prednisone can slow the rate of muscle deterioration in Duchenne MD and help children retain strength and prolong independent walking by as much as several years. However, these medicines have side effects such as weight gain, facial changes, loss of linear (height) growth, and bone fragility that can be especially troubling in children. Immunosuppressive drugs such as cyclosporine and azathioprine can delay some damage to dying muscle cells. Drugs that may provide short-term relief from myotonia (muscle spasms and weakness) include mexiletine; phenytoin; baclofen, which blocks signals sent from the spinal cord to contract the muscles; dantrolene, which interferes with the process of muscle contraction; and quinine. (Drugs for myotonia may not be effective in myotonic MD but work well for myotonia congenita, a genetic neuromuscular disorder characterized by the slow relaxation of the muscles.) Respiratory infections may be treated with antibiotics.

Physical therapy can help prevent deformities, improve movement, and keep muscles as flexible and strong as possible. Options include passive stretching, postural correction, and exercise. A program is developed to meet the individual's needs. Therapy should begin as soon as possible following diagnosis, before there is joint or muscle tightness.

- Passive stretching can increase joint flexibility and prevent contractures that restrict movement and cause loss of function. When done correctly, passive stretching is not painful. The therapist or other trained health professional slowly moves the joint as far as possible and maintains the position for about 30 seconds. The movement is repeated several times during the session. Passive stretching on children may be easier following a warm bath or shower.

- Regular, moderate exercise can help people with MD maintain range of motion and muscle strength, prevent muscle atrophy, and delay the development of contractures. Individuals with a weakened diaphragm can learn coughing and deep breathing exercises that are designed to keep the lungs fully expanded.

- Postural correction is used to counter the muscle weakness, contractures, and spinal irregularities that force individuals with MD into uncomfortable positions. When possible, individuals should sit upright, with feet at a 90-degree angle to the floor. Pillows and foam wedges can help keep the person upright, distribute weight evenly, and cause the legs to straighten. Armrests should be at the proper height to provide support and prevent leaning.

- Support aids such as wheelchairs, splints and braces, other orthopedic appliances, and overhead bed bars (trapezes) can help maintain mobility. Braces are used to help stretch muscles and provide support while keeping the person ambulatory. Spinal supports can help delay scoliosis. Night splints, when used in conjunction with passive stretching, can delay contractures. Orthotic devices such as standing frames and swivel walkers help people remain standing or walking for as long as possible, which promotes better circulation and improves calcium retention in bones.

- Repeated low-frequency bursts of electrical stimulation to the thigh muscles may produce a slight increase in strength in some boys with Duchenne MD, though this therapy has not been proven to be effective.

Occupational therapy may help some people deal with progressive weakness and loss of mobility. Some individuals may need to learn new job skills or new ways to perform tasks while other persons may need to change jobs. Assistive technology may include modifications to home and workplace settings and the use of motorized wheelchairs, wheelchair accessories, and adaptive utensils.

Speech therapy may help individuals whose facial and throat muscles have weakened. Individuals can learn to use special communication devices, such as a computer with voice synthesizer

Dietary changes have not been shown to slow the progression of MD. Proper nutrition is essential, however, for overall health. Limited mobility or inactivity resulting from muscle weakness can contribute to obesity, dehydration, and constipation. A high-fiber, high-protein, low-calorie diet combined with recommended fluid intake may help. Feeding techniques can help people with MD who have a swallowing disorder and find it difficult to pass from or liquid from the mouth to the stomach.

Corrective surgery is often performed to ease complications from MD.

- Tendon or muscle-release surgery is recommended when a contracture becomes severe enough to lock a joint or greatly impair movement. The procedure, which involves lengthening a tendon or muscle to free movement, is usually performed under general anesthesia. Rehabilitation includes the use of braces and physical therapy to strengthen muscles and maintain the restored range of motion. A period of immobility is often needed after these orthopedic procedures, thus the benefits of the procedure should be weighed against the risk of this period of immobility, as the latter may lead to a setback.

- Individuals with either Emery-Dreifuss or myotonic dystrophy may require a pacemaker at some point to treat cardiac problems.

- Surgery to reduce the pain and postural imbalance caused by scoliosis may help some individuals. Scoliosis occurs when the muscles that support the spine begin to weaken and can no longer keep the spine straight. The spinal curve, if too great, can interfere with breathing and posture, causing pain. One or more metal rods may need to be attached to the spine to increase strength and improve posture. Another option is spinal fusion, in which bone is inserted between the vertebrae in the spine and allowed to grow, fusing the vertebrae together to increase spinal stability.

- People with myotonic dystrophy often develop cataracts, a clouding of the lens of the eye that blocks light. Cataract surgery involves removing the cloudy lens to improve the person's ability to see.

What Is the Prognosis?

The prognosis varies according to the type of MD and the speed of progression. Some types are mild and progress very slowly, allowing normal life expectancy, while others are more severe and result in functional disability and loss of ambulation. Life expectancy often depends on the degree of muscle weakness, as well as the presence and severity of respiratory and/or cardiac complications.

Section 32.6

Spinal Muscular Atrophy

This section contains text excerpted from the following sources: Text
beginning with the heading "What Is Spinal Muscular Atrophy?"
is excerpted from "Spinal Muscular Atrophy," Genetic Home
Reference (GHR), National Institutes of Health (NIH), March 21,
2016; Text under the heading "What Causes SMA?" is excerpted
from "Friedreich's Ataxia Fact Sheet," National Institute of
Neurological Disorders and Stroke (NINDS), February 19, 2016.

What Is Spinal Muscular Atrophy (SMA)?

Spinal muscular atrophy is a genetic disorder that affects the control of muscle movement. It is caused by a loss of specialized nerve
cells, called motor neurons, in the spinal cord and the part of the brain
that is connected to the spinal cord (the brainstem). The loss of motor
neurons leads to weakness and wasting (atrophy) of muscles used for
activities such as crawling, walking, sitting up, and controlling head
movement. In severe cases of spinal muscular atrophy, the muscles
used for breathing and swallowing are affected. There are many types
of spinal muscular atrophy distinguished by the pattern of features,
severity of muscle weakness, and age when the muscle problems begin.

Type I spinal muscular atrophy (also called Werdnig-Hoffman
disease) is a severe form of the disorder that is evident at birth or
within the first few months of life. Affected infants are developmen-
tally delayed; most are unable to support their head or sit unassisted.
Children with this type have breathing and swallowing problems that
may lead to choking or gagging.

Type II spinal muscular atrophy is characterized by muscle weakness that develops in children between ages 6 and 12 months. Children with type II can sit without support, although they may need
help getting to a seated position. Individuals with this type of spinal
muscular atrophy cannot stand or walk unaided.

Type III spinal muscular atrophy (also called Kugelberg-Welander
disease or juvenile type) has milder features that typically develop
between early childhood and adolescence. Individuals with type III
spinal muscular atrophy can stand and walk unaided, but walking

and climbing stairs may become increasingly difficult. Many affected individuals will require wheelchair assistance later in life.

The signs and symptoms of type IV spinal muscular atrophy often occur after age 30. Affected individuals usually experience mild to moderate muscle weakness, tremor, twitching, or mild breathing problems. Typically, only muscles close to the center of the body (proximal muscles), such as the upper arms and legs, are affected in type IV spinal muscular atrophy.

The features of X-linked spinal muscular atrophy appear in infancy and include severe muscle weakness and difficulty breathing. Children with this type often have joint deformities (contractures) that impair movement. In severe cases, affected infants are born with broken bones. Poor muscle tone before birth may contribute to the contractures and broken bones seen in these children.

Spinal muscular atrophy, lower extremity, dominant (SMA-LED) is characterized by leg muscle weakness that is most severe in the thigh muscles (quadriceps). This weakness begins in infancy or early childhood and progresses slowly. Affected individuals often have a waddling or unsteady walk and have difficulty rising from a seated position and climbing stairs.

An adult-onset form of spinal muscular atrophy that begins in early to mid-adulthood affects the proximal muscles and is characterized by muscle cramping of the limbs and abdomen, weakness in the leg muscles, involuntary muscle contractions, tremors, and a protrusion of the abdomen thought to be related to muscle weakness. Some affected individuals experience difficulty swallowing and problems with bladder and bowel function.

How Common Is Spinal Muscular Atrophy?

Spinal muscular atrophy affects 1 in 6,000 to 1 in 10,000 people.

What Genes Are Related to Spinal Muscular Atrophy?

Mutations in the *SMN1, UBA1, DYNC1H1,* and *VAPB* genes cause spinal muscular atrophy. Extra copies of the *SMN2* gene modify the severity of spinal muscular atrophy.

The *SMN1* and *SMN2* genes provide instructions for making a protein called the survival motor neuron (SMN) protein. The SMN protein is important for the maintenance of specialized nerve cells called motor neurons. Motor neurons are located in the spinal cord and the brainstem; they control muscle movement. Most functional

SMN protein is produced from the *SMN1* gene, with a small amount produced from the *SMN2* gene. Several different versions of the SMN protein are produced from the *SMN2* gene, but only one version is full size and functional.

Mutations in the *SMN1* gene cause spinal muscular atrophy types I, II, III, and IV. *SMN1* gene mutations lead to a shortage of the SMN protein. Without SMN protein, motor neurons die, and nerve impulses are not passed between the brain and muscles. As a result, some muscles cannot perform their normal functions, leading to weakness and impaired movement.

Some people with type II, III, or IV spinal muscular atrophy have three or more copies of the *SMN2* gene in each cell. Having multiple copies of the *SMN2* gene can modify the course of spinal muscular atrophy. The additional SMN proteins produced from the extra copies of the *SMN2* gene can help replace some of the SMN protein that is lost due to mutations in the *SMN1* gene. In general, symptoms are less severe and begin later in life as the number of copies of the *SMN2* gene increases.

Mutations in the *UBA1* gene cause X-linked spinal muscular atrophy. The *UBA1* gene provides instructions for making the ubiquitin-activating enzyme E1. This enzyme is involved in a process that targets proteins to be broken down (degraded) within cells. *UBA1* gene mutations lead to reduced or absent levels of functional enzyme, which disrupts the process of protein degradation. A buildup of proteins in the cell can cause it to die; motor neurons are particularly susceptible to damage from protein buildup.

The *DYNC1H1* gene provides instructions for making a protein that is part of a group (complex) of proteins called dynein. This complex is found in the fluid inside cells (cytoplasm), where it is part of a network that moves proteins and other materials. In neurons, dynein moves cellular materials away from the junctions between neurons (synapses) to the center of the cell. This process helps transmit chemical messages from one neuron to another. *DYNC1H1* gene mutations that cause SMA-LED disrupt the function of the dynein complex. As a result, the movement of proteins, cellular structures, and other materials within cells are impaired. A decrease in chemical messaging between neurons that control muscle movement is thought to contribute to the muscle weakness experienced by people with SMA-LED. It is unclear why this condition affects only the lower extremities.

The adult-onset form of spinal muscular atrophy is caused by a mutation in the *VAPB* gene. The *VAPB* gene provides instructions for making a protein that is found in cells throughout the body.

Researchers suggest that this protein may play a role in preventing the buildup of unfolded or misfolded proteins within cells. It is unclear how a *VAPB* gene mutation leads to the loss of motor neurons. An impaired *VAPB* protein might cause misfolded and unfolded proteins to accumulate and impair the normal function of motor neurons.

Other types of spinal muscular atrophy that primarily affect the lower legs and feet and the lower arms and hands are caused by the dysfunction of neurons in the spinal cord. When spinal muscular atrophy shows this pattern of signs and symptoms, it is also known as distal hereditary motor neuropathy. The various types of this condition are caused by mutations in other genes.

What Causes SMA?

SMA is caused by defects in the gene *SMN1*, which makes a protein that is important for the survival of motor neurons (SMN protein). In SMA, insufficient levels of the SMN protein lead to degeneration of the lower motor neurons, producing weakness and wasting of the skeletal muscles. This weakness is often more severe in the trunk and upper leg and arm muscles than in muscles of the hands and feet.

How Is It Inherited?

SMA disorders in children are inherited in an autosomal recessive manner. Autosomal recessive means the child must inherit a copy of the defective gene from both parents. These parents are likely to be asymptomatic (without symptoms of the disease). Autosomal recessive diseases often affect more than one person in the same generation (siblings or cousins).

Kennedy disease, an adult form of SMA is X-linked inherited, which means the mother carries the defective gene on one of her X chromosomes and passes the disorder along to her sons. Males inherit an X chromosome from their mother and a Y chromosome from their father, while females inherit an X chromosome from each parent. Daughters have a 50 percent chance of inheriting their mother's faulty X chromosome and a safe X chromosome from their father, which would make them asymptomatic carriers of the mutation.

What Are the Types of SMA?

SMA in children is classified into three types, based on ages of onset, severity, and progression of symptoms. All three types are caused by defects in the *SMN1* gene.

1. **SMA type I,** also called **Werdnig-Hoffmann disease** or **infantile-onset SMA**, is evident by the time a child is 6 months old. Symptoms may include hypotonia (severely reduced muscle tone), diminished limb movements, lack of tendon reflexes, fasciculations, tremors, swallowing and feeding difficulties, and impaired breathing. Some children also develop scoliosis (curvature of the spine) or other skeletal abnormalities. Affected children never sit or stand and the vast majority usually die of respiratory failure before the age of 2. However, the survival rate in individuals with SMA type I has increased in recent years, in relation to the growing trend toward more proactive clinical care.

2. Symptoms of **SMA type II**, the intermediate form, usually begin between 6 and 18 months of age. Children may be able to sit without support but are unable to stand or walk unaided, and may have respiratory difficulties, including an increased risk of respiratory infections. The progression of disease is variable. Life expectancy is reduced but some individuals live into adolescence or young adulthood.

3. Symptoms of **SMA type III (Kugelberg-Welander disease)** appear between 2 and 17 years of age and include abnormal gait; difficulty running, climbing steps, or rising from a chair; and a fine tremor of the fingers. The lower extremities are most often affected. Complications include scoliosis and joint contractures—chronic shortening of muscles or tendons around joints, caused by abnormal muscle tone and weakness, which prevents the joints from moving freely. Individuals with SMA type III may be prone to respiratory infections, but with care may have a normal lifespan.

Other forms of SMA include:

- **Congenital SMA with arthrogryposis** (persistent contracture of joints with fixed abnormal posture of the limb) is a rare disorder. Manifestations include severe contractures, scoliosis, chest deformity, respiratory problems, unusually small jaws, and drooping of the upper eyelids.

- **Kennedy disease**, also known as **progressive spinobulbar muscular atrophy,** may first be recognized between 15 and 60 years of age. The onset of symptoms varies and includes weakness and atrophy of the facial, jaw, and tongue muscles, leading to problems with chewing, swallowing, and changes in speech. Early symptoms may include muscle pain and fatigue. Weakness in arm and leg muscles closest to the trunk of the body develops over time, with muscle atrophy and fasciculations. Individuals with Kennedy disease also develop sensory loss in the feet and hands. Nerve conduction studies confirm that nearly all individuals have a sensory neuropathy (pain from sensory nerve inflammation or degeneration). Affected individuals may have enlargement of the male breasts or develop noninsulin-dependent diabetes mellitus.

How Is SMA Diagnosed?

A blood test is available that can indicate whether there are deletions or mutations of the *SMN1* gene. This test identifies at least 95 percent of SMA Types I, II, and III. Other diagnostic tests may include electromyography (which records the electrical activity from the brain and/or spinal cord to a peripheral nerve root found in the arms and legs that controls muscles during contraction and at rest), nerve conduction velocity studies (which measure electrical energy by assessing the nerve's ability to send a signal), muscle biopsy (used to diagnose neuromuscular disorders and may also reveal if a person is a carrier of a defective gene that could be passed on to children), and laboratory tests of blood, urine, and other substances.

Are There Treatments for SMA?

There is no cure for SMA. Treatment consists of managing the symptoms and preventing complications.

Muscle relaxants such as baclofen, tizanidine, and the benzodiazepines may reduce spasticity. Botulinum toxin may be used to treat jaw spasms or drooling. Excessive saliva can be treated with amitriptyline, glycopyolate, and atropine or by botulinum injections into the salivary glands. Antidepressants may be helpful in treating depression.

Physical therapy, occupational therapy, and rehabilitation may help to improve posture, prevent joint immobility, and slow muscle weakness and atrophy. Stretching and strengthening exercises may help reduce spasticity, increase range of motion, and keeps circulation flowing. Some individuals require additional therapy for speech, chewing, and swallowing difficulties. Applying heat may relieve muscle pain. Assistive devices such as supports or braces, orthotics, speech synthesizers, and wheelchairs may help some people retain independence.

Proper nutrition and a balanced diet are essential to maintaining weight and strength. People who cannot chew or swallow may require insertion of a feeding tube. Non-invasive ventilation at night can prevent apnea in sleep, and some individuals may also require assisted ventilation due to muscle weakness in the neck, throat, and chest during daytime.

What Is the Prognosis?

Prognosis varies depending on the type of SMA. Some forms of SMA are fatal. The course of Kennedy disease varies but is generally slowly progressive. Individuals tend to remain ambulatory until late in the disease. The life expectancy for individuals with Kennedy disease is usually normal. People with SMA may appear to be stable for long periods, but improvement should not be expected.

Chapter 33

Noonan Syndrome

What Is Noonan Syndrome?

Noonan syndrome is a condition that affects many areas of the body. It is characterized by mildly unusual facial characteristics, short stature, heart defects, bleeding problems, skeletal malformations, and many other signs and symptoms.

People with Noonan syndrome have distinctive facial features such as a deep groove in the area between the nose and mouth (philtrum), widely spaced eyes that are usually pale blue or blue-green in color, and low-set ears that are rotated backward. Affected individuals may have a high arch in the roof of the mouth (high-arched palate), poor alignment of the teeth, and a small lower jaw (micrognathia). Many children with Noonan syndrome have a short neck and both children and adults may have excess neck skin (also called webbing) and a low hairline at the back of the neck.

Approximately 50 to 70 percent of individuals with Noonan syndrome have short stature. At birth, they are usually of normal length and weight, but growth slows over time. Abnormal levels of growth hormone may contribute to the slow growth.

This chapter contains text excerpted from the following sources: Text beginning with the heading "What Is Noonan Syndrome?" is excerpted from "Noonan Syndrome," Genetic Home Reference (GHR), National Institutes of Health (NIH), March 14, 2016; Text under the heading "What Are the Symptoms of Noonan Syndrome?" is excerpted from "Learning about Noonan Syndrome," National Human Genome Research Institute (NHGRI), December 23, 2013.

Individuals with Noonan syndrome often have either a sunken chest (pectus excavatum) or a protruding chest (pectus carinatum). Some affected people may also have an abnormal side-to-side curvature of the spine (scoliosis).

Most people with Noonan syndrome have a heart defect. The most common heart defect is a narrowing of the valve that controls blood flow from the heart to the lungs (pulmonary valve stenosis). Some affected individuals have hypertrophic cardiomyopathy, which is a thickening of the heart muscle that forces the heart to work harder to pump blood.

A variety of bleeding disorders have been associated with Noonan syndrome. Some people may have excessive bruising, nosebleeds, or prolonged bleeding following injury or surgery. Women with a bleeding disorder typically have excessive bleeding during menstruation (menorrhagia) or childbirth.

Adolescent males with Noonan syndrome typically experience delayed puberty. Affected individuals go through puberty starting at age 13 or 14 and have a reduced pubertal growth spurt. Most males with Noonan syndrome have undescended testicles (cryptorchidism), which may be related to delayed puberty or to infertility (inability to father a child) later in life. Females with Noonan syndrome typically have normal puberty and fertility.

Noonan syndrome can cause a variety of other signs and symptoms. Most children diagnosed with Noonan syndrome have normal intelligence, but a small percentage has special educational needs, and some have intellectual disability. Some affected individuals have vision or hearing problems. Infants with Noonan syndrome may be born with puffy hands and feet caused by a buildup of fluid (lymphedema), which can go away on its own. Affected infants may also have feeding problems, which typically get better by age 1 or 2. Older individuals can also develop lymphedema, usually in the ankles and lower legs.

How Common Is Noonan Syndrome?

Noonan syndrome occurs in approximately 1 in 1,000 to 2,500 people.

What Genes Are Related to Noonan Syndrome?

Mutations in the *PTPN11, SOS1, RAF1, KRAS, NRAS,* and *BRAF* genes cause Noonan syndrome.

Most cases of Noonan syndrome result from mutations in one of three genes, *PTPN11, SOS1*, or *RAF1. PTPN11* gene mutations account for approximately 50 percent of all cases of Noonan syndrome. *SOS1* gene mutations account for 10 to 15 percent and *RAF1* gene mutations account for 5 to 10 percent of Noonan syndrome cases. About 2 percent of people with Noonan syndrome have mutations in the *KRAS* gene and usually have a more severe or atypical form of the disorder. It is not known how many cases are caused by mutations in the *BRAF* or *NRAS* genes, but it is likely a very small proportion. The cause of Noonan syndrome in the remaining 20 percent of people with this disorder is unknown.

The *PTPN11, SOS1, RAF1, KRAS, NRAS,* and *BRAF* genes all provide instructions for making proteins that are important in signaling pathways needed for the proper formation of several types of tissue during development. These proteins also play roles in cell division, cell movement, and cell differentiation (the process by which cells mature to carry out specific functions). Mutations in any of the genes listed above cause the resulting protein to be continuously active, rather than switching on and off in response to cell signals. This constant activation disrupts the regulation of systems that control cell growth and division, leading to the characteristic features of Noonan syndrome.

Is Noonan Syndrome Inherited?

Noonan syndrome is inherited in families in an autosomal dominant pattern. This means that a person who has Noonan syndrome has one copy of an altered gene that causes the disorder. In about one-third to two-thirds of families one of the parents also has Noonan syndrome. The parent who has Noonan syndrome has a 1 in 2 (50 percent) chance to pass on the altered gene to a child who will be affected; and a 1 in 2 (50 percent) chance to pass on the normal version of the gene to a child who will not have Noonan syndrome. In many individuals who have Noonan syndrome, the altered gene happens for the first time in them, and neither of the parents has Noonan syndrome. This is called a de novo mutation. The chance for these parents to have another child with Noonan syndrome is very small (less than 1 percent).

What Are the Symptoms of Noonan Syndrome?

Symptoms of Noonan syndrome may include the following:

- A characteristic facial appearance.

- Short stature.

- Heart defect present at birth (congenital heart defect).

- A broad or webbed neck.

- Minor eye problems such as strabismus in up to 95 percent of individuals.

- Bleeding problems such as a history of abnormal bleeding or bruising.

- An unusual chest shape with widely-spaced and low set nipples.

- Developmental delay of varying degrees, but usually mild.

- In males, undescended testes (cryptorchidism).

How Is Noonan Syndrome Diagnosed?

The diagnosis of Noonan syndrome is based on the person's clinical symptoms and signs. The specialist examines the person looking for the specific features of Noonan syndrome.

Individuals who have Noonan syndrome have normal chromosome studies. Four genes-*PTPN11, SOS1, RADF1,* and *KRAS*-are the only genes that are known to be associated with Noonan syndrome. Approximately 50 percent of individuals with Noonan syndrome have mutations in the *PTPN11* gene. Twenty percent of those with Noonan Syndrome have mutations in the *SOS1.* Mutations in the *RAF1* gene account for between 10 and 15 percent of Noonan syndrome cases. About 5 percent of people with Noonan syndrome have mutations in the *KRAS* gene and usually have a more severe or atypical form of the disorder. The cause of Noonan syndrome in the remaining 10 to 15 percent of people with this disorder is not yet known.

What Is the Treatment for Noonan Syndrome?

Treatment for individuals who have Noonan syndrome is based on their particular symptoms. Heart problems are treated in the same way as they are for individuals in the general population. Early intervention programs are used to help with developmental disabilities, when present. Bleeding problems that can be present in Noonan syndrome may have a variety of causes and are treated according to their cause. Growth problems may be caused by lack of growth hormone and may be treated with growth hormone treatment. Symptoms such as heart problems are followed on a regular basis.

Chapter 34

Porphyria

What Is Porphyria?

Porphyria is a group of disorders caused by abnormalities in the chemical steps that lead to heme production. Heme is a vital molecule for all of the body's organs, although it is most abundant in the blood, bone marrow, and liver. Heme is a component of several iron-containing proteins called hemoproteins, including hemoglobin (the protein that carries oxygen in the blood).

Researchers have identified several types of porphyria, which are distinguished by their genetic cause and their signs and symptoms. Some types of porphyria, called cutaneous porphyrias, primarily affect the skin. Areas of skin exposed to the sun become fragile and blistered, which can lead to infection, scarring, changes in skin coloring (pigmentation), and increased hair growth. Cutaneous porphyrias include congenital erythropoietic porphyria, erythropoietic protoporphyria, hepatoerythropoietic porphyria, and porphyria cutanea tarda.

Other types of porphyria, called acute porphyrias, primarily affect the nervous system. These disorders are described as "acute" because their signs and symptoms appear quickly and usually last a short

This chapter contains text excerpted from the following sources: Text beginning with the heading "What Is Porphyria?" is excerpted from "Porphyria," Genetics Home Reference (GHR), National Institutes of Health (NIH), March 14, 2016; Text under the heading "What Are the Types of Porphyria?" is excerpted from "Porphyria," National Institute of Diabetes and Digestive and Kidney Diseases (NIDDK), February 2014.

time. Episodes of acute porphyria can cause abdominal pain, vomiting, constipation, and diarrhea. During an episode, a person may also experience muscle weakness, seizures, fever, and mental changes such as anxiety and hallucinations. These signs and symptoms can be life-threatening, especially if the muscles that control breathing become paralyzed. Acute porphyrias include acute intermittent porphyria and ALAD deficiency porphyria. Two other forms of porphyria, hereditary coproporphyria and variegate porphyria, can have both acute and cutaneous symptoms.

The porphyrias can also be split into erythropoietic and hepatic types, depending on where damaging compounds called porphyrins and porphyrin precursors first build up in the body. In erythropoietic porphyrias, these compounds originate in the bone marrow. Erythropoietic porphyrias include erythropoietic protoporphyria and congenital erythropoietic porphyria. Health problems associated with erythropoietic porphyrias include a low number of red blood cells (anemia) and enlargement of the spleen (splenomegaly). The other types of porphyrias are considered hepatic porphyrias. In these disorders, porphyrins and porphyrin precursors originate primarily in the liver, leading to abnormal liver function and an increased risk of developing liver cancer.

Environmental factors can strongly influence the occurrence and severity of signs and symptoms of porphyria. Alcohol, smoking, certain drugs, hormones, other illnesses, stress, and dieting or periods without food (fasting) can all trigger the signs and symptoms of some forms of the disorder. Additionally, exposure to sunlight worsens the skin damage in people with cutaneous porphyrias.

How Common Is Porphyria?

The exact prevalence of porphyria is unknown, but it probably ranges from 1 in 500 to 1 in 50,000 people worldwide. Overall, porphyria cutanea tarda is the most common type of porphyria. For some forms of porphyria, the prevalence is unknown because many people with a genetic mutation associated with the disease never experience signs or symptoms.

Acute intermittent porphyria is the most common form of acute porphyria in most countries. It may occur more frequently in northern European countries, such as Sweden, and in the United Kingdom. Another form of the disorder, hereditary coproporphyria, has been reported mostly in Europe and North America. Variegate porphyria is most common in the Afrikaner population of South Africa; about 3 in 1,000 people in this population have the genetic change that causes this form of the disorder.

What Genes Are Related to Porphyria?

Each form of porphyria results from mutations in one of these genes: *ALAD, ALAS2, CPOX, FECH, HMBS, PPOX, UROD,* or *UROS.*

The genes related to porphyria provide instructions for making the enzymes needed to produce heme. Mutations in most of these genes reduce enzyme activity, which limits the amount of heme the body can produce. As a result, compounds called porphyrins and porphyrin precursors, which are formed during the process of heme production, can build up abnormally in the liver and other organs. When these substances accumulate in the skin and interact with sunlight, they cause the cutaneous forms of porphyria. The acute forms of the disease occur when porphyrins and porphyrin precursors build up in and damage the nervous system.

One type of porphyria, porphyria cutanea tarda, results from both genetic and nongenetic factors. About 20 percent of cases are related to mutations in the *UROD* gene. The remaining cases are not associated with UROD gene mutations and are classified as sporadic. Many factors contribute to the development of porphyria cutanea tarda. These include an increased amount of iron in the liver, alcohol consumption, smoking, hepatitis C or HIV infection, or certain hormones. Mutations in the *HFE* gene (which cause an iron overload disorder called hemochromatosis) are also associated with porphyria cutanea tarda. Other, as-yet-unidentified genetic factors may also play a role in this form of porphyria.

What Are the Types of Porphyria?

Each of the eight types of porphyria corresponds to low levels of a specific enzyme in the heme biosynthetic pathway. Experts often classify porphyrias as acute or cutaneous based on the symptoms a person experiences:

- Acute porphyrias affect the nervous system. They occur rapidly and last only a short time.

- Cutaneous porphyrias affect the skin.

Two types of acute porphyrias, hereditary coproporphyria and variegate porphyria, can also have cutaneous symptoms.

Experts also classify porphyrias as erythropoietic or hepatic:

- In erythropoietic porphyrias, the body overproduces porphyrins, mainly in the bone marrow.

- In hepatic porphyrias, the body overproduces porphyrins and porphyrin precursors, mainly in the liver.

Table 34.1 lists each type of porphyria, the deficient enzyme responsible for the disorder, and the main location of porphyrin buildup.

Table 34.1. Types of Porphyria

Type of Porphyria	Deficient Enzyme	Main Location of Porphyrin Buildup
delta-aminolevulinate-dehydratase deficiency porphyria	delta-aminolevulinic acid dehydratase	liver
acute intermittent porphyria	porphobilinogen deaminase	liver
hereditary coproporphyria	coproporphyrinogen oxidase	liver
variegate porphyria	protoporphyrinogen oxidase	liver
congenital erythropoietic porphyria	uroporphyrinogen III cosynthase	bone marrow
porphyria cutanea tarda	uroporphyrinogen decarboxylase (~75% deficiency)	liver
hepatoerythropoietic porphyria	uroporphyrinogen decarboxylase (~90% deficiency)	bone marrow
erythropoietic protoporphyria*	ferrochelatase (~75% deficiency)	bone marrow
Protoporphyria XLPP is a variant of erythropoietic protoporphyria.		

What Causes Porphyria?

Most porphyrias are inherited disorders. Scientists have identified genes for all eight enzymes in the heme biosynthetic pathway. Most porphyrias result from inheriting an abnormal gene, also called a gene mutation, from one parent. Some porphyrias, such as congenital erythropoietic porphyria, hepatoerythropoietic porphyria, and erythropoietic protoporphyria, occur when a person inherits two abnormal genes, one from each parent. The likeliness of a person passing the abnormal gene or genes to the next generation depends on the type of porphyria.

Porphyria cutanea tarda is usually an acquired disorder, meaning factors other than genes cause the enzyme deficiency. This type of porphyria can be triggered by

- too much iron

- use of alcohol or estrogen

- smoking

- chronic hepatitis C—a long-lasting liver disease that causes inflammation, or swelling, of the liver

- HIV—the virus that causes AIDS

- abnormal genes associated with hemochromatosis—the most common form of iron overload disease, which causes the body to absorb too much iron

For all types of porphyria, symptoms can be triggered by

- use of alcohol

- smoking

- use of certain medications or hormones

- exposure to sunlight

- stress

- dieting and fasting

What Are the Symptoms of Porphyria?

Some people with porphyria-causing gene mutations have latent porphyria, meaning they have no symptoms of the disorder. Symptoms of cutaneous porphyrias include

- over sensitivity to sunlight

- blisters on exposed areas of the skin

- itching and swelling on exposed areas of the skin

Symptoms of acute porphyrias include

- pain in the abdomen—the area between the chest and hips

- pain in the chest, limbs, or back

- nausea and vomiting

- constipation—a condition in which an adult has fewer than three bowel movements a week or a child has fewer than two bowel movements a week, depending on the person

- urinary retention—the inability to empty the bladder completely

- confusion

- hallucinations

- seizures and muscle weakness

Symptoms of acute porphyrias can develop over hours or days and last for days or weeks. These symptoms can come and go over time, while symptoms of cutaneous porphyrias tend to be more continuous. Porphyria symptoms can vary widely in severity.

How Is Porphyria Diagnosed?

A health care provider diagnoses porphyria with blood, urine, and stool tests. These tests take place at a health care provider's office or a commercial facility. A blood test involves drawing blood and sending the sample to a lab for analysis. For urine and stool tests, the patient collects a sample of urine or stool in a special container. A health care provider tests the samples in the office or sends them to a lab for analysis. High levels of porphyrins or porphyrin precursors in blood, urine, or stool indicate porphyria. A health care provider may also recommend DNA testing of a blood sample to look for known gene mutations that cause porphyrias.

How Is Porphyria Treated?

Treatment for porphyria depends on the type of porphyria the person has and the severity of the symptoms.

Acute Porphyrias

A health care provider treats acute porphyrias with heme or glucose loading to decrease the liver's production of porphyrins and porphyrin precursors. A patient receives heme intravenously once a day for 4 days. Glucose loading involves giving a patient a glucose solution by mouth or intravenously. Heme is usually more effective and is the

410

treatment of choice unless symptoms are mild. In rare instances, if symptoms are severe, a health care provider will recommend liver transplantation to treat acute porphyria.

In liver transplantation, a surgeon removes a diseased or an injured liver and replaces it with a healthy, whole liver or a segment of a liver from another person, called a donor. A patient has liver transplantation surgery in a hospital under general anesthesia. Liver transplantation can cure liver failure.

Cutaneous Porphyrias

The most important step a person can take to treat a cutaneous porphyria is to avoid sunlight as much as possible. Other cutaneous porphyrias are treated as follows:

- **Porphyria cutanea tarda.** A health care provider treats porphyria cutanea tarda by removing factors that tend to activate the disease and by performing repeated therapeutic phlebotomies to reduce iron in the liver. Therapeutic phlebotomy is the removal of about a pint of blood from a vein in the arm. A technician performs the procedure at a blood donation center, such as a hospital, clinic, or bloodmobile. A patient does not require anesthesia. Another treatment approach is low-dose hydroxychloroquine tablets to reduce porphyrins in the liver.

- **Erythropoietic protoporphyria.** People with erythropoietic protoporphyria may be given beta-carotene or cysteine to improve sunlight tolerance, though these medications do not lower porphyrin levels. Experts recommend hepatitis A and B vaccines and avoiding alcohol to prevent protoporphyric liver failure. A health care provider may use liver transplantation or a combination of medications to treat people who develop liver failure. Unfortunately, liver transplantation does not correct the primary defect, which is the continuous overproduction of protoporphyria by bone marrow. Successful bone marrow transplantations may successfully cure erythropoietic protoporphyria. A health care provider only considers bone marrow transplantation if the disease is severe and leading to secondary liver disease.

- **Congenital erythropoietic porphyria and hepatoerythropoietic porphyria.** People with congenital erythropoietic porphyria or hepatoerythropoietic porphyria may need surgery to remove the spleen or blood transfusions to treat anemia.

A surgeon removes the spleen in a hospital, and a patient receives general anesthesia. With a blood transfusion, a patient receives blood through an intravenous (IV) line inserted into a vein. A technician performs the procedure at a blood donation center, and a patient does not need anesthesia.

Secondary Porphyrinurias

Conditions called secondary porphyrinurias, such as disorders of the liver and bone marrow, as well as a number of drugs, chemicals, and toxins are often mistaken for porphyria because they lead to mild or moderate increases in porphyrin levels in the urine. Only high—not mild or moderate—levels of porphyrin or porphyrin precursors lead to a diagnosis of porphyria.

Eating, Diet, and Nutrition

People with an acute porphyria should eat a diet with an average-to-high level of carbohydrates. The recommended dietary allowance for carbohydrates is 130 g per day for adults and children 1 year of age or older; pregnant and breastfeeding women need higher intakes. People should avoid limiting intake of carbohydrates and calories, even for short periods of time, as this type of dieting or fasting can trigger symptoms. People with an acute porphyria who want to lose weight should talk with their health care providers about diets they can follow to lose weight gradually.

People undergoing therapeutic phlebotomies should drink plenty of milk, water, or juice before and after each procedure. A healthcare provider may recommend vitamin and mineral supplements for people with a cutaneous porphyria.

Chapter 35

Retinoblastoma

General Information about Retinoblastoma

Retinoblastoma Is a Disease in Which Malignant (Cancer) Cells Form in the Tissues of the Retina

The retina is the nerve tissue that lines the inside of the back of the eye. The retina senses light and sends images to the brain by way of the optic nerve.

Although retinoblastoma may occur at any age, it usually occurs in children younger than 5 years, most often younger than 2 years. The cancer may be in one eye (unilateral) or in both eyes (bilateral). Retinoblastoma rarely spreads from the eye to nearby tissue or other parts of the body.

Retinoblastoma Occurs in Heritable and Nonheritable Forms

A child is thought to have the heritable form of retinoblastoma when one of the following is true:

- There is a family history of retinoblastoma.

- There is a certain mutation (change) in the RB1 gene. The mutation in the RB1 gene may be passed from the parent to the child

This chapter includes text excerpted from "Retinoblastoma Treatment–Patient Version (PDQ®)," National Cancer Institute (NCI), February 23, 2016.

or it may occur in the egg or sperm before conception or soon after conception.

- There is more than one tumor in the eye or there is a tumor in both eyes.
- There is a tumor in one eye and the child is younger than 1 year.

After diagnosis and treatment in a child with heritable retinoblastoma, new tumors may continue to form for a few years. Regular eye exams to check for new tumors are usually done every 2 to 4 months for at least 28 months.

Nonheritable retinoblastoma is retinoblastoma that is not the heritable form. Most cases of retinoblastoma are the nonheritable form.

Treatment for Both Forms of Retinoblastoma Should Include Genetic Counseling

Parents should receive genetic counseling (a discussion with a trained professional about genetic diseases) to discuss whether genetic testing is needed and the risk of retinoblastoma for the child's brothers or sisters.

A Child Who Has Heritable Retinoblastoma Has an Increased Risk of Trilateral Retinoblastoma and Other Cancers

A child with heritable retinoblastoma has an increased risk of a pineal tumor in the brain. When retinoblastoma and a brain tumor occur at the same time it is called trilateral retinoblastoma. The brain tumor is usually diagnosed between 20 and 36 months of age. Regular screening using MRI (magnetic resonance imaging) every 6 months for 5 years may be done for a child thought to have heritable retinoblastoma or for a child with retinoblastoma in one eye and a family history of the disease. CT scans (computerized tomography) should not be used for routine screening to avoid exposing the child to ionizing radiation.

Heritable retinoblastoma also increases the child's risk of other types of cancer such as lung cancer, bladder cancer, or melanoma in later years. Regular follow-up exams are important.

Signs and Symptoms of Retinoblastoma Include "White Pupil" and Eye Pain or Redness

These and other signs and symptoms may be caused by retinoblastoma or by other conditions. Check with a doctor if your child has any of the following:

- Pupil of the eye appears white instead of red when light shines into it. This may be seen in flash photographs of the child. Pain or redness in the eye.

- Eyeball is larger than normal.

- Colored part of the eye and pupil look cloudy.

- Eyes appear to be looking in different directions (lazy eye).

Tests That Examine the Retina Are Used to Detect (Find) and Diagnose Retinoblastoma

The following tests and procedures may be used:

- **Physical exam and history:** An exam of the body to check general signs of health, including checking for signs of disease, such as lumps or anything else that seems unusual. A history of the patient's health habits and past illnesses and treatments will also be taken. The doctor will ask if there is a family history of retinoblastoma.

- **Eye exam with dilated pupil:** An exam of the eye in which the pupil is dilated (opened wider) with medicated eye drops to allow the doctor to look through the lens and pupil to the retina. The inside of the eye, including the retina and the optic nerve, is examined with a light. Depending on the age of the child, this exam may be done under anesthesia.

There are several types of eye exams that are done with the pupil dilated:

- **Ophthalmoscopy:** An exam of the inside of the back of the eye to check the retina and optic nerve using a small magnifying lens and a light.

- **Slit-lamp biomicroscopy:** An exam of the inside of the eye to check the retina, optic nerve, and other parts of the eye using a strong beam of light and a microscope.

- **Fluorescein angiography:** A procedure to look at blood vessels and the flow of blood inside the eye. An orange fluorescent dye called fluorescein is injected into a blood vessel in the arm and goes into the bloodstream. As the dye travels through blood vessels of the eye, a special camera takes pictures of the retina and choroid to find any blood vessels that are blocked or leaking.

- **Ultrasound exam of the eye:** A procedure in which high-energy sound waves (ultrasound) are bounced off the internal tissues of the eye to make echoes. Eye drops are used to numb the eye and a small probe that sends and receives sound waves is placed gently on the surface of the eye. The echoes make a picture of the inside of the eye and the distance from the cornea to the retina is measured. The picture, called a sonogram, shows on the screen of the ultrasound monitor. The picture can be printed to be looked at later.

- **MRI (magnetic resonance imaging):** A procedure that uses a magnet, radio waves, and a computer to make a series of detailed pictures of areas inside the body, such as the eye. This procedure is also called nuclear magnetic resonance imaging (NMRI).

- **CT scan (CAT scan):** A procedure that makes a series of detailed pictures of areas inside the body, such as the eye, taken from different angles. The pictures are made by a computer linked to an X-ray machine. A dye may be injected into a vein or swallowed to help the organs or tissues show up more clearly. This procedure is also called computed tomography, computerized tomography, or computerized axial tomography.

- **Bone scan:** A procedure to check if there are rapidly dividing cells, such as cancer cells, in the bone. A very small amount of radioactive material is injected into a vein and travels through the bloodstream. The radioactive material collects in the bones and is detected by a scanner that also takes a picture of the body. Areas of bone with cancer show up brighter in the picture because they take up more radioactive material than normal bone cells do.

Retinoblastoma can usually be diagnosed without a biopsy.

When retinoblastoma is in one eye, it sometimes forms in the other eye. Exams of the unaffected eye are done until it is known if the retinoblastoma is the heritable form.

Certain Factors Affect Prognosis (Chance of Recovery) and Treatment Options

The prognosis (chance of recovery) and treatment options depend on the following:

- Whether the cancer is in one or both eyes.

- The size and number of tumors.

- Whether the tumor has spread to the area around the eye, to the brain, or to other parts of the body.

- Whether there are symptoms at the time of diagnosis, for trilateral retinoblastoma.

- The age of the patient.

- How likely it is that vision can be saved in one or both eyes.

- Whether a second type of cancer has formed.

Stages of Retinoblastoma

After Retinoblastoma Has Been Diagnosed, Tests Are Done to Find out If Cancer Cells Have Spread within the Eye or to Other Parts of the Body

The process used to find out if cancer has spread within the eye or to other parts of the body is called staging. The information gathered from the staging process determines the stage of the disease. It is important to know the stage in order to plan treatment.

The following tests and procedures may be used in the staging process:

- **Eye exam with dilated pupil:** An exam of the eye in which the pupil is dilated (opened wider) with medicated eye drops to allow the doctor to look through the lens and pupil to the retina. The inside of the eye, including the retina and the optic nerve, is examined using a light. Depending on the age of the child, this exam may be done under anesthesia.

- **Ultrasound exam:** A procedure in which high-energy sound waves (ultrasound) are bounced off internal tissues or organs and make echoes. The echoes form a picture of body tissues called a sonogram. The picture can be printed to be looked at later.

- **CT scan (CAT scan):** A procedure that makes a series of detailed pictures of areas inside the body taken from different angles. The pictures are made by a computer linked to an X-ray machine. A dye may be injected into a vein or swallowed to help the organs or tissues show up more clearly. This procedure is also called computed tomography, computerized tomography, or computerized axial tomography.

- **MRI (magnetic resonance imaging):** A procedure that uses a magnet, radio waves, and a computer to make a series of detailed pictures of areas inside the body. This procedure is also called nuclear magnetic resonance imaging (NMRI).

- **Bone scan:** A procedure to check if there are rapidly dividing cells, such as cancer cells, in the bone. A very small amount of radioactive material is injected into a vein and travels through the bloodstream. The radioactive material collects in the bones and is detected by a scanner that also takes a picture of the body. Areas of bone with cancer show up brighter in the picture because they take up more radioactive material than normal bone cells do.

- **Bone marrow aspiration and biopsy:** The removal of bone marrow and a small piece of bone by inserting a hollow needle into the hipbone or breastbone. A pathologist views the bone marrow under a microscope to look for signs of cancer. A bone marrow aspiration and biopsy is done if the doctor thinks the cancer has spread outside of the eye.

- **Lumbar puncture:** A procedure used to collect cerebrospinal fluid (CSF) from the spinal column. This is done by placing a needle between two bones in the spine and into the CSF around the spinal cord and removing a sample of the fluid. The sample of CSF is checked under a microscope for signs that the cancer has spread to the brain and spinal cord. This procedure is also called an LP or spinal tap.

The International Retinoblastoma Staging System (IRSS) May Be Used for Staging Retinoblastoma

There are several staging systems for retinoblastoma. The IRSS stages are based on how much cancer remains after surgery to remove the tumor and whether the cancer has spread.

Stage 0

The tumor is in the eye only. The eye has not been removed and the tumor was treated without surgery.

Stage I

The tumor is in the eye only. The eye has been removed and no cancer cells remain.

Stage II

The tumor is in the eye only. The eye has been removed and there are cancer cells left that can be seen only with a microscope.

Stage III

Stage III is divided into stages IIIa and IIIb:

- In stage IIIa, cancer has spread from the eye to tissues around the eye socket.
- In stage IIIb, cancer has spread from the eye to lymph nodes near the ear or in the neck.

Stage IV

Stage IV is divided into stages IVa and IVb:

- In stage IVa, cancer has spread to the blood but not to the brain or spinal cord. One or more tumors may have spread to other parts of the body such as the bone or liver.
- In stage IVb, cancer has spread to the brain or spinal cord. It also may have spread to other parts of the body.

Treatment for Retinoblastoma Depends on Whether It Is Intraocular (within the Eye) or Extraocular (Outside the Eye)

Intraocular Retinoblastoma

In intraocular retinoblastoma, cancer is found in one or both eyes and may be in the retina only or may also be in other parts of the eye such as the choroid, ciliary body, or part of the optic nerve. Cancer has not spread to tissues around the outside of the eye or to other parts of the body.

Extraocular Retinoblastoma (Metastatic)

In extraocular retinoblastoma, cancer has spread beyond the eye. It may be found in tissues around the eye (orbital retinoblastoma) or it may have spread to the central nervous system (brain and spinal cord) or to other parts of the body such as the liver, bones, bone marrow, or lymph nodes

There Are Three Ways That Cancer Spreads in the Body

Cancer can spread through tissue, the lymph system, and the blood:

- **Tissue.** The cancer spreads from where it began by growing into nearby areas.

- **Lymph system.** The cancer spreads from where it began by getting into the lymph system. The cancer travels through the lymph vessels to other parts of the body.

- **Blood.** The cancer spreads from where it began by getting into the blood. The cancer travels through the blood vessels to other parts of the body.

Cancer May Spread from Where It Began to Other Parts of the Body

When cancer spreads to another part of the body, it is called metastasis. Cancer cells break away from where they began (the primary tumor) and travel through the lymph system or blood.

- **Lymph system**. The cancer gets into the lymph system, travels through the lymph vessels, and forms a tumor (metastatic tumor) in another part of the body.

- **Blood**. The cancer gets into the blood, travels through the blood vessels, and forms a tumor (metastatic tumor) in another part of the body.

The metastatic tumor is the same type of cancer as the primary tumor. For example, if retinoblastoma spreads to the bone, the cancer cells in the bone are actually retinoblastoma cells. The disease is metastatic retinoblastoma, not bone cancer.

Treatment Option Overview

There Are Different Types of Treatment for Patients with Retinoblastoma

Different types of treatment are available for patients with retinoblastoma. Some treatments are standard (the currently used treatment), and some are being tested in clinical trials. A treatment clinical trial is a research study meant to help improve current treatments or obtain information on new treatments for patients with cancer. When clinical trials show that a new treatment is better than the standard treatment, the new treatment may become the standard treatment.

Because cancer in children is rare, taking part in a clinical trial should be considered. Some clinical trials are open only to patients who have not started treatment.

Children with Retinoblastoma Should Have Their Treatment Planned by a Team of Health Care Providers Who Are Experts in Treating Cancer in Children

The goals of treatment are to save the child's life, to save vision and the eye, and to prevent serious side effects. Treatment will be overseen by a pediatric oncologist, a doctor who specializes in treating children with cancer. The pediatric oncologist works with other health care providers who are experts in treating children with eye cancer and who specialize in certain areas of medicine. These may include a pediatric ophthalmologist (children's eye doctor) who has a lot of experience in treating retinoblastoma and the following specialists:

- Pediatric surgeon
- Radiation oncologist
- Pediatrician
- Pediatric nurse specialist
- Rehabilitation specialist
- Psychologist
- Social worker
- Geneticist or genetic counselor

Some Cancer Treatments Cause Side Effects Months or Years after Treatment Has Ended

Side effects from cancer treatment that begin during or after treatment and continue for months or years are called late effects.

Late effects of treatment for retinoblastoma may include the following:

- Physical problems such as seeing or hearing problems or, if the eye is removed, a change in the shape and size of the bone around the eye.

- Changes in mood, feelings, thinking, learning, or memory.

- Second cancers (new types of cancer), such as lung and bladder cancers, osteosarcoma, soft tissue sarcoma, or melanoma.

The following risk factors may increase the risk of having another cancer:

- Having the heritable form of retinoblastoma.

- Past treatment with radiation therapy, especially before age 1 year.

- Having a previous second cancer.

It is important to talk with your child's doctors about the effects cancer treatment can have on your child. Regular follow-up by health professionals who are experts in diagnosing and treating late effects is important.

Six Types of Standard Treatment Are Used

1. Surgery (enucleation)

Enucleation is surgery to remove the eye and part of the optic nerve. The eye will be checked with a microscope to see if there are any signs that the cancer is likely to spread to other parts of the body. Enucleation is done if there is little or no chance that vision can be saved and when the tumor is large, did not respond to treatment, or comes back after treatment. The patient will be fitted for an artificial eye.

Close follow-up is needed for 2 years or more to check for signs of recurrence in the area around the affected eye and to check the other eye.

2. Radiation therapy

Radiation therapy is a cancer treatment that uses high-energy X-rays or other types of radiation to kill cancer cells or keep them from growing. There are two types of radiation therapy. External radiation therapy uses a machine outside the body to send radiation toward the cancer. Internal radiation therapy uses a radioactive substance sealed in needles, seeds, wires, plaques, or catheters that are placed directly into or near the cancer.

Methods of radiation therapy used to treat retinoblastoma include the following:

- **Intensity-modulated radiation therapy (IMRT):** A type of 3-dimensional (3-D) radiation therapy that uses a computer to make pictures of the size and shape of the tumor. Thin beams of radiation of different intensities (strengths) are aimed at the tumor from many angles. This type of radiation therapy causes less damage to healthy tissue near the tumor.

- **Stereotactic radiation therapy:** Radiation therapy that uses a rigid head frame attached to the skull to aim high-dose radiation beams directly at the tumors, causing less damage to nearby healthy tissue. This is also called stereotactic external-beam radiation and stereotaxic radiation therapy.

- **Proton beam radiation therapy:** Radiation therapy that uses protons made by a special machine. A proton is a type of high-energy radiation that is different from an X-ray.

- **Plaque radiotherapy:** Radioactive seeds are attached to one side of a disk, called a plaque, and placed directly on the outside wall of the eye near the tumor. The side of the plaque with the seeds on it faces the eyeball, aiming radiation at the tumor. The plaque helps protect other nearby tissue from the radiation.

The way the radiation therapy is given depends on how the cancer responded to other treatments and whether cancer has spread to other parts of the body.

3. Cryotherapy

Cryotherapy is a treatment that uses an instrument to freeze and destroy abnormal tissue. This type of treatment is also called cryosurgery.

4. Thermotherapy

Thermotherapy is the use of heat to destroy cancer cells. Thermotherapy may be given using a laser beam aimed through the dilated pupil or onto the outside of the eyeball. Thermotherapy may be used alone for small tumors or combined with chemotherapy for larger tumors. This treatment is a type of laser therapy.

5. Chemotherapy

Chemotherapy is a cancer treatment that uses drugs to stop the growth of cancer cells, either by killing the cells or by stopping them from dividing. The way the chemotherapy is given depends on the stage of the cancer and where the cancer is in the body.

There are different types of chemotherapy:

- **Systemic chemotherapy:** When chemotherapy is taken by mouth or injected into a vein or muscle, the drugs enter the bloodstream and can reach cancer cells throughout the body. Systemic chemotherapy is given to shrink the tumor (chemoreduction) and avoid surgery to remove the eye. After chemoreduction, other treatments may include radiation therapy, cryotherapy, laser therapy, or regional chemotherapy. Systemic chemotherapy may also be given to kill any cancer cells that are left after the initial treatment or to patients with retinoblastoma that occurs outside the eye. Treatment given after the initial treatment, to lower the risk that the cancer will come back, is called adjuvant therapy.

- **Regional chemotherapy:** When chemotherapy is placed directly into the cerebrospinal fluid (intrathecal chemotherapy), an organ (such as the eye), or a body cavity, the drugs mainly affect cancer cells in those areas. Several types of regional chemotherapy are used to treat retinoblastoma.

  - **Ophthalmic artery infusion chemotherapy:** Ophthalmic artery infusion chemotherapy carries anticancer drugs directly to the eye. A catheter is put into an artery that leads to the eye and the anticancer drug is given through the catheter. After the drug is given, a small balloon may be inserted into the artery to block it and keep most of the anticancer drug trapped near the tumor. This type of chemotherapy may be given as the initial treatment when the tumor is in one eye only or when the tumor has not responded to other types of treatment. Ophthalmic artery infusion chemotherapy is given at special retinoblastoma treatment centers.

  - **Subtenon chemotherapy:** Subtenon chemotherapy is the use of drugs injected through the membrane covering the muscles and nerves at the back of the eyeball. It is usually combined with systemic chemotherapy and local treatment (such as radiation therapy, cryotherapy, or thermotherapy) in order to avoid surgery to remove the eye.

- **Intravitreal chemotherapy:** Intravitreal chemotherapy is the injection of anticancer drugs directly into the vitreous (fluid) inside in the eye. It is used to treat cancer that has spread to the vitreous that has not responded to treatment or has come back after treatment.

6. High-Dose Chemotherapy with Stem Cell Rescue

High-dose chemotherapy with stem cell rescue is a way of giving high doses of chemotherapy and replacing blood—forming cells destroyed by the cancer treatment. Stem cells (immature blood cells) are removed from the blood or bone marrow of the patient and are frozen and stored. After the chemotherapy is completed, the stored stem cells are thawed and given back to the patient through an infusion. These reinfused stem cells grow into (and restore) the body's blood cells.

Chapter 36

Rett Syndrome

What Is Rett Syndrome?

Rett syndrome is a neurodevelopmenal disorder that affects girls almost exclusively. It is characterized by normal early growth and development followed by a slowing of development, loss of purposeful use of the hands, distinctive hand movements, slowed brain and head growth, problems with walking, seizures, and intellectual disability.

The disorder was identified by Dr. Andreas Rett, an Austrian physician who first described it in a journal article in 1966. It was not until after a second article about the disorder, published in 1983 by Swedish researcher Dr. Bengt Hagberg, that the disorder was generally recognized.

The course of Rett syndrome, including the age of onset and the severity of symptoms, varies from child to child. Before the symptoms begin, however, the child generally appears to grow and develop normally, although there are often subtle abnormalities even in early infancy, such as loss of muscle tone (hypotonia), difficulty feeding, and jerkiness in limb movements. Then, gradually, mental and physical symptoms appear. As the syndrome progresses, the child loses purposeful use of her hands and the ability to speak. Other early symptoms may include problems crawling or walking and diminished eye contact. The loss of functional use of the hands is followed by compulsive hand

This chapter includes text excerpted from "Rett Syndrome Fact Sheet," National Institute of Neurological Disorders and Stroke (NINDS), July 27, 2015.

movements such as wringing and washing. The onset of this period of regression is sometimes sudden.

Apraxia—the inability to perform motor functions—is perhaps the most severely disabling feature of Rett syndrome, interfering with every body movement, including eye gaze and speech.

Children with Rett syndrome often exhibit autistic-like behaviors in the early stages. Other symptoms may include walking on the toes, sleep problems, a wide-based gait, teeth grinding and difficulty chewing, slowed growth, seizures, cognitive disabilities, and breathing difficulties while awake such as hyperventilation, apnea (breath holding), and air swallowing.

What Are the Stages of the Disorder?

Scientists generally describe four stages of Rett syndrome.

Stage I, called early onset, typically begins between 6 and 18 months of age. This stage is often overlooked because symptoms of the disorder may be somewhat vague, and parents and doctors may not notice the subtle slowing of development at first. The infant may begin to show less eye contact and have reduced interest in toys. There may be delays in gross motor skills such as sitting or crawling. Hand-wringing and decreasing head growth may occur, but not enough to draw attention. This stage usually lasts for a few months but can continue for more than a year.

Stage II, or the rapid destructive stage, usually begins between ages 1 and 4 and may last for weeks or months. Its onset may be rapid or gradual as the child loses purposeful hand skills and spoken language. Characteristic hand movements such as wringing, washing, clapping, or tapping, as well as repeatedly moving the hands to the mouth often begin during this stage. The child may hold the hands clasped behind the back or held at the sides, with random touching, grasping, and releasing. The movements continue while the child is awake but disappear during sleep. Breathing irregularities such as episodes of apnea and hyperventilation may occur, although breathing usually improves during sleep. Some girls also display autistic-like symptoms such as loss of social interaction and communication. Walking may be unsteady and initiating motor movements can be difficult. Slowed head growth is usually noticed during this stage.

Stage III, or the plateau or pseudo-stationary stage, usually begins between ages 2 and 10 and can last for years. Apraxia, motor problems, and seizures are prominent during this stage. However, there may be improvement in behavior, with less irritability, crying, and autistic-like features. A girl in stage III may show more interest in her surroundings and her alertness, attention span, and communication skills may improve. Many girls remain in this stage for most of their lives.

Stage IV, or the late motor deterioration stage, can last for years or decades. Prominent features include reduced mobility, curvature of the spine (scoliosis) and muscle weakness, rigidity, spasticity, and increased muscle tone with abnormal posturing of an arm, leg, or top part of the body. Girls who were previously able to walk may stop walking. Cognition, communication, or hand skills generally do not decline in stage IV. Repetitive hand movements may decrease and eye gaze usually improves.

What Causes Rett Syndrome?

Nearly all cases of Rett syndrome are caused by a mutation in the methyl CpG binding protein 2, or *MECP2* gene. Scientists identified the gene—which is believed to control the functions of many other genes—in 1999. The *MECP2* gene contains instructions for the synthesis of a protein called methyl cytosine binding protein 2 (MeCP2), which is needed for brain development and acts as one of the many biochemical switches that can either increase gene expression or tell other genes when to turn off and stop producing their own unique proteins. Because the *MECP2* gene does not function properly in individuals with Rett syndrome, insufficient amounts or structurally abnormal forms of the protein are produced and can cause other genes to be abnormally expressed.

Not everyone who has an *MECP2* mutation has Rett syndrome. Scientists have identified mutations in the *CDKL5* and *FOXG1* genes in individuals who have atypical or congenital Rett syndrome, but they are still learning how those mutations cause the disorder. Scientists believe the remaining cases may be caused by partial gene deletions, mutations in other parts of the *MECP2* gene, or additional genes that have not yet been identified, and they continue to look for other causes.

Is Rett Syndrome Inherited?

Although Rett syndrome is a genetic disorder, less than 1 percent of recorded cases are inherited or passed from one generation to the next. Most cases are spontaneous, which means the mutation occurs randomly. However, in some families of individuals affected by Rett syndrome, there are other female family members who have a mutation of their *MECP2* gene but do not show clinical symptoms. These females are known as "asymptomatic female carriers."

Who Gets Rett Syndrome?

Rett syndrome is estimated to affect one in every 10,000 to 15,000 live female births and in all racial and ethnic groups worldwide. Prenatal testing is available for families with an affected daughter who has an identified *MECP2* mutation. Since the disorder occurs spontaneously in most affected individuals, however, the risk of a family having a second child with the disorder is less than 1 percent.

Genetic testing is also available for sisters of girls with Rett syndrome who have an identified *MECP2* mutation to determine if they are asymptomatic carriers of the disorder, which is an extremely rare possibility.

The *MECP2* gene is found on a person's X chromosome, one of the two sex chromosomes. Girls have two X chromosomes, but only one is active in any given cell. This means that in a girl with Rett syndrome only a portion of the cells in the nervous system will use the defective gene. Some of the child's brain cells use the healthy gene and express normal amounts of the protein.

The severity of Rett syndrome in girls is in part a function of the percentage of their cells that express a normal copy of the *MECP2* gene. If the active X chromosome that is carrying the defective gene is turned off in a large proportion of cells, the symptoms will be mild, but if a larger percentage of cells have the X chromosome with the normal *MECP2* gene turned off, onset of the disorder may occur earlier and the symptoms may be more severe.

The story is different for boys who have a *MECP2* mutation known to cause Rett syndrome in girls. Because boys have only one X chromosome (and one Y chromosome) they lack a backup copy that could compensate for the defective one, and they have no protection from the harmful effects of the disorder. Boys with such a defect frequently do not show clinical features of Rett syndrome but experience severe problems when they are first born and die shortly after birth. A very small number of boys may have a different mutation in the *MECP2* gene or a sporadic mutation after conception that can cause some degree of intellectual disability and developmental problems.

How Is Rett Syndrome Diagnosed?

Doctors clinically diagnose Rett syndrome by observing signs and symptoms during the child's early growth and development, and conducting ongoing evaluations of the child's physical and neurological status. Scientists have developed a genetic test to complement the clinical diagnosis, which involves searching for the *MECP2* mutation on the child's X chromosome.

A pediatric neurologist, clinical geneticist, or developmental pediatrician should be consulted to confirm the clinical diagnosis of Rett syndrome. The physician will use a highly specific set of guidelines that are divided into three types of clinical criteria: main, supportive, and exclusion. The presence of any of the exclusion criteria negates a diagnosis of classic Rett syndrome.

Examples of main diagnostic criteria or symptoms include partial or complete loss of acquired purposeful hand skills, partial or complete loss of acquired spoken language, repetitive hand movements (such has hand wringing or squeezing, clapping or rubbing), and gait abnormalities, including toe-walking or an unsteady, wide-based, stiff-legged walk.

Supportive criteria are not required for a diagnosis of Rett syndrome but may occur in some individuals. In addition, these symptoms—which vary in severity from child to child—may not be observed in very young girls but may develop with age. A child with supportive criteria but none of the essential criteria does not have Rett syndrome. Supportive criteria include scoliosis, teeth-grinding, small cold hands and feet in relation to height, abnormal sleep patterns, abnormal muscle tone, inappropriate laughing or screaming, intense eye communication, and diminished response to pain.

In addition to the main diagnostic criteria, a number of specific conditions enable physicians to rule out a diagnosis of Rett syndrome. These are referred to as exclusion criteria. Children with any one of the following criteria do not have Rett syndrome: brain injury secondary to trauma, neurometabolic disease, severe infection that causes neurological problems; and grossly abnormal psychomotor development in the first 6 months of life.

Is Treatment Available?

There is no cure for Rett syndrome. Treatment for the disorder is symptomatic—focusing on the management of symptoms—and supportive, requiring a multidisciplinary approach. Medication may be needed for breathing irregularities and motor difficulties, and anticonvulsant drugs may be used to control seizures. There should be regular monitoring for scoliosis and possible heart abnormalities.

Occupational therapy can help children develop skills needed for performing self-directed activities (such as dressing, feeding, and practicing arts and crafts), while physical therapy and hydrotherapy may prolong mobility. Some children may require special equipment and aids such as braces to arrest scoliosis, splints to modify hand movements, and nutritional programs to help them maintain adequate weight. Special academic, social, vocational, and support services may be required in some cases.

What Is the Outlook for Those with Rett Syndrome?

Despite the difficulties with symptoms, many individuals with Rett syndrome continue to live well into middle age and beyond. Because the disorder is rare, very little is known about long-term prognosis and life expectancy. While there are women in their 40s and 50s with the disorder, currently it is not possible to make reliable estimates about life expectancy beyond age 40.

Chapter 37

Tuberous Sclerosis

What Is Tuberous Sclerosis?

Tuberous sclerosis—also called tuberous sclerosis complex (TSC)—is a rare, multi-system genetic disease that causes benign tumors to grow in the brain and on other vital organs such as the kidneys, heart, eyes, lungs, and skin. It usually affects the central nervous system and results in a combination of symptoms including seizures, developmental delay, behavioral problems, skin abnormalities, and kidney disease.

The disorder affects as many as 25,000 to 40,000 individuals in the United States and about 1 to 2 million individuals worldwide, with an estimated prevalence of one in 6,000 newborns. TSC occurs in all races and ethnic groups, and in both genders.

Many TSC patients show evidence of the disorder in the first year of life. However, clinical features can be subtle initially, and many signs and symptoms take years to develop. As a result, TSC can be unrecognized or misdiagnosed for years.

What Causes Tuberous Sclerosis?

TSC is caused by defects, or mutations, on two genes-*TSC1* and *TSC2*. Only one of the genes needs to be affected for TSC to be present.

This chapter includes text excerpted from "Tuberous Sclerosis Fact Sheet," National Institute of Neurological Disorders and Stroke (NINDS), January 21, 2016.

The *TSC1* gene, discovered in 1997, is on chromosome 9 and produces a protein called hamartin. The *TSC2* gene, discovered in 1993, is on chromosome 16 and produces the protein tuberin. Scientists believe these proteins act in a complex as growth suppressors by inhibiting the activation of a master, evolutionarily conserved kinase called mTOR. Loss of regulation of mTOR occurs in cells lacking either hamartin or tuberin, and this leads to abnormal differentiation and development, and to the generation of enlarged cells, as are seen in TSC brain lesions.

Is TSC Inherited?

Although some individuals inherit the disorder from a parent with TSC, most cases occur as sporadic cases due to new, spontaneous mutations in *TSC1* or *TSC2*. In this situation, neither parent has the disorder or the faulty gene(s). Instead, a faulty gene first occurs in the affected individual.

In familial cases, TSC is an autosomal dominant disorder, which means that the disorder can be transmitted directly from parent to child. In those cases, only one parent needs to have the faulty gene in order to pass it on to a child. If a parent has TSC, each offspring has a 50 percent chance of developing the disorder. Children who inherit TSC may not have the same symptoms as their parent and they may have either a milder or a more severe form of the disorder.

Rarely, individuals acquire TSC through a process called gonadal mosaicism. These patients have parents with no apparent defects in the two genes that cause the disorder. Yet these parents can have a child with TSC because a portion of one of the parent's reproductive cells (sperm or eggs) can contain the genetic mutation without the other cells of the body being involved. In cases of gonadal mosaicism, genetic testing of a blood sample might not reveal the potential for passing the disease to offspring.

What Are the Signs and Symptoms of TSC?

TSC can affect many different systems of the body, causing a variety of signs and symptoms. Signs of the disorder vary depending on which system and which organs are involved. The natural course of TSC varies from individual to individual, with symptoms ranging from very mild to quite severe. In addition to the benign tumors that frequently occur in TSC, other common symptoms include seizures, cognitive impairment, behavior problems, and skin abnormalities. Tumors can grow in nearly any organ, but they most commonly occur in the brain, kidneys, heart, lungs, and skin. Malignant tumors are rare in TSC. Those that do occur primarily affect the kidneys.

Brain Involvement in TSC. Three types of brain lesions are seen in TSC: *cortical tubers,* for which the disease is named, generally form on the surface of the brain but may also appear in the deep areas of the brain: *subependymal nodules* (SEN), which form in the walls of the ventricles—the fluid-filled cavities of the brain; and *subependymal giant-call* astrocytomas (SEGA), which develop from SEN and grow such that they may block the flow of fluid within the brain, causing a buildup of fluid and pressure and leading to headaches and blurred vision.

TSC usually causes the greatest problems for those affected and their family members through effects on brain function. Most individuals with TSC will have seizures at some point during their life. Seizures of all types may occur, including infantile spasms; tonic-clonic seizures (also known as grand mal seizures); or tonic, akinetic, atypical absence, myoclonic, complex partial or generalized squires. Infantile spasms can occur as soon as the day of birth and are often difficult to recognize. Seizures can also be difficult to control by medication, and sometimes surgery or other measures are used.

About one-half to two-thirds of individuals with TSC have developmental delays ranging from mild learning disabilities to severe impairment. Behavior problems, including aggression, sudden rage, attention deficit hyperactivity disorder, acting out, obsessive-compulsive disorder, and repetitive, destructive, or self-harming behavior occur in children with TSC and can be difficult to manage. About one-third of children with TSC meet criteria for autism spectrum disorder.

Kidney problems such as cysts and angiomyolipomas occur in an estimated 70 to 80 percent of individuals with TSC, usually occurring between ages 15 and 30. Cysts are usually small, appear in limited numbers, and cause no serious problems. Approximately 2 percent of individuals with TSC develop large numbers of cysts in a pattern similar to polycystic kidney disease during childhood. In these cases, kidney function is compromised and kidney failure occurs. In rare instances, the cysts may bleed, leading to blood loss and anemia.

Angiomyolipomas-benign growths consisting of fatty tissue and muscle cells-are the most common kidney lesions in TSC. These growths are seen in the majority of individuals with TSC, but are also found in about one of every 300 people without TSC. Angiomyolipomas caused by TSC are usually found in both kidneys and in most cases they produce no symptoms. However, they can sometimes grow so large that they cause pain or kidney failure. Bleeding from angiomyolipomas may also occur, causing both pain and weakness. If severe bleeding does not stop naturally, there may severe blood loss, resulting in profound anemia and a life-threatening drop in blood pressure, warranting urgent medical attention.

Other rare kidney problems include renal cell carcinoma, developing from an angiomyolipoma, and oncocytomas, benign tumors unique to individuals with TSC.

Tumors called *cardiac rhabdomyomas* are often found in the hearts of infants and young children with TSC, and they are often seen on prenatal fetus ultrasound exams. If the tumors are large or there are multiple tumors, they can block circulation and cause death. However, if they do not cause problems at birth-when in most cases they are at their largest size-they usually become smaller with time and do not affect the individual in later life.

Benign tumors called *phakomas* are sometimes found in the eyes of individuals with TSC, appearing as white patches on the retina. Generally they do not cause vision loss or other vision problems, but they can be used to help diagnose the disease.

Additional tumors and cysts may be found in other areas of the body, including the liver, lung, and pancreas. Bone cysts, rectal polyps, gum fibromas, and dental pits may also occur.

A wide variety of skin abnormalities may occur in individuals with TSC. Most cause no problems but are helpful in diagnosis. Some cases may cause disfigurement, necessitating treatment. The most common skin abnormalities include:

- Hypomelanic macules, which are white or lighter patches of skin that may appear anywhere on the body and are caused by a lack of skin pigment or melanin-the substance that gives skin its color.

- Reddish spots or bumps called *facial angiofibromas* (also called adenoma sebaceum), which appear on the face (sometimes resembling acne) and consist of blood vessels and fibrous tissue.

- Raised, discolored areas on the forehead called forehead plaques, which are common and unique to TSC and may help doctors diagnose the disorder.

- Areas of thick leathery, pebbly skin called shagreen patches, usually found on the lower back or nape of the neck.

- Small fleshy tumors called ungual *orsubungual fibromas* that grow around and under the toenails or fingernails and may need to be surgically removed if they enlarge or cause bleeding. These usually appear later in life, ages 20 - 50.

- Other skin features that are not unique to individuals with TSC, including *molluscum fibrosum* or skin tags, which typically occur across the back of the neck and shoulders, café au lait spots or flat brown marks, and poliosis, a tuft or patch of white hair that may appear on the scalp or eyelids.

Lung lesions are present in about one-third of adult women with TSC and are much less commonly seen in men. Lung lesions include lymphangioleiomyomatosis (LAM) and multinodular multifocal pneumocyte hyperplasia (MMPH). LAM is a tumor-like disorder in which cells proliferate in the lungs, and there is lung destruction with cyst formation. There is a range of symptoms with LAM, with many TSC individuals having no symptoms, while others suffer with breathlessness, which can progress and be severe. MMPH is a more benign tumor that occurs in men and women equally.

How Is TSC Diagnosed?

The diagnosis of TSC is based upon clinical criteria. In many cases the first clue to recognizing TSC is the presence of seizures or delayed development. In other cases, the first sign may be white patches on the skin (hypomelanotic macules) or the identification of cardiac tumor rhabdomyoma.

Diagnosis of the disorder is based on a careful clinical exam in combination with computed tomography (CT) or magnetic resonance imaging (MRI) of the brain, which may show tubers in the brain, and an ultrasound of the heart, liver, and kidneys, which may show tumors in those organs. Doctors should carefully examine the skin for the wide variety of skin features, the fingernails and toenails for ungual fibromas, the teeth and gums for dental pits and/or gum fibromas, and the eyes for retinal lesions. A Wood's lamp or ultraviolet light may be used to locate the hypomelantic macules which are sometimes hard to see on infants and individuals with pale or fair skin. Because of the wide variety of signs of TSC, it is best if a doctor experienced in the diagnosis of TSC evaluates a potential patient.

In infants TSC may be suspected if the child has cardiac rhabdomyomas or seizures (infantile spasms) at birth. With a careful examination of the skin and brain, it may be possible to diagnose TSC in a very young infant. However, many children are not diagnosed until later in life when their seizures begin and other symptoms such as facial angiofibromas appear.

How Is TSC Treated?

There is no cure for TSC, although treatment is available for a number of the symptoms. Antiepileptic drugs may be used to control seizures. Vigabatrin is a particularly useful medication in TSC, and has been approved by the U.S. Food and Drug Administration (FDA) for treatment of infantile spams in TSC, although it has significant side effects. The FDA has approved the drug everolimus (Afinitor®) to treat subependymal giant cell astrocytomas (SEGA brain tumors) and angiomyolipoma kidney tumors. Specific medications may be prescribed for behavior problems. Intervention programs including special schooling and occupational therapy may benefit individuals with special needs and developmental issues. Surgery may be needed in case of complications connected to tubers, SEN or SEGA, as well as in risk of hemorrhage from kidney tumors. Respiratory insufficiency due to LAM can be treated with supplemental oxygen therapy or lung transplantation if severe.

Because TSC is a lifelong condition, individuals need to be regularly monitored by a doctor to make sure they are receiving the best possible treatments. Due to the many varied symptoms of TSC, care by a clinician experienced with the disorder is recommended.

Basic laboratory studies have revealed insight into the function of the TSC genes and has led to recent use of rapamycin and related drugs for treating some manifestations of TSC. Rapamycin has been shown to be effective in treating SEGA, the brain tumor seen in TSC. However, its benefit for a variety of other aspects of and tumors seen in people with TSC is less certain, and clinical trials looking at the benefit carefully are continuing. Rapamycin and related drugs are not yet approved by the FDA for any purpose in individuals with TSC.

What Is the Prognosis?

The prognosis for individuals with TSC is highly variable and depends on the severity of symptoms. Those individuals with mild symptoms usually do well and have a normal life expectancy, while paying attention to TSC-specific issues. Individuals who are severely affected can suffer from severe mental retardation and persistent epilepsy.

All individuals with TSC are at risk for life-threatening conditions related to the brain tumors, kidney lesions, or LAM. Continued monitoring by a physician experienced with TSC is important. With appropriate medical care, most individuals with the disorder can look forward to normal life expectancy.

Chapter 38

Vision Disorders

Chapter Contents

Section 38.1

Color Vision Deficiency

This chapter contains text excerpted from the following sources:
Text beginning with the heading "What Is Color Vision Deficiency?"
is excerpted from "Color Vision Deficiency," Genetics Home
Reference (GHR), National Institutes of Health (NIH), March 14,
2016; Text under the heading "Who Gets Color Blindness?"
is excerpted from "Facts about Color Blindness," National
Eye Institute (NEI), February 2015.

What Is Color Vision Deficiency?

Color vision deficiency (sometimes called color blindness) represents a group of conditions that affect the perception of color. Red-green color vision defects are the most common form of color vision deficiency. Affected individuals have trouble distinguishing between some shades of red, yellow, and green. Blue-yellow color vision defects (also called tritan defects), which are rarer, cause problems with differentiating shades of blue and green and cause difficulty distinguishing dark blue from black. These two forms of color vision deficiency disrupt color perception but do not affect the sharpness of vision (visual acuity).

A less common and more severe form of color vision deficiency called blue cone monochromacy causes very poor visual acuity and severely reduced color vision. Affected individuals have additional vision problems, which can include increased sensitivity to light (photophobia), involuntary back-and-forth eye movements (nystagmus), and near-sightedness (myopia). Blue cone monochromacy is sometimes considered to be a form of achromatopsia, a disorder characterized by a partial or total lack of color vision with other vision problems.

How Common Is Color Vision Deficiency?

Red-green color vision defects are the most common form of color vision deficiency. This condition affects males much more often than females. Among populations with Northern European ancestry, it occurs in about 1 in 12 males and 1 in 200 females. Red-green color vision defects have a lower incidence in almost all other populations studied.

Blue-yellow color vision defects affect males and females equally. This condition occurs in fewer than 1 in 10,000 people worldwide.

Blue cone monochromacy is rarer than the other forms of color vision deficiency, affecting about 1 in 100,000 people worldwide. Like red-green color vision defects, blue cone monochromacy affects males much more often than females.

What Genes Are Related to Color Vision Deficiency?

Mutations in the *OPN1LW, OPN1MW,* and *OPN1SW* genes cause the forms of color vision deficiency described above. The proteins produced from these genes play essential roles in color vision. They are found in the retina, which is the light-sensitive tissue at the back of the eye. The retina contains two types of light receptor cells, called rods and cones, that transmit visual signals from the eye to the brain. Rods provide vision in low light. Cones provide vision in bright light, including color vision. There are three types of cones, each containing a specific pigment (a photopigment called an opsin) that is most sensitive to particular wavelengths of light. The brain combines input from all three types of cones to produce normal color vision.

The *OPN1LW, OPN1MW,* and *OPN1SW* genes provide instructions for making the three opsin pigments in cones. The opsin made from the OPN1LW gene is more sensitive to light in the yellow/orange part of the visible spectrum (long-wavelength light), and cones with this pigment are called long-wavelength-sensitive or L cones. The opsin made from the *OPN1MW* gene is more sensitive to light in the middle of the visible spectrum (yellow/green light), and cones with this pigment are called middle-wavelength-sensitive or M cones. The opsin made from the *OPN1SW* gene is more sensitive to light in the blue/violet part of the visible spectrum (short-wavelength light), and cones with this pigment are called short-wavelength-sensitive or S cones.

Genetic changes involving the *OPN1LW* or *OPN1MW* gene cause red-green color vision defects. These changes lead to an absence of L or M cones or to the production of abnormal opsin pigments in these cones that affect red-green color vision. Blue-yellow color vision defects result from mutations in the *OPN1SW* gene. These mutations lead to the premature destruction of S cones or the production of defective S cones. Impaired S cone function alters perception of the color blue, making it difficult or impossible to detect differences between shades of blue and green and causing problems with distinguishing dark blue from black.

Blue cone monochromacy occurs when genetic changes affecting the *OPN1LW* and *OPN1MW* genes prevent both L and M cones from functioning normally. In people with this condition, only S cones are functional, which leads to reduced visual acuity and poor color vision. The loss of L and M cone function also underlies the other vision problems in people with blue cone monochromacy.

Some problems with color vision are not caused by gene mutations. These nonhereditary conditions are described as acquired color vision deficiencies. They can be caused by other eye disorders, such as diseases involving the retina, the nerve that carries visual information from the eye to the brain (the optic nerve), or areas of the brain involved in processing visual information. Acquired color vision deficiencies can also be side effects of certain drugs, such as chloroquine (which is used to treat malaria), or result from exposure to particular chemicals, such as organic solvents.

Who Gets Color Blindness?

As many as 8 percent of men and 0.5 percent of women with Northern European ancestry have the common form of red-green color blindness.

Men are much more likely to be color blind than women because the genes responsible for the most common, inherited color blindness are on the X chromosome. Males only have one X chromosome, while females have two X chromosomes. In females, a functional gene on only one of the X chromosomes is enough to compensate for the loss on the other. This kind of inheritance pattern is called X-linked, and primarily affects males. Inherited color blindness can be present at birth, begin in childhood, or not appear until the adult years.

How Do We See Color?

What color is a strawberry? Most of us would say red, but do we all see the same red? Color vision depends on our eyes and brain working together to perceive different properties of light.

We see the natural and artificial light that illuminates our world as white, although it is actually a mixture of colors that, perceived on their own, would span the visual spectrum from deep blue to deep red. You can see this when rain separates sunlight into a rainbow or a glass prism separates white light into a multi-color band. The color of light is determined by its wavelength. Longer wavelength corresponds to red light and shorter wavelength corresponds to blue light.

Strawberries and other objects reflect some wavelengths of light and absorb others. The reflected light we perceive as color. So, a strawberry is red because its surface is only reflecting the long wavelengths we see as red and absorbing the others. An object appears white when it reflects all wavelengths and black when it absorbs all wavelengths.

Vision begins when light enters the eye and the cornea and lens focus it onto the retina, a thin layer of tissue at the back of the eye that contains millions of light-sensitive cells called photoreceptors. Some photoreceptors are shaped like rods and some are shaped like cones. In each eye there are many more rods than cones – approximately 120 million rods compared to only 6 million cones. Rods and cones both contain photopigment molecules that undergo a chemical change when they absorb light. This chemical change acts like an on-switch, triggering electrical signals that are then passed from the retina to the visual parts of the brain.

Rods and cones are different in how they respond to light. Rods are more responsive to dim light, which makes them useful for night vision. Cones are more responsive to bright light, such as in the day-time when light is plentiful.

Another important difference is that all rods contain only one photopigment, while cones contain one of three different photopigments. This makes cones sensitive to long (red), medium (green), or short (blue) wavelengths of light. The presence of three types of photopigments, each sensitive to a different part of the visual spectrum, is what gives us our rich color vision.

Humans are unusual among mammals for our trichromatic vision – named for the three different types of photopigments we have. Most mammals, including dogs, have just two photopigment types. Other creatures, such as butterflies, have more than three. They may be able to see colors we can only imagine.

Most of us have a full set of the three different cone photopigments and so we share a very similar color vision experience, but because the human eye and brain together translate light into color, each of us sees colors differently. The differences may be slight. Your blue may be more blue than someone else's, or in the case of color blindness, your red and green may be someone else's brown.

What Are the Different Types of Color Blindness?

The most common types of color blindness are inherited. They are the result of defects in the genes that contain the instructions for making the photopigments found in cones. Some defects alter the

445

photopigment's sensitivity to color, for example, it might be slightly more sensitive to deeper red and less sensitive to green. Other defects can result in the total loss of a photopigment. Depending on the type of defect and the cone that is affected problems can arise with red, green, or blue color vision.

Red-Green Color Blindness

The most common types of hereditary color blindness are due to the loss or limited function of red cone (known as protan) or green cone (deutran) photopigments. This kind of color blindness is commonly referred to as red-green color blindness.

- **Protanomaly**: In males with protanomaly, the red cone photopigment is abnormal. Red, orange, and yellow appear greener and colors are not as bright. This condition is mild and doesn't usually interfere with daily living. Protanomaly is an X-linked disorder estimated to affect 1 percent of males.

- **Protanopia**: In males with protanopia, there are no working red cone cells. Red appears as black. Certain shades of orange, yellow, and green all appear as yellow. Protanopia is an X-linked disorder that is estimated to affect 1 percent of males.

- **Deuteranomaly**: In males with deuteranomaly, the green cone photopigment is abnormal. Yellow and green appear redder and it is difficult to tell violet from blue. This condition is mild and doesn't interfere with daily living. Deuteranomaly is the most common form of color blindness and is an X-linked disorder affecting 5 percent of males.

- **Deuteranopia**: In males with deuteranopia, there are no working green cone cells. They tend to see reds as brownish-yellow and greens as beige. Deuteranopia is an X-linked disorder that affects about 1 percent of males.

Blue-Yellow Color Blindness

Blue-yellow color blindness is rarer than red-green color blindness. Blue-cone (tritan) photopigments are either missing or have limited function.

- **Tritanomaly**: People with tritanomaly have functionally limited blue cone cells. Blue appears greener and it can be difficult to tell yellow and red from pink. Tritanomaly is extremely rare. It is an autosomal dominant disorder affecting males and females equally.

- **Tritanopia**: People with tritanopia, also known as blue-yellow color blindness, lack blue cone cells. Blue appears green and yellow appears violet or light grey. Tritanopia is an extremely rare autosomal recessive disorder affecting males and females equally.

Complete Color Blindness

People with complete color blindness (monochromacy) don't experience color at all and the clearness of their vision (visual acuity) may also be affected.

There are two types of monochromacy:

1. **Cone monochromacy:** This rare form of color blindness results from a failure of two of the three cone cell photopigments to work. There is red cone monochromacy, green cone monochromacy, and blue cone monochromacy. People with cone monochromacy have trouble distinguishing colors because the brain needs to compare the signals from different types of cones in order to see color. When only one type of cone works, this comparison isn't possible. People with blue cone monochromacy, may also have reduced visual acuity, near-sightedness, and uncontrollable eye movements, a condition known as nystagmus. Cone monochromacy is an autosomal recessive disorder.

2. **Rod monochromacy or achromatopsia:** This type of monochromacy is rare and is the most severe form of color blindness. It is present at birth. None of the cone cells have functional photopigments. Lacking all cone vision, people with rod monochromacy see the world in black, white, and gray. And since rods respond to dim light, people with rod monochromacy tend to be photophobic—very uncomfortable in bright environments. They also experience nystagmus. Rod monochromacy is an autosomal recessive disorder.

How Is Color Blindness Diagnosed?

Eye care professionals use a variety of tests to diagnose color blindness. These tests can quickly diagnose specific types of color blindness.

The **Ishihara Color Test** is the most common test for red-green color blindness. The test consists of a series of colored circles, called Ishihara plates, each of which contains a collection of dots in different colors and sizes. Within the circle are dots that form a shape clearly visible to those with normal color vision, but invisible or difficult to see for those with red-green color blindness.

The **newer Cambridge Color Test** uses a visual array similar to the Ishihara plates, except displayed on a computer monitor. The goal is to identify a C shape that is different in color from the background. The "C" is presented randomly in one of four orientations. When test-takers see the "C," they are asked to press one of four keys that correspond to the orientation.

The **anomaloscope** uses a test in which two different light sources have to be matched in color. Looking through the eyepiece, the viewer sees a circle. The upper half is a yellow light that can be adjusted in brightness. The lower half is a combination of red and green lights that can be mixed in variable proportions. The viewer uses one knob to adjust the brightness of the top half, and another to adjust the color of the lower half. The goal is to make the upper and lower halves the same brightness and color.

The **HRR Pseudoisochromatic Color Test** is another red-green color blindness test that uses color plates to test for color blindness.

The Farnsworth-Munsell 100 Hue Test uses a set of blocks or pegs that are roughly the same color but in different hues (shades of the color). The goal is to arrange them in a line in order of hue. This test measures the ability to discriminate subtle color changes. It is used by industries that depend on the accurate color perception of its employees, such as graphic design, photography, and food quality inspection.

The **Farnsworth Lantern Test** is used by the U.S. military to determine the severity of color blindness. Those with mild forms pass the test and are allowed to serve in the armed forces.

Are There Treatments for Color Blindness?

There is no cure for color blindness. However, people with red-green color blindness may be able to use a special set of lenses to help them perceive colors more accurately. These lenses can only be used outdoors under bright lighting conditions. Visual aids have also been developed to help people cope with color blindness. There are iPhone and iPad apps, for example, that help people with color blindness discriminate among colors. Some of these apps allow users to snap a photo and tap it anywhere on the image to see the color of that area. More sophisticated apps allow users to find out both color and shades of color. These kinds of apps can be helpful in selecting ripe fruits such as bananas, or finding complementary colors when picking out clothing.

How Does Color Blindness Affect Daily Life?

Color blindness can make it difficult to read color-coded information such as bar graphs and pie charts. This can be particularly troubling for children who aren't yet diagnosed with color blindness, since educational materials are often color-coded. Children with red-green color blindness may also have difficulty reading a green chalkboard when yellow chalk is used. Art classes, which require selecting appropriate colors of paint or crayons, may be challenging.

Color blindness can go undetected for some time since children will often try to hide their disorder. It's important to have children tested, particularly boys, if there is a family history of color blindness. Many school systems offer vision screening tests that include color blindness testing. Once a child is diagnosed, he or she can learn to ask for help with tasks that require color recognition.

Simple everyday tasks like cooking meat to the desired color or selecting ripe produce can be a challenge for adults. Children might find food without bright color as less appetizing. Traffic lights pose challenges, since they have to be read by the position of the light. Since most lights are vertical, with green on bottom and red on top, if a light is positioned horizontally, a color blind person has to do a quick mental rotation to read it. Reading maps or buying clothes that match colors can also be difficult. However, these are relatively minor inconveniences and most people with color blindness learn to adapt.

Section 38.2

Early-Onset Glaucoma

This section includes text excerpted from "Early-Onset Glaucoma," Genetics Home Reference (GHR), National Institutes of Health (NIH), March 14, 2016.

What Is Early-Onset Glaucoma?

Glaucoma is a group of eye disorders in which the optic nerves connecting the eyes and the brain are progressively damaged. This damage can lead to reduction in side (peripheral) vision and eventual blindness. Other signs and symptoms may include bulging eyes, excessive tearing, and abnormal sensitivity to light (photophobia). The term "early-onset glaucoma" may be used when the disorder appears before the age of 40.

In most people with glaucoma, the damage to the optic nerves is caused by increased pressure within the eyes (intraocular pressure). Intraocular pressure depends on a balance between fluid entering and leaving the eyes.

Usually glaucoma develops in older adults, in whom the risk of developing the disorder may be affected by a variety of medical conditions including high blood pressure (hypertension) and diabetes mellitus, as well as family history. The risk of early-onset glaucoma depends mainly on heredity.

Structural abnormalities that impede fluid drainage in the eye may be present at birth and usually become apparent during the first year of life. Such abnormalities may be part of a genetic disorder that affects many body systems, called a syndrome. If glaucoma appears before the age of 5 without other associated abnormalities, it is called primary congenital glaucoma.

Other individuals experience early onset of primary open-angle glaucoma, the most common adult form of glaucoma. If primary open-angle glaucoma develops during childhood or early adulthood, it is called juvenile open-angle glaucoma.

How Common Is Early-Onset Glaucoma?

Primary congenital glaucoma affects approximately 1 in 10,000 people. Its frequency is higher in the Middle East. Juvenile open-angle glaucoma affects about 1 in 50,000 people. Primary open-angle glaucoma is much more common after the age of 40, affecting about 1 percent of the population worldwide.

What Genes Are Related to Early-Onset Glaucoma?

Approximately 10 percent to 33 percent of people with juvenile open-angle glaucoma have mutations in the *MYOC* gene. *MYOC* gene mutations have also been detected in some people with primary congenital glaucoma. The *MYOC* gene provides instructions for producing a protein called myocilin. Myocilin is found in certain structures of the eye, called the trabecular meshwork and the ciliary body, that regulate the intraocular pressure.

Researchers believe that myocilin functions together with other proteins as part of a protein complex. Mutations may alter the protein in such a way that the complex cannot be formed. Defective myocilin that is not incorporated into functional complexes may accumulate in the trabecular meshwork and ciliary body. The excess protein may prevent sufficient flow of fluid from the eye, resulting in increased intraocular pressure and causing the signs and symptoms of early-onset glaucoma.

Between 20 percent and 40 percent of people with primary congenital glaucoma have mutations in the *CYP1B1* gene. *CYP1B1* gene mutations have also been detected in some people with juvenile open-angle glaucoma. The *CYP1B1* gene provides instructions for producing a form of the cytochrome P450 protein. Like myocilin, this protein is found in the trabecular meshwork, ciliary body, and other structures of the eye.

It is not well understood how defects in the *CYP1B1* protein cause signs and symptoms of glaucoma. Recent studies suggest that the defects may interfere with the early development of the trabecular meshwork. In the clear covering of the eye (the cornea), the *CYP1B1* protein may also be involved in a process that regulates the secretion of fluid inside the eye. If this fluid is produced in excess, the high intraocular pressure characteristic of glaucoma may develop.

The *CYP1B1* protein may interact with myocilin. Individuals with mutations in both the *MYOC* and *CYP1B1* genes may develop glaucoma at an earlier age and have more severe symptoms than do those with mutations in only one of the genes. Mutations in other genes may also be involved in early-onset glaucoma.

How Do People Inherit Early-Onset Glaucoma?

Early-onset glaucoma can have different inheritance patterns. Primary congenital glaucoma is usually inherited in an autosomal recessive pattern, which means both copies of the gene in each cell have mutations. Most often, the parents of an individual with an autosomal recessive condition each carry one copy of the mutated gene, but do not show signs and symptoms of the condition.

Juvenile open-angle glaucoma is inherited in an autosomal dominant pattern, which means one copy of the altered gene in each cell is sufficient to cause the disorder. In some families, primary congenital glaucoma may also be inherited in an autosomal dominant pattern.

Section 38.3

X-Linked Juvenile Retinoschisis

This section includes text excerpted from "X-Linked Juvenile Retinoschisis," Genetics Home Reference (GHR), National Institutes of Health (NIH), March 14, 2016.

What Is X-Linked Juvenile Retinoschisis?

X-linked juvenile retinoschisis is a condition characterized by impaired vision that begins in childhood and occurs almost exclusively in males. This disorder affects the retina, which is a specialized light-sensitive tissue that lines the back of the eye. Damage to the retina impairs the sharpness of vision (visual acuity) in both eyes. Typically, X-linked juvenile retinoschisis affects cells in the central area of the retina called the macula. The macula is responsible for sharp central vision, which is needed for detailed tasks such as reading, driving, and recognizing faces. X-linked juvenile retinoschisis is one type of a broader disorder called macular degeneration, which disrupts the normal functioning of the macula. Occasionally, side (peripheral) vision is affected in people with X-linked juvenile retinoschisis.

X-linked juvenile retinoschisis is usually diagnosed when affected boys start school and poor vision and difficulty with reading become apparent. In more severe cases, eye squinting and involuntary movement of the eyes (nystagmus) begin in infancy. Other early features of X-linked juvenile retinoschisis include eyes that do not look in the same direction (strabismus) and farsightedness (hyperopia). Visual acuity often declines in childhood and adolescence but then stabilizes throughout adulthood until a significant decline in visual acuity typically occurs in a man's fifties or sixties. Sometimes, severe complications develop, such as separation of the retinal layers (retinal detachment) or leakage of blood vessels in the retina (vitreous hemorrhage). These eye abnormalities can further impair vision or cause blindness.

How Common Is X-Linked Juvenile Retinoschisis?

The prevalence of X-linked juvenile retinoschisis is estimated to be 1 in 5,000 to 25,000 men worldwide.

What Genes Are Related to X-Linked Juvenile Retinoschisis?

Mutations in the RS1 gene cause most cases of X-linked juvenile retinoschisis. The *RS1* gene provides instructions for making a protein called retinoschisin, which is found in the retina. Studies suggest that retinoschisin plays a role in the development and maintenance of the retina. The protein is probably involved in the organization of cells in the retina by attaching cells together (cell adhesion).

RS1 gene mutations result in a decrease in or complete loss of functional retinoschisin, which disrupts the maintenance and organization of cells in the retina. As a result, tiny splits (schisis) or tears form in the retina. This damage often forms a "spoke-wheel" pattern in the macula, which can be seen during an eye examination. In half of affected individuals, these abnormalities can occur in the area of the macula, affecting visual acuity, in the other half of cases the schisis occurs in the sides of the retina, resulting in impaired peripheral vision.

Some individuals with X-linked juvenile retinoschisis do not have a mutation in the *RS1* gene. In these individuals, the cause of the disorder is unknown.

How Do People Inherit X-Linked Juvenile Retinoschisis?

This condition is inherited in an X-linked recessive pattern. The gene associated with this condition is located on the X chromosome, which is one of the two sex chromosomes. In males (who have only one X chromosome), one altered copy of the gene in each cell is sufficient to cause the condition. In females (who have two X chromosomes), a mutation would have to occur in both copies of the gene to cause the disorder. Because it is unlikely that females will have two altered copies of this gene, males are affected by X-linked recessive disorders much more frequently than females.

A characteristic of X-linked inheritance is that fathers cannot pass X-linked traits to their sons.

Chapter 39

Wilson Disease

What Is Wilson Disease?

Wilson disease is an inherited disorder in which excessive amounts of copper accumulate in the body, particularly in the liver, brain, and eyes. The signs and symptoms of Wilson disease usually first appear between the ages of 6 and 45, but they most often begin during the teenage years. The features of this condition include a combination of liver disease and neurological and psychiatric problems.

Liver disease is typically the initial feature of Wilson disease in affected children and young adults; individuals diagnosed at an older age usually do not have symptoms of liver problems, although they may have very mild liver disease. The signs and symptoms of liver disease include yellowing of the skin or whites of the eyes (jaundice), fatigue, loss of appetite, and abdominal swelling.

Nervous system or psychiatric problems are often the initial features in individuals diagnosed in adulthood and commonly occur in young adults with Wilson disease. Signs and symptoms of these problems can include clumsiness, tremors, difficulty walking, speech problems, impaired thinking ability, depression, anxiety, and mood swings.

This chapter contains text excerpted from the following sources: Text beginning with the heading "What Is Wilson Disease?" is excerpted from "Wilson Disease," Genetics Home Reference (GHR), National Institutes of Health (NIH), March 14, 2016; Text under the heading "What Causes Wilson Disease?" is excerpted from "Wilson Disease," National Institute of Diabetes and Digestive and Kidney Diseases (NIDDK), July 2014.

In many individuals with Wilson disease, copper deposits in the front surface of the eye (the cornea) form a green-to-brownish ring, called the Kayser-Fleischer ring, that surrounds the colored part of the eye. Abnormalities in eye movements, such as a restricted ability to gaze upwards, may also occur.

How Common Is Wilson Disease?

Wilson disease is a rare disorder that affects approximately 1 in 30,000 individuals.

What Genes Are Related to Wilson Disease?

Wilson disease is caused by mutations in the *ATP7B* gene. This gene provides instructions for making a protein called copper-transporting ATPase 2, which plays a role in the transport of copper from the liver to other parts of the body. Copper is necessary for many cellular functions, but it is toxic when present in excessive amounts. The copper-transporting ATPase 2 protein is particularly important for the elimination of excess copper from the body. Mutations in the *ATP7B* gene prevent the transport protein from functioning properly. With a shortage of functional protein, excess copper is not removed from the body. As a result, copper accumulates to toxic levels that can damage tissues and organs, particularly the liver and brain.

Research indicates that a normal variation in the *PRNP* gene may modify the course of Wilson disease. The PRNP gene provides instructions for making prion protein, which is active in the brain and other tissues and appears to be involved in transporting copper. Studies have focused on the effects of a *PRNP* gene variation that affects position 129 of the prion protein. At this position, people can have either the protein building block (amino acid) methionine or the amino acid valine. Among people who have mutations in the *ATP7B* gene, it appears that having methionine instead of valine at position 129 of the prion protein is associated with delayed onset of symptoms and an increased occurrence of neurological symptoms, particularly tremors. Larger studies are needed, however, before the effects of this *PRNP* gene variation on Wilson disease can be established.

What Causes Wilson Disease?

Wilson disease is caused by an inherited autosomal recessive mutation, or change, in the *ATP7B* gene. In an autosomal recessive disease, the child has to inherit the gene mutation from both parents to have an increased likelihood for the disease. The chance of a child inheriting autosomal recessive mutations from both parents with a gene mutation is 25 percent, or one in four. If only one parent carries the mutated gene, the child will not get the disease, although the child may inherit one copy of the gene mutation. The child is called a "carrier" of the disease and can pass the gene mutation to the next generation. Genetic testing is a procedure that identifies changes in a patient's genes and can show whether a parent or child is a carrier of a mutated gene. Autosomal recessive diseases are typically not seen in every generation of an affected family.

The Figure 39.1 shows the chance of inheriting an autosomal recessive mutation from parents who both carry the mutated gene.

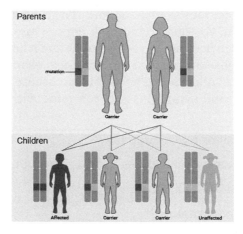

Figure 39.1. *Autosomal Recessive*

The chance of a child inheriting autosomal recessive mutations from both parents with a gene mutation is 25 percent, or one in four.

Who Is More Likely to Develop Wilson Disease?

Men and women develop Wilson disease at equal rates. About one in 30,000 people have Wilson disease. Symptoms usually appear between ages 5 and 35; however, new cases have been reported in people ages 3 to 72.*

A person's risk of being a carrier or having Wilson disease increases when his or her family has a known history of Wilson disease. Some people may not know about a family history of the condition because the mutation is often passed to a child by a parent who is a carrier. A person's chances of having Wilson disease increase if a healthcare provider has diagnosed one or both parents with the condition.

* Rosencrantz R, Schilsky M. Wilson disease: pathogenesis and clinical considerations in diagnosis and treatment. Seminars in Liver Disease. 2011;31:245–259.

What Are the Signs and Symptoms of Wilson Disease?

The signs and symptoms of Wilson disease vary, depending on what organs of the body are affected. Wilson disease is present at birth; however, the signs and symptoms of the disease do not appear until the copper builds up in the liver, the brain, or other organs.

When people have signs and symptoms, they usually affect the liver, the central nervous system, or both. The central nervous system includes the brain, the spinal cord, and nerves throughout the body. Sometimes a person does not have symptoms and a healthcare provider discovers the disease during a routine physical exam or blood test, or during an illness. Children can have Wilson disease for several years before any signs and symptoms occur. People with Wilson disease may have

- liver-related signs and symptoms

- central nervous system-related signs and symptoms

- mental health-related signs and symptoms

- other signs and symptoms

Liver-related Signs and Symptoms

People with Wilson disease may develop signs and symptoms of chronic, or long lasting, liver disease:

- weakness

- fatigue, or feeling tired

- loss of appetite

- nausea

- vomiting

- weight loss

- pain and bloating from fluid accumulating in the abdomen

- edema—swelling, usually in the legs, feet, or ankles and less often in the hands or face

- itching

- Spider like blood vessels, called spider angiomas, near the surface of the skin

- muscle cramps

- jaundice, a condition that causes the skin and whites of the eyes to turn yellow

Some people with Wilson disease may not develop signs or symptoms of liver disease until they develop acute liver failure—a condition that develops suddenly.

Central Nervous System-related Signs and Symptoms

Central nervous system-related symptoms usually appear in people after the liver has retained a lot of copper; however, signs and symptoms of liver disease may not be present. Central nervous system-related symptoms occur most often in adults and sometimes occur in children. Signs and symptoms include

- tremors or uncontrolled movements

- muscle stiffness

- problems with speech, swallowing, or physical coordination

A healthcare provider may refer people with these symptoms to a neurologist—a doctor who specializes in nervous system diseases.

Mental Health-related Signs and Symptoms

Some people will have mental health-related signs and symptoms when copper builds up in the central nervous system. Signs and symptoms may include

- personality changes

- depression

- feeling anxious, or nervous, about most things

- psychosis—when a person loses contact with reality

Other Signs and Symptoms

Other signs and symptoms of Wilson disease may include

- anemia, a condition in which red blood cells are fewer or smaller than normal, which prevents the body's cells from getting enough oxygen

- arthritis, a condition in which a person has pain and swelling in one or more joints

- high levels of amino acids, protein, uric acid, and carbohydrates in urine

- low platelet or white blood cell count

- osteoporosis, a condition in which the bones become less dense and more likely to fracture

Kayser-Fleischer Rings

Kayser-Fleischer rings result from a buildup of copper in the eyes and are the most unique sign of Wilson disease. During an eye exam, a healthcare provider will see a rusty-brown ring around the edge of the iris and in the rim of the cornea. The iris is the colored part of the eye surrounding the pupil. The cornea is the transparent outer membrane or layer that covers the eye.

People with Wilson disease who show signs of nervous system damage usually have Kayser-Fleischer rings. However, the rings are present in only 40 to 66 percent of people with signs of liver damage alone.

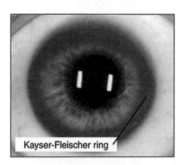

Figure 39.2. *Kayser-Fleischer Ring*

What Are the Complications of Wilson Disease?

People who have Wilson disease that is not treated or diagnosed early can have serious complications, such as

- cirrhosis—scarring of the liver
- kidney damage—as liver function decreases, the kidneys may be damaged
- persistent nervous system problems when nervous system symptoms do not resolve
- liver cancer—hepatocellular carcinoma is a type of liver cancer that can occur in people with cirrhosis
- liver failure—a condition in which the liver stops working properly
- death, if left untreated

How Is Wilson Disease Diagnosed?

A healthcare provider may use several tests and exams to diagnose Wilson disease, including the following:

- medical and family history
- physical exam
- blood tests
- urine tests
- liver biopsy
- imaging tests

Healthcare providers typically see the same symptoms of Wilson disease in other conditions, and the symptoms of Wilson disease do not occur together often, making the disease difficult to diagnose.

How Is Wilson Disease Treated?

Medications

A healthcare provider will prescribe medications to treat Wilson disease. The medications have different actions that healthcare providers use during different phases of the treatment.

Chelating agents. Chelating agents are medications that remove extra copper from the body by releasing it from organs into the bloodstream. Once the cooper is in the bloodstream, the kidneys then filter the copper and pass it into the urine. A healthcare provider usually recommends chelating agents at the beginning of treatment. A potential side effect of chelating agents is that nervous system symptoms may become worse during treatment. The two medications available for this type of treatment include

trientine (Syprine)—the risk for side effects and worsening nervous system symptoms appears to be lower with trientine than d-penicillamine. Researchers are still studying the side effects; however, some healthcare providers prefer to prescribe trientine as the first treatment of choice because it appears to be safer.

d-penicillamine—people taking d-penicillamine may have other reactions or side effects, such as

- fever

- a rash

- kidney problems

- bone marrow problems

A healthcare provider will prescribe a lower dose of a chelating agent to women who are pregnant to reduce the risk of birth defects. A healthcare provider should consider future screening on any newborn whose parent has Wilson disease.

Zinc. A healthcare provider will prescribe zinc for patients who do not have symptoms, or after a person has completed successful treatment using a chelating agent and symptoms begin to improve. Zinc, taken by mouth as zinc salts such as zinc acetate (Galzin), blocks the digestive tract's absorption of copper from food. Although most people taking zinc usually do not experience side effects, some people may experience stomach upset. A healthcare provider may prescribe zinc for children with Wilson disease who show no symptoms. Women may take the full dosage of zinc safely during pregnancy.

Maintenance, or long term, treatment begins when symptoms improve and tests show that copper is at a safe level. Maintenance treatment typically includes taking zinc or a lower dose of a chelating agent. A healthcare provider closely monitors the person and reviews regular blood and urine tests to ensure maintenance treatment controls the copper level in the body.

Treatment for people with Wilson disease who have no symptoms may include a chelating agent or zinc in order to prevent symptoms from developing and stop or slow disease progression.

People with Wilson disease will take medications for the rest of their lives. Follow-up and adherence to the healthcare provider's treatment plan is necessary to manage symptoms and prevent organ damage.

Changes in Eating, Diet, and Nutrition

People with Wilson disease should reduce their dietary copper intake by avoiding foods that are high in copper, such as

- shellfish
- liver
- mushrooms
- nuts
- chocolate

People should not eat these foods during the initial treatment and talk with the healthcare provider to discuss if they are safe to eat in moderation during maintenance treatment.

People with Wilson disease whose tap water runs through copper pipes or comes from a well should check the copper levels in the tap water. Water that sits in copper pipes may pick up copper residue, but running water lowers the level to within acceptable limits. People with Wilson disease should not use copper containers or cookware to store or prepare food or drinks.

To help ensure coordinated and safe care, people should discuss their use of complementary and alternative medical practices, including their use of vitamins and dietary supplements, with their healthcare provider. If the healthcare provider recommends taking any type of supplement or vitamin, a pharmacist can recommend types that do not contain copper.

People should talk with a healthcare provider about diet changes to reduce copper intake.

Liver Transplant

A liver transplant may be necessary in people when

- cirrhosis leads to liver failure
- acute liver failure happens suddenly
- treatment is not effective

A liver transplant is an operation to remove a diseased or an injured liver and replace it with a healthy one from another person, called a donor. A successful transplant is a life-saving treatment for people with liver failure.

Most liver transplants are successful. About 85 percent of transplanted livers are functioning after 1 year. Liver transplant surgery provides a cure for Wilson disease in most cases.

How Can Wilson Disease Be Prevented?

A person cannot prevent Wilson disease; however, people with a family history of Wilson disease, especially those with an affected sibling or parent, should talk with a healthcare provider about testing. A healthcare provider may be able to diagnose Wilson disease before symptoms appear. Early diagnosis and treatment of Wilson disease can reduce or even prevent organ damage.

People with a family history of the disease may also benefit from genetic testing that can identify one or more gene mutations. A healthcare provider may refer a person with a family history of Wilson disease to a geneticist—a doctor who specializes in genetic diseases.

Points to Remember

- Wilson disease is a genetic disease that prevents the body from removing extra copper.

- Normally, the liver filters extra copper and releases it into bile. In Wilson disease, the liver does not filter copper correctly and copper builds up in the liver, brain, eyes, and other organs.

- Wilson disease is caused by an inherited autosomal recessive mutation, or change, in the *ATP7B* gene. In an autosomal recessive disease, the child has to inherit the gene mutation from both parents to have an increased likelihood for the disease.

- The signs and symptoms of Wilson disease vary, depending on what organs of the body are affected. People with Wilson disease may have

  - liver-related signs and symptoms

  - central nervous system-related signs and symptoms

  - mental health-related signs and symptoms

  - other signs and symptoms

- A healthcare provider will treat Wilson disease with a lifelong effort to reduce and control the amount of copper in the body. Treatment may include

- medicationschanges in eating, diet, and nutrition
- a liver transplant
- People with Wilson disease should reduce their dietary copper intake by avoiding foods that are high in copper, such as
  - shellfish
  - liver
  - mushrooms
  - nuts
  - chocolate
- A person cannot prevent Wilson disease; however, people with a family history of Wilson disease, especially those with an affected sibling or parent, should talk with a healthcare provider about testing.

Part Three

Chromosome Abnormalities

Chapter 40

Angelman Syndrome

What Is Angelman Syndrome?

Angelman syndrome is a complex genetic disorder that primarily affects the nervous system. Characteristic features of this condition include delayed development, intellectual disability, severe speech impairment, and problems with movement and balance (ataxia). Most affected children also have recurrent seizures (epilepsy) and a small head size (microcephaly). Delayed development becomes noticeable by the age of 6 to 12 months, and other common signs and symptoms usually appear in early childhood.

Children with Angelman syndrome typically have a happy, excitable demeanor with frequent smiling, laughter, and hand-flapping movements. Hyperactivity, a short attention span, and a fascination with water are common. Most affected children also have difficulty sleeping and need less sleep than usual.

With age, people with Angelman syndrome become less excitable, and the sleeping problems tend to improve. However, affected individuals continue to have intellectual disability, severe speech impairment, and seizures throughout their lives. Adults with Angelman syndrome have distinctive facial features that may be described as "coarse." Other common features include unusually fair skin with light-colored hair and an abnormal side-to-side curvature of the spine (scoliosis). The life expectancy of people with this condition appears to be nearly normal.

This chapter includes text excerpted from "Angelman Syndrome," Genetics Home Reference (GHR), National Institutes of Health (NIH), March 14, 2016.

How Common Is Angelman Syndrome?

Angelman syndrome affects an estimated 1 in 12,000 to 20,000 people.

What Are the Genetic Changes Related to Angelman Syndrome?

Many of the characteristic features of Angelman syndrome result from the loss of function of a gene called *UBE3A*. People normally inherit one copy of the *UBE3A* gene from each parent. Both copies of this gene are turned on (active) in many of the body's tissues. In certain areas of the brain, however, only the copy inherited from a person's mother (the maternal copy) is active. This parent-specific gene activation is caused by a phenomenon called genomic imprinting. If the maternal copy of the *UBE3A* gene is lost because of a chromosomal change or a gene mutation, a person will have no active copies of the gene in some parts of the brain.

Several different genetic mechanisms can inactivate or delete the maternal copy of the *UBE3A* gene. Most cases of Angelman syndrome (about 70 percent) occur when a segment of the maternal chromosome 15 containing this gene is deleted. In other cases (about 11 percent), Angelman syndrome is caused by a mutation in the maternal copy of the *UBE3A* gene.

In a small percentage of cases, Angelman syndrome results when a person inherits two copies of chromosome 15 from his or her father (paternal copies) instead of one copy from each parent. This phenomenon is called paternal uniparental disomy. Rarely, Angelman syndrome can also be caused by a chromosomal rearrangement called a translocation, or by a mutation or other defect in the region of DNA that controls activation of the *UBE3A* gene. These genetic changes can abnormally turn off (inactivate) *UBE3A* or other genes on the maternal copy of chromosome 15.

The causes of Angelman syndrome are unknown in 10 to 15 percent of affected individuals. Changes involving other genes or chromosomes may be responsible for the disorder in these cases.

In some people who have Angelman syndrome, the loss of a gene called *OCA2* is associated with light-colored hair and fair skin. The *OCA2* gene is located on the segment of chromosome 15 that is often deleted in people with this disorder. However, loss of the *OCA2* gene does not cause the other signs and symptoms of Angelman syndrome. The protein produced from this gene helps determine the coloring (pigmentation) of the skin, hair, and eyes.

Can Angelman Syndrome Be Inherited?

Most cases of Angelman syndrome are not inherited, particularly those caused by a deletion in the maternal chromosome 15 or by paternal uniparental disomy. These genetic changes occur as random events during the formation of reproductive cells (eggs and sperm) or in early embryonic development. Affected people typically have no history of the disorder in their family.

Rarely, a genetic change responsible for Angelman syndrome can be inherited. For example, it is possible for a mutation in the *UBE3A* gene or in the nearby region of DNA that controls gene activation to be passed from one generation to the next.

Chapter 41

Cri-du-Chat Syndrome

What Is Cri-du-Chat Syndrome?

Cri-du-chat (cat's cry) syndrome, also known as 5p- (5p minus) syndrome, is a chromosomal condition that results when a piece of chromosome 5 is missing. Infants with this condition often have a high-pitched cry that sounds like that of a cat. The disorder is characterized by intellectual disability and delayed development, small head size (microcephaly), low birth weight, and weak muscle tone (hypotonia) in infancy. Affected individuals also have distinctive facial features, including widely set eyes (hypertelorism), low-set ears, a small jaw, and a rounded face. Some children with cri-du-chat syndrome are born with a heart defect.

How Common Is Cri-du-Chat Syndrome?

Cri-du-chat syndrome occurs in an estimated 1 in 20,000 to 50,000 newborns. This condition is found in people of all ethnic backgrounds.

This chapter contains text excerpted from the following sources: Text beginning with the heading "What Is Cri-du-Chat Syndrome?" is excerpted from "Cri-du-Chat Syndrome" Genetics Home Reference (GHR), National Institutes of Health (NIH), March 14, 2016; Text under the heading "What Causes Cri-du-Chat Syndrome?" is excerpted from "Learning about Cri-du-Chat Syndrome," National Human Genome Research Institute (NHGRI), April 18, 2013.

What Are the Genetic Changes Related to Cri-du-Chat Syndrome?

Cri-du-chat syndrome is caused by a deletion of the end of the short (p) arm of chromosome 5. This chromosomal change is written as 5p-. The size of the deletion varies among affected individuals; studies suggest that larger deletions tend to result in more severe intellectual disability and developmental delay than smaller deletions.

The signs and symptoms of cri-du-chat syndrome are probably related to the loss of multiple genes on the short arm of chromosome 5. Researchers believe that the loss of a specific gene, *CTNND2*, is associated with severe intellectual disability in some people with this condition. They are working to determine how the loss of other genes in this region contributes to the characteristic features of cri-du-chat syndrome.

Can Cri-du-Chat Syndrome Be Inherited?

Most cases of cri-du-chat syndrome are not inherited. The deletion occurs most often as a random event during the formation of reproductive cells (eggs or sperm) or in early fetal development. Affected people typically have no history of the disorder in their family.

About 10 percent of people with cri-du-chat syndrome inherit the chromosome abnormality from an unaffected parent. In these cases, the parent carries a chromosomal rearrangement called a balanced translocation, in which no genetic material is gained or lost. Balanced translocations usually do not cause any health problems; however, they can become unbalanced as they are passed to the next generation. Children who inherit an unbalanced translocation can have a chromosomal rearrangement with extra or missing genetic material. Individuals with cri-du-chat syndrome who inherit an unbalanced translocation are missing genetic material from the short arm of chromosome 5, which results in the intellectual disability and health problems characteristic of this disorder.

What Are the Symptoms of Cri-du-Chat Syndrome?

The symptoms of cri-du-chat syndrome vary among individuals. The variability of the clinical symptoms and developmental delays may be related to the size of the deletion of the 5p arm.

The clinical symptoms of cri-du-chat syndrome usually include a high-pitched cat-like cry, mental retardation, delayed development, distinctive facial features, small head size (microcephaly), widely-spaced eyes (hypertelorism), low birth weight and weak muscle tone (hypotonia) in infancy. The cat-like cry typically becomes less apparent with time.

Most individuals who have cri-du-chat syndrome have difficulty with language. Half of children learn sufficient verbal skills to communicate. Some individuals learn to use short sentences, while others express themselves with a few basic words, gestures, or sign language.

Other characteristics may include feeding difficulties, delays in walking, hyperactivity, scoliosis, and significant retardation. A small number of children are born with serious organ defects and other life-threatening medical conditions, although most individuals with cri-du-chat syndrome have a normal life expectancy.

Both children and adults with this syndrome are usually friendly and happy, and enjoy social interaction.

How Is Cri-du-Chat Syndrome Diagnosed?

The diagnosis of cri-du-chat syndrome is generally made in the hospital at birth. A healthcare provider may note the clinical symptoms associated with the condition. The cat-like cry is the most prominent clinical feature in newborn children and is usually diagnostic for the cri-du-chat syndrome.

Additionally, analysis of the individual's chromosomes may be performed. The missing portion (deletion) of the short arm of chromosome 5 may be seen on a chromosome analysis. If not, a more detailed type of genetic test called FISH analysis may be needed to reveal the deletion.

What Is the Treatment for Cri-du-Chat Syndrome?

No specific treatment is available for this syndrome. Children born with this genetic condition will most likely require ongoing support from a team made up of the parents, therapists, and medical and educational professionals to help the child achieve his or her maximum potential. With early and consistent educational intervention, as well as physical and language therapy, children with cri-du-chat syndrome are capable of reaching their fullest potential and can lead full and meaningful lives.

Chapter 42

Down Syndrome and Other Trisomy Disorders

Chapter Contents

Section 42.1

Down Syndrome

This section contains text excerpted from the following sources:
Text beginning with the heading "What Is Down Syndrome?" is
excerpted from "Facts about Down Syndrome," Centres for
Disease Control and Prevention (CDC), March 3, 2016; Text under
the heading "What Are Common Symptoms of Down Syndrome?"
is excerpted from "Down Syndrome: Condition Information,"
Eunice Kennedy Shriver National Institute of Child Health and
Human Development (NICHD), January 17, 2014.

What Is Down Syndrome?

Down syndrome is a condition in which a person has an extra chromosome. Chromosomes are small "packages" of genes in the body. They determine how a baby's body forms during pregnancy and how the baby's body functions as it grows in the womb and after birth. Typically, a baby is born with 46 chromosomes. Babies with Down syndrome have an extra copy of one of these chromosomes, chromosome 21. A medical term for having an extra copy of a chromosome is 'trisomy.' Down syndrome is also referred to as Trisomy 21. This extra copy changes how the baby's body and brain develop, which can cause both mental and physical challenges for the baby.

Even though people with Down syndrome might act and look similar, each person has different abilities. People with Down syndrome usually have an IQ (a measure of intelligence) in the mildly-to-moderately low range and are slower to speak than other children.

Types of Down Syndrome

There are three types of Down syndrome. People often can't tell the difference between each type without looking at the chromosomes because the physical features and behaviors are similar.

1. **Trisomy 21:** About 95% of people with Down syndrome have Trisomy 21. With this type of Down syndrome, each cell in the body has 3 separate copies of chromosome 21 instead of the usual 2 copies.

2. **Translocation Down syndrome:** This type accounts for a small percentage of people with Down syndrome (about 3%). This occurs when an extra part or a whole extra chromosome 21 is present, but it is attached or "trans-located" to a different chromosome rather than being a separate chromosome 21.

3. **Mosaic Down syndrome:** This type affects about 2% of the people with Down syndrome. Mosaic means mixture or combination. For children with mosaic Down syndrome, some of their cells have 3 copies of chromosome 21, but other cells have the typical two copies of chromosome 21. Children with mosaic Down syndrome may have the same features as other children with Down syndrome. However, they may have fewer features of the condition due to the presence of some (or many) cells with a typical number of chromosomes.

What Are Common Symptoms of Down Syndrome?

The symptoms of Down syndrome vary from person to person, and people with Down syndrome may have different problems at different times of their lives.

Physical Symptoms

Common physical signs of Down syndrome include

- Decreased or poor muscle tone
- Short neck, with excess skin at the back of the neck
- Flattened facial profile and nose
- Small head, ears, and mouth
- Upward slanting eyes, often with a skin fold that comes out from the upper eyelid and covers the inner corner of the eye
- White spots on the colored part of the eye (called Brushfield spots)
- Wide, short hands with short fingers
- A single, deep, crease across the palm of the hand
- A deep groove between the first and second toes

In addition, physical development in children with Down syndrome is often slower than development of children without Down syndrome. For example, because of poor muscle tone, a child with Down syndrome may be slow to learn to turn over, sit, stand, and walk. Despite these delays, children with Down syndrome can learn to participate in physical exercise activities like other children. It may take children with Down syndrome longer than other children to reach developmental milestones, but they will eventually meet many of these milestones.

Intellectual and Developmental Symptoms

Cognitive impairment, problems with thinking and learning, is common in people with Down syndrome and usually ranges from mild to moderate. Only rarely is Down syndrome associated with severe cognitive impairment.

Other common cognitive and behavioral problems may include

- Short attention span
- Poor judgment
- Impulsive behavior
- Slow learning
- Delayed language and speech development

Most children with Down syndrome develop the communication skills they need, although it might take longer for them to do so compared with other children. Early, ongoing speech and language interventions to encourage expressive language and improve speech are particularly helpful.

Parents and families of children with Down syndrome can connect with other families and people with Down syndrome from around the world to learn more and share information. The NICHD-led DS-Connect® is a safe and secure registry to help families and researchers identify similarities and differences in the physical and developmental symptoms and milestones of people with Down syndrome and guide future research.

Associated Conditions and Disorders

People with Down syndrome are at increased risk for a range of other health conditions, including autism spectrum disorders, problems with hormones and glands, hearing loss, vision problems, and heart abnormalities.

What Causes Down Syndrome?

Down syndrome is caused by a random error in cell division that results in the presence of an extra copy of chromosome 21.

The type of error is called nondisjunction. Usually when one cell divides in two, pairs of chromosomes are split so that one of the pair goes to one cell, and the other from the pair goes to the other cell. In nondisjunction, something goes wrong and both chromosomes from one pair go into one cell and no chromosomes for that pair go into the other cell.

Most of the time, the error occurs at random during the formation of an egg or sperm. To date, no behavioral activity of the parents or environmental factor is known to cause Down syndrome.

After much research on these cell division errors, researchers know that:

- In more than 90% of cases, the extra copy of chromosome 21 comes from the mother in the egg.

- In about 4% of the cases, the father provides the extra copy of chromosome 21 through the sperm.

- In the remaining cases, the error occurs after fertilization, as the embryo grows.

How Many People Are Affected by or at Risk for Down Syndrome?

According to the Centers for Disease Control and Prevention, approximately 6,000 babies are born in the United States each year with Down syndrome, or approximately 1 out of every 691 live births.

Down syndrome is the most frequent chromosomal cause of mild to moderate intellectual disability, and it occurs in all ethnic and economic groups. Currently, more than 400,000 people are living with Down syndrome in the United States, according to the National Down Syndrome Society.

Researchers know some, but not all, of the risk factors for Down syndrome. For example, parents who have a child with Down syndrome or another chromosomal disorder, or who have a chromosomal disorder themselves, are more likely to have a child with Down syndrome.

In the United States, demographic factors also affect the risk for a child to be born with Down syndrome. These factors include geographic region, maternal education, marital status, and Hispanic ethnicity.

Maternal Age and Risk for Down Syndrome

Because the likelihood that an egg will contain an extra copy of chromosome 21 increases significantly as a woman ages, older women are much more likely than younger women to give birth to an infant with Down syndrome. Although women older than 35 years of age make up less than 15% of all births in the United States each year, about 40% of babies with Down syndrome are born to women in this age group.

This likelihood increases as age increases. Following are the rates of Down syndrome for select ages:

- At age 25, the likelihood is 1 in 1,300

- At age 30, the likelihood is 1 in 900

- At age 35, the likelihood is 1 in 350

- At age 42, the likelihood is 1 in 55

- At age 49, the likelihood is 1 in 25

How Do Health Care Providers Diagnose Down Syndrome?

Health care providers can check for Down syndrome during pregnancy or after a child is born. There are two types of tests for Down syndrome during pregnancy:

1. **A prenatal screening test**. This test can show an increased likelihood that a fetus has Down syndrome, but it cannot determine Down syndrome is definitely present. If a screening test shows an increased likelihood, a diagnostic test can be ordered

2. **A prenatal diagnostic test**. This test can determine with certainty that Down syndrome is present. Diagnostic tests carry a slightly greater risk to the fetus than do screening tests.

The American Congress of Obstetricians and Gynecologists (ACOG) recommends that all pregnant women be offered a Down syndrome screening test.

Prenatal Screening for Down Syndrome

There are several options for Down syndrome prenatal screening. These include:

- A blood test and an ultrasound test during the first trimester of pregnancy. This is the most accepted approach for screening during the first trimester. A blood test enables a healthcare provider to check for "markers," such as certain proteins, in the mother's blood that suggest an increased likelihood of Down syndrome. Then the health care provider does an ultrasound test, which uses high-frequency sound waves to create images. An ultrasound can detect fluid at the back of a fetus's neck, which sometimes indicates Down syndrome. The ultrasound test is called measurement of nuchal translucency. During the first trimester, this combined method results in more effective or comparable detection rates than methods used during the second trimester.

- A blood test during the second trimester of pregnancy. As in the first trimester, a blood test enables a healthcare provider to check for markers in the mother's blood. A triple screen looks for levels of three different markers; a quadruple screen looks for levels of four different markers.

- A combined test (sometimes called an integrated test). This approach uses both a blood test and an ultrasound during the first trimester as well as a second-trimester blood test. Health care providers then combine all these results to produce one Down syndrome risk rating.

If a woman is pregnant with twins or triplets, a blood test will not be as reliable because the substances from a Down syndrome fetus may be harder to detect.

Prenatal Diagnostic Testing for Down Syndrome

If a screening test suggests the likelihood of Down syndrome, a diagnostic test can be performed. ACOG recommends that pregnant women of all ages be given the option of skipping the screening test and getting a diagnostic test first. Until recently, only women over age 35 and other at-risk women were offered this option because diagnostic tests carry a slight risk of miscarriage. Before having diagnostic testing, a pregnant woman and her family may want to meet with a genetic counselor to discuss their family history and the risks and benefits of testing in their specific situation.

Diagnostic testing for Down syndrome involves removing a sample of genetic material. After it is removed, the sample is checked for extra material from chromosome 21, which may indicate that a fetus has Down syndrome. Parents usually get the results of the test a week or two later.

The following procedures are used to extract samples.

- **Amniocentesis**. A health care provider takes a sample of amniotic fluid, which is then tested for the extra chromosome. This test cannot be done until week 14 to 18 of the pregnancy.

- **Chorionic villus sampling (CVS).** A health care provider takes a sample of cells from a part of the placenta, which is the organ that connects a woman and her fetus, and then tests the sample for the extra chromosome. This test is done between weeks 9 and 11 of pregnancy.

- **Percutaneous umbilical blood sampling (PUBS).** A health care provider takes a sample of fetal blood in the umbilical cord through the uterus. The blood is then tested for the extra chromosome. PUBS is the most accurate diagnostic method and can confirm the results of CVS or amniocentesis. However, PUBS cannot be performed until later in the pregnancy, during the 18th to 22nd week.

Prenatal diagnostic testing does involve some risk to the mother and fetus, including risk of miscarriage that ranges from less than 1% to 2%. If you and your family are considering prenatal diagnostic testing for Down syndrome, discuss all the risks and benefits with your healthcare provider.

Chromosomal Testing of Maternal Blood

A pregnant woman who is at risk for having an infant with Down syndrome also can have a chromosomal test using her blood. A mother's blood carries DNA from the fetus, which may show extra chromosome 21 material.

A more invasive test then would usually confirm the blood test.

Testing and In Vitro Fertilization (IVF)

Another approach to diagnosis is used in conjunction with in vitro fertilization (IVF). Preimplantation genetic diagnosis (PGD) allows clinicians to detect chromosome imbalances or other genetic conditions in a fertilized egg before it is implanted into the uterus.

This technique is useful mostly for couples who are at risk of passing on a variety of genetic conditions, including X-linked disorders, as well as couples who have suffered repeated spontaneous pregnancy losses, sub-fertile couples, or those at risk for single-gene disorders.

Those interested in PGD should have genetic counseling and should consider close monitoring and additional testing during their pregnancies, given some increased risk of chromosomal abnormalities arising secondary to the in vitro fertilization process.

Diagnosis of Down Syndrome after Birth

A diagnosis of Down syndrome after birth is often based initially on physical signs of the syndrome.

But because individuals with Down syndrome may not have these symptoms, and because many of these symptoms are common in the general population, the health care provider will take a sample of the baby's blood to confirm the diagnosis. The blood sample is analyzed to determine the number of the baby's chromosomes.

What Are Common Treatments for Down Syndrome?

There is no single, standard treatment for Down syndrome. Treatments are based on each individual's physical and intellectual needs as well as his or her personal strengths and limitations. People with Down syndrome can receive proper care while living at home and in the community.

A child with Down syndrome likely will receive care from a team of health professionals, including, but not limited to, physicians, special educators, speech therapists, occupational therapists, physical therapists, and social workers. All professionals who interact with children with Down syndrome should provide stimulation and encouragement.

People with Down syndrome are at a greater risk for a number of health problems and conditions than are those who do not have Down syndrome. Many of these associated conditions may require immediate care right after birth, occasional treatment throughout childhood and adolescence, or long-term treatments throughout life. For example, an infant with Down syndrome may need surgery a few days after birth to correct a heart defect; or a person with Down syndrome may have digestive problems that require a lifelong special diet.

Children, teens, and adults with Down syndrome also need the same regular medical care as those without the condition, from well-baby visits and routine vaccinations as infants to reproductive counseling and cardiovascular care later in life. Like other people, they also benefit from regular physical activity and social activities.

Early Intervention and Educational Therapy

"Early intervention" refers to a range of specialized programs and resources that professionals provide to very young children with Down syndrome and their families. These professionals may include special educators, speech therapists, occupational therapists, physical therapists, and social workers.

Research indicates that early intervention improves outcomes for children with Down syndrome. This assistance can begin shortly after birth and often continues until a child reaches age 3. After that age, most children receive interventions and treatment through their local school district.

Most children with Down syndrome are eligible for free, appropriate public education under federal law. Public Law 105-17 (2004) states that the Individuals with Disabilities Education Act (IDEA) makes it possible for children with disabilities to get free educational services and devices to help them learn as much as they can. Each child is entitled to these services from birth through the end of high school, or until age 21, whichever comes first. Most early intervention programs fall under this legislation.

The National Early Childhood Technical Assistance Center, run by the U.S. Department of Education, provides information and resources for parents and families looking for early intervention programs.

The law also states that each child must be taught in the least restrictive environment that is appropriate. This statement does not mean that each child will be placed in a regular classroom. Instead, educators will work to provide an environment that best fits the child's needs and skills.

The following information may be helpful for those considering educational assistance programs for a child with Down syndrome:

- The child must have certain cognitive or learning deficits to be eligible for free special education programs. Parents can contact a local school principal or special education coordinator to learn how to have a child examined to see if he or she qualifies for services under the IDEA.

- If a child qualifies for special services, a team of people will work together to design an Individualized Educational Plan (IEP) for the child. The team may include parents or caregivers, teachers, a school psychologist, and other specialists in child development or education. The IEP includes specific learning goals for that child, based on his or her needs and capabilities. The team also decides how best to carry out the IEP.

- Children with Down syndrome may attend a school for children with special needs. Parents may have a choice between a school where most of the children do not have disabilities and one for children with special needs. Educators and health care providers can help families with the decision about what environment is best. Integration into a regular school has become much more common in recent decades, and IDEA requires that public schools work to maximize a child's access to typical learning experiences and interactions.

Treatment Therapies

A variety of therapies can be used in early intervention programs and throughout a person's life to promote the greatest possible development, independence, and productivity. Some of these therapies are listed below.

- **Physical therapy** includes activities and exercises that help build motor skills, increase muscle strength, and improve posture and balance.

  - Physical therapy is important, especially early in a child's life, because physical abilities lay the foundation for other skills. The ability to turn over, crawl, and reach helps infants learn about the world around them and how to interact with it.

  - A physical therapist also can help a child with Down syndrome compensate for physical challenges, such as low muscle tone, in ways that avoid long-term problems. For example, a physical therapist might help a child establish an efficient walking pattern, rather than one that might lead to foot pain.

- **Speech-language therapy** can help children with Down syndrome improve their communication skills and use language more effectively.

  - Children with Down syndrome often learn to speak later than their peers. A speech-language therapist can help them develop the early skills necessary for communication, such as imitating sounds. The therapist also may help an infant breastfeed because breastfeeding can strengthen muscles that are used for speech.

  - In many cases, children with Down syndrome understand language and want to communicate before they can speak.

A speech-language therapist can help a child use alternate means of communication, such as sign language and pictures, until he or she learns to speak.

- Learning to communicate is an ongoing process, so a person with Down syndrome also may benefit from speech and language therapy in school as well as later in life. The therapist may help with conversation skills, pronunciation skills, understanding what is read (called comprehension), and learning and remembering words.

- **Occupational therapy** helps find ways to adjust everyday tasks and conditions to match a person's needs and abilities.

  - This type of therapy teaches self-care skills such as eating, getting dressed, writing, and using a computer.

  - An occupational therapist might offer special tools that can help improve everyday functioning, such as a pencil that is easier to grip.

  - At the high school level, an occupational therapist could help teenagers identify jobs, careers, or skills that match their interests and strengths.

- **Emotional and behavioral therapies** work to find useful responses to both desirable and undesirable behaviors. Children with Down syndrome may become frustrated because of difficulty communicating, may develop compulsive behaviors, and may have Attention Deficit Hyperactivity Disorder and other mental health issues. These types of therapists try to understand why a child is acting out, create ways and strategies for avoiding or preventing these situations from occurring, and teach better or more positive ways to respond to situations.

  - A psychologist, counselor, or other mental health professional can help a child deal with emotions and build coping and interpersonal skills.

  - The changes in hormone levels that adolescents experience during puberty can cause them to become more aggressive. Behavioral therapists can help teenagers recognize their intense emotions and teach them healthy ways to reach a feeling of calmness.

- Parents may also benefit from guidance on how to help a child with Down syndrome manage day-to-day challenges and reach his or her full potential.

Drugs and Supplements

Some people with Down syndrome take amino acid supplements or drugs that affect their brain activity. However, many of the recent clinical trials of these treatments were poorly controlled and revealed adverse effects from these treatments. Since then, newer psychoactive drugs that are much more specific have been developed. No controlled clinical studies of these medications for Down syndrome have demonstrated their safety and efficacy, however.

Many studies of drugs to treat symptoms of dementia in Down syndrome have included only a few participants. The results of these studies have not shown clear benefits of these drugs, either. Similarly, studies of antioxidants for dementia in Down syndrome have shown that these supplements are safe, but not effective.

Assistive Devices

More and more often, interventions for children with Down syndrome involve assistive devices—any type of material, equipment, tool, or technology that enhances learning or makes tasks easier to complete. Examples include amplification devices for hearing problems, bands that help with movement, special pencils to make writing easier, touchscreen computers, and computers with large-letter keyboards.

What Conditions or Disorders Are Commonly Associated with Down Syndrome?

In addition to intellectual and developmental disabilities, children with Down syndrome are at an increased risk for certain health problems. However, each individual with Down syndrome is different, and not every person will have serious health problems. Many of these associated conditions can be treated with medication, surgery, or other interventions.

Some of the conditions that occur more often among children with Down syndrome include:

- **Heart defects.** Almost one-half of babies with Down syndrome have congenital heart disease (CHD), the most common type of birth defect. CHD can lead to high blood pressure in the lungs, an inability of the heart to effectively and efficiently pump blood, and cyanosis (blue-tinted skin caused by reduced oxygen in the blood). For this reason, the American Academy of Pediatrics (AAP) Committee on Genetics recommends infants with Down syndrome receive an echocardiogram (a sound "picture" of the heart) and an evaluation from a pediatric cardiologist. Sometimes, the heart defect can be detected before birth, but testing after birth is more accurate. Some heart defects are minor and may be treated with medication, but others require immediate surgery.

- **Vision problems.** More than 60% of children with Down syndrome have vision problems, including cataracts (clouding of the eye lens) that may be present at birth. The risk of cataract increases with age. Other eye problems that are more likely in children with Down syndrome are near-sightedness, "crossed" eyes, and rapid, involuntary eye movements. Glasses, surgery, or other treatments usually improve vision. The AAP recommends that infants with Down syndrome be examined by a pediatric eye specialist during the newborn period, and then have vision exams regularly as recommended.

- **Hearing loss.** About 70% to 75% of children with Down syndrome have some hearing loss, sometimes because of problems with ear structures. The AAP recommends that babies with Down syndrome be screened for hearing loss at birth and have regular follow-up hearing exams. Many inherited hearing problems can be corrected. Children with Down syndrome also tend to get a lot of ear infections. These should be treated quickly to prevent possible hearing loss.

- **Infections.** People with Down syndrome are 12 times more likely to die from untreated and unmonitored infections than other people. Down syndrome often causes problems in the immune system that can make it difficult for the body to fight off infections, so even seemingly minor infections should be treated quickly and monitored continuously. Caregivers also should make sure that children with Down syndrome receive all recommended immunizations to help prevent certain infections. Infants with Down syndrome have a 62-fold higher rate of pneumonia, especially in the first year after birth, than do infants without Down syndrome, for example.

- **Hypothyroidism.** The thyroid is a gland that makes hormones the body uses to regulate things such as temperature and energy. Hypothyroidism, when the thyroid makes little or no thyroid hormone, occurs more often in children with Down syndrome than in children without Down syndrome. Taking thyroid hormone by mouth, throughout life, can successfully treat the condition. A child may have thyroid problems at birth or may develop them later, so healthcare providers recommend a thyroid examination at birth, at 6 months, and annually throughout life. Routine newborn screening may detect hypothyroidism at birth. However, some state newborn screening programs only screen for hypothyroidism one way, by measuring free thyroxine (T4) in the blood. Because many infants with Down syndrome have normal T4, they should be screened for levels of thyroid stimulating hormone (TSH) in these states as well.

- **Blood disorders.** Children with Down syndrome are 10 to 15 times more likely than other children to develop leukemia, which is cancer of the white blood cells. Children with leukemia should receive appropriate cancer treatment, which may include chemotherapy. Those with Down syndrome are also more likely to have anemia (low iron in the blood) and polycythemia (high red blood cell levels), among other blood disorders. These conditions may require additional treatment and monitoring.

- **Hypotonia (poor muscle tone).** Poor muscle tone and low strength contribute to the delays in rolling over, sitting up, crawling, and walking that are common in children with Down syndrome. Despite these delays, children with Down syndrome can learn to participate in physical activities like other children.

- **Poor muscle tone**, combined with a tendency for the tongue to stick out, can also make it difficult for an infant with Down syndrome to feed properly, regardless of whether they are breastfed or fed from a bottle. Infants may need nutritional supplements to ensure they are getting all the nutrients they need. Parents can work with breastfeeding experts and pediatric nutritionists to ensure proper nutrition. In some cases, the weak muscles can cause problems along the digestive tract, leading to various digestive problems, from difficulty swallowing to constipation. Families may need to work with a gastroenterologist to overcome these problems.

- **Problems with the upper part of the spine.** One or two of
  every ten children with Down syndrome has misshapen bones
  in the upper part of the spine, underneath the base of the skull.
  These misshaped bones can press on the spinal cord and increase
  the risk for injury. It is important to determine if these spinal
  problems (called atlantoaxial instability) are present before the
  child has any surgery because certain movements required for
  anesthesia or surgery could cause permanent injury. In addition,
  some sports have an increased risk of spinal injury, so possible precautions should be discussed with a child's health care provider.

- **Disrupted sleep patterns and sleep disorders.** Many children with Down syndrome have disrupted sleep patterns and
  often have obstructive sleep apnea, which causes significant
  pauses in breathing during sleep. A child's health care provider
  may recommend a sleep study in a special sleep lab to detect
  problems and determine possible solutions. It might be necessary to remove the tonsils or to use a continuous positive airway
  pressure device to create airflow during sleep.

- **Gum disease and dental problems.** Children with Down
  syndrome may develop teeth more slowly than other children,
  develop teeth in a different order, develop fewer teeth, or have
  misaligned teeth compared to children who do not have Down
  syndrome. Gum disease (periodontal disease), a more serious
  health issue, may develop for a number of reasons, including
  poor oral hygiene. Healthcare providers recommend visiting the
  dentist within 6 months of the appearance of the child's first
  tooth or by the time the child is 1 year old.

- **Epilepsy.** Children with Down syndrome are more likely to have
  epilepsy, a condition characterized by seizures, than those without Down syndrome. The risk for epilepsy increases with age,
  but seizures usually occur either during the first 2 years of life
  or after the third decade of life. Almost one-half of people with
  Down syndrome who are older than age 50 have epilepsy. Seizures can usually be treated and controlled well with medication.

- **Digestive problems.** Digestive problems range from structural
  defects in the digestive system or its organs, to problems digest-
  ing certain types of foods or food ingredients. Treatments for
  these problems vary based on the specific problem. Some structural defects require surgery. Some people with Down syndrome
  have to eat a special diet throughout their lifetime.

- **Celiac disease.** People with celiac disease experience intestinal problems when they eat gluten, a protein in wheat, barley, and rye. Because children with Down syndrome are more likely to have celiac disease, healthcare providers recommend testing for it at age 2 or even younger if the child is having celiac symptoms.

- **Mental health and emotional problems.** Children with Down syndrome may experience behavioral and emotional problems, including anxiety, depression, and Attention Deficit Hyperactivity Disorder. They might also display repetitive movements, aggression, autism, psychosis, or social withdrawal. Although they are not more likely to experience these problems, they are more likely to have difficulty coping with the problems in positive ways, especially during adolescence. Treatments may include working with a behavioral specialist and taking medications.

The conditions listed above are ones that are commonly found in children with Down syndrome. Adults with Down syndrome may have many of these as well as additional health issues.

Is There a Cure for Down Syndrome?

At present, there is no cure for Down syndrome. However, researchers are exploring a number of ways to address and correct many aspects of the syndrome.

For example, *Eunice Kennedy Shriver* National Institute of Child Health and Human Development (NICHD) researchers have used mouse models to test treatments for preventing the intellectual and developmental disabilities associated with Down syndrome. One study found that mice with Down syndrome who were treated in the womb with specific chemicals had no delay in achieving several developmental milestones. Another study found that specific chemicals prevented learning deficits in adult mice who had Down syndrome.

What Are the Health Issues for Adults with Down Syndrome?

The life expectancy for people with Down syndrome has increased substantially in the last few decades, to an average age of 50 years and beyond. In addition to living longer, people with Down syndrome now live fuller, richer lives than ever before as family members and contributors to their community. Many adults with Down syndrome form meaningful relationships and eventually marry. Now that people with Down syndrome are living longer, the needs of adults with Down syndrome are receiving greater attention. With assistance from family and caretakers, many adults with Down syndrome have developed the skills required to hold jobs and to live independently well into later adult life.

Increased life expectancy in individuals with Down syndrome puts them at risk as they age for developing mental health issues, such as depression. Death of parents, changes in caregivers, and medical issues often contribute to such changes in mental health. Individuals with Down syndrome seem to respond well to treatment with medication, but it is important that they follow instructions for taking these medications closely.

Premature aging is a characteristic of adults with Down syndrome, as is dementia, memory loss, and impaired judgment similar to that occurring in individuals with Alzheimer disease. Although much has been learned about Alzheimer disease as it affects individuals with Down syndrome, effective treatments and diagnostic tools that can identify early stages of dementia or the symptoms of mild cognitive impairment are still needed. Currently, changes in behavior may be the best indicators of dementia in people with Down syndrome. Families should look for associations between the type of behavior, how often the behavior occurs, when the behavior occurs, and the persistence of specific behaviors as a way to check for dementia and memory loss in a person with Down syndrome. Family members and caretakers may need to step in if the individual begins to lose the skills required for independent living.

Other medical issues associated with aging in individuals with Down syndrome include high cholesterol (which can be treated with medications), obesity, metabolic syndrome, diabetes, cataracts and other visual problems, and early menopause. In contrast, individuals with Down syndrome appear to be "protected" from certain diseases that are common in the elderly: they do not develop hardening of the arteries; they have fewer solid tumor cancers (for example, breast cancer), and they have low blood pressure.

Longitudinal studies of aging in Down syndrome (some ongoing for more than 25 years) reveal that healthy aging occurs in most individuals with Down syndrome if they continue to receive routine medical care and attention to their special needs.

Section 42.2

Triple X Syndrome

This section includes text excerpted from "Triple X
Syndrome," Genetics Home Reference (GHR), National
Institutes of Health (NIH), March 14, 2016.

What Is Triple X Syndrome?

Triple X syndrome, also called trisomy X or 47,XXX, is characterized
by the presence of an additional X chromosome in each of a female's
cells. Although females with this condition may be taller than average, this chromosomal change typically causes no unusual physical
features. Most females with triple X syndrome have normal sexual
development and are able to conceive children.

Triple X syndrome is associated with an increased risk of learning
disabilities and delayed development of speech and language skills.
Delayed development of motor skills (such as sitting and walking),
weak muscle tone (hypotonia), and behavioral and emotional difficulties are also possible, but these characteristics vary widely among
affected girls and women. Seizures or kidney abnormalities occur in
about 10 percent of affected females.

How Common Is Triple X Syndrome?

This condition occurs in about 1 in 1,000 newborn girls. Five to 10
girls with triple X syndrome are born in the United States each day.

What Are the Genetic Changes Related to Triple X Syndrome?

People normally have 46 chromosomes in each cell. Two of the 46
chromosomes, known as X and Y, are called sex chromosomes because
they help determine whether a person will develop male or female sex
characteristics. Females typically have two X chromosomes (46,XX),
and males have one X chromosome and one Y chromosome (46,XY).

Triple X syndrome results from an extra copy of the X chromosome in each of a female's cells. As a result of the extra X chromosome, each cell has a total of 47 chromosomes (47,XXX) instead of the usual 46. An extra copy of the X chromosome is associated with tall stature, learning problems, and other features in some girls and women.

Some females with triple X syndrome have an extra X chromosome in only some of their cells. This phenomenon is called 46,XX/47,XXX mosaicism.

Can Triple X Syndrome Be Inherited?

Most cases of triple X syndrome are not inherited. The chromosomal change usually occurs as a random event during the formation of reproductive cells (eggs and sperm). An error in cell division called nondisjunction can result in reproductive cells with an abnormal number of chromosomes. For example, an egg or sperm cell may gain an extra copy of the X chromosome as a result of nondisjunction. If one of these atypical reproductive cells contributes to the genetic makeup of a child, the child will have an extra X chromosome in each of the body's cells.

46,XX/47,XXX mosaicism is also not inherited. It occurs as a random event during cell division in early embryonic development. As a result, some of an affected person's cells have two X chromosomes (46,XX), and other cells have three X chromosomes (47,XXX).

Section 42.3

Trisomy 13 (Patau Syndrome)

This section includes text excerpted from "Trisomy 13,"
Genetics Home Reference (GHR), National Institutes
of Health (NIH), March 14, 2016.

What Is Trisomy 13?

Trisomy 13, also called Patau syndrome, is a chromosomal condition associated with severe intellectual disability and physical abnormalities in many parts of the body. Individuals with trisomy 13 often have heart defects, brain or spinal cord abnormalities, very small or poorly developed eyes (microphthalmia), extra fingers or toes, an opening in the lip (a cleft lip) with or without an opening in the roof of the mouth (a cleft palate), and weak muscle tone (hypotonia). Due to the presence of several life-threatening medical problems, many infants with trisomy 13 die within their first days or weeks of life. Only five percent to 10 percent of children with this condition live past their first year.

How Common Is Trisomy 13?

Trisomy 13 occurs in about 1 in 16,000 newborns. Although women of any age can have a child with trisomy 13, the chance of having a child with this condition increases as a woman gets older.

What Are the Genetic Changes Related to Trisomy 13?

Most cases of trisomy 13 result from having three copies of chromosome 13 in each cell in the body instead of the usual two copies. The extra genetic material disrupts the normal course of development, causing the characteristic features of trisomy 13.

Trisomy 13 can also occur when part of chromosome 13 becomes attached (translocated) to another chromosome during the formation of reproductive cells (eggs and sperm) or very early in fetal development. Affected people have two normal copies of chromosome 13, plus an extra copy of chromosome 13 attached to another chromosome. In rare cases, only part of chromosome 13 is present in three copies. The physical signs and symptoms in these cases may be different than those found in full trisomy 13.

A small percentage of people with trisomy 13 have an extra copy of chromosome 13 in only some of the body's cells. In these people, the condition is called mosaic trisomy 13. The severity of mosaic trisomy 13 depends on the type and number of cells that have the extra chromosome. The physical features of mosaic trisomy 13 are often milder than those of full trisomy 13.

Can Trisomy 13 Be Inherited?

Most cases of trisomy 13 are not inherited and result from random events during the formation of eggs and sperm in healthy parents. An error in cell division called nondisjunction results in a reproductive cell with an abnormal number of chromosomes. For example, an egg or sperm cell may gain an extra copy of chromosome 13. If one of these atypical reproductive cells contributes to the genetic makeup of a child, the child will have an extra chromosome 13 in each cell of the body.

Translocation trisomy 13 can be inherited. An unaffected person can carry a rearrangement of genetic material between chromosome 13 and another chromosome. These rearrangements are called balanced translocations because there is no extra material from chromosome 13. A person with a balanced translocation involving chromosome 13 has an increased chance of passing extra material from chromosome 13 to their children.

Section 42.4

Trisomy 18 (Edwards Syndrome)

This section includes text excerpted from "Trisomy 18,"
Genetics Home Reference (GHR), National Institutes
of Health (NIH), March 14, 2016.

What Is Trisomy 18?

Trisomy 18, also called Edwards syndrome, is a chromosomal condition associated with abnormalities in many parts of the body. Individuals with trisomy 18 often have slow growth before birth (intrauterine growth retardation) and a low birth weight. Affected individuals may have heart defects and abnormalities of other organs that develop before birth. Other features of trisomy 18 include a small, abnormally shaped head; a small jaw and mouth; and clenched fists with overlapping fingers. Due to the presence of several life-threatening medical problems, many individuals with trisomy 18 die before birth or within their first month. Five to 10 percent of children with this condition live past their first year, and these children often have severe intellectual disability.

How Common Is Trisomy 18?

Trisomy 18 occurs in about 1 in 5,000 live-born infants; it is more common in pregnancy, but many affected fetuses do not survive to term. Although women of all ages can have a child with trisomy 18, the chance of having a child with this condition increases as a woman gets older.

What Are the Genetic Changes Related to Trisomy 18?

Most cases of trisomy 18 result from having three copies of chromosome 18 in each cell in the body instead of the usual two copies. The extra genetic material disrupts the normal course of development, causing the characteristic features of trisomy 18.

Approximately 5 percent of people with trisomy 18 have an extra copy of chromosome 18 in only some of the body's cells. In these people, the condition is called mosaic trisomy 18. The severity of mosaic trisomy 18 depends on the type and number of cells that have the extra chromosome. The development of individuals with this form of trisomy 18 may range from normal to severely affected.

Very rarely, part of the long (q) arm of chromosome 18 becomes attached (translocated) to another chromosome during the formation of reproductive cells (eggs and sperm) or very early in embryonic development. Affected individuals have two copies of chromosome 18, plus the extra material from chromosome 18 attached to another chromosome. People with this genetic change are said to have partial trisomy 18. If only part of the q arm is present in three copies, the physical signs of partial trisomy 18 may be less severe than those typically seen in trisomy 18. If the entire q arm is present in three copies, individuals may be as severely affected as if they had three full copies of chromosome 18.

Can Trisomy 18 Be Inherited?

Most cases of trisomy 18 are not inherited, but occur as random events during the formation of eggs and sperm. An error in cell division called nondisjunction results in a reproductive cell with an abnormal number of chromosomes. For example, an egg or sperm cell may gain an extra copy of chromosome 18. If one of these atypical reproductive cells contributes to the genetic makeup of a child, the child will have an extra chromosome 18 in each of the body's cells.

Mosaic trisomy 18 is also not inherited. It occurs as a random event during cell division early in embryonic development. As a result, some of the body's cells have the usual two copies of chromosome 18, and other cells have three copies of this chromosome.

Partial trisomy 18 can be inherited. An unaffected person can carry a rearrangement of genetic material between chromosome 18 and another chromosome. This rearrangement is called a balanced translocation because there is no extra material from chromosome 18. Although they do not have signs of trisomy 18, people who carry this type of balanced translocation are at an increased risk of having children with the condition.

Chapter 43

Fragile X Syndrome

What Is Fragile X Syndrome?

Fragile X syndrome is a genetic condition that causes a range of developmental problems including learning disabilities and cognitive impairment. Usually, males are more severely affected by this disorder than females.

Affected individuals usually have delayed development of speech and language by age 2. Most males with fragile X syndrome have mild to moderate intellectual disability, while about one-third of affected females are intellectually disabled. Children with fragile X syndrome may also have anxiety and hyperactive behavior such as fidgeting or impulsive actions. They may have attention deficit disorder (ADD), which includes an impaired ability to maintain attention and difficulty focusing on specific tasks. About one-third of individuals with fragile X syndrome have features of autism spectrum disorders that affect communication and social interaction. Seizures occur in about 15 percent of males and about 5 percent of females with fragile X syndrome.

This chapter contains text excerpted from the following sources: Text beginning with the heading "What Is Fragile X Syndrome?" is excerpted from "Fragile X Syndrome," Genetics Home Reference (GHR), National Institute of Health (NIH), March 14, 2016; Text under the heading "How Is a Change in the FMR1 Gene Related to Fragile X and Associated Disorders?" is excerpted from "Fragile X Syndrome: Condition Information," *Eunice Kennedy Shriver* National Institute of Child Health and Human Development (NICHD), October 29, 2013.

Most males and about half of females with fragile X syndrome have characteristic physical features that become more apparent with age. These features include a long and narrow face, large ears, a prominent jaw and forehead, unusually flexible fingers, flat feet, and in males, enlarged testicles (macroorchidism) after puberty.

How Common Is Fragile X Syndrome?

Fragile X syndrome occurs in approximately 1 in 4,000 males and 1 in 8,000 females.

What Genes Are Related to Fragile X Syndrome?

Mutations in the *FMR1* gene cause fragile X syndrome. The *FMR1* gene provides instructions for making a protein called FMRP. This protein helps regulate the production of other proteins and plays a role in the development of synapses, which are specialized connections between nerve cells. Synapses are critical for relaying nerve impulses.

Nearly all cases of fragile X syndrome are caused by a mutation in which a DNA segment, known as the CGG triplet repeat, is expanded within the *FMR1* gene. Normally, this DNA segment is repeated from 5 to about 40 times. In people with fragile X syndrome, however, the CGG segment is repeated more than 200 times. The abnormally expanded CGG segment turns off (silences) the *FMR1* gene, which prevents the gene from producing FMRP. Loss or a shortage (deficiency) of this protein disrupts nervous system functions and leads to the signs and symptoms of fragile X syndrome.

Males and females with 55 to 200 repeats of the CGG segment are said to have an *FMR1* gene premutation. Most people with a premutation are intellectually normal. In some cases, however, individuals with a premutation have lower than normal amounts of FMRP. As a result, they may have mild versions of the physical features seen in fragile X syndrome (such as prominent ears) and may experience emotional problems such as anxiety or depression. Some children with a premutation may have learning disabilities or autistic-like behavior. The premutation is also associated with an increased risk of disorders called fragile X-associated primary ovarian insufficiency (FXPOI) and fragile X-associated tremor/ataxia syndrome (FXTAS).

How Do People Inherit Fragile X Syndrome?

Fragile X syndrome is inherited in an X-linked dominant pattern. A condition is considered X-linked if the mutated gene that causes the disorder is located on the X chromosome, one of the two sex chromosomes. (The Y chromosome is the other sex chromosome.) The inheritance is dominant if one copy of the altered gene in each cell is sufficient to cause the condition. X-linked dominant means that in females (who have two X chromosomes), a mutation in one of the two copies of a gene in each cell is sufficient to cause the disorder. In males (who have only one X chromosome), a mutation in the only copy of a gene in each cell causes the disorder. In most cases, males experience more severe symptoms of the disorder than females.

In women, the *FMR1* gene premutation on the X chromosome can expand to more than 200 CGG repeats in cells that develop into eggs. This means that women with the premutation have an increased risk of having a child with fragile X syndrome. By contrast, the premutation in men does not expand to more than 200 repeats as it is passed to the next generation. Men pass the premutation only to their daughters. Their sons receive a Y chromosome, which does not include the *FMR1* gene.

What Causes Fragile X Syndrome?

Fragile X results from a change or mutation in the Fragile X Mental Retardation 1 (*FMR1*) gene, which is found on the X chromosome. The gene normally makes a protein called Fragile X Mental Retardation Protein, or FMRP. This protein is important for creating and maintaining connections between cells in the brain and nervous system. The mutation causes the body to make only a little bit or none of the protein, which often causes the symptoms of fragile X syndrome.

Not everyone with the mutated *FMR1* gene has symptoms of fragile X syndrome, because the body may still be able to make FMRP. A few things affect how much FMRP the body can make:

- **The size of the mutation.** Some people have a smaller mutation (a lower number of repeats) in their *FMR1* gene, while others have big mutations (a large number of repeats) in the gene. If the mutation is small, the body may be able to make some of the protein. Having the protein available makes the symptoms milder.

- **The number of cells that have the mutation.** Because not every cell in the body is exactly the same, some cells might have the *FMR1* mutation while others do not. This situation is called mosaicism. If the mutation is in most of the body's cells, the person will probably have symptoms of fragile X syndrome. If the mutation is in only some of the cells, the person might not have any symptoms at all or only mild symptoms.

- **Being female.** Females have two X chromosomes (XX), while males have only one. In females, if the *FMR1* gene on one X chromosome has the mutation, the *FMR1* gene on the other X chromosome might not have the mutation. Even if one of the female's genes has a very large mutation, the body can usually make at least some FMRP, leading to milder symptoms.

How Many People Are Affected by Fragile X Syndrome?

Although fragile X syndrome is relatively rare, premutations in the FMR1 gene are relatively common. A study of 6,747 people found that 1 in 151 women and 1 in 468 men had the premutation. People with the premutation might not have any symptoms of fragile X. However, the premutation can sometimes expand in the next generation, which can cause fragile X syndrome.

What Are the Symptoms of Fragile X Syndrome?

People with fragile X syndrome do not all have the same signs and symptoms, but they do have some things in common. Symptoms are often milder in females than in males.

- **Intelligence and learning.** Many people with fragile X syndrome have problems with intellectual functioning.

  - These problems can range from the mild, such as learning disorders or problems with mathematics, to the severe, such as an intellectual or developmental disability.

  - The syndrome may affect the ability to think, reason, and learn.

  - Because many people with fragile X syndrome also have attention disorders, hyperactivity, anxiety, and language-processing problems, a person with fragile X syndrome may have more capabilities than his or her IQ (intelligence quotient) score suggests.

- **Physical.** Most infants and younger children with fragile X syndrome don't have any specific physical features of this syndrome. When these children start to go through puberty, however, many will begin to develop certain features that are typical of those with fragile X syndrome.

  - These features include a narrow face, large head, large ears, flexible joints, flat feet, and a prominent forehead.

- These physical signs become more obvious with age.

- **Behavioral, social, and emotional.** Most children with fragile X syndrome have some behavioral challenges.

  - They may be afraid or anxious in new situations.

  - They may have trouble making eye contact with other people.

  - Boys, especially, may have trouble paying attention or be aggressive.

  - Girls may be shy around new people. They may also have attention disorders and problems with hyperactivity.

- **Speech and language.** Most boys with fragile X syndrome have some problems with speech and language.

- They may have trouble speaking clearly, may stutter, or may leave out parts of words. They may also have problems understanding other people's social cues, such as tone of voice or specific types of body language.

  - Girls usually do not have severe problems with speech or language.

  - Some children with fragile X syndrome begin talking later than typically developing children. Most will talk eventually, but a few might stay nonverbal throughout their lives.

- **Sensory.** Many children with fragile X syndrome are bothered by certain sensations, such as bright light, loud noises, or the way certain clothing feels on their bodies.

  - These sensory issues might cause them to act out or display behavior problems.

How Do Health Care Providers Diagnose Fragile X Syndrome?

Health care providers often use a blood sample to diagnose fragile X syndrome. The health care provider will take a sample of blood and will send it to a laboratory, which will determine what form of the *FMR1* gene is present.

Prenatal Testing (During Pregnancy)

Pregnant women who have an *FMR1* premutation or full mutation may pass that mutated gene on to their children. A prenatal test allows healthcare providers to detect the mutated gene in the developing fetus. This important information helps families and providers to prepare for fragile X syndrome and to intervene as early as possible.

Possible types of prenatal tests include:

- **Amniocentesis**. A health care provider takes a sample of amniotic fluid, which is then tested for the *FMR1* mutation.

- **Chorionic villus V sampling.** A health care provider takes a sample of cells from the placenta, which is then tested for the FMR1 mutation.

Because prenatal testing involves some risk to the mother and fetus, if you or a family member is considering prenatal testing for fragile X syndrome,, discuss all the risks and benefits with your healthcare provider.

Prenatal testing is not very common, and many parents do not know they carry the mutation. Therefore, parents usually start to notice symptoms in their children when they are infants or toddlers. The average age at diagnosis is 36 months for boys and 42 months for girls.

Diagnosis of Children

Many parents first notice symptoms of delayed development in their infants or toddlers. These symptoms may include delays in speech and language skills, social and emotional difficulties, and being sensitive to certain sensations. Children may also be delayed in or have problems with motor skills such as learning to walk.

A health care provider can perform developmental screening to determine the nature of delays in a child. If a health care provider suspects the child has fragile X syndrome, he/she can refer parents to a clinical geneticist, who can perform a genetic test for fragile X syndrome.

What Are the Treatments for Fragile X Syndrome?

There is no single treatment for fragile X syndrome, but there are treatments that help minimize the symptoms of the condition. Individuals with fragile X syndrome who receive appropriate education, therapy services, and medications have the best chance of using all of their individual capabilities and skills. Even those with an intellectual or developmental disability can learn to master many self-help skills.

Early intervention is important. Because a young child's brain is still forming, early intervention gives children the best start possible and the greatest chance of developing a full range of skills. The sooner a child with fragile X syndrome gets treatment, the more opportunity there is for learning.

Educational Treatments

Most children with fragile X syndrome can benefit from special education services that are tailored to their particular strengths and weaknesses. Educational treatments should take the child's specific symptoms of fragile X syndrome into account to promote the best learning environment.

Eligibility for Special Education

Most children with fragile X syndrome are eligible for free, appropriate public education under federal law. Although a medical diagnosis does not guarantee access to special education services, most children with fragile X syndrome will have certain cognitive or learning deficits that makes them eligible for services. Parents can contact a local school principal or special education coordinator to learn how to have a child examined to see if he or she qualifies for services under the Individuals with Disabilities Education Act.

Suggestions for Working with Individuals with Fragile X Syndrome

Everyone with fragile X syndrome is unique. However, those with this disorder often share some particular behaviors and intellectual characteristics. For example, children with fragile X syndrome can easily become overwhelmed by crowds, noise, and touch. Other common characteristics include weak abstract thinking skills and poor quantitative (measuring and counting) skills. However, these children often have unique strengths as well, including visual memory. By taking these unique strengths and weaknesses into account, teachers can promote the best learning for these children.

Suggestions

- Know the learning style of the individual.
- Develop a consistent daily schedule or routine.

- Use visual signs (pictures, sign language, logos, words) and concrete examples or materials to present ideas, concepts, steps, etc.

- Prepare the individual for any changes in routine by explaining these changes ahead of time, possibly by using visual signs.

- Include functional goals with academic goals; for instance, teach the individual the names of different pieces of clothing as well as how to dress himself/herself.

- Provide opportunities for the child to be active and move around.

- Use computers and interactive educational software.

- Provide a quiet place where the child can first retreat and then regroup.

What Type of Classroom

In general, there are three options for the classroom placement of a child with Fragile X, based on that child's specific abilities and needs:

- Full inclusion in a regular classroom

- Inclusion with "pull-out" services

- Full-time special education classroom

- Placement decisions should be based on each child's needs and abilities.

Individualized Educational Plan (IEP)

If a child with fragile X syndrome qualifies for special services, a team of people will work together to design an IEP for the child. The team may include parents or caregivers, teachers, a school psychologist, and other specialists in child development or education. The IEP includes specific learning goals for that child, based on his or her needs and capabilities. The team also decides how best to carry out the IEP. It reaches a consensus on classroom placement for the child, determines any devices or special assistance the child needs, and identifies the specialists who will work with the child.

The special services team should evaluate the child on a regular basis. The team can chart progress and decide whether changes in treatment are needed (for instance, changes to the IEP, in classroom placement, or in the services provided).

Therapy Treatments

A variety of professionals can help individuals with fragile X syndrome and their families manage the symptoms of the disorder. Those with fragile X might benefit from services provided by several different specialists:

- **Speech-language therapists** can help people with fragile X syndrome improve their pronunciation of words and sentences, slow down their speech, and use language more effectively.

- **Occupational therapists** help find ways to adjust tasks and conditions to match a person's needs and abilities.

- **Physical therapists** design activities and exercises that help build motor control and improve posture and balance.

- **Behavioral therapists** try to understand why someone with fragile X syndrome acts out, and they create ways and strategies for avoiding or preventing these situations from occurring while also teaching better or more positive ways to respond to situations.

To this point, the food and Drug Administration (FDA) has not approved any drugs specifically for the treatment of fragile X syndrome or its symptoms. But in many cases, medications are used to treat certain symptoms of fragile X syndrome, as shown in the chart below. The *Eunice Kennedy Shriver* National Institute of Child Health and Human Development (NICHD) does not endorse or support the use of any of these medications in treating the symptoms of fragile X syndrome, or for other conditions for which the medications are not FDA approved.

Medication is most effective when paired with therapy designed to teach new coping or behavioral skills. Not every medication helps every child.

Please note that some of these medications carry serious risks. Others may make symptoms worse at first, or they may take several weeks to become effective. Doctors may have to try different dosages or combinations of medications to find the most effective plan. Families, caregivers, and doctors need to work together to ensure that a medication is working and that the medication plan is safe.

This table is meant for reference ONLY and should not take the place of a health care provider's advice. Discuss any questions about medication with a health care provider.

Table 43.1. Medications for Fragile X Syndrome

Symptoms	Generic Medication (Brand Name in Parentheses)
Seizures Mood instability	• Carbamazepine (Tegretol) • Valproic acid or Divalproex (Depakote) • Lithium carbonate • Gabapentin (Neurontin) • Lamotrigine (Lamictal) • Topiramate (Topamax), Tiagabine (Gabitril), and Vigabatrin (Sabril) • Phenobarbital and Primidone (Mysoline) • Phenytoin (Dilantin)
Attention deficit (with or without hyperactivity)	• Methylphenidate (Ritalin, Concerta) and Dextroamphetamine (Adderall, Dexedrine) • L-acetylcarnitine • Venlafaxine (Effexor) and Nefazodone (Serzone) • Amantadine (Symmetrel) • Folic acid
Hyperarousal Sensory overstimulation (often occurs with ADD/ADHD)	• Clonidine (Catapres TTS patches) • Guanfacine (Tenex)
Aggression Intermittent explosive disorder Obsessive-compulsive disorder (often occurs with anxiety and/or depression)	• Fluoxetine (Prozac) • Sertraline (Zoloft) and Citalopram (Celexa) • Paroxetine (Paxil) • Fluvoxamine (Luvox) • Risperidone (Risperdal) • Quetiapine (Seroquel) • Olanzapine (Zyprexa)
Sleep disturbances	• Trazodone • Melatonin

ADD: attention deficit disorder; ADHD: attention deficit hyperactivity disorder; TTS: transdermal therapeutic system.

Are There Specific Disorders or Conditions Associated with Fragile X Syndrome?

Among the other conditions associated with fragile X syndrome are the following:

• **Autism spectrum disorder.** From 30% to 50% of people with fragile X syndrome also meet the criteria for autism spectrum disorder.

- **Mitral valve prolapse.** In mitral valve prolapse, a heart condition, the valve that separates the upper and lower left chambers of the heart does not work properly. This condition is usually not life-threatening, but in severe cases, surgery might be required to correct the problem.

- **Seizures.** Between 6% and 20% of children with fragile X syndrome have seizures. Seizures associated with the syndrome are more common in boys than in girls.

How Does the FMR1 Gene Change as It Is Passed from Parent to Child?

The repeats in the promoter part of the *FMR1* gene are unstable, and sometimes the number of repeats increases from one generation to the next.

A premutation gene is less stable than a full mutation gene. So as it passes from parent to child, a premutation gene might expand to become a full mutation gene. The chances of expansion depend on the number of repeats in the promoter of the premutation gene:

Normal

FMR1 genes that have 5 to 44 CGG repeats in the promoter are considered normal. When these genes are passed from parent to child, the number of repeats does not increase or decrease.

Intermediate

FMR1 genes with 45 to 54 CGG repeats in the promoter are considered intermediate, or borderline. An intermediate gene may expand from one generation to the next, depending on which parent has the gene.

Mother to Child

About 14% of the time, when a mother passes an intermediate gene to her child, the CGG repeats increase to a number seen with premutations. Research shows that an intermediate gene will not become a full mutation gene in one generation, and so a mother with an intermediate gene will not have a child with a full mutation.

Father to Child

When intermediate genes are transmitted from father to child, they are generally stable and do not increase to premutations.

Premutations

Premutation (55 to 199 CGG repeats) *FMR1* genes can expand to a full mutation from one generation to the next. The risk of expansion depends on which parent has the gene and the number of repeats in that gene.

Mother to Child

An *FMR1* gene from the mother with 100 CGG repeats is very likely to expand to a full mutation when passed to the child. An *FMR1* gene from the mother with 70 to 79 CGG repeats has about a 30% chance of expanding to a full mutation in one generation.

Father to Child

Premutations passed from father to child have almost no chance of expanding to full mutations.

Chapter 44

Klinefelter Syndrome

What Is Klinefelter Syndrome?

Klinefelter syndrome is a chromosomal condition that affects male physical and cognitive development. Its signs and symptoms vary among affected individuals.

Affected individuals typically have small testes that do not produce as much testosterone as usual. Testosterone is the hormone that directs male sexual development before birth and during puberty. A shortage of testosterone can lead to delayed or incomplete puberty, breast enlargement (gynecomastia), reduced facial and body hair, and an inability to have biological children (infertility). Some affected individuals also have genital differences including undescended testes (cryptorchidism), the opening of the urethra on the underside of the penis (hypospadias), or an unusually small penis (micropenis).

Older children and adults with Klinefelter syndrome tend to be taller than their peers. Compared with unaffected men, adults with Klinefelter syndrome have an increased risk of developing breast cancer and a chronic inflammatory disease called systemic lupus erythematosus. Their chance of developing these disorders is similar to that of women in the general population.

This chapter contains text excerpted from the following sources: Text beginning with the heading "What Is Klinefelter Syndrome?" is excerpted from "Klinefelter Syndrome," Genetics Home Reference (GHR), National Institutes of Health (NIH), March 14, 2016; Text under the heading "What Causes Klinefelter Syndrome (KS)?" is excerpted from "Klinefelter Syndrome (KS): Condition Information," *Eunice Kennedy Shriver* National Institute of Child Health and Human Development (NICHD), October 25, 2013.

Children with Klinefelter syndrome may have learning disabilities and delayed speech and language development. They tend to be quiet, sensitive, and unassertive, but personality characteristics vary among affected individuals.

How Common Is Klinefelter Syndrome?

Klinefelter syndrome affects 1 in 500 to 1,000 newborn males. Most variants of Klinefelter syndrome are much rarer, occurring in 1 in 50,000 or fewer newborns.

Researchers suspect that Klinefelter syndrome is underdiagnosed because the condition may not be identified in people with mild signs and symptoms. Additionally, the features of the condition vary and overlap significantly with those of other conditions.

What Are the Genetic Changes Related to Klinefelter Syndrome?

Klinefelter syndrome is a condition related to the X and Y chromosomes (the sex chromosomes). People typically have two sex chromosomes in each cell: females have two X chromosomes (46,XX), and males have one X and one Y chromosome (46,XY). Most often, Klinefelter syndrome results from the presence of one extra copy of the X chromosome in each cell (47,XXY). Extra copies of genes on the X chromosome interfere with male sexual development, often preventing the testes from functioning normally and reducing the levels of testosterone. Most people with an extra X chromosome have the features described above, although some have few or no associated signs and symptoms.

Some people with features of Klinefelter syndrome have more than one extra sex chromosome in each cell (for example, 48,XXXY or 49,XXXXY). These conditions, which are often called variants of Klinefelter syndrome, tend to cause more severe signs and symptoms than classic Klinefelter syndrome. In addition to affecting male sexual development, variants of Klinefelter syndrome are associated with intellectual disability, distinctive facial features, skeletal abnormalities, poor coordination, and severe problems with speech. As the number of extra sex chromosomes increases, so does the risk of these health problems.

Some people with features of Klinefelter syndrome have the extra X chromosome in only some of their cells; in these individuals, the condition is described as mosaic Klinefelter syndrome (46,XY/47,XXY). Individuals with mosaic Klinefelter syndrome may have milder signs and symptoms, depending on how many cells have an additional X chromosome.

Can Klinefelter Syndrome Be Inherited?

Klinefelter syndrome and its variants are not inherited; these chromosomal changes usually occur as random events during the formation of reproductive cells (eggs and sperm) in a parent. An error in cell division called nondisjunction results in a reproductive cell with an abnormal number of chromosomes. For example, an egg or sperm cell may gain one or more extra copies of the X chromosome as a result of nondisjunction. If one of these atypical reproductive cells contributes to the genetic makeup of a child, the child will have one or more extra X chromosomes in each of the body's cells.

Mosaic 46,XY/47,XXY is also not inherited. It occurs as a random event during cell division early in fetal development. As a result, some of the body's cells have one X chromosome and one Y chromosome (46,XY), and other cells have an extra copy of the X chromosome (47,XXY).

What Causes Klinefelter Syndrome (KS)?

The extra chromosome results from a random error that occurs when a sperm or egg is formed; this error causes an extra X cell to be included each time the cell divides to form new cells. In very rare cases, more than one extra X or an extra Y is included.

How Many People Are Affected by or at Risk for Klinefelter Syndrome (KS)?

Researchers estimate that 1 male in about 500 newborn males has an extra X chromosome, making KS among the most common chromosomal disorders seen in all newborns. The likelihood of a third or fourth X is much rarer:

Prevalence of Klinefelter syndrome variants

Scientists are not sure what factors increase the risk of KS. The error that produces the extra chromosome occurs at random, meaning the error is not hereditary or passed down from parent to child. Research suggests that older mothers might be slightly more likely to have a son with KS. However, the extra X chromosome in KS comes from the father about one-half of the time.

What Are Common Symptoms of Klinefelter Syndrome (KS)?

Because XXY males do not really appear different from other males and because they may not have any or have mild symptoms, XXY males often don't know they have KS.

In other cases, males with KS may have mild or severe symptoms. Whether or not a male with KS has visible symptoms depends on many factors, including how much testosterone his body makes, if he is mosaic (with both XY and XXY cells), and his age when the condition is diagnosed and treated.

KS symptoms fall into these main categories:

Physical Symptoms

Many physical symptoms of KS result from low testosterone levels in the body. The degree of symptoms differs based on the amount of testosterone needed for a specific age or developmental stage and the amount of testosterone the body makes or has available.

During the first few years of life, when the need for testosterone is low, most XXY males do not show any obvious differences from typical male infants and young boys. Some may have slightly weaker muscles, meaning they might sit up, crawl, and walk slightly later than average. For example, on average, baby boys with KS do not start walking until age 18 months.

After age 5 years, when compared to typically developing boys, boys with KS may be slightly:

- Taller

- Fatter around the belly

- Clumsier

- Slower in developing motor skills, coordination, speed, and muscle strength

Puberty for boys with KS usually starts normally. But because their bodies make less testosterone than non-KS boys, their pubertal development may be disrupted or slow. In addition to being tall, KS boys may have:

- Smaller testes and penis

- Breast growth (about one-third of teens with KS have breast growth)

- Less facial and body hair

- Reduced muscle tone

- Narrower shoulders and wider hips

- Weaker bones, greater risk for bone fractures

- Decreased sexual interest

- Lower energy

- Reduced sperm production

An adult male with KS may have these features:

- **Infertility**: Nearly all men with KS are unable to father a biologically-related child without help from a fertility specialist.

- Small testes, with the possibility of testes shrinking slightly after the teen years

- Lower testosterone levels, which lead to less muscle, hair, and sexual interest and function

- Breasts or breast growth (called gynecomastia)

In some cases, breast growth can be permanent, and about 10% of XXY males need breast-reduction surgery.

Language and Learning Symptoms

Most males with KS have normal intelligence quotients (IQs) and successfully complete education at all levels. (IQ is a frequently used intelligence measure, but does not include emotional, creative, or other types of intelligence.) Between 25% and 85% of all males with KS have some kind of learning or language-related problem, which makes it more likely that they will need some extra help in school. Without this help or intervention, KS males might fall behind their classmates as schoolwork becomes harder.

KS males may experience some of the following learning and language-related challenges:

- **A delay in learning to talk.** Infants with KS tend to make only a few different vocal sounds. As they grow older, they may have difficulty saying words clearly. It might be hard for them to distinguish differences between similar sounds.

- **Trouble using language to express their thoughts and needs.** Boys with KS might have problems putting their thoughts, ideas, and emotions into words. Some may find it hard to learn and remember some words, such as the names of common objects.

- **Trouble processing what they hear**. Although most boys with KS can understand what is being said to them, they might take longer to process multiple or complex sentences. In some cases, they might fidget or "tune out" because they take longer to process the information. It might also be difficult for KS males to concentrate in noisy settings. They might also be less able to understand a speaker's feelings from just speech alone.

- **Reading difficulties.** Many boys with KS have difficulty understanding what they read (called poor reading comprehension). They might also read more slowly than other boys.

By adulthood, most males with KS learn to speak and converse normally, although they may have a harder time doing work that involves extensive reading and writing.

Social and Behavioral Symptoms

Many of the social and behavioral symptoms in KS may result from the language and learning difficulties. For instance, boys with KS who have language difficulties might hold back socially and could use help building social relationships.

Boys with KS, compared to typically developing boys, tend to be:

- Quieter

- Less assertive or self-confident

- More anxious or restless

- Less physically active

- More helpful and eager to please

- More obedient or more ready to follow directions

In the teenage years, boys with KS may feel their differences more strongly. As a result, these teen boys are at higher risk of depression, substance abuse, and behavioral disorders. Some teens might withdraw, feel sad, or act out their frustration and anger.

As adults, most men with KS have lives similar to those of men without KS. They successfully complete high school, college, and other levels of education. They have successful and meaningful careers and professions. They have friends and families.

Contrary to research findings published several decades ago, males with KS are no more likely to have serious psychiatric disorders or to get into trouble with the law.

Symptoms of Poly-X KS

Males with poly-X Klinefelter syndrome have more than one extra X chromosome, so their symptoms might be more pronounced than in males with KS. In childhood, they may also have seizures, crossed eyes, constipation, and recurrent ear infections. Poly-KS males might also show slight differences in other physical features.

Some common additional symptoms for several poly-X Klinefelter syndromes are listed below.

48,XXYY

- Long legs
- Little body hair
- Lower IQ, average of 60 to 80 (normal IQ is 90 to 110)
- Leg ulcers and other vascular disease symptoms
- Extreme shyness, but also sometimes aggression and impulsiveness

48,XXXY (or tetrasomy)

- Eyes set further apart
- Flat nose bridge
- Arm bones connected to each other in an unusual way
- Short
- Fifth (smallest) fingers curve inward (clinodactyly)
- Lower IQ, average 40 to 60
- Immature behavior

49,XXXXY (or pentasomy)

- Low IQ, usually between 20 and 60
- Small head
- Short

- Upward-slanted eyes
- Heart defects, such as when the chambers do not form properly
- High feet arches
- Shy, but friendly
- Difficulty with changing routines

What Are the Treatments for Symptoms in Klinefelter Syndrome (KS)?

It's important to remember that because symptoms can be mild, many males with KS are never diagnosed or treated.

The earlier in life that KS symptoms are recognized and treated, the more likely it is that the symptoms can be reduced or eliminated. It is especially helpful to begin treatment by early puberty. Puberty is a time of rapid physical and psychological change, and treatment can successfully limit symptoms. However, treatment can bring benefits at any age.

The type of treatment needed depends on the type of symptoms being treated.

Treating Physical Symptoms

For Low Testosterone

About one-half of XXY males' chromosomes have low testosterone levels. These levels can be raised by taking supplemental testosterone. Testosterone treatment can:

- Improve muscle mass
- Deepen the voice
- Promote growth of facial and body hair
- Help the reproductive organs to mature
- Build and maintain bone strength and help prevent osteoporosis in later years
- Produce a more masculine appearance, which can also help relieve anxiety and depression
- Increase focus and attention

There are various ways to take testosterone:

- Injections or shots, every 2 to 3 weeks

- Pills

- Through the skin, also called transdermal; current methods include wearing a testosterone patch or rubbing testosterone gel on the skin

Males taking testosterone treatment should work closely with an endocrinologist, a doctor who specializes in hormones and their functions, to ensure the best outcome from testosterone therapy.

Not all males with XXY condition benefit from testosterone therapy. For males whose testosterone level is low to normal, the benefits of taking testosterone are less clear than for when testosterone is very low. Side effects, although generally mild, can include acne, skin rashes from patches or gels, breathing problems (especially during sleep), and higher risk of an enlarged prostate gland or prostate cancer in older age. In addition, testosterone supplementation will not increase testicular size, decrease breast growth, or correct infertility.

Although the majority of boys with KS grow up to live as males, some develop atypical gender identities. For these males, supplemental testosterone may not be suitable. Gender identity should be discussed with healthcare specialists before starting treatment.

For Enlarged Breasts

No approved drug treatment exists for this condition of over-developed breast tissue, termed gynecomastia. Some healthcare providers recommend surgery—called mastectomy—to remove or reduce the breasts of XXY males.

When adult men have breasts, they are at higher risk for breast cancer than other men and need to be checked for this condition regularly. The mastectomy lowers the risk of cancer and can reduce the social stress associated with XXY males having enlarged breasts.

Because it is a surgical procedure, mastectomy carries a variety of risks. XXY males who are thinking about mastectomy should discuss all the risks and benefits with their healthcare provider.

For Infertility

Between 95% and 99% of XXY men are infertile because they do not produce enough sperm to fertilize an egg naturally. But, sperm are found in more than 50% of men with KS.

Advances in assistive reproductive technology (ART) have made it possible for some men with KS to conceive. One type of ART, called testicular sperm extraction with intracytoplasmic sperm injection (TESE-ICSI), has shown success for XXY males. For this procedure, a surgeon removes sperm from the testes and places one sperm into an egg.

Like all ART, TESE-ICSI carries both risks and benefits. For instance, it is possible that the resulting child might have the XXY condition. In addition, the procedure is expensive and is often is not covered by health insurance plans. Importantly, there is no guarantee the procedure will work.

Studies suggest that collecting sperm from adolescent XXY males and freezing the sperm until later might result in more pregnancies during subsequent fertility treatments. This is because although XXY males may make some healthy sperm during puberty, this becomes more difficult as they leave adolescence and enter adulthood.

Treating Language and Learning Symptoms

Some, but not all, children with KS have language development and learning delays. They might be slow to learn to talk, read, and write, and they might have difficulty processing what they hear. But various interventions, such as speech therapy and educational assistance, can help to reduce and even eliminate these difficulties. The earlier treatment begins, the better the outcomes.

Parents might need to bring these types of problems to the teacher's attention. Because these boys can be quiet and cooperative in the classroom, teachers may not notice the need for help.

Boys and men with KS can benefit by visiting therapists who are experts in areas such as coordination, social skills, and coping. XXY males might benefit from any or all of the following:

- **Physical therapists** design activities and exercises to build motor skills and strength and to improve muscle control, posture, and balance.

- **Occupational therapists** help build skills needed for daily functioning, such as social and play skills, interaction and conversation skills, and job or career skills that match interests and abilities.

- **Behavioral therapists** help with specific social skills, such as asking other kids to play and starting conversations. They can also teach productive ways of handling frustration, shyness, anger, and other emotions that can arise from feeling "different."

- **Mental health therapists** or counselors help males with KS find ways to cope with feelings of sadness, depression, self-doubt, and low self-esteem. They can also help with substance abuse problems. These professionals can also help families deal with the emotions of having a son with KS.

- **Family therapists** provide counseling to a man with KS, his spouse, partner, or family. They can help identify relationship problems and help patients develop communication skills and understand other people's needs.

Parents of XXY males have also mentioned that taking part in **physical activities at low-key levels**, such as karate, swimming, tennis, and golf, were helpful in improving motor skills, coordination, and confidence.

With regard to education, some boys with KS will qualify to receive state-sponsored special needs services to address their developmental and learning symptoms. But, because these symptoms may be mild, many XXY males will not be eligible for these services. Families can contact a local school district official or special education coordinator to learn more about whether XXY males can receive the following free services:

- The Early Intervention Program for Infants and Toddlers with Disabilities is required by two national laws, the Individuals with Disabilities and Education Improvement Act (IDEIA) and the Individuals with Disabilities Education Act (IDEA). Every state operates special programs for children from birth to age 3, helping them develop in areas such as behavior, development, communication, and social play.

- An Individualized Education Plan (IEP) for school is created and administered by a team of people, starting with parents and including teachers and school psychologists. The team works together to design an IEP with specific academic, communica- tion, motor, learning, functional, and socialization goals, based on the child's educational needs and specific symptoms.

Treating Social and Behavioral Symptoms

Many of the professionals and methods for treating learning and language symptoms of the XXY condition are similar to or the same as the ones used to address social and behavioral symptoms.

For instance, boys with KS may need help with social skills and interacting in groups. Occupational or behavioral therapists might be able to assist with these skills. Some school districts and health centers might also offer these types of skill-building programs or classes.

In adolescence, symptoms such as lack of body hair could make XXY males uncomfortable in school or other social settings, and this discomfort can lead to depression, substance abuse, and behavioral problems or "acting out." They might also have questions about their masculinity or gender identity. In these instances, consulting a psychologist, counselor, or psychiatrist may be helpful.

Contrary to research results released decades ago, current research shows that XXY males are no more likely than other males to have serious psychiatric disorders or to get into trouble with the law.

How Do HealthCare Providers Diagnose Klinefelter Syndrome (KS)?

The only way to confirm the presence of an extra chromosome is by a karyotype test. A healthcare provider will take a small blood or skin sample and send it to a laboratory, where a technician inspects the cells under a microscope to find the extra chromosome. A karyotype test shows the same results at any time in a person's life.

Tests for chromosome disorders, including KS, may be done before birth. To obtain tissue or liquid for this test, a pregnant woman undergoes chorionic villus sampling or amniocentesis. These types of prenatal testing carry a small risk for miscarriage and are not routinely conducted unless the woman has a family history of chromosomal disorders, has other medical problems, or is above 35 years of age.

Factors That Influence When KS Is Diagnosed

Because symptoms can be mild, some males with KS are never diagnosed.

Several factors affect whether and when a diagnosis occurs:

- Few newborns and boys are tested for or diagnosed with KS.

- Although newborns in the United States are screened for some conditions, they are not screened for XXY or other sex-chromosome differences.

- In childhood, symptoms can be subtle and overlooked easily. Only about 1 in 10 males with KS is diagnosed before puberty.

- Sometimes, visiting a healthcare provider will not produce a diagnosis. Some symptoms, such as delayed early speech, might be treated successfully without further testing for KS.

- Most XXY diagnoses occur at puberty or in adulthood.

- Puberty brings a surge in diagnoses as some males (or their parents) become concerned about slow testes growth or breast development and consult a healthcare provider.

- Many men are diagnosed for the first time in fertility clinics. Among men seeking help for infertility, about 15% have KS.

Is There a Cure for Klinefelter Syndrome (KS)?

At present, there is no way to remove chromosomes from cells to "cure" the XXY condition.

But many symptoms can be successfully treated, minimizing the impact the condition has on length and quality of life. Most adult XXY men have full independence and have friends, families, and normal social relationships. They live about as long as other men, on average.

Are There Disorders or Conditions Associated with KS?

Males with KS are at higher risk for some other health conditions, for reasons that are not fully understood. But these risks can be minimized by paying attention to symptoms and treating them appropriately.

Associated conditions include:

- **Autoimmune disorders**, such as type 1 diabetes, rheumatoid arthritis, hypothyroidism, and lupus. In these disorders, the immune cells attack parts of the body instead of protecting them.

- **Breast cancer**. Males with KS have a higher risk of developing this cancer, although still a lower risk than females'. XXY males should pay attention to any changes in their breasts, such as lumps or any leakage from the nipple, and should see their healthcare provider right away if they have any concerns.

- **Venous disease,** or diseases of the arteries and veins. Some of these include:

- Varicose veins

- Deep vein thrombosis, a blood clot in a deep vein

- Pulmonary embolism, a blockage of an artery in the lungs

To reduce their risk, males can keep a normal body weight; get regular, moderate physical activity; quit smoking; and avoid sitting or standing in the same position for long periods of time. If venous diseases develop, they can be treated in different ways, depending on their severity. For instance, some treatments include wearing compression socks and others require taking blood thinner medications.

- **Tooth decay**. Almost one-half of men with KS have taurodontism, a dental problem in which the teeth have larger-than-normal chambers for holding pulp (the soft tissue that contains nerve endings and blood vessels) and shorter-than-normal tooth roots, both of which make it easier for tooth decay to develop. Regular dental check-ups and good oral hygiene habits will help prevent, catch, and treat problems.

- **Osteoporosis,** in which bones lose calcium, become brittle, and break more easily, may develop over time in KS males who have low testosterone levels for long periods of time. Testosterone treatment; regular, moderate physical activity; and eating a healthy diet can decrease the risk of osteoporosis. If the disease develops, medications can help limit its severity.

Can KS Lead to Cancer?

Compared with the general male population, men with KS may have a higher chance over time of getting breast cancer, non-Hodgkin lymphoma, and lung cancer. There are ways to reduce this risk, such as removing the breasts and avoiding use of tobacco products. In general, XXY males are also at lower risk for prostate cancer.

If I Have KS, Will I Be Able to Get a Woman Pregnant?

It is possible that an XXY male could get a woman pregnant naturally. Although sperm are found in more than 50% of men with KS, low sperm production could make conception very difficult.

A few men with KS have recently been able to father a biologically related child by undergoing assisted fertility services, specifically, a procedure called testicular sperm extraction with intracytoplasmic sperm injection (TESE-ICSI). TESE-ICSI, this carries a slightly higher risk of chromosomal disorders in the child, including having an extra X.

Chapter 45

Prader-Willi Syndrome

What Is Prader-Willi Syndrome?

Prader-Willi syndrome is a complex genetic condition that affects many parts of the body. In infancy, this condition is characterized by weak muscle tone (hypotonia), feeding difficulties, poor growth, and delayed development. Beginning in childhood, affected individuals develop an insatiable appetite, which leads to chronic overeating (hyperphagia) and obesity. Some people with Prader-Willi syndrome, particularly those with obesity, also develop type 2 diabetes mellitus (the most common form of diabetes).

People with Prader-Willi syndrome typically have mild to moderate intellectual impairment and learning disabilities. Behavioral problems are common, including temper outbursts, stubbornness, and compulsive behavior such as picking at the skin. Sleep abnormalities can also occur. Additional features of this condition include distinctive facial features such as a narrow forehead, almond-shaped eyes, and a triangular mouth; short stature; and small hands and feet. Some people with Prader-Willi syndrome have unusually fair skin and light-colored

This chapter contains text excerpted from the following sources: Text beginning with the heading "What Is Prader-Willi Syndrome?" is excerpted from "Prader-Willi Syndrome," Genetics Home Reference (GHR), National Institutes of Health (NIH), March 14, 2016; Text under the heading "What Are the Symptoms of Prader-Willi Syndrome (PWS)?" is excerpted from "Prader-Willi Syndrome (PWS): Condition Information," *Eunice Kennedy Shriver* National Institute of Child Health and Human Development (NICHD), January 14, 2014.

hair. Both affected males and affected females have underdeveloped genitals. Puberty is delayed or incomplete, and most affected individuals are unable to have children (infertile).

How Common Is Prader-Willi Syndrome?

Prader-Willi syndrome affects an estimated 1 in 10,000 to 30,000 people worldwide.

What Are the Genetic Changes Related to Prader-Willi Syndrome?

Prader-Willi syndrome is caused by the loss of function of genes in a particular region of chromosome 15. People normally inherit one copy of this chromosome from each parent. Some genes are turned on (active) only on the copy that is inherited from a person's father (the paternal copy). This parent-specific gene activation is caused by a phenomenon called genomic imprinting.

Most cases of Prader-Willi syndrome (about 70 percent) occur when a segment of the paternal chromosome 15 is deleted in each cell. People with this chromosomal change are missing certain critical genes in this region because the genes on the paternal copy have been deleted, and the genes on the maternal copy are turned off (inactive). In another 25 percent of cases, a person with Prader-Willi syndrome has two copies of chromosome 15 inherited from his or her mother (maternal copies) instead of one copy from each parent. This phenomenon is called maternal uniparental disomy. Rarely, Prader-Willi syndrome can also be caused by a chromosomal rearrangement called a translocation, or by a mutation or other defect that abnormally turns off (inactivates) genes on the paternal chromosome 15.

It appears likely that the characteristic features of Prader-Willi syndrome result from the loss of function of several genes on chromosome 15. Among these are genes that provide instructions for making molecules called small nucleolar RNAs (snoRNAs). These molecules have a variety of functions, including helping to regulate other types of RNA molecules. (RNA molecules play essential roles in producing proteins and in other cell activities.) Studies suggest that the loss of a particular group of snoRNA genes, known as the SNORD116 cluster, may play a major role in causing the signs and symptoms of Prader-Willi syndrome. However, it is unknown how a missing SNORD116 cluster could contribute to intellectual disability, behavioral problems, and the physical features of the disorder.

In some people with Prader-Willi syndrome, the loss of a gene called *OCA2* is associated with unusually fair skin and light-colored hair. The *OCA2* gene is located on the segment of chromosome 15 that is often deleted in people with this disorder. However, loss of the *OCA2* gene does not cause the other signs and symptoms of Prader-Willi syndrome. The protein produced from this gene helps determine the coloring (pigmentation) of the skin, hair, and eyes.

Researchers are studying other genes on chromosome 15 that may also be related to the major signs and symptoms of this condition.

Can Prader-Willi Syndrome Be Inherited?

Most cases of Prader-Willi syndrome are not inherited, particularly those caused by a deletion in the paternal chromosome 15 or by maternal uniparental disomy. These genetic changes occur as random events during the formation of reproductive cells (eggs and sperm) or in early embryonic development. Affected people typically have no history of the disorder in their family.

Rarely, a genetic change responsible for Prader-Willi syndrome can be inherited. For example, it is possible for a genetic change that abnormally inactivates genes on the paternal chromosome 15 to be passed from one generation to the next.

What Are the Symptoms of Prader-Willi Syndrome (PWS)?

Scientists think that the symptoms of PWS may be caused by a problem in a portion of the brain called the hypothalamus. The hypothalamus lies in the base of the brain. When it works normally, it controls hunger or thirst, body temperature, pain, and when it is time to awaken and to sleep. Problems with the hypothalamus can affect various body functions and pathways, leading to a variety of symptoms.

Individuals with PWS may have mild to severe symptoms, which often include:

Feeding and Metabolic Symptoms

An important early symptom of PWS is an infant's inability to suck, which affects the ability to feed. Nearly all infants with PWS need help with feeding. Infants may require feeding support for several months. Without assistance, they will not grow. Nursing systems with one-way valves and manual sucking assistive devices, similar to those used with cleft palate (such as bottles with special nipples for babies who do not have the sucking reflex), often are needed. Occasionally, feeding tubes are required, but generally for no more than the first 6 months after birth. The infants may need fewer calories because of the reduced metabolism associated with PWS and may not demand feeding on their own. Frequent weight checks will help in adjusting the infant's diet to maintain a suitable weight gain.

As the infants grow into toddlers and children, compulsive overeating replaces the need for feeding support. Because the metabolic rate of individuals with PWS is lower than normal, their caloric intake must be restricted to maintain a healthy weight, often to 60% of the caloric requirement of comparably sized children without the syndrome.

Feeding and metabolic symptoms persist into adulthood. Unless individuals with PWS live in environments that limit access to food (such as locked cabinets and a locked refrigerator), they will eat uncontrollably, even food that is rotten or sitting in the garbage. Uncontrollable eating can cause choking, a ruptured esophagus, and blockages in the digestive system. It can also lead to extreme weight gain and morbid obesity. Because of their inability to stop eating, people with PWS are at increased risk for diabetes, trouble breathing during sleep, and other health risks. For these reasons, people with PWS need to be monitored by a healthcare professional their entire lives.

Physical Symptoms

Many physical symptoms of PWS arise from poor regulation of various hormones, including growth hormone, thyroid hormone, and possibly adrenalin. Individuals with PWS grow slowly and experience delays in reaching physical activity milestones (e.g., standing, walking).

Children with PWS tend to be substantially shorter than other children of similar age. They may have small hands and feet and a curvature of the back, called scoliosis. In addition, they frequently have difficulty making their eyes work together to focus, a condition called strabismus.

Infants with PWS are often born with underdeveloped sex organs, including a small penis and scrotum or a small clitoris and vaginal lips. Most individuals with PWS are infertile.

Intellectual Symptoms

Individuals with PWS have varying levels of intellectual disabilities. Learning disabilities are common, as are delays in starting to talk and in the development of language.

Behavioral and Psychiatric Symptoms

Imbalances in hormone levels may contribute to behavioral and psychiatric problems. Behavioral problems may include temper tantrums, extreme stubbornness, obsessive-compulsive symptoms, picking the skin, and general trouble in controlling emotions. The individual will often repeat questions or statements. Sleep disturbances may include excessive daytime sleepiness and disruptions of sleep. Many individuals with PWS have a high pain threshold.

Stages of PWS Symptoms

The appearance of PWS symptoms occurs in two recognized stages:

Stage 1 (Infancy to age 2 years)

- "Floppiness" and poor muscle tone
- Weak cries and a weak sucking reflex
- Inability to breastfeed, which may require feeding support, such as tube feeding
- Developmental delays
- Small genital organs

Stage 2 (Ages 2 to 8)

- Unable to feel satisfied with normal intake of food
- Inability to control eating, which can lead to overeating if not monitored
- Food-seeking behaviors
- Low metabolism
- Weight gain and obesity
- Daytime sleepiness and sleep problems
- Intellectual disabilities
- Small hands and feet
- Short stature
- Curvature of the spine (scoliosis)
- High pain threshold

Behavioral problems, including the display of obsessive-compulsive symptoms, picking the skin, and difficulty controlling emotions
Small genitals, often resulting in infertility in later life.

How Many People Are Affected / at Risk for Prader-Willi Syndrome (PWS)?

Prader-Willi syndrome, which occurs in about one in every 15,000 to 25,000 live births, is the most common genetic disorder that can lead to life-threatening obesity in children. Boys and girls are equally affected.

Scientists do not know what increases the risk for Prader-Willi syndrome. The genetic error that leads to Prader-Willi syndrome occurs at random, usually around the time of conception or during early fetal development. The syndrome is usually not hereditary.

Genetic testing can identify the chance that a second sibling will develop Prader-Willi syndrome, a possibility that is usually less than 1%.

What Causes Prader-Willi Syndrome (PWS)?

Prader-Willi syndrome is caused by genetic changes on an "unstable" region of chromosome 15 that affects the regulation of gene expression, or how genes turn on and off. This part of the chromosome is called unstable because it is prone to being shuffled around by the cell's genetic machinery before the chromosome is passed on from parent to child.

The genetic changes that cause Prader-Willi syndrome occur in a portion of the chromosome, referred to as the Prader-Willi critical region (PWCR), around the time of conception or during early fetal development. This region was identified in 1990 using genetic DNA probes. Although Prader-Willi syndrome is genetic, it usually is not inherited and generally develops due to deletions or partial deletions on chromosome 15.

Specific changes to the chromosome can include the following:

- **Deletions**. A section of a chromosome may be lost or deleted, along with the functions that this section supported. About 65% to 75% of Prader-Willi syndrome cases result from the loss of function of several genes in one region of the father's chromosome 15, due to deletion. The corresponding mother's genes on chromosome 15 are always inactive and thus cannot make up for the deletion on the father's chromosome 15. The missing paternal genes normally play a fundamental role in regulating hunger and fullness.

- **Maternal uniparental disomy**. A cell usually contains one set of chromosomes from the father and another set from the mother. In ordinary cases, a child has two chromosome 15s, one from each parent. In 20% to 30% of Prader-Willi syndrome cases, the child has two chromosome 15s from the mother and none from the father. Because genes located in the PWCR are normally inactive in the chromosome that comes from the mother, the child's lack of active genes in this region leads to Prader-Willi syndrome.

- **An imprinting center defect**. Genes in the PWCR on the chromosome that came from the mother are normally inactivated, due to a process known as "imprinting" that affects whether the cell is able to "read" a gene or not. In less than 5% of Prader-Willi syndrome cases, the chromosome 15 inherited from the father is imprinted in the same way as the mother's. This can be caused by a small deletion in a region of the father's chromosome that controls the imprinting process, called the imprinting center. In these cases, both of the child's copies of chromosome 15 have inactive PWCRs, leading to Prader-Willi syndrome.

How Do HealthCare Providers Diagnose Prader-Willi Syndrome (PWS)?

In many cases of Prader-Willi syndrome, diagnosis is prompted by physical symptoms in the newborn.

If a newborn is unable to suck or feed for a few days and has a "floppy" body and weak muscle tone, a healthcare provider may conduct genetic testing for Prader-Willi syndrome. Formal diagnostic criteria for recognizing Prader-Willi syndrome depend on the age of the individual-specifically, whether the third birthday has been reached. Before age 3, the most important symptom is extremely poor muscle tone, called hypotonia, which makes infants feel floppy. In affected children 3 years of age and older, other symptoms become apparent, such as obesity, intellectual delays, learning disabilities, or behavior problems, especially connected with food and eating.

- **Children younger than 3 years** must have at least four major criteria and at least one minor criterion for a Prader-Willi syndrome diagnosis.

- **Those older than 3 years** must have at least five major criteria and at least three minor criteria for a diagnosis of Prader-Willi syndrome.

Major Clinical Criteria of Prader-Willi Syndrome

- Extremely weak muscles in the body's torso

- Difficulty sucking, which improves after the first few months

- Feeding difficulties and/or failure to grow, requiring feeding assistance, such as feeding tubes or special nipples to aid in sucking

- Beginning of rapid weight gain, between ages 1 and 6, resulting in severe obesity

- Excessive, uncontrollable overeating

- Specific facial features, including narrow forehead and down-turned mouth

- Reduced development of the genital organs, including small genitalia (vaginal lips and clitoris in females and small scrotum and penis in males); incomplete and delayed puberty; infertility

- Developmental delays, mild-to-moderate intellectual disability, multiple learning disabilities

Minor Clinical Criteria of Prader-Willi Syndrome

- Decreased movement and noticeable fatigue during infancy

- Behavioral problems-specifically, temper tantrums, obsessive-compulsive behavior, stubbornness, rigidity, stealing, and lying (especially related to food)

- Sleep problems, including daytime sleepiness and sleep disruption

- Short stature, compared with other members of the family, noticeable by age 15

- Light color of skin, eyes, and hair

- Small hands and feet in comparison to standards for height and age

- Narrow hands

- Nearsightedness and/or difficulty focusing both eyes at the same time
- Thick saliva
- Poor pronunciation
- Picking of the skin

Additional Findings

- High pain threshold
- Inability to vomit
- Curvature of the spine (scoliosis)
- Earlier-than-usual activity in the adrenal glands, which can lead to early puberty
- Especially brittle bones

Genetic testing must confirm the Prader-Willi syndrome diagnosis. More than 99% of individuals with Prader-Willi syndrome have an abnormality within a specific area of chromosome 15. Early diagnosis is best because it enables affected individuals to begin early intervention/special needs programs and treatment specifically for Prader-Willi symptoms.

Genetic testing can confirm the chance that a sibling might be born with Prader-Willi syndrome. Prenatal diagnosis also is available for at-risk pregnancies-that is, pregnancies among women with a family history of Prader-Willi syndrome abnormalities.

Genetic Counseling and Testing of At-Risk Relatives

Genetic counseling and testing provide individuals and families with information about the nature, inheritance, and implications of genetic disorders so that they can make informed medical and personal decisions about having children. Genetic counseling helps people understand their risks. The risk of occurrence in siblings of patients with Prader-Willi syndrome depends on what caused the disorder to occur.

Is There a Cure for Prader-Willi Syndrome (PWS)?

Prader-Willi syndrome has no cure. However, early diagnosis and treatment may help prevent or reduce the number of challenges that individuals with Prader-Willi syndrome may experience, and which may be more of a problem if diagnosis or treatment is delayed.

What Are the Treatments for Prader-Willi Syndrome (PWS)?

Parents can enroll infants with PWS in early intervention programs. However, even if a PWS diagnosis is delayed, treatments are valuable at any age.

The types of treatment depend on the individual's symptoms. The healthcare provider may recommend the following:

- **Use of special nipples or tubes for feeding difficulties**. Difficulty in sucking is one of the most common symptoms of newborns with Prader-Willi syndrome. Special nipples or tubes are used for several months to feed newborns and infants who are unable to suck properly, to make sure that the infant is fed adequately and grows. To ensure that the child is growing properly, the healthcare provider will monitor height, weight, and body mass index (BMI) monthly during infancy.

- **Strict supervision of daily food intake**. Once overeating starts between ages 2 and 4 years, supervision will help to minimize food hoarding and stealing and prevent rapid weight gain and severe obesity. Parents should lock refrigerators and all cabinets containing food. No medications have proven beneficial in reducing food-seeking behavior.

A well-balanced, low-calorie diet and regular exercise are essential and must be maintained for the rest of the individual's life. People with PWS rarely need more than 1,000 to 1,200 calories per day. Height, weight, and BMI should be monitored every 6 months during the first 10 years of life after infancy and once a year after age 10 for the rest of the person's life to make sure he or she is maintaining a healthy weight. Ongoing consultation with a dietitian to guarantee adequate vitamin and mineral intake, including calcium and vitamin D, might be needed.

- **Growth Hormone (GH) therapy**. GH therapy has been demonstrated to increase height, lean body mass, and mobility; decrease fat mass; and improve movement and flexibility in individuals with PWS from infancy through adulthood. When given early in life, it also may prevent or reduce behavioral difficulties. Additionally, GH therapy can help improve speech, improve abstract reasoning, and often allow information to be processed more quickly. It also has been shown to improve sleep quality and resting energy expenditure. GH therapy usually is started during infancy or at diagnosis with PWS. This therapy often continues during adulthood at 20% to 25% of the recommended dose for children.

- **Treatment of eye problems by a pediatric ophthalmologist**. Many infants have trouble getting their eyes to focus together. These infants should be referred to a pediatric ophthalmologist who has expertise in working with infants with disabilities.

- **Treatment of curvature of the spine by an orthopedist**. An orthopedist should evaluate and treat, if necessary, curvature of the spine (scoliosis). Treatment will be the same as that for people with scoliosis who do not have PWS.

- **Sleep studies and treatment**. Sleep disorders are common with PWS. Treating a sleep disorder can help improve the quality of sleep. The same treatments that healthcare providers use with the general population can apply to individuals with PWS.

- **Physical therapy**. Muscle weakness is a serious problem among individuals with PWS. For children younger than age 3, physical therapy may increase muscular strength and help such children achieve developmental milestones. For older children, daily exercise will help build lean body mass.

- **Behavioral therapy**. People with PWS have difficulty controlling their emotions. Using behavioral therapy can help. Stubbornness, anger, and obsessive-compulsive behavior, including obsession with food, should be handled with behavioral management programs using firm limit-setting strategies. Structure and routines also are advised.

- **Medications**. Medications, especially serotonin reuptake inhibitors (SRIs), may reduce obsessive-compulsive symptoms. SRIs also may help manage psychosis.

- **Early interventions / Special needs programs**. Individuals with PWS have varying degrees of intellectual difficulty and learning disabilities. Early intervention programs, including speech therapy for delays in acquiring language and for difficulties with pronunciation, should begin as early as possible and continue throughout childhood.

- **Special education is almost always necessary for school-age children.** Groups that offer training in social skills may also prove beneficial. An individual aide is often useful in helping PWS children focus on schoolwork.

- **Sex hormone treatments and/or corrective surgery**. These treatments are used to treat small genitals (penis, scrotum, clitoris).

- **Replacement of sex hormones.** Replacement of sex hormones during puberty may result in development of adequate secondary sex characteristics (e.g., breasts, pubic hair, a deeper voice).

- **Placement in group homes during adulthood.** Group homes offer necessary structure and supervision for adults with PWS, helping them avoid compulsive eating, severe obesity, and other health problems.

Are There Disorders or Conditions Associated with PWS?

Several other disorders and conditions are associated with PWS:

- Obesity and secondary problems due to extreme obesity
  - Diabetes
  - Sleep apnea
- Obsessive-compulsive disorder
- Infertility
- Autism spectrum disorders

Does PWS Affect Pregnancy?

Until recently, experts believed that people with PWS were infertile. However, because several pregnancies have occurred in women with PWS, birth control should be considered.

Inheritance of PWS and Angelman Syndrome

PWS could affect the offspring of someone with the syndrome, depending on how the individual developed the disorder and the individual's sex. The offspring could be at risk of being born with PWS or with Angelman syndrome. Angelman syndrome, like PWS, results from defects in one region of chromosome 15. The two syndromes both involve missing or silenced genes in this region, called the Prader-Willi critical region (PWCR). This section of the chromosome is "imprinted," and the genes involved in Angelman syndrome and PWS have different sex-specific imprinting patterns. This is the reason why the sex of the parent with PWS affects which disorder the offspring is at risk to inherit.

Deletion

If a mother with PWS developed the syndrome because of the deletion of a section of one of her two copies of chromosome 15, her child will have a 50% risk of being born with Angelman syndrome. That is, if the mother with PWS passes on her chromosome 15 with the deletion, the child will have Angelman syndrome. This is because the father's genes in this region that are linked to Angelman syndrome are normally inactivated; thus, the child will have no active copies of these genes, causing Angelman syndrome. If the mother passes on her normal copy of chromosome 15, the child will not be born with Angelman syndrome or PWS.

In the case of a father with PWS who has a deletion in chromosome 15, there is a 50% chance that he will pass on the affected chromosome to his child, leading to PWS. This is because a mother's genes that are linked to PWS are normally inactivated; thus, the child will have no active copies of these genes.

Because fertility is so rare in individuals with PWS, only one case of a mother with a deletion passing on Angelman syndrome to her child has been reported. No cases have been reported of a father who had PWS because of a deletion passing on PWS to his child, but it is possible.

Uniparental Disomy

No case of either syndrome in the child of an individual with PWS through uniparental disomy (two copies of chromosome 15 from the mother and none from the father) has ever been reported, but they are theoretically possible. Inheritance could happen in three different ways, but all require the parent with PWS passing on both copies of his or her chromosome 15, which is unlikely.

If the offspring also receives a copy of chromosome 15 from the other parent and none of these three copies is lost, this condition will be fatal before birth.

If the parent with PWS is the mother and the offspring ends up with only two copies of chromosome 15 during development, the child will probably be born with PWS because he or she has inherited two inactivated copies of the genes in the PWCR.

If the parent with PWS is the father and the offspring ends up with only two copies of chromosome 15 during development, the child will probably be born with Angelman syndrome. This is because the genes related to Angelman syndrome in the chromosome inherited from the mother are inactivated, and thus the child does not have any working copies of these genes, causing Angelman syndrome.

Imprinting Center Defect

No cases have been reported of a parent who has PWS because of an imprinting center defect passing on PWS to his/her child. However, there is a theoretical possibility of this happening.

Chapter 46

Smith-Magenis Syndrome

What Is Smith-Magenis Syndrome?

Smith-Magenis syndrome is a developmental disorder that affects many parts of the body. The major features of this condition include mild to moderate intellectual disability, delayed speech and language skills, distinctive facial features, sleep disturbances, and behavioral problems.

How Common Is Smith-Magenis Syndrome?

Smith-Magenis syndrome affects at least 1 in 25,000 individuals worldwide. Researchers believe that many people with this condition are not diagnosed, however, so the true prevalence may be closer to 1 in 15,000 individuals.

What Are the Genetic Changes Related to Smith-Magenis Syndrome?

Most people with Smith-Magenis syndrome have a deletion of genetic material from a specific region of chromosome 17. Although

This chapter contains text excerpted from the following sources: Text begins with the heading "What Is Smith-Magenis Syndrome?" is excerpted from "Smith-Magenis Syndrome," Genetics Home Reference (GHR), National Institutes of Health (NIH), March 14, 2016; Text under the heading "What Are the Signs and Symptoms of Smith-Magenis Syndrome?" is excerpted from "Smith-Magenis Syndrome," National Center for Advancing Translational Sciences (NCATS), August 22, 2014.

this region contains multiple genes, researchers believe that the loss of one particular gene, *RAI1*, in each cell is responsible for most of the characteristic features of this condition. The loss of other genes in the deleted region may help explain why the features of Smith-Magenis syndrome vary among affected individuals.

A small percentage of people with Smith-Magenis syndrome have a mutation in the *RAI1* gene instead of a chromosomal deletion. Although these individuals have many of the major features of the condition, they are less likely than people with a chromosomal deletion to have short stature, hearing loss, and heart or kidney abnormalities.

The *RAI1* gene provides instructions for making a protein whose function is unknown. Mutations in one copy of this gene lead to the production of a nonfunctional version of the *RAI1* protein or reduce the amount of this protein that is produced in cells. Researchers are uncertain how changes in this protein result in the physical, mental, and behavioral problems associated with Smith-Magenis syndrome.

Can Smith-Magenis Syndrome Be Inherited?

Smith-Magenis syndrome is typically not inherited. This condition usually results from a genetic change that occurs during the formation of reproductive cells (eggs or sperm) or in early fetal development. Most often, people with Smith-Magenis syndrome have no history of the condition in their family.

What Are the Signs and Symptoms of Smith-Magenis Syndrome?

Most people with Smith-Magenis syndrome have a broad, square-shaped face with deep-set eyes, full cheeks, and a prominent lower jaw. The middle of the face and the bridge of the nose often appear flattened. The mouth tends to turn downward with a full, outward-curving upper lip. These facial differences can be subtle in early childhood, but they usually become more distinctive in later childhood and adulthood. Dental abnormalities are also common in affected individuals.

Disrupted sleep patterns are characteristic of Smith-Magenis syndrome, typically beginning early in life. Affected people may be very sleepy during the day, but have trouble falling asleep and awaken several times each night.

People with Smith-Magenis syndrome have affectionate, engaging personalities, but most also have behavioral problems. These include frequent temper tantrums and outbursts, aggression, anxiety, impulsiveness, and difficulty paying attention. Self-injury, including biting, hitting, head banging, and skin picking, is very common. Repetitive self-hugging is a behavioral trait that may be unique to Smith-Magenis syndrome. People with this condition also compulsively lick their fingers and flip pages of books and magazines (a behavior known as 'lick and flip').

Other signs and symptoms of Smith-Magenis syndrome include short stature, abnormal curvature of the spine (scoliosis), reduced sensitivity to pain and temperature, and a hoarse voice. Some people with this disorder have ear abnormalities that lead to hearing loss. Affected individuals may have eye abnormalities that cause nearsightedness (myopia) and other vision problems. Although less common, heart and kidney defects also have been reported in people with Smith-Magenis syndrome.

What Causes Smith-Magenis Syndrome?

Most people with Smith-Magenis syndrome have a deletion of genetic material from a specific region of chromosome 17. Although this region contains multiple genes, researchers believe that the loss of one particular gene, *RAI1*, is responsible for most of the characteristic features of this condition. The loss of other genes in the deleted region may explain why there is variability in features among affected individuals.

A small percentage of people with Smith-Magenis syndrome have just a mutation in the *RAI1* gene (not a deletion of the larger part of the chromosome). Although these individuals have many of the major features of the condition, they are less likely than people with a chromosomal deletion to have short stature, hearing loss, and heart or kidney abnormalities.

Chapter 47

Turner Syndrome

What Is Turner Syndrome?

Turner syndrome is a chromosomal condition that affects development in females. The most common feature of Turner syndrome is short stature, which becomes evident by about age 5. An early loss of ovarian function (ovarian hypofunction or premature ovarian failure) is also very common. The ovaries develop normally at first, but egg cells (oocytes) usually die prematurely and most ovarian tissue degenerates before birth. Many affected girls do not undergo puberty unless they receive hormone therapy, and most are unable to conceive (infertile). A small percentage of females with Turner syndrome retain normal ovarian function through young adulthood.

About 30 percent of females with Turner syndrome have extra folds of skin on the neck (webbed neck), a low hairline at the back of the neck, puffiness or swelling (lymphedema) of the hands and feet, skeletal abnormalities, or kidney problems. One third to one half of individuals with Turner syndrome are born with a heart defect, such as a narrowing of the large artery leaving the heart (coarctation of the aorta) or abnormalities of the valve that connects the aorta with the heart (the aortic valve). Complications associated with these heart defects can be life-threatening.

This chapter contains text excerpted from the following sources: Text beginning with the heading "What Is Turner Syndrome?" is excerpted from "Turner Syndrome," Genetics Home Reference (GHR), National Institutes of Health (NIH), March 14, 2016; Text under the heading "What Are the Signs and Symptoms of Turner Syndrome?" is excerpted from "Turner Syndrome," National Center for Advancing Translational Sciences (NCATS), January 11, 2016

Most girls and women with Turner syndrome have normal intelligence. Developmental delays, nonverbal learning disabilities, and behavioral problems are possible, although these characteristics vary among affected individuals.

How Common Is Turner Syndrome?

This condition occurs in about 1 in 2,500 newborn girls worldwide, but it is much more common among pregnancies that do not survive to term (miscarriages and stillbirths).

What Are the Genetic Changes Related to Turner Syndrome?

Turner syndrome is related to the X chromosome, which is one of the two sex chromosomes. People typically have two sex chromosomes in each cell: females have two X chromosomes, while males have one X chromosome and one Y chromosome. Turner syndrome results when one normal X chromosome is present in a female's cells and the other sex chromosome is missing or structurally altered. The missing genetic material affects development before and after birth.

About half of individuals with Turner syndrome have monosomy X, which means each cell in the individual's body has only one copy of the X chromosome instead of the usual two sex chromosomes. Turner syndrome can also occur if one of the sex chromosomes is partially missing or rearranged rather than completely absent. Some women with Turner syndrome have a chromosomal change in only some of their cells, which is known as mosaicism. Women with Turner syndrome caused by X chromosome mosaicism are said to have mosaic Turner syndrome.

Researchers have not determined which genes on the X chromosome are associated with most of the features of Turner syndrome. They have, however, identified one gene called SHOX that is important for bone development and growth. The loss of one copy of this gene likely causes short stature and skeletal abnormalities in women with Turner syndrome.

Can Turner Syndrome Be Inherited?

Most cases of Turner syndrome are not inherited. When this condition results from monosomy X, the chromosomal abnormality occurs as a random event during the formation of reproductive cells (eggs and sperm) in the affected person's parent. An error in cell division called nondisjunction can result in reproductive cells with an abnormal number of chromosomes. For example, an egg or sperm cell may lose a sex chromosome as a result of nondisjunction. If one of these atypical reproductive cells contributes to the genetic makeup of a child, the child will have a single X chromosome in each cell and will be missing the other sex chromosome.

Mosaic Turner syndrome is also not inherited. In an affected individual, it occurs as a random event during cell division in early fetal development. As a result, some of an affected person's cells have the usual two sex chromosomes, and other cells have only one copy of the X chromosome. Other sex chromosome abnormalities are also possible in females with X chromosome mosaicism.

Rarely, Turner syndrome caused by a partial deletion of the X chromosome can be passed from one generation to the next.

What Are the Signs and Symptoms of Turner Syndrome?

There are various signs and symptoms of Turner syndrome, which can range from very mild to more severe. Short stature is the most common feature and usually becomes apparent by age 5. In early childhood, frequent middle ear infections are common and can lead to hearing loss in some cases. Most affected girls do not produce the necessary sex hormones for puberty, so they don't have a pubertal growth spurt, start their periods or develop breasts without hormone treatment. While most affected women are infertile, pregnancy is possible with egg donation and assisted reproductive technology. Intelligence is usually normal, but developmental delay, learning disabilities, and/ or behavioral problems are sometimes present.

Additional symptoms of Turner syndrome may include:

- a wide, webbed neck
- a low or indistinct hairline in the back of the head
- swelling (lymphedema) of the hands and feet
- broad chest and widely spaced nipples
- arms that turn out slightly at the elbow
- congenital heart defects or heart murmur
- scoliosis (curving of the spine) or other skeletal abnormalities
- kidney problems

- an underactive thyroid gland

- a slightly increased risk to develop diabetes, especially if older or overweight

- osteoporosis due to a lack of estrogen, (usually prevented by hormone replacement therapy).

What Causes Turner Syndrome?

Turner syndrome is caused by partial or complete loss of one of the X chromosomes in cells of females. Females without Turner syndrome have 2 full X chromosome in all of their cells (and males have one X chromosome and one Y chromosome). The missing genetic material affects development before and after birth.

Most females with Turner syndrome are missing a full X chromosome in all of their cells (also called monosomy X). This form results from a random error in an egg or sperm cell prior to conception.

Some females with Turner syndrome have two X chromosomes, but one of them is missing a piece (has a deletion). Depending on the specific gene(s) that are missing, the features of Turner syndrome may result. A deletion may occur sporadically (not inherited) or may be inherited from a parent.

Mosaic Turner syndrome (when some cells have one X chromosome and some have two sex chromosomes) is caused by a random error in early fetal development (shortly after conception).

It is still unclear exactly which genes on the X chromosome are associated with each feature of Turner syndrome. It is known that the *SHOX* gene on the X chromosome is important for growth and bone development. A missing copy of this gene is thought to result in the short stature and skeletal abnormalities in many affected women.

What Is the Long-Term Outlook for People with Turner Syndrome?

The long-term outlook (prognosis) for people with Turner syndrome is typically good. Life expectancy is slightly shorter than average but may be improved by addressing and treating associated chronic illnesses, such as obesity and hypertension. Regular checkups have shown substantial improvements in the quality and length of life for women with Turner syndrome. While almost all women are infertile, pregnancy with donor eggs and assisted reproductive technology is possible. Even with growth hormone therapy, most affected people are shorter than average.

Chapter 48

22q11.2 Deletion Syndrome

What Is 22q11.2 Deletion Syndrome?

22q11.2 deletion syndrome is a disorder caused by the deletion of a small piece of chromosome 22. The deletion occurs near the middle of the chromosome at a location designated q11.2.

22q11.2 deletion syndrome has many possible signs and symptoms that can affect almost any part of the body. The features of this syndrome vary widely, even among affected members of the same family. Common signs and symptoms include heart abnormalities that are often present from birth, an opening in the roof of the mouth (a cleft palate), and distinctive facial features. People with 22q11.2 deletion syndrome often experience recurrent infections caused by problems with the immune system, and some develop autoimmune disorders such as rheumatoid arthritis and Graves disease in which the immune system attacks the body's own tissues and organs. Affected individuals may also have breathing problems, kidney abnormalities, low levels of calcium in the blood (which can result in seizures), a decrease in blood platelets (thrombocytopenia), significant feeding difficulties, gastrointestinal problems, and hearing loss. Skeletal differences are

This chapter contains text excerpted from the following sources: Text beginning with the heading "What Is 22q11.2 Deletion Syndrome?" is excerpted from "22q11.2 Deletion Syndrome," Genetics Home Reference (GHR), National Institutes of Health (NIH), March 21, 2016; Text under the heading "What Are the Signs and Symptoms of 22q11.2 Deletion Syndrome?" is excerpted from "22q11.2 Deletion Syndrome," National Center for Advancing Translational Sciences (NCATS), July 20 2015.

possible, including mild short stature and, less frequently, abnormalities of the spinal bones.

Many children with 22q11.2 deletion syndrome have developmental delays, including delayed growth and speech development, and learning disabilities. Later in life, they are at an increased risk of developing mental illnesses such as schizophrenia, depression, anxiety, and bipolar disorder. Additionally, affected children are more likely than children without 22q11.2 deletion syndrome to have attention deficit hyperactivity disorder (ADHD) and developmental conditions such as autism spectrum disorders that affect communication and social interaction.

Because the signs and symptoms of 22q11.2 deletion syndrome are so varied, different groupings of features were once described as separate conditions. Doctors named these conditions DiGeorge syndrome, velocardiofacial syndrome (also called Shprintzen syndrome), and conotruncal anomaly face syndrome. In addition, some children with the 22q11.2 deletion were diagnosed with the autosomal dominant form of Opitz G/BBB syndrome and Cayler cardiofacial syndrome. Once the genetic basis for these disorders was identified, doctors determined that they were all part of a single syndrome with many possible signs and symptoms. To avoid confusion, this condition is usually called 22q11.2 deletion syndrome, a description based on its underlying genetic cause.

How Common Is 22q11.2 Deletion Syndrome?

22q11.2 deletion syndrome affects an estimated 1 in 4,000 people. However, the condition may actually be more common than this estimate because doctors and researchers suspect it is underdiagnosed due to its variable features. The condition may not be identified in people with mild signs and symptoms, or it may be mistaken for other disorders with overlapping features.

What Are the Genetic Changes Related to 22q11.2 Deletion Syndrome?

Most people with 22q11.2 deletion syndrome are missing a sequence of about 3 million DNA building blocks (base pairs) on one copy of chromosome 22 in each cell. This region contains 30 to 40 genes, many of which have not been well characterized. A small percentage of affected individuals have shorter deletions in the same region. This condition is described as a contiguous gene deletion syndrome because it results from the loss of many genes that are close together.

Researchers are working to identify all of the genes that contribute to the features of 22q11.2 deletion syndrome. They have determined that the loss of a particular gene on chromosome 22, *TBX1*, is probably responsible for many of the syndrome's characteristic signs (such as heart defects, a cleft palate, distinctive facial features, hearing loss, and low calcium levels). Some studies suggest that a deletion of this gene may contribute to behavioral problems as well. The loss of another gene, *COMT*, in the same region of chromosome 22 may also help explain the increased risk of behavioral problems and mental illness. The loss of additional genes in the deleted region likely contributes to the varied features of 22q11.2 deletion syndrome.

Can 22q11.2 Deletion Syndrome Be Inherited?

The inheritance of 22q11.2 deletion syndrome is considered autosomal dominant because a deletion in one copy of chromosome 22 in each cell is sufficient to cause the condition. Most cases of 22q11.2 deletion syndrome are not inherited, however. The deletion occurs most often as a random event during the formation of reproductive cells (eggs or sperm) or in early fetal development. Affected people typically have no history of the disorder in their family, though they can pass the condition to their children. In about 10 percent of cases, a person with this condition inherits the deletion in chromosome 22 from a parent. In inherited cases, other family members may be affected as well.

What Are the Signs and Symptoms of 22q11.2 Deletion Syndrome?

Signs and symptoms of 22q11.2 deletion syndrome vary greatly from person to person, even among affected people in the same family. Symptoms may include:

- Heart defects (74% of individuals)

- Palatal abnormalities (69% of individuals)

- Characteristic facial features (e.g., elongated face, almond-shaped eyes, wide nose, and small ears)

- Learning difficulties (70-90% of individuals)

- Immune system problems (75% of individuals)

- Low levels of calcium (50% of individuals)

- Significant feeding problems (30% of individuals)

- Kidney anomalies (37% of individuals)

- Hearing loss

- Laryngotracheoesophageal anomalies

- Growth hormone deficiency

- Autoimmune disorders (e.g., thrombocytopenia, juvenile rheumatoid arthritis, overactive thyroid, vitiligo, neutropenia, and hemolytic anemia)

- Seizures

- Skeletal abnormalities (e.g., extra fingers, toes, or ribs, wedge-shaped spinal bones, craniosynostosis)

- Psychiatric illness

- Eye abnormalities (e.g., ptosis, coloboma, cataract, and strabismus)

- Central nervous system abnormalities

- Gastrointestinal anomalies

- Preauricular tags

- Abnormal growths (e.g., hepatoblastoma, renal cell carcinoma, Wilm's tumor, and neuroblastoma)

What Causes 22q11.2 Deletion Syndrome?

22q11.2 deletion syndrome is caused by a missing piece (deletion) of part of chromosome 22 in each cell. The deletion occurs near the middle of the chromosome at a location designated q11.2.

Most people with 22q11.2 deletion syndrome are missing a piece of the chromosome that contains about 30 to 40 genes, many of which have not been well characterized. Some affected people have smaller deletions. Researchers are working to learn more about all of the genes that contribute to the features of 22q11.2 deletion syndrome. The deletion of a particular gene, *TBX1*, is probably responsible for many of the syndrome's characteristic signs (such as heart defects, a cleft palate, distinctive facial features, hearing loss, and low calcium levels). Loss of this gene may also contribute to behavioral problems. The loss of another gene, *COMT*, may also cause increased risk of behavioral problems and mental illness in affected people. The other genes that are deleted likely contribute to the various features of 22q11.2 deletion syndrome.

What Is the Long-Term Outlook for People with 22q11.2 Deletion Syndrome?

There is a wide range of symptoms and severity among people with 22q11.2 deletion syndrome. The long-term outlook (prognosis) for each person therefore depends on the specific signs and symptoms each affected person has.

The exact mortality rate for 22q11.2 deletion syndrome is not known, but the rate of death in childhood is rare and is largely due to heart disease. Congenital heart defects occur in 74% of affected people and account for over 90% of deaths. One study estimated the childhood mortality rate to be 4%. This rate is lower than the rate seen in older studies, and may reflect better cardiac care in recent years. The rare people with complete thymic aplasia and absent T cells have a high mortality rate, but this occurs in less than 1% of affected people.

Data on adults has been hard to collect. The adult mortality rate is higher than the rest of the adult population, but the exact rate is not known. The causes of premature death in adults are likely multifactorial and include both cardiac and noncardiac factors. There does not appear to be a single cause of death in adults with 22q11.2 deletion syndrome.

Chapter 49

Williams Syndrome

What Is Williams Syndrome (WS)?

Williams syndrome is a developmental disorder that affects many parts of the body. This condition is characterized by mild to moderate intellectual disability or learning problems, unique personality characteristics, distinctive facial features, and heart and blood vessel (cardiovascular) problems.

People with Williams syndrome typically have difficulty with visual-spatial tasks such as drawing and assembling puzzles, but they tend to do well on tasks that involve spoken language, music, and learning by repetition (rote memorization). Affected individuals have outgoing, engaging personalities and tend to take an extreme interest in other people. Attention deficit disorder (ADD), problems with anxiety, and phobias are common among people with this disorder.

Young children with Williams syndrome have distinctive facial features including a broad forehead, a short nose with a broad tip, full cheeks, and a wide mouth with full lips. Many affected people have dental problems such as teeth that are small, widely spaced, crooked, or missing. In older children and adults, the face appears longer and more gaunt.

This chapter contains text excerpted from the following sources: Text beginning with the heading "What Is Williams Syndrome?" is excerpted from "Williams Syndrome" Genetics Home Reference (GHR), National Institutes of Health (NIH), March 21, 2016; Text under the heading "Is There Any Treatment?" is excerpted from "NINDS Williams Syndrome Information Page," National Institute of Neurological Disorders and Stroke (NINDS), June 30, 2015.

A form of cardiovascular disease called supravalvular aortic stenosis (SVAS) occurs frequently in people with Williams syndrome. Supravalvular aortic stenosis is a narrowing of the large blood vessel that carries blood from the heart to the rest of the body (the aorta). If this condition is not treated, the aortic narrowing can lead to shortness of breath, chest pain, and heart failure. Other problems with the heart and blood vessels, including high blood pressure (hypertension), have also been reported in people with Williams syndrome.

Additional signs and symptoms of Williams syndrome include abnormalities of connective tissue (tissue that supports the body's joints and organs) such as joint problems and soft, loose skin. Affected people may also have increased calcium levels in the blood (hypercalcemia) in infancy, developmental delays, problems with coordination, and short stature. Medical problems involving the eyes and vision, the digestive tract, and the urinary system are also possible.

How Common Is Williams Syndrome?

Williams syndrome affects an estimated 1 in 7,500 to 10,000 people.

What Are the Genetic Changes Related to Williams Syndrome?

Williams syndrome is caused by the deletion of genetic material from a specific region of chromosome 7. The deleted region includes 26 to 28 genes, and researchers believe that a loss of several of these genes probably contributes to the characteristic features of this disorder.

CLIP2, ELN, GTF2I, GTF2IRD1, and *LIMK1* are among the genes that are typically deleted in people with Williams syndrome. Researchers have found that loss of the ELN gene is associated with the connective tissue abnormalities and cardiovascular disease (specifically supravalvular aortic stenosis) found in many people with this disease. Studies suggest that deletion of *CLIP2, GTF2I, GTF2IRD1, LIMK1,* and perhaps other genes may help explain the characteristic difficulties with visual-spatial tasks, unique behavioral characteristics, and other cognitive difficulties seen in people with Williams syndrome. Loss of the *GTF2IRD1* gene may also contribute to the distinctive facial features often associated with this condition.

Researchers believe that the presence or absence of the *NCF1* gene on chromosome 7 is related to the risk of developing hypertension in people with Williams syndrome. When the *NCF1* gene is included in the part of the chromosome that is deleted, affected individuals are less likely to develop hypertension. Therefore, the loss of this gene appears to be a protective factor. People with Williams syndrome whose *NCF1* gene is not deleted have a higher risk of developing hypertension.

The relationship between other genes in the deleted region of chromosome 7 and the signs and symptoms of Williams syndrome is under investigation or unknown.

Can Williams Syndrome Be Inherited?

Most cases of Williams syndrome are not inherited but occur as random events during the formation of reproductive cells (eggs or sperm) in a parent of an affected individual. These cases occur in people with no history of the disorder in their family.

Williams syndrome is considered an autosomal dominant condition because one copy of the altered chromosome 7 in each cell is sufficient to cause the disorder. In a small percentage of cases, people with Williams syndrome inherit the chromosomal deletion from a parent with the condition.

Is There Any Treatment?

There is no cure for Williams syndrome, nor is there a standard course of treatment. Because WS is an uncommon and complex disorder, multidisciplinary clinics have been established at several centers in the United States. Treatments are based on an individual's particular symptoms. People with WS require regular cardiovascular monitoring for potential medical problems, such as symptomatic narrowing of the blood vessels, high blood pressure, and heart failure.

What Is the Prognosis?

The prognosis for individuals with WS varies. Some degree of impaired intellect is found in most people with the disorder. Some adults are able to function independently, complete academic or vocational school, and live in supervised homes or on their own; most live with a caregiver. Parents can increase the likelihood that their child will be able to live semi-independently by teaching self-help skills early. Early intervention and individualized educational programs designed with the distinct cognitive and personality profiles of WS in mind also help individuals maximize their potential. Medical complications associated with the disorder may shorten the lifespans of some individuals with WS.

Part Four

Complex Disorders with Genetic and Environmental Components

Chapter 50

Addiction and Genetics

Chapter Contents

561

Section 50.1

Genetics of Alcohol Use Disorders

This section includes text excerpted from "Genetics of
Alcohol Use Disorder," National Institute on Alcohol Abuse and
Alcoholism (NIAAA), May 17, 2012. Reviewed April 2016.

How Do Genes Influence Alcoholism?

Alcoholism often seems to run in families, and we may hear about
scientific studies of an "alcoholism gene." Genetics certainly influence
our likelihood of developing alcoholism, but the story isn't so simple.

Research shows that genes are responsible for about half of the risk
for alcoholism. Therefore, genes alone do not determine whether someone will become an alcoholic. Environmental factors, as well as gene
and environment interactions account for the remainder of the risk.

Multiple genes play a role in a person's risk for developing alcoholism. There are genes that increase a person's risk, as well as those that
may decrease that risk, directly or indirectly. For instance, some people
of Asian descent carry a gene variant that alters their rate of alcohol
metabolism, causing them to have symptoms like flushing, nausea,
and rapid heartbeat when they drink. Many people who experience
these effects avoid alcohol, which helps protect them from developing
alcoholism.

As we have learned more about the role genes play in our health,
researchers have discovered that different factors can alter the expression of our genes. This field is called epigenetics. Scientists are learning
more and more about how epigenetics can affect our risk for developing
alcoholism.

Can Our Genes Affect Alcohol Treatment?

Scientists are also exploring how genes may influence the effectiveness of treatments for alcoholism. For instance, the drug naltrexone
has been shown to help some, but not all, alcohol-dependent patients
to reduce their drinking. Research has shown that alcoholic patients
with variations in a specific gene respond positively to treatment with

the drug, while those without the specific gene do not. A fuller understanding of how genes influence treatment outcomes will help doctors prescribe the treatment that is most likely to help each patient.

What Is NIAAA Doing to Learn More?

National Institute on Alcohol Abuse and Alcoholism (NIAAA) has funded the Collaborative Studies on Genetics of Alcoholism (COGA) since 1989, with the goal of identifying the specific genes that influence alcoholism. In addition, NIAAA funds investigators' research in this important field, and also has an in-house research emphasis on the interaction of genes and the environment. NIAAA is committed to learning more about how genes affect alcohol use and abuse so that treatment— and prevention efforts—can continue to be developed and improved.

Section 50.2

Odds of Quitting Smoking Are Affected by Genetics

This section includes text excerpted from "Odds of
Quitting Smoking Affected by Genetics," National Institutes
of Health (NIH), May 30, 2012. Reviewed May 2016.

Genetics can help determine whether a person is likely to quit smoking on his or her own or need medication to improve the chances of success, according to research published in today's American Journal of Psychiatry. Researchers say the study moves health care providers a step closer to one day providing more individualized treatment plans to help patients quit smoking.

The study was supported by multiple components of the National Institutes of Health, including the National Institute on Drug Abuse (NIDA), the National Human Genome Research Institute, the National Cancer Institute, and the Clinical and Translational Science Awards program, administered by the National Center for Advancing Translational Sciences.

"This study builds on our knowledge of genetic vulnerability to nicotine dependence, and will help us tailor smoking cessation strategies accordingly," said NIDA Director Nora D. Volkow, M.D. "It also highlights the potential value of genetic screening in helping to identify individuals early on and reduce their risk for tobacco addiction and its related negative health consequences."

Researchers focused on specific variations in a cluster of nicotinic receptor genes, CHRNA5-CHRNA3-CHRNB4, which prior studies have shown contribute to nicotine dependence and heavy smoking. Using data obtained from a previous study supported by the National Heart Lung and Blood Institute, researchers showed that individuals carrying the high-risk form of this gene cluster reported a 2-year delay in the median quit age compared to those with the low-risk genes. This delay was attributable to a pattern of heavier smoking among those with the high risk gene cluster. The researchers then conducted a clinical trial, which confirmed that persons with the high-risk genes were more likely to fail in their quit attempts compared to those with the low-risk genes when treated with placebo. However, medications approved for nicotine cessation (such as nicotine replacement therapies or bupropion) increased the likelihood of abstinence in the high risk groups. Those with the highest risk had a three-fold increase in their odds of being abstinent at the end of active treatment compared to placebo, indicating that these medications may be particularly beneficial for this population.

"We found that the effects of smoking cessation medications depend on a person's genes," said first author Li-Shiun Chen, M.D., of the Washington University School of Medicine, St. Louis. "If smokers have the risk genes, they don't quit easily on their own and will benefit greatly from the medications. If smokers don't have the risk genes, they are likely to quit successfully without the help of medications such as nicotine replacement or bupropion."

According to the Centers for Disease Control and Prevention (link is external), tobacco use is the single most preventable cause of disease, disability, and death in the United States. Smoking or exposure to secondhand smoke results in more than 440,000 preventable deaths each year — about 1 in 5 U.S. deaths overall. Another 8.6 million live with a serious illness caused by smoking. Despite these well-documented health costs, over 46 million U.S. adults continue to smoke cigarettes.

Chapter 51

Alzheimer Disease and Genetics

Chapter Contents

Section 51.1

Genes Related to Alzheimer Disease

This section includes text excerpted from "Alzheimer
Disease," Genetics Home Reference (GHR), National
Institutes of Health (NIH), March 21, 2016.

What Is Alzheimer Disease?

Alzheimer disease is a degenerative disease of the brain that causes dementia, which is a gradual loss of memory, judgment, and ability to function. This disorder usually appears in people older than age 65, but less common forms of the disease appear earlier in adulthood.

Memory loss is the most common sign of Alzheimer disease. Forgetfulness may be subtle at first, but the loss of memory worsens over time until it interferes with most aspects of daily living. Even in familiar settings, a person with Alzheimer disease may get lost or become confused. Routine tasks such as preparing meals, doing laundry, and performing other household chores can be challenging. Additionally, it may become difficult to recognize people and name objects. Affected people increasingly require help with dressing, eating, and personal care.

As the disorder progresses, some people with Alzheimer disease experience personality and behavioral changes and have trouble interacting in a socially appropriate manner. Other common symptoms include agitation, restlessness, withdrawal, and loss of language skills. People with this disease usually require total care during the advanced stages of the disease. Affected individuals usually survive 8 to 10 years after the appearance of symptoms, but the course of the disease can range from 1 to 25 years. Death usually results from pneumonia, malnutrition, or general body wasting (inanition).

Alzheimer disease can be classified as early-onset or late-onset. The signs and symptoms of the early-onset form appear before age 65, while the late-onset form appears after age 65. The early-onset form is much less common than the late-onset form, accounting for less than 5 percent of all cases of Alzheimer disease.

How Common Is Alzheimer Disease?

Alzheimer disease currently affects an estimated 2.4 million to 4.5 million Americans. Because the risk of developing Alzheimer disease increases with age and more people are living longer, the number of people with this disease is expected to increase significantly in coming decades.

What Genes Are Related to Alzheimer Disease?

Most cases of early-onset Alzheimer disease are caused by gene mutations that can be passed from parent to child. Researchers have found that this form of the disorder can result from mutations in one of three genes: *APP*, *PSEN1*, or *PSEN2*. When any of these genes is altered, large amounts of a toxic protein fragment called amyloid beta peptide are produced in the brain. This peptide can build up in the brain to form clumps called amyloid plaques, which are characteristic of Alzheimer disease. A buildup of toxic amyloid beta peptide and amyloid plaques may lead to the death of nerve cells and the progressive signs and symptoms of this disorder.

Some evidence indicates that people with Down syndrome have an increased risk of developing Alzheimer disease. Down syndrome, a condition characterized by intellectual disability and other health problems, occurs when a person is born with an extra copy of chromosome 21 in each cell. As a result, people with Down syndrome have three copies of many genes in each cell, including the *APP* gene, instead of the usual two copies. Although the connection between Down syndrome and Alzheimer disease is unclear, the production of excess amyloid beta peptide in cells may account for the increased risk. People with Down syndrome account for less than 1 percent of all cases of Alzheimer disease.

The causes of late-onset Alzheimer disease are less clear. The late-onset form does not clearly run in families, although clusters of cases have been reported in some families. This disorder is probably related to variations in one or more genes in combination with lifestyle and environmental factors. A gene called APOE has been studied extensively as a risk factor for the disease. In particular, a variant of this gene called the e4 allele seems to increase an individual's risk for developing late-onset Alzheimer disease. Researchers are investigating many additional genes that may play a role in Alzheimer disease risk.

How Do People Inherit Alzheimer Disease?

The early-onset form of Alzheimer disease is inherited in an autosomal dominant pattern, which means one copy of the altered gene in each cell is sufficient to cause the disorder. In most cases, an affected person inherits the altered gene from one affected parent.

The inheritance pattern of late-onset Alzheimer disease is uncertain. People who inherit one copy of the *APOE* e4 allele have an increased chance of developing the disease; those who inherit two copies of the allele are at even greater risk. It is important to note that people with the *APOE* e4 allele inherit an increased risk of developing Alzheimer disease, not the disease itself. Not all people with Alzheimer disease have the e4 allele, and not all people who have the e4 allele will develop the disease.

Section 51.2

Genetics of Alzheimer Risk

This section includes text excerpted from "Alzheimer Disease Genetics Fact Sheet," National Institute on Aging (NIA), National Institutes of Health (NIH), March 22, 2016.

Genetics of Alzheimer Disease

Some diseases are caused by a genetic mutation, or permanent change in one or more specific genes. If a person inherits from a parent a genetic mutation that causes a certain disease, then he or she will usually get the disease. Sickle cell anemia, cystic fibrosis, and early-onset familial Alzheimer disease are examples of inherited genetic disorders.

In other diseases, a genetic variant may occur. A single gene can have many variants. Sometimes, this difference in a gene can cause a disease directly. More often, a variant plays a role in increasing or decreasing a person's risk of developing a disease or condition. When a genetic variant increases disease risk but does not directly cause a disease, it is called a genetic risk factor.

Identifying genetic variants may help researchers find the most effective ways to treat or prevent diseases such as Alzheimer's in an individual. This approach, called precision medicine, takes into account individual variability in genes, environment, and lifestyle for each person.

Alzheimer Disease Genetics

Alzheimer disease is an irreversible, progressive brain disease. It is characterized by the development of amyloid plaques and neuro-fibrillary, or tau, tangles; the loss of connections between nerve cells (neurons) in the brain; and the death of these nerve cells. There are two types of Alzheimer—early-onset and late-onset. Both types have a genetic component.

Early-Onset Alzheimer Disease

Early-onset Alzheimer disease occurs in people age 30 to 60 and represents less than 5 percent of all people with Alzheimer. Most cases are caused by an inherited change in one of three genes, resulting in a typle known as early-onset familial Alzheimer disease, or FAD. For others, the disease appears to develop without any specific, known cause.

A child whose biological mother or father carries a genetic mutation for early-onset FAD has a 50/50 chance of inheriting that mutation. If the mutation is in fact inherited, the child has a very strong probability of developing early-onset FAD.

Early-onset FAD is caused by any one of a number of different single-gene mutations on chromosomes 21, 14, and

1. Each of these mutations causes abnormal proteins to be formed. Mutations on chromosome 21 cause the formation of abnormal amyloid precursor protein (APP). A mutation on chromosome 14 causes abnormal presenilin 1 to be made, and a mutation on chromosome 1 leads to abnormal presenilin.

2. Each of these mutations plays a role in the breakdown of APP, a protein whose precise function is not yet fully understood. This breakdown is part of a process that generates harmful forms of amyloid plaques, a hallmark of the disease.

Critical research findings about early-onset Alzheimer have helped identify key steps in the formation of brain abnormalities typical of the more common late-onset form of Alzheimer disease.

Genetics studies have helped explain why the disease develops in people at various ages.

NIA-supported scientists are continuing research into early-onset disease through the Dominantly Inherited Alzheimer Network (DIAN), an international partnership to study families with early-onset FAD. By observing the Alzheimer-related brain changes that occur in these families long before symptoms of memory loss or cognitive issues appear, scientists hope to gain insight into how and why the disease develops in both its early- and late-onset forms.

In addition, an NIA-supported clinical trial in Colombia, South America, is testing the effectiveness of an amyloid-clearing drug in symptom-free volunteers at high risk of developing early-onset FAD.

Late-Onset Alzheimer Disease

Most people with Alzheimer disease have the late-onset form of the disease, in which symptoms become apparent in the mid-60s and later. The causes of late-onset Alzheimer disease are not yet completely understood, but they likely include a combination of genetic, environmental, and lifestyle factors that affect a person's risk for developing the disease.

Researchers have not found a specific gene that directly causes the late-onset form of the disease. However, one genetic risk factor— having one form of the apolipoprotein E (*APOE*) gene on chromosome 19—does increase a person's risk. APOE comes in several different forms, or alleles:

- APOE ε2 is relatively rare and may provide some protection against the disease. If Alzheimer disease occurs in a person with this allele, it usually develops later in life than it would in someone with the *APOE ε4* gene.

- APOE ε3, the most common allele, is believed to play a neutral role in the disease—neither decreasing nor increasing risk.

- APOE ε4 increases risk for Alzheimer disease and is also associated with an earlier age of disease onset. A person has zero, one, or two APOE ε4 alleles. Having more APOE ε4 alleles increases the risk of developing Alzheimer disease.

APOE ε4 is called a risk-factor gene because it increases a person's risk of developing the disease. However, inheriting an APOE ε4 allele does not mean that a person will definitely develop Alzheimer. Some people with an APOE ε4 allele never get the disease, and others who develop Alzheimer do not have any APOE ε4 alleles.

Using a relatively new approach called genome-wide association study (GWAS), researchers have identified a number of regions of interest in the genome (an organism's complete set of DNA, including all of its genes) that may increase a person's risk for late-onset Alzheimer to varying degrees. By 2015, they had confirmed 33 regions of interest in the Alzheimer genome.

A method called whole genome sequencing determines the complete DNA sequence of a person's genome at a single time. Another method called whole exome sequencing looks at the parts of the genome that directly code for the proteins. Using these two approaches, researchers can identify new genes that contribute to or protect against disease risk. Recent discoveries have led to new insights about biological pathways involved in Alzheimer and may one day lead to effective interventions.

Genetic Testing

A blood test can identify which APOE alleles a person has, but results cannot predict who will or will not develop Alzheimer disease. It is unlikely that genetic testing will ever be able to predict the disease with 100 percent accuracy, researchers believe, because too many other factors may influence its development and progression.

Currently, APOE testing is used in research settings to identify study participants who may have an increased risk of developing Alzheimer. This knowledge helps scientists look for early brain changes in participants and compare the effectiveness of treatments for people with different APOE profiles. Most researchers believe that APOE testing is useful for studying Alzheimer disease risk in large groups of people but not for determining any one person's risk.

Genetic testing is used by researchers conducting clinical trials and by physicians to help diagnose early-onset Alzheimer disease. However, genetic testing is not otherwise recommended.

Section 51.3

Alzheimer Disease: Putting the Pieces Together with Integrative Genomics

This section includes text excerpted from "Alzheimer Disease: Putting the Pieces Together with Integrative Genomics," National Human Genome Research Institute (NHGRI), August 21, 2013.

Alzheimer disease—a neurological disorder causing progressive dementia, disorientation and behavioral changes—will affect more than 5 million Americans this year. While five percent of those with Alzheimer disease develop it between the ages of 30-65 as a result of any one of several rare, inherited, single-gene mutations, the large majority of affected individuals develop a non-familial form after the age of 65, called late-onset Alzheimer disease(LOAD).

In comparison to the early-onset form, the underlying cause of LOAD is much more complex; it is thought to be caused by a combination of several genetic and nongenetic risk factors. Genetic risk factors refer to common human genetic variations, or alleles, that increase a person's chance of developing a disease without directly causing it. While each risk factor is not sufficient to cause the disease on its own, multiple risk factors can combine their modest individual effects to develop LOAD.

Though advancing age is currently the strongest known risk factor for LOAD, the most influential genetic factor to be identified is one of three common alleles for the gene apolipoprotein E (*APOE*) that is referred to as *APOE4*. A person who inherits the *APOE4* allele from only one parent has a threefold increase in LOAD risk, whereas a person that inherits *APOE4* from both parents is ten times more likely to develop LOAD. Despite this strong association, it has remained unclear how *APOE4* contributes to the disease. July's Genome Advance of the Month describes a study, published in the August 1, 2013, issue of Nature, which combined several genomic methods to identify important regulatory processes that link the common genetic variation *APOE4* to the development of LOAD.

The team of researchers from Columbia University began their investigation by using publically available data that contained gene expression measurements from a specific region of autopsied brains called the cerebral cortex, which is responsible for controlling the intellectual functions (learning, memory, etc.) that are affected in Alzheimer disease. The gene expression measurements provided a record of the number of times each gene sequence is copied or 'transcribed' into messenger RNA (a code that contains instructions for making the protein) within the cerebral cortex, allowing the researchers to see whether the presence of *APOE4* causes brain cells to express higher or lower levels of certain genes.

To this end, they compared the expression level of all genes in the genome that had been transcribed into messenger RNA (transcriptome) in the cerebral cortex of *APOE4*-negative, healthy individuals to that of both *APOE4*-negative LOAD patients and *APOE4*-positive, healthy individuals. This comparison allowed the team to examine the effects of LOAD disease and the *APOE4* allele on gene expression independently of one another. Interestingly, many of the gene expression changes found in healthy *APOE4* carriers matched the gene expression changes seen in LOAD patients. This suggests that individuals that carry the *APOE4* allele have a specific set of gene expression changes in their brain that promotes LOAD (*APOE4*/LOAD expression profile), thereby increasing their risk of developing the disease.

To identify key regulatory genes that may be responsible for initiating this transcriptome-wide change in gene expression, the researchers performed a second analysis that focused on changes in co-expression, or simultaneous expression, of gene pairs. An instance of a change in co-expression would be if expression of both gene A and gene B were normally high in *APOE4*-negative tissue, but *APOE4*-positive tissue showed low expression of gene A and high expression of gene B. If gene A's co-expression with several other genes was also changed, this would suggest gene A is an important regulatory gene.

Using this approach, the researchers sought to determine which genes were most altered in their co-expression with the set of genes in the *APOE4*/LOAD expression profile. The two most highly ranked candidate genes were *RNF219*, which has been associated with changes in cognitive performance, and *SV2A*, which is a well-described regulator of protein transport in brain cells. Several subsequent experiments performed in human cells verified that these two genes also play critical regulatory roles in the processing and transport of amyloid precursor protein (APP) within brain cells that contain *APOE4*. This is extremely relevant as a small portion of APP is cut off to generate a smaller protein fragment called amyloid beta, which is known to accumulate and form clumps in the brain cells of Alzheimer patients as well as *APOE4* carriers. Taken together, these identified regulatory genes link the common genetic risk factor *APOE4* to the disease-causing brain changes seen in LOAD.

Although researchers are still missing a few pieces in this puzzle, the work presented here has significantly advanced understanding of the genetic mechanisms that increase LOAD risk. Not only did this study determine that the *APOE4* allele increases an individual's risk of LOAD through a specific set of gene expression changes, but it also identified two genes that play an important role in regulating *APOE4*-dependent amyloid beta production. Overall, these impressive results provide a major steppingstone for future Alzheimer research and demonstrate the power of an integrative genomics approach when it's applied to the study of complex, multifactorial diseases like LOAD.

Chapter 52

Allergic Asthma and Genetics

What Is Allergic Asthma?

Asthma is a breathing disorder characterized by inflammation of the airways and recurrent episodes of breathing difficulty. These episodes, sometimes referred to as asthma attacks, are triggered by irritation of the inflamed airways. In allergic asthma, the attacks occur when substances known as allergens are inhaled, causing an allergic reaction. Allergens are harmless substances that the body's immune system mistakenly reacts to as though they are harmful. Common allergens include pollen, dust, animal dander, and mold. The immune response leads to the symptoms of asthma. Allergic asthma is the most common form of the disorder.

A hallmark of asthma is bronchial hyperresponsiveness, which means the airways are especially sensitive to irritants and respond excessively. Because of this hyperresponsiveness, attacks can be triggered by irritants other than allergens, such as physical activity, respiratory infections, or exposure to tobacco smoke, in people with allergic asthma.

An asthma attack is characterized by tightening of the muscles around the airways (bronchoconstriction), which narrows the airway

This chapter includes text excerpted from "Allergic Asthma," Genetics Home Reference (GHR), National Institutes of Health (NIH), March 21, 2016.

and makes breathing difficult. Additionally, the immune reaction can lead to swelling of the airways and overproduction of mucus. During an attack, an affected individual can experience chest tightness, wheezing, shortness of breath, and coughing. Over time, the muscles around the airways can become enlarged (hypertrophied), further narrowing the airways.

Some people with allergic asthma have another allergic disorder, such as hay fever (allergic rhinitis) or food allergies. Asthma is sometimes part of a series of allergic disorders, referred to as the atopic march. Development of these conditions typically follows a pattern, beginning with eczema (atopic dermatitis), followed by food allergies, then hay fever, and finally asthma. However, not all individuals with asthma have progressed through the atopic march, and not all individuals with one allergic disease will develop others.

How Common Is Allergic Asthma?

Approximately 235 million people worldwide have asthma. In the United States, the condition affects an estimated 8 percent of the population. In nearly 90 percent of children and 50 percent of adults with asthma, the condition is classified as allergic asthma.

What Genes Are Related to Allergic Asthma?

The cause of allergic asthma is complex. It is likely that a combination of multiple genetic and environmental factors contribute to development of the condition. Doctors believe genes are involved because having a family member with allergic asthma or another allergic disorder increases a person's risk of developing asthma.

Studies suggest that more than 100 genes may be associated with allergic asthma, but each seems to be a factor in only one or a few populations. Many of the associated genes are involved in the body's immune response. Others play a role in lung and airway function.

There is evidence that an unbalanced immune response underlies allergic asthma. While there is normally a balance between type 1 (or Th1) and type 2 (or Th2) immune reactions in the body, many individuals with allergic asthma predominantly have type 2 reactions. Type 2 reactions lead to the production of immune proteins called IgE antibodies and the generation of other factors that predispose to bronchial hyperresponsiveness. Normally, the body produces IgE antibodies in response to foreign invaders, particularly parasitic worms. For unknown reasons, in susceptible individuals, the body reacts to an allergen as if it is harmful, producing IgE antibodies specific to it. Upon later encounters with the allergen, IgE antibodies recognize it, which stimulates an immune response, causing bronchoconstriction, airway swelling, and mucus production.

Not everyone with a variation in one of the allergic asthma-associated genes develops the condition; exposure to certain environmental factors also contributes to its development. Studies suggest that these exposures trigger epigenetic changes to the DNA. Epigenetic changes modify DNA without changing the DNA sequence. They can affect gene activity and regulate the production of proteins, which may influence the development of allergies in susceptible individuals.

How Do People Inherit Allergic Asthma?

Allergic asthma can be passed through generations in families, but the inheritance pattern is unknown. People with mutations in one or more of the associated genes inherit an increased risk of allergic asthma, not the condition itself. Because allergic asthma is a complex condition influenced by genetic and environmental factors, not all people with a mutation in an asthma-associated gene will develop the disorder.

Chapter 53

Cancer and Genetics

Chapter Contents

Section 53.1

Cancer and Genetics

This section includes text excerpted from "The Genetics
of Cancer," U.S. Department of Health and Human
Services (HHS), April 22, 2015.

Genetic Changes and Cancer

Cancer is a genetic disease—that is, cancer is caused by certain
changes to genes that control the way our cells function, especially
how they grow and divide. These changes include mutations in the
DNA that makes up our genes.

Genetic changes that increase cancer risk can be inherited from
our parents if the changes are present in germ cells, which are the
reproductive cells of the body (eggs and sperm). Such changes, called
germline changes, are found in every cell of the offspring.

Cancer-causing genetic changes can also be acquired during one's
lifetime, as the result of errors that occur as cells divide during a person's lifetime or exposure to substances, such as certain chemicals in
tobacco smoke, and radiation, such as ultraviolet rays from the sun,
that damage DNA.

Genetic changes that occur after conception are called somatic (or
acquired) changes. They can arise at any time during a person's life.
The number of cells in the body that carry such changes depends on
when the changes occur during a person's lifetime.

In general, cancer cells have more genetic changes than normal
cells. But each person's cancer has a unique combination of genetic
alterations. Some of these changes may be the result of cancer, rather
than the cause. As the cancer continues to grow, additional changes
will occur. Even within the same tumor, cancer cells may have different genetic changes.

Hereditary Cancer Syndromes

Inherited genetic mutations play a major role in about 5 to 10 percent of all cancers. Researchers have associated mutations in specific

genes with more than 50 hereditary cancer syndromes, which are disorders that may predispose individuals to developing certain cancers.

Genetic tests can tell whether a person from a family that shows signs of such a syndrome has one of these mutations. These tests can also show whether family members without obvious disease have inherited the same mutation as a family member who carries a cancer-associated mutation.

Many experts recommend that genetic testing for cancer risk be considered when someone has a personal or family history that suggests an inherited cancer risk condition, as long as the test results can be adequately interpreted (that is, they can clearly tell whether a specific genetic change is present or absent) and when the results provide information that will help guide a person's future medical care.

Cancers that are not caused by inherited genetic mutations can sometimes appear to "run in families." For example, a shared environment or lifestyle, such as tobacco use, can cause similar cancers to develop among family members. However, certain patterns in a family—such as the types of cancer that develop, other non-cancer conditions that are seen, and the ages at which cancer develops—may suggest the presence of a hereditary cancer syndrome.

Even if a cancer-predisposing mutation is present in a family, not everyone who inherits the mutation will necessarily develop cancer. Several factors influence the outcome in a given person with the mutation, including the pattern of inheritance of the cancer syndrome.

Here are examples of genes that can play a role in hereditary cancer syndromes.

- The most commonly mutated gene in all cancers is TP53, which produces a protein that suppresses the growth of tumors. In addition, germline mutations in this gene can cause Li-Fraumeni syndrome, a rare, inherited disorder that leads to a higher risk of developing certain cancers.

- Inherited mutations in the BRCA1 and BRCA2 genes are associated with hereditary breast and ovarian cancer syndrome, which is a disorder marked by an increased lifetime risk of breast and ovarian cancers in women. Several other cancers have been associated with this syndrome, including pancreatic and prostate cancers, as well as male breast cancer.

- Another gene that produces a tumor suppressor protein is PTEN. Mutations in this gene are associated with Cowden syndrome, an inherited disorder that increases the risk of breast, thyroid, endometrial, and other types of cancer

Genetic Test Results

Genetic tests are usually requested by a person's doctor or other health care provider. Genetic counseling can help people consider the risks, benefits, and limitations of genetic testing in their particular situations.

The results of genetic tests can be positive, negative, or uncertain. A genetic counselor, doctor, or other health care professional trained in genetics can help an individual or family understand their test results. These professionals can also help explain the incidental findings that a test may yield, such as a genetic risk factor for a disease that is unrelated to the reason for administering the test. And they can clarify the implications of test results for other family members.

Medical test results are normally included in a person's medical records, particularly if a doctor or other health care provider has ordered the test or has been consulted about the test results. Therefore, people considering genetic testing should understand that their results may become known to other people or organizations that have legitimate, legal access to their medical records, such as their insurance company or employer, if their employer provides the patient's health insurance as a benefit.

However, legal protections are in place to prevent genetic discrimination. The Genetic Information Nondiscrimination Act of 2008 is a federal law that prohibits discrimination based on genetic information in determining health insurance eligibility or rates and suitability for employment. In addition, because a person's genetic information is considered health information, it is covered by the Privacy Rule of the Health Information Portability and Accountability Act of 1996.

Clinical DNA Sequencing

Until recently, most genetic testing for cancer focused on testing for individual inherited mutations. But, as more efficient and cheaper DNA sequencing technologies have become available, sequencing of an individual's entire genome or the DNA of an individual's tumor is becoming more common.

Clinical DNA sequencing can be useful in detecting many genetic mutations at one time. Targeted multiple-gene panels test for many inherited mutations or somatic mutations at the same time. These panels can include different genes and be tailored to individual tumor types. Targeted gene panels limit the data to be analyzed and include only known genes, which makes the interpretation more straightforward than in broader approaches that assess the whole genome (or tumor genome) or significant parts of it. Multiple-gene panel tests are becoming increasingly common in genetic testing for hereditary cancer syndromes.

Tumor sequencing can identify somatic mutations that may be driving the growth of particular cancers. It can also help doctors sort out which therapies may work best against a particular tumor. For instance, patients whose lung tumors harbor certain mutations may benefit from drugs that target these particular changes.

Testing tumor DNA may reveal a mutation that has not previously been found in that tumor type. But if that mutation occurs in another tumor type and a targeted therapy has been developed for the alteration, the treatment may be effective in the "new" tumor type as well.

Tumor sequencing can also identify germline mutations. Indeed, in some cases, the genetic testing of tumors has shown that a patient's cancer could be associated with a hereditary cancer syndrome that the family was not aware of.

As with testing for specific mutations in hereditary cancer syndromes, clinical DNA sequencing has implications that patients need to consider. For example, they may learn incidentally about the presence of germline mutations that may cause other diseases, in them or in their family members.

Section 53.2

Breast Cancer and Heredity

This section includes text excerpted from "Breast Cancer,"
Genetics Home Reference (GHR), National Institutes
of Health (NIH), March 21, 2016.

What Is Breast Cancer?

Breast cancer is a disease in which certain cells in the breast become abnormal and multiply uncontrollably to form a tumor. Although breast cancer is much more common in women, this form of cancer can also develop in men. In both women and men, the most common form of breast cancer begins in cells lining the milk ducts (ductal cancer). In women, cancer can also develop in the glands that produce milk (lobular cancer). Most men have little or no lobular tissue, so lobular cancer in men is very rare.

In its early stages, breast cancer usually does not cause pain and may exhibit no noticeable symptoms. As the cancer progresses, signs and symptoms can include a lump or thickening in or near the breast; a change in the size or shape of the breast; nipple discharge, tenderness, or retraction (turning inward); and skin irritation, dimpling, or scaliness. However, these changes can occur as part of many different conditions. Having one or more of these symptoms does not mean that a person definitely has breast cancer.

In some cases, cancerous tumors can invade surrounding tissue and spread to other parts of the body. If breast cancer spreads, cancerous cells most often appear in the bones, liver, lungs, or brain. Tumors that begin at one site and then spread to other areas of the body are called metastatic cancers.

A small percentage of all breast cancers cluster in families. These cancers are described as hereditary and are associated with inherited gene mutations. Hereditary breast cancers tend to develop earlier in life than noninherited (sporadic) cases, and new (primary) tumors are more likely to develop in both breasts.

How Common Is Breast Cancer?

Breast cancer is the second most commonly diagnosed cancer in women. (Only skin cancer is more common.) About one in eight women in the United States will develop invasive breast cancer in her lifetime. Researchers estimate that more than 230,000 new cases of invasive breast cancer will be diagnosed in U.S. women in 2015.

Male breast cancer represents less than 1 percent of all breast cancer diagnoses. Scientists estimate that about 2,300 new cases of breast cancer will be diagnosed in men in 2015.

Particular gene mutations associated with breast cancer are more common among certain geographic or ethnic groups, such as people of Ashkenazi (central or eastern European) Jewish heritage and people of Norwegian, Icelandic, or Dutch ancestry.

What Genes Are Related to Breast Cancer?

Cancers occur when a buildup of mutations in critical genes—those that control cell growth and division or repair damaged DNA—allow cells to grow and divide uncontrollably to form a tumor. In most cases of breast cancer, these genetic changes are acquired during a person's lifetime and are present only in certain cells in the breast. These changes, which are called somatic mutations, are not inherited. Somatic mutations in many different genes have been found in breast cancer cells. Less commonly, gene mutations present in essentially all of the body's cells increase the risk of developing breast cancer. These genetic changes, which are classified as germline mutations, are usually inherited from a parent. In people with germline mutations, changes in other genes, together with environmental and lifestyle factors, also influence whether a person will develop breast cancer.

Some breast cancers that cluster in families are associated with inherited mutations in particular genes, such as *BRCA1* or *BRCA2*. These genes are described as "high penetrance" because they are associated with a high risk of developing breast cancer, ovarian cancer, and several other types of cancer in women who have mutations. Men with mutations in these genes also have an increased risk of developing several forms of cancer, including breast cancer. The proteins produced from the *BRCA1* and *BRCA2* genes are involved in fixing damaged DNA, which helps to maintain the stability of a cell's genetic information. They are described as tumor suppressors because they

585

help keep cells from growing and dividing too fast or in an uncontrolled way. Mutations in these genes impair DNA repair, allowing potentially damaging mutations to persist in DNA. As these defects accumulate, they can trigger cells to grow and divide without control or order to form a tumor.

A significantly increased risk of breast cancer is also a feature of several rare genetic syndromes. These include Cowden syndrome, which is most often caused by mutations in the *PTEN* gene; hereditary diffuse gastric cancer, which results from mutations in the *CDH1* gene; Li-Fraumeni syndrome, which is usually caused by mutations in the *TP53* gene; and Peutz-Jeghers syndrome, which typically results from mutations in the *STK11* gene. The proteins produced from these genes act as tumor suppressors. Mutations in any of these genes can allow cells to grow and divide unchecked, leading to the development of a cancerous tumor. Like *BRCA1* and *BRCA2*, these genes are considered "high penetrance" because mutations greatly increase a person's chance of developing cancer. In addition to breast cancer, mutations in these genes increase the risk of several other types of cancer over a person's lifetime. Some of the conditions also include other signs and symptoms, such as the growth of noncancerous (benign) tumors.

Mutations in dozens of other genes have been studied as possible risk factors for breast cancer. These genes are described as "low penetrance" or "moderate penetrance" because changes in each of these genes appear to make only a small or moderate contribution to overall breast cancer risk. Some of these genes provide instructions for making proteins that interact with the proteins produced from the *BRCA1* or *BRCA2* genes. Others act through different pathways. Researchers suspect that the combined influence of variations in these genes may significantly impact a person's risk of developing breast cancer.

In many families, the genetic changes associated with hereditary breast cancer are unknown. Identifying additional genetic risk factors for breast cancer is an active area of medical research.

In addition to genetic changes, researchers have identified many personal and environmental factors that contribute to a person's risk of developing breast cancer. These factors include gender, age, ethnic background, a history of previous breast cancer, certain changes in breast tissue, and hormonal and reproductive factors. A history of breast cancer in closely related family members is also an important risk factor, particularly if the cancer occurred in early adulthood.

How Do People Inherit Breast Cancer?

Most cases of breast cancer are not caused by inherited genetic factors. These cancers are associated with somatic mutations in breast cells that are acquired during a person's lifetime, and they do not cluster in families.

In hereditary breast cancer, the way that cancer risk is inherited depends on the gene involved. For example, mutations in the *BRCA1* and *BRCA2* genes are inherited in an autosomal dominant pattern, which means one copy of the altered gene in each cell is sufficient to increase a person's chance of developing cancer. Although breast cancer is more common in women than in men, the mutated gene can be inherited from either the mother or the father.

In the other syndromes discussed above, the gene mutations that increase cancer risk also have an autosomal dominant pattern of inheritance. It is important to note that people inherit an increased likelihood of developing cancer, not the disease itself. Not all people who inherit mutations in these genes will ultimately develop cancer.

In many cases of breast cancer that clusters in families, the genetic basis for the disease and the mechanism of inheritance are unclear.

Section 53.3

Colon Cancer and Heredity

This section contains text excerpted from the following sources:
Text under the heading "Why Is It Important to Know Your Family
Health History?" is excerpted from "Have You or a Family Member
Had Colorectal (Colon) Cancer?" Centers for Disease Control
and Prevention, March 23, 2016; Text under the heading "What
Do We Know about Heredity and Colon Cancer?" is excerpted
from "Learning about Colon Cancer," National Human Genome
Research Institute, March 22, 2012. Reviewed May 2016.

Having a family health history of colorectal (colon) cancer can make you more likely to get colorectal cancer yourself. If you have close family members with colorectal cancer, collect your family health history of colorectal and other cancers, and share this information with your doctor.

If you have had colorectal cancer, make sure that your family members know about your diagnosis, especially if you have Lynch syndrome.

Why Is It Important to Know Your Family Health History?

If you have a family health history of colorectal cancer, your doctor may consider your family health history when deciding which colorectal cancer screening might be right for you. For example, if you have a close family member who had colorectal cancer at a young age or have multiple close family members with colorectal cancer, your doctor may recommend screening starting at a younger age, being done more frequently, and using colonoscopy only instead of other tests. In some cases, your doctor may recommend that you have genetic counseling, and a genetic counselor may recommend genetic testing based on your family health history.

When collecting your family health history, be sure to include your close relatives: parents, brothers, sisters, children, grandparents, aunts, uncles, nieces, and nephews. List any cancers that each relative had and at what age he or she was diagnosed. For relatives who have died, list age and cause of death.

In some cases, colorectal cancer is caused by an inherited genetic condition called Lynch syndrome, also known as hereditary nonpolyposis colorectal cancer or HNPCC. About 3% (1 in 30) of colorectal cancer cases are due to Lynch syndrome. People with Lynch syndrome are much more likely to develop colorectal cancer, especially at a younger age (before 50), and women with Lynch syndrome are much more likely to get endometrial (uterine) cancer. People with Lynch syndrome also have an increased chance of getting other cancers, including ovarian, stomach, liver, kidney, brain, and skin cancer. If you or your family members are found to have Lynch syndrome, your doctor can help you take steps to reduce your risk of getting cancer in the future or to find it early if you get it.

What Is Lynch Syndrome and Why Is It Important to Know If You Have It?

Lynch syndrome is hereditary, meaning that it is caused by an inherited genetic changes, or mutations, that can be passed from parents to children. If you are diagnosed with Lynch syndrome, your parents, children, sisters, and brothers have a 50% (1 in 2) chance of having this condition. Your other close relatives are also at increased risk of having Lynch syndrome.

After surgery to remove colorectal cancer, tumor tissue samples are often screened to see if the tumor could have been caused by Lynch syndrome. In some cases, additional testing is needed to know for sure if the tumor was caused by Lynch syndrome. If you have had colorectal cancer in the last few years, your tumor may have been checked for Lynch syndrome. Genetic counseling and testing for Lynch syndrome also might be recommended for you if:

- You were diagnosed with colorectal cancer in the past
- You have been diagnosed with endometrial cancer (especially before age 50)
- You have several family members with colorectal or other cancers associated with Lynch syndrome
- You have a family member with Lynch syndrome

If you have been diagnosed with Lynch syndrome, talk to your doctor about your increased chances of getting the other cancers caused by Lynch syndrome. Be sure to let your family members know if you have Lynch syndrome. Once a mutation that causes Lynch syndrome is found in one person in a family, other family members can then be tested for that mutation to find out if they have Lynch syndrome.

What Do We Know about Heredity and Colon Cancer?

Colon cancer, a malignant tumor of the large intestine, affects both men and women. In the United States, approximately 160,000 new cases of colorectal cancer are diagnosed each year.

The majority of colon cancer cases are sporadic, which means a genetic mutation may happen in that individual person. However, approximately 5 percent of individuals with colon cancer have a hereditary form, which means that they have inherited a mutation from one of their parents that causes the disease. In those families, the chance of developing colon cancer is significantly higher than in the average person. These hereditary cancers typically occur at an earlier age than sporadic (non-inherited) cases of colon cancer. The risk of inheriting these mutated genes from an affected parent is 50 percent for both males and females.

Scientists have discovered several genes contributing to a susceptibility to two types of colon cancer:

1. **FAP (familial adenomatous polyposis)**

   So far, only one gene has been discovered that leads to FAP: the APC gene, located on human chromosome 5. However, over

300 different mutations have been identified in this APC gene. Individuals with this syndrome develop many polyps in their colon. People who inherit mutations in this gene have a nearly 100 percent chance of developing colon cancer by age 40.

2. **HNPCC (hereditary nonpolyposis colon cancer) also called Lynch Syndrome**

   Individuals with an HNPCC gene mutation have an estimated 80 percent lifetime risk of developing colon or rectal cancer. However, these cancers account for only three to five percent of all colorectal cancers. So far, five HNPCC genes have been discovered:

   - MSH2 on chromosome 2

   - MLH1 on chromosome 3

   - PMS2 on chromosome 7

   - MSH6 on chromosome 2

   - PMS1 on chromosome 2

Mutations in MSH2 and MLH1 are the most common mutations that cause HNPCC. A mutation in PMS1 was originally reported in a single family with HNPCC, however, this mutation was not found in all members of the family who had developed the disease. For this reason, the role of PMS1 in HNPCC is currently being questioned.

The genes that cause HNPCC and FAP were relatively easy to discover because they exert strong effects. Other genes that cause susceptibility to colon cancer are harder to discover because the cancers are caused by a number of genes, each of which individually exerts a weak effect.

Is There a Test for Hereditary Colon Cancer?

Gene testing can identify individuals who carry the more common gene mutations associated with FAP or HPNCC, such as those listed above. However, these tests may not identify all gene mutations that cause FAP or HNPCC. In some families, additional mutations may be present that cause the FAP or HNPCC, which cannot be detected by the commonly used gene tests.

The test for FAP syndrome involves examining DNA in blood cells called lymphocytes (white blood cells), looking for mutations in the APC gene. No treatment to reduce cancer risk is currently available for people with APC mutations that are associated with FAP. But for those who test positive, frequent surveillance can detect the cancer at an early, more treatable stage. Because of the early age at which this syndrome appears, the test may be offered to children under the age of 18 if they have a parent known to carry the mutated APC gene.

Researchers hope that an easier test, which is currently experimental, will become available for common use in three to five years. This new test looks for cancer cells with the APC mutation in a stool sample.

Genetic testing for HNPCC involves looking for mutations in four of the five genes identified that are associated with HNPCC – MLH1, MSH2, MSH6, and PMS2.

Individuals in families at high risk of genetic predisposition may consider testing. Genetic counselors can help individuals make decisions regarding testing.

Section 53.4

Gynecologic Cancers and Heredity

This section includes text excerpted from "Genetics of Breast and Gynecologic Cancers–Health Professional Version (PDQ®)," National Cancer Institute (NCI), March 4, 2016.

Ovarian cancer is the fifth most deadly cancer in women. An estimated 60,050 new cases of endometrial cancer are expected in 2016, with an estimated 10,470 deaths.

A possible genetic contribution to both breast and ovarian cancer risk is indicated by the increased incidence of these cancers among women with a family history, and by the observation of some families in which multiple family members are affected with breast and/or ovarian cancer, in a pattern compatible with an inheritance of autosomal dominant cancer susceptibility. Formal studies of families (linkage analysis) have subsequently proven the existence of autosomal dominant predispositions to breast and ovarian cancer and have led to the identification of several highly penetrant genes as the cause of inherited cancer risk in many families. Mutations in these genes are rare in the general population and are estimated to account for no more than 5% to 10% of breast and ovarian cancer cases overall. It is likely that other genetic factors contribute to the etiology of some of these cancers.

Risk Factors for Ovarian Cancer

Family History including Inherited Cancer Genes

Although reproductive, demographic, and lifestyle factors affect risk of ovarian cancer, the single greatest ovarian cancer risk factor is a family history of the disease. A large meta-analysis of 15 published studies estimated an odds ratio of 3.1 for the risk of ovarian cancer associated with at least one FDR with ovarian cancer.

Age

Ovarian cancer incidence rises in a linear fashion from age 30 years to age 50 years and continues to increase, though at a slower rate, thereafter. Before age 30 years, the risk of developing epithelial ovarian cancer is remote, even in hereditary cancer families.

Reproductive History

Nulliparity is consistently associated with an increased risk of ovarian cancer, including among *BRCA1/BRCA2* mutation carriers, yet a meta-analysis could only identify risk-reduction in women with four or more live births. Risk may also be increased among women who have used fertility drugs, especially those who remain nulligravid. Several studies have reported a risk reduction in ovarian cancer after OC pill use in *BRCA1/BRCA2* mutation carriers; a risk reduction has also been shown after tubal ligation in BRCA1 carriers, with a statistically significant decreased risk of 22% to 80% after the procedure. On the other hand, evidence is growing that the use of menopausal HRT is associated with an increased risk of ovarian cancer, particularly in long-time users and users of sequential estrogen-progesterone schedules.

Surgical History

Bilateral tubal ligation and hysterectomy are associated with reduced ovarian cancer risk, including in *BRCA1/BRCA2* mutation carriers. Ovarian cancer risk is reduced more than 90% in women with documented *BRCA1* or *BRCA2* mutations who chose risk-reducing salpingo-oophorectomy. In this same population, risk-reducing oophorectomy also resulted in a nearly 50% reduction in the risk of subsequent breast cancer.

Oral Contraceptives

Use of OCs for 4 or more years is associated with an approximately 50% reduction in ovarian cancer risk in the general population. A majority of, but not all, studies also support OCs being protective among *BRCA1/ BRCA2* mutation carriers. A meta-analysis of 18 studies including 13,627 *BRCA* mutation carriers reported a significantly reduced risk of ovarian cancer (SRR, 0.50; 95% CI, 0.33–0.75) associated with OC use.

Risk Factors for Endometrial Cancer

Family History including Inherited Cancer Genes

Although the hyperestrogenic state is the most common predisposing factor for endometrial cancer, family history also plays a significant role in a woman's risk for disease. Approximately 3% to 5% of uterine cancer cases are attributable to a hereditary cause, with the main hereditary endometrial cancer syndrome being Lynch syndrome (LS), an autosomal dominant genetic condition with a population prevalence of 1 in 300 to 1 in 1,000 individuals.

Age

Age is an important risk factor for endometrial cancer. Most women with endometrial cancer are diagnosed after menopause. Only 15% of women are diagnosed with endometrial cancer before age 50 years, and fewer than 5% are diagnosed before age 40 years. Women with LS tend to develop endometrial cancer at an earlier age, with the median age at diagnosis of 48 years.

Reproductive History

Reproductive factors such as multiparity, late menarche, and early menopause decrease the risk of endometrial cancer because of the lower cumulative exposure to estrogen and the higher relative exposure to progesterone.

Hormones

Hormonal factors that increase the risk of type I endometrial cancer are better understood. All endometrial cancers share a predominance of estrogen relative to progesterone. Prolonged exposure to estrogen or unopposed estrogen increases the risk of endometrial cancer. Endogenous exposure to estrogen can result from obesity, polycystic ovary syndrome (PCOS), and nulliparity, while exogenous estrogen can result from taking unopposed estrogen or tamoxifen. Unopposed estrogen increases the risk of developing endometrial cancer by two-fold to twentyfold, proportional to the duration of use. Tamoxifen, a selective estrogen receptor modulator, acts as an estrogen agonist on the endometrium while acting as an estrogen antagonist in breast tissue, and increases the risk of endometrial cancer. In contrast, oral contraceptives, the levonorgestrel-releasing intrauterine system, and combination estrogen-progesterone hormone replacement therapy all reduce the risk of endometrial cancer through the antiproliferative effect of progesterone acting on the endometrium.

Autosomal Dominant Inheritance of Breast and Gynecologic Cancer Predisposition

Autosomal dominant inheritance of breast and gynecologic cancers is characterized by transmission of cancer predisposition from generation to generation, through either the mother's or the father's side of the family, with the following characteristics:

- Inheritance risk of 50%. When a parent carries an autosomal dominant genetic predisposition, each child has a 50:50 chance of inheriting the predisposition. Although the risk of inheriting the predisposition is 50%, not everyone with the predisposition will develop cancer because of incomplete penetrance and/or gender-restricted or gender-related expression.

- Both males and females can inherit and transmit an autosomal dominant cancer predisposition. A male who inherits a cancer predisposition can still pass the altered gene on to his sons and daughters.

Breast and ovarian cancer are components of several autosomal dominant cancer syndromes. The syndromes most strongly associated with both cancers are the BRCA1 or BRCA2 mutation syndromes. Breast cancer is also a common feature of Li-Fraumeni syndrome due to TP53 mutations and of Cowden syndrome due to PTEN mutations. Other genetic syndromes that may include breast cancer as an associated feature include heterozygous carriers of the ataxia telangiectasia gene and Peutz-Jeghers syndrome. Ovarian cancer has also been associated with LS, basal cell nevus (Gorlin) syndrome (OMIM), and multiple endocrine neoplasia type 1 (OMIM). LS is mainly associated with colorectal cancer and endometrial cancer, although several studies have demonstrated that patients with LS are also at risk of developing transitional cell carcinoma of the ureters and renal pelvis; cancers of the stomach, small intestine, liver and biliary tract, brain, breast, prostate, and adrenal cortex; and sebaceous skin tumors (Muir-Torre syndrome).

Germline mutations in the genes responsible for these autosomal dominant cancer syndromes produce different clinical phenotypes of characteristic malignancies and, in some instances, associated nonmalignant abnormalities.

The family characteristics that suggest hereditary cancer predisposition include the following:

- Multiple cancers within a family.

- Cancers typically occur at an earlier age than in sporadic cases (defined as cases not associated with genetic risk).

- Two or more primary cancers in a single individual. These could be multiple primary cancers of the same type (e.g., bilateral breast cancer) or primary cancer of different types (e.g., breast cancer and ovarian cancer in the same individual or endometrial and colon cancer in the same individual).

- Cases of male breast cancer. The inheritance risk for autosomal dominant genetic conditions is 50% for both males and females, but the differing penetrance of the genes may result in some unaffected individuals in the family.

There are no pathognomonic features distinguishing breast and ovarian cancers occurring in BRCA1 or BRCA2 mutation carriers from those occurring in noncarriers. Breast cancers occurring in BRCA1 mutation carriers are more likely to be ER-negative, progesterone receptor–negative, HER2/neu receptor–negative (i.e., triple-negative breast cancers), and have a basal phenotype. BRCA1-associated ovarian cancers are more likely to be high-grade and of serous histopathology.

Some pathologic features distinguish LS mutation carriers from noncarriers. The hallmark feature of endometrial cancers occurring in LS is mismatch repair (MMR) defects, including the presence of microsatellite instability (MSI), and the absence of specific MMR proteins. In addition to these molecular changes, there are also histologic changes including tumor-infiltrating lymphocytes, peritumoral lymphocytes, undifferentiated tumor histology, lower uterine segment origin, and synchronous tumors.

Section 53.5

Lung Cancer and Heredity

This section includes text excerpted from "Lung cancer," Genetics Home Reference (GHR), National Institutes of Health (NIH), March 21, 2016.

What Is Lung Cancer?

Lung cancer is a disease in which certain cells in the lungs become abnormal and multiply uncontrollably to form a tumor. Lung cancer may or may not cause signs or symptoms in its early stages. Some people with lung cancer have chest pain, frequent coughing, breathing problems, trouble swallowing or speaking, blood in the mucus, loss of appetite and weight loss, fatigue, or swelling in the face or neck. Lung cancer occurs most often in adults in their sixties or seventies. Most people who develop lung cancer have a history of long-term tobacco smoking; however, the condition can occur in people who have never smoked.

Lung cancer is generally divided into two types, small cell lung cancer and non-small cell lung cancer, based on the size of the affected cells when viewed under a microscope. Non-small cell lung cancer accounts for 85 percent of lung cancer, while small cell lung cancer accounts for the remaining 15 percent.

Small cell lung cancer grows quickly and often spreads to other tissues (metastasizes), most commonly to the adrenal glands (small hormone-producing glands located on top of each kidney), liver, brain, and bones. In more than half of cases, the small cell lung cancer has spread beyond the lung at the time of diagnosis. After diagnosis, most people with small cell lung cancer survive for about one year; less than seven percent survive 5 years.

Non-small cell lung cancer is divided into three main subtypes: adenocarcinoma, squamous cell carcinoma, and large cell lung carcinoma. Adenocarcinoma arises from the cells that line the small air sacs (alveoli) located throughout the lungs. Squamous cell carcinoma arises from the squamous cells that line the passages leading from the windpipe to the lungs (bronchi). Large cell carcinoma describes non-small cell lung cancers that do not appear to be adenocarcinomas or squamous cell carcinomas. As the name suggests, the tumor cells are large when viewed under a microscope. The 5-year survival rate for people with non-small cell lung cancer is usually between 11 and 17 percent; it can be lower or higher depending on the subtype and stage of the cancer.

How Common Is Lung Cancer?

In the United States, it is estimated that more than 221,000 people develop lung cancer each year. An estimated 72 to 80 percent of lung cancer cases occur in tobacco smokers.

Approximately 6.6 percent of individuals will develop lung cancer during their lifetime. It is the leading cause of cancer deaths, accounting for an estimated 27 percent of all cancer deaths in the United States.

What Genes Are Related to Lung Cancer?

Cancers occur when genetic mutations build up in critical genes, specifically those that control cell growth and division or the repair of damaged DNA. These changes allow cells to grow and divide uncontrollably to form a tumor. In nearly all cases of lung cancer, these genetic changes are acquired during a person's lifetime and are present only in certain cells in the lung. These changes, which are called somatic mutations, are not inherited. Somatic mutations in many different genes have been found in lung cancer cells.

Mutations in the *EGFR* and *KRAS* genes are estimated to be present in up to half of all lung cancer cases. These genes each provide instructions for making a protein that is embedded within the cell membrane. When these proteins are turned on (activated) by binding to other molecules, signaling pathways are triggered within cells that promote cell growth and division (proliferation).

Mutations in either the *EGFR* or *KRAS* gene lead to the production of a protein that is constantly turned on (constitutively activated). As a result, cells are signaled to constantly proliferate, leading to tumor formation. When these gene changes occur in cells in the lungs, lung cancer develops.

Mutations in many other genes have each been found in a small proportion of cases.

In addition to genetic changes, researchers have identified many personal and environmental factors that expose individuals to cancer-causing compounds (carcinogens) and increase the rate at which somatic mutations occur, contributing to a person's risk of developing lung cancer. The greatest risk factor is long-term tobacco smoking, which increases a person's risk of developing lung cancer 20-fold. Other risk factors include exposure to air pollution, radon, asbestos, or secondhand smoke; long-term use of hormone replacement therapy for menopause; and a history of lung disease such as tuberculosis, emphysema, or chronic bronchitis. A history of lung cancer in closely related family members is also an important risk factor; however, because relatives with lung cancer were likely smokers, it is unclear whether the increased risk of lung cancer is the result of genetic factors or exposure to secondhand smoke.

How Do People Inherit Lung Cancer?

Most cases of lung cancer are not related to inherited gene changes. These cancers are associated with somatic mutations that occur only in certain cells in the lung.

When lung cancer is related to inherited gene changes, the cancer risk is inherited in an autosomal dominant pattern, which means one copy of the altered gene in each cell is sufficient to increase a person's chance of developing cancer. It is important to note that people inherit an increased risk of cancer, not the disease itself. Not all people who inherit mutations in these genes will develop lung cancer.

Section 53.6

Genetic Risk for Prostate Cancer

This section includes text excerpted from "Prostate Cancer," Genetics Home Reference (GHR), National Institutes of Health (NIH), April 2015.

Prostate cancer is a common disease that affects men, usually in middle age or later. In this disorder, certain cells in the prostate become abnormal and multiply without control or order to form a tumor. The prostate is a gland that surrounds the male urethra and helps produce semen, the fluid that carries sperm.

Early prostate cancer usually does not cause pain, and most affected men exhibit no noticeable symptoms. Men are often diagnosed as the result of health screenings, such as a blood test for a substance called prostate specific antigen (PSA) or a medical procedure called a digital rectal exam. As the tumor grows larger, signs and symptoms can include difficulty starting or stopping the flow of urine, a feeling of not being able to empty the bladder completely, blood in the urine or semen, or pain with ejaculation. However, these changes can also occur with many other genitourinary conditions. Having one or more of these symptoms does not necessarily mean that a man has prostate cancer.

The severity and outcome of prostate cancer varies widely. Early-stage prostate cancer can usually be treated successfully, and some older men have prostate tumors that grow so slowly that they may never cause health problems during their lifetime, even without treatment. In other men, however, the cancer is much more aggressive; in these cases, prostate cancer can be life-threatening.

Some cancerous tumors can invade surrounding tissue and spread to other parts of the body. Tumors that begin at one site and then spread to other areas of the body are called metastatic cancers. The signs and symptoms of metastatic cancer depend on where the disease has spread. If prostate cancer spreads, cancerous cells most often appear in the lymph nodes, bones, lungs, liver, or brain. Bone metastases of prostate cancer most often cause pain in the lower back, pelvis, or hips.

- A small percentage of all prostate cancers cluster in families. These hereditary cancers are associated with inherited gene mutations. Hereditary prostate cancers tend to develop earlier in life than non-inherited (sporadic) cases.

Frequency

About 1 in 7 men will be diagnosed with prostate cancer at some time during their life. In addition, studies indicate that many older men have undiagnosed prostate cancer that is non-aggressive and unlikely to cause symptoms or affect their lifespan. While most men who are diagnosed with prostate cancer do not die from it, this common cancer is still the second leading cause of cancer death among men in the United States.

More than 60 percent of prostate cancers are diagnosed after age 65, and the disorder is rare before age 40. In the United States, African Americans have a higher risk of developing prostate cancer than do men of other ethnic backgrounds, and they also have a higher risk of dying from the disease.

Genetic Changes

Cancers occur when genetic mutations build up in critical genes, specifically those that control cell growth and division or the repair of damaged DNA. These changes allow cells to grow and divide uncontrollably to form a tumor. In most cases of prostate cancer, these genetic changes are acquired during a man's lifetime and are present only in certain cells in the prostate. These changes, which are called somatic mutations, are not inherited. Somatic mutations in many different genes have been found in prostate cancer cells. Less commonly, genetic changes present in essentially all of the body's cells increase the risk of developing prostate cancer. These genetic changes, which are classified as germline mutations, are usually inherited from a parent. In people with germline mutations, changes in other genes, together with environmental and lifestyle factors, also influence whether a person will develop prostate cancer.

Inherited mutations in particular genes, such as *BRCA1*, *BRCA2*, and *HOXB13*, account for some cases of hereditary prostate cancer. Men with mutations in these genes have a high risk of developing prostate cancer and, in some cases, other cancers during their lifetimes. In addition, men with *BRCA2* or *HOXB13* gene mutations may have a higher risk of developing life-threatening forms of prostate cancer.

The proteins produced from the *BRCA1* and *BRCA2* genes are involved in fixing damaged DNA, which helps to maintain the stability of a cell's genetic information. For this reason, the BRCA1 and BRCA2 proteins are considered to be tumor suppressors, which means that they help keep cells from growing and dividing too fast or in an uncontrolled way. Mutations in these genes impair the cell's ability to fix damaged DNA, allowing potentially damaging mutations to persist. As these defects accumulate, they can trigger cells to grow and divide uncontrollably and form a tumor.

The *HOXB13* gene provides instructions for producing a protein that attaches (binds) to specific regions of DNA and regulates the activity of other genes. On the basis of this role, the protein produced from the *HOXB13* gene is called a transcription factor. Like BRCA1 and BRCA2, the *HOXB13* protein is thought to act as a tumor suppressor. *HOXB13* gene mutations may result in impairment of the protein's tumor suppressor function, resulting in the uncontrolled cell growth and division that can lead to prostate cancer.

Inherited variations in dozens of other genes have been studied as possible risk factors for prostate cancer. Some of these genes provide instructions for making proteins that interact with the proteins produced from the *BRCA1, BRCA2,* or *HOXB13* genes. Others act as tumor suppressors through different pathways. Changes in these genes probably make only a small contribution to overall prostate cancer risk. However, researchers suspect that the combined influence of variations in many of these genes may significantly impact a person's risk of developing this form of cancer.

In many families, the genetic changes associated with hereditary prostate cancer are unknown. Identifying additional genetic risk factors for prostate cancer is an active area of medical research.

In addition to genetic changes, researchers have identified many personal and environmental factors that may contribute to a person's risk of developing prostate cancer. These factors include a high-fat diet that includes an excess of meat and dairy and not enough vegetables, a largely inactive (sedentary) lifestyle, obesity, excessive alcohol use, or exposure to certain toxic chemicals. A history of prostate cancer in closely related family members is also an important risk factor, particularly if the cancer occurred at an early age.

Inheritance Pattern

Many cases of prostate cancer are not related to inherited gene changes. These cancers are associated with somatic mutations that occur only in certain cells in the prostate.

When prostate cancer is related to inherited gene changes, the way that cancer risk is inherited depends on the gene involved. For example, mutations in the *BRCA1, BRCA2,* and *HOXB13* genes are inherited in an autosomal dominant pattern, which means one copy of the altered gene in each cell is sufficient to increase a person's chance of developing cancer. In other cases, the inheritance of prostate cancer risk is unclear. It is important to note that people inherit an increased risk of cancer, not the disease itself. Not all people who inherit mutations in these genes will develop cancer.

Chapter 54

Crohn Disease and Genetics

What Is Crohn Disease?

Crohn disease is a complex, chronic disorder that primarily affects the digestive system. This condition typically involves abnormal inflammation of the intestinal walls, particularly in the lower part of the small intestine (the ileum) and portions of the large intestine (the colon). Inflammation can occur in any part of the digestive system, however. The inflamed tissues become thick and swollen, and the inner surface of the intestine may develop open sores (ulcers).

Crohn disease most commonly appears in a person's late teens or twenties, although the disease can appear at any age. Signs and symptoms tend to flare up multiple times throughout life. The most common features of this condition are persistent diarrhea, abdominal pain and cramping, loss of appetite, weight loss, and fever. Some people with Crohn disease have chronic bleeding from inflamed tissues in the intestine; over time, this bleeding can lead to a low number of

---

This chapter contains text excerpted from the following sources: Text beginning with the heading "What Is Crohn Disease?" is excerpted from "Crohn Disease," Genetics Home Reference (GHR), National Institutes of Health (NIH), March 21, 2016; Text under the heading "What Causes Crohn's Disease?" is excerpted from "Crohn's Disease," National Institute of Diabetes and Digestive and Kidney Diseases (NIDDK), September 2014.

603

red blood cells (anemia). In some cases, Crohn disease can also cause medical problems affecting the joints, eyes, or skin.

Intestinal blockage is a common complication of Crohn disease. Blockages are caused by swelling or a buildup of scar tissue in the intestinal walls. Some affected individuals also develop fistulae, which are abnormal connections between the intestine and other tissues. Fistulae occur when ulcers break through the intestinal wall to form passages between loops of the intestine or between the intestine and nearby structures (such as the bladder, vagina, or skin).

Crohn disease is one common form of inflammatory bowel disease (IBD). Another type of IBD, ulcerative colitis, also causes chronic inflammation of the intestinal lining. Unlike Crohn disease, which can affect any part of the digestive system, ulcerative colitis typically causes inflammation only in the colon. In addition, the two disorders involve different patterns of inflammation.

How Common Is Crohn Disease?

Crohn disease is most common in western Europe and North America, where it affects 100 to 150 in 100,000 people. About one million Americans are currently affected by this disorder. Crohn disease occurs more often in whites and people of eastern and central European (Ashkenazi) Jewish descent than among people of other ethnic backgrounds.

What Are the Genetic Changes Related to Crohn Disease?

Crohn disease is related to chromosomes 5 and 10.

Variations of the *ATG16L1, IRGM*, and NOD2 genes increase the risk of developing Crohn disease.

The *IL23R* gene is associated with Crohn disease.

A variety of genetic and environmental factors likely play a role in causing Crohn disease. Although researchers are studying risk factors that may contribute to this complex disorder, many of these factors remain unknown. Cigarette smoking is thought to increase the risk of developing this disease, and it may also play a role in periodic flare-ups of signs and symptoms.

Studies suggest that Crohn disease may result from a combination of certain genetic variations, changes in the immune system, and the presence of bacteria in the digestive tract. Recent studies have identified variations in specific genes, including *ATG16L1, IL23R, IRGM,* and *NOD2*, that influence the risk of developing Crohn disease. These genes provide instructions for making proteins that are involved in immune system function. Variations in any of these genes may disrupt the ability of cells in the intestine to respond normally to bacteria. An abnormal immune response to bacteria in the intestinal walls may lead to chronic inflammation and the digestive problems characteristic of Crohn disease.

Researchers have also discovered genetic variations in certain regions of chromosome 5 and chromosome 10 that appear to contribute to Crohn disease risk. One area of chromosome 5, known as the *IBD5* locus, contains several genetic changes that may increase the risk of developing this condition. Other regions of chromosome 5 and chromosome 10 identified in studies of Crohn disease risk are known as "gene deserts" because they include no known genes. Instead, these regions may contain stretches of DNA that regulate nearby genes. Additional research is needed to determine how genetic variations in these chromosomal regions are related to a person's chance of developing Crohn disease.

What Causes Crohn Disease?

The exact cause of Crohn disease is unknown. Researchers believe the following factors may play a role in causing Crohn disease:

- autoimmune reaction
- genes
- environment

Autoimmune reaction. Scientists believe one cause of Crohn disease may be an autoimmune reaction—when a person's immune system attacks healthy cells in the body by mistake. Normally, the immune system protects the body from infection by identifying and destroying bacteria, viruses, and other potentially harmful foreign substances. Researchers believe bacteria or viruses can mistakenly trigger the immune system to attack the inner lining of the intestines. This immune system response causes the inflammation, leading to symptoms.

Genes. Crohn disease sometimes runs in families. Research has shown that people who have a parent or sibling with Crohn disease may be more likely to develop the disease. Researchers continue to study the link between genes and Crohn disease.

Environment. Some studies suggest that certain things in the environment may increase the chance of a person getting Crohn disease, although the overall chance is low. Nonsteroidal anti-inflammatory drugs, antibiotics, and oral contraceptives may slightly increase the chance of developing Crohn disease. A high-fat diet may also slightly increase the chance of getting Crohn disease.

Some people incorrectly believe that eating certain foods, stress, or emotional distress can cause Crohn disease. Emotional distress and eating certain foods do not cause Crohn disease. Sometimes the stress of living with Crohn disease can make symptoms worse. Also, some people may find that certain foods can trigger or worsen their symptoms.

Who Is More Likely to Develop Crohn Disease?

Crohn disease can occur in people of any age. However, it is more likely to develop in people

- between the ages of 20 and 29

- who have a family member, most often a sibling or parent, with IBD

- who smoke cigarettes

What Are the Signs and Symptoms of Crohn Disease?

The most common signs and symptoms of Crohn disease are

- diarrhea

- abdominal cramping and pain

- weight loss

Other general signs and symptoms include

- feeling tired

- nausea or loss of appetite

- fever

- anemia—a condition in which the body has fewer red blood cells than normal

Signs and symptoms of inflammation outside of the intestines include

- joint pain or soreness

- eye irritation

- skin changes that involve red, tender bumps under the skin

The symptoms a person experiences can vary depending on the severity of the inflammation and where it occurs.

Chapter 55

Mental Illness and Genetics

Chapter Contents

Section 55.1

Familial Recurrence of Mental Illness

This section includes text excerpted from "Common
Genetic Factors Found in 5 Mental Disorders," National
Institutes of Health (NIH), March 18, 2013.

Common Genetic Factors Found in 5 Major Mental Disorders

Major mental disorders traditionally thought to be distinct share
certain genetic glitches, according to a new study. The finding may
point to better ways to diagnose and treat these conditions.

Scientists have long recognized that many psychiatric disorders tend
to run in families, suggesting potential genetic roots. Such disorders
include autism, attention deficit hyperactivity disorder (ADHD), bipolar
disorder, major depression and schizophrenia. Symptoms can overlap
and so distinguishing among these 5 major psychiatric syndromes can be
difficult. Their shared symptoms suggest they may also share similarities
at the biological level. In fact, recent studies have turned up limited evidence of shared genetic risk factors, such as for schizophrenia and bipolar
disorder, autism and schizophrenia, and depression and bipolar disorder.

To take a broader look, an international research consortium conducted an analysis that incorporated data from genome-wide association studies (GWAS) of the 5 major disorders. This type of study
involves scanning through thousands of genetic markers in search of
tiny variations that appear more often in people who have a particular condition than in those who don't. The research received primary
funding from NIH's National Institute of Mental Health (NIMH), along
with other NIH components.

As reported in the *Lancet*, the scientists screened for evidence of ill-
ness-associated genetic variation among over 33,000 patients. All had
been diagnosed with at least 1 of the 5 disorders. A comparison group
included about 28,000 people who had no major psychiatric diagnosis.

The analysis revealed variations significantly associated with all 5
disorders. These included variations in 2 genes that code for the cellular
machinery that helps regulate the flow of calcium into neurons. Variation

in one of these, called *CACNA1C*, had previously been linked to bipolar disorder, schizophrenia and major depression. *CACNA1C* is known to affect brain circuitry involved in emotion, thinking, attention and memory—functions that can be disrupted in mental illnesses. Variation in another calcium channel gene, called *CACNB2*, was also linked to the 5 disorders.

In addition, the researchers discovered illness-linked variation for all 5 disorders in certain regions of chromosomes 3 and 10. Each of these sites spans several genes, and causal factors haven't yet been pinpointed. The suspect region along chromosome 3 had the strongest links to the disorders. This region also harbors certain variations previously linked to bipolar disorder and schizophrenia.

"Although statistically significant, each of these genetic associations individually can account for only a small amount of risk for mental illness," says study co-author Dr. Jordan Smoller of Massachusetts General Hospital. Because of this, the variations couldn't yet be used to predict or diagnose specific conditions. But these results may help researchers move closer to making more accurate diagnoses. They may also help lead to a better understanding of the factors that cause these major mental disorders.

Section 55.2

Genetic Links in Obsessive Compulsive Disorder (OCD)

This section includes text excerpted from "Obsessive Compulsive Disorder," National Institute of Mental Health (NIMH), January 2016.

What Is Obsessive Compulsive Disorder?

Obsessive Compulsive Disorder (OCD) is a common, chronic and long-lasting disorder in which a person has uncontrollable, reoccurring thoughts (obsessions) and behaviors (compulsions) that he or she feels the urge to repeat over and over.

Signs and Symptoms

People with OCD may have symptoms of obsessions, compulsions, or both. These symptoms can interfere with all aspects of life, such as work, school, and personal relationships.

Obsessions are repeated thoughts, urges, or mental images that cause anxiety. Common symptoms include:

- fear of germs or contamination
- unwanted forbidden or taboo thoughts involving sex, religion, and harm
- aggressive thoughts towards others or self
- having things symmetrical or in a perfect order

Compulsions are repetitive behaviors that a person with OCD feels the urge to do in response to an obsessive thought. Common compulsions include:

- excessive cleaning and/or handwashing
- ordering and arranging things in a particular, precise way
- repeatedly checking on things, such as repeatedly checking to see if the door is locked or that the oven is off
- compulsive counting

Not all rituals or habits are compulsions. Everyone double checks things sometimes. But a person with OCD generally:

- Can't control his or her thoughts or behaviors, even when those thoughts or behaviors are recognized as excessive
- Spends at least 1 hour a day on these thoughts or behaviors
- Doesn't get pleasure when performing the behaviors or rituals, but may feel brief relief from the anxiety the thoughts cause
- Experiences significant problems in their daily life due to these thoughts or behaviors

Some individuals with OCD also have a tic disorder. Motor tics are sudden, brief, repetitive movements, such as eye blinking and other eye movements, facial grimacing, shoulder shrugging, and head or shoulder jerking. Common vocal tics include repetitive throat-clearing, sniffing, or grunting sounds.

Symptoms may come and go, ease over time, or worsen. People with OCD may try to help themselves by avoiding situations that trigger their obsessions, or they may use alcohol or drugs to calm themselves. Although most adults with OCD recognize that what they are doing doesn't make sense, some adults and most children may not realize that their behavior is out of the ordinary. Parents or teachers typically recognize OCD symptoms in children.

If you think you have OCD, talk to your doctor about your symptoms. If left untreated, OCD can interfere in all aspects of life.

Risk Factors

OCD is a common disorder that affects adults, adolescents, and children all over the world. Most people are diagnosed by about age 19, typically with an earlier age of onset in boys than in girls, but onset after age 35 does happen.

The causes of OCD are unknown, but risk factors include:

Genetics

Twin and family studies have shown that people with first-degree relatives (such as a parent, sibling, or child) who have OCD are at a higher risk for developing OCD themselves. The risk is higher if the first-degree relative developed OCD as a child or teen. Ongoing research continues to explore the connection between genetics and OCD and may help improve OCD diagnosis and treatment.

Brain Structure and Functioning

Imaging studies have shown differences in the frontal cortex and subcortical structures of the brain in patients with OCD. There appears to be a connection between the OCD symptoms and abnormalities in certain areas of the brain, but that connection is not clear. Research is still underway. Understanding the causes will help determine specific, personalized treatments to treat OCD.

Environment

People who have experienced abuse (physical or sexual) in childhood or other trauma are at an increased risk for developing OCD.

In some cases, children may develop OCD or OCD symptoms following a streptococcal infection—this is called Pediatric Autoimmune Neuropsychiatric Disorders Associated with Streptococcal Infections (PANDAS).

Treatments and Therapies

OCD is typically treated with medication, psychotherapy or a combination of the two. Although most patients with OCD respond to treatment, some patients continue to experience symptoms.

Sometimes people with OCD also have other mental disorders, such as anxiety, depression, and body dysmorphic disorder, a disorder in which someone mistakenly believes that a part of their body is abnormal. It is important to consider these other disorders when making decisions about treatment.

Medication

Serotonin reuptake inhibitors (SRIs) and selective serotonin reuptake inhibitors (SSRIs) are used to help reduce OCD symptoms. Examples of medications that have been proven effective in both adults and children with OCD include clomipramine, which is a member of an older class of "tricyclic" antidepressants, and several newer "selective serotonin reuptake inhibitors" (SSRIs), including:

- fluoxetine

- fluvoxamine

- sertraline

SRIs often require higher daily doses in the treatment of OCD than of depression, and may take 8 to 12 weeks to start working, but some patients experience more rapid improvement.

If symptoms do not improve with these types of medications, research shows that some patients may respond well to an antipsychotic medication (such as risperidone). Although research shows that an antipsychotic medication may be helpful in managing symptoms for people who have both OCD and a tic disorder, research on the effectiveness of antipsychotics to treat OCD is mixed.

If you are prescribed a medication, be sure you:

- Talk with your doctor or a pharmacist to make sure you understand the risks and benefits of the medications you're taking.

- Do not stop taking a medication without talking to your doctor first. Suddenly stopping a medication may lead to "rebound" or worsening of OCD symptoms. Other uncomfortable or potentially dangerous withdrawal effects are also possible.

- Report any concerns about side effects to your doctor right away. You may need a change in the dose or a different medication.

- Report serious side effects to the U.S. Food and Drug Administration (FDA) MedWatch Adverse Event Reporting program online at http://www.fda.gov/Safety/MedWatch or by phone at 1-800-332-1088. You or your doctor may send a report.

Other medications have been used to treat OCD, but more research is needed to show the benefit for these options.

Psychotherapy

Psychotherapy can be an effective treatment for adults and children with OCD. Research shows that certain types of psychotherapy, including cognitive behavior therapy (CBT) and other related therapies (e.g., habit reversal training) can be as effective as medication for many individuals. Research also shows that a type of CBT called Exposure and Response Prevention (EX/RP) is effective in reducing compulsive behaviors in OCD, even in people who did not respond well to SRI medication. For many patients EX/RP is the add-on treatment of choice when SRIs or SSRIs medication does not effectively treat OCD symptoms.

Other Treatment Options

NIMH is supporting research into new treatment approaches for people whose OCD does not respond well to the usual therapies. These new approaches include combination and add-on (augmentation) treatments, as well as novel techniques such as deep brain stimulation (DBS).

Finding Treatment

For general information on mental health and to locate treatment services in your area, call the Substance Abuse and Mental Health Services Administration (SAMHSA) Treatment Referral Helpline at 1-800-662-HELP (4357). SAMHSA also has a Behavioral Health Treatment Locator on its website that can be searched by location.

Section 55.3

Genetic Links in Schizophrenia and Bipolar Disorder

This section includes text excerpted from "New Data Reveal Extent of Genetic Overlap Between Major Mental Disorders," National Institute of Mental Health (NIMH), August 12, 2013.

Schizophrenia, Bipolar Disorder Share the Most Common Genetic Variation

The largest genome-wide study of its kind has determined how much five major mental illnesses are traceable to the same common inherited genetic variations. Researchers funded in part by the National Institutes of Health found that the overlap was highest between schizophrenia and bipolar disorder; moderate for bipolar disorder and depression and for ADHD and depression; and low between schizophrenia and autism. Overall, common genetic variation accounted for 17–28 percent of risk for the illnesses.

"Since our study only looked at common gene variants, the total genetic overlap between the disorders is likely higher," explained Naomi Wray, Ph.D., University of Queensland, Brisbane, Australia, who co-led the multi-site study by the Cross Disorders Group of the Psychiatric Genomics Consortium (PGC), which is supported by the NIH's National Institute of Mental Health (NIMH). "Shared variants with smaller effects, rare variants, mutations, duplications, deletions, and gene-environment interactions also contribute to these illnesses."

Dr. Wray, Kenneth Kendler, M.D., of Virginia Commonwealth University, Richmond, Jordan Smoller, M.D., of Massachusetts General Hospital, Boston, and other members of the PGC group report on their findings August 11, 2013, in the journal *Nature Genetics*.

"Such evidence quantifying shared genetic risk factors among traditional psychiatric diagnoses will help us move toward classification that will be more faithful to nature," said Bruce Cuthbert, Ph.D., director of the NIMH Division of Adult Translational Research and Treatment Development and coordinator of the Institute's Research

Domain Criteria (RDoC) project, which is developing a mental disorders classification system for research based more on underlying causes.

Earlier this year, PGC researchers—more than 300 scientists at 80 research centers in 20 countries—reported the first evidence of overlap between all five disorders. People with the disorders were more likely to have suspect variation at the same four chromosomal sites. But the extent of the overlap remained unclear. In the new study, they used the same genome-wide information and the largest data sets currently available to estimate the risk for the illnesses attributable to any of hundreds of thousands of sites of common variability in the genetic code across chromosomes. They looked for similarities in such genetic variation among several thousand people with each illness and compared them to controls—calculating the extent to which pairs of disorders are linked to the same genetic variants.

The overlap in heritability attributable to common genetic variation was about 15 percent between schizophrenia and bipolar disorder, about 10 percent between bipolar disorder and depression, about 9 percent between schizophrenia and depression, and about 3 percent between schizophrenia and autism.

The newfound molecular genetic evidence linking schizophrenia and depression, if replicated, could have important implications for diagnostics and research, say the researchers. They expected to see more overlap between ADHD and autism, but the modest schizophrenia-autism connection is consistent with other emerging evidence.

The study results also attach numbers to molecular evidence documenting the importance of heritability traceable to common genetic variation in causing these five major mental illnesses. Yet this still leaves much of the likely inherited genetic contribution to the disorders unexplained—not to mention non-inherited genetic factors. For example, common genetic variation accounted for 23 percent of schizophrenia, but evidence from twin and family studies estimate its total heritability at 81 percent. Similarly, the gaps are 25 percent vs. 75 percent for bipolar disorder, 28 percent vs. 75 percent for ADHD, 14 percent vs. 80 percent for autism, and 21 percent vs. 37 percent for depression.

Among other types of genetic inheritance known to affect risk and not detected in this study are contributions from rare variants not associated with common sites of genetic variation. However, the researchers say that their results show clearly that more illness-linked common variants with small effects will be discovered with the greater statistical power that comes with larger sample sizes.

"It is encouraging that the estimates of genetic contributions to mental disorders trace those from more traditional family and twin studies. The study points to a future of active gene discovery for mental disorders" said Thomas Lehner, Ph.D., chief of the NIMH Genomics Research Branch, which funds the project.

Chapter 56

Diabetes and Genetics

What Is Diabetes?

Diabetes is a complex group of diseases with a variety of causes. People with diabetes have high blood glucose, also called high blood sugar or hyperglycemia.

Diabetes is a disorder of metabolism—the way the body uses digested food for energy. The digestive tract breaks down carbohydrates—sugars and starches found in many foods—into glucose, a form of sugar that enters the bloodstream. With the help of the hormone insulin, cells throughout the body absorb glucose and use it for energy. Diabetes develops when the body doesn't make enough insulin or is not able to use insulin effectively, or both.

Insulin is made in the pancreas, an organ located behind the stomach. The pancreas contains clusters of cells called islets. Beta cells within the islets make insulin and release it into the blood.

If beta cells don't produce enough insulin, or the body doesn't respond to the insulin that is present, glucose builds up in the blood instead of being absorbed by cells in the body, leading to prediabetes or diabetes. Prediabetes is a condition in which blood glucose levels or A1C levels—which reflect average blood glucose levels—are higher than normal but not high enough to be diagnosed as diabetes. In diabetes, the body's cells are starved of energy despite high blood glucose levels.

This chapter includes text excerpted from "Causes of Diabetes," National Institute of Diabetes and Digestive and Kidney Diseases (NIDDK), June 2014.

Over time, high blood glucose damages nerves and blood vessels, leading to complications such as heart disease, stroke, kidney disease, blindness, dental disease, and amputations. Other complications of diabetes may include increased susceptibility to other diseases, loss of mobility with aging, depression, and pregnancy problems. No one is certain what starts the processes that cause diabetes, but scientists believe genes and environmental factors interact to cause diabetes in most cases.

The two main types of diabetes are type 1 diabetes and type 2 diabetes. A third type, gestational diabetes, develops only during pregnancy. Other types of diabetes are caused by defects in specific genes, diseases of the pancreas, certain drugs or chemicals, infections, and other conditions. Some people show signs of both type 1 and type 2 diabetes.

What Causes Type 1 Diabetes?

Type 1 diabetes is caused by a lack of insulin due to the destruction of insulin-producing beta cells in the pancreas. In type 1 diabetes—an autoimmune disease—the body's immune system attacks and destroys the beta cells. Normally, the immune system protects the body from infection by identifying and destroying bacteria, viruses, and other potentially harmful foreign substances. But in autoimmune diseases, the immune system attacks the body's own cells. In type 1 diabetes, beta cell destruction may take place over several years, but symptoms of the disease usually develop over a short period of time.

Type 1 diabetes typically occurs in children and young adults, though it can appear at any age. In the past, type 1 diabetes was called juvenile diabetes or insulin-dependent diabetes mellitus.

Latent autoimmune diabetes in adults (LADA) may be a slowly developing kind of type 1 diabetes. Diagnosis usually occurs after age 30. In LADA, as in type 1 diabetes, the body's immune system destroys the beta cells. At the time of diagnosis, people with LADA may still produce their own insulin, but eventually most will need insulin shots or an insulin pump to control blood glucose levels.

Genetic Susceptibility

Heredity plays an important part in determining who is likely to develop type 1 diabetes. Genes are passed down from biological parent to child. Genes carry instructions for making proteins that are needed for the body's cells to function. Many genes, as well as interactions among genes, are thought to influence susceptibility to and protection from type 1 diabetes. The key genes may vary in different population groups. Variations in genes that affect more than 1 percent of a population group are called gene variants.

Certain gene variants that carry instructions for making proteins called human leukocyte antigens (HLAs) on white blood cells are linked to the risk of developing type 1 diabetes. The proteins produced by *HLA* genes help determine whether the immune system recognizes a cell as part of the body or as foreign material. Some combinations of *HLA* gene variants predict that a person will be at higher risk for type 1 diabetes, while other combinations are protective or have no effect on risk.

While *HLA* genes are the major risk genes for type 1 diabetes, many additional risk genes or gene regions have been found. Not only can these genes help identify people at risk for type 1 diabetes, but they also provide important clues to help scientists better understand how the disease develops and identify potential targets for therapy and prevention.

Genetic testing can show what types of *HLA* genes a person carries and can reveal other genes linked to diabetes. However, most genetic testing is done in a research setting and is not yet available to individuals. Scientists are studying how the results of genetic testing can be used to improve type 1 diabetes prevention or treatment.

Risk Factors for Type 2 Diabetes

People who develop type 2 diabetes are more likely to have the following characteristics:

- age 45 or older

- overweight or obese

- physically inactive

- parent or sibling with diabetes

- family background that is African American, Alaska Native, American Indian, Asian American, Hispanic/Latino, or Pacific Islander American

- history of giving birth to a baby weighing more than 9 pounds

- history of gestational diabetes

- high blood pressure—140/90 or above—or being treated for high blood pressure

- high-density lipoprotein (HDL), or good, cholesterol below 35 milligrams per deciliter (mg/dL), or a triglyceride level above 250 mg/dL

- polycystic ovary syndrome, also called PCOS

- prediabetes—an A1C level of 5.7 to 6.4 percent; a fasting plasma glucose test result of 100–125 mg/dL, called impaired fasting glucose; or a 2-hour oral glucose tolerance test result of 140–199, called impaired glucose tolerance

- acanthosis nigricans, a condition associated with insulin resistance, characterized by a dark, velvety rash around the neck or armpits

- history of CVD

The American Diabetes Association (ADA) recommends that testing to detect prediabetes and type 2 diabetes be considered in adults who are overweight or obese and have one or more additional risk factors for diabetes. In adults without these risk factors, testing should begin at age 45.

What Causes Gestational Diabetes?

Scientists believe gestational diabetes is caused by the hormonal changes and metabolic demands of pregnancy together with genetic and environmental factors.

Insulin Resistance and Beta Cell Dysfunction

Hormones produced by the placenta and other pregnancy-related factors contribute to insulin resistance, which occurs in all women during late pregnancy. Insulin resistance increases the amount of insulin needed to control blood glucose levels. If the pancreas can't produce enough insulin due to beta cell dysfunction, gestational diabetes occurs.

As with type 2 diabetes, excess weight is linked to gestational diabetes. Overweight or obese women are at particularly high risk for gestational diabetes because they start pregnancy with a higher need for insulin due to insulin resistance. Excessive weight gain during pregnancy may also increase risk.

Family History

Having a family history of diabetes is also a risk factor for gestational diabetes, suggesting that genes play a role in its development.

Genetics may also explain why the disorder occurs more frequently in African Americans, American Indians, and Hispanics/Latinos. Many gene variants or combinations of variants may increase a woman's risk for developing gestational diabetes. Studies have found several gene variants associated with gestational diabetes, but these variants account for only a small fraction of women with gestational diabetes.

Future Risk of Type 2 Diabetes

Because a woman's hormones usually return to normal levels soon after giving birth, gestational diabetes disappears in most women after delivery. However, women who have gestational diabetes are more likely to develop gestational diabetes with future pregnancies and develop type 2 diabetes. Women with gestational diabetes should be tested for persistent diabetes 6 to 12 weeks after delivery and at least every 3 years thereafter.

Also, exposure to high glucose levels during gestation increases a child's risk for becoming overweight or obese and for developing type 2 diabetes later on. The result may be a cycle of diabetes affecting multiple generations in a family. For both mother and child, maintaining a healthy body weight and being physically active may help prevent type 2 diabetes.

Other Types and Causes of Diabetes

Other types of diabetes have a variety of possible causes.

Genetic Mutations Affecting Beta Cells, Insulin, and Insulin Action

Some relatively uncommon forms of diabetes known as monogenic diabetes are caused by mutations, or changes, in a single gene. These mutations are usually inherited, but sometimes the gene mutation occurs spontaneously. Most of these gene mutations cause diabetes by reducing beta cells' ability to produce insulin.

The most common types of monogenic diabetes are neonatal diabetes mellitus (NDM) and MODY. NDM occurs in the first 6 months of life. MODY is usually found during adolescence or early adulthood but sometimes is not diagnosed until later in life.

Other rare genetic mutations can cause diabetes by damaging the quality of insulin the body produces or by causing abnormalities in insulin receptors.

Other Genetic Diseases

Diabetes occurs in people with Down syndrome, Klinefelter syndrome, and Turner syndrome at higher rates than the general population. Scientists are investigating whether genes that may predispose people to genetic syndromes also predispose them to diabetes.

The genetic disorders cystic fibrosis and hemochromatosis are linked to diabetes. Cystic fibrosis produces abnormally thick mucus, which blocks the pancreas. The risk of diabetes increases with age in people with cystic fibrosis. Hemochromatosis causes the body to store too much iron. If the disorder is not treated, iron can build up in and damage the pancreas and other organs.

Damage to or Removal of the Pancreas

Pancreatitis, cancer, and trauma can all harm the pancreatic beta cells or impair insulin production, thus causing diabetes. If the damaged pancreas is removed, diabetes will occur due to the loss of the beta cells.

Endocrine Diseases

Endocrine diseases affect organs that produce hormones. Cushing's syndrome and acromegaly are examples of hormonal disorders that can cause prediabetes and diabetes by inducing insulin resistance. Cushing's syndrome is marked by excessive production of cortisol—sometimes called the "stress hormone." Acromegaly occurs when the body produces too much growth hormone. Glucagonoma, a rare tumor of the pancreas, can also cause diabetes. The tumor causes the body to produce too much glucagon. Hyperthyroidism, a disorder that occurs when the thyroid gland produces too much thyroid hormone, can also cause elevated blood glucose levels.

Autoimmune Disorders

Rare disorders characterized by antibodies that disrupt insulin action can lead to diabetes. This kind of diabetes is often associated with other autoimmune disorders such as lupus erythematosus. Another rare autoimmune disorder called stiff-man syndrome is associated with antibodies that attack the beta cells, similar to type 1 diabetes.

Medications and Chemical Toxins

Some medications, such as nicotinic acid and certain types of diuretics, anti-seizure drugs, psychiatric drugs, and drugs to treat human immunodeficiency virus (HIV), can impair beta cells or disrupt insulin action. Pentamidine, a drug prescribed to treat a type of pneumonia, can increase the risk of pancreatitis, beta cell damage, and diabetes. Also, glucocorticoids—steroid hormones that are chemically similar to naturally produced cortisol—may impair insulin action. Glucocorticoids are used to treat inflammatory illnesses such as rheumatoid arthritis, asthma, lupus, and ulcerative colitis.

Many chemical toxins can damage or destroy beta cells in animals, but only a few have been linked to diabetes in humans. For example, dioxin—a contaminant of the herbicide Agent Orange, used during the Vietnam War—may be linked to the development of type 2 diabetes. In 2000, based on a report from the Institute of Medicine, the U.S. Department of Veterans Affairs (VA) added diabetes to the list of conditions for which Vietnam veterans are eligible for disability compensation. Also, a chemical in a rat poison no longer in use has been shown to cause diabetes if ingested. Some studies suggest a high intake of nitrogen-containing chemicals such as nitrates and nitrites might increase the risk of diabetes. Arsenic has also been studied for possible links to diabetes.

Lipodystrophy

Lipodystrophy is a condition in which fat tissue is lost or redistributed in the body. The condition is associated with insulin resistance and type 2 diabetes.

Points to Remember

- Diabetes is a complex group of diseases with a variety of causes. Scientists believe genes and environmental factors interact to cause diabetes in most cases.

- People with diabetes have high blood glucose, also called high blood sugar or hyperglycemia. Diabetes develops when the body doesn't make enough insulin or is not able to use insulin effectively, or both.

- Insulin is a hormone made by beta cells in the pancreas. Insulin helps cells throughout the body absorb and use glucose for energy. If the body does not produce enough insulin or cannot use insulin effectively, glucose builds up in the blood instead of being absorbed by cells in the body, and the body is starved of energy.

- Prediabetes is a condition in which blood glucose levels or A1C levels are higher than normal but not high enough to be diagnosed as diabetes. People with prediabetes can substantially reduce their risk of developing diabetes by losing weight and increasing physical activity.

- The two main types of diabetes are type 1 diabetes and type 2 diabetes. Gestational diabetes is a third form of diabetes that develops only during pregnancy.

- Type 1 diabetes is caused by a lack of insulin due to the destruction of insulin-producing beta cells. In type 1 diabetes—an autoimmune disease—the body's immune system attacks and destroys the beta cells.

- Type 2 diabetes—the most common form of diabetes—is caused by a combination of factors, including insulin resistance, a condition in which the body's muscle, fat, and liver cells do not use insulin effectively. Type 2 diabetes develops when the body can no longer produce enough insulin to compensate for the impaired ability to use insulin.

- Scientists believe gestational diabetes is caused by the hormonal changes and metabolic demands of pregnancy together with genetic and environmental factors. Risk factors for gestational diabetes include being overweight and having a family history of diabetes.

- Monogenic forms of diabetes are relatively uncommon and are caused by mutations in single genes that limit insulin production, quality, or action in the body.

- Other types of diabetes are caused by diseases and injuries that damage the pancreas; certain chemical toxins and medications; infections; and other conditions.

Chapter 57

Heart Disease and Genetics

Chapter Contents

Section 57.1

Heart Disease and Genetic Risk

This section includes text excerpted from "Heart Disease," Centers
for Disease Control and Prevention (CDC), August 10, 2015.

About Heart Disease

The term "heart disease" refers to several types of heart conditions. The most common type of heart disease in the United States
is coronary artery disease, which affects the blood flow to the heart.
Decreased blood flow can cause a heart attack.

Heart Disease Risk Factors

Several health conditions, your lifestyle, and your age and family
history can increase your risk for heart disease. These are called risk
factors. About half of all Americans (47%) have at least one of the three
key risk factors for heart disease: high blood pressure, high cholesterol,
and smoking.

Some of the risk factors for heart disease cannot be controlled, such
as your age or family history. But you can take steps to lower your risk
by changing the factors you can control.

Conditions That Increase Risk for Heart Disease

Several medical conditions can increase your risk for heart disease.
If you have one of these conditions, you can take steps to control it
and lower your risk.

High Blood Pressure

High blood pressure is a major risk factor for heart disease. It is a
medical condition that occurs when the pressure of the blood in your
arteries and other blood vessels is too high. The high pressure, if not
controlled, can affect your heart and other major organs of your body,
including your kidneys and brain.

High blood pressure is often called a "silent killer" because many people do not notice symptoms to signal high blood pressure. Lowering blood pressure by changes in lifestyle or by medication can reduce your risk for heart disease and heart attack.

High Cholesterol

Cholesterol is a waxy, fat-like substance made by the liver or found in certain foods. Your liver makes enough for your body's needs, but we often get more cholesterol from the foods we eat. If we take in more cholesterol than the body can use, the extra cholesterol can build up in the walls of the arteries, including those of the heart. This leads to narrowing of the arteries and can decrease the blood flow to the heart, brain, kidneys, and other parts of the body.

Some cholesterol is "good," and some is "bad." High cholesterol is the term used for high levels of low-density lipoprotein, or LDL, which are considered "bad" because they can lead to heart disease. A higher level of high-density lipoprotein cholesterol, or HDL, is considered "good" because it provides some protection against heart disease.

A blood test can detect the amount of cholesterol and triglycerides (a related kind of fat) in your blood.

Diabetes

Diabetes mellitus also increases the risk for heart disease. Your body needs glucose (sugar) for energy. Insulin is a hormone made in the pancreas that helps move glucose from the food you eat to your body's cells. If you have diabetes, your body doesn't make enough insulin, can't use its own insulin as well as it should, or both.

Diabetes causes sugars to build up in the blood. The risk of death from heart disease for adults with diabetes is two to four times higher than adults who do not have diabetes. Talk to your doctor about ways to manage diabetes and control other risk factors.

Heart Disease Behavior

Your lifestyle choices can increase your risk for heart disease and heart attack. To reduce your risk, your doctor may recommend changes to your lifestyle. The good news is that healthy behaviors can lower your risk for heart disease.

Unhealthy Diet

Diets high in saturated fats, trans fat, and cholesterol have been linked to heart disease and related conditions, such as atherosclerosis. Also, too much salt (sodium) in the diet can raise blood pressure levels.

Physical Inactivity

Not getting enough physical activity can lead to heart disease. It also can increase the chances of having other medical conditions that are risk factors, including obesity, high blood pressure, high cholesterol, and diabetes. Regular physical activity can lower your risk for heart disease.

Obesity

Obesity is excess body fat. Obesity is linked to higher "bad" cholesterol and triglyceride levels and to lower "good" cholesterol levels. In addition to heart disease, obesity can also lead to high blood pressure and diabetes. Talk to your health care team about a plan to reduce your weight to a healthy level.

Too Much Alcohol

Drinking too much alcohol can raise blood pressure levels and the risk for heart disease. It also increases levels of triglycerides, a form of cholesterol, which can harden your arteries.

- Women should have no more than 1 drink a day.
- Men should have no more than 2 drinks a day.

Tobacco Use

Tobacco use increases the risk for heart disease and heart attack. Cigarette smoking can damage the heart and blood vessels, which increases your risk for heart conditions such as atherosclerosis and heart attack. Also, nicotine raises blood pressure, and carbon monoxide reduces the amount of oxygen that your blood can carry. Exposure to other people's secondhand smoke can increase the risk for heart disease even for nonsmokers.

Family History and Other Characteristics That Increase Risk for Heart Disease

Family members share genes, behaviors, lifestyles, and environments that can influence their health and their risk for disease. Heart disease can run in a family, and your risk for heart disease can increase based on your age, and your race, or ethnicity.

Genetics and Family History

When members of a family pass traits from one generation to another through genes, that process is called heredity.

Genetic factors likely play some role in high blood pressure, heart disease, and other related conditions. However, it is also likely that people with a family history of heart disease share common environments and other potential factors that increase their risk.

The risk for heart disease can increase even more when heredity combines with unhealthy lifestyle choices, such as smoking cigarettes and eating an unhealthy diet.

Other Characteristics

Both men and women can have heart disease. Some other characteristics that you cannot control, like your age, sex, and race or ethnicity, can affect your risk for heart disease.

- **Age**. Your risk for heart disease increases as you get older.

- **Sex**. Heart disease was the number one killer of both men and women in 2013.

- **Race or ethnicity**. In 2013 heart disease was the leading cause of death in the United States for non-Hispanic whites, non-Hispanic blacks, and American Indians. For Hispanics, and Asian Americans and Pacific Islanders, heart disease is second only to cancer as a cause of death.

Section 57.2

Coronary Artery Disease and Genetic Risk

This section includes text excerpted from "Coronary
Heart Disease," National Heart, Lung, and Blood
Institute (NHLBI), October 23, 2015.

What Is Coronary Heart Disease?

Coronary heart disease (CHD) is a disease in which a waxy substance called plaque builds up inside the coronary arteries. These arteries supply oxygen-rich blood to your heart muscle.

When plaque builds up in the arteries, the condition is called atherosclerosis. The buildup of plaque occurs over many years.

Over time, plaque can harden or rupture (break open). Hardened plaque narrows the coronary arteries and reduces the flow of oxygen-rich blood to the heart.

If the plaque ruptures, a blood clot can form on its surface. A large blood clot can mostly or completely block blood flow through a coronary artery. Over time, ruptured plaque also hardens and narrows the coronary arteries.

Overview

If the flow of oxygen-rich blood to your heart muscle is reduced or blocked, angina or a heart attack can occur.

Angina is chest pain or discomfort. It may feel like pressure or squeezing in your chest. The pain also can occur in your shoulders, arms, neck, jaw, or back. Angina pain may even feel like indigestion.

A heart attack occurs if the flow of oxygen-rich blood to a section of heart muscle is cut off. If blood flow isn't restored quickly, the section of heart muscle begins to die. Without quick treatment, a heart attack can lead to serious health problems or death.

Over time, CHD can weaken the heart muscle and lead to heart failure and arrhythmias. Heart failure is a condition in which your heart can't pump enough blood to meet your body's needs. Arrhythmias are problems with the rate or rhythm of the heartbeat.

Outlook

Lifestyle changes, medicines, and medical procedures can help prevent or treat coronary heart disease. These treatments may reduce the risk of related health problems.

What Causes Coronary Heart Disease?

Research suggests that coronary heart disease (CHD) starts when certain factors damage the inner layers of the coronary arteries. These factors include:

- Smoking
- High levels of certain fats and cholesterol in the blood
- High blood pressure
- High levels of sugar in the blood due to insulin resistance or diabetes
- Blood vessel inflammation

Plaque might begin to build up where the arteries are damaged. The buildup of plaque in the coronary arteries may start in childhood.

Over time, plaque can harden or rupture (break open). Hardened plaque narrows the coronary arteries and reduces the flow of oxygen-rich blood to the heart. This can cause angina (chest pain or discomfort).

If the plaque ruptures, blood cell fragments called platelets stick to the site of the injury. They may clump together to form blood clots.

Blood clots can further narrow the coronary arteries and worsen angina. If a clot becomes large enough, it can mostly or completely block a coronary artery and cause a heart attack.

Who Is at Risk for Coronary Heart Disease?

In the United States, coronary heart disease (CHD) is a leading cause of death for both men and women. Each year, about 370,000 Americans die from coronary heart disease. Certain traits, conditions, or habits may raise your risk for CHD. The more risk factors you have, the more likely you are to develop the disease. You can control many risk factors, which may help prevent or delay CHD.

Major Risk Factors

- **Unhealthy blood cholesterol levels**. This includes high LDL cholesterol (sometimes called "bad" cholesterol) and low HDL cholesterol (sometimes called "good" cholesterol).

- **High blood pressure**. Blood pressure is considered high if it stays at or above 140/90 mmHg over time. If you have diabetes or chronic kidney disease, high blood pressure is defined as 130/80 mmHg or higher. (The mmHg is millimeters of mercury—the units used to measure blood pressure.)

- **Smoking**. Smoking can damage and tighten blood vessels, lead to unhealthy cholesterol levels, and raise blood pressure. Smoking also can limit how much oxygen reaches the body's tissues.

- **Insulin resistance**. This condition occurs if the body can't use its own insulin properly. Insulin is a hormone that helps move blood sugar into cells where it's used for energy. Insulin resistance may lead to diabetes.

- **Diabetes**. With this disease, the body's blood sugar level is too high because the body doesn't make enough insulin or doesn't use its insulin properly.

- **Overweight or obesity**. The terms "overweight" and "obesity" refer to body weight that's greater than what is considered healthy for a certain height.

- **Metabolic syndrome**. Metabolic syndrome is the name for a group of risk factors that raises your risk for CHD and other health problems, such as diabetes and stroke.

- **Lack of physical activity**. Being physically inactive can worsen other risk factors for CHD, such as unhealthy blood cholesterol levels, high blood pressure, diabetes, and overweight or obesity.

- **Unhealthy diet.** An unhealthy diet can raise your risk for CHD. Foods that are high in saturated and trans fats, cholesterol, sodium, and sugar can worsen other risk factors for CHD.

- **Older age**. Genetic or lifestyle factors cause plaque to build up in your arteries as you age. In men, the risk for coronary heart disease increases starting at age 45. In women, the risk for coronary heart disease increases starting at age 55.

- **A family history** of early coronary heart disease is a risk factor for developing coronary heart disease, specifically if a father or brother is diagnosed before age 55, or a mother or sister is diagnosed before age 65.

Although older age and a family history of early heart disease are risk factors, it doesn't mean that you'll develop CHD if you have one or both. Controlling other risk factors often can lessen genetic influences and help prevent CHD, even in older adults.

Emerging Risk Factors

Researchers continue to study other possible risk factors for CHD. High levels of a protein called C-reactive protein (CRP) in the blood may raise the risk of CHD and heart attack. High levels of CRP are a sign of inflammation in the body. Inflammation is the body's response to injury or infection. Damage to the arteries' inner walls may trigger inflammation and help plaque grow.

Research is under way to find out whether reducing inflammation and lowering CRP levels also can reduce the risk of CHD and heart attack. High levels of triglycerides in the blood also may raise the risk of CHD, especially in women. Triglycerides are a type of fat.

Other Risks Related to Coronary Heart Disease

Other conditions and factors also may contribute to CHD, including:

- **Sleep apnea**. Sleep apnea is a common disorder in which you have one or more pauses in breathing or shallow breaths while you sleep. Untreated sleep apnea can increase your risk for high blood pressure, diabetes, and even a heart attack or stroke.

- **Stress**. Research shows that the most commonly reported "trigger" for a heart attack is an emotionally upsetting event, especially one involving anger.

- **Alcohol**. Heavy drinking can damage the heart muscle and worsen other CHD risk factors. Men should have no more than two drinks containing alcohol a day. Women should have no more than one drink containing alcohol a day.

- **Preeclampsia**. This condition can occur during pregnancy. The two main signs of preeclampsia are a rise in blood pressure and excess protein in the urine. Preeclampsia is linked to an increased lifetime risk of heart disease, including CHD, heart attack, heart failure, and high blood pressure.

Section 57.3

Researchers Discover Underlying Genetics, Marker for Stroke, Cardiovascular Disease

This section includes text excerpted from "Researchers Discover Underlying Genetics, Marker for Stroke, Cardiovascular Disease," National Institutes of Health (NIH), March 20, 2014.

Scientists studying the genomes of nearly 5,000 people have pinpointed a genetic variant tied to an increased risk for stroke, and have also uncovered new details about an important metabolic pathway that plays a major role in several common diseases. Together, their findings may provide new clues to underlying genetic and biochemical influences in the development of stroke and cardiovascular disease, and may also help lead to new treatment strategies.

"Our findings have the potential to identify new targets in the prevention and treatment of stroke, cardiovascular disease and many other common diseases," said Stephen R. Williams, Ph.D., a postdoctoral fellow at the University of Virginia Cardiovascular Research Center and the University of Virginia Center for Public Health Genomics, Charlottesville.

Dr. Williams, Michele Sale, Ph.D., associate professor of medicine, Brad Worrall, M.D., professor of neurology and public health sciences, all at the University of Virginia, and their team reported their findings March 20, 2014 in PLoS Genetics. The investigators were supported by the National Human Genome Research Institute (NHGRI) Genomics and Randomized Trials Network (GARNET) program.

Stroke is the fourth leading cause of death and a major cause of adult disability in this country, yet its underlying genetics have been difficult to understand. Numerous genetic and environmental factors can contribute to a person having a stroke. "Our goals were to break down the risk factors for stroke," Dr. Williams said.

The researchers focused on one particular biochemical pathway called the folate one-carbon metabolism (FOCM) pathway. They knew that abnormally high blood levels of the amino acid homocysteine are associated with an increased risk of common diseases such as stroke, cardiovascular disease and dementia. Homocysteine is a breakdown product of methionine, which is part of the FOCM pathway. The same pathway can affect many important cellular processes, including the methylation of proteins, DNA and RNA. DNA methylation is a mechanism that cells use to control which genes are turned on and off, and when.

But clinical trials of homocysteine-lowering therapies have not prevented disease, and the genetics underlying high homocysteine levels–and methionine metabolism gone awry–are not well defined.

Dr. Williams and his colleagues conducted genome-wide association studies of participants from two large long-term projects: the Vitamin Intervention for Stroke Prevention (VISP), a trial looking at ways to prevent a second ischemic stroke, and the Framingham Heart Study (FHS), which has followed the cardiovascular health and disease in a general population for decades. They also measured methionine metabolism—the ability to convert methionine to homocysteine—in both groups. In all, they studied 2,100 VISP participants and 2,710 FHS subjects.

In a genome-wide association study, researchers scan the genome to identify specific genomic variants associated with a disease. In this case, the scientists were trying to identify variants associated with a trait—the ability to metabolize methionine into homocysteine.

Investigators identified variants in five genes in the FOCM pathway that were associated with differences in a person's ability to convert methionine to homocysteine. They found that among the five genes, one—the ALDH1L1 gene—was also strongly associated with stroke in the Framingham study. When the gene is not working properly, it has been associated with a breakdown in a normal cellular process called programmed cell death, and cancer cell survival.

They also made important discoveries about the methionine-homocysteine process. "GNMT produces a protein that converts methionine to homocysteine. Of the five genes that we identified, it was the one most significantly associated with this process," Dr. Williams said. "The analyses suggest that differences in GNMT are the major drivers behind the differences in methionine metabolism in humans."

"It's striking that the genes are in the same pathway, so we know that the genomic variants affecting that pathway contribute to the variability in disease and risk that we're seeing," he said. "We may have found how genetic information controls the regulation of GNMT."

The group determined that the five genes accounted for 6 percent of the difference in individuals' ability to process methionine into homocysteine among those in the VISP trial. The genes also accounted for

13 percent of the difference in those participants in the FHS, a remarkable result given the complex nature of methionine metabolism and its impact on cerebrovascular risk. In many complex diseases, genomic variants often account for less than 5 percent of such differences.

"This is a great example of the kinds of successful research efforts coming out of the GARNET program," said program director Ebony Madden, Ph.D. "GARNET scientists aim to identify variants that affect treatment response by doing association studies in randomized trials. These results show that variants in genes are associated with the differences in homocysteine levels in individuals."

The association of the ALDH1L1 gene variant with stroke is just one example of how the findings may potentially lead to new prevention efforts, and help develop new targets for treating stroke and heart disease, Dr. Williams said.

"As genome sequencing becomes more widespread, clinicians may be able to determine if a person's risk for abnormally high levels of homocysteine is elevated," he said. "Changes could be made to an individual's diet because of a greater risk for stroke and cardiovascular disease."

The investigators plan to study the other four genes in the pathway to try to better understand their potential roles in stroke and cardiovascular disease risk.

Chapter 58

Hypertension and Genetics

Description of High Blood Pressure

High blood pressure is a common disease in which blood flows through blood vessels (arteries) at higher than normal pressures.

Measuring Blood Pressure

Blood pressure is the force of blood pushing against the walls of the arteries as the heart pumps blood. High blood pressure, sometimes called hypertension, happens when this force is too high. Health care workers check blood pressure readings the same way for children, teens, and adults. They use a gauge, stethoscope or electronic sensor, and a blood pressure cuff. With this equipment, they measure:

- **Systolic Pressure:** blood pressure when the heart beats while pumping blood

This chapter contains text excerpted from the following sources: Text under the heading "Description of High Blood Pressure?" is excerpted from "High Blood Pressure," National Heart, Lung, and Blood Institute (NHLBI), September 10, 2015; Text under the heading "Family History and Other Characteristics That Increase Risk for High Blood Pressure" is excerpted from "Family History and Other Characteristics That Increase Risk for High Blood Pressure," Centers for Disease Control and Prevention, July 7, 2014; Text under the heading "Pulmonary Arterial Hypertension" is excerpted from "Pulmonary Arterial Hypertension," Genetics Home Reference (GHR), January 2016.

- **Diastolic Pressure:** blood pressure when the heart is at rest between beats

Health care workers write blood pressure numbers with the systolic number above the diastolic number.
For example:
118/76 mmHg
People read "118 over 76"
millimeters of mercury.

Normal Blood Pressure

Normal blood pressure for adults is defined as a systolic pressure below 120 mmHg and a diastolic pressure below 80 mmHg. It is normal for blood pressures to change when you sleep, wake up, or are excited or nervous. When you are active, it is normal for your blood pressure to increase. However, once the activity stops, your blood pressure returns to your normal baseline range.

Blood pressure normally rises with age and body size. Newborn babies often have very low blood pressure numbers that are considered normal for babies, while older teens have numbers similar to adults.

Abnormal Blood Pressure

Abnormal increases in blood pressure are defined as having blood pressures higher than 120/80 mmHg. The following table outlines and defines high blood pressure severity levels.

Stages of High Blood Pressure in Adults

Table 58.1. Systolic and Diastolic Pressures

Stages	Systolic		Diastolic
Prehypertension	120–139	OR	80–89
High blood pressure Stage 1	140–159	OR	90–99
High blood pressure Stage 2	160 or higher	OR	100 or higher

The ranges in the table are blood pressure guides for adults who do not have any short-term serious illnesses. **People with diabetes or chronic kidney disease should keep their blood pressure below 130/80 mmHg.**

640

Although blood pressure increases seen in prehypertension are less than those used to diagnose high blood pressure, prehypertension can progress to high blood pressure and should be taken seriously. Over time, consistently high blood pressure weakens and damages your blood vessels, which can lead to complications.

Types of High Blood Pressure

There are two main types of high blood pressure: primary and secondary high blood pressure.

1. Primary High Blood Pressure

Primary, or essential, high blood pressure is the most common type of high blood pressure. This type of high blood pressure tends to develop over years as a person ages.

2. Secondary High Blood Pressure

Secondary high blood pressure is caused by another medical condition or use of certain medicines. This type usually resolves after the cause is treated or removed.

Causes of High Blood Pressure

Changes, either from genes or the environment, in the body's normal functions may cause high blood pressure, including changes to kidney fluid and salt balances, the renin-angiotensin-aldosterone system, sympathetic nervous system activity, and blood vessel structure and function.

Biology and High Blood Pressure

Researchers continue to study how various changes in normal body functions cause high blood pressure. The key functions affected in high blood pressure include:

- Kidney fluid and salt balances
- Renin-angiotensin-aldosterone system
- Sympathetic nervous system activity
- Blood vessel structure and function

Kidney Fluid and Salt Balances

The kidneys normally regulate the body's salt balance by retaining sodium and water and excreting potassium. Imbalances in this kidney function can expand blood volumes, which can cause high blood pressure.

Renin-Angiotensin-Aldosterone System

The renin-angiotensin-aldosterone system makes angiotensin and aldosterone hormones. Angiotensin narrows or constricts blood vessels, which can lead to an increase in blood pressure. Aldosterone controls how the kidneys balance fluid and salt levels. Increased aldosterone levels or activity may change this kidney function, leading to increased blood volumes and high blood pressure.

Sympathetic Nervous System Activity

The sympathetic nervous system has important functions in blood pressure regulation, including heart rate, blood pressure, and breathing rate. Researchers are investigating whether imbalances in this system cause high blood pressure.

Blood Vessel Structure and Function

Changes in the structure and function of small and large arteries may contribute to high blood pressure. The angiotensin pathway and the immune system may stiffen small and large arteries, which can affect blood pressure.

Genetic Causes of High Blood Pressure

Much of the understanding of the body systems involved in high blood pressure has come from genetic studies. High blood pressure often runs in families. Years of research have identified many genes and other mutations associated with high blood pressure, some in the renal salt regulatory and renin-angiotensin-aldosterone pathways. However, these known genetic factors only account for 2 to 3 percent of all cases. Emerging research suggests that certain DNA changes during fetal development also may cause the development of high blood pressure later in life.

Environmental Causes of High Blood Pressure

Environmental causes of high blood pressure include unhealthy lifestyle habits, being overweight or obese, and medicines.

Unhealthy Lifestyle Habits

Unhealthy lifestyle habits can cause high blood pressure, including:

- High dietary sodium intake and sodium sensitivity
- Drinking excess amounts of alcohol
- Lack of physical activity

Overweight and Obesity

Research studies show that being overweight or obese can increase the resistance in the blood vessels, causing the heart to work harder and leading to high blood pressure.

Medicines

Prescription medicines such as asthma or hormone therapies, including birth control pills and estrogen, and over-the-counter medicines such as cold relief medicines may cause this form of high blood pressure. This happens because medicines can change the way your body controls fluid and salt balances, cause your blood vessels to constrict, or impact the renin-angiotensin-aldosterone system leading to high blood pressure.

Other Medical Causes of High Blood Pressure

Other medical causes of high blood pressure include other medical conditions such as chronic kidney disease, sleep apnea, thyroid problems, or certain tumors. This happens because these other conditions change the way your body controls fluids, sodium, and hormones in your blood, which leads to secondary high blood pressure.

Risk Factors for High Blood Pressure

Anyone can develop high blood pressure; however, age, race or ethnicity, being overweight, gender, lifestyle habits, and a family history of high blood pressure can increase your risk for developing high blood pressure.

Age

Blood pressure tends to rise with age. About 65 percent of Americans age 60 or older have high blood pressure. However, the risk for prehypertension and high blood pressure is increasing for children and teens, possibly due to the rise in the number of overweight children and teens.

Race / Ethnicity

High blood pressure is more common in African American adults than in Caucasian or Hispanic American adults. Compared with these ethnic groups, African Americans:

- Tend to get high blood pressure earlier in life.
- Often, on average, have higher blood pressure numbers.
- Are less likely to achieve target blood pressure goals with treatment.

Overweight

You are more likely to develop prehypertension or high blood pressure if you're overweight or obese. The terms "overweight" and "obese" refer to body weight that's greater than what is considered healthy for a certain height.

Gender

Before age 55, men are more likely than women to develop high blood pressure. After age 55, women are more likely than men to develop high blood pressure.

Lifestyle Habits

Unhealthy lifestyle habits can raise your risk for high blood pressure, and they include:

- Eating too much sodium or too little potassium
- Lack of physical activity
- Drinking too much alcohol
- Stress

Family History and Other Characteristics That Increase Risk for High Blood Pressure

Family members share genes, behaviors, lifestyles, and environments that can influence their health and their risk for disease. High blood pressure can run in a family, and your risk for high blood pressure can increase based on your age and your race or ethnicity.

Genetics and Family History

When members of a family pass traits from one generation to another through genes, that process is called heredity.

Genetic factors likely play some role in high blood pressure, heart disease, and other related conditions. However, it is also likely that people with a family history of high blood pressure share common environments and other potential factors that increase their risk.

The risk for high blood pressure can increase even more when heredity combines with unhealthy lifestyle choices, such as smoking cigarettes and eating an unhealthy diet.

Family health history is a record of the diseases and health conditions that people in your family have had. Family health history is a useful tool for understanding health risks and preventing disease. To help people collect and organize their family history information, CDC's Office of Public Health Genomics collaborated with the Surgeon General and other federal agencies to develop a Web-based tool called "My Family Health Portrait."

Other Characteristics

Both men and women can have high blood pressure. Some other characteristics that you cannot control—like your age, race, or ethnicity—can affect your risk for high blood pressure.

Age. Because your blood pressure tends to rise as you get older, your risk for high blood pressure increases with age. About 9 of 10 Americans will develop high blood pressure during their lifetimes.

Sex. Women are about as likely as men to develop high blood pressure at some point during their lives.

Race or ethnicity. Blacks develop high blood pressure more often than whites, Hispanics, Asians, Pacific Islanders, American Indians, or Alaska Natives. Compared to whites, blacks also develop high blood pressure earlier in life.

Pulmonary Arterial Hypertension

Pulmonary arterial hypertension is a progressive disorder characterized by abnormally high blood pressure (hypertension) in the pulmonary artery, the blood vessel that carries blood from the heart to the lungs. Pulmonary arterial hypertension is one form of a broader condition known as pulmonary hypertension. Pulmonary hypertension occurs when most of the very small arteries throughout the lungs narrow in diameter, which increases the resistance to blood flow through the lungs. To overcome the increased resistance, blood pressure increases in the pulmonary artery and in the right ventricle of the heart, which is the chamber that pumps blood into the pulmonary artery. Ultimately, the increased blood pressure can damage the right ventricle of the heart.

Signs and symptoms of pulmonary arterial hypertension occur when increased blood pressure cannot fully overcome the elevated resistance. As a result, the flow of oxygenated blood from the lungs to the rest of the body is insufficient. Shortness of breath (dyspnea) during exertion and fainting spells are the most common symptoms of pulmonary arterial hypertension. People with this disorder may experience additional symptoms, particularly as the condition worsens. Other symptoms include dizziness, swelling (edema) of the ankles or legs, chest pain, and a rapid heart rate.

Frequency

In the United States, about 1,000 new cases of pulmonary arterial hypertension are diagnosed each year. This disorder is twice as common in females as in males.

Genetic Changes

Mutations in the BMPR2 gene are the most common genetic cause of pulmonary arterial hypertension. This gene plays a role in regulating the number of cells in certain tissues. Researchers suggest that a mutation in this gene promotes cell division or prevents cell death, resulting in an overgrowth of cells in small arteries throughout the lungs. As a result, these arteries narrow in diameter, which increases the resistance to blood flow. Blood pressure in the pulmonary artery and the right ventricle of the heart increases to overcome the increased resistance to blood flow.

Mutations in several additional genes have also been found to cause pulmonary arterial hypertension, but they are much less common causes of the disorder than are BMPR2 gene mutations. Variations in other genes may increase the risk of developing pulmonary arterial hypertension or modify the course of the disease (usually making it more severe). Changes in as-yet-unidentified genes may also be associated with this condition.

Although pulmonary arterial hypertension often occurs on its own, it can also be part of syndromes that affect many parts of the body. For example, this condition is occasionally found in people with systemic scleroderma, systemic lupus erythematosus, critical congenital heart disease, or Down syndrome.

Researchers have also identified nongenetic factors that increase the risk of developing pulmonary arterial hypertension. These include certain drugs used as appetite suppressants and several illegal drugs, such as cocaine and methamphetamine. Pulmonary arterial hypertension is also a rare complication of certain infectious diseases, including HIV and schistosomiasis.

Inheritance Pattern

Pulmonary arterial hypertension is usually sporadic, which means it occurs in individuals with no known family history of the disorder. These non-familial cases are described as idiopathic pulmonary arterial hypertension. About 20 percent of these cases are caused by mutations in one of the genes known to be associated with the disease, but most of the time a causative gene mutation has not been identified.

Inherited cases of this disorder are known as familial pulmonary arterial hypertension. When the condition is inherited, it most often has an autosomal dominant pattern of inheritance, which means one copy of an altered gene in each cell is sufficient to cause the disorder. However, many people with an altered gene never develop pulmonary arterial hypertension; this phenomenon is called reduced penetrance.

Other Names for This Condition

- Ayerza syndrome
- familial primary pulmonary hypertension
- FPPH
- idiopathic pulmonary hypertension
- PAH
- PPH
- PPHT
- primary pulmonary hypertension
- sporadic primary pulmonary hypertension

Chapter 59

Heredity and Movement Disorders

Chapter Contents

Section 59.1

Genetics of Essential Tremor

This section contains text excerpted from the following sources: Text beginning with the heading "What Is Essential Tremor?" is excerpted from "Essential Tremor," Genetics Home Reference (GHR), National Institutes of Health (NIH), March 21, 2016; Text under the heading "Is There Any Treatment?" is excerpted from "NINDS Essential Tremor Information Page," National Institute of Neurological Disorders and Stroke (NINDS), April 25, 2013.

What Is Essential Tremor?

Essential tremor is a movement disorder that causes involuntary, rhythmic shaking (tremor), especially in the hands. It is distinguished from tremor that results from other disorders or known causes, such as Parkinson disease or head trauma. Essential tremor usually occurs alone, without other neurological signs or symptoms. However, some experts think that essential tremor can include additional features, such as mild balance problems.

Essential tremor usually occurs with movements and can occur during many different types of activities, such as eating, drinking, or writing. Essential tremor can also occur when the muscles are opposing gravity, such as when the hands are extended. It is usually not evident at rest.

In addition to the hands and arms, muscles of the trunk, face, head, and neck may also exhibit tremor in this disorder; the legs and feet are less often involved. Head tremor may appear as a "yes-yes" or "no-no" movement while the affected individual is seated or standing. In some people with essential tremor, the tremor may affect the voice (vocal tremor).

Essential tremor does not shorten the lifespan. However, it may interfere with fine motor skills such as using eating utensils, writing, shaving, or applying makeup, and in some cases these and other activities of daily living can be greatly impaired. Symptoms of essential tremor may be aggravated by emotional stress, anxiety, fatigue, hunger, caffeine, cigarette smoking, or temperature extremes.

Essential tremor may appear at any age but is most common in the elderly. Some studies have suggested that people with essential tremor have a higher than average risk of developing neurological conditions including Parkinson disease or sensory problems such as hearing loss, especially in individuals whose tremor appears after age 65.

How Common Is Essential Tremor?

Essential tremor is a common disorder, affecting up to 10 million people in the United States. Estimates of its prevalence vary widely because several other disorders, as well as other factors such as certain medications, can result in similar tremors. In addition, mild cases are often not brought to medical attention, or may not be detected in clinical exams that do not include the particular circumstances in which an individual's tremor occurs. Severe cases are often misdiagnosed as Parkinson disease.

What Genes Are Related to Essential Tremor?

The causes of essential tremor are unknown. Researchers are studying several areas (loci) on particular chromosomes that may be linked to essential tremor, but no specific genetic associations have been confirmed. Several genes as well as environmental factors likely help determine an individual's risk of developing this complex condition. The specific changes in the nervous system that account for the signs and symptoms of essential tremor are unknown.

How Do People Inherit Essential Tremor?

Essential tremor can be passed through generations in families, but the inheritance pattern varies. In most affected families, essential tremor appears to be inherited in an autosomal dominant pattern, which means one copy of an altered gene in each cell is sufficient to cause the disorder, although no genes that cause essential tremor have been identified. In other families, the inheritance pattern is unclear. Essential tremor may also appear in people with no history of the disorder in their family.

In some families, some individuals have essential tremor while others have other movement disorders, such as involuntary muscle tensing (dystonia). The potential genetic connection between essential tremor and other movement disorders is an active area of research.

Is There Any Treatment?

There is no definitive cure for essential tremor. Symptomatic drug therapy may include propranolol or other beta blockers and primidone, an anticonvulsant drug. Eliminating tremor "triggers" such as caffeine and other stimulants from the diet is often recommended. Physical and occupational therapy may help to reduce tremor and improve coordination and muscle control for some individuals. Deep brain stimulation uses a surgically implanted, battery-operated medical device called a neurostimulator to deliver electrical stimulation to targeted areas of the brain that control movement, temporarily blocking the nerve signals that cause tremor. Other surgical intervention is effective but may have side effects.

What Is the Prognosis?

Although essential tremor is not life-threatening, it can make it harder to perform daily tasks and is embarrassing to some people. Tremor frequency may decrease as the person ages, but the severity may increase, affecting the person's ability to perform certain tasks or activities of daily living. In many people the tremor may be mild throughout life.

Section 59.2

Parkinson Disease: Genetic Links

This section includes text excerpted from "Parkinson's Disease:
Hope Through Research," National Institute of Neurological
Disorders and Stroke (NINDS), March 21, 2016.

What Is Parkinson Disease?

Parkinson disease (PD) is a degenerative disorder of the central nervous system that belongs to a group of conditions called movement disorders. It is both chronic, meaning it persists over a long period of time, and progressive, meaning its symptoms grow worse over time.

As nerve cells (neurons) in parts of the brain become impaired or die, people may begin to notice problems with movement, tremor, stiffness in the limbs or the trunk of the body, or impaired balance. As these symptoms become more pronounced, people may have difficulty walking, talking, or completing other simple tasks. Not everyone with one or more of these symptoms has PD, as the symptoms appear in other diseases as well.

The precise cause of PD is unknown, although some cases of PD are hereditary and can be traced to specific genetic mutations. Most cases are sporadic—that is, the disease does not typically run in families. It is thought that PD likely results from a combination of genetic susceptibility and exposure to one or more unknown environmental factors that trigger the disease.

PD is the most common form of parkinsonism, in which disorders of other causes produce features and symptoms that closely resemble Parkinson disease. While most forms of parkinsonism have no known cause, there are cases in which the cause is known or suspected or where the symptoms result from another disorder.

No cure for PD exists today, but research is ongoing and medications or surgery can often provide substantial improvement with motor symptoms.

What Causes the Disease?

Parkinson disease occurs when nerve cells, or neurons, in the brain die or become impaired. Although many brain areas are affected, the most common symptoms result from the loss of neurons in an area near the base of the brain called the *substantia nigra*. Normally, the neurons in this area produce an important brain chemical known as *dopamine*. Dopamine is a chemical messenger responsible for transmitting signals between the substantia nigra and the next "relay station" of the brain, the *corpus striatum*, to produce smooth, purposeful movement. Loss of dopamine results in abnormal nerve firing patterns within the brain that cause impaired movement.

Studies have shown that most people with Parkinson have lost 60 to 80 percent or more of the dopamine-producing cells in the substantia nigra by the time symptoms appear, and that people with PD also have loss of the nerve endings that produce the *neurotransmitter* norepinephrine. Norepinephrine, which is closely related to dopamine, is the main chemical messenger of the sympathetic nervous system, the part of the nervous system that controls many automatic functions of the body, such as pulse and blood pressure. The loss of norepinephrine might explain several of the non-motor features seen in PD, including fatigue and abnormalities of blood pressure regulation.

The affected brain cells of people with PD contain Lewy bodies— deposits of the protein alpha-synuclein. Researchers do not yet know why Lewy bodies form or what role they play in the disease. Some research suggests that the cell's protein disposal system may fail in people with PD, causing proteins to build up to harmful levels and trigger cell death. Additional studies have found evidence that clumps of protein that develop inside brain cells of people with PD may contribute to the death of neurons. Some researchers speculate that the protein buildup in Lewy bodies is part of an unsuccessful attempt to protect the cell from the toxicity of smaller aggregates, or collections, of synuclein.

Genetics. Scientists have identified several genetic mutations associated with PD, including the alpha-synuclein gene, and many more genes have been tentatively linked to the disorder. Studying the genes responsible for inherited cases of PD can help researchers understand both inherited and sporadic cases. The same genes and proteins that are altered in inherited cases may also be altered in sporadic cases by environmental toxins or other factors. Researchers also hope that discovering genes will help identify new ways of treating PD.

Environment. Exposure to certain toxins has caused parkinsonian symptoms in rare circumstances (such as exposure to MPTP, an illicit drug, or in miners exposed to the metal manganese). Other still-unidentified environmental factors may also cause PD in genetically susceptible individuals.

Mitochondria. Several lines of research suggest that mitochondria may play a role in the development of PD. Mitochondria are the energy-producing components of the cell and abnormalities in the mitochondria are major sources of free radicals—molecules that damage membranes, proteins, DNA, and other parts of the cell. This damage is often referred to as oxidative stress. Oxidative stress-related changes, including free radical damage to DNA, proteins, and fats, have been detected in the brains of individuals with PD. Some mutations that affect mitochondrial function have been identified as causes of PD.

While mitochondrial dysfunction, oxidative stress, inflammation, toxins, and many other cellular processes may contribute to PD, the actual cause of the cell loss death in PD is still undetermined.

What Genes Are Linked to Parkinson Disease?

Several genes have been definitively linked to PD. The first to be identified was alpha-synuclein. In the 1990s, researchers at National Institutes of Health and other institutions studied the genetic profiles of a large Italian family and three Greek families with familial PD and found that their disease was related to a mutation in this gene. They found a second alpha-synuclein mutation in a German family with PD. These findings prompted studies of the role of alpha-synuclein in PD, which led to the discovery that Lewy bodies seen in all cases of PD contain alpha-synuclein protein. This discovery revealed the link between hereditary and sporadic forms of the disease.

In 2003, researchers studying inherited PD discovered that the disease in one large family was caused by a triplication of the normal alpha-synuclein gene on one copy of chromosome 4 (a chromosome is a threadlike structure of a protein and the genetic material DNA). This triplication caused people in the affected family to produce too much of the normal alpha-synuclein. This study showed that an excess of the normal form of synuclein could result in PD, just as the abnormal form does.

Other genes linked to PD include parkin, *DJ-1, PINK1,* and *LRRK2*. *DJ-1* and *PINK1* cause rare, early-onset forms of PD. The parkin gene is translated into a protein that normally helps cells break down and recycle proteins. *DJ-1* normally helps regulate gene activity and protect cells from oxidative stress. *PINK1* codes for a protein active in mitochondria. Mutations in this gene appear to increase susceptibility to cellular stress.

Mutations in *LRRK2* were originally identified in several English and Basque families as a cause of a late-onset PD. Subsequent studies have identified mutations of this gene in other families with PD as well as in a small percentage of people with apparently sporadic PD. *LRRK2* mutations are a major cause of PD in North Africa and the Middle East.

Another interesting association is with the *GBA* gene, which makes the enzyme glucocerebrosidase. Mutations in both *GBA* genes cause Gaucher disease (in which fatty acids, oils, waxes, and steroids accumulate in the brain), but different changes in this gene are associated with an increased risk for Parkinson disease as well. Investigators seek to understand what this association can tell us about PD risk factors and potential treatments.

Who Gets Parkinson Disease?

Estimates suggest that about 50,000 Americans are diagnosed with PD each year, although some estimates are much higher. Getting an accurate count of the number of cases is difficult because many people in the early stages of the disease may assume their symptoms are the result of normal aging and do not seek medical attention. Diagnosis is sometimes complicated by the fact that other conditions may produce symptoms of PD and there is no definitive test for the disease. People with PD may sometimes be told by their doctors that they have other disorders, and people with PD-like diseases may be incorrectly diagnosed as having PD.

PD affects about 50 percent more men than women, and the reasons for this discrepancy are unclear. While PD occurs in people throughout the world, a number of studies have found a higher incidence in developed countries. Other studies have found an increased risk in people who live in rural areas with increased pesticide use. However, those apparent risks are not fully characterized.

One clear risk factor for PD is age. The average age of onset is 60 years, and the incidence rises significantly with advancing age. However, about 5 to 10 percent of people with PD have "early-onset" disease that begins before the age of 50. Some early-onset cases are linked to specific gene mutations such as parkin. People with one or more close relatives who have PD have an increased risk of developing the disease themselves, but the total risk is still about 2 to 5 percent unless the family has a known gene mutation for the disease. An estimated 15 to 25 percent of people with PD have a known relative with the disease.

In very rare cases, parkinsonian symptoms may appear in people before the age of 20. This condition is called juvenile parkinsonism. It often begins with *dystonia* and *bradykinesia*, and the symptoms often improve with levodopa medication.

What Are the Symptoms of the Disease?

The four primary symptoms of PD are:

1. **Tremor**. The tremor associated with PD has a characteristic appearance. Typically, the tremor takes the form of a rhythmic back-and-forth motion at a rate of 4–6 beats per second. It may involve the thumb and forefinger and appear as a "pill rolling" tremor. Tremor often begins in a hand, although sometimes a foot or the jaw is affected first. It is most obvious when the hand is at rest or when a person is under stress. Tremor

usually disappears during sleep or improves with intentional movement. It is usually the first symptom that causes people to seek medical attention.

2. **Rigidity**. Rigidity, or a resistance to movement, affects most people with PD. The muscles remain constantly tense and contracted so that the person aches or feels stiff. The rigidity becomes obvious when another person tries to move the individual's arm, which will move only in ratchet-like or short, jerky movements known as "cogwheel" rigidity.

3. **Bradykinesia**. This slowing down of spontaneous and automatic movement is particularly frustrating because it may make simple tasks difficult. The person cannot rapidly perform routine movements. Activities once performed quickly and easily—such as washing or dressing—may take much longer. There is often a decrease in facial expressions.

4. **Postural instability**. Postural instability, or impaired balance, causes affected individuals to fall easily.

PD does not affect everyone the same way, and the rate of progression and the particular symptoms differ among individuals.

PD symptoms typically begin on one side of the body. However, the disease eventually affects both sides. Even after the disease involves both sides of the body, the symptoms are often less severe on one side than on the other.

Friends or family members may be the first to notice changes in someone with early PD. They may see that the person's face lacks expression and animation (known as "masked face") or that the person moves more slowly.

Early symptoms of PD may be subtle and occur gradually. Affected people may feel mild tremors or have difficulty getting out of a chair. Activities may take longer to complete than in the past and individuals may note some stiffness in addition to slowness. They may notice that they speak too softly or that their handwriting is slow and looks cramped or small. This very early period may last a long time before the more classical and obvious motor (movement) symptoms appear.

As the disease progresses, the symptoms of Parkinson disease may begin to interfere with daily activities. Affected individuals may not be able to hold utensils steady or they may find that the shaking makes reading a newspaper difficult. People with PD often develop a so-called parkinsonian gait that includes a tendency to lean forward, taking small quick steps as if hurrying (called festination), and reduced swinging in one or both arms. They may have trouble initiating movement (start hesitation), and they may stop suddenly as they walk (freezing).

A number of other symptoms may accompany PD, and some can be treated with medication or physical therapy.

- **Depression**. This common disorder may appear early in the course of the disease, even before other symptoms are noticed. Some people lose their motivation and become dependent on family members. Fortunately, depression typically can be treated successfully with antidepressant medications such as amytriptyline or fluoxetine.

- **Emotional changes**. Some people with PD become fearful and insecure, while others may become irritable or uncharacteristically pessimistic.

- **Difficulty with swallowing and chewing**. Muscles used in swallowing may work less efficiently in later stages of the disease. Food and saliva may collect in the mouth and back of the throat, which can result in choking or drooling. These problems may also make it difficult to get adequate nutrition. Speech-language therapists, occupational therapists (who help people learn new ways to perform activities of daily living), and dieticians can often help with these problems.

- **Speech changes**. About half of all individuals with PD have speech difficulties that may be characterized as speaking too softly or in a monotone. Some may hesitate before speaking, slur, or speak too fast. A speech therapist may be able to help these individuals reduce some of these problems.

- **Urinary problems or constipation**. In some people with PD, bladder and bowel problems can occur due to the improper functioning of the autonomic nervous system, which is responsible for regulating smooth muscle activity. Medications can effectively treat some of these symptoms.

- **Skin problems**. In PD, the skin on the face may become oily, particularly on the forehead and at the sides of the nose. The scalp may become oily too, resulting in dandruff. In other cases, the skin can become very dry. Standard treatments for skin problems can help.

- **Sleep problems**. Sleep problems are common in PD and include difficulty staying asleep at night, restless sleep, nightmares and emotional dreams, and drowsiness or sudden sleep onset during the day. Another common problem is "REM behavior disorder," in which people act out their dreams, potentially resulting in injury to themselves or their bed partners. The medications used to treat PD may contribute to some of these sleep issues. Many of these problems respond to specific therapies.

- **Dementia or other cognitive problems**. Some people with PD may develop memory problems and slow thinking. Cognitive problems become more severe in late stages of PD, and a diagnosis of Parkinson disease dementia (PDD) may be given. Memory, social judgment, language, reasoning, or other mental skills may be affected. There is currently no way to halt PD dementia, but drugs such as rivastigmine, donepezil, or memantine may help. The medications used to treat the motor symptoms of PD may cause confusion and hallucinations.

- **Orthostatic hypotension**. Orthostatic hypotension is a sudden drop in blood pressure when a person stands up from a lying-down or seated position. This may cause dizziness, lightheadedness, and, in extreme cases, loss of balance or fainting. Studies have suggested that, in PD, this problem results from a loss of nerve endings in the sympathetic nervous system that controls heart rate, blood pressure, and other automatic functions in the body. The medications used to treat PD may also contribute to this symptom. Orthostatic hypotension may improve by increasing salt intake. Physicians treating the disorder may also reduce anti-hypertension drug dosage or by prescribing medications such as fludrocortisone.

- **Muscle cramps and dystonia**. The rigidity and lack of normal movement associated with PD often causes muscle cramps, especially in the legs and toes. Massage, stretching, and applying heat may help with these cramps. PD can also be associated with dystonia—sustained muscle contractions that cause forced or twisted positions. Dystonia in PD is often caused by fluctuations in the body's level of dopamine. Management strategies may involve adjusting medications.

- **Pain**. Many people with PD develop aching muscles and joints because of the rigidity and abnormal postures often associated with the disease. Treatment with levodopa and other dopaminergic drugs often alleviates these pains to some extent. Certain exercises may help.

- **Fatigue and loss of energy**. Many people with PD often have fatigue, especially late in the day. Fatigue may be associated with depression or sleep disorders, but it may also result from muscle stress or from overdoing activity when the person feels well. Fatigue may also result from akinesia—trouble initiating or carrying out movement. Exercise, good sleep habits, staying mentally active, and not forcing too many activities in a short time may help to alleviate fatigue.

- **Sexual dysfunction**. Because of its effects on nerve signals from the brain, PD may cause sexual dysfunction. PD-related depression or use of certain medications may also cause decreased sex drive and other problems. People should discuss these issues with their physician as they may be treatable.

Hallucinations, delusions, and other psychotic symptoms can be caused by the drugs prescribed for PD. Reducing PD medications dosages or changing medications may be necessary if hallucinations occur. If such measures are not effective, doctors sometimes prescribe drugs called atypical antipsychotics, which include clozapine and quetiapine. The typical antipsychotic drugs, which include haloperidol, worsen the motor symptoms of PD and should not be used.

Chapter 60

Genetic Factors in Obesity

Adult Obesity Causes and Consequences

Obesity is a complex health issue to address. Obesity results from a combination of causes and contributing factors, including individual factors such as behavior and genetics. Behaviors can include dietary patterns, physical activity, inactivity, medication use, and other exposures. Additional contributing factors in our society include the food and physical activity environment, education and skills, and food marketing and promotion.

Obesity is a serious concern because it is associated with poorer mental health outcomes, reduced quality of life, and the leading causes of death in the United States and worldwide, including diabetes, heart disease, stroke, and some types of cancer.

Behavior

Healthy behaviors include a healthy diet pattern and regular physical activity. Energy balance of the number of calories consumed from

---

This chapter contains text excerpted from the following sources: Text under the heading "Adult Obesity Causes and Consequences" is excerpted from "Adult Obesity Causes & Consequences," Centers for Disease Control and Prevention (CDC), June 16, 2015.; Text under the heading "Behavior, Environment, and Genetic Factors All Have a Role in Causing People to Be Overweight and Obese" is excerpted from "Behavior, Environment, and Genetic Factors All Have a Role in Causing People to Be Overweight and Obese," Centers for Disease Control and Prevention (CDC)May 10, 2013.

foods and beverages with the number of calories the body uses for activity plays a role in preventing excess weight gain. A healthy diet pattern follows the Dietary Guidelines for Americans which emphasizes eating whole grains, fruits, vegetables, lean protein, low-fat and fat-free dairy products and drinking water. The Physical Activity Guidelines for Americans recommends adults do at least 150 minutes of moderate intensity activity or 75 minutes of vigorous intensity activity, or a combination of both, along with 2 days of strength training per week.

Having a healthy diet pattern and regular physical activity is also important for long term health benefits and prevention of chronic diseases such as Type 2 diabetes and heart disease.

Community Environment

People and families may make decisions based on their environment or community. For example, a person may choose not to walk or bike to the store or to work because of a lack of sidewalks or safe bike trails. Community, home, child care, school, health care, and workplace settings can all influence people's daily behaviors. Therefore, it is important to create environments in these locations that make it easier to engage in physical activity and eat a healthy diet.

Other Factors: Diseases and Drugs

Some illnesses may lead to obesity or weight gain. These may include Cushing disease, and polycystic ovary syndrome. Drugs such as steroids and some antidepressants may also cause weight gain. The science continues to emerge on the role of other factors in energy balance and weight gain such as chemical exposures and the role of the microbiome.

A health care provider can help you learn more about your health habits and history in order to tell you whether behaviors, illnesses, medications, and/or psychological factors are contributing to weight gain or making weight loss hard.

Consequences of Obesity

Health Consequences

People who are obese, compared to those with a normal or healthy weight, are at increased risk for many serious diseases and health conditions, including the following:

- All-causes of death (mortality)
- High blood pressure (Hypertension)
- High LDL cholesterol, low HDL cholesterol, or high levels of tri-glycerides (Dyslipidemia)
- Type 2 diabetes
- Coronary heart disease
- Stroke
- Gallbladder disease
- Osteoarthritis (a breakdown of cartilage and bone within a joint)
- Sleep apnea and breathing problems
- Some cancers (endometrial, breast, colon, kidney, gallbladder, and liver)
- Low quality of life
- Mental illness such as clinical depression, anxiety, and other mental disorders
- Body pain and difficulty with physical functioning

Economic and Societal Consequences

Obesity and its associated health problems have a significant economic impact on the U.S. healthcare system. Medical costs associated with overweight and obesity may involve direct and indirect costs. Direct medical costs may include preventive, diagnostic, and treatment services related to obesity. Indirect costs relate to morbidity and mortality costs including productivity. Productivity measures include 'absenteeism' (costs due to employees being absent from work for obesity-related health reasons) and 'presenteeism' (decreased productivity of employees while at work) as well as premature mortality and disability.

National Estimated Costs of Obesity

The medical care costs of obesity in the United States are high. In 2008 dollars, these costs were estimated to be $147 billion.

The annual nationwide productive costs of obesity obesity-related absenteeism range between $3.38 billion ($79 per obese individual) and $6.38 billion ($132 per obese individual).

In addition to these costs, data shows implications of obesity on recruitment by the armed forces. An assessment was performed of the percentage of the U.S. military-age population that exceeds the U.S. Army's current active duty enlistment standards for weight-for-height and percent body fat, using data from the National Health and Nutrition Examination Surveys. In 2007-2008, 5.7 million men and 16.5 million women who were eligible for military service exceeded the Army's enlistment standards for weight and body fat.

Behavior, Environment, and Genetic Factors All Have a Role in Causing People to Be Overweight and Obese

Obesity results from the energy imbalance that occurs when a person consumes more calories than their body burns. Obesity is a serious public health problem because it is associated with some of the leading causes of death in the United States and worldwide, including diabetes, heart disease, stroke, and some types of cancer.

Do Genes Have a Role in Obesity?

In recent decades, obesity has reached epidemic proportions in populations whose environments promote physical inactivity and increased consumption of high-calorie foods. However, not all people living in such environments will become obese, nor will all obese people have the same body fat distribution or suffer the same health problems. These differences can be seen in groups of people with the same racial or ethnic background and even within families. Genetic changes in human populations occur too slowly to be responsible for the obesity epidemic. Nevertheless, the variation in how people respond to the same environment suggests that genes do play a role in the development of obesity.

How Could Genes Influence Obesity?

Genes give the body instructions for responding to changes in its environment. Studies of resemblances and differences among family members, twins, and adoptees offer indirect scientific evidence that a sizable portion of the variation in weight among adults is due to genetic factors. Other studies have compared obese and non-obese people for variation in genes that could influence behaviors (such as a drive to overeat, or a tendency to be sedentary) or metabolism (such as a diminished capacity to use dietary fats as fuel, or an increased tendency to store body fat). These studies have identified variants in several genes that may contribute to obesity by increasing hunger and food intake.

Rarely, a clear pattern of inherited obesity within a family is caused by a specific variant of a single gene (monogenic obesity). Most obesity, however, probably results from complex interactions among multiple genes and environmental factors that remain poorly understood (multifactorial obesity).

The "Thrifty Genotype" Hypothesis

Any explanation of the obesity epidemic has to consider both genetics and the environment. One explanation that is often cited is the mismatch between today's environment and "energy-thrifty genes" that multiplied in the distant past, when food sources were unpredictable. In other words, according to the "thrifty genotype" hypothesis, the same genes that helped our ancestors survive occasional famines are now being challenged by environments in which food is plentiful year round.

Can Public Health Genomics Help?

Currently, genetic tests are not useful for guiding personal diet or physical activity plans. Research on genetic variation that affects response to changes in diet and physical activity is still at an early stage. Doing a better job of explaining obesity in terms of genes and environment factors could help encourage people who are trying to reach and maintain a healthy weight.

What about Family History?

Health care practitioners routinely collect family health history to help identify people at high risk of obesity-related diseases such as diabetes, cardiovascular diseases, and some forms of cancer. Family health history reflects the effects of shared genetics and environment among close relatives. Families can't change their genes but they can change the family environment to encourage healthy eating habits and physical activity. Those changes can improve the health of family members—and improve the family health history of the next generation.

How Can You Tell If You or Your Family Members Are Overweight?

Most health care practitioners use the Body Mass Index (BMI) to determine whether a person is overweight.

Chapter 61

Stroke: Genetic Links

What Is a Stroke?

A stroke occurs if the flow of oxygen-rich blood to a portion of the brain is blocked. Without oxygen, brain cells start to die after a few minutes. Sudden bleeding in the brain also can cause a stroke if it damages brain cells.

If brain cells die or are damaged because of a stroke, symptoms occur in the parts of the body that these brain cells control. Examples of stroke symptoms include sudden weakness; paralysis or numbness of the face, arms, or legs (paralysis is an inability to move); trouble speaking or understanding speech; and trouble seeing.

A stroke is a serious medical condition that requires emergency care. A stroke can cause lasting brain damage, long-term disability, or even death.

If you think you or someone else is having a stroke, call 9–1–1 right away. Do not drive to the hospital or let someone else drive you. Call an ambulance so that medical personnel can begin life-saving treatment on the way to the emergency room. During a stroke, every minute counts.

This chapter contains text excerpted from the following sources: Text beginning with the heading "What Is a Stroke?" is excerpted from "What Is a Stroke?" National Heart, Lung, and Blood Institute (NHLBI), October 28, 2015; Text under the heading "Family History and Other Characteristics That Increase Risk for Stroke" is excerpted from "Stroke," Centers for Disease Control and Prevention (CDC), March 17, 2014.

Overview

The two main types of stroke are ischemic and hemorrhagic. Ischemic is the more common type of stroke.

An ischemic stroke occurs if an artery that supplies oxygen-rich blood to the brain becomes blocked. Blood clots often cause the blockages that lead to ischemic strokes.

A hemorrhagic stroke occurs if an artery in the brain leaks blood or ruptures. The pressure from the leaked blood damages brain cells. High blood pressure and aneurysms* are examples of conditions that can cause hemorrhagic strokes.

Another condition that's similar to a stroke is a transient ischemic attack, also called a TIA or "mini-stroke." A TIA occurs if blood flow to a portion of the brain is blocked only for a short time. Thus, damage to the brain cells isn't permanent.

Like ischemic strokes, TIAs often are caused by blood clots. Although TIAs are not full-blown strokes, they greatly increase the risk of having a stroke. If you have a TIA, it's important for your doctor to find the cause so you can take steps to prevent a stroke.

Both strokes and TIAs require emergency care.

* Aneurysms are balloon-like bulges in an artery that can stretch and burst.

Outlook

Stroke is a leading cause of death in the United States. Many factors can raise your risk of having a stroke. Talk with your doctor about how you can control these risk factors and help prevent a stroke.

If you have a stroke, prompt treatment can reduce damage to your brain and help you avoid lasting disabilities. Prompt treatment also may help prevent another stroke.

Researchers continue to study the causes and risk factors for stroke. They're also finding new and better treatments and new ways to help the brain repair itself after a stroke.

What Causes a Stroke?

Ischemic Stroke and Transient Ischemic Attack

An ischemic stroke or transient ischemic attack (TIA) occurs if an artery that supplies oxygen-rich blood to the brain becomes blocked. Many medical conditions can increase the risk of ischemic stroke or TIA.

For example, atherosclerosis is a disease in which a fatty substance called plaque builds up on the inner walls of the arteries. Plaque hardens and narrows the arteries, which limits the flow of blood to tissues and organs (such as the heart and brain).

Plaque in an artery can crack or rupture. Blood platelets, which are disc-shaped cell fragments, stick to the site of the plaque injury and clump together to form blood clots. These clots can partly or fully block an artery.

Plaque can build up in any artery in the body, including arteries in the heart, brain, and neck. The two main arteries on each side of the neck are called the carotid arteries. These arteries supply oxygen-rich blood to the brain, face, scalp, and neck.

When plaque builds up in the carotid arteries, the condition is called carotid artery disease. Carotid artery disease causes many of the ischemic strokes and TIAs that occur in the United States.

An embolic stroke (a type of ischemic stroke) or TIA also can occur if a blood clot or piece of plaque breaks away from the wall of an artery. The clot or plaque can travel through the bloodstream and get stuck in one of the brain's arteries. This stops blood flow through the artery and damages brain cells.

Heart conditions and blood disorders also can cause blood clots that can lead to a stroke or TIA. For example, atrial fibrillation, or AF, is a common cause of embolic stroke.

In AF, the upper chambers of the heart contract in a very fast and irregular way. As a result, some blood pools in the heart. The pooling increases the risk of blood clots forming in the heart chambers.

An ischemic stroke or TIA also can occur because of lesions caused by atherosclerosis. These lesions may form in the small arteries of the brain, and they can block blood flow to the brain.

Hemorrhagic Stroke

Sudden bleeding in the brain can cause a hemorrhagic stroke. The bleeding causes swelling of the brain and increased pressure in the skull. The swelling and pressure damage brain cells and tissues.

Examples of conditions that can cause a hemorrhagic stroke include high blood pressure, aneurysms, and arteriovenous malformations (AVMs).

"Blood pressure" is the force of blood pushing against the walls of the arteries as the heart pumps blood. If blood pressure rises and stays high over time, it can damage the body in many ways.

Aneurysms are balloon-like bulges in an artery that can stretch and burst. AVMs are tangles of faulty arteries and veins that can rupture within the brain. High blood pressure can increase the risk of hemorrhagic stroke in people who have aneurysms or AVMs.

Family History and Other Characteristics That Increase Risk for Stroke

Family members share genes, behaviors, lifestyles, and environments that can influence their health and their risk for disease. Stroke risk can be higher in some families than in others, and your risk for stroke can increase based on your age, sex, and race or ethnicity.

Genetics and Family History

When members of a family pass traits from one generation to another through genes, that process is called heredity.

Genetic factors likely play some role in high blood pressure, stroke, and other related conditions. Several genetic disorders can cause a stroke, including sickle cell disease. It also is likely that people with a family history of stroke share common environments and other potential factors that increase their risk.

The risk for stroke can increase even more when heredity combines with unhealthy lifestyle choices, such as smoking cigarettes and eating an unhealthy diet.

Other Characteristics

Both men and women can have a stroke. Some other characteristics that you cannot control, like your age, sex, and race or ethnicity, can affect your risk for stroke:

- **Age**. Age is the single most important risk factor for stroke. The older you are, the more likely you are to have a stroke. The chance of having a stroke about doubles every 10 years after age 55. Although stroke is common among the elderly, many people younger than 65 years also have strokes.

- **Sex**. Stroke is more common in men than in women for most age groups. But women of all ages are more likely to die from stroke than are men. Pregnancy and use of birth control pills pose special stroke risks for women.

- **Race or ethnicity**. Blacks, Hispanics, American Indians, and Alaska Natives have a greater chance of having a stroke than do non-Hispanic whites or Asians. The risk of having a first stroke is nearly twice as high for blacks than for whites. Blacks are also more likely to die from stroke than are whites.

The good news is that most strokes can be prevented by working with your healthcare team to reduce your risk.

Chapter 62

Tourette Syndrome and Genetics

What Is Tourette Syndrome?

Tourette syndrome is a complex disorder characterized by repetitive, sudden, and involuntary movements or noises called tics. Tics usually appear in childhood, and their severity varies over time. In most cases, tics become milder and less frequent in late adolescence and adulthood.

Tourette syndrome involves both motor tics, which are uncontrolled body movements, and vocal or phonic tics, which are outbursts of sound. Some motor tics are simple and involve only one muscle group. Simple motor tics, such as rapid eye blinking, shoulder shrugging, or nose twitching, are usually the first signs of Tourette syndrome. Motor tics also can be complex (involving multiple muscle groups), such as jumping, kicking, hopping, or spinning.

Vocal tics, which generally appear later than motor tics, also can be simple or complex. Simple vocal tics include grunting, sniffing, and throat-clearing.

This chapter contains text excerpted from the following sources: Text beginning with the heading "What Is Tourette Syndrome?" is excerpted from "Tourette Syndrome," Genetics Home Reference (GHR), National Institutes of Health (NIH), March 21, 2016; Text under the heading "What Causes TS?" is excerpted from "Tourette Syndrome Fact Sheet," National Institute of Neurological Disorders and Stroke (NINDS), April 16, 2014.

In addition to frequent tics, people with Tourette syndrome are at risk for associated problems including attention deficit hyperactivity disorder (ADHD), obsessive-compulsive disorder (OCD), anxiety, depression, and problems with sleep.

How Common Is Tourette Syndrome?

Although the exact incidence of Tourette syndrome is uncertain, it is estimated to affect 1 to 10 in 1,000 children. This disorder occurs in populations and ethnic groups worldwide, and it is more common in males than in females.

What Genes Are Related to Tourette Syndrome?

A variety of genetic and environmental factors likely play a role in causing Tourette syndrome. Most of these factors are unknown, and researchers are studying risk factors before and after birth that may contribute to this complex disorder. Scientists believe that tics may result from changes in brain chemicals (neurotransmitters) that are responsible for producing and controlling voluntary movements.

Mutations involving the *SLITRK1* gene have been identified in a small number of people with Tourette syndrome. This gene provides instructions for making a protein that is active in the brain. The *SLITRK1* protein probably plays a role in the development of nerve cells, including the growth of specialized extensions (axons and dendrites) that allow each nerve cell to communicate with nearby cells. It is unclear how mutations in the *SLITRK1* gene can lead to this disorder.

Most people with Tourette syndrome do not have a mutation in the *SLITRK1* gene. Because mutations have been reported in so few people with this condition, the association of the *SLITRK1* gene with this disorder has not been confirmed. Researchers suspect that changes in other genes, which have not been identified, are also associated with Tourette syndrome.

How Do People Inherit Tourette Syndrome?

The inheritance pattern of Tourette syndrome is unclear. Although the features of this condition can cluster in families, many genetic and environmental factors are likely to be involved. Among family members of an affected person, it is difficult to predict who else may be at risk of developing the condition.

Tourette syndrome was previously thought to have an autosomal dominant pattern of inheritance, which suggests that one mutated copy of a gene in each cell would be sufficient to cause the condition. Several decades of research have shown that this is not the case. Almost all cases of Tourette syndrome probably result from a variety of genetic and environmental factors, not changes in a single gene.

What Causes TS?

Although the cause of TS is unknown, current research points to abnormalities in certain brain regions (including the basal ganglia, frontal lobes, and cortex), the circuits that interconnect these regions, and the neurotransmitters (dopamine, serotonin, and norepinephrine) responsible for communication among nerve cells. Given the often complex presentation of TS, the cause of the disorder is likely to be equally complex.

What Are the Symptoms?

Tics are classified as either simple or complex. Simple motor tics are sudden, brief, repetitive movements that involve a limited number of muscle groups. Some of the more common simple tics include eye blinking and other eye movements, facial grimacing, shoulder shrugging, and head or shoulder jerking. Simple vocalizations might include repetitive throat-clearing, sniffing, or grunting sounds.

Complex tics are distinct, coordinated patterns of movements involving several muscle groups. Complex motor tics might include facial grimacing combined with a head twist and a shoulder shrug. Other complex motor tics may actually appear purposeful, including sniffing or touching objects, hopping, jumping, bending, or twisting. Simple vocal tics may include throat-clearing, sniffing/snorting, grunting, or barking.

More complex vocal tics include words or phrases. Perhaps the most dramatic and disabling tics include motor movements that result in self-harm such as punching oneself in the face or vocal tics including coprolalia (uttering socially inappropriate words such as swearing) or echolalia (repeating the words or phrases of others). However, coprolalia is only present in a small number (10 to 15 percent) of individuals with TS.

Some tics are preceded by an urge or sensation in the affected muscle group, commonly called a premonitory urge. Some with TS will describe a need to complete a tic in a certain way or a certain number of times in order to relieve the urge or decrease the sensation.

Tics are often worse with excitement or anxiety and better during calm, focused activities. Certain physical experiences can trigger or worsen tics, for example tight collars may trigger neck tics, or hearing another person sniff or throat-clear may trigger similar sounds. Tics do not go away during sleep but are often significantly diminished.

What Is the Course of TS?

Tics come and go over time, varying in type, frequency, location, and severity. The first symptoms usually occur in the head and neck area and may progress to include muscles of the trunk and extremities. Motor tics generally precede the development of vocal tics and simple tics often precede complex tics. Most patients experience peak tic severity before the mid-teen years with improvement for the majority of patients in the late teen years and early adulthood. Approximately 10-15 percent of those affected have a progressive or disabling course that lasts into adulthood.

What Disorders Are Associated with TS?

Many individuals with TS experience additional neurobehavioral problems that often cause more impairment than the tics themselves. These include inattention, hyperactivity and impulsivity (attention deficit hyperactivity disorder—ADHD); problems with reading, writing, and arithmetic; and obsessive-compulsive symptoms such as intrusive thoughts/worries and repetitive behaviors. For example, worries about dirt and germs may be associated with repetitive hand-washing, and concerns about bad things happening may be associated with ritualistic behaviors such as counting, repeating, or ordering and arranging.

People with TS have also reported problems with depression or anxiety disorders, as well as other difficulties with living, that may or may not be directly related to TS. In addition, although most individuals with TS experience a significant decline in motor and vocal tics in late adolescence and early adulthood, the associated neurobehavioral conditions may persist. Given the range of potential complications, people with TS are best served by receiving medical care that provides a comprehensive treatment plan.

How Is TS Diagnosed?

TS is a diagnosis that doctors make after verifying that the patient has had both motor and vocal tics for at least 1 year. The existence of other neurological or psychiatric conditions can also help doctors arrive at a diagnosis. Common tics are not often misdiagnosed by knowledgeable clinicians. However, atypical symptoms or atypical presentations (for example, onset of symptoms in adulthood) may require specific specialty expertise for diagnosis. There are no blood, laboratory, or imaging tests needed for diagnosis. In rare cases, neuroimaging studies, such as magnetic resonance imaging (MRI) or computerized tomography (CT), electroencephalogram (EEG) studies, or certain blood tests may be used to rule out other conditions that might be confused with TS when the history or clinical examination is atypical.

It is not uncommon for patients to obtain a formal diagnosis of TS only after symptoms have been present for some time. The reasons for this are many. For families and physicians unfamiliar with TS, mild and even moderate tic symptoms may be considered inconsequential, part of a developmental phase, or the result of another condition. For example, parents may think that eye blinking is related to vision problems or that sniffing is related to seasonal allergies. Many patients are self-diagnosed after they, their parents, other relatives, or friends read or hear about TS from others.

How Is TS Treated?

Because tic symptoms often do not cause impairment, the majority of people with TS require no medication for tic suppression. However, effective medications are available for those whose symptoms interfere with functioning. Neuroleptics (drugs that may be used to treat psychotic and non-psychotic disorders) are the most consistently useful medications for tic suppression; a number are available but some are more effective than others (for example, haloperidol and pimozide).

Unfortunately, there is no one medication that is helpful to all people with TS, nor does any medication completely eliminate symptoms. In addition, all medications have side effects. Many neuroleptic side effects can be managed by initiating treatment slowly and reducing the dose when side effects occur. The most common side effects of neuroleptics include sedation, weight gain, and cognitive dulling. Neurological side effects such as tremor, dystonic reactions (twisting movements or postures), parkinsonian-like symptoms, and other dyskinetic (involuntary) movements are less common and are readily managed with dose reduction.

Discontinuing neuroleptics after long-term use must be done slowly to avoid rebound increases in tics and withdrawal dyskinesias. One form of dyskinesia called tardive dyskinesia is a movement disorder distinct from TS that may result from the chronic use of neuroleptics. The risk of this side effect can be reduced by using lower doses of neuroleptics for shorter periods of time.

Other medications may also be useful for reducing tic severity, but most have not been as extensively studied or shown to be as consistently useful as neuroleptics. Additional medications with demonstrated efficacy include alpha-adrenergic agonists such as clonidine and guanfacine. These medications are used primarily for hypertension but are also used in the treatment of tics. The most common side effect from these medications that precludes their use is sedation. However, given the lower side effect risk associated with these medications, they are often used as first-line agents before proceeding to treatment with neuroleptics.

Effective medications are also available to treat some of the associated neurobehavioral disorders that can occur in patients with TS. Recent research shows that stimulant medications such as methylphenidate and dextroamphetamine can lessen ADHD symptoms in people with TS without causing tics to become more severe. However, the product labeling for stimulants currently contraindicates the use of these drugs in children with tics/TS and those with a family history of tics. Scientists hope that future studies will include a thorough discussion of the risks and benefits of stimulants in those with TS or a family history of TS and will clarify this issue. For obsessive-compulsive symptoms that significantly disrupt daily functioning, the serotonin reuptake inhibitors (clomipramine, fluoxetine, fluvoxamine, paroxetine, and sertraline) have been proven effective in some patients.

Behavioral treatments such as awareness training and competing response training can also be used to reduce tics. A recent NIH-funded, multi-center randomized control trial called Cognitive Behavioral Intervention for Tics, or CBIT, showed that training to voluntarily move in response to a premonitory urge can reduce tic symptoms. Other behavioral therapies, such as biofeedback or supportive therapy, have not been shown to reduce tic symptoms. However, supportive therapy can help a person with TS better cope with the disorder and deal with the secondary social and emotional problems that sometimes occur.

What Is the Prognosis?

Although there is no cure for TS, the condition in many individuals improves in the late teens and early 20s. As a result, some may actually become symptom-free or no longer need medication for tic suppression. Although the disorder is generally lifelong and chronic, it is not a degenerative condition. Individuals with TS have a normal life expectancy. TS does not impair intelligence. Although tic symptoms tend to decrease with age, it is possible that neurobehavioral disorders such as ADHD, OCD, depression, generalized anxiety, panic attacks, and mood swings can persist and cause impairment in adult life.

Part Five

Genetic Research

Chapter 63

The Human Genome Project

What Is a Genome?

A genome is an organism's complete set of DNA, including all of its genes. Each genome contains all of the information needed to build and maintain that organism. In humans, a copy of the entire genome—more than 3 billion DNA base pairs—is contained in all cells that have a nucleus.

What Was the Human Genome Project and Why Has It Been Important?

The Human Genome Project was an international research effort to determine the sequence of the human genome and identify the genes that it contains. The Project was coordinated by the National Institutes of Health and the U.S. Department of Energy. Additional contributors included universities across the United States and international partners in the United Kingdom, France, Germany, Japan, and China. The Human Genome Project formally began in 1990 and was completed in 2003, two years ahead of its original schedule.

The work of the Human Genome Project has allowed researchers to begin to understand the blueprint for building a person. As researchers learn more about the functions of genes and proteins, this knowledge will have a major impact in the fields of medicine, biotechnology, and the life sciences.

This chapter includes text excerpted from "The Human Genome Project," Genetics Home Reference (GHR), National Institutes of Health (NIH), March 21, 2016.

What Were the Goals of the Human Genome Project?

The main goals of the Human Genome Project were to provide a complete and accurate sequence of the 3 billion DNA base pairs that make up the human genome and to find all of the estimated 20,000 to 25,000 human genes. The Project also aimed to sequence the genomes of several other organisms that are important to medical research, such as the mouse and the fruit fly.

In addition to sequencing DNA, the Human Genome Project sought to develop new tools to obtain and analyze the data and to make this information widely available. Also, because advances in genetics have consequences for individuals and society, the Human Genome Project committed to exploring the consequences of genomic research through its Ethical, Legal, and Social Implications (ELSI) program.

What Did the Human Genome Project Accomplish?

In April 2003, researchers announced that the Human Genome Project had completed a high-quality sequence of essentially the entire human genome. This sequence closed the gaps from a working draft of the genome, which was published in 2001. It also identified the locations of many human genes and provided information about their structure and organization. The Project made the sequence of the human genome and tools to analyze the data freely available via the Internet.

In addition to the human genome, the Human Genome Project sequenced the genomes of several other organisms, including brewers' yeast, the roundworm, and the fruit fly. In 2002, researchers announced that they had also completed a working draft of the mouse genome. By studying the similarities and differences between human genes and those of other organisms, researchers can discover the functions of particular genes and identify which genes are critical for life.

What Were Some of the Ethical, Legal, and Social Implications Addressed by the Human Genome Project?

The Ethical, Legal, and Social Implications (ELSI) program was founded in 1990 as an integral part of the Human Genome Project. The mission of the ELSI program was to identify and address issues raised by genomic research that would affect individuals, families, and society. A percentage of the Human Genome Project budget at the National Institutes of Health (NIH) and the U.S. Department of Energy was devoted to ELSI research.

The ELSI program focused on the possible consequences of genomic research in four main areas:

1. Privacy and fairness in the use of genetic information, including the potential for genetic discrimination in employment and insurance.

2. The integration of new genetic technologies, such as genetic testing, into the practice of clinical medicine.

3. Ethical issues surrounding the design and conduct of genetic research with people, including the process of informed consent.

4. The education of healthcare professionals, policy makers, students, and the public about genetics and the complex issues that result from genomic research.

Chapter 64

Pharmacogenomics

What Is Pharmacogenomics?

Pharmacogenomics is the study of how genes affect a person's response to drugs. This relatively new field combines pharmacology (the science of drugs) and genomics (the study of genes and their functions) to develop effective, safe medications and doses that will be tailored to a person's genetic makeup.

Many drugs that are currently available are "one size fits all," but they don't work the same way for everyone. It can be difficult to predict who will benefit from a medication, who will not respond at all, and who will experience negative side effects (called adverse drug reactions). Adverse drug reactions are a significant cause of hospitalizations and deaths in the United States. With the knowledge gained from the Human Genome Project, researchers are learning how inherited differences in genes affect the body's response to medications. These genetic differences will be used to predict whether a medication will be effective for a particular person and to help prevent adverse drug reactions.

This chapter contains text excerpted from the following sources: Text beginning with the heading "What Is Pharmacogenomics?" is excerpted from "What is pharmacogenomics?" Genetics Home Reference (GHR), National Institutes of Health (NIH), March 21, 2016; Text under the heading "What Role Do Genes Play in How Medicines Work?" is excerpted from "Pharmacogenomics Fact Sheet," National Institute of General Medical Sciences (NIGMS), March 2015; Text under the heading "What Might Pharmacogenomics Mean for You?" is excerpted from "Frequently Asked Questions about Pharmacogenomics," National Human Genome Research Institute (NHGRI), February 14, 2014.

The field of pharmacogenomics is still in its infancy. Its use is currently quite limited, but new approaches are under study in clinical trials. In the future, pharmacogenomics will allow the development of tailored drugs to treat a wide range of health problems, including cardiovascular disease, Alzheimer disease, cancer, HIV/AIDS, and asthma.

What Role Do Genes Play in How Medicines Work?

Just as our genes determine our hair and eye color, they are partially responsible for how our bodies respond to medications.

Genes are instructions, written in DNA, for building protein molecules. Different people can have different versions—slightly different DNA sequences—of the same gene. Some of these variations are common and some are rare. Some are relevant for health, such as those associated with a tendency to develop certain diseases.

Pharmacogenomics looks at variations in genes for proteins that influence drug responses. Such proteins include a number of liver enzymes that convert medications into their active or inactive forms. Even small differences in the genetic sequences of these enzymes can have a big impact on a drug's safety or effectiveness.

One example involves a liver enzyme known as *CYP2D6*. This enzyme acts on a quarter of all prescription drugs, including the painkiller codeine, which it converts into the drug's active form, morphine. The *CYP2D6* gene exists in more than 160 different versions, many of which vary by only a single difference in their DNA sequence, although some have larger changes. The majority of these variants don't affect drug responses.

Some people have hundreds or even thousands of copies of the *CYP2D6* gene (typically, people have two copies of each gene). Those with extra copies of this gene manufacture an overabundance of *CYP2D6* enzyme molecules and metabolize the drug very rapidly. As a result, codeine may be converted to morphine so quickly and completely that a standard dose of the drug can be an overdose.

On the other end of the spectrum, some variants of *CYP2D6* result in a nonfunctional enzyme. People with these variants metabolize codeine slowly, if at all, so they might not experience much pain relief. For these people, doctors might prescribe a different type of pain reliever.

How Is Pharmacogenomics Affecting Drug Design, Development and Prescribing Guidelines?

The U.S. Food and Drug Administration (FDA), which monitors the safety of all drugs in the United States, has included pharmacogenomic information on the labels of more than 150 medications. This information—which can cover dosage guidance, possible side effects or differences in effectiveness for people with certain genomic variations—can help doctors tailor their drug prescriptions for individual patients.

Pharmaceutical companies are beginning to use pharmacogenomic knowledge to develop and market drugs for people with specific genetic profiles. Studying a drug only in those likely to benefit from it could speed up and streamline its development and maximize its therapeutic benefit.

Additionally, if scientists can identify the genetic basis for certain serious side effects, drugs could be prescribed only to people who are not at risk for them. As a result, potentially lifesaving medications, which otherwise might be taken off the market because they pose a risk for some people, could still be available to those who could benefit from them.

How Is Pharmacogenomics Affecting Medical Treatment?

Doctors base the majority of their drug prescriptions on clinical factors, such as a patient's age, weight, sex, and liver and kidney function. For a small subset of drugs, researchers have identified genetic variations that influence how people respond. In these cases, doctors can use the pharmacogenomic information to select the best medication and identify people who need an unusually high or low dose.

What Might Pharmacogenomics Mean for You?

Until recently, drugs have been developed with the idea that each drug works pretty much the same in everybody. But genomic research has changed that "one size fits all" approach and opened the door to more personalized approaches to using and developing drugs.

Depending on your genetic makeup, some drugs may work more or less effectively for you than they do in other people. Likewise, some drugs may produce more or fewer side effects in you than in someone else. In the near future, doctors will be able to routinely use information about your genetic makeup to choose those drugs and drug doses that offer the greatest chance of helping you.

Pharmacogenomics may also help to save you time and money. By using information about your genetic makeup, doctors soon may be able to avoid the trial-and-error approach of giving you various drugs that are not likely to work for you until they find the right one. Using pharmacogenomics, the "best-fit" drug to help you can be chosen from the beginning.

How Is Pharmacogenomic Information Being Used Today?

Doctors are starting to use pharmacogenomic information to prescribe drugs, but such tests are routine for only a few health problems. However, given the field's rapid growth, pharmacogenomics is soon expected to lead to better ways of using drugs to manage heart disease, cancer, asthma, depression and many other common diseases.

One current use of pharmacogenomics involves people infected with the human immunodeficiency virus (HIV). Before prescribing the antiviral drug abacavir (Ziagen), doctors now routinely test HIV-infected patients for a genetic variant that makes them more likely to have a bad reaction to the drug.

Another example is the breast cancer drug trastuzumab (Herceptin). This therapy works only for women whose tumors have a particular genetic profile that leads to overproduction of a protein called HER2.

The U.S. Food and Drug Administration (FDA) also recommends genetic testing before giving the chemotherapy drug mercaptopurine (Purinethol) to patients with acute lymphoblastic leukemia. Some people have a genetic variant that interferes with their ability to process the drug. This processing problem can cause severe side effects and increase risk of infection, unless the standard dose is adjusted according to the patient's genetic makeup.

The FDA also advises doctors to test colon cancer patients for certain genetic variants before administering irinotecan (Camptosar), which is part of a combination chemotherapy regimen. The reasoning is that patients with one particular variant may not be able to clear the drug from their bodies as quickly as others, resulting in severe diarrhea and increased infection risk. Such patients may need to receive lower doses of the drug.

What Other Uses of Pharmacogenomics Are Being Studied?

Much research is underway to understand how genomic information can be used to develop more personalized and cost-effective strategies for using drugs to improve human health.

In 2007, the FDA revised the label on the common blood-thinning drug warfarin (Coumadin) to explain that a person's genetic makeup might influence response to the drug. Some doctors have since begun using genetic information to adjust warfarin dosage. Still, more research is needed to conclusively determine whether warfarin dosing that includes genetic information is better than the current trial-and-error approach.

The FDA also is considering genetic testing for another blood-thinner, clopidogrel bisulfate (Plavix), used to prevent dangerous blood clots. Researchers have found that Plavix may not work well in people with a certain genetic variant.

Cancer is another very active area of pharmacogenomic research. Studies have found that the chemotherapy drugs, gefitinib (Iressa) and erlotinib (Tarceva), work much better in lung cancer patients whose tumors have a certain genetic change. On the other hand, research has shown that the chemotherapy drugs cetuximab (Erbitux) and panitumumab (Vecitibix) do not work very well in the 40 percent of colon cancer patients whose tumors have a particular genetic change.

Pharmacogenomics may also help to quickly identify the best drugs to treat people with certain mental health disorders. For example, while some patients with depression respond to the first drug they are given, many do not, and doctors have to try another drug. Because each drug takes weeks to take its full effect, patients' depression may grow worse during the time spent searching for a drug that helps.

Recently, researchers identified genetic variations that influence the response of depressed people to citalopram (Celexa), which belongs to a widely used class of antidepressant drugs called selective serotonin re-uptake inhibitors (SSRIs). Clinical trials are now underway to learn whether genetic tests that predict SSRI response can improve patients' outcomes.

Can Pharmacogenomics Be Used to Develop New Drugs?

Yes. Besides improving the ways in which existing drugs are used, genome research will lead to the development of better drugs. The goal is to produce new drugs that are highly effective and do not cause serious side effects.

Until recently, drug developers usually used an approach that involved screening for chemicals with broad action against a disease. Researchers are now using genomic information to find or design drugs aimed at subgroups of patients with specific genetic profiles. In addition, researchers are using pharmacogenomic tools to search for drugs that target specific molecular and cellular pathways involved in disease.

Pharmacogenomics may also breathe new life into some drugs that were abandoned during the development process. For example, development of the beta-blocker drug bucindolol (Gencaro) was stopped after two other beta-blocker drugs won FDA approval to treat heart failure. But interest in Gencaro revived after tests showed that the drug worked well in patients with two genetic variants that regulate heart function. If Gencaro is approved by the FDA, it could become the first new heart drug to require a genetic test before prescription.

Chapter 65

Gene Therapy

Chapter Contents

Section 65.1

What Is Gene Therapy?

This section includes text excerpted from "Gene Therapy,"
Genetics Home Reference (GHR), National Institutes of
Health (NIH), March 21, 2016.

What Is Gene Therapy?

Gene therapy is an experimental technique that uses genes to treat
or prevent disease. In the future, this technique may allow doctors to
treat a disorder by inserting a gene into a patient's cells instead of
using drugs or surgery. Researchers are testing several approaches
to gene therapy, including:

- Replacing a mutated gene that causes disease with a healthy
  copy of the gene.

- Inactivating, or "knocking out," a mutated gene that is functioning improperly.

- Introducing a new gene into the body to help fight a disease.

Although gene therapy is a promising treatment option for a number of diseases (including inherited disorders, some types of cancer,
and certain viral infections), the technique remains risky and is still
under study to make sure that it will be safe and effective. Gene therapy is currently only being tested for the treatment of diseases that
have no other cures.

How Does Gene Therapy Work?

Gene therapy is designed to introduce genetic material into cells
to compensate for abnormal genes or to make a beneficial protein. If a
mutated gene causes a necessary protein to be faulty or missing, gene
therapy may be able to introduce a normal copy of the gene to restore
the function of the protein.

A gene that is inserted directly into a cell usually does not function.
Instead, a carrier called a vector is genetically engineered to deliver

the gene. Certain viruses are often used as vectors because they can deliver the new gene by infecting the cell. The viruses are modified so they can't cause disease when used in people. Some types of virus, such as retroviruses, integrate their genetic material (including the new gene) into a chromosome in the human cell. Other viruses, such as adenoviruses, introduce their DNA into the nucleus of the cell, but the DNA is not integrated into a chromosome.

The vector can be injected or given intravenously (by IV) directly into a specific tissue in the body, where it is taken up by individual cells. Alternately, a sample of the patient's cells can be removed and exposed to the vector in a laboratory setting. The cells containing the vector are then returned to the patient. If the treatment is successful, the new gene delivered by the vector will make a functioning protein.

Researchers must overcome many technical challenges before gene therapy will be a practical approach to treating disease. For example, scientists must find better ways to deliver genes and target them to particular cells. They must also ensure that new genes are precisely controlled by the body.

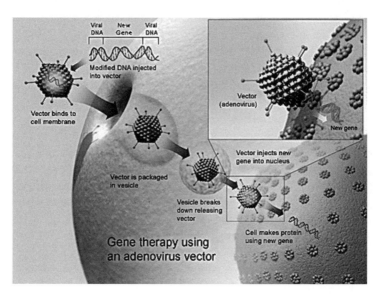

Figure 65.1. *Gene Therapy Using an Adenovirus Vector*

- A new gene is injected into an adenovirus vector, which is used to introduce the modified DNA into a human cell. If the treatment is successful, the new gene will make a functional protein.

Is Gene Therapy Safe?

Gene therapy is under study to determine whether it could be used to treat disease. Current research is evaluating the safety of gene therapy; future studies will test whether it is an effective treatment option. Several studies have already shown that this approach can have very serious health risks, such as toxicity, inflammation, and cancer. Because the techniques are relatively new, some of the risks may be unpredictable; however, medical researchers, institutions, and regulatory agencies are working to ensure that gene therapy research is as safe as possible.

Comprehensive federal laws, regulations, and guidelines help protect people who participate in research studies (called clinical trials). The U.S. Food and Drug Administration (FDA) regulates all gene therapy products in the United States and oversees research in this area. Researchers who wish to test an approach in a clinical trial must first obtain permission from the FDA. The FDA has the authority to reject or suspend clinical trials that are suspected of being unsafe for participants.

The National Institutes of Health (NIH) also plays an important role in ensuring the safety of gene therapy research. NIH provides guidelines for investigators and institutions (such as universities and hospitals) to follow when conducting clinical trials with gene therapy. These guidelines state that clinical trials at institutions receiving NIH funding for this type of research must be registered with the NIH Office of Biotechnology Activities. The protocol, or plan, for each clinical trial is then reviewed by the NIH Recombinant DNA Advisory Committee (RAC) to determine whether it raises medical, ethical, or safety issues that warrant further discussion at one of the RAC's public meetings.

An Institutional Review Board (IRB) and an Institutional Biosafety Committee (IBC) must approve each gene therapy clinical trial before it can be carried out. An IRB is a committee of scientific and medical advisors and consumers that reviews all research within an institution. An IBC is a group that reviews and approves an institution's potentially hazardous research studies. Multiple levels of evaluation and oversight ensure that safety concerns are a top priority in the planning and carrying out of gene therapy research.

What Are the Ethical Issues Surrounding Gene Therapy?

Because gene therapy involves making changes to the body's set of basic instructions, it raises many unique ethical concerns.

The ethical questions surrounding gene therapy include:

- How can "good" and "bad" uses of gene therapy be distinguished?

- Who decides which traits are normal and which constitute a disability or disorder?

- Will the high costs of gene therapy make it available only to the wealthy?

- Could the widespread use of gene therapy make society less accepting of people who are different?

- Should people be allowed to use gene therapy to enhance basic human traits such as height, intelligence, or athletic ability?

Current gene therapy research has focused on treating individuals by targeting the therapy to body cells such as bone marrow or blood cells. This type of gene therapy cannot be passed on to a person's children. Gene therapy could be targeted to egg and sperm cells (germ cells), however, which would allow the inserted gene to be passed onto future generations. This approach is known as germline gene therapy.

The idea of germline gene therapy is controversial. While it could spare future generations in a family from having a particular genetic disorder, it might affect the development of a fetus in unexpected ways or have long-term side effects that are not yet known. Because people who would be affected by germline gene therapy are not yet born, they can't choose whether to have the treatment. Because of these ethical concerns, the U.S. Government does not allow federal funds to be used for research on germline gene therapy in people.

Is Gene Therapy Available to Treat My Disorder?

Gene therapy is currently available only in a research setting. The U.S. Food and Drug Administration (FDA) has not yet approved any gene therapy products for sale in the United States.

Hundreds of research studies (clinical trials) are under way to test gene therapy as a treatment for genetic conditions, cancer, and HIV/AIDS. If you are interested in participating in a clinical trial, talk with your doctor or a genetics professional about how to participate.

Section 65.2

Tackling the Thorny Side of Gene Therapy

This section contains text excerpted from the following sources: Text
under the heading "NIH Researchers Tackle Thorny Side of Gene
Therapy" is excerpted from "NIH Researchers Tackle Thorny Side
of Gene Therapy," National Human Genome Research Institute
(NHGRI), January 20, 2015; Text under the heading "Gene Therapy
Approach for Ovarian Cancer Shows Encouraging Signs in Animal
Model" is excerpted from "Gene Therapy Approach for Ovarian
Cancer Shows Encouraging Signs in Animal Model,"
National Cancer Institute (NCI), August 14, 2015.

NIH Researchers Tackle Thorny Side of Gene Therapy

*Pre-clinical studies in mice reveal ways to reduce cancer risk with
modified treatment*

National Institutes of Health researchers have uncovered a key factor
in understanding the elevated cancer risk associated with gene therapy.
They conducted research on mice with a rare disease similar to one in
humans, hoping their findings may eventually help improve gene therapy for humans. Researchers at the National Human Genome Research
Institute (NHGRI), part of NIH, published their research in the January
20, 2015, online issue of the *Journal of Clinical Investigation.*

"Effective and safe gene therapies have the potential to dramatically reverse diseases that are life-threatening for affected children,"
said NHGRI Scientific Director Dan Kastner, M.D., Ph.D. "This study
is an important step in developing gene therapies that can be safely
used to benefit patients."

Toxic side effects actually are rarely observed by researchers who
have designed gene therapies using an adeno-associated virus (AAV)
as a vector to deliver the corrected gene to a specific point in the cell's
DNA. AAVs are small viruses that infect humans but do not cause
disease. A vector is a DNA molecule of AAV used as a vehicle to carry
corrected genetic material into a cell. AAV viruses are uniquely suited
for gene therapy applications.

But one prior study did find an association between AAV and the
occurrence of liver cancer. The present research addresses this problem

in gene therapy for an inherited disease in children called methylmalonic acidemia, or MMA. For 10 years, NHGRI researchers have worked toward a gene therapy to treat MMA. The condition affects as many as 1 in 67,000 children born in the United States. Affected children are unable to properly metabolize certain amino acids consumed in their diet, which can damage a number of organs and lead to kidney failure. MMA patients also suffer from severe metabolic instability, failure to thrive, intellectual and physical disabilities, pancreatitis, anemia, seizures, vision loss, and strokes. The most common therapy is a restrictive diet, but doctors must resort to dialysis or kidney or liver transplants when the disease progresses.

In prior MMA gene therapy studies, researchers showed that mice bred to develop the condition could be restored to health by AAV gene therapy injection shortly after birth. The mice in the study survived into adulthood and were free from the effects of MMA.

"The corrected gene delivered by AAV is the most effective therapy we have developed so far to treat MMA," said Charles Venditti, M.D., Ph.D., senior author and investigator in NHGRI's Genetic and Molecular Biology Branch. "However, we have identified an important safety parameter related to the AAV gene therapy in our mouse models that is critical to understand before we move to human patient trials."

Now, in a long-term follow-up of the treated mice—after mice reached about two years of age—the researchers documented a 50–70 percent higher occurrence of liver cancer in AAV-treated mice compared with a 10 percent liver cancer rate in untreated mice. Dr. Venditti's team determined that the AAV vector triggered the cancer. The research team performed additional experiments to detect where in the mouse genome the AAV vector delivered the corrected gene and how that related to any cancer development. In many mice that developed liver cancer, the AAV vector targeted a region of the mouse genome called Rian, near a gene called Mir341 that codes for a microRNA molecule. MicroRNAs are small, non-coding RNA molecules involved in the regulation of gene expression. When the AAV was inserted near Mir341, the vector caused elevated expression of the gene, which the researchers believe contributed to the occurrence of liver cancer in the mice. The authors note that Mir341 is found in the mouse genome, however, it is not present in humans.

When the researchers used an alternate AAV vector to deliver the corrected gene in a study of just 10 mice, that vector did not insert where it would elevate the expression of nearby genes and it did not cause liver cancer. The researchers found that this modification was a safer gene therapy.

"These studies will help us move forward to develop safer gene therapy for methylmalonic acidemia," said Randy Chandler, Ph.D., lead author and NHGRI staff scientist. "Most of the AAV integrations that caused liver cancer landed in a gene that is not found in the human genome, which suggests that the cancers we observed after AAV gene therapy may have been a mouse-specific phenomenon. However, these studies do convincingly demonstrate that AAV can be a cancer-causing agent, which argues for further studies."

The researchers also observed that lower doses of AAV resulted in reduced rates of liver cancer compared to a control group of mice. Their data showed that the rate of cancer dropped in proportion to the dose of the AAV.

Dr. Venditti hopes that methodologies described in his team's research will be used by others to study the toxicity of AAV vectors in their preclinical trials.

Gene Therapy Approach for Ovarian Cancer Shows Encouraging Signs in Animal Model

A single injection of a gene therapy viral vector can deliver effective and long-lasting levels of a protein that inhibits the growth of some mouse tumors derived from patients with recurrent ovarian cancer, according to a study published in the Proceedings of the National Academy of Sciences.

Mullerian inhibiting substance (MIS) is a protein produced in the male testis during early development. In the developing male fetus, precursor cells that would become the fallopian tubes, uterus, cervix, and vagina of a female, express receptors to MIS, which causes these tissues to regress.

"We hypothesized that since ovarian cancer cells still express the receptors to MIS, why not use the hormone that causes regression in the fetus to target these cells?" asked David Pépin, Ph.D., of Massachusetts General Hospital and lead author of the study. "Cancer cells often behave a lot like cells in early development."

MIS has been of interest to researchers as a potential anticancer agent for several decades. Manufacturing MIS in the lab, however, has proven to be particularly difficult, and not enough could be produced to test this hypothesis in preclinical studies, explained the study's senior author, Patricia Donahoe, M.D., also of Massachusetts General Hospital. However, in 2013, Drs. Donahoe and Pépin published a study in which they were able to engineer a slightly modified version of MIS that produced a better yield and a more biologically active version of the protein.

In the new study, the researchers first tested the engineered MIS in cell lines from patients with recurrent ovarian cancer. Seeing positive responses, they introduced this modified MIS into a virus capable of coaxing target cells to produce the protein (that is, a viral vector). The viral vector, called AAV9—designed by study co-author Guangping Gao, Ph.D., director of the Gene Therapy Program at the University of Massachusetts—allowed them to deliver the gene for modified MIS into mouse tissues which, in turn, produced the therapeutic protein.

"The AAV9 does not hit the tumor directly," explained Dr. Donahoe. "It gets expressed in muscle and other organs, and so the patients themselves become a bioreactor for the production of MIS, which then acts on the tumor."

Growth of tumors in three of the five mice tested—all of which had implanted tumors from patients with recurrent ovarian cancer—was significantly inhibited by MIS.

These results are especially encouraging given the high mortality rate for ovarian cancer and the current lack of therapeutic options, said Dr. Pépin. "For the most part, we have been using the same chemotherapy for the last 20 years."

Dr. Pépin envisions ultimately using the gene therapy in concert with chemotherapy. MIS inhibits the growth of ovarian cancer cells, he said, and other studies suggest that it also seems to be particularly good at inhibiting cancer stem cells.

"While chemotherapy is effective against the bulk of the tumor, it largely spares or even stimulates some cancer stem cells, the very cells responsive to MIS, suggesting a mechanism for synergy."

Advantages of the gene therapy include the fact that "we can get a permanent expression of the therapeutic protein at levels that would otherwise be difficult to achieve with injected proteins," said Dr. Pépin. There was also no evidence of side effects, he added. Furthermore, the AAV9 vector does not integrate into the host genome, so there is no risk of it disrupting a gene or causing cancer, he explained.

"It's much safer than previous gene therapy viruses," he said.

Drs. Donahoe and Pépin are currently seeking commercial partners to produce the AAV9 gene therapy to test in a clinical trial.

Section 65.3

Gene Therapy and Children

Gene therapy carries the promise of cures for many diseases and for types of medical treatment that didn't seem possible until recently. With its potential to eliminate and prevent hereditary diseases such as cystic fibrosis and hemophilia and its use as a possible cure for heart disease, AIDS, and cancer, gene therapy is a potential medical miracle-worker.

But what about gene therapy for children? There's a fair amount of risk involved, so thus far only seriously ill kids or those with illnesses that can't be cured by standard medical treatments have been involved in clinical trials using gene therapy.

As those studies continue, gene therapy may soon offer hope for children with serious illnesses that don't respond to conventional therapies.

About Genes

Our genes help make us unique. Inherited from our parents, they go far in determining our physical traits — like eye color and the color and texture of our hair. They also determine things like whether babies will be male or female, the amount of oxygen blood can carry, and the likelihood of getting certain diseases.

Genes are composed of strands of a molecule called DNA and are located in single file within the chromosomes. The genetic message is encoded by the building blocks of the DNA, which are called nucleotides. Approximately 3 billion pairs of nucleotides are in the chromosomes of a human cell, and each person's genetic makeup has a unique sequence of nucleotides. This is mainly what makes us different from one another.

Scientists believe that every human has about 25,000 genes per cell. A mutation, or change, in any one of these genes can result in a disease, physical disability, or shortened life span. These mutations can be passed from one generation to another, inherited just like a mother's curly hair or a father's brown eyes. Mutations also can occur spontaneously in some cases, without having been passed on by a parent. With gene therapy, the treatment or elimination of inherited diseases or physical conditions due to these mutations could become a reality.

Gene therapy involves the manipulation of genes to fight or prevent diseases. Put simply, it introduces a "good" gene into a person who has a disease caused by a "bad" gene.

Two Types of Gene Therapy

The two forms of gene therapy are:

1. **Somatic gene therapy**, which involves introducing a "good" gene into targeted cells to treat the patient — but not the patient's future children because these genes do not get passed along to offspring. In other words, even though some of the patient's genes may be altered to treat a disease, it won't change the chance that the disease will be passed on to the patient's children. This is the more common form of gene therapy being done.

2. **Germline gene therapy**, which involves modifying the genes in egg or sperm cells, which will then pass any genetic changes to future generations. Experimenting with this type of therapy, scientists injected fragments of DNA into fertilized mouse eggs. The mice grew into adults and their offspring had the new gene. Scientists found that certain growth and fertility problems could be corrected with this therapy, which led them to think that the same could be true for humans. Although it has potential for preventing inherited disease, germline gene therapy is controversial and very little research is being done, for technical and ethical reasons.

Possible Effects of Gene Therapy

Currently, gene therapy is done only through clinical trials, which often take years to complete. After new drugs or procedures are tested in laboratories, clinical trials are conducted with human patients under strictly controlled circumstances. Such trials usually last 2 to 4 years and go through several phases of research. In the United States, the

U.S. Food and Drug Administration (FDA) must then approve the new therapy for the marketplace, which can take another 2 years.

The most active research being done in gene therapy for kids has been for genetic disorders (like cystic fibrosis). Other gene therapy trials involve children with severe immunodeficiencies, such as adenosine deaminase (ADA) deficiency (a rare genetic disease that makes kids prone to serious infection), sickle cell anemia, thalassemia, hemophilia, and those with familial hypercholesterolemia (extremely high levels of serum cholesterol).

Gene therapy does have risks and limitations. The viruses and other agents used to deliver the "good" genes can affect more than the cells for which they're intended. If a gene is added to DNA, it could be put in the wrong place, which could potentially cause cancer or other damage.

Genes also can be "overexpressed," meaning they can drive the production of so much of a protein that they can be harmful. Another risk is that a virus introduced into one person could be transmitted to others or into the environment.

Gene therapy trials in children present an ethical dilemma, according to some gene therapy experts. Kids with an altered gene may have mild or severe effects and the severity often can't be determined in infants. So just because some kids appear to have a genetic problem doesn't mean they'll be substantially affected by it, but they'll have to live with the knowledge of that problem.

Kids could be tested for disorders if there is a medical treatment or a lifestyle change that could be beneficial—or if knowing they don't carry the gene reduces the medical surveillance needed. For example, finding out a child doesn't carry the gene for a disorder that runs in the family might mean that he or she doesn't have to undergo yearly screenings or other regular exams.

The Future of Gene Therapy

To cure genetic diseases, scientists must first determine which gene or set of genes causes each disease. The Human Genome Project and other international efforts have completed the initial work of sequencing and mapping virtually all of the 25,000 genes in the human cell. This research will provide new strategies to diagnose, treat, cure, and possibly prevent human diseases.

Although this information will help scientists determine the genetic basis of many diseases, it will be a long time before diseases actually can be treated through gene therapy.

Gene therapy's potential to revolutionize medicine in the future is exciting, and hopes are high for its role in curing and preventing childhood diseases. One day it may be possible to treat an unborn child for a genetic disease even before symptoms appear.

Scientists hope that the human genome mapping will help lead to cures for many diseases and that successful clinical trials will create new opportunities.

Chapter 66

Precision Medicine Initiative Cohort Program

What Is the Precision Medicine Initiative?

In his State of the Union address President Obama announced that he's launching the Precision Medicine Initiative (PMI)—a bold new research effort to revolutionize how we improve health and treat disease. The PMI aims to leverage advances in genomics, emerging methods for managing and analyzing large data sets while protecting privacy, and health information technology to accelerate biomedical discoveries.

When Can I Sign up to Join the Precision Medicine Initiative Cohort Program?

We anticipate enrollment for the Precision Medicine Initiative Cohort Program will begin sometime in 2016. Before we begin enrollment, we need to solidify the details for this historic program. NIH will widely publicize when enrollment is ready to begin, and we hope you will sign up.

Can Anyone Sign Up?

Yes, anyone living in the United States will be able to participate.

This chapter includes text excerpted from "Precision Medicine Initiative Cohort Program," National Institutes of Health (NIH), February 29, 2016.

What Would Be Expected of Me If I Enroll in the Precision Medicine Initiative Cohort Program?

Volunteers will be asked to share data including data from their electronic health records and health survey information. Participants may be asked to provide health data on lifestyle habits and environmental exposures as well. Participants will also undergo a standard baseline physical exam and provide a biological sample such as blood, urine, or saliva.

Will My Health Information Be Safe? How Do You Plan to Ensure Privacy? What about Data Security?

Privacy and security are critically important. The White House has developed a set of privacy principles and released for public comment a security framework.

Maintaining data security and privacy will be paramount to maintaining participants' trust and engagement in the Precision Medicine Initiative Cohort Program. The Precision Medicine Initiative Cohort Program will engage teams of privacy experts and employ rigorous security testing models, develop participant education with regard to privacy and potential re-identification risk, and clearly articulate response plans in the case of a privacy breach. The Precision Medicine Initiative Working Group made recommendations for security and privacy of individual information, including establishing safeguards against unintended release of data and penalties for the unauthorized re-identification of participants. These recommendations are intended to ensure the proper use of the data and to set the foundation of trust between participants, researchers, and governance.

Will I Get Access to Results and Data from the Study?

Yes. It is important for participants to have the highest levels of access to their study results, along with summarized results from across the cohort, and will be provided with tools to make sense of the results. The Precision Medicine Initiative Cohort Program will ensure this is done ethically and responsibly.

Will the Cohort Accept Children?

Yes. The Precision Medicine Initiative Cohort Program is expected to reflect the broad diversity of the United States, including all life stages.

How Long Will It Take to Develop a National Research Cohort of One Million U.S. Volunteers?

NIH aims to begin enrolling participants in 2016 and reach one million volunteers within three to four years, but hopes to continue to enroll participants well beyond one million participants.

What Do We Hope to Learn?

The Precision Medicine Initiative Working Group developed a set of high-value scientific opportunities based on input from four public workshops and two requests for information. A large-scale cohort of 1 million or more participants who contribute genetic, environmental, and lifestyle information over a long period of time will allow researchers to:

- develop ways to measure risk for a range of diseases based on environmental exposures, genetic factors, and interactions between the two;

- identify the causes of individual differences in response to commonly used drugs (commonly referred to as pharmacogenomics);

- discover biological markers that signal increased or decreased risk of developing common diseases;

- use mobile health (mHealth) technologies to correlate activity, physiological measures and environmental exposures with health outcomes;

- develop new disease classifications and relationships;

- empower study participants with data and information to improve their own health; and

- create a platform to enable trials of targeted therapies.

Which Diseases Will Be Studied?

This large-scale cohort will not be focused on a specific disease, but instead will be a broad resource for researchers working on a variety of important health questions. Researchers have already seen successful precision medicine approaches in treating certain types of cancers. This cohort will seek to extend that success to many other diseases, including common diseases such as diabetes, heart disease, Alzheimer's, obesity, and mental illnesses, as well as rare diseases. Importantly, the cohort will focus not just on disease, but also on ways to increase an individual's chances of remaining healthy throughout their life.

How Long Before We See the Results of Precision Medicine in the Form of New Treatments or Preventions?

Precision medicine is an approach to disease prevention and treatment that takes into account individual variability in genes, environment and lifestyle to aid in the development of individualized care. This is not a new area of science. While we have seen some great progress, it can take many years to understand the contribution of a single unique variable on a given disease or treatment. It will take even more time to develop new treatments and methods of disease prevention. By launching a study of the size and scope proposed here, we hope to accelerate our understanding of disease onset and progression, treatment response, and health outcomes.

When will the First Set of Funding Awards for Building the Scientific Network and Infrastructure Be Made?

The NIH will be issuing the first awards to establish the building blocks for this critical resource in February 2016. NIH expects to make significant headway toward building the cohort infrastructure through awards made in fiscal year 2016 when it issues additional awards to support a coordinating center, biobank, and participants technologies center, and to establish healthcare provider organization enrollment centers. These additional awards will be made in June/July 2016.

How Can I Participate in the Precision Medicine Initiative Cohort Program Prior to 2016?

We are looking to a broad range of stakeholders to learn about new or expanded initiatives and programs aimed at enabling new ways to improve health and treat disease—and ways to use this information to inform our precision medicine efforts going forward.

Chapter 67

Genomic Medicine

What Is Genomic Medicine?

NHGRI defines genomic medicine as *"an emerging medical discipline that involves using genomic information about an individual as part of their clinical care (e.g., for diagnostic or therapeutic decision-making) and the health outcomes and policy implications of that clinical use."* Already, genomic medicine is making an impact in the fields of oncology, pharmacology, rare and undiagnosed diseases, and infectious disease.

The nation's investment in the Human Genome Project (HGP) was grounded in the expectation that knowledge generated as a result of that extraordinary research effort would be used to advance our understanding of biology and disease and to improve health. In the years since the HGP's completion there has been much excitement about the potential for so-called 'personalized medicine' to reach the clinic. More recently, a report from the National Academy of Sciences has called for the adoption of 'precision medicine,' where genomics, epigenomics, environmental exposure, and other data would be used to more accurately guide individual diagnosis. Genomic medicine, as defined above, can be considered a subset of precision medicine.

The translation of new discoveries to use in patient care takes many years. Based on discoveries over the past 5 to 10 years, genomic medicine is beginning to fuel new approaches in certain medical

This chapter includes text excerpted from "Genomic Medicine," National Human Genome Research Institute (NHGRI), March 31, 2015.

specialties. Oncology, in particular, is at the leading edge of incorporating genomics, as diagnostics for genetic and genomic markers are increasingly included in cancer screening, and to guide tailored treatment strategies.

How Do We Get There?

It has often been estimated that it takes, on average, 17 years to translate a novel research finding into routine clinical practice. This time lag is due to a combination of factors, including the need to validate research findings, the fact that clinical trials are complex and take time to conduct and then analyze, and because disseminating information and educating healthcare workers about a new advance is not an overnight process.

Once sufficient evidence has been generated to demonstrate a benefit to patients, or "clinical utility," professional societies and clinical standards groups will use that evidence to determine whether to incorporate the new test into clinical practice guidelines. This determination will also factor in any potential ethical and legal issues, as well economic factors such as cost-benefit ratios.

The NHGRI Genomic Medicine Working Group (GMWG) has been gathering expert stakeholders in a series of Genomic Medicine meetings to discuss issues surrounding the adoption of genomic medicine. Particularly, the GMWG draws expertise from researchers at the cutting edge of this new medical specialty, with the aim of better informing future translational research at NHGRI. Additionally the working group provides guidance to the National Advisory Council on Human Genome Research (NACHGR) and NHGRI in other areas of genomic medicine implementation, such as outlining infrastructural needs for adoption of genomic medicine, identifying related efforts for future collaborations, and reviewing progress overall in genomic medicine implementation.

Examples of Genomic Medicines

Translational

- The causes of intellectual disability are often unknown, but a team in The Netherlands has used diagnostic exome sequencing of 100 affected individuals and their unaffected parents in order to uncover novel candidate genes and mutations that cause severe intellectual disability.

- Colorectal cancers with a particular mutation can benefit from treatment with aspirin post-diagnosis. Aspirin (and other non-steroidal anti-inflammatory drugs) decrease the activity of a signaling pathway called PI3K. Between 15 and 20 percent of colorectal cancer patients have a mutation in a gene called *PIK3CA* that makes a protein that's part of the PI3K pathway, and it has been discovered that regular aspirin treatment is associated with increased survival compared to colorectal cancer patients who have the non-mutated version of *PIK3CA*.

- Currently, every baby born in the United States is tested at birth for between 29 and 50 severe, inherited, treatable genetic diseases through a public health program called newborn screening. Whole genome sequencing would enable clinicians to look for mutations across the entire genome simultaneously for a much larger number of diseases or conditions. Rapid whole genome sequencing has been shown to provide a useful differential diagnosis within 50 hours for children in the neonatal intensive care unit.

- Researchers at Stanford University in California have been developing a new test to detect when a transplanted heart may be rejected by the recipient. Currently, the only way to detect the onset of rejection is by performing an invasive tissue biopsy. This novel approach only requires blood samples, and detects the levels of cell-free circulating DNA from the donor organ in the recipient's blood stream. This circulating DNA from the donor can be elevated for up to five months before rejection can be detected by biopsy, and the level of DNA correlates with the severity of the rejection event (i.e., more circulating DNA signals a more severe event).

- Cell-free circulating DNA is also being explored as a biomarker for cancers. As tumor cells die they release fragments of their mutated DNA into the bloodstream. Sequencing this DNA can give insights into the tumor and possible treatments, and even be used to monitor tumor progression (as an alternative to invasive biopsies).

Clinical

- Pharmacogenomics involves using an individual's genome to determine whether or not a particular therapy, or dose of therapy, will be effective. Currently, more than 100 FDA-approved drugs have pharmacogenomics information in their labels, in diverse fields such as analgesics, antivirals, cardiovascular drugs, and anti-cancer therapeutics.

- FDA has also cleared or approved 45 human genetic tests, and more than 100 nucleic acid-based tests for microbial pathogens.

- DNA sequencing is being used to investigate infectious disease outbreaks, including Ebola virus, drug-resistant strains of *Staphylococcus aureas and Klebsiella pneumoniae,* as well as food poisoning following contamination with Escherichia coli. Sequencing has also recently been used to diagnose bacterial meningoencephalitis, rapidly identifying the correct therapeutic agent for the patient.

- Cystic fibrosis is one of the most common genetic diseases, caused by mutations in a gene called *CTFR.* More than 900 different *CTFR* mutations that cause cystic fibrosis have been identified to date. Approximately four percent of cases are caused by a mutation known as G551D, and now a drug called ivacaftor has been developed that is extraordinarily effective [nejm. org] at treating this disease in individuals with this particular mutation.

- Whole genome sequencing or whole exome sequencing (where only the protein-coding exons within genes, rather than the entire genome, are sequenced), has been used to help doctors diagnose-and in some extraordinary cases to identify available treatments-in rare disease cases. For example, Alexis and Noah Beery, a pair of Californian twins, were misdiagnosed with cerebral palsy, but DNA sequencing pointed to a new diagnosis, as well as a treatment, to which both children are responding well. Another patient who was misdiagnosed (for 30 years) with cerebral palsy was also found to have a treatable dopa-responsive dystonia thanks to whole exome sequencing. In another case, a young boy in Wisconsin, Nic Volker, was able to be cured of an extreme form of inflammatory bowel disease after his genome sequence revealed that a bone marrow transplant would likely be life-saving.

- The translation of new genomic medicine discoveries is already making a difference to patient care.

Part Six

Information for Parents
of Children with
Genetic Disorders

Chapter 68

Birth Defects

Facts about Birth Defects

Birth defects are common, costly, and critical conditions that affect 1 in every 33 babies born in the United States each year.

Birth Defects Are Common

Every 4 ½ minutes, a baby is born with a birth defect in the United States. That means nearly 120,000 babies are affected by birth defects each year.

Birth defects are structural changes present at birth that can affect almost any part or parts of the body (e.g., heart, brain, foot). They may affect how the body looks, works, or both. Birth defects can vary from mild to severe. The well-being of each child affected with a birth defect depends mostly on which organ or body part is involved and how much it is affected. Depending on the severity of the defect and what body part is affected, the expected lifespan of a person with a birth defect may or may not be affected.

This chapter contains text excerpted from the following sources: Text beginning with the heading "Facts about Birth Defects" is excerpted from "Birth Defects," Centers for Disease Control and Prevention (CDC), September 21, 2015; Text under the heading "What Are the Types of Genetic Tests?" is excerpted from "What Are the Types of Genetic Tests?" U.S. Department of Health and Human Services (HHS), May 17, 2016.

Identifying Birth Defects

A birth defect can be found before birth, at birth, or any time after birth. Most birth defects are found within the first year of life. Some birth defects (such as cleft lip) are easy to see, but others (such as heart defects or hearing loss) are found using special tests, such as echocardiograms (an ultrasound picture of the heart), X-rays or hearing tests.

Causes

Birth defects can occur during any stage of pregnancy. Most birth defects occur in the first 3 months of pregnancy, when the organs of the baby are forming. This is a very important stage of development. However, some birth defects occur later in pregnancy. During the last six months of pregnancy, the tissues and organs continue to grow and develop.

For some birth defects, like fetal alcohol syndrome, we know the cause. But for most birth defects, we don't know what causes them. For most birth defects, we think they are caused by a complex mix of factors. These factors include our genes (information inherited from our parents), our behaviors, and things in the environment. But, we don't fully understand how these factors might work together to cause birth defects.

While we still have more work to do, we have learned a lot about birth defects through past research. For example, some things might increase the chances of having a baby with a birth defect, such as:

- Smoking, drinking alcohol, or taking certain "street" drugs during pregnancy.

- Having certain medical conditions, such as being obese or having uncontrolled diabetes before and during pregnancy.

- Taking certain medications, such as isotretinoin (a drug used to treat severe acne).

- Having someone in your family with a birth defect. To learn more about your risk of having a baby with a birth defect, you can talk with a clinical geneticist or a genetic counselor.

- Being an older mother, typically over the age of 34 years.

Having one or more of these risks doesn't mean you'll have a pregnancy affected by a birth defect. Also, women can have a baby born with a birth defect even when they don't have any of these risks. It is important to talk to your doctor about what you can do to lower your risk.

Prevention

Not all birth defects can be prevented. But, there are things that a woman can do before and during pregnancy to increase her chance of having a healthy baby:

- Be sure to see your healthcare provider regularly and start prenatal care as soon as you think you might be pregnant.
- Get 400 micrograms (mcg) of folic acid every day, starting at least one month before getting pregnant.
- Don't drink alcohol, smoke, or use "street" drugs.
- Talk to a healthcare provider about any medications you are taking or thinking about taking. This includes prescription and over-the-counter medications and dietary or herbal supplements. Don't stop or start taking any type of medication without first talking with a doctor.
- Learn how to prevent infections during pregnancy.
- If possible, be sure any medical conditions are under control, before becoming pregnant. Some conditions that increase the risk for birth defects include diabetes and obesity.

What Are the Types of Genetic Tests?

Genetic testing can provide information about a person's genes and chromosomes. Available types of testing include:

Newborn Screening

Newborn screening is used just after birth to identify genetic disorders that can be treated early in life. Millions of babies are tested each year in the United States. All states currently test infants for phenylketonuria (a genetic disorder that causes intellectual disability if left untreated) and congenital hypothyroidism (a disorder of the thyroid gland). Most states also test for other genetic disorders.

Diagnostic Testing

Diagnostic testing is used to identify or rule out a specific genetic or chromosomal condition. In many cases, genetic testing is used to confirm

719

a diagnosis when a particular condition is suspected based on physical signs and symptoms. Diagnostic testing can be performed before birth or at any time during a person's life, but is not available for all genes or all genetic conditions. The results of a diagnostic test can influence a person's choices about health care and the management of the disorder.

Carrier Testing

Carrier testing is used to identify people who carry one copy of a gene mutation that, when present in two copies, causes a genetic disorder. This type of testing is offered to individuals who have a family history of a genetic disorder and to people in certain ethnic groups with an increased risk of specific genetic conditions. If both parents are tested, the test can provide information about a couple's risk of having a child with a genetic condition.

Prenatal Testing

Prenatal testing is used to detect changes in a fetus's genes or chromosomes before birth. This type of testing is offered during pregnancy if there is an increased risk that the baby will have a genetic or chromosomal disorder. In some cases, prenatal testing can lessen a couple's uncertainty or help them make decisions about a pregnancy. It cannot identify all possible inherited disorders and birth defects, however.

Preimplantation Testing

Preimplantation testing, also called preimplantation genetic diagnosis (PGD), is a specialized technique that can reduce the risk of having a child with a particular genetic or chromosomal disorder. It is used to detect genetic changes in embryos that were created using assisted reproductive techniques such as in-vitro fertilization. In-vitro fertilization involves removing egg cells from a woman's ovaries and fertilizing them with sperm cells outside the body. To perform preimplantation testing, a small number of cells are taken from these embryos and tested for certain genetic changes. Only embryos without these changes are implanted in the uterus to initiate a pregnancy.

Predictive and Presymptomatic Testing

Predictive and presymptomatic types of testing are used to detect gene mutations associated with disorders that appear after birth, often later in life. These tests can be helpful to people who have a family member with a genetic disorder, but who have no features of the disorder themselves at the time of testing. Predictive testing can identify mutations that increase a person's risk of developing disorders with a genetic basis, such as certain types of cancer. Presymptomatic testing can determine whether a person will develop a genetic disorder, such as hereditary hemochromatosis (an iron overload disorder), before any signs or symptoms appear. The results of predictive and presymptomatic testing can provide information about a person's risk of developing a specific disorder and help with making decisions about medical care.

Chapter 69

Safety and Children with Disabilities

Keeping Children with Disabilities Safe

We all want to keep our children safe and secure and help them to be happy and healthy. Preventing injuries and harm is not very different for children with disabilities compared to children without disabilities. However, finding the right information and learning about the kinds of risks children might face at different ages is often not easy for parents of children with disabilities. Each child is different—and the general recommendations that are available to keep children safe should be tailored to fit your child's skills and abilities.

What Can We Do?

Parents or caregivers can talk to their child's doctor or healthcare professional about how to keep him or her safe. Your child's teacher or child care provider might also have some good ideas. Once you have ideas about keeping your child safe, make a safety plan and share it with your child and other adults who might be able to help if needed.

***

This chapter includes text excerpted from "Safety and Children with Disabilities," Centers for Disease Control and Prevention (CDC), March 15, 2016.

Here are some things to think about when making a safety plan for your child:

Moving Around and Handling Things

Does your child have challenges with moving around and handling things around them?

Sometimes children are faced with unsafe situations, especially in new places. Children who have limited ability to move, see, hear, or make decisions, and children who do not feel or understand pain might not realize that something is unsafe, or might have trouble getting away.

Take a look around the place where your child will be to make sure every area your child can reach is safe for your child. Check your child's clothing and toys–are they suitable for his or her abilities, not just age and size? For example, clothing and toys that are meant for older children might have strings that are not safe for a child who cannot easily untangle themselves, or toys might have small parts that are not safe for children who are still mouthing toys.

Safety Equipment

Do you have the right kind of safety equipment?

Safety equipment is often developed for age and size, and less for ability. For example, a major cause of child death is motor vehicle crashes. Keeping your child safe in the car is important. When choosing the right car seat, you might need to consider whether your child has difficulties sitting up or sitting still in the seat, in addition to your child's age, height, and weight. If you have a child with disabilities, talk to your healthcare professional about the best type of car seat or booster seat and the proper seat position for your child. You can also ask a certified child passenger safety technician who is trained in special needs.

Other examples of special safety equipment include:

- Life jackets may need to be specially fitted for your child.

- Smoke alarms that signal with a light and vibration may be better in a home where there is a child who cannot hear.

- Hand rails and safety bars can be put into homes to help a child who has difficulty moving around or a child who is at risk for falling.

Speak to your healthcare professional about the right equipment for your child and have this equipment ready and available before you may need it.

Talking and Understanding

Does your child have problems with talking or understanding?

Children who have problems communicating might have limited ability to learn about safety and danger. For example, children who cannot hear might miss spoken instructions. Children who have trouble understanding or remembering might not learn about safety as easily as other children. Children who have a hard time communicating might not be able to ask questions about safety. Adults might think that children with disabilities are aware of dangers when they actually are not.

Parents and caregivers may need to find different ways to teach their children about safety, such as:

- Showing them what to do

- Using pretend play to rehearse

- Practicing on a regular basis

Parents and caregivers may need to find different ways to let their children communicate that they are in danger. For example, teaching your child to use a whistle, bell, or alarm can alert others to danger. Tell adults who take care of your child about the ways to communicate with your child if there is any danger.

It's also useful to contact your local fire department and explain any special circumstances you have, so that they don't have to rely on the child or others to explain their special needs in case of an emergency.

Making Decisions

Does your child have problems with making decisions?

Children might have limited ability to make decisions either because of developmental delays or limits in their thinking skills, or in their ability to stop themselves from doing things that they want, but should not do.

For example, children with attention-deficit/hyperactivity disorder (ADHD) or fetal alcohol spectrum disorders (FASDs) might be very impulsive and fail to think about the results of their actions. People often put more dangerous things higher up, so that little children cannot reach them. Your older child might be able to reach something that he or she is not ready to handle safely. Check your child's environment, particularly new places.

Some children might also have problems distinguishing when situations and people are safe or dangerous. They might not know what to do. Parents and caregivers can give children specific instructions on how to behave in certain situations that might become dangerous.

Moving and Exploring

Does your child have enough chances to move and explore?

Children with disabilities often need some extra protection. But just like all children, they also need to move and explore so that they can develop healthy bodies and minds.

Some parents of children with special needs worry about their children needing extra protection. It is not possible to protect children from every bump and bruise. Exploring can help children learn what's safe and what might be difficult or dangerous. Being fit and healthy can help children stay safe, and an active lifestyle is important for long-term health.

Children with disabilities might find it hard to take part in sports and active play–for example, equipment may need to be adjusted, coaches may need extra information and support to help a child with a disability, or a communication problem may make it more difficult for some children to play as part of a team.

Talk to your child's teachers, potential coaches, care providers, or health professional about ways to find the right balance between being safe and being active.

Chapter 70

Early Intervention: An Overview

What Is Early Intervention?

Early intervention is a system of services that **helps babies and toddlers with developmental delays or disabilities**. Early intervention focuses on helping eligible babies and toddlers learn the basic and brand-new skills that typically develop during the first three years of life, such as:

- physical (reaching, rolling, crawling, and walking);
- cognitive (thinking, learning, solving problems);
- communication (talking, listening, understanding);
- social/emotional (playing, feeling secure and happy); and
- self-help (eating, dressing).

Examples of early intervention services: If an infant or toddler has a disability or a developmental delay in one or more of these developmental areas, that child will likely be eligible for early intervention services.

This chapter includes text excerpted from "Overview of Early Intervention," U.S. Department of Education (ED), March 2014.

Those services will be tailored to meet the child's individual needs and may include:

- Assistive technology (devices a child might need)
- Audiology or hearing services
- Speech and language services
- Counseling and training for a family
- Medical services
- Nursing services
- Nutrition services
- Occupational therapy
- Physical therapy
- Psychological services

Services may also be provided to address the **needs and priorities of the child's family**. Family-directed services are meant to help family members understand the special needs of their child and how to enhance his or her development.

Who's Eligible for Early Intervention?

Early intervention is intended for infants and toddlers who have a *developmental delay* or *disability*. Eligibility is determined by evaluating the child (with parents' consent) to see if the little one does, in fact, have a delay in development or a disability. Eligible children can receive early intervention services from birth through the third birthday (and sometimes beyond).

For some children, from birth: Sometimes it is known from the moment a child is born that early intervention services will be essential in helping the child grow and develop. Often this is so for children who are diagnosed at birth with a specific condition or who experience significant prematurity, very low birth weight, illness, or surgery soon after being born. Even before heading home from the hospital, this child's parents may be given a *referral* to their local early intervention office.

For others, because of delays in development: Some children have a relatively routine entry into the world, but may develop more slowly than others, experience setbacks, or develop in ways that seem very different from other children. For these children, a visit with a developmental pediatrician and a thorough evaluation may lead to an early intervention referral.

Parents don't have to wait for a referral to early intervention, however. If you're concerned about your child's development, you may contact your local program directly and ask to have your child evaluated. That evaluation is provided free of charge.

However a child comes to be referred, evaluated, and determined eligible, early intervention services provide vital support so that children with developmental needs can thrive and grow.

What's a Developmental Delay?

The term "developmental delay" is an important one in early intervention. Broadly speaking, it means that a child is delayed in some area of development. There are five areas in which development may be affected:

1. Cognitive development

2. Physical development, including vision and hearing

3. Communication development

4. Social or emotional development

5. Adaptive development

Developmental milestones: Think of all the baby skills that can fall under any one of those developmental areas! Babies and toddlers have a lot of new skills to learn, so it's always of concern when a child's development seems slow or more difficult than would normally be expected.

Definition of "developmental delay" Part C of IDEA **broadly** defines the term "developmental delay." But the exact meaning of the term varies from state to state, because each state defines the term for itself, including:

• describing the evaluation and assessment procedures that will be used to measure a child's development in **each** of the five developmental areas; and

• specifying the level of delay in functioning (or other comparable criteria) that constitutes a developmental delay in **each** of the five developmental areas.

If You're Concerned about a Baby or Toddler's Development

It's not uncommon for parents and family members to become concerned when their beautiful baby or growing toddler doesn't seem to be developing according to the normal schedule of "baby" **milestones**.

"He hasn't rolled over yet."

"The little girl next door is already sitting up on her own!"

"She should be saying a few words by now."

Sound familiar? While it's true that children develop differently, at their own pace, and that the range of what's "normal" development is quite broad, it's hard not to worry and wonder.

What to Do

If you think that your child is not developing at the same pace or in the same way as most children his or her age, it is often a good idea to talk first to your child's pediatrician. Explain your concerns. Tell the doctor what you have observed with your child. Your child may have a disability or a developmental delay, or he or she may be at risk of having a disability or delay.

You can also get in touch with your community's early intervention program, and ask to have your little one evaluated to see if he or she has a developmental delay or disability. **This evaluation is free of charge**, won't hurt your child, and looks at his or her basic skills. Based on that evaluation, your child may be eligible for early intervention services, which will be designed to address your child's special needs or delays.

How to Get in Touch with Your Community's Early Intervention Program

There are several ways to connect with the EI program in your community. Try any of these suggestions:

- Contact the Pediatrics branch in a local hospital and ask where you should call to find out about early intervention services in your area.

- Ask your pediatrician for a referral to the local early intervention system.

What to Say to the Early Intervention Contact Person

Explain that you are concerned about your child's development. Say that you think your child may need early intervention services.

Explain that you would like to have your child evaluated under Part C of IDEA.

Referral: Write down any information the contact person gives you. You will probably be referred to either your community's early intervention program or to what is known as *Child Find*. Child Find operates in every state to identify babies and toddlers who need early intervention services because of developmental delays or disability. You can use the Parent's Record-Keeping Worksheet to keep track of this important information. In fact, in general, it's a good idea to write down the names and phone numbers of everyone you talk to as you move through the early intervention process.

The Evaluation and Assessment Process

Service coordinator

Once connected with either Child Find or your community's early intervention program, you'll be assigned a service coordinator who will explain the early intervention process and help you through the next steps in that process. The service coordinator will serve as your single point of contact with the early intervention system.

Screening and / or Evaluation

One of the first things that will happen is that your child will be evaluated to see if, indeed, he or she has a developmental delay or disability. (In some states, there may be a preliminary step called screening to see if there's cause to suspect that a baby or toddler has a disability or developmental delay.) The family's service coordinator will explain what's involved in the *screening* and/or evaluation and ask for your permission to proceed. You must provide your *written consent* before screening and/or evaluation may take place.

The evaluation group will be made up of qualified people who have different areas of training and experience. Together, they know about children's speech and language skills, physical abilities, hearing and vision, and other important areas of development. They know how to work with children, even very young ones, to discover if a child has a problem or is developing within normal ranges. Group members may evaluate your child together or individually. As part of the evaluation, the team will observe your child, ask your child to do things, talk to you and your child, and use other methods to gather information. These procedures will help the team find out how your child functions in the five areas of development.

Exceptions for Diagnosed Physical or Mental Conditions

It's important to note that an evaluation of your child won't be necessary if he or she is automatically eligible due to a diagnosed physical or mental condition that has a high probability of resulting in a developmental delay. Such conditions include but aren't limited to chromosomal abnormalities; genetic or congenital disorders; sensory impairments; inborn errors of metabolism; disorders reflecting disturbance of the development of the nervous system; congenital infections; severe attachment disorders; and disorders secondary to exposure to toxic substances, including fetal alcohol syndrome. Many states have policies that further specify what conditions automatically qualify an infant or toddler for early intervention (e.g., Down syndrome, Fragile X syndrome).

Determining Eligibility

The results of the evaluation will be used to determine your child's eligibility for early intervention services. You and a team of professionals will meet and review all of the data, results, and reports. The people on the team will talk with you about whether your child meets the criteria under IDEA and state policy for having a developmental delay, a diagnosed physical or mental condition, or being at risk for having a substantial delay. If so, your child is generally found to be eligible for services.

Initial assessment of the child. With parental consent, in depth assessment must now be conducted to determine your child's unique needs and the early intervention services appropriate to address those needs. Initial assessment will include reviewing the results of the evaluation, personal observation of your child, and identifying his or her needs in each developmental area.

Initial assessment of the family. With approval of the family members involved, assessments of family members are also conducted to identify the resources, concerns, and priorities of the family related to enhancing the development of your child. The family-directed assessment is voluntary on the part of each family member participating in the assessment and is based on information gathered through an assessment tool and also through an interview with those family members who elect to participate.

Who Pays for All This?

Under IDEA, evaluations and assessments are provided at no cost to parents. They are funded by state and federal monies.

Writing the IFSP

Having collected a great deal of information about your child and family, it's now possible for the team (including you as parents) to sit down and write an individualized plan of action for your child and family. This plan is called the **Individualized Family Service Plan,** or **IFSP**. It is a very important document, and you, as parents, are important members of the team that develops it. Each state has specific guidelines for the IFSP. Your service coordinator can explain what the IFSP guidelines are in your state.

Guiding principles: The IFSP is a written document that, among other things, outlines the early intervention services that your child and family will receive. One guiding principal of the IFSP is that the family is a child's greatest resource, that a young child's needs are closely tied to the needs of his or her family. The best way to support children and meet their needs is to support and build upon the individual strengths of their family. So, **the IFSP is a whole family plan** with the parents as major contributors in its development. Involvement of other team members will depend on what the child needs. These other team members could come from several agencies and may include medical people, therapists, child development specialists, social workers, and others.

What Info Is Included in an IFSP?

Your child's IFSP must include the following:

- Your child's present physical, cognitive, communication, social/ emotional, and adaptive development levels and needs

- Family information (with your agreement), including the resources, priorities, and concerns of you, as parents, and other family members closely involved with the child

- The major results or outcomes expected to be achieved for your child and family

- The specific services your child will be receiving

- Where in the natural environment (e.g., home, community) the services will be provided (if the services will not be provided in the natural environment, the IFSP must include a statement justifying why not)

- When and where your son or daughter will receive services

- The number of days or sessions he or she will receive each service and how long each session will last

- Who will pay for the services

- The name of the service coordinator overseeing the implementation of the IFSP

- The steps to be taken to support your child's transition out of early intervention and into another program when the time comes.

The IFSP may also identify services your family may be interested in, such as financial information or information about raising a child with a disability.

Informed parental consent: The IFSP must be fully explained to you, the parents, and your suggestions must be considered. You must give written consent for each service to be provided. If you do not give your consent in writing, your child will not receive that service.

Reviewing and updating the IFSP: The IFSP is reviewed every six months and is updated at least once a year. This takes into account that children can learn, grow, and change quickly in just a short period of time.

Timeframes for All This

When the early intervention system receives a referral about a child with a suspected disability or developmental delay, a time clock starts running. Within *45 days,* the early intervention system must complete the critical steps discussed thus far:

- screening (if used in the state),

- initial evaluation of the child,

- initial assessments of the child and family, and

- writing the IFSP (if the child has been found eligible).

That's a tall order, but important, given how quickly children grow and change. When a baby or toddler has developmental issues, they need to be addressed as soon as possible. So—45 days, that's the timeframe from referral to completion of the IFSP for an eligible child.

Who Pays for the Services?

Whether or not you, as parents, will have to pay for any services for your child depends on the policies of your state. Check with your service coordinator. Your state's system of payments must be available in writing and given to you, so there are no surprises or unexpected bills later.

What's Free to Families

Under Part C of IDEA, the following services must be provided **at no** cost to families:

- Child Find services;

- evaluations and assessments;

- the development and review of the IFSP; and

- service coordination.

When Services Are Not Free

Depending on your state's policies, you may have to pay for certain other services. You may be charged a **"sliding-scale" fee,** meaning the fees are based on what you earn. Some services may be covered by your health insurance, by Medicaid, or by Indian Health Services. The Part C system may ask for your permission to access your public or private insurance in order to pay for the early intervention services your child receives. In most cases, the early intervention system may **not** use your health care insurance (private or public) **without your express, written consent.** If you do not give such consent, the system may **not** limit or deny you or your child services.

Every effort is made to provide services to all infants and toddlers who need help, regardless of family income. Services cannot be denied to a child just because his or her family is not able to pay for them.

Chapter 71

Education of Children with Special Needs

Chapter Contents

Section 71.1

Individualized Education Programs

This section contains text excerpted from the following sources: Text beginning with the heading "Overview" is excerpted from "The Short-And-Sweet IEP Overview," U.S. Department of Education (ED), March 2013; Text under the heading "When the IEP Team Meets" is excerpted from "When the IEP Team Meets," U.S. Department of Education (ED), March 2015.

Overview

An Individualized Education Program (IEP) is a written statement of the educational program designed to meet a child's individual needs. Every child who receives special education services must have an IEP. That's why the process of developing this vital document is of great interest and importance to educators, administrators, and families alike. Here's a crash course on the IEP.

What' are the IEP's purposes?

The IEP has two general purposes:

1. to set reasonable learning goals for a child, and

2. to state the services that the school district will provide for the child.

Who develops the IEP?

The IEP is developed by a team of individuals that includes key school staff and the child's parents. The team meets, reviews the assessment information available about the child, and designs an educational program to address the child's educational needs that result from his or her disability.

When is the IEP developed?

An IEP meeting must be held **within 30 calendar days** after it is determined, through a full and individual evaluation, that a child has one of the disabilities listed in IDEA and needs special education and related services. A child's IEP must also be reviewed at least annually thereafter to determine whether the annual goals are being achieved and must be revised as appropriate.

What's in an IEP?

Each child's IEP must contain specific information, as listed within IDEA, our nation's special education law. This includes (but is not limited to):

- the child's **present levels of academic achievement and functional performance,** describing how the child is currently doing in school and how the child's disability affects his or her involvement and progress in the general curriculum

- annual **goals** for the child, meaning what parents and the school team think he or she can reasonably accomplish in a year

- the **special education and related services** to be provided to the child, including supplementary aids and services (such as a communication device) and changes to the program or supports for school personnel

- how much of the school day the child will be educated separately from nondisabled children or not participate in extracurricular or other nonacademic activities such as lunch or clubs

- how (and if) the child is to participate in state and district-wide assessments, including what modifications to tests the child needs

- when services and modifications will begin, how often they will be provided, where they will be provided, and how long they will last

- how school personnel will measure the child's progress toward the annual goals.

Can students be involved in developing their own IEPs?

Yes, they certainly can be! IDEA actually requires that the student be invited to any IEP meeting where transition services will be discussed. These are services designed to help the student plan for his or her transition to adulthood and life after high school.

When the IEP Team Meets

IEP teams are made up of individuals who bring different perspectives and expertise to the table. Pooling their knowledge, team members set out to craft an individualized response to a specific child's needs, taking into account that same child's strengths and talents. There's a lot of information shared at IEP meetings, and a lot of discussion. The end product is the child's individualized education program.

First, we'll start with an overview of key points about IEP meetings. Then, we'll take a longer look at specific aspects of these meetings that will help you be an active partner in this critical activity.

Overview of the First IEP Meeting

After a child is found eligible for special education and related services, a meeting must be held within 30 days to develop to the IEP. The school system must notify the child's parents of when and where the meeting will take place, so they have the opportunity to attend and participate.

Who Develops the Child's IEP?

Many people come together to develop a child's IEP. This group is called the IEP team and includes most of the same types of individuals who were involved in the child's initial evaluation. Team members will include:

- the child's parents;

- at least one regular education teacher, if the child is (or may be) participating in the regular education environment;

- at least one of the child's special education teachers or special education providers;

- a representative of the public agency (school system) who (a) is qualified to provide or supervise the provision of special education, (b) knows about the general curriculum; and (c) knows about the resources the school system has available;

- an individual who can interpret the evaluation results and talk about what instruction may be necessary for the child;

- the child, when appropriate;

- representatives from any other agencies that may be responsible for paying for or providing transition services (if the child is 16 years or, if appropriate, younger); and

- other individuals (invited by parents or the school) who have knowledge or special expertise about the child. For example, a relative who is close to the child, a child care provider, or related services personnel.

What's in an IEP?

Let's take a quick look at what type of information an IEP must contain. This will show the scope of what the IEP team must discuss as part of developing a child's IEP. It's also the meeting's intended outcome—what the team wants to accomplish. It may take more than one meeting to write the IEP, especially when you consider the breadth and depth of the information the IEP must include:

- the child's present levels of academic achievement and functional performance, describing how the child is currently doing in school and how the child's disability affects his or her involvement and progress in the general curriculum

- annual goals for the child, meaning what parents and the school team think he or she can reasonably accomplish in a year

- the special education and related services to be provided to the child, including supplementary aids and services (such as a communication device) and changes to the program or supports for school personnel

- how much of the school day the child will be educated separately from nondisabled children or not participate in extracurricular or other nonacademic activities such as lunch or clubs (called extent of nonparticipation)

- how (and if) the child is to participate in state and district-wide assessments, including what modifications to tests the child needs

- service delivery details, such as when services and modifications will begin, how often they will be provided, where they will be provided, and how long they will last

- how school personnel will measure the child's progress toward the annual goals.

You'll notice that we've linked each of these components to a page where you can find a full explanation of what IDEA requires and what the IEP team will discuss. These are all part of the IEP Contents page, so we won't repeat that information here. Rather, we're going to focus the discussion on key additional issues team members will need to consider as they write the child's IEP.

741

What Happens at an IEP Meeting?

During the IEP meeting, the different members of the IEP team share their thoughts and suggestions. If this is the first IEP meeting after the child's evaluation, the team may go over the evaluation results, so the child's strengths and needs will be clear. These results will help the team decide what special help the child needs in school.

After the various team members (including the parent) have shared their thoughts and concerns about the child, the group will have a better idea of that child's strengths and needs. This will allow the team to discuss and decide on the statements associated with each IEP's component listed above, especially:

- the "present levels" statement;

- the educational and other goals that are appropriate for the child; and

- the type of special education services the child needs; and

- what related services are necessary to help the child benefit from his or her special education.

The team must also make decisions about whether or not any of the "special factors" identified in IDEA need to be considered, including the child's needs for *assistive technology.*

Goals, special education services, and related services are all discussed as part of the IEP Contents page. We would refer you there to learn much more about each of these IEP components and the discussions that the IEP team will have as part of specifying each in the IEP. These are critical parts of an IEP, so the IEP team will probably spend a lot of time focused on how the child's needs can be addressed through the goals that are written and the special education and related services that are appropriate for the child.

Special Factors to Consider

Depending on the needs of the child, the IEP team may also discuss the special factors listed below:

- **If the child's behavior's interferes with his or her learning or the learning of others:** The IEP team will talk about strategies and supports to address the child's behavior.

- **If the child has limited proficiency in English:** The IEP team will talk about the child's language needs as these needs relate to his or her IEP.

- **If the child is blind or visually impaired:** The IEP team must provide for instruction in Braille or the use of Braille, unless it determines after an appropriate evaluation that the child does not need this instruction.

- **If the child has communication needs:** The IEP team must consider those needs.

- **If the child is deaf or hard of hearing:** The IEP team will consider the child's language and communication needs. This includes opportunities to communicate directly with classmates and school staff in his or her usual method of communication (for example, sign language).

- **If the child needs assistive technology devices and services.**

May a Member of the Team Be Excused from a Meeting?

Yes, certain members of the IEP team may be excused from an IEP meeting *under specific conditions.* These conditions will vary depending on whether or the team member's area of expertise is going to be discussed or modified in the meeting.

When the member's area of expertise is not going to be discussed or modified. When a member of the team whose area of expertise is not going to be discussed or modified at the meeting, he or she may be excused from attending on one condition: **The parent *and* the school system must *both* agree in writing that the member's attendance is not necessary.**

This provision was added to IDEA during its 2004 reauthorization. Interestingly, the provision **only applies to certain members of the team**—the ones who are required IEP team members. To be specific, this means:

- the child's regular education teacher (if the child is, or may be participating in the regular education environment);

- the child's special education teacher, or where appropriate, the child's special education provider;

- a representative of the public agency, who is qualified to provide, or supervise the provision of, specially designed instruction; and

- an individual who can interpret the instructional implications of evaluation results.

Simply put: Each of these team members may be excused from an IEP meeting if (a) his or her area of expertise is **not** going to be discussed or modified at the meeting; **and** (b) the parent and school system **both agree in writing** that the member's attendance is not necessary.

What about other team members?

A written agreement between the parent and school is **not** required to excuse an IEP team member who has knowledge or special expertise regarding the child, such as a related service provider. This is because that individual attends the meeting at the discretion of the parents or the public agency and is not a required team member.

When the member's area of expertise is going to be discussed or modified. Even though a member's area of expertise is going to be discussed at the meeting, it may still be possible for that member to be excused from attending. But certain conditions must be met—specifically:

- The parent, in writing, and the public agency consent to the excusal; and

- The member submits input into the development of the IEP prior to the meeting. This input must be in writing and is submitted to the parent and the IEP team

What Happens if the Member's Absence Inhibits Development of the IEP?

The Department of Education (2006) offers an instructive perspective on how excusal is intended to work, including how to avoid having a member's absence slow down or inhibit IEP development.

The IEP Team is expected to act in the best interest of the child. As with any IEP Team meeting, if additional information is needed to finalize an appropriate IEP, there is nothing in the Act that prevents an IEP Team from reconvening after the needed information is obtained, as long as the IEP is developed in a timely manner.

The parent can request an additional IEP Team meeting at any time and does not have to agree to excuse an IEP Team member. Likewise, if a parent learns at the IEP Team meeting that a required participant will not be at the meeting, the parent can agree to continue with the meeting and request an additional meeting if more information is needed, or request that the meeting be rescheduled.

Additionally, as the Department points out:

- Parents who want to confer with an excused team member may ask to do so before agreeing or consenting to excuse the member from attending the meeting.

- School systems may not routinely or unilaterally excuse IEP team members from meetings as parent agreement or consent is required in each instance.

- Schools systems need to carefully consider whether it makes sense to offer to hold the IEP team meeting when a particular member isn't attending or whether it would be better to reschedule the meeting so that person could attend and participate in the discussion.

An LEA that routinely excuses team members from attending IEP meetings would not be in compliance with the requirements of the Act, and, therefore, would be subject to the state's monitoring and enforcement provisions.

It is up to each public agency to determine the individual in the LEA with the authority to make the agreement (or provide consent) with the parent to excuse a team member for the meeting. The designated individual must have the authority to bind the LEA to the agreement with the parent or provide consent on behalf of the LEA.

Putting It All Together—and in Writing

As you can see, there are a lot of important matters to talk about in an IEP meeting! Based on those discussions, the IEP team will then write the child's IEP, bearing in mind that it must include specific types of information, including a statement of the child's present level of academic achievement and functional performance, annual goals, the special education services that will be provided, and much more.

The resultant IEP will then guide how services are provided to the child in the coming year. Before the school system can provide the child with special education for the first time, parents must give written consent.

Parents are entitled to a copy of their child's IEP at no charge, and all school personnel responsible in some way for implementing the IEP must know what their roles and obligations are and be given access to the child's IEP.

Deciding Placement

Placement—where the child receives his or her special education and related services—is a complicated issue and is the subject of a suite of pages called Placement Issues. It's also the subject of an entire module in the Building the Legacy training curriculum (Module 15, LRE Decision Making). While we refer you to both of these sources of detailed information, this summary remark puts placement within its proper context:

Placement is directly connected to the child's IEP, is based on the child's IEP, must be decided by a knowledgeable group of persons, including the child's parents, but is not necessarily decided by the IEP team.

Who decides placement, based on what? The IEP forms the basis for the placement decision, which is made by a group of persons, including the child's parents, and other persons knowledgeable about the child, the meaning of evaluation data, and placement options.

As the summary remark above indicates, the placement group may or may not be the IEP team, but in all cases, the parents are members of that group and participate in making the determination of placement for their child.

Placement can be in a range of settings—in the regular classroom, a special education class, a pull-out program, or a separate school.

Section 71.2

What Parents Can Ask and Do to Help Children Thrive at School

This section contains text excerpted from "I Have a Question...," U.S. Department of Education (ED), 2014.

As a parent or caregiver, you have a key role in your child's education—you can help bridge your child's transition from home to school, and give him or her the best chance at success in learning and in life.

While your child's education begins at home, this tool provides you with a set of questions to ask, and important issues to consider when approaching your child's teachers, principals and counselors about his or her development. As a parent or caregiver, it can be hard to know how to support your child's learning, but asking your child's educators the right questions is a good place to start.

Quality: Is My Child Getting a Great Education?

- How will you keep me informed about how my child is doing on a regular basis? How can we work together if my child falls behind?

- Is my child on grade level, and on track to be ready for college and a career? How do I know?

Ready for Success: Will My Child Be Prepared to Succeed in Whatever Comes Next?

- How will you measure my child's progress and ability in subjects including reading, math, science, the arts, social and emotional development, and other activities?

- How much time will my child spend preparing for and taking state and district tests? How will my child's teacher and I know how to use the results to help my child make progress?

Safe and Healthy: Is My Child Safe and Cared for at School?

- What programs are in place to ensure that the school is a safe, nurturing and positive environment? What are the discipline and bullying policies at the school?

- Are the meals and snacks provided healthy? How much time is there for recess and/or exercise?

Great Teachers: Is My Child Engaged and Learning Every Day?

- How do I know my child's teachers are effective?

- How much time do teachers get to collaborate with one another?

- What kind of professional development is available to teachers here?

Equity and Fairness: Does My Child, and Every Child at My Child's School or Program, Have the Opportunity to Succeed and Be Treated Fairly?

- How does the school make sure that all students are treated fairly? (For example, are there any differences in suspension/ expulsion rates by race or gender?)

- Does the school offer all students access to the classes they need to prepare them for success, including English language learners and students with special needs (for example, Algebra I and II, gifted and talented classes, science labs, AP or IB classes, art, music)?

What's Next?

What Do I Do If My Child Is Not Getting Educated According to the Known High Standards for His or Her Grade Level and in View of His or Her Future?

- Keep asking questions of the teacher, principal, other parents and education experts, including questions about your school choices.

- Find other parents who have the same concerns and work together toward improving the conditions.

- Talk to the counselor, school advisory group, PTA, parent liaison or other school or program staff. They may share your concerns or be able to help you.

- Bring your concerns to the school district office, chancellor or superintendent.

- Attend public meetings and school board meetings, and tell your story.

- Consult the resources provided at the end of this guide.

Advice from Teachers: Here Are Some Ways Teachers Suggest Parents Can Help Support Their Child's Success in School.

- Set high expectations for your child.

- Make sure your child is in school every day and on time. Attendance matters!

- Work collaboratively with your child's teachers and talk to them about goals and expectations for your child.

- Talk to your child each day about what he or she is doing in school and discuss what he or she learned.

- Encourage your child to complete assignments, and see that she or he finishes them.

- Attend parent-teacher conferences.

- Participate in family engagement and volunteer opportunities.

Section 71.3

Preparing for College: What Students with Disabilities Need to Know

This section contains text excerpted from "Guide to Student Transition Planning," Disability.gov, April 8, 2014.

What Is Transition Planning?

The National Collaborative on Workforce and Development (NCWD) for Youth defines transition planning as:

"...a coordinated set of activities for a student with a disability that: A) Is designed within an outcome-oriented process, that promotes movement from school-to-post-school activities, including post-secondary education, vocational training, integrated employment (including supported employment), continuing and adult education, adult services, independent living, or community participation; B) Is based upon the individual student's needs, taking into account the student's preferences and interests; and C) Includes instruction, related services, special education, community experiences, the development of employment and other post-school adult living objectives, and when appropriate, the acquisition of daily living skills and functional vocational evaluation."

The transition planning process should begin around middle school and continue throughout high school. The student, his or her parents or guardians, teachers and school counselors should work together to develop a plan for life after high school. This plan should take into account the student's strengths, preferences and interests, as well as any accommodations needs and other key factors. The types of questions to think about are similar to what any student would need to address, with a few additional considerations:

- What types of things interest this student? Is he or she creative and thinking about going into the arts? Is there an interest in a particular field, such as journalism or mathematics?

- Is the student thinking about going to college? If so, which type of school would be a good fit (community college, in-state four-year University, out-of-state university, etc.)?

- Is the student thinking about training for a trade? If so, what schools or programs are available? Which would be a good fit for him/her?

- Which standardized tests does the student need to take to apply for colleges or technical/trade schools? Will the student need any accommodations while taking these tests?

- What types of accommodations would the student need in college or at technical/trade school?

- What are the student's financial needs? Does he or she want to apply for student aid? Which types of aid would be best (e.g., loans, grants, scholarships)? When are the applications due? What information needs to be provided?

- Which type of living situation is the student interested in (e.g., at home, college dorm, on his/her own) and what types of accommodations will the student need?

- Is the student interested in going directly into the workforce? What job training, internship or apprenticeship opportunities are available?

Where Can I Learn about Options for Life after High School?

After graduating from high school, there are a wide range of options for your future; choosing your path is a big decision. Some options include:

- Going to college;

- Attending a trade or technical school;

- Participating in a job training or internship program;
- Volunteering; or
- Getting a job.

What Laws Protect Students' Educational Rights during the Transition Process?

- The Individuals with Disabilities Education Act's (IDEA) definition of transition services is, "a coordinated set of activities for a student with a disability that:
  - Are focused on improving the academic and functional achievement of the student to facilitate movement from school to post-school activities;
  - Are based on the individual student's needs, taking into account his/her strengths, preferences and interests; and
  - Include instruction, related services, community experiences, the development of employment and other post-school adult living objectives, and, if appropriate, acquisition of daily living skills and functional vocational evaluation."

- Transition planning should be included as a part of a student's Individualized Education Program (IEP) or Individualized Learning Plan once the student has turned 16, or at a younger age if determined appropriate by the IEP Team. The IEP should include "measurable post-secondary goals based upon age-appropriate transition assessments related to training, education, employment and, where appropriate, independent living skills," as well as transition services needed to assist the student in reaching those goals. Some schools also work with local businesses to offer work-based learning opportunities, such as youth apprenticeships, paid and unpaid work experience, job shadowing, mentoring and community service. Check with your guidance counselors or teachers to find out which work-based learning opportunities are available through your high school. Read "IEP and Transition Planning" or "Transition Goals in the IEP" to learn more.

- Legal protections after high school (including accommodations): it's important to understand that the IDEA does not apply to students after they graduate from high school. Protections for

post-high school students are provided by the Americans with
Disabilities Act (ADA) and Section 504 of the Rehabilitation
Act, and students must meet certain criteria to be eligible for
accommodations. A college, university or trade/technical school
may not provide the same accommodations a student received
in high school. Students should discuss their accommodations
needs with the disability student service office or a student
adviser at the college, university or trade school they are
interested in attending. For more information, read the U.S.
Department of Education's guide "Students with Disabilities
Preparing for Post-Secondary Education: Know Your Rights
and Responsibilities" and the HEATH Resource Center's "Transitioning from High School to College: A Spotlight on Section
504."

- Testing: ADA Title III regulations prohibit discrimination by
  "any private entity that offers examinations or courses related to
  applications, licensing, certification or credentialing for secondary or post-secondary education, professional or trade purposes."
  These regulations require that any request for documentation
  must be reasonable and limited to the need for the modification,
  accommodation, or auxiliary aid or service requested. Entities
  must give considerable weight to documentation of past modifications, accommodations or auxiliary aids, or services received
  in similar testing situations, or those provided in response to an
  IEP or under Section 504 of the Rehabilitation Act. Learn about
  accommodations available for people with disabilities taking the
  GED test.

- Employment rights: the ADA also provides protections for
  employees who need assistive technology as a "reasonable
  accommodation." Section 508 of the Rehabilitation Act protects
  federal employees' access to information and electronic technology. Learn more about the laws and regulations that protect
  employees and job seekers with disabilities by reading Disabil-
  ity.gov's "What Are My Legal Rights on the Job as a Person with
  a Disability?" The U.S. Equal Employment Opportunity Commission's (EEOC) fact sheet "Job Applicants and the Americans
  with Disabilities Act" provides information about what questions employers can and cannot ask about your disability on job
  applications and during the interview process and what types of
  accommodations employers must provide to job applicants with
  disabilities.

How Do I Plan for the Transition to College or a Trade or Technical School?

Many high school graduates with disabilities choose to continue their education by attending college. There are several things to consider about going to college, including what is the right school, what sort of living situation is best (e.g., at home, in a dorm), whether or not to apply for student aid, which type of aid (grants, loans, scholarships) to apply for, etc. The following resources can help begin the college planning process:

Planning for College or Trade School

- "A Practical Guide for People with Disabilities Who Want to Go to College" offers tips and ideas to help students with disabilities plan for college. The guide addresses topics such as finding the right school, applying for financial aid and determining what accommodations are needed.

- The U.S. Department of Education's College Navigator tool helps students choose the right school based on location, programs and tuition.

- The HEATH Resource Center's College Application Process online training provides information to help students with disabilities understand the college admissions process and outlines some of the differences between high school and college. The Center also offers free online trainings about preparing to take the SAT or ACT and how to write a college application essay.

- "College Planning for Students with Disabilities" is a handbook that guides students with disabilities through the important steps and considerations necessary to prepare for college. It covers issues such as self-advocacy and a student's legal rights and responsibilities.

- ISEEK's Tips to Prepare for College webpage offers practical advice for students from middle school through adult learners on steps to take to prepare for college.

- The KnowHow2Go website offers information and resources for middle and high school students and Veterans and military members about planning for college, including making a plan, exploring your interests and how to pay for college. It includes the 4 Steps to College online tool.

- The Education Quest Foundation's Students Transitioning to College webpage offers information on managing money, selecting a major and what to expect from the first year of college.

- The U.S. Department of Education's "Funding Your Education: The Guide to Student Financial Aid" provides information for students and families about federal student aid to pay for college, technical or training school or other post-secondary education. The guide explains the application process; the various federal loans, grants and work-study programs available; and how to apply for federal student aid. Find in-depth information about financial aid by reading Disability.gov's "Guide to Student Financial Aid." Financial Aid for Students with Disabilities" offers additional information for paying for college or trade school.

- Affordable Colleges Online offers information about post-secondary education options for every budget. Use the website's search tool to find affordable options. The "Guide to Online Learning for Students with Disabilities" provides information about distance learning for students with disabilities. Learn how to work with student disability services to get accommodations and assistive technology for students with hearing, vision, cognitive or physical disabilities.

- Some colleges and universities offer programs specifically designed for students with intellectual and developmental disabilities. Examples of these types of programs include the George Mason University LIFE program, Temple University's Academy for Adult Learning and Virginia Commonwealth University's ACE-IT in College program. There are also college programs specifically for students with autism spectrum disorders, including Asperger Syndrome.

- Think College offers additional college planning resources for people with intellectual disabilities and their parents. Use the site's college search tool to find college programs for students with intellectual disabilities. The student section offers advice from college students about how college is different from high school, tips for success and information about financial aid options, including scholarships, grants and loans.

- The Guide for College Students Living with a Chronic Condition has information and resources about topics like balancing school work while managing a chronic illness, financial aid options and returning to school after treatment.

- The University of Minnesota Institute on Community Integration offers Student Stories with advice from students with intellectual disabilities on how to successfully make the transition to college.

- "Navigating College – A Handbook on Self Advocacy for Students with Autism" is a handbook from the Autistic Self Advocacy Network for current and future college students with autism. It discusses getting accommodations in college, disability disclosure and advocating for yourself. Also includes information on living independently, staying healthy while in college and dealing with social issues. Read the Navigating College blog to learn more. The Autism Society of America also has the "Preparing to Experience College Living" guide for students with autism moving from high school to higher education.

- Learning Disabilities (LD) Online offers resources for students with learning disabilities who want to go to college. The website includes information about taking standardized tests and entrance exams, such as the SATs. The National Center for Learning Disabilities offers additional information about post-high school options for students with LD. The College Programs for Students with Learning Disabilities webpage offers a list of colleges that offer programs specially designed for students with LD.

- The PACER Center's "Off to College: Tips for Students with Visual Impairments" offers tips and helpful hints for students with visual impairments getting ready to go to college, as does the Texas School for the Blind and Visually Impaired.

- PepNet 2 provides information on equality for students who are deaf or hard of hearing during college entrance exams and other tests.

- Use the Career OneStop online tool to learn about education and training programs that offer certificates or diplomas in a variety of fields, or browse programs by occupation.

Making the Transition to College or Trade School

The college experience is very different from high school, and there are steps students with disabilities can take to make the transition easier. Be sure to meet with your college or university's disabled student services office to discuss your accommodations needs and ways they can help students with disabilities get the most out of their time at school. The resources below can also help make the transition from high school to college smoother.

- The Going to College website offers high school students with disabilities tools and resources to help identify their strengths and learning styles, discover what to expect at college and learn how to prepare for higher education. The site's Getting Accommodations section has information to help students get the accommodations they need while in college.

- The U.S. Department of Education's publication "Students with Disabilities Preparing for Post-Secondary Education: Know Your Rights and Responsibilities" offers information on how legal rights and protections for students with disabilities change after high school. It includes information on accommodations, including for those needed for test taking.

- The National Collaborative on Workforce and Disability (NCWD) for youth's "Making My Way through College" helps students with disabilities prepare for and succeed in college. Also has information on moving from college to the workforce.

- The HEATH Resource offers an online training about accommodations for college students.

- Graduates in Science, Technology, Engineering and Math (STEM) fields are in high demand. The need for qualified workers in STEM fields is growing, and jobs in these fields are also often high paying. In fact, the top 10 bachelor degree majors with the highest median earnings are all in STEM fields. Efforts are being made to make sure students with disabilities have opportunities in STEM fields. Examples include the U.S. Department of Labor High School/High Tech program, the American Association for the Advancement of Science Entry Point Internship Program, and the University of Washington Disabilities, Opportunities, Internetworking and Technology (DO-IT) Center.

Chapter 72

Transitional Planning

Chapter Contents

Section 72.1

Transitioning to the Workplace

This section contains text excerpted from "Guide to Student
Transition Planning," Disability.gov, April 8, 2014.

Where Can I Find Information about Vocational Rehabilitation and Other Job Training Programs?

- Vocational rehabilitation (VR) agencies: are federally-funded
agencies located in every state that provide job training and
placement services for people with disabilities. VR professionals
work with people with disabilities to help them find and keep
jobs that fit their abilities and interests. They also provide information about job accommodations and supports. Some states
have separate VR programs for people who are blind or visually
impaired or deaf or hard of hearing.

- Some VR agencies help pay for certain job-related things, such
as schooling, job training programs, text books and other supplies. The services available from VR agencies vary from state to
state. State VR agencies can provide information about the programs they offer, eligibility and applying for services.

- Job Corps: is a U.S. Department of Labor program that provides
free education and job training to help young people train for a
career, earn a high school diploma or GED and find and keep a
good job. To be eligible, a person must be between 16-24 years
old and qualify as low income. Read the FAQs or learn about the
types of jobs for which students can train. Find a Job Corps program or call 1-800-733-5627 for more information.

- American Job Centers: are centers located in communities
across the country that help job seekers learn about job training
programs and find employment resources. Visit the American
Job Center website or call 1-877-872-5627 (TTY: 1-877-889-5627)
to find a local Job Center. The online tool has information about
education and training programs that offer certificates or diplomas in a variety of professions.

- Apprenticeship: is one of the oldest forms of training. It involves training on the job under the direction of a master or senior worker to learn a skill or trade. The U.S. Department of Labor's Apprenticeship tool kit offers information on apprenticeship basics, how young people can prepare for apprenticeship programs and how to increase the participation of youth with disabilities in these programs. Find apprenticeship opportunities in your state by visiting the U.S. Department of Labor website.

- Local Independent Living Centers (ILC): may provide job coaching, training and other career services.

- Disability.gov's "Where Can I Get Information about Job Training Programs?": provides additional resources about job training programs and services.

- Volunteering & National Service Programs: like AmeriCorps provide students with real-life work experience through volunteering. AmeriCorps is a program run by the Corporation for National & Community Service. AmeriCorps members volunteer at local or national organizations and agencies that address critical community needs in education, public safety, health and the environment. Most AmeriCorps members receive student loan deferment and training and may receive a living allowance and health insurance. After AmeriCorps members complete their service, they also receive a Segal AmeriCorps Education Award to help pay for college, graduate school, vocational training or to repay student loans.

- Visit the All for Good search engine to find volunteer opportunities in your area, or visit Disability.gov's Volunteering section for additional resources.

Where Can I Find Information about Going to Work?

- "A Guide for School to Work Transition" covers topics such as Vocational Rehabilitation and working while receiving disability benefits.

- The Center for Parent Information and Resources offers a variety of resources about making the transition from school to the workforce, including information about reasonable accommodations and job coaching.

- Disability.gov's Where Can High School and College Students Get Help with Their Job Search? section includes resources that can help young people begin their job search.

- The HEATH Resource Center's online training about the job application process helps young people learn about job search, application, and interview processes and identify resources and strategies for finding employment. The Center also offers a training about interview skills.

- The I'm Determined website offers resources for young people, parents and educators about school to work transition topics. The "Transition to Employment Guide" includes examples of questions to consider regarding employment for students with disabilities. Information is broken up by age range.

- Career Opportunities for Students with Disabilities is a job posting and college student resume database system. Students can use the site to find employment opportunities and employers can use it to find qualified students with disabilities.

- Work-based learning opportunities: such as internships, job shadowing, and on-the-job training, give students an introduction to the world of work and are an important step toward getting to a job in their chosen career field. The National Consortium on Leadership & Disability for Youth's guide, "Internships – the On-Ramp to Employment: A Guide for Students with Disabilities" provides step-by-step information on how students with disabilities can find internships. Many government agencies, and the White House, offer internship programs. Visit Disability. gov's Mentoring and Internship Programs section to find more internship opportunities.

- Summer jobs or part-time employment: can be an important part of a student's transition process. They help young people with disabilities gain valuable work experience and learn skills that can help them after they graduate. The White House's Youth Jobs + campaign works with businesses, nonprofit organizations and government agencies to develop employment opportunities for low-income and disconnected youth. Visit Youth. Jobs to find employment opportunities. Youth.gov also has information about youth employment, as well as other resources for students with disabilities.

- Supported employment: helps people with disabilities with on-the-job supports, such as job coaches, help getting job accommodations and additional training. Nonprofit organizations like Easter Seals and The Arc often offer supported employment programs for people with disabilities. The National Alliance on Mental Illness (NAMI) offers information about supported employment for people with mental health disabilities.

- Job accommodations: reasonable accommodations are supports or assistive technology that help people with disabilities do their job. Job accommodations could be a change in a person's schedule that allows for breaks, time off to get treatments, only working a certain amount of hours or Personal Assistance Services.

- They could also be technology, devices or a change in work environment (such as widening doorways or raising desks). The Americans with Disabilities Act (ADA) requires that employers provide reasonable accommodations if they are necessary for the employee to do his or her job, unless it would cause the company "undue hardship" to do so. The U.S. Department of Defense Computer/Electronic Accommodations Program (CAP) offers a series of videos with examples of various types of job accommodations.

- NCWD for Youth's "The 411 on Disability Disclosure: A Workbook for Youth with Disabilities" and accompanying video offer tips and advice for young people and the adults that work with them so they can make informed decisions about whether or not to disclose their disability. It provides information to help them understand how that decision may impact their education, employment, and social lives. The workbook also has exercises to help young people practice disclosing their disability. NCWD for Youth offers a fact sheet about the role of families and advocates in disclosure. Youth service providers may wish to read, "Advising Youth with Disabilities on Disclosure: Tips for Service Providers."

- The Employer Assistance & Resource Network's (EARN) "Disability Disclosure: What You Need to Know" discusses disclosing a disability and providing accommodations for people with disabilities in college and in the workplace. Students, job seekers, employees and employers can learn about disclosure, the rights of people with disabilities under the ADA and reasonable accommodations for people with disabilities in the Job

- Accommodation Network's (JAN) guide, "Disability Disclosure and Interviewing Techniques for Persons with Disabilities" and the U.S. Department of Labor's fact sheet "Youth, Disclosure

761

and the Workplace Why, When, What and How," provide additional information about disclosure. Young people with mental illness may wish to read "Self-Disclosure and Its Impact on Individuals Who Receive Mental Health Services" and "Entering the World of Work: What Youth with Mental Health Needs Should Know about Accommodations."

- Employment laws and regulations: learn about the laws and regulations that protect employees and jobseekers by reading the What Are My Legal Rights on the Job as a Person with a Disability? section of Disability.gov's Guide to Employment. The U.S. Equal Employment Opportunity Commission's (EEOC) fact sheet "Job Applicants and the Americans with Disabilities Act" provides information about what questions employers can and cannot ask about a job candidate's disability on job applications and during the interview process, and what types of accommodations employers must provide to job applicants with disabilities.

- The U.S. Equal Employment Opportunity Commission's (EEOC) Youth at Work website has information and resources, including a video and classroom guides, to educate working-age students about different types of workplace discrimination, including disability discrimination.

- Resumes and interviewing: writing clear and concise resumes and cover letters and developing strong interviewing skills are vitally important when looking for a job.

- Self-employment: starting a small business is another option for young people with disabilities. Being self-employed can help avoid transportation barriers or a lengthy commute to a job.

Living Independently and Advocating for Yourself

- Independent Living basically means that people with disabilities have the same opportunities to live, work and socialize that people without disabilities have. Independent living focuses on people with disabilities living in the community, either by themselves or with others – not in institutions. There are many things to take into consideration when making decisions about living independently after graduating from high school or college. Local Independent Living Centers (ILC) can be a great way to learn about programs and services to help find employment, develop independent living skills and meet other people with disabilities.

- The following resources may also help with some of the choices young people with disabilities will need to make, such as where to live, how to manage personal assistance services (PAS) and how to learn to advocate for themselves.

- The "Living Independently Toolkit": helps people with intellectual and developmental disabilities think about their life, future plans, needs and happiness. They can use the guide to answer questions about community, health, home and work and find out about next steps to take.

- The Center for Parent Information and Resources: offers information and resources about independent living, including how young people can get help determining their independent living needs.

- The I'm Determined! website: offers detailed information about independent living and community participation for students and young adults with disabilities. Information is broken up by age range.

- The Apartment: Resources for Independent Living: offers information and resources about transportation, finances and finding place to live.

- The National Youth Leadership Network (NYLN): promotes leadership development, education, employment, independent living, health and wellness among young people with disabilities.

- Personal Assistance Services (PAS): provide people with disabilities help with activities of daily living (ADLs), such as bathing, dressing and cooking, so they can remain independent. People who provide these services are sometimes called personal care attendants. Young people with disabilities who require help with ADLs or currently use PAS should consider how this will impact them as they move into adulthood. "Making the Move to Managing Your Own Personal Assistance Services (PAS): A Toolkit for Youth with Disabilities Transitioning to Adulthood" explains the differences between job-related and personal PAS, helps youth establish transition goals and provides information on how to cover the cost of PAS care. Spinal Cord Injury Info

763

Sheet provides details about the use of personal care attendants by people with spinal cord injuries.

- Workplace PAS help employees with disabilities perform their job duties. Examples of workplace PAS include helping an employee with a cognitive disability with making decisions or reading memos to an employee who is blind. Workplace PAS can be considered a "reasonable accommodation" under the Americans with Disabilities Act (ADA).

- Transportation: is also a critical part of independent living. Young people with disabilities need to explore options for getting to school, work and participating in the community. Travel training is a way to help people with disabilities learn to navigate public transportation systems. These services are offered through transportation providers, state and local government agencies and nonprofit organizations, such as Independent Living Centers. Travel training is sometimes used in conjunction with orientation and mobility training for people who are blind or have low vision. Easter Seals Project ACTION's guide, "Travel Training for Student Success: The Route to Achieving Post-Secondary Student Outcomes," provides secondary school educators with resources to support young adults' needs for public transportation through travel training. Read Disability.gov's "Guide to Transportation" for more information about transportation options.

- Self-advocacy: as people with disabilities move into adulthood, there will be more and more instances where they will have to express their needs and wants, and perhaps stand up for their rights, in order to get services and assistance. Self-advocacy helps people with disabilities learn how to do this.

- "Taking Action: A Step by Step Guide to Self-Advocacy" is a guide from the United Spinal Association that provides information to help people with disabilities become effective self-advocates and get the services, accommodations and information they need and want. The guide includes a section about filing complaints if a person feels his or her rights have been violated.

- The Self-Advocacy Online website has informational videos, listings of self-advocacy groups by state and stories from people who have overcome bullying, gone to college and improved their lives using self-advocacy.

- The National Gateway to Self-Determination website has resources, training and information about self-determination and self-advocacy for people with intellectual and developmental disabilities.

- The Arc's Self-Determination Scale helps young adults with cognitive disabilities determine their strengths and interests.

- The I'm Determined! website offers additional information, divided by age range, on self-determination.

Section 72.2

Assisting Disabled Youth with Job Search and Retention

This section includes text excerpted from "Disability Employment," U.S. Office of Personnel Management (OPM), July 26, 2010. Reviewed on April 2016.

Job Seekers

The Federal Government is actively recruiting and hiring persons with disabilities. We offer a variety of exciting jobs, competitive salaries, excellent benefits, and opportunities for career advancement.

Hiring people with disabilities into Federal jobs is fast and easy. People with disabilities can be appointed to Federal jobs non-competitively through a process called Schedule A. Learn how to be considered for Federal jobs under the noncompetitive process. People with disabilities may also apply for jobs through the traditional or competitive process.

Getting a Job

Most Federal agencies have a Selective Placement Program Coordinator, a Special Emphasis Program Manager (SEPM) for Employment of Adults with Disabilities, or equivalent, who helps to recruit, hire and accommodate people with disabilities at that agency.

Find a Selective Placement Program Coordinator

Most Federal agencies have a Selective Placement Program Coordinator, a Special Emphasis Program Manager (SEPM) for Employment of Adults with Disabilities, or equivalent, who helps to recruit, hire and accommodate people with disabilities at that agency.

Reasonable Accommodations

The Federal Government may provide you reasonable accommodation in appropriate cases. Requests are considered on a case-by-case basis.

Federal Agencies

As the Nation's largest employer, the Federal Government has a special responsibility to lead by example in including people with disabilities in the workforce. This website contains important information for federal agencies to use in recruiting, hiring, and retaining individuals with disabilities and targeted disabilities.

Background

On July 26, 2010, President Obama issued Executive Order 13548, which provides that the Federal Government, as the Nation's largest employer, must become a model for the employment of individuals with disabilities. The order directs Executive departments and agencies (agencies) to improve their efforts to employ Federal workers with disabilities and targeted disabilities through increased recruitment, hiring, and retention of these individuals. This is not only the right thing to do, but it is also good for the Government, as it increases the potential pool of highly qualified people from which the Federal Government draws its talent. Importantly, the Executive Order adopts the goal set forth in Executive Order 13163 of hiring 100,000 people with disabilities into the Federal Government over 5 years, including individuals with targeted disabilities.

The Executive Order also instructed the Director of the Office of Personnel Management (OPM), in consultation with the Secretary of Labor, the Chair of the Equal Employment Opportunity Commission (EEOC), and the Director of the Office of Management and Budget (OMB), to design model recruitment and hiring strategies for agencies to facilitate their employment of people with disabilities.

In addition to the Executive Order, federal agencies are obligated under the Rehabilitation Act of 1973, as amended to affirmatively employ people with disabilities. The specific requirements of this obligation are spelled out in the Equal Employment Opportunity Commission Management Directive (MD) 715.

Recruiting

This section contains recruiting information and resources for selective placement program coordinators, human resources professionals, managers and hiring officials.

Hiring

There are two types of hiring processes. In the non-competitive hiring process, agencies use a special authority (Schedule A) to hire persons with disabilities without requiring them to compete for the job. In the competitive process, applicants compete with each other through a structured process.

Retention

Retention is essential to making the investment of identifying and hiring people pay off. Learn helpful practices for retaining people with disabilities.

Providing Accommodation

In order to meet their accommodation obligations, agencies should think creatively about ways to make their workplace more accessible and create an environment where their employees who have disabilities can thrive. Here are some suggestions that relate specifically to reasonable accommodation issues.

Chapter 73

Government Benefits
for Children and Adults
with Disabilities

Chapter Contents

Section 73.1

Facts about Social Security's Disability Program

This section includes text excerpted from "The Facts about
Social Security's Disability Program," Social Security
Administration (SSA), March 2016.

Social Security Disability Insurance Is Coverage That Workers Earn

Social Security disability is a social insurance program under which
workers earn coverage for benefits, by working and paying Social Security taxes on their earnings. The program provides benefits to disabled
workers and to their dependents. For those who can no longer work
due to a disability, our disability program is there to replace some of
their lost income.

The Social Security Act Defines Disability Very Strictly

Eligibility rules for Social Security's disability program differ from
those of private plans or other government agencies. Social Security
doesn't provide temporary or partial disability benefits, like workers'
compensation or veterans' benefits do. To receive disability benefits, a
person must meet the definition of disability under the Social Security
Act (Act). A person is disabled under the Act if he or she can't work due
to a severe medical condition that has lasted, or is expected to last, at
least one year or result in death. The person's medical condition must
prevent him or her from doing work that he or she did in the past, and
it must prevent the person from adjusting to other work. Because the
Act defines disability so strictly, Social Security disability beneficiaries
are among the most severely impaired in the country. In fact, Social
Security disability beneficiaries are more than three times as likely
to die in a year as other people the same age. Among those who start
receiving disability benefits at the age of 55, 1-in-5 men and 1-in-7
women die within five years of the onset of their disabilities.

Disability Is Unpredictable and Can Happen to Anyone at Any Age

Fifty-six million Americans, or 1-in-5, live with disabilities. Thirty-eight million disabled Americans, or 1-in-10, live with severe disabilities. Disability is something many Americans, especially younger people, think can only affect the lives of other people. Tragically, thousands of young people are seriously injured or killed, often as the result of traumatic events. Many serious medical conditions, such as cancer or mental illness, can affect the young as well as the elderly. The sobering fact for 20-year-olds, insured for disability benefits, is that more than 1-in-4 of them becomes disabled before reaching retirement age. As a result, they may need to rely on the Social Security disability benefits for income support. Our disability benefits provide a critical source of financial support to people when they need it most.

Social Security Disability Payments Are Modest

At the beginning of 2016, Social Security paid an average monthly disability benefit of $1,166. That is barely enough to keep a beneficiary above the 2015 poverty level ($11,770 annually). For many beneficiaries, their monthly disability payment represents most of their income. Even these modest payments can make a huge difference in the lives of people who can no longer work. They allow people to meet basic needs and the needs of their families.

As Experts Projected for Decades, the Number of People Qualifying for Social Security Disability Benefits Has Increased

For 60 years, Social Security disability has helped increasing numbers of workers and their families replace lost income. Several factors have contributed to this increase, which the Social Security Trustees and our actuaries have projected for decades. The primary factors contributing to the increase are:

- The baby boomers (people born in 1946 through 1965) reached their most disability prone years between 1990 and 2011; and

- More women have joined the workforce in the past few decades and have worked consistently enough to qualify for benefits if they become disabled. Despite the increase, the 9 million or so people getting a Social Security disability benefit represent just a small subset of Americans living with disabilities.

Social Security Works Aggressively to Prevent, Detect, and Prosecute Fraud

Social Security, along with the Office of the Inspector General, aggressively identifies and prosecutes those who commit fraud. Our zero tolerance approach has resulted in a fraud incidence rate that is a fraction of one percent. One of our most effective measures to guard against fraud is the Cooperative Disability Investigations program.

Under the program, we investigate suspicious disability claims early, before making a decision to award benefits. In effect, we proactively stop fraud before it happens. In fiscal year 2012, with the help of state and local law enforcement, the program reported nearly $340 million in projected savings to the disability programs. This resulted in a return on investment of $17 for each $1 spent.

Eradicating fraud is a team effort. We need people who suspect something to say something. If you suspect fraud, please contact the Office of the Inspector General at 1-800-269-0271 or visit us at http:// oig.ssa.gov and click on Report Fraud, Waste, or Abuse.

Section 73.2

FAQs on Social Security's Disability Program

This section includes text excerpted from "Disability.gov's Guide to Disability Benefits," Disability.gov, September 7, 2013.

Am I Eligible for Social Security Disability Benefits?

What the Social Security Administration (SSA) Means By "Disabled"?

SSA's definition of "disability" is very strict. SSA pays benefits only for total disability, meaning when a person cannot engage in substantial gainful activity (SGA). No benefits are paid for partial or short-term disability.

SSA pays monthly cash disability benefits through two programs:

1. **Social Security Disability Insurance (SSDI):** SSDI benefits are for people who have worked for a certain amount of time and paid Social Security taxes during that period.

2. **Supplemental Security Income (SSI):** SSI benefits are for people who are low income and are age 65 or older or blind or have a disability.

To receive SSDI or SSI benefits, you must:

- Not be able to do the work that you did before;
- Not be able to do other kinds of work because of your medical condition(s); and
- Have a disability that has lasted or is expected to last for at least one year or to result in death.

Even if your doctor says that you have a disability, you cannot get Social Security disability benefits unless your medical records show that you meet SSA's requirements. Read more about this definition of disability and how SSA makes a decision on disability claims.

Disability payments cannot begin until you have been disabled continuously for five full calendar months; payments are made starting with the sixth full month after the date your disability began. After you receive disability benefits for 24 months, you are automatically enrolled in Medicare. You will not receive Social Security benefits for any month in the waiting period.

Compassionate Allowances

The Compassionate Allowances program lets SSA quickly make decisions and pay benefits on claims filed by individuals with serious diseases and medical conditions, which automatically meet SSA's disability standards.

What's the Difference between Social Security Disability Insurance (SSDI) and Supplemental Security Income (SSI)?

The Social Security Administration (SSA) manages the Social Security Disability Insurance (SSDI) and Supplemental Security Income (SSI) programs. While both of these programs offer cash benefits for people with disabilities, the eligibility requirements for each are different.

What Is SSDI?

SSDI is funded through payroll taxes. To get SSDI, you must be an adult between the ages of 18 and 64 and have earned a certain number of "work credits" by working and paying into the Social Security system for a certain amount of time. After you receive SSDI for two years, you'll become automatically eligible for Medicare.

Under SSDI, the spouse and children of a person with a disability are eligible to receive partial dependent benefits even if they don't have a disability themselves.

Social Security disability benefits are paid after you have been disabled continuously throughout a period of five full calendar months. Disability benefits are paid beginning with the sixth full month after the date your disability began. You're not entitled to benefits for any month during this five-month waiting period. The amount of the monthly benefit after the waiting period is based upon how much you've earned while working.

What Is SSI?

SSI is a program that is strictly need-based, according to income and assets, and is funded by general fund taxes. To meet the SSI income requirements, you must have limited income and resources.

An adult or child who has a disability must meet all of the following requirements:

- Have limited income;

- Have limited resources;

- Be a U.S. citizen or national or in one of certain categories of aliens; and

- Live in the United States or Northern Mariana Islands.

The monthly payment is based strictly on financial need and varies up to the maximum federal benefit rate. Some states add money to federal SSI payments. Approval for benefits generally takes three to six months. Once you're approved for SSI, you'll get benefits retroactive to the date of your application.

If you have a disability which prevents you from working, and you appear to meet all other eligibility requirements, it is possible to get SSI earlier. Sometimes on the day you apply.

In most states, people who get SSI are automatically eligible for Medicaid.

What Do I Need to Apply for Social Security Disability Benefits?

Before You Apply

- Use SSA's Benefits Eligibility Screening Tool (BEST) to find out if you may be eligible for Social Security benefits.

- Read the Adult Disability Starter Kit fact sheet to learn about the application process and what you need to know before you apply for Social Security disability benefits.

- Watch SSA's video series on applying for disability benefits. It addresses topics such as SSA's definition of "disabled," medical evidence required to apply, and the appeals process.

- Learn more about the medical evidence required to apply for disability benefits by reading "Disability Evaluation Under Social Security: Evidentiary Requirements" or visiting Disability.gov's "Medical Documentation for Social Security Disability Applications" section.

When You Apply

- If the results from BEST show that you may be eligible for Social Security benefits, you can apply online. Before you begin, review the Adult Disability Checklist.

- You will need to fill out the Disability Benefit Application and Adult Disability Report; then, complete the Authorization to Disclose Information Form (SSA-827). This form can be completed electronically as part of the Adult Disability Report.

- If you don't want to apply online or if you have questions about the process, call SSA at 1-800-772-1213 (TTY: 1-800-325-0778), Monday through Friday from 7 a.m–7 p.m. Eastern Time to make an appointment to apply for benefits. You can also contact your local Social Security office for assistance.

How Do I Apply for Social Security Disability Benefits for My Child?

Supplemental Security Income (SSI)

Children under age 18 may get SSI benefits if they have a disability and their family has little or no income and resources.

The Social Security Administration (SSA) has a very strict definition of disability for children. It includes the following:

- The child must have a physical or mental condition(s) that very seriously limits his or her activities; and

- The condition(s) must last, or be expected to last, at least one year or result in death.

To apply for disability benefits for a child under age 18, you will need to complete an Application for SSI and a Child Disability Report.

Social Security Disability Insurance (SSDI)

If you receive SSDI, your children may also qualify for benefits, even if they don't have a disability. The child can be a biological child, adopted child, stepchild or dependent grandchild. To qualify, the child must be under age 18, or age 18–19 and a full-time high school student.

The SSDI program also pays benefits to adults who have a disability that began before age 22. SSA considers this SSDI benefit as a "child's" benefit, because it is paid on the parent's Social Security record.

In order for a child with a disability to receive benefits as a dependent on a parent's record after age 18, the following rules apply:

- The disability must have started before age 22; and

- He or she must meet the definition of disability for adults.

To apply for SSDI child's benefits, contact SSA at 1-800-772-1213 (TTY: 1-800-325-0778), Monday through Friday from 7 a.m–7 p.m. Eastern Time to make an appointment to apply for benefits. You can also contact your local Social Security office for assistance.

Where Do I Apply for Disability Benefits for Wounded Warriors?

Disability benefits from the Social Security Administration (SSA) for wounded warriors are different than those paid by the U.S. Department of Veterans Affairs (VA) and the U.S. Department of Defense (DoD). You will need to complete a separate application.

SSA expedites claims for military service members who became disabled while on active military service on or after October 1, 2001, regardless of where the disability occurs.

To apply for benefits online, visit SSA's Wounded Warriors web-page. You can also call SSA at 1-800-772-1213 (TTY: 1-800-325-0778), Monday through Friday from 7 a.m–7 p.m. Eastern Time or contact your local Social Security office for assistance.

How Do I Apply for Temporary Disability Benefits?

The Social Security Administration does not pay temporary dis-ability benefits. However, there are disability compensation programs, such as workers' compensation, that provide wage replacement ben-efits, medical treatment, vocational rehabilitation and other benefits to workers or their dependents who are injured on the job or have an occupational disease.

The U.S. Department of Labor's Office of Workers' Compensation Programs has fact sheets to answer frequently asked questions. Workers injured while employed by private companies or state and local govern-ment agencies should contact their State Workers' Compensation Board.

Some states make temporary cash payments to individuals who cannot work because of sickness or injury that was not caused by their job. Contact your state's Department of Labor to find out what assistance is offered in your state.

How Can I Check the Status of My Disability Benefits Application?

If you have already applied for Social Security disability benefits, you can check the status of your application online.

Please allow five days from the date you originally filed your appli-cation before you use this service. You can also contact your local Social Security Administration (SSA) office.

What Do I Do If My Claim Is Denied?

If your application for Social Security disability benefits is denied, you have the right to appeal a decision on your claim. You can file an appeal:

- Online–you will need to have your Notice of Decision before you begin;

- By phone at 1-800-772-1213 (TTY: 1-800-325-0778); or

- At your local Social Security Administration (SSA) office.

General Information

- Your name, Social Security Number, address and phone number;

- Your Notice of Decision;

- If you have a representative, his or her name, address and phone number; and

- The name, address and phone number of a friend or relative who knows about your medical condition.

Medical Information (Since You Last Filed a Disability Claim or Appeal)

- Description of any changes and new medical conditions;

- The name, address, phone number, type of treatment and visit dates for all doctors, hospitals and clinics;

- The names of medicines (over-the-counter and prescription) you are currently taking, who prescribed them and any side effects; and

- The name, location and date of all medical tests you have had and who ordered them.

Are There Any Programs That Help People Receiving Disability Benefits Return to Work?

If you're receiving Social Security Disability Insurance (SSDI) or Supplemental Security Income (SSI) benefits, the Social Security Administration (SSA) has work incentives programs that can help you go back to work. These work incentives include:

- Continued cash benefits for a period of time while you work;

- Continued Medicare or Medicaid for a period of time while you work; and

- Help with education, training and vocational rehabilitation to start a new line of work.

Ticket to Work

SSA's Ticket to Work (TTW) program helps people who receive SSDI or SSI return to work, or begin working if they've never done so. Anyone ages 18 to 64 who receives SSDI or SSI benefits because of his or her disability is eligible to participate. For more information about the TTW program call 1-866-968-7842 (TTY: 1-866-833-2967) Monday–Friday from 8 a.m–8 p.m. Eastern Time, or search for help in your state on the ChooseWork website.

What Is a Trial Work Period?

SSA's trial work period allows you to test your ability to work while still receiving your full Social Security benefits for at least nine months.

During the trial work period, you will receive SSI and SSDI your full benefit amount, no matter how much you earn, as long as you report your work activity and continue to have a disability. In 2016, a trial work month is any month in which a person's total earnings are over $810. For people who are self-employed, a trail work month is any month in which a person earns more than $810 after expenses or works more than 80 hours. The trial work period continues until you have worked nine months within a 60-month period. If you're able to work after this time period, your benefits will eventually stop.

What Is the Extended Period of Eligibility?

After the trial work period, you have 36 months during which you can work and still receive benefits for any month your earnings are not what SSA calls "substantial gainful activity" (SGA). For 2016, you can earn up to $1,130 a month ($1,820 for people who are blind) without losing your benefits.

SSI Employment Supports

SSA also offers employment supports specifically for people who receive SSI. Examples of these include the Earned Income Exclusion, the Plan to Achieve Self-Support (PASS) and Medicaid While Working.

How Will Working Affect My Social Security Disability Benefits?

Substantial Gainful Activity (SGA)

To be eligible for disability benefits, you must not be able to participate in what's called SGA. If you work and make more than a certain amount a month, the Social Security Administration (SSA) considers you to be participating in SGA. For 2016, you can earn as much as $1,130 ($1,820 if you're blind) without losing your benefits.

Reporting Your Earnings

Be aware that if you go back to work, you will need to report your income to SSA. To report your earnings call SSA's main number (1-800-772-1213) or call, visit or write your local Social Security office.

Do You Want to Work and Keep Your Benefits?

If you get SSI or SSDI, the Ticket to Work (TTW) program and other work incentive programs can help you return to work.

Work incentives include:

- Continued cash benefits for a period of time while you work;

- Continued Medicare or Medicaid for a period of time while you work; and

- Help with education, training and rehabilitation to start a new line of work.

Anyone ages 18 through 64 who receives SSDI or SSI benefits because of his or her disability is eligible to participate in the TTW program.

How Do I Report Fraud or Misuse of Social Security Benefits or Social Security Numbers?

A variety of situations may be considered fraud, waste or abuse against Social Security, such as:

- Making false statements on claims;

- Concealing facts or events which affect eligibility for Social Security benefits;

- Misuse of benefits by a representative payee;

- Buying or selling counterfeit or legitimate Social Security cards; and

- Social Security Number misuse.

To report fraud, waste or abuse of Social Security disability benefits, file a Fraud Reporting Form.

Part Seven

Additional Help and Information

Chapter 74

Glossary of Terms Related to Genetic Disorders

akinesia: Trouble initiating or carrying out movements.

allele: A form of a gene. Each person receives two alleles of a gene, one from each biological parent. This combination is one factor among many that influence a variety of processes in the body. On chromosome 19, the apolipoprotein E (APOE) gene has three common alleles: ε2, ε3, and ε4.

amino acids: A set of twenty different molecules used to build proteins. Proteins consist of one or more chains of amino acids called polypeptides. The sequence of the amino acid chain causes the polypeptide to fold into a shape that is biologically active. The amino acid sequences of proteins are encoded in the genes.

apert syndrome: One of a group of genetic disorders, called acrocephalosyndactyly, characterized by malformations of the skull, face, hands, and feet. Apert syndrome is an autosomal dominant trait due to a mutation in a gene called FGFR2 (fibroblast growth factor receptor 2).

The terms in this glossary were excerpted from the "Talking Glossary of Genetic Terms," National Human Genome Research Institute (NHGRI), National Institutes of Health (NIH). The complete text of this document is available online at http://www.genome.gov/glossary/index.cfm. Last accessed May 23, 2016.

apolipoprotein E (APOE) gene: A gene on chromosome 19 involved in making a protein that helps carry cholesterol and other types of fat in the bloodstream. The APOE ε4 allele is the major known risk-factor gene for late-onset Alzheimer disease.

apoptosis: The process of programmed cell death. It is used during early development to eliminate unwanted cells. In adults, apoptosis is used to rid the body of cells that have been damaged beyond repair. Apoptosis also plays a role in preventing cancer. If apoptosis is for some reason prevented, it can lead to uncontrolled cell division and the subsequent development of a tumor.

atrophy: A decrease in size or wasting away of a body part or tissue.

autosomal dominant: A pattern of inheritance characteristic of some genetic diseases. "Autosomal" means that the gene in question is located on one of the numbered, or non-sex, chromosomes. "Dominant" means that a single copy of the disease-associated mutation is enough to cause the disease.

autosomal recessive: A pattern of inheritance in which both parents carry and pass on a defective gene to their child.

autosome: Any of the numbered chromosomes, as opposed to the sex chromosomes. Humans have twenty-two pairs of autosomes and one pair of sex chromosomes (the X and Y). Autosomes are numbered roughly in relation to their sizes. That is, Chromosome 1 has approximately 2,800 genes, while chromosome 22 has approximately 750 genes.

base pair: Two chemical bases bonded to one another forming a "rung of the DNA ladder." The DNA molecule consists of two strands that wind around each other like a twisted ladder. Each strand has a backbone made of alternating sugar (deoxyribose) and phosphate groups. Attached to each sugar is one of four bases--adenine (A), cytosine (C), guanine (G), or thymine (T). The two strands are held together by hydrogen bonds between the bases, with adenine forming a base pair with thymine, and cytosine forming a base pair with guanine.

beta-blockers: A class of medications also known as beta-adrenergic blockers that affect the body's response to certain nerve impulses. This, in turn, decreases the rate and force of the heart's contractions, which lowers blood pressure and reduces the heart's demand for oxygen. In addition to treating high blood pressure, beta-blockers may be used for angina, and to prevent heart attacks, migraine headaches, and glaucoma.

biopsy: A procedure in which tissue or other material is removed from the body and studied for signs of disease.

birth defect: An abnormality present at birth. Also called a congenital defect, it can be caused by a genetic mutation, an unfavorable environment during pregnancy, or a combination of both. The effect of a birth defect can be mild, severe, or incompatible with life.

bradykinesia: Gradual loss of spontaneous movement.

BRCA1 **and** *BRCA2***:** The first two genes found to be associated with inherited forms of breast cancer. Both genes normally act as tumor suppressors, meaning that they help regulate cell division. When these genes are rendered inactive due to mutation, uncontrolled cell growth results, leading to breast cancer. Women with mutations in either gene have a much higher risk for developing breast cancer than women without mutations in the genes.

cancer: A group of diseases characterized by uncontrolled cell growth. Cancer begins when a single cell mutates, resulting in a breakdown of the normal regulatory controls that keep cell division in check.

candidate gene: A gene whose chromosomal location is associated with a particular disease or other phenotype. Because of its location, the gene is suspected of causing the disease or other phenotype.

carrier: A person who carries a gene for a recessive genetic disorder. The person has the potential to pass the disorder on to his or her child, but is not personally affected by the disorder.

cell: The basic building block of living things. An adult human body is estimated to contain between 10 and 100 trillion cells.

centromere: A constricted region of a chromosome that separates it into a short arm (p) and a long arm (q).

chondrodysplasias: Once referred to as dwarfism. A group of genetic disorders, often caused by a single gene variation that affects the structure or metabolism of the bone, cartilage, or connective tissue.

chromosome: An organized package of DNA found in the nucleus of the cell. Different organisms have different numbers of chromosomes. Humans have 23 pairs of chromosomes--22 pairs of numbered chromosomes, called autosomes, and one pair of sex chromosomes, X and Y.

codominance: A relationship between two versions of a gene. Individuals receive one version of a gene, called an allele, from each parent. If the alleles are different, the dominant allele usually will be expressed, while the effect of the other allele, called recessive, is masked. In codominance, however, neither allele is recessive and the phenotypes of both alleles are expressed.

codon: A trinucleotide sequence of DNA or RNA that corresponds to a specific amino acid. There are sixty-four different codons: sixty-one specify amino acids while the remaining three are used as stop signals.

collagen: The principal protein of the skin, bones, cartilage, tendons, and other connective tissues.

contracture: Chronic shortening of a muscle or tendon that limits movement of a bony joint, such as the elbow.

copy number variation (CNV): When the number of copies of a particular gene varies from one individual to the next. The extent to which copy number variation contributes to human disease is not yet known. It has long been recognized that some cancers are associated with elevated copy numbers of particular genes.

corpus striatum: A part of the brain that helps regulate motor activities.

creatine kinase: A protein needed for the chemical reactions that produce energy for muscle contractions; high levels in the blood indicate muscle damage.

cutis laxa: Latin for loose or lax skin, cutis laxa refers to an extremely rare connective tissue disorder in which the skin lacks elasticity and hangs in loose folds. Caused by underlying genetic defects in connective tissue structure, the disorder can also result in serious problems with vocal cords, bones, cartilage, blood vessels, and vital internal organs.

deep brain stimulation: A treatment that uses an electrode implanted into part of the brain to stimulate it in a way that temporarily inactivates some of the signals it produces.

deletion: A type of mutation involving the loss of genetic material. It can be small, involving a single missing DNA base pair, or large, involving a piece of a chromosome.

DNA (deoxyribonucleic acid): The chemical name for the molecule that carries genetic instructions in all living things. The DNA molecule consists of two strands that wind around one another to form a shape known as a double helix. Each strand has a backbone made of alternating sugar (deoxyribose) and phosphate groups. Attached to each sugar is one of four bases--adenine (A), cytosine (C), guanine (G), and thymine (T). The two strands are held together by bonds between the bases; adenine bonds with thymine, and cytosine bonds with guanine. The sequence of the bases along the backbones serves as instructions for assembling protein and RNA molecules.

DNA replication: The process by which a molecule of DNA is duplicated. When a cell divides, it must first duplicate its genome so that each daughter cell winds up with a complete set of chromosomes.

DNA sequencing: A laboratory technique used to determine the exact sequence of bases (A, C, G, and T) in a DNA molecule. The DNA base sequence carries the information a cell needs to assemble protein and RNA molecules. DNA sequence information is important to scientists investigating the functions of genes.

dominant: A genetic trait (or genetically transmitted disorder) that is evident when only one copy of the gene for that trait is present. Most dominant traits are due to genes on the autosomes (nonsex chromosomes). They affect males and females equally.

dopamine: A chemical messenger, deficient in the brains of people with PD, that transmits impulses from one nerve cell to another.

double helix: The description of the structure of a DNA molecule. A DNA molecule consists of two strands that wind around each other like a twisted ladder.

duplication: A type of mutation that involves the production of one or more copies of a gene or region of a chromosome. Gene duplication is an important mechanism by which evolution occurs.

dural ectasia: An enlargement of the dura, a primary membrane of connective tissue that covers the spine and contains the spinal fluid. Common in people with Marfan syndrome, dural ectasia occurs mainly in the lower spine and can cause low back pain, abdominal pain, headaches, leg pain, and perineal pain and numbness.

dyskinesias: Abnormal involuntary twisting and writhing movements that can result from long-term use of high doses of levodopa.

dystonia: Involuntary muscle contractions that cause slow repetitive movements or abnormal postures.

dystrophin: A protein that helps maintain the shape and structure of muscle fibers.

Ehlers-Danlos syndrome (EDS): A heritable connective tissue disease characterized by easy bruising, joint laxity (the ability to bend beyond normal range of motion), lax skin, and tissue weakness.

electromyography: A recording and study of the electrical properties of skeletal muscle.

epidermolysis bullosa (EB): A potentially disabling, disfiguring, and sometimes lethal connective tissue disorder caused by defects of several proteins in the skin, resulting in skin blistering. Some forms of the disease may involve the gastrointestinal tract, the pulmonary system, muscles, or the bladder.

epigenetics: An emerging field of science that studies heritable changes caused by the activation and deactivation of genes without any change in the underlying DNA sequence of the organism.

exon: The portion of a gene that codes for amino acids.

fibroblast: The most common type of cell found in connective tissue. Fibroblasts secrete collagen proteins that are used to maintain a structural framework for many tissues. They also play an important role in healing wounds.

fibrodysplasia ossificans progressiva (FOP): An extremely rare disorder in which a genetic mutation causes fibrous tissue such as muscles, tendons, and ligaments to ossify, or turn to bone, when damaged. The disease is also characterized by a deformity of the big toe.

first-degree relative: A family member who shares about 50 percent of their genes with a particular individual in a family. This includes parents, offspring, and siblings.

fluorescence in situ hybridization (FISH): A laboratory technique for detecting and locating a specific DNA sequence on a chromosome. The technique relies on exposing chromosomes to a small DNA sequence called a probe that has a fluorescent molecule attached to it. The probe sequence binds to its corresponding sequence on the chromosome.

frameshift mutation: A type of mutation involving the insertion or deletion of a nucleotide in which the number of deleted base pairs is not divisible by three. This is important because the cell reads a gene in groups of three bases. Each group of three bases corresponds to one of 20 different amino acids used to build a protein. If a mutation disrupts this reading frame, then the entire DNA sequence following the mutation will be read incorrectly.

gene expression: The process by which the information encoded in a gene is used to direct the assembly of a protein molecule. The cell reads the sequence of the gene in groups of three bases. Each group of three bases (codon) corresponds to one of twenty different amino acids used to build the protein.

gene regulation: The process of turning genes on and off. Gene regulation ensures that the appropriate genes are expressed at the proper times.

gene therapy: An experimental technique for treating disease by altering the patient's genetic material. Most often, gene therapy works by introducing a healthy copy of a defective gene into the patient's cells.

gene: A basic unit of heredity. Genes direct a cell to make proteins and guide almost every aspect of a cell's construction, operation, and repair.

genetic counseling: The professional interaction between a healthcare provider with specialized knowledge of genetics and an individual or family. The genetic counselor determines whether a condition in the family may be genetic and estimates the chances that another relative may be affected.

genetic marker: A DNA sequence with a known physical location on a chromosome. Genetic markers can help link an inherited disease with the responsible gene.

genetic mutation: A permanent change in a gene that can be passed on to children. The rare, early-onset familial form of Alzheimer disease is associated with mutations in genes on chromosomes 21, 14, and 1.

genetic risk factor: A change in a gene that increases a person's risk of developing a disease.

genetic screening: The process of testing a population for a genetic disease in order to identify a subgroup of people that either have the disease or the potential to pass it on to their offspring.

genetic testing: The use of a laboratory test to look for genetic variations associated with a disease. The results of a genetic test can be used to confirm or rule out a suspected genetic disease or to determine the likelihood of a person passing on a mutation to their offspring.

genetic variant: A change in a gene that may increase or decrease a person's risk of developing a disease or condition.

genome: An organism's complete set of DNA, including all of its genes. Each genome contains all of the information needed to build and maintain that organism.

genomics: The study of the entire genome of an organism.

glycoprotein: A molecule that has a protein and a carbohydrate component.

heritable: Capable of being transmitted from parent to child through genes.

heterozygous: Having inherited different forms of a particular gene from each parent.

homocystinuria: A genetically transmitted disease in which an enzyme deficiency permits the buildup of the amino acid homocyteine. The result, if not treated, can be mental retardation, blood vessel disease, and atherosclerosis (hardening of the arteries).

insertion: A type of mutation involving the addition of genetic material.

karyotype: An individual's collection of chromosomes.

linkage: The close association of genes or other DNA sequences on the same chromosome.

linkage studies: Tests conducted among family members to determine how a genetic trait is passed on through generations.

locus: The specific physical location of a gene or other DNA sequence on a chromosome, like a genetic street address.

lordosis: An abnormal forward curving of the spine.

mapping: The process of making a representative diagram cataloging the genes and other features of a chromosome and showing their relative locations.

marfan syndrome: A heritable disorder of connective tissue resulting from mutations in the gene that specifies the genetic code for fibrillin-1, a protein important to connective tissue. The disorder is characterized by excessively long leg bones and long "spider-like" fingers. Other problems include skeletal malformations, abnormal position of the lens of the eye, and enlargement at the beginning part of the aorta, the major vessel carrying blood away from the heart. If left untreated, an enlarged aorta can lead to hemorrhage and even death.

marker: A DNA sequence with a known physical location on a chromosome. Markers can help link an inherited disease with the responsible genes.

merosin: A protein found in the connective tissue that surrounds muscle fibers.

missense mutation: When the change of a single base pair causes the substitution of a different amino acid in the resulting protein. This amino acid substitution may have no effect, or it may render the protein nonfunctional.

mitochondrial DNA: The small circular chromosome found inside mitochondria. The mitochondria are organelles found in cells that are the sites of energy production.

mitosis: A cellular process that replicates chromosomes and produces two identical nuclei in preparation for cell division.

monosomy: The state of having a single copy of a chromosome pair instead of the usual two copies found in diploid cells. Monosomy can be partial if a portion of the second chromosome copy is present. Monosomy, or partial monosomy, is the cause of some human diseases such as Turner syndrome and Cri-du-Chat syndrome.

muscle wasting: A decrease in muscle strength and size.

mutations: Changes in genes that can occur randomly or as a result of some factor in the environment.

myoglobin: An oxygen—binding protein in muscle cells that generates energy by turning glucose into carbon dioxide and water.

myopathy: Any disorder of muscle tissue or muscles.

myotonia: An inability to relax muscles following a sudden contraction.

neuropathy: Nervous system disease or dysfunction that may cause symptoms including muscle weakness, loss of muscle bulk, muscle cramps and spasms, and pain.

neurotransmitters: Chemicals which carry messages from one nerve cell, or neuron, to another.

newborn screening: Testing performed on newborn babies to detect a wide variety of disorders. Typically, testing is performed on a blood sample obtained from a heel prick when the baby is two or three days old.

nonsense mutation: The substitution of a single base pair that leads to the appearance of a stop codon where previously there was a codon specifying an amino acid. The presence of this premature stop codon results in the production of a shortened, and likely nonfunctional, protein.

osteogenesis imperfecta: A condition that results from mutation in two genes that make type I collagen, a protein important to bones and teeth. These mutations cause the body to either make too little collagen or poor-quality collagen. The result includes bones that fracture easily, low muscle mass, and joints and ligaments that move beyond their intended range of motion.

parkinsonian gait: A characteristic way of walking that includes a tendency to lean forward; small, quick steps as if hurrying forward (called festination); and reduced swinging of the arms.

parkinsonism: A term referring to a group of conditions that are characterized by four typical symptoms—tremor, rigidity, postural instability, and bradykinesia.

personalized medicine: An emerging practice of medicine that uses an individual's genetic profile to guide decisions made in regard to the prevention, diagnosis, and treatment of disease. Knowledge of a patient's genetic profile can help doctors select the proper medication or therapy and administer it using the proper dose or regimen.

Pfeiffer syndrome: Also called type V acrocephalosyndactyly, Pfeiffer syndrome is one of a group of genetic disorders characterized by malformations of the skull, face, hands, and feet. Like the more common Apert syndrome, Pfeiffer syndrome is caused by a mutation in the FGFR2 (fibroblast growth factor receptor 2) gene.

pharmacogenomics: A branch of pharmacology concerned with using DNA and amino acid sequence data to inform drug development and testing. An important application of pharmacogenomics is correlating individual genetic variation with drug responses.

phenotype: An individual's observable traits, such as height, eye color, and blood type.

point mutation: When a single base pair is altered. Point mutations can have one of three effects. First, the base substitution can be a silent mutation where the altered codon corresponds to the same amino acid. Second, the base substitution can be a missense mutation where the altered codon corresponds to a different amino acid. Or third, the base substitution can be a nonsense mutation where the altered codon corresponds to a stop signal.

polymorphism: One of two or more variants of a particular DNA sequence. The most common type of polymorphism involves variation at a single base pair. Polymorphisms can also be much larger in size and involve long stretches of DNA. Called a single nucleotide polymorphism, or SNP (pronounced snip), scientists are studying how SNPs in the human genome correlate with disease, drug response, and other phenotypes.

postural instability: Impaired balance that causes a tendency to lean forward or backward and to fall easily.

protein: A substance that determines the physical and chemical characteristics of a cell and therefore of an organism. Proteins are essential to all cell functions and are created using genetic information.

proteoglycans: A class of glycoproteins that perform various functions and serve as the "filler" substance between the cells. An inability to break down proteoglycans is characteristic of a series of genetic disorders called mucopolysaccharidoses.

pseudohypertrophy: A condition in which muscles may be enlarged by an accumulation of fat and connective tissue, causing them to look larger and healthier than they actually are.

pseudoxanthoma elasticum (PXE): A rare disorder of degeneration of the elastic fibers with tiny areas of calcification in the skin, the back of the eyes (retinae), and the blood vessels. Pseudoxanthoma elasticum typically causes skin abnormalities, eye abnormalities that can lead to blindness, atherosclerosis (hardening of the arteries), mitral valve prolapse, and fragile blood vessels that can lead to problems with circulation and abnormal bleeding into internal organs, including the bowel. Pseudoxanthoma elasticum is inherited either as an autosomal recessive or as an autosomal dominant trait.

recessive: A genetic trait or disorder that is usually expressed when only two copies of a gene for that trait, one from each parent, are present.

recombinant DNA (rDNA): A technology that uses enzymes to cut and paste together DNA sequences of interest. The recombined DNA sequences can be placed into vehicles called vectors that ferry the DNA into a suitable host cell where it can be copied or expressed.

retrovirus: A virus that uses RNA as its genetic material. When a retrovirus infects a cell, it makes a DNA copy of its genome that is inserted into the DNA of the host cell. There are a variety of different retroviruses that cause human diseases such as some forms of cancer and acquired immunodeficiency syndrome (AIDS).

ribosome: A cellular particle made of RNA and protein that serves as the site for protein synthesis in the cell. The ribosome reads the sequence of the messenger RNA (mRNA) and, using the genetic code, translates the sequence of RNA bases into a sequence of amino acids.

rigidity: A symptom of the disease in which muscles feel stiff and display resistance to movement even when another person tries to move the affected part of the body, such as an arm.

RNA (ribonucleic acid): A molecule similar to DNA. Unlike DNA, RNA is single-stranded. An RNA strand has a backbone made of alternating sugar (ribose) and phosphate groups. Attached to each sugar is one of four bases—adenine (A), uracil (U), cytosine (C), or guanine (G). Different types of RNA exist in the cell: messenger RNA (mRNA), ribosomal RNA (rRNA), and transfer RNA (tRNA).

scoliosis: An abnormal lateral, or sideways, curving of the spine.

sex chromosome: A type of chromosome that participates in sex determination. Humans and most other mammals have two sex chromosomes, the X and the Y. Females have two X chromosomes in their cells, while males have both X and a Y chromosomes in their cells.

sex linked: A trait in which a gene is located on a sex chromosome. In humans, the term generally refers to traits that are influenced by genes on the X chromosome.

somatic cell: Any cell of the body except sperm and egg cells. Somatic cells are diploid, meaning that they contain two sets of chromosomes, one inherited from each parent.

stem cell: A cell with the potential to form many of the different cell types found in the body. When stem cells divide, they can form more stem cells or other cells that perform specialized functions.

substantia nigra: Movement-control center in the brain where loss of dopamine-producing nerve cells triggers the symptoms of PD; substantia nigra means "black substance," so called because the cells in this area are dark.

substitution: A type of mutation where one base pair is replaced by a different base pair. The term also refers to the replacement of one amino acid in a protein with a different amino acid.

susceptibility: A condition of the body that increases the likelihood that the individual will develop a particular disease. Susceptibility is influenced by a combination of genetic and environmental factors.

syndrome: A collection of recognizable traits or abnormalities that tend to occur together and are associated with a specific disease.

telomere: The end of a chromosome. Telomeres are made of repetitive sequences of non-coding DNA that protect the chromosome from damage. Each time a cell divides, the telomeres become shorter. Eventually, the telomeres become so short that the cell can no longer divide.

trait: A specific characteristic of an organism. Traits can be determined by genes or the environment, or more commonly by interactions between them. The genetic contribution to a trait is called the genotype. The outward expression of the genotype is called the phenotype.

transcription: The process of making an RNA copy of a gene sequence. This copy, called a messenger RNA (mRNA) molecule, leaves the cell nucleus and enters the cytoplasm, where it directs the synthesis of the protein, which it encodes.

transfer RNA (tRNA): small RNA molecule that participates in protein synthesis. Each tRNA molecule has two important areas:a trinucleotide region called the anticodon and a region for attaching a specific amino acid. During translation, each time an amino acid is added to the growing chain, a tRNA molecule forms base pairs with its complementary sequence on the messenger RNA (mRNA) molecule, ensuring that the appropriate amino acid is inserted into the protein.

translation: The process of translating the sequence of a messenger RNA (mRNA) molecule to a sequence of amino acids during protein synthesis.

translocation: A type of chromosomal abnormality in which a chromosome breaks and a portion of it reattaches to a different chromosome.

tremor: Shakiness or trembling, often in a hand, which in PD is usually most apparent when the affected part is at rest.

X chromosome: One of two sex chromosomes.

X-linked recessive: A pattern of disease inheritance in which the mother carries the affected gene on the chromosome that determines the child's sex and passes it to her son.

Y chromosome: One of two sex chromosomes.

Chapter 75

Sources of Further Help and Information Related to Genetic Disorders

General

Eunice Kennedy Shriver *National Institute of Child Health and Human Development (NICHD)*
P.O. Box 3006
Rockville, MD 20847
Toll-Free: 800-370-2943
Toll-Free TTY: 888-320-6942
Toll-Free Fax: 866-760-5947
Website: www.nichd.nih.gov
E-mail: NICHDInformation
ResourceCenter@mail.nih.gov

Genetics Home Reference
Toll-Free TTY: 866-569-1162
Website: ghr.nlm.nih.gov

National Digestive Diseases Information Clearinghouse
2 Information Way
Bethesda, MD 20892-3570
Toll-Free: 800-891-5389
Fax: 703-738-4929
Website: www.niddk.nih.gov/
health-information/health-
topics/digestive-diseases/Pages/
default.aspx
E-mail: nddic@info.niddk.nih.gov

National Heart, Lung, and Blood Institute, National Institutes of Health, NHLBI Health Information Center
P.O. Box 30105
Bethesda, MD 20824-0105
Phone: 301-592-8573
Fax: 301-592-8563
Website: www.nhlbi.nih.gov
E-mail: nhlbiinfo@nhlbi.nih.gov

National Human Genome Research Institute, Communications and Public Liaison Branch, National Institutes of Health
Bldg. 31, Rm. 4B09
9000 Rockville Pike
Bethesda, MD 20892-2152
Phone: 301-402-0911
Fax: 301-402-2218
Website: www.genome.gov
E-mail: egreen@mail.nih.gov.

National Institute of Arthritis and Musculoskeletal and Skin Diseases (NIAMS), Information Clearinghouse, National Institutes of Health
1 AMS Cir.
Bethesda, MD 20892-3675
Toll-Free: 877-22-NIAMS
(877-226-4267)
Phone: 301-495-4484
TTY: 301-565-2966
Fax: 301-718-6366
Website: www.niams.nih.gov
E-mail: NIAMSinfo@mail.nih.gov

National Institute of Diabetes and Digestive and Kidney Diseases (NIDDK), Office of Communications & Public Liaison
Bldg. 31, Rm. 9A06
31 Center Dr., MSC 2560
Bethesda, MD 20892-2560
Phone: 301-496-3583
Website: www2.niddk.nih.gov
E-mail: nddic@info.niddk.nih.gov

National Institute of General Medical Sciences, Office of Communications & Public Liaison
45 Center Dr.
MSC 6200
Bethesda, MD 20892-6200
Phone: 301-496-7301
Website: www.nigms.nih.gov
E-mail: info@nigms.nih.gov

National Institute of Neurological Disorders and Stroke, Office of Communications, National Institutes of Health Neurological Institute
P.O. Box 5801
Bethesda, MD 20824
Toll-Free: 800-352-9424
Phone: 301-496-5751
Website: www.ninds.nih.gov
E-mail: NEXT@ninds.nih.gov

The Nemours Foundation
Website: www.kidshealth.org
E-mail: info@KidsHealth.org

Rare Diseases Clinical Research Network
Website: www.
rarediseasesnetwork.epi.usf.edu
E-mail: GopalR@mail.nih.gov

Albinism

National Organization for Albinism and Hypopigmentation (NOAH)
P.O. Box 959
East Hampstead, NH
03826-0959
Toll-Free: 800-473-2310 (U.S. and Canada)
Phone: 603-887-2310
Toll-Free Fax: 800-648-2310
Website: www.albinism.org
E-mail: webmaster@albinism.org

Angelman Syndrome

Angelman Syndrome Association
P.O. Box 554
Sutherland, NSW 2232
Australia
Website: www.
angelmansyndrome.org
E-mail: wildkellie@gmail.com

Angelman Syndrome Foundation
4255 Westbrook Dr.
Ste. 219
Aurora, IL 60504
Toll-Free: 800-432-6435
Phone: 630-978-4245
Fax: 630-978-7408
Website: www.angelman.org
E-mail: info@angelman.org

Canadian Angelman Syndrome Society
P.O. Box 37
Priddis, Alberta T0L 1W0
Canada
Phone: 403-931-2415
Fax: 403-931-4237
Website: www.angelmancanada.
org
E-mail: janzentd@telus.net

Blood Disorders

American Hemochromatosis Society, Inc.
4044 W.Lake Mary Blvd.
Unit #104 PMB 416
Lake Mary, FL 32746-2012
Toll-Free: 888-655-IRON
(888-655-4766)
Phone: 407-829-4488
Fax: 407-333-1284
Website: www.americanhs.org
E-mail: mail@americanhs.org

Canadian Fanconi Anemia Research Fund
P.O. Box 38157
Toronto, ON M5N 3A9
Canada
Phone: 416-489-6393
Fax: 416-489-6393
Website: www.fanconicanada.org
E-mail: admin@fanconicanada.
org

Fanconi Anemia Research Fund, Inc.
1801 Willamette St.
Ste. 200
Eugene, OR 97401
Toll-Free: 888-FANCONI
(888-326-2664)
Phone: 541-687-4658
Fax: 541-687-0548
Website: www.fanconi.org
E-mail: info@fanconi.org

Iron Disorders Institute
P.O. Box 675
Taylors, SC 29687
Website: www.irondisorders.org
E-mail: info@irondisorders.org

National Hemophilia Foundation
116 W.32nd St.
11th Fl.
New York, NY 10001
Phone: 212-328-3700
Fax: 212-328-3777
Website: www.hemophilia.org

Sickle Cell Disease Association of America
231 E. Baltimore St.
Ste. 800
Baltimore, MD 21202
Toll-Free: 800-421-8453
Phone: 410-528-1555
Fax: 410-528-1495
Website: www.sicklecelldisease.
org
E-mail: scdaa@sicklecelldisease.
org

CHARGE Syndrome

CHARGE Syndrome Foundation, Inc.
141 Middle Neck Rd.
Sands Point, NY 11050
Toll Free: 800-442-7604
Phone: 516-684-4720
Fax: 516-883-9060
Website: www.chargesyndrome.
org
E-mail: info@chargesyndrome.
org

Connective Tissue Disorders

Canadian Marfan Association (CMA), Centre Plaza Postal Outlet
128 Queen St. S.
P.O. Box 42257
Mississauga, ON L5M 4Z0
Canada
Toll-Free: 866-722-1722
Phone: 905-826-3223
Fax: 905-826-2125
Website: www.gadacanada.ca/
E-mail: info@marfan.ca

Ehlers-Danlos National Foundation (EDNF)
1760 Old Meadow Rd.
Ste. 500
McLean, VA 22102
Phone: 703-506-2892
Fax: 703-506-3266
Website: www.ednf.org
E-mail: ednfstaff@ednf.org

National Marfan Foundation (NMF)
22 Manhasset Ave.
Port Washington NY 11050
Toll-Free: 800-862-7326
Phone: 516-883-8712
Fax: 516-883-8040
Website: www.marfan.org
E-mail: staff@marfan.org

Osteogenesis Imperfecta Foundation
804 W.Diamond Ave.
Ste. 210
Gaithersburg, MD 20878
Toll-Free: 800-981-2663
Phone: 301-947-0083
Fax: 301-947-0456
Website: www.oif.org
E-mail: bonelink@oif.org

Cornelia de Lange Syndrome Foundation
302 W.Main St.
#100
Avon, CT 06001
Toll-Free: 800-753-2357 or
800-223-8355
Phone: 860-676-8166 or
860-676-8255
Fax: 860-676-8337
Website: www.cdlsusa.org
E-mail: info@cdlsusa.org

Cystic Fibrosis

Cystic Fibrosis Foundation
6931 Arlington Rd.
2nd Fl.
Bethesda, MD 20814
Toll free: 800-FIGHT CF
(800-344-4823)
Phone: 301-951-4422
Fax: 301-951-6378
Website: www.cff.org
E-mail: info@cff.org

Fragile X Syndrome

FRAXA Research Foundation
10 Prince Pl.
Newburyport, MA 01950
Phone: 978-462-1866
Website: www.fraxa.org

National Fragile X Foundation
1615 Bonanza St.
Ste. 202
Walnut Creek, CA 94596
Toll-Free: 800-688-8765
Fax: 925-938-9315
Website: www.fragilex.org
E-mail: natlfx@fragilex.org

Gene Therapy

American Society of Gene & Cell Therapy
555 E. Wells St.
Ste. 1100
Milwaukee, WI 53202
Phone: 414-278-1341
Fax: 414-276-3349
Website: www.asgct.org
E-mail: info@asgct.org

Huntington Disease

Huntington's Disease Society of America
505 Eighth Ave.
Ste. 902
New York, NY 10018
Toll-Free: 800-345-HDSA
(800-345-4372)
Phone: 212-242-1968
Fax: 212-239-3430
Website: www.hdsa.org
E-mail: hdsainfo@hdsa.org

Jewish Genetic Disorders

Center for Jewish Genetics
30 S. Wells
Chicago, IL 60606
Phone: 312-357-4718
Website: www.jewishgenetics.
org
E-mail: jewishgeneticsctr@juf.
org

Leukodystrophy

United Leukodystrophy Foundation
224 N. Second St.
Ste. 2
DeKalb, IL 60115
Toll-Free: 800-728-5483
Phone: 815-748-3211
Fax: 815-748-0844
Website: www.ulf.org
E-mail: office@ulf.org

Lipid Storage Diseases

Batten Disease Support and Research Association
1175 Dublin Rd.
Columbus, OH 43215
Toll-Free: 800-448-4570
Toll-Free Fax: 866-648-8718
Website: www.bdsra.org
E-mail: bdsra1@bdsra.org

Canadian Fabry Association
1707 W.7th Ave.
Unit #314
Vancouver, BC V6J 5E9
Canada
Website: www.fabrycanada.com
E-mail: President@fabrycanada.
com

Children's Brain Disease Foundation
Parnassus Heights Medical
Bldg., Ste. 900
San Francisco, CA 94117
Phone: 415-665-3003
Fax: 415-665-3003

Children's Gaucher Research Fund
8110 Warren Ct.
Granite Bay, CA 95746
Phone: 916-797-3700
Fax: 916-797-3707
Website: www.childrensgaucher.
org
E-mail: research@
childrensgaucher.org

Fabry Support & Information Group
108 N.E. 2nd St.
Ste. C, P.O. Box 510
Concordia, MO 64020-0510
Phone: 660-463-1355
Website: www.fabry.org
E-mail: info@fabry.org

Nathan's Battle Foundation [For Batten Disease Research]
459 State Rd. 135 S.
Greenwood, IN 46142
Phone: 317-888-7396
Fax: 317-888-0504
Website: www.nathansbattle.com
E-mail: pmilto@indy.net

National Fabry Disease Foundation
4301 Connecticut Ave. N.W.
Ste. 404
Washington, DC 20008-2369
Toll-Free: 800-651-9131
Fax: 919-932-7786
Website: www.fabrydisease.org
E-mail: info@fabrydisease.org

National Gaucher Foundation
2227 Idlewood Rd.
Ste. 6
Tucker, GA 30084
Toll-Free: 800-504-3189
Fax: 920-563-0931
Website: www.gaucherdisease.org
E-mail: ngf@gaucherdisease.org

National Niemann-Pick Disease Foundation, Inc.
401 Madison Ave.
Ste. B, P.O. Box 49
Fort Atkinson, WI 53538
Toll-Free: 877-CURE-NPC
(877-287-3672)
Phone: 920-563-0930
Website: www.nnpdf.org
E-mail: nnpdf@nnpdf.org

National Tay-Sachs and Allied Diseases Association
2001 Beacon St., Ste. 204
Boston, MA 02135
Toll-Free: 800-90-NTSAD
(800-906-8723)
Fax: 617-277-0134
Website: www.ntsad.org
E-mail: info@ntsad.org

Mitochondrial Diseases

Australian Mitochondrial Disease Foundation
9-13 Young St.
Ste. 4, Level 6
Sydney NSW 2000
Australia
Fax: 412-793-6477
Website: www.amdf.org.au
E-mail: info@amdf.org.au

United Mitochondrial Disease Foundation
8085 Saltsburg Rd., Ste. 201
Pittsburgh, PA 15239
Toll-Free: 888-317-UMDF
(888-317-8633)
Phone: 412-793-8077
Website: www.umdf.org
E-mail: info@umdf.org

*Neurofibromatosis Acoustic
Neuroma Association*
600 Peachtree Parkway, Ste. 108
Cumming, GA 30041-6899
Toll-Free: 877-200-8211
Phone: 770-205-8211
Toll-Free Fax: 877-202-0239
Fax: 770-205-0239
Website: www.anausa.org
E-mail: info@anausa.org

*Children's Tumor
Foundation*
95 Pine St., 16th Fl.
New York, NY 10005-1703
Toll-Free: 800-323-7938
Phone: 212-344-6633
Fax: 212-747-0004
Website: www.ctf.org
E-mail: info@ctf.org

Neurofibromatosis Network
213 S. Wheaton Ave.
Wheaton, IL 60187
Toll-Free: 800-942-6825
Phone: 630-510-1115
Fax: 630-510-8508
Website: www.nfnetwork.org
E-mail: admin@nfnetwork.org

Neuromuscular Disorders

*Charcot-Marie-Tooth
Association (CMTA)*
P.O. Box 105
Glenolden, PA 19036
Toll-Free: 800-606-CMTA
(800-606-2682)
Phone: 610-499-9264
Fax: 610-499-9267
Website: www.cmtausa.org
E-mail: info@cmtausa.org

*Coalition to Cure Calpain 3
(C3)*
15 Compo Parkway
Westport, CT 06880
Phone: 203-221-1611
Fax: 734-668-4755
Website: www.curecalpain3.org
E-mail: info@curecalpain3.org

Cure CMD
P.O. Box 701
Olathe, KS 66051
Toll-Free: 866-400-3626
Website: www.curecmd.org
E-mail: info@curecmd.com

*Facioscapulohumeral
Muscular Dystrophy (FSH)
Society*
450 Bedford St.
Lexington, MA 02420
Phone: 781-301-6060
Fax: 781-862-1116
Website: www.fshsociety.org
E-mail: info@fshsociety.org

*Families of Spinal Muscular
Atrophy*
925 Busse Rd.
Elk Grove Village, IL 60007
Toll-Free: 800-886-1762
Phone: 847-367-7620
Fax: 847-367-7623
Website: www.curesma.org
E-mail: info@fsma.org

Friedreich's Ataxia Research Alliance (FARA)
533 W. Uwchlan Ave.
Downingtown, PA 19335
Phone: 484-879-6160
Fax: 484-872-1402
Website: www.CureFA.org
E-mail: info@CureFA.org

Hereditary Neuropathy Foundation, Inc.
432 Park Ave. S.
4th Fl.
New York, NY 10016
Toll-Free: 855-HELPCMT
(855-435-7268)
Phone: 212-722-8396
Fax: 917-591-2758
Website: www.hnf-cure.org
E-mail: info@hnf-cure.org

Jain Foundation
2310 130th Ave. N.E.
Ste. B101
Bellevue, WA 98005
Phone: 425-882-1440
Fax: 425-658-1703
Website: www.jain-foundation.org
E-mail: ehwang@jain-foundation.org

Muscular Dystrophy Association (MDA)
3300 E. Sunrise Dr.
Tucson, AZ 85718-3208
Toll-Free: 800-572-1717
Phone: 520-529-2000
Fax: 520-529-5300
Website: www.mda.org
E-mail: mda@mdausa.org

Muscular Dystrophy Family Fund
P.O. Box 776
Carmel, IN 46082
Phone: 317-249-8488 or
317-615-9140
Fax: 317-853-6743
Website: www.mdff.org

Myotonic Dystrophy Foundation
P.O. Box 29543
Sunland, CA 94129
Toll-Free: 866-968-6642
Phone: 415-800-7777
Website: www.myotonic.org
E-mail: info@myotonic.org

National Ataxia Foundation (NAF)
2600 Fernbrook Lane N.
Ste. 119
Minneapolis, MN 55447-4752
Phone: 763-553-0020
Fax: 763-553-0167
Website: www.ataxia.org
E-mail: naf@ataxia.org

Neuropathy Association
60 E. 42nd St.
Ste. 942
New York, NY 10165-0999
Toll-Free: 888-PN-FACTS
(888-763-2287)
Phone: 212-692-0662
Fax: 212-692-0668
Website: www.foundationforpn.org
E-mail: info@neuropathy.org

Parent Project Muscular Dystrophy (PPMD)
401 Hackensack Ave.
9th Fl.
Hackensack, NJ 07601
Toll-Free: 800-714-KIDS
(800-714-5437)
Phone: 201-250-8440
Fax: 201-250-8435
Website: www.parentprojectmd.org
E-mail: info@parentprojectmd.org

Spastic Paraplegia Foundation
7700 Leesburg Pike
Ste. 123
Falls Church, VA 22043
Toll-Free: 877-SPF-GIVE
(877-773-4483)
Fax: 877-SPF-GIVE
(877-773-4483)
Website: www.sp-foundation.org
E-mail: information@sp-foundation.org

Spinal Muscular Atrophy Foundation
888 Seventh Ave.
Ste. 400
New York, NY 10019
Toll-Free: 877-FUND-SMA
(877-386-3762)
Phone: 646-253-7100
Fax: 212-247-3079
Website: www.smafoundation.org

Porphyria

American Porphyria Foundation
4900 Woodway
Ste. 780
Houston, TX 77056–1837
Toll-Free: 866-APF-3635
(866-273-3635)
Phone: 713-266-9617
Fax: 713-840-9552
Website: www.porphyriafoundation.com
E-mail: porphyrus@aol.com

The Porphyrias Consortium, Consortium Project Coordinator, Mount Sinai School of Medicine, Department of Genetics and Genomic Sciences
1425 Madison Ave., 14-75A
New York, NY 10029
Toll-Free: 866-322-7968
Phone: 212-659-6779
Fax: 212-659-6780
Website: www.fpwr.org
E-mail: grants@fpwr.org

Prader-Willi Syndrome

Foundation for Prader-Willi Research
5455 Wilshire Blvd.
Ste. 2020
Los Angeles, CA 90036
Toll-Free: 888-322-5487
Phone: 760-536-3027
Website: www.fpwr.org

*Prader-Willi Syndrome
Association (USA)*
8588 Potter Park Dr.
Ste. 500
Sarasota, FL 34238
Toll-Free: 800-926-4797
Phone: 941-312-0400
Fax: 941-312-0142
Website: www.pwsausa.org
E-mail: jheinemann@pwsausa.
org

Retinoblastoma

*Retinoblastoma
International*
18030 Brookhurst St.
Box 408
Fountain Valley, CA 92708
Website: www.retinoblastoma.
net
E-mail: info@retinoblastoma.net

Rett Syndrome

*International Rett Syndrome
Foundation*
4600 Devitt Dr.
Cincinnati, OH 45246
Toll-Free: 800-818-7388
Phone: 513-874-3020
Fax: 513-874-2520
Website: www.rettsyndrome.org
E-mail: admin@rettsyndrome.
org

*Rett Syndrome Research
Trust*
67 Under Cliff Rd.
Trumbull, CT 06611
Phone: 203-445-0041
Fax: 203-445-9234
Website: www.rsrt.org
E-mail: monica@rsrt.org

Smith-Magenis Syndrome

*PRISMS, Inc. (Parents and
Researchers Interested in
Smith-Magenis Syndrome)*
21800 Town Center Plaza
Ste. 266A-633
Sterling, VA 20164
Phone: 972-231-0035
Fax: 972-499-1832
Website: www.prisms.org
E-mail: hgraf@prisms.org

SMS Research Foundation
18620 S.W. 39th St.
Miramar, FL 33029
Phone: 203-450-9022
Website: www.
smsresearchfoundation.org
E-mail: info@
smsresearchfoundation.org

Trisomy Disorders

*National Association for
Down Syndrome (NADS)*
P.O. Box 206
Wilmette, IL 60091
Phone: 630-325-9112
Website: www.nads.org
E-mail: info@nads.org

National Down Syndrome Congress
30 Mansell Ct.
Ste. 108
Roswell, GA 30076
Toll-Free: 800-232-NDSC
(800-232-6372)
Phone: 770-604-9500
Website: www.ndsccenter.org
E-mail: info@ndsccenter.org

National Down Syndrome Society
666 Broadway
8th Fl.
New York, NY 10012
Toll-Free: 800-221-4602
Fax: 770-604-9898
Website: www.ndss.org
E-mail: info@ndss.org

Trisomy 18 Foundation
4491 Cheshire Stn. Plaza
Ste. 157
Dale City, VA 22193
Phone: 810-867-4211
Website: www.trisomy18.org
E-mail: T18info@trisomy18.org

Tuberous Sclerosis

Tuberous Sclerosis Alliance
801 Roeder Rd.
Ste. 750
Silver Spring, MD 20910-4467
Toll-Free: 800-225-6872
Phone: 301-562-9890
Fax: 301-562-9870
Website: www.tsalliance.org
E-mail: info@tsalliance.org

Tuberous Sclerosis Canada
92 Caplan Ave.
Ste. 125
Barrie, ON L9N 0Z7
Canada
Toll-Free: 888-223-2410
Website: www.tscanada.ca
E-mail: TSCanadaST@gmail.com

Urea Cycle Disorders

National Urea Cycle Disorders Foundation
Toll-Free: 800-38-NUCDF
(800-386-8233)
Website: www.nucdf.org
E-mail: info@nucdf.org

Vision Disorders

Glaucoma Associates of Texas
10740 N. Central Expy.
Ste. 300
Dallas, TX 75231
Phone: 214-360-0000
Fax: 214-739-8562
Website: www.glaucomaassociates.com
E-mail: ablankenship@glaucomaassociates.com

Glaucoma Research Foundation
251 Post St., Ste. 600
San Francisco, CA 94108
Toll-Free: 800-826-6693
Phone: 415-986-3162
Fax: 415-986-3763
Website: www.glaucoma.org
E-mail: question@glaucoma.org

Williams Syndrome

Williams Syndrome Association
570 Kirts Blvd.
Ste. 223
Troy, MI 48084-4156
Toll-Free: 800-806-1871
Phone: 248-244-2229
Fax: 248-244-2230
Website: www.williams-syndrome.org
E-mail: info@williams-syndrome.org

Wilson Disease

Wilson Disease Association
5572 N. Diversey Blvd.
Milwaukee, WI 53217
Toll-Free: 866-961-0533
Phone: 414-961-0533
Fax: 414-962-3886
Website: www.wilsonsdisease.org
E-mail: info@wilsonsdisease.org

Index

Index

813